THE HANDBOOK OF FINANCIAL MODELING

A PRACTICAL APPROACH TO CREATING AND IMPLEMENTING VALUATION PROJECTION MODELS

Jack Avon

Jason & Vicky
remember your dreams
Make them be
Jack Avon

Apress®

The Handbook of Financial Modeling: A Practical Approach to Creating and Implementing Valuation Projection Models

ISBN-13 (pbk): 978-1-4302-6205-3

ISBN-13 (electronic): 978-1-4302-6206-0

President and Publisher: Paul Manning
Lead Editor: Jeff Olson
Developmental Editor: Ralph Moore

Coordinating Editor: Rita Fernando
Copy Editor: Jennifer Sharpe
Compositor: SPi Global
Indexer: SPi Global
Cover Designer: Anna Ishchenko

Distributed to the book trade worldwide by Springer Science+Business Media New York, 233 Spring Street, 6th Floor, New York, NY 10013. Phone 1-800-SPRINGER, fax (201) 348-4505, e-mail `orders-ny@springer-sbm.com`, or visit `www.springeronline.com`. Apress Media, LLC is a California LLC and the sole member (owner) is Springer Science + Business Media Finance Inc (SSBM Finance Inc). SSBM Finance Inc is a Delaware corporation.

For information on translations, please e-mail `rights@apress.com`, or visit `www.apress.com`.

Apress and friends of ED books may be purchased in bulk for academic, corporate, or promotional use. eBook versions and licenses are also available for most titles. For more information, reference our Special Bulk Sales–eBook Licensing web page at `www.apress.com/bulk-sales`.

Any source code or other supplementary materials referenced by the author in this text is available to readers at `www.apress.com`. For detailed information about how to locate your book's source code, go to `www.apress.com/source-code/`.

Apress Business: The Unbiased Source of Business Information

Apress business books provide essential information and practical advice, each written for practitioners by recognized experts. Busy managers and professionals in all areas of the business world—and at all levels of technical sophistication—look to our books for the actionable ideas and tools they need to solve problems, update and enhance their professional skills, make their work lives easier, and capitalize on opportunity.

Whatever the topic on the business spectrum—entrepreneurship, finance, sales, marketing, management, regulation, information technology, among others—Apress has been praised for providing the objective information and unbiased advice you need to excel in your daily work life. Our authors have no axes to grind; they understand they have one job only—to deliver up-to-date, accurate information simply, concisely, and with deep insight that addresses the real needs of our readers.

It is increasingly hard to find information—whether in the news media, on the Internet, and now all too often in books—that is even-handed and has your best interests at heart. We therefore hope that you enjoy this book, which has been carefully crafted to meet our standards of quality and unbiased coverage.

We are always interested in your feedback or ideas for new titles. Perhaps you'd even like to write a book yourself. Whatever the case, reach out to us at editorial@apress.com and an editor will respond swiftly. Incidentally, at the back of this book, you will find a list of useful related titles. Please visit us at www.apress.com to sign up for newsletters and discounts on future purchases.

The Apress Business Team

This book is dedicated to my beautiful wife Jenny and children Luke, Thandiwe, and Nathaniel for giving me their unconditional support, encouragement, and the time and space to write this book. I also would like to thank my parents Roger and Esnat who have always supported me and continue to encourage me to stretch myself creatively and intellectually.

Contents

About the Author

Jack Avon is the director and principal consultant at Isys Systems (Ringwood) Ltd., a financial modeling and analysis company in the United Kingdom. He has broad industry experience with integrating in-house systems with Microsoft Excel and Access and developing custom models and management information systems. Mr. Avon has consulted in financial modeling since 1997 and has worked with clients in banking, media, telecommunications, transportation, construction, oil, gas, and the public sector. He is the founder of the Association of Financial Modelers, has a background in finance and IT, and is an avid photographer. Mr. Avon lives in Surrey with his wife and three children.

Acknowledgments

I would like to express my sincere gratitude to the many people who saw me through this book—to all those who provided support, talked things over, read, wrote, offered comments, allowed me to quote their remarks and assisted in the editing, proofreading, and design.

I would like to thank Ralph Moore for the sterling work of reviewing and challenging me on the writing throughout the review. I would also like to thank Rita Fernando for the coordination of all matters concerned with the book and for keeping me to my schedules and providing assistance throughout the book writing. Above all I want to thank my wife Jenny who gave me the encouragement and conviction to follow my path and who has put so much of her life on hold to give me support and reassurance. Nothing I do would be possible without her.

Thanks also to the rest of my family who continually supported and encouraged me to discover my port of call in life. It was a difficult journey for them, but they persevered with me and in particular my father Roger, who has made so many sacrifices to give me the best in life unconditionally.

I would also like to thank Nicky Turner for her quiet inspirations to me during the writing of this book. She has always kept my corner.

A mention should also go to Tony Turner who sadly cannot see this book, but I treasure his belief and confidence in me and my career from the moment he met me. May you see and read this book Tony wherever you are.

To my children Luke, Thandiwe, and Nathaniel who give me reason to do better and remind me of how fortunate I am.

I would like to thank Simon Williams and the team at Operis and Sarah Hothersall at Lyquidity for their unconditional faith in the book and for helping me in the process of selecting and editing the material.

Thanks to Jeff Olson, Ralph Moore, Jennifer Sharpe, Rita Fernando, and the Apress team for giving me this great opportunity to express a subject that gives me so much joy. Finally, I would like to thank Morgan Ertel for her belief in me and for making this happen.

Introduction

This book is written from the perspective of a financial modeler and so gives some insight into the thinking and approach that modelers will find themselves in. This is quite deliberate, because I believe that what is missing from many financial modeling sources is the insight into what it's really like to be a modeler.

There are varying opinions about how a financial model should look. One reason is because modeling is a relatively recent practice. The majority of modeling is also Excel-based, which means it has a built-in, flexible approach. Anyone who uses Excel will tell you there are usually several different ways of achieving the same result.

Another reason why so many approaches exist is that there is a series of modeling methodologies which, while embodying the virtues of best practice, nonetheless have fundamentally different philosophical views about modeling.

Financial models are developed predominantly in Microsoft Excel and as a result tend to conform to the Microsoft Office user experience. So why should there be such a disparity in people's views of models? Part of the problem is that it is not that easy to describe a model. Sure, it's possible to describe theoretical models and what they should like, but an actual working model is a completely different game altogether. The real reason models are generally difficult to understand is because modeling is about building a representation of a business, project, or even a process and creating scenarios and sensitivities of possible outcomes that could arise when certain variables are manipulated. There are a couple of distinct types of businesses, each type with unusual challenges, and each challenge may be a project, and each project may have many different processes. As a result, no two models will ever be same. Over the years, I have found that the best way to describe a financial model is to describe the physical business or project because that is what the model will represent.

It has been becoming increasingly evident in recent years that the demands and therefore the requirements of the financial modeler have been greatly expanded from the typical spreadsheet jockeys of yesteryear. The playing field has changed, and modelers are now seasoned professionals in their own right and come from areas such as accounting, engineering, and legal.

Modelers are expected to be commercially savvy as well as analytical. In addition, while modeling requires a certain amount of hands-on development, the modern-day financial modeler should also be comfortable with presenting and communicating to all levels of business. Your typical modeler today is not just someone who has a strong appreciation of information technology (IT) but has other skills such as project management, change control, financial and commercial acumen, stakeholder management, and communication skills.

Finally, there is a high expectation that modelers are highly skilled with Excel (and to some extent Microsoft Access, particularly for data analytics). While touted as a spreadsheet application, Microsoft Excel is so much more. In the right hands, it's a serious development tool with very powerful analysis features. As the versions of Excel have improved since Excel 2000, it has become a respected development platform in its own right. Applications written using Excel are now often found alongside those written using Visual Basic for Applications (VBA) code, C++, .NET, and so on, as part of many corporations' core suite of business-critical applications. Indeed, Excel is sometimes used for the client end of web-based applications, made particularly easy with Excel XML import/export features.

My hope for you as you read this book is that you acquire an inside understanding of modeling, its challenges, and its issues. I also hope that you become more aware of the numerous possibilities of how to model but don't feel restricted to following one methodology. Maybe along the way, as you read this book, you will begin to feel comfortable with calling yourself a financial modeler.

CHAPTER

1

Financial Modeling: An Overview

This chapter serves as a background to financial modeling by providing a definition and describing the financial modeling environment.

Financial Modeling: A Definition

Modeling is a specific discipline that often but not exclusively uses spreadsheets. Financial modeling is, in fact, a part of financial analysis and emphasizes the interpretation and output of inputs and variables. A suitable definition should mention processes, variables, and quantitative relations, hence the following definition:

> *Financial modeling is a theoretical construction of a project, process, or transaction in a spreadsheet that deals with the identification of key drivers and variables and a set of logical and quantitative relationships between them.*

Microsoft Excel as the Modeler's Tool

Financial modeling is very closely linked with the history of spreadsheets, specifically the development of Microsoft Excel. Over time, spreadsheets have become the primary tool for the flexible manipulation of data, and Excel is the dominant spreadsheet tool. Of course, there are a number of other modeling software programs, including Oracle Essbase, MoSes, and SAS Financial Management, that primarily aid in financial analytics. One aspect that almost all these proprietary software programs lack, however, is flexibility. The result has been a boon for Excel, as it has filled the gap due not only to its flexibility but also because of its relatively low learning curve.

The other reason for Excel's success as a modeler's tool is due to the success of the Microsoft Office suite. MS Office is arguably the most dominant and widely used suite of applications in software history. As its dominance has increased, so has the number of applications it offers and the versatility of those applications. For modelers, being able to design and build models in Excel, write Visual Basic for Applications (VBA) code, and integrate the code (VBA macros) into the larger Visual Basic suite to create custom software applications, is a real benefit that is unparalleled. Modelers can also link their models to a data store by using Access, which can be integrated together with SQL server, and then create dynamic, data-driven presentations through PowerPoint. They can then take these PowerPoint presentations and produce automated documentation and user manuals in MS Word all in one place.

Functional spreadsheet applications were first developed in the 1980s with the release of Lotus 1-2-3. Microsoft Excel for Windows was first released in 1987 as Excel 2.0. The very first version was Excel 1.0, which was released in 1985 and was an Apple Mac version only. It was not until the release of Microsoft Excel 95 that spreadsheet applications became widely used within the business world. It was also at this point that financial modeling began to emerge as a bona fide discipline around the world. Since the release of Microsoft Excel 95, spreadsheet application functionality has improved at an exponential rate, providing model developers with the tools to construct increasingly sophisticated models.

Today, modeling is recognized for its ability to enable business decision-making and solve often complex questions about the future. The demand for experienced modelers has risen steadily over time. This trend will continue for some years to come because more and more businesses are realizing that an experienced financial modeler can provide significant added value to any process, business, or project.

In order to meet the increasingly complex demands of model users, financial modelers have significantly improved their modeling skills, not only by being technical modelers but by being experts in business in their own right. Hence, it's quite noticeable that modelers are increasingly coming from professions such as accounting and engineering.

Note Excel Versions to Date

Excel 1.0

This version was released by Microsoft in September 1985. This was not a serious modeling tool at this stage and therefore lacked most of the common functionality that we associate with Excel applications today.

Excel 5.0 (Version 5)

This version was released in 1993 and gave us the first look at Visual Basic for Applications (VBA).

Excel 95 (Version 7)

Released in 1995, Excel 95 was a reworked, 32-bit version of Excel 5.0. Although there was little change from previous versions, this version was noticeably more stable and had better integration with the other Microsoft Office applications.

Excel 97 (Version 8)

This version was released in 1997 and was a major upgrade. Significant changes included a full VBA editor with separate code modules, user forms, and class modules. One of the most useful enhancements for VBA programmers was the introduction of Event Procedures. The entire structure of Command Bars (menus and toolbars) was completely changed and enhanced. On the user interface side of Excel, Conditional Formatting and Data Validation were added.

Excel 2000 (Version 9)

Released in 1999, an updated version of the VBA language (VBA6) was introduced, incorporating modeless user forms and some much needed new language functions such as Join and Split. Excel 2000 was the first version to support the COM Add-in model, which allowed users to write add-ins that could work in any Office applications.

Excel 2002 (Version 10)

Released in 2001, there were no substantial changes on the VBA component of excel. On the user interface side, Smart Tags and the Formula Evaluation tool were probably the most prominent additions. The overall appearance of Excel was modified to provide a softer color palette, and the ability to recover corrupt files was substantially improved.

Excel 2003 (Version 11)

This version only had some minor enhancements but did include the introduction of XML.

Excel 2007 (Version 12)

Released in 2007, this version was a major upgrade from the previous version. Similar to other updated Microsoft Office products, Excel 2007 used the new ribbon menu system. This was different from what users were familiar with, but the number of mouse clicks needed to reach a given functionality was generally less. For example, removing grid lines only required two mouse clicks. Most business users would agree that the replacement of the straightforward menu system with the more convoluted ribbon dramatically reduced productivity in the beginning, although this method is now accepted as being more intuitive.

Excel 2010 (Version 14)

Released in 2009, this version featured a few enhancements but was more about making Excel an online application. Excel 2010 was designed to enable working through cloud services. Even with the enablement of cloud services to promote collaborative working, there still remains the central issue that Excel is a single-user environment and therefore cloud has not had the impact that could have been gained were it a multi-user application.

Excel 2013 (Version 15)

This version was released in August 2012 and included minor enhancements, such as the increased smoothness of the user interface and the enhancement of the display of graphics.

Where Are Financial Models Used?

When we talk about financial modeling, we are really looking at quite a range of tasks, including data analysis, scenario analysis, financial management, information processing, software development, and project management. Models are very specific to each situation and will often contain confidential information. As a result, there are very few physical examples of financial models available in the public domain.

Financial models are used in the finance departments of most organizations, but particularly are employed in these areas:

- Investment banking: Risk modeling, option pricing models, and various quantitative models
- Insurance: Insolvency models, actuarial models, risk models (Monte Carlo simulations)
- Retail banking: Funding models (models that can assess client viability by using a number of metrics), credit models
- Corporate finance: Capital budgeting models, cost of capital, financial statement analysis, governance models (SOX compliance testing)
- Governments and institutions: Econometric analysis-based models (used to forecast the socioeconomy in a country or region), macroeconomic models (used to analyze the like effect of government policy decisions on variables such as foreign exchange rates, interest rates, disposable income, and the gross national product)
- Outsourcing and BPO (business process outsourcing): Cost modeling, price and margin models, bid models

There are differing types of financial models, depending on their objectives and goals, such as the following:

- Transactions: Used in acquisitions, divestments
- Investments: Used in capital projects such as procuring new equipment and property development.
- Corporate finance: Used to assist in deciding the best capital/corporate structure of a company
- Project financing: Used by banks to show if borrowers will be able to meet repayments and stay within the covenants set by the bank
- Joint venture: Used to calculate returns to various parties at various exit times

The following figures are from a commercial bid model that was designed and built for a large telecommunications organization in order to understand the profits, losses, and cash flows for their outsourcing deals. As such, Figure 1-1 to Figure 1-4 should provide a visual as to what the parts of a specific type of financial model may look like.

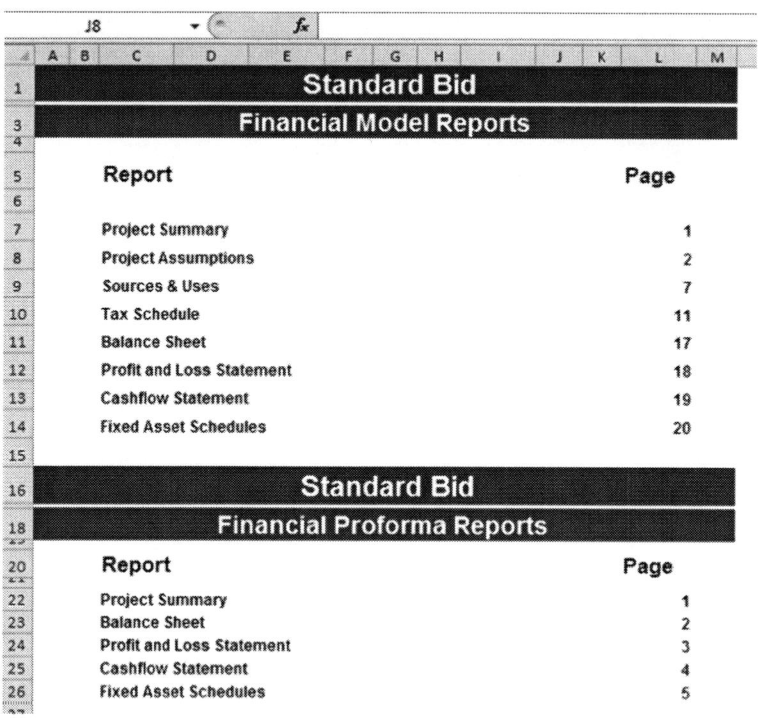

Figure 1-1. This figure shows the cover of a bid model

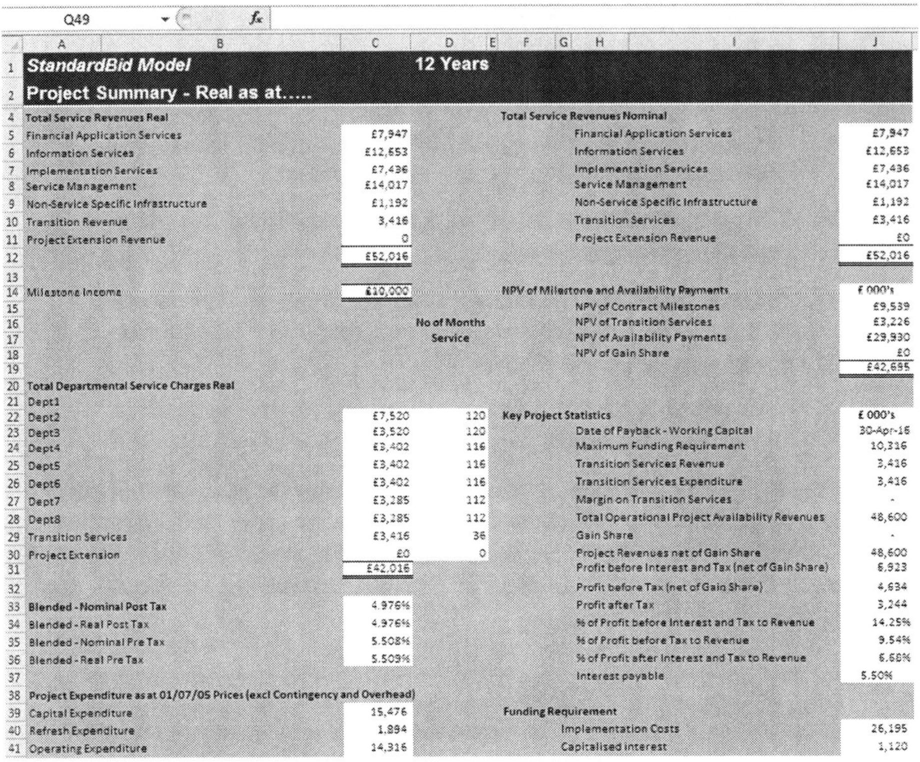

Q49 *fx*

	A–B	C	D	F–I	J
1	*StandardBid Model*		12 Years		
2	Project Summary - Real as at.....				
4	**Total Service Revenues Real**			**Total Service Revenues Nominal**	
5	Financial Application Services	£7,947		Financial Application Services	£7,947
6	Information Services	£12,653		Information Services	£12,653
7	Implementation Services	£7,436		Implementation Services	£7,436
8	Service Management	£14,017		Service Management	£14,017
9	Non-Service Specific Infrastructure	£1,192		Non-Service Specific Infrastructure	£1,192
10	Transition Revenue	3,416		Transition Services	£3,416
11	Project Extension Revenue	0		Project Extension Revenue	£0
12		£52,016			£52,016
13					
14	Milestone Income	£10,000		**NPV of Milestone and Availability Payments**	£ 000's
15				NPV of Contract Milestones	£9,539
16			No of Months	NPV of Transition Services	£3,226
17			Service	NPV of Availability Payments	£29,930
18				NPV of Gain Share	£0
19					£42,695
20	**Total Departmental Service Charges Real**				
21	Dept1				
22	Dept2	£7,520	120	**Key Project Statistics**	£ 000's
23	Dept3	£3,520	120	Date of Payback - Working Capital	30-Apr-16
24	Dept4	£3,402	116	Maximum Funding Requirement	10,316
25	Dept5	£3,402	116	Transition Services Revenue	3,416
26	Dept6	£3,402	116	Transition Services Expenditure	3,416
27	Dept7	£3,285	112	Margin on Transition Services	-
28	Dept8	£3,285	112	Total Operational Project Availability Revenues	48,600
29	Transition Services	£3,416	36	Gain Share	-
30	Project Extension	£0	0	Project Revenues net of Gain Share	48,600
31		£42,016		Profit before Interest and Tax (net of Gain Share)	6,923
32				Profit before Tax (net of Gain Share)	4,634
33	**Blended - Nominal Post Tax**	4.976%		Profit after Tax	3,244
34	Blended - Real Post Tax	4.976%		% of Profit before Interest and Tax to Revenue	14.25%
35	Blended - Nominal Pre Tax	5.508%		% of Profit before Tax to Revenue	9.54%
36	Blended - Real Pre Tax	5.509%		% of Profit after Interest and Tax to Revenue	6.68%
37				Interest payable	5.50%
38	**Project Expenditure as at 01/07/05 Prices (excl Contingency and Overhead)**				
39	Capital Expenditure	15,476		**Funding Requirement**	
40	Refresh Expenditure	1,894		Implementation Costs	26,195
41	Operating Expenditure	14,316		Capitalised interest	1,120

Figure 1-2. This figure depicts a summary from a bid model

H16 fx 61.0343887900609

	A / B	C	D	E	F	G	H
1	**Standard Bid Model**						
2	**Profit and Loss Account**						
3	**Real as at......** Financial Years						
5							
6	FY (01/04 - 31/03)		01/04/05	01/10/05	01/04/06	01/10/06	01/04/07
7		Total	30/09/05	31/03/06	30/09/06	31/03/07	30/09/07
8			1	2	3	4	5
9	PROFIT & LOSS ACCOUNT						
10							
11	Turnover						
12	*Availability Payments*						
13	Financial Advisory Services	4,447	-	-	-	-	51
14	Information Services	7,153	-	-	-	-	82
15	Implementation Services	6,436	-	-	-	-	73
16	SSC Services	5,355	-	-	-	-	61
17	Service Management	14,017	-	-	-	-	160
18	Programme Management	1,192	-	-	-	-	14
19	*Milestone payments*						
20	Financial Advisory Services	3,500	-	480	1,449	1,220	258
21	Information Services	5,500	-	565	1,558	505	133
22	Implementation Services	1,000	-	2	7	15	435
23	SSC Services	-	-	-	-	-	-
24	Service Management	-	-	-	-	-	-
25	Programme Management	-	-	-	-	-	-
26	Transition Services Income	3,416	-	362	723	723	703
27	Project Extension	-	-	-	-	-	-
28	Charges to 3rd parties	-	-	-	-	-	-
29	Lease Receipts WIP	-	-	-	-	-	-
31	**Total Turnover**	52,016	-	1,410	3,737	2,463	1,969
34							
35	Operating Costs						
36	Non-Recurring Pay	5,159	-	737	1,665	1,268	527
37	Non-Recurring Non-Pay	13,103	-	1,578	4,840	2,837	1,862
38	Recurring Pay	11,780	-	35	152	385	562
39	Recurring Non-Pay	8,363	-	75	363	301	224
40	Non-Recurring Pay - Refresh	425	-	-	-	-	-
41	Non-Recurring Non-Pay - Refresh	1,727	-	-	-	-	-
42	Amortisation of Capitalised Interest	1,120	-	-	-	6	19
43	Transition Services Expenditure	3,416	-	362	723	723	703
44	Project Extension	-	-	-	-	-	-
45	Depreciation	-	-	-	-	-	-
46	Lease Rentals	-	-	-	-	-	-
48	**Total Operating Costs**	45,093	-	2,786	7,743	5,519	3,897

Figure 1-3. This figure is a sample of the profit and loss (income statement) from a bid model

V89

	A	B	C	D	E	F	G	H
1	Standard Bid Model							
2	Cash flow							
3	Real as at.....		Financial Years					
5		FY (01/04 - 31/03)		01/04/05	01/10/05	01/04/06	01/10/06	01/04/07
6			Total	30/09/05	31/03/06	30/09/06	31/03/07	30/09/07
7				1	2	3	4	5
9	CASH FLOW STATEMENT							
10								
11		Operating Revenue (Turnover)						
12		*Availability Payments*						
13		Financial Advisory Services	4,447	-	-	-	-	51
14		Information Services	7,153	-	-	-	-	82
15		Implementation Services	6,436	-	-	-	-	73
16		SSC Services	5,355	-	-	-	-	61
17		Service Management	14,017	-	-	-	-	160
18		Programme Management	1,192	-	-	-	-	14
19		*Milestone payments*	-					
20		Financial Advisory Services	3,500	-	480	1,449	1,220	258
21		Information Services	5,500	-	565	1,558	505	133
22		Implementation Services	1,000	-	2	7	15	435
23		SSC Services	-	-	-	-	-	-
24		Service Management	-	-	-	-	-	-
25		Programme Management	-	-	-	-	-	-
26		Transition Services	3,416	-	362	723	723	703
27		Project Extension	-	-	-	-	-	-
28		Charges to 3rd parties	-	-	-	-	-	-
29		Lease Receipts	-	-	-	-	-	-
31		Total Operating Income	52,016	-	1,410	3,737	2,463	1,969
34								
35								
36		Total operating costs	45,093	-	2,786	7,743	5,519	3,897
38		Profit before Tax and Interest	6,923	-	(1,377)	(4,006)	(3,056)	(1,928)
40								
41		add back: depreciation & other non-cash items	1,120	-	-	-	6	19
42		(increase)/decrease in stock	-	-	-	-	-	-
43		(increase)/decrease in debtors	(0)	-	-	-	-	88
44		increase/(decrease) in creditors	0	-	382	172	(212)	(80)
45								
47		Net Cash Inflows from Operating Activities	8,044	-	(994)	(3,835)	(3,263)	(2,076)

Figure 1-4. A sample cash flow from an bid model

The Role of the Financial Modeler

Financial modelers are primarily responsible for the design and build of the model. They also are expected to manage the financial modeling process—from the start of the project to when the model is delivered and in use. (This process is discussed in greater detail in Chapter 4.)

As mentioned previously, financial modelers come from a number of different professions, but by and large the majority are actually accountants. One of the reasons why the accounting profession is a breeding ground for modelers is that much of financial modeling requires the modeler to have a good grasp of a large host of financial concepts. However, this is by no means the main requirement for being a professional financial modeler. More importantly perhaps is the modeler's ability to quickly assimilate large amounts of information and then filter that information to accurately identify underlying issues.

Ironically, despite the importance of effective data processing in financial modeling, not all modelers are skilled in this regard. In fact, how modelers process and then interpret information is very much dependent upon their experience. For example, modelers who lack business and industry experience will often make fundamental data processing mistakes. If you are a modeler lacking in experience, take heart. Having a profoundly analytical and questioning nature and being able to ask the right people the right questions to fill in your knowledge of a given project will also serve you well. Lastly, modelers should also be comfortable communicating to people of any background and at any level in an organization. When communicating, remember to abide by the three C's: be *clear*, be *concise*, and *cut to the chase*.

Those who do not have a formal accounting background should not let this stop them from considering a career as a modeler. It is certainly an advantage to have an accounting background, but many modelers are not accountants and have found that they are not in any way hindered in their work.

Note Accountants use Excel for financial calculations and to generate financial statements and financial metrics. By and large, these statements are casually called financial models, but this misconception could not be further from the truth. A financial model is not just a series of financial statements. It also involves interactions between variables, relationships of key drivers, presenting scenarios, and looking at aspects like "what if."

CHAPTER

2

Financial Modeling Best Practices

Often clients will commission me to look at their existing financial models and make recommendations as to how the models can be expanded or adapted to accommodate changes in their business. Sometimes I am even asked to completely rebuild a model because it does not fit the purpose for which it was built. In almost all of these models that need rebuilding, the lack of good planning is very apparent—especially once the model's structural features are examined. This chapter will give insight into those features and in doing so will equip you with a layer of knowledge about what makes a good financial model.

What Are the Best Practices of Financial Modeling?

There are a number of financial modeling techniques or methods that have withstood the rigor of time. These modeling techniques that have endured time are recognized as part of modeling best practices. You will often hear the phrase "best practice financial modeling." In fact, if you type this phrase into your web search browser, you will find links to several organizations and white papers on the topic. A more accurate term, however, would be "best practices," because essentially it is a series of methods that each by its own merit constitutes a good way to model.

Therefore, for this book, "best practices" refers to a number of ideals and methods that help with modeling. I generally use the analogy of a chef. While there are several types of chefs and they each have their own distinct style, they all largely prescribe to a similar set of practices and have a similar set of core skills that they adopt when preparing food.

In my experience, the majority of people who use models as end users have never seen a model built to best practices, let alone a fully functional financial model. Why would I make such a bold statement? The reality is that the term "model" is quite general and is used today to describe anything that is performed in Excel. For example, if it's a financial worksheet or workbook, it tends to be termed a "model." The result is that with literally hundreds of millions of financial worksheets out there, a very small portion are out-and-out financial models.

Clear differences exist between a best practice financial model and a general financial model, such as the level of documentation in the model or the ease of usability. When working with clients, I introduce customers to a best practice financial model this way. I open two models for the clients to review, one which is a best practice model and the other is a general model. Then I ask them to identify which one is the best practice model. It does not matter who the customer is, the result is always the same: the best practice model is always chosen correctly. The next section will highlight these fundamental best practices and will also provide examples.

Keep the Constituents Separate

Separating the inputs, calculations, and outputs is a mandatory requirement—this is possibly the single most quoted principle of financial modeling. There are clear reasons for these separations. Separating the modeling stages ensures that the number of errors that otherwise would have been made due to the user's lack of understanding of the model can be cut down.

Separating the inputs and outputs assists with auditing and tracking, which ultimately gives the model credibility as it provides transparency to outputs (the financial statements). The separation is essential and is an indicator that the model has been developed by someone who understands financial modeling. Being able to identify inputs of a spreadsheet is crucial for understanding the effect on the outputs, such as what the outputs are based on.

It is also important that inputs can be used to perform "what if" analysis on outputs. Models lack these separations due to lack of planning, and unfortunately for all who will use them these models are very likely to have any number of acute errors. My colleagues and I at Isys Systems use our benchmark error testing to assess the likelihood of finding serious errors during model audits. Our clients are almost always shocked when we inform them of the frequency and types of errors we have encountered. We find significant errors on at least 98% of all audits that we perform. The main reason for this appalling error rate is that the models have not been planned, designed, and built as financial models, nor have they been built by bona fide financial modelers.

Here is a list of several ways to separate inputs from the calculations and outputs:

- Use different colors. For example, use a yellow cell fill for inputs and a gray cell fill for calculations and outputs. This is usually suitable for very small models.
- Use different areas of a single worksheet. For example, label an area "Inputs" at the top of the worksheet and "Calculations" below the inputs with the outputs below the calculations. This is usually suitable for relatively simple models.
- Use different worksheets for the inputs, calculations, and outputs for medium and large models.

Tip You could create a special style in Excel and apply it to all input cells. This way, you could change the parameters of the style at any time, and it would automatically apply to all relevant cells.

Take a look at the worksheet in Figure 2-1. Notice that there are inputs, calculations, and outputs. How would you know by looking at the worksheet which are inputs, calculations, and outputs?

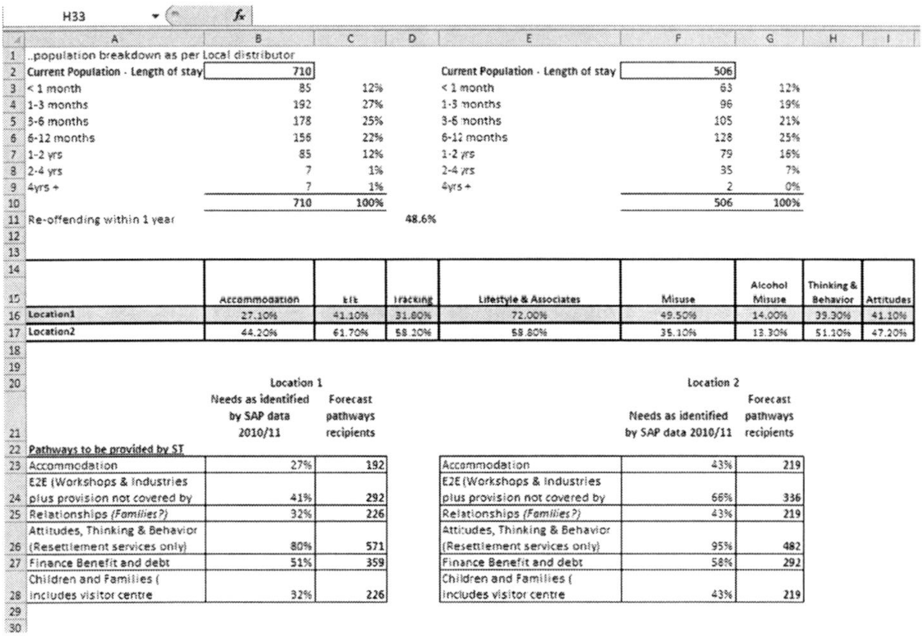

H33

	A	B	C	D	E	F	G
1	..population breakdown as per Local distributor						
2	Current Population - Length of stay	710			Current Population - Length of stay	506	
3	< 1 month	85	12%		< 1 month	63	12%
4	1-3 months	192	27%		1-3 months	96	19%
5	3-6 months	178	25%		3-6 months	105	21%
6	6-12 months	156	22%		6-12 months	128	25%
7	1-2 yrs	85	12%		1-2 yrs	79	16%
8	2-4 yrs	7	1%		2-4 yrs	35	7%
9	4yrs +	7	1%		4yrs +	2	0%
10		710	100%			506	100%
11	Re-offending within 1 year			48.6%			

	A	Accommodation	E1E	Tracking	Lifestyle & Associates	Misuse	Alcohol Misuse	Thinking & Behavior	Attitudes
16	Location1	27.10%	41.10%	31.80%	72.00%	49.50%	14.00%	39.30%	41.10%
17	Location2	44.20%	61.70%	58.20%	58.80%	35.10%	13.30%	51.10%	47.20%

	Location 1	Needs as identified by SAP data 2010/11	Forecast pathways recipients	Location 2	Needs as identified by SAP data 2010/11	Forecast pathways recipients
22	Pathways to be provided by ST					
23	Accommodation	27%	192	Accommodation	43%	219
24	E2E (Workshops & Industries plus provision not covered by	41%	292	E2E (Workshops & Industries plus provision not covered by	66%	336
25	Relationships *(Families?)*	32%	226	Relationships *(Families?)*	43%	219
26	Attitudes, Thinking & Behavior (Resettlement services only)	80%	571	Attitudes, Thinking & Behavior (Resettlement services only)	95%	482
27	Finance Benefit and debt	51%	359	Finance Benefit and debt	58%	292
28	Children and Families (includes visitor centre	32%	226	Children and Families (includes visitor centre	43%	219

Figure 2-1. This spreadsheet model design does not separate the inputs, calculations, and outputs

This worksheet would be referred to as model by non-modelers, but it is not a financial model. Why? The lack of organization is the clue, and I will let you in on a secret. The single most important part of any model is not the inputs or calculations but the outputs. Why? Because ultimately the validity of a financial model will always be judged on its ability to produce the output that are required by the clients. In Figure 2-1, it's not clear which part of the worksheet are the inputs, nor which are the outputs. Because of the lack of organization, this worksheet presents numerous questions concerning its credentials as a financial model.

Contrast the spreadsheet in Figure 2-1 with the one shown in Figure 2-2, which shows how the inputs, calculations, and outputs can be separated in one worksheet.

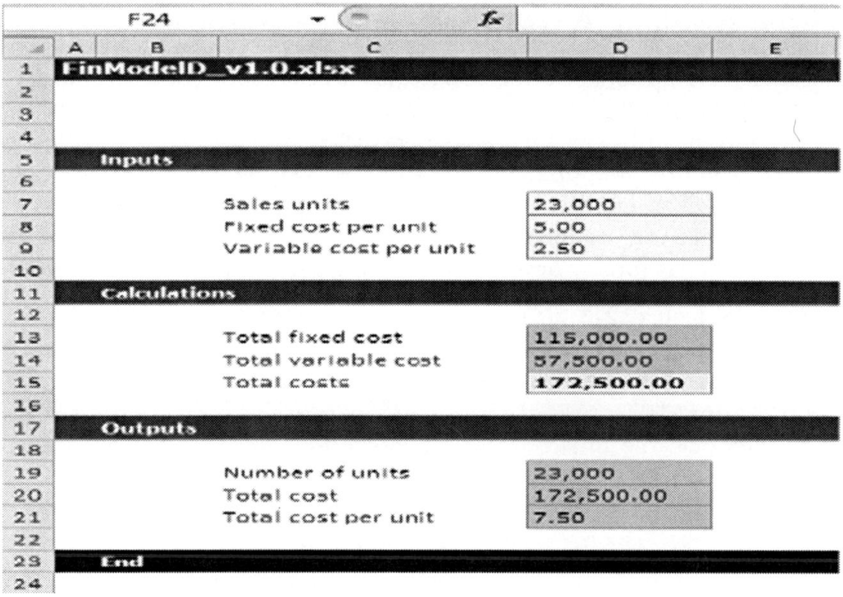

Figure 2-2. This spreadsheet model design separates the inputs, calculations, and outputs

The spreadsheet in Figure 2-2 uses color styles to distinguish between inputs cells and calculations cells. The use of color styles to provide visual cues in models is a recurring theme in models and is part of the modeling styles. Colors give guidance to users as to what actions they are required to take and where for instance using a pale yellow color on a cell is sign that a user input is required in that cell. They also can inform users that a cell has a calculation function and that they should leave it alone. If you intend to follow best practice, use colors to provide visual cues to your users. Also be sure to include a style sheet in the model that defines the significance of the colors. (Cover style sheets will be discussed later in Chapter 13, How to Capture Document and Track Assumptions in Your Model.)

With larger and more complex models, it is often good practice and more practical to display outputs in a separate worksheet. For instance, you may need to provide a balance sheet, income statement, and statement of cash flows each on a worksheet of their own.

Reduce Implicit Assumptions to a Minimum

Sometimes assumptions will get built into the structure of the model. For example, an assumption that the inflation rate of 4% will start from Year 2 could be implicit in having the repayment calculations start from the second time period in the model. Even so, a better way would be to model this assumption with an explicit input so that the user can quickly see how much the inflation rate is in each year and can vary the rate if needed. This would make the formulas more complex, but the model would be more adaptable.

For example, Figure 2-3 clearly shows the inflation rate of 4% in Year 2. Thereafter, it is also stated in each year. In this figure, the inflation has been made explicit and therefore is unlikely to cause confusion to the user. This is an important modeling practice to include because any assumptions that may have an effect on the final outputs of the model will be clear, apparent, and easily read.

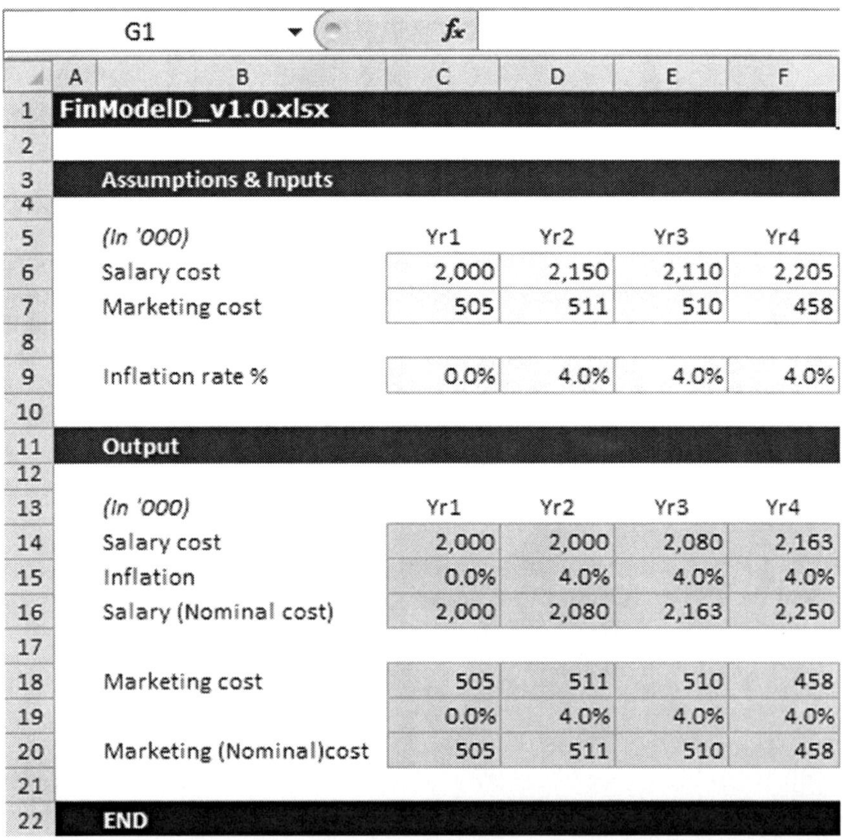

G1 fx

	A	B	C	D	E	F
1	FinModelD_v1.0.xlsx					
2						
3		Assumptions & Inputs				
4						
5		*(In '000)*	Yr1	Yr2	Yr3	Yr4
6		Salary cost	2,000	2,150	2,110	2,205
7		Marketing cost	505	511	510	458
8						
9		Inflation rate %	0.0%	4.0%	4.0%	4.0%
10						
11		Output				
12						
13		*(In '000)*	Yr1	Yr2	Yr3	Yr4
14		Salary cost	2,000	2,000	2,080	2,163
15		Inflation	0.0%	4.0%	4.0%	4.0%
16		Salary (Nominal cost)	2,000	2,080	2,163	2,250
17						
18		Marketing cost	505	511	510	458
19			0.0%	4.0%	4.0%	4.0%
20		Marketing (Nominal)cost	505	511	510	458
21						
22		END				

Figure 2-3. The inflation rates are explicit and clearly shown in each year in this model

Note Implicit means something is not directly expressed, or rather it is expressed indirectly and is therefore not apparent. Explicit means something is clearly expressed and leaves nothing to conjecture and is therefore clearly defined or formulated. Not all assumptions can be made explicit, so it is important to find a balance between the model's flexibility and complexity. The main principle is that the modeler should always make a conscious decision about whether assumptions should be implicitly or explicitly modeled.

Avoid Using Constants Inside Formulas

It is best to steer clear from using constants inside formulas as they are a cause of major errors in models. You should use constants inside formulas only for very obvious things that never change, such as there being 12 months in a year. Any less straightforward constants usually warrant being separated out just to make clear that they exist. For example, if you are creating a model to analyze the costs within every department in an organization, the number of departments in the organization would be fixed and this would be situation where that number could be used a constant.

Tip Ironically, the way that constants are used in models is an indication as to the competency of the modeler. In general, a seasoned modeler will never place constants within a formula. Test it out for yourself if you have the opportunity to audit or view a financial model. Check for these constants in formulas and see how many you find; a sound model will contain fewer than 10 instances of constants in formula.

In Figure 2-4, the contract duration is 60 months, and a contract end date is needed. One way would be to create a formula based on the constant that there are always either 30 days or 31 days in a month, except for February. The number 30.44 days could be used, but as I later demonstrate, it is far from ideal. In Figure 2-4, the contract end date will be January 1, 2018.

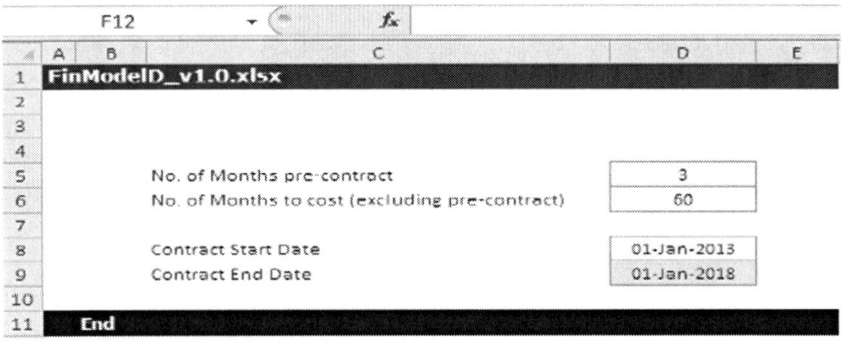

Figure 2-4. A constant has been used in this formula and will now need careful attention

Read through the following formula:

=(D6 * 30.44)+D8, that is 60 Month x 30.44 days + Start Date

The problems associated with using a constant number such as 30.44 days can wreak havoc. Once such a constant has been plugged in, model users must be aware of its use and that it is static. For example, with this model, there will be synchronization issues during a leap year. In addition, in this case, the use of 30.44 days is far too rudimentary. If you multiply this constant number by 12 months, the answer is 365.28 days which if used in models will cause issues with date timings. For an alternative method, see how the contract end date differs in Figure 2-5.

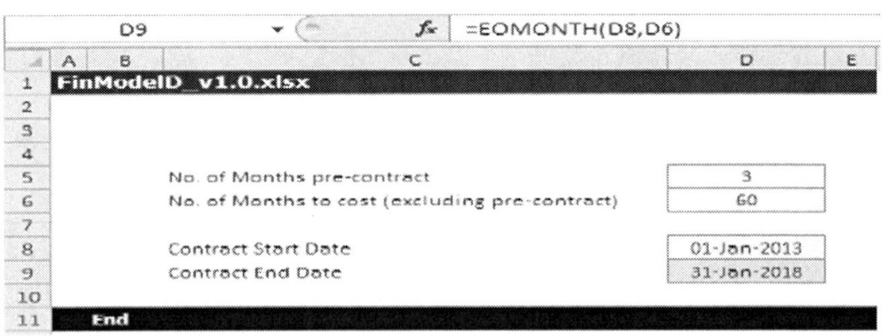

Figure 2-5. A function has been used to avoid placing a constant in the formula.

In Figure 2-5, this model uses a built-in Excel function that handles months with the EOMONTH (start date, the number of months after the date formula), as it allows the modeler to use months and days consistently and unambiguously. One of the challenges for a modeler is to find ways of avoiding constants in formula while as the same time keeping the model simple.

Let Inputs Drive Your Models, Not Calculations

The assumptions that you develop for the model should be guided by the final users' thinking. It is very easy to base assumptions purely from the modeler's point of view, which then leads to models that just don't match what the final users expect. This is a frequent and potentially dangerous trap to fall in for many reasons, and it will invariably highlight weaknesses in the modeler's understanding of the subject. Beware of this trap because it verges in the realms of professional negligence. When modeling, all assumptions can be traced and documented to the sponsor of the model.

Tip Consider this scenario. You have been asked to develop a model that calculates staff salary increases every year (indexation). The sponsor of the model has provided you with a salary rate. As a modeler, be sure to use that rate and resist the temptation to create your own rates to save time or to make it easier on yourself. If you do, you put yourself at risk of misrepresentation. If the model is used to make critical business decisions and there is a fundamental issue with the salary rates, you will be able to demonstrate that the rates were supplied by the sponsor and avoid some serious legal challenges.

If there are many different types of assumptions, put them on the assumption's sheet in separate small tables with their own headings. Create groups by using tables and labels for sections and subsections. A good approach is to apply indentation to make the logical hierarchy obvious or use grouping to separate headings. By modeling in this way, you will ensure that the user's wishes are being considered.

The diagram on assumptions in Figure 2-6 is a snapshot of part of the assumption register from a very complex IT financial model. But notice that for every assumption line, there is a requirement to provide an assumption owner and also a reference. While this may seem like overkill (particularly on a small model), my advice to any financial modeler is to never neglect the assumption register. This is your insurance policy against potential litigation should the assignment get out of your control and go off-course.

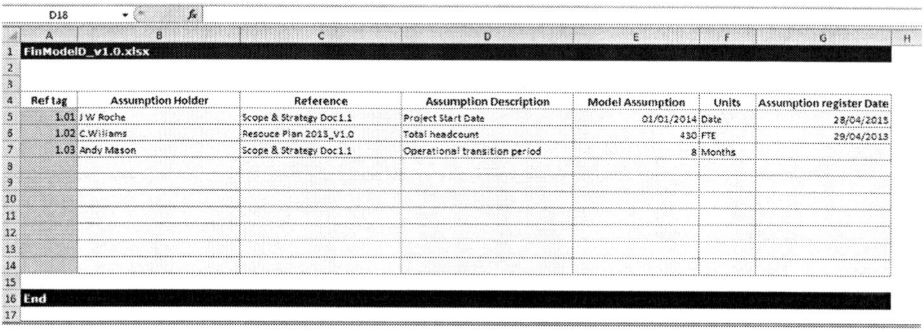
FinModelD_v1.0.xlsx

Ref tag	Assumption Holder	Reference	Assumption Description	Model Assumption	Units	Assumption register Date
1.01	J W Roche	Scope & Strategy Doc1.1	Project Start Date	01/01/2014	Date	28/04/2013
1.02	C.Williams	Resouce Plan 2013_V1.0	Total headcount	430	FTE	29/04/2013
1.03	Andy Mason	Scope & Strategy Doc1.1	Operational transition period	8	Months	

End

Figure 2-6. This is a snapshot of an assumption register. These registers should not be complex, but should who supplied the assumption and give reference where it is used

Have Only One Input for Each Assumption

A very common mistake in models is that of creating multiple input assumptions for the same variable across the model. Duplicating input assumptions will require the user to change a given input in several places. Critically, if the user is unaware of all the changes that are required or forgets to make the changes, then the model will have some flawed inputs, dramatically increasing the risk of error.

The duplication of assumption inputs is common while building large complex models that have multiple modelers. To reduce the possibility of this type of problem, make sure model documentation begins from the design stage and follows through the building and testing stages. Ideally there should be a change control mechanism implemented during the building. If that is not yet possible, consider having a checklist with additions and changes made to the model. When there is more than one modeler, this checklist should be filled out by each modeler daily.

Duplicating assumption inputs is not restricted only to large models. It can also occur when there is a lack of planning on a complex model. I come across this situation regularly during model audits. This occurs because the focus has been on creating calculations prior to understanding the inputs. Then as the complexity of the model becomes greater, the calculations become less adequate to handle the complexity. The modeler will then often lose track of which inputs interact with which calculations and from then on duplication can start to occur. From the model audit aspect, these types of errors are particularly difficult to find. It usually involves a process of elimination to get to the root cause, although fixing the errors is relatively simple.

To avoid the mistake of duplicating assumptions, develop the practice of documenting the assumptions. Instead of just recording where the assumptions came from, also include where it is being used and where it is ending up. This step does mean that the model process will take longer, but the rewards far outweigh the potential heartache of having to recover an assumption input that has complex links.

Figure 2-6 demonstrates a typical assumption register from a model that gives details of where the assumption came from (assumption holder and reference). Take note of the ref tag column. By attaching a unique tag to every assumption, you should then use this tag reference in the model every time that assumption is used. Typically if you leave the first column blank, you can then use this to attach the ref tag. By applying this method, it then becomes quite simple to track where each assumption has ended up and how many times it has been used, which will also expose any duplication of an assumption.

Specify Measurement Units for All Input Assumptions

Model users should be able to understand the measurement unit for every input assumption. These units should be obvious to modelers, but they should not assume that everyone who sees the model over its lifetime will be equally informed. To avoid confusion and especially if a large number of units are involved, designate a separate column for measurement units. This step also helps to avoid errors with the conversion of units. You will be amazed how often measurements are omitted in models and become the cause of confusion. Typically, the measurements can range from anything to currencies, dates, volumes, or resources (usually Full Time Equivalents quoted as FTE).

The Logical Flow of Calculations and Circularity

Formulas should take their parameters from rows above and columns to the left, as this makes the organization of the model more logical. Figure 2-7 illustrates how the model data should reflect how a person can "read" the information as a book, without the need to skip pages and return.

Figure 2-7. Fundamentally, all data must move from left to right and then downward

When the top-down flow cannot be maintained, for example, due to a logical circularity, repeat the relevant rows twice. The ones at the top will refer further down and include the word "circular" in the description. Then the rows at the bottom will be calculated in the usual way from data above and also should have the word "circular." This will make the circularity clear to any user of the model. Nevertheless, always consider if it is possible to use a different approach or to change the input assumptions to avoid circularities, as they usually make models more difficult to use and update. Sometimes, it is preferable to create a macro that would copy and paste values to break the circularity rather than to allow circular references in Excel.

A common area for a logical circularity occurs when calculating interest payments from a calculation, as in Figure 2-8.

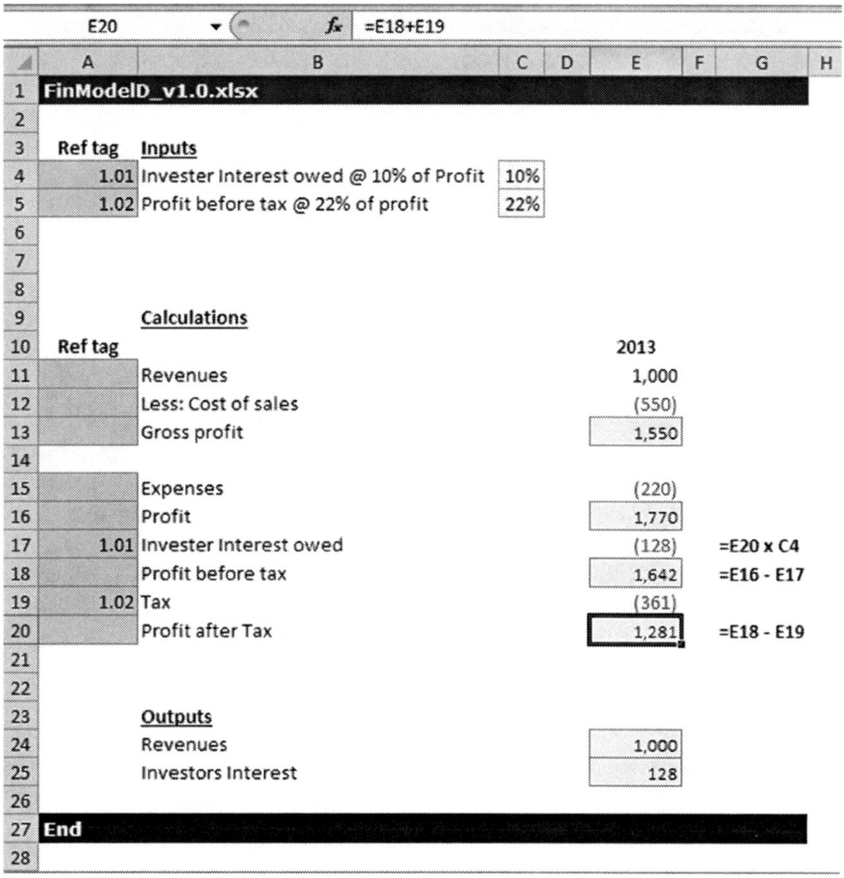

E20 fx =E18+E19

	A	B	C	D	E	F	G	H
1	FinModelD_v1.0.xlsx							
2								
3	Ref tag	Inputs						
4	1.01	Invester Interest owed @ 10% of Profit	10%					
5	1.02	Profit before tax @ 22% of profit	22%					
6								
7								
8								
9		Calculations						
10	Ref tag				2013			
11		Revenues			1,000			
12		Less: Cost of sales			(550)			
13		Gross profit			1,550			
14								
15		Expenses			(220)			
16		Profit			1,770			
17	1.01	Invester Interest owed			(128)		=E20 x C4	
18		Profit before tax			1,642		=E16 - E17	
19	1.02	Tax			(361)			
20		Profit after Tax			1,281		=E18 - E19	
21								
22								
23		Outputs						
24		Revenues			1,000			
25		Investors Interest			128			
26								
27	End							
28								

Figure 2-8. To calculate the interest owed, this figure shows that there is circularity on the profit after tax

Figure 2-8 includes a profit statement and what interest must be paid to an investor. The circularity occurs because the interest to the investor is calculated by using the profit after tax (profit after investor interest is paid). You can see that E17 is formula-based on E20 x the investor percentage, which is 10%. As a result, an endless loop is created. There are a number of options on how you can work with circularity, including these two ways:

- Go to Excel Options. In the Formula section, check the Enable iterative calculation option, as in Figure 2-9.

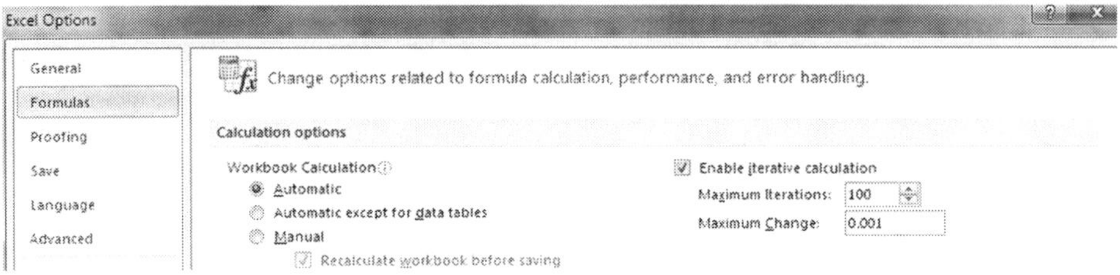

Figure 2-9. Select the option to enable iterative calculations when working with circularity

- Use VBA code (Visual Basic for Applications) to clean out the interest calculation cell every time you enact the code.

Which of these options you choose depends on what is acceptable to your end user. However, consider that it is really a false economy if you choose to enable iterative calculations (the first option). With this option, the circularity will still exist even if you allow iteration in the model. Therein lies the problem. Even though things may appear fine on your workstation, the circularity is likely to kick in again once the model is transferred or opened on a different workstation because the iteration option would not be enabled. When this occurs, it is possible that files could be corrupted and Excel would automatically close down or freeze the screen.

Note I would urge you to avoid circularities at all costs. Not only do they complicate the model, they also help to induce a certain lack of confidence about the ability of the modeler to the end user. As a result, the user's confidence in the model is destroyed. Examine the different ways of working around circularities. The one we most often use at Isys Systems is to create some VBA macro that allows the circularity to be hard-coded out.

Use Consistent Formulas Across Rows

When working with models, it is extremely important to use consistent formulas across the rows. When this principle is not followed, problems and errors will likely occur. For every calculation row, input a single formula and copy it across all the columns. Avoid using a different formula somewhere in the middle of a row. Doing so dramatically increases the risk of error at the development stage and also during any subsequent updates. If inconsistent formulas cannot be avoided, the relevant spreadsheet areas should be clearly marked with color and comments. Even so, such situations indicate a weakness in the model design.

The main concern with inconsistent rows is that users will assume they are consistent. At some point, they will end up trying to copy a formula across or down several cells at one go, thereby overwriting all the unique formulas you have created and plunging the model into generating errors.

Tip Sometimes it will seem impossible to keep this consistency across rows. Once this consistency is broken, however, the model is then vulnerable to errors during its lifetime. These errors will likely end up as the end users' problem. When faced with a dilemma over row or column consistency, ask yourself, "Can I break this into separate columns or rows?" Usually, you can.

In Figure 2-10a and Figure 2-10b, the consistency in row 7 can clearly be seen between column D and column E. But by the time we get to column H in Figure 2-10c, you can see that the formula has subtly changed (the minus "1" on the end is missing). It is no longer the same as the previous columns and has lost its consistency. To compound this problem, there are no visual cues or comments provided to the user to give any warning of this consistency issue.

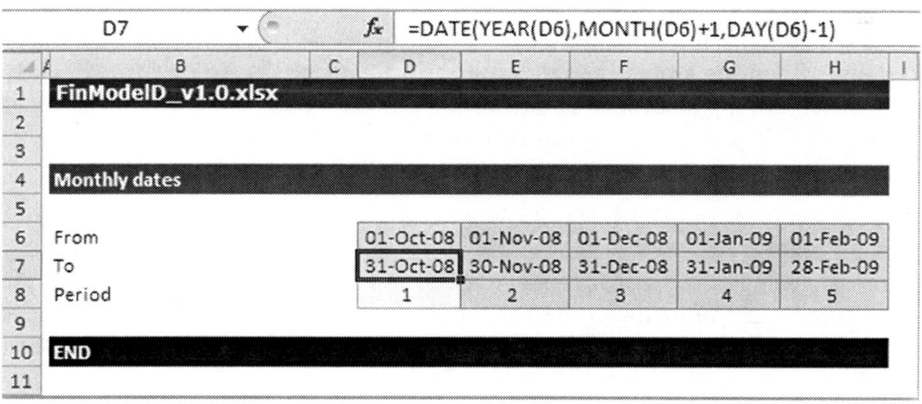

Figure 2-10a. In this figure, column D is the starting formula

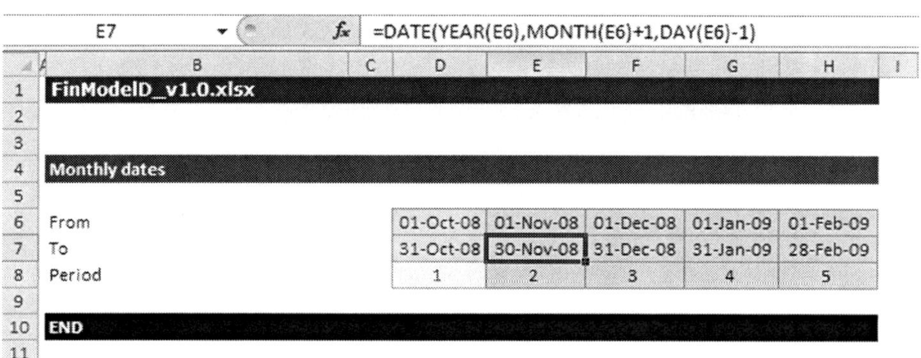

Figure 2-10b. In this figure, the formula in column E is consistent with the formula in column D

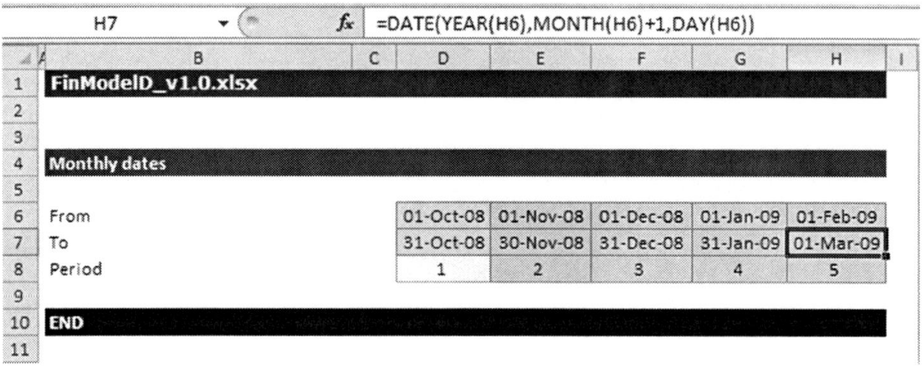

Figure 2-10c. In this figure, the formula in column H is not consistent with previous columns

This situation is not uncommon in financial models and will usually occur because the modeler has chosen to jump straight into creating a formula without considering the design of the model. When performing model reviews or audits, this process is critical to look for and eliminate purely because an inconsistent formula is such a common cause for harm in financial models.

The alternative solutions for dealing with inconsistent formulas all evolve around making the user of the model understand what is happening. From my point of view, avoid inconsistency at all cost. However, if you must break the consistency of the formula, then use colors to highlight the cells where the formula is different (as in Figure 2-10d) and incorporate that into the style sheet (previously shown in Figure 2-2).

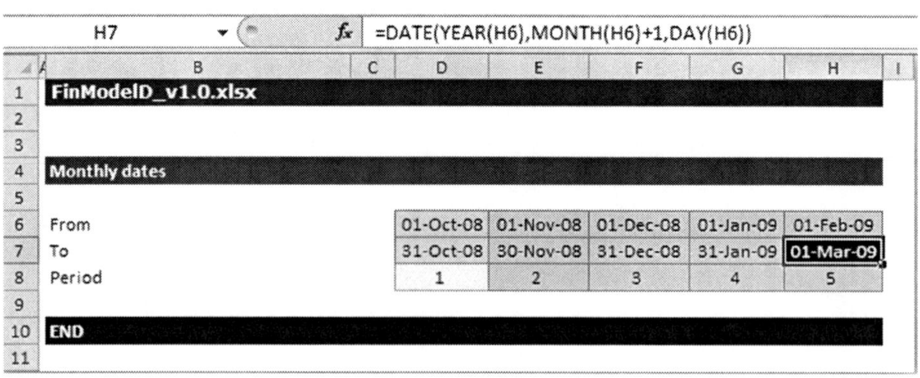

Figure 2-10d. In this figure, the cell with the inconsistent formula in column H is now clearly highlighted

Avoid Mixing Time Periods of Different Lengths

Often the modeler is required to calculate short-term and long-term projections with different granularity. For example, a requirement might be to produce monthly forecasts for the first two years and yearly projections for a number of years after that. The temptation is sometimes to create monthly columns, followed by yearly columns (see Figure 2-11). Such a design decision should be avoided. You would either need to remember to change formulas in the middle of every row, or you would need to make the formulas very complex to take care of the different period lengths correctly. Both options are likely to lead to problems over the model lifetime because it will become very difficult to create totals without making errors.

J1

	A	B	C	D	E	F	G	H
1	FinModelD_v1.0.xlsx							
2								
3	Ref tag		Oct-11	Nov-11	Dec-11	2012	2013	2014
4		Profit	120	140	85	1,240	1,320	1,430
5	1.02	Less: Cost of Sales	(45)	(56)	(34)	(745)	(790)	(775)
6		Gross profit	75	84	51	495	530	655
7								
8	END							
9								

Figure 2-11. The mixture of years and months for the dates in this figure will likely create problems for the end users

My recommended approach is to build the entire model using the smallest required granularity (that is, monthly in the case of Figure 2-11). You can always aggregate monthly columns into annual ones on a separate summary sheet. With Excel 2003 or earlier versions, it is impossible to build the entire model on the smallest required granularity due to column number restrictions. Instead, use distinct sheets to model time intervals of different lengths. Fortunately, there are no longer limitations on the number of columns in Excel 2010.

Tip This date granularity is typical of modeling problems that occur very frequently. If there's any situation that can cause a model to be completely ripped and rebuilt, it is this date situation. Therefore, it is best to figure out how you will overcome dates. If you build your model in months, even if you are reporting in quarters or annually, you can always aggregate up.

Figure 2-12 is an excerpt from a timeline from a back-office operations model. The timeline is a part of the model that acts as a calendar, and it allows users to move dates and times flexibly while still keeping the model base structure. Note that the timeline will always have the smallest date length, in this case months, and then into financial quarters and also years. This format allows the modeler to base the model calculations on months and then extrapolate these to financial quarters and annual periods when required with ease.

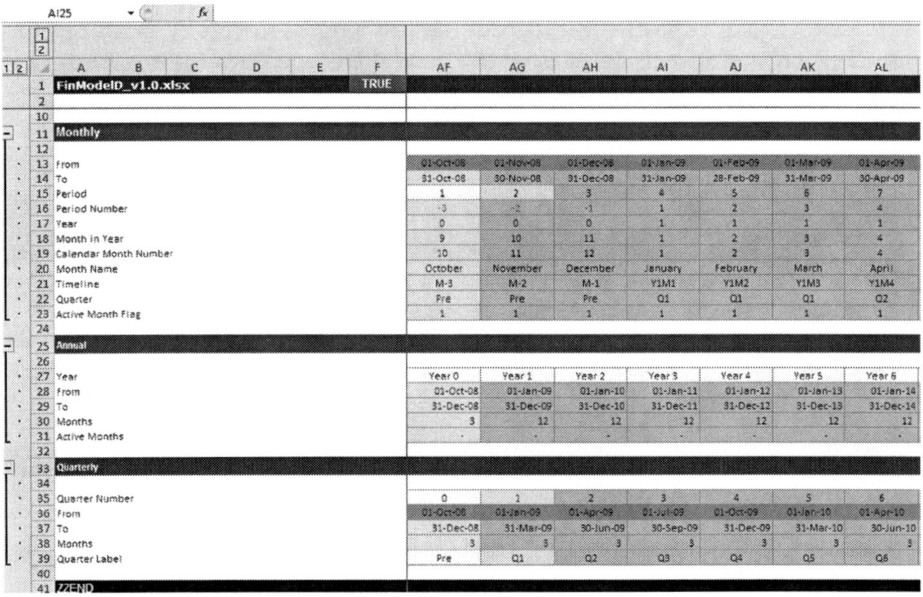

	A	AF	AG	AH	AI	AJ	AK	AL
1	FinModelD_v1.0.xlsx TRUE							
2								
10								
11	Monthly							
12								
13	From	01-Oct-08	01-Nov-08	01-Dec-08	01-Jan-09	01-Feb-09	01-Mar-09	01-Apr-09
14	To	31-Oct-08	30-Nov-08	31-Dec-08	31-Jan-09	28-Feb-09	31-Mar-09	30-Apr-09
15	Period	1	2	3	4	5	6	7
16	Period Number	-3	-2	-1	1	2	3	4
17	Year	0	0	0	1	1	1	1
18	Month in Year	9	10	11	1	2	3	4
19	Calendar Month Number	10	11	12	1	2	3	4
20	Month Name	October	November	December	January	February	March	April
21	Timeline	M-3	M-2	M-1	Y1M1	Y1M2	Y1M3	Y1M4
22	Quarter	Pre	Pre	Pre	Q1	Q1	Q1	Q2
23	Active Month Flag	1	1	1	1	1	1	1
24								
25	Annual							
26								
27	Year	Year 0	Year 1	Year 2	Year 3	Year 4	Year 5	Year 6
28	From	01-Oct-08	01-Jan-09	01-Jan-10	01-Jan-11	01-Jan-12	01-Jan-13	01-Jan-14
29	To	31-Dec-08	31-Dec-09	31-Dec-10	31-Dec-11	31-Dec-12	31-Dec-13	31-Dec-14
30	Months	3	12	12	12	12	12	12
31	Active Months	-	-	-	-	-	-	-
32								
33	Quarterly							
34								
35	Quarter Number	0	1	2	3	4	5	6
36	From	01-Oct-08	01-Jan-09	01-Apr-09	01-Jul-09	01-Oct-09	01-Jan-10	01-Apr-10
37	To	31-Dec-08	31-Mar-09	30-Jun-09	30-Sep-09	31-Dec-09	31-Mar-10	30-Jun-10
38	Months	3	3	3	3	3	3	3
39	Quarter Label	Pre	Q1	Q2	Q3	Q4	Q5	Q6
40								
41	ZZEND							

Figure 2-12. This figure depicts the timeline (time intervals) worksheet in a model

Break Up Long Formulas into Simple Pieces

It is best not to reduce the number of cells used by trying to condense too many calculations into a single formula. Writing long and complex formulas that nobody can understand is generally the mark of bad modeling practice.

Try to instead split a complex calculation into smaller pieces and utilize as many rows as required. Usually the more separate calculations you use, the easier it will be to follow and understand the model. With this format, more logical elements will be labeled and the resulting formulas will be much simpler.

Tip If your formula becomes lengthy because you have to repeat some part of it several times, consider creating a defined name for that part. Remember that defined names in Excel can refer not only to cells and ranges, but can also contain formulas. If a formula includes relative references, change it accordingly, depending on where the defined name is used. Defined names refer to a cell or a group of cells that are given a specific name (defined), which then enables the modeler to use that group of cells by referencing the name. They are also called range names.

When creating a formula, keep things as simple as possible; you should spare a thought for the auditor or the person who will use the model. Remember, modeling is not a competition; no one will praise the modeler for having complex formulas, particularly not auditors. The message should be simple and consistent.

Include Automatic Error Checks

A good quality financial model will always have various error traps and checks built into its logic. These help to ensure internal consistency of inputs, calculations, and outputs. Most often such checks represent simple formulas that return zero in case of success and a nonzero value in case of error. For example, to check that a balance sheet balances across all time periods, you should add a row that would subtract total assets from total liabilities. It is a good idea to use different formatting for that row, such as italics or a red font.

Tip Good practice is to provide a consolidation worksheet where all the error checks are catalogued in a dashboard, allowing the user to identify where any errors occur and also the overall model integrity.

Figure 2-13 shows a worksheet in a model. Notice at the top of the sheet the black band with a green cell containing the text "TRUE." By incorporating error checks throughout the model, you can even create sheet-specific checks so that the model user will know if the model is error-free visually just by looking at a worksheet. In comparison, an error would have produced a red cell containing the text "FALSE."

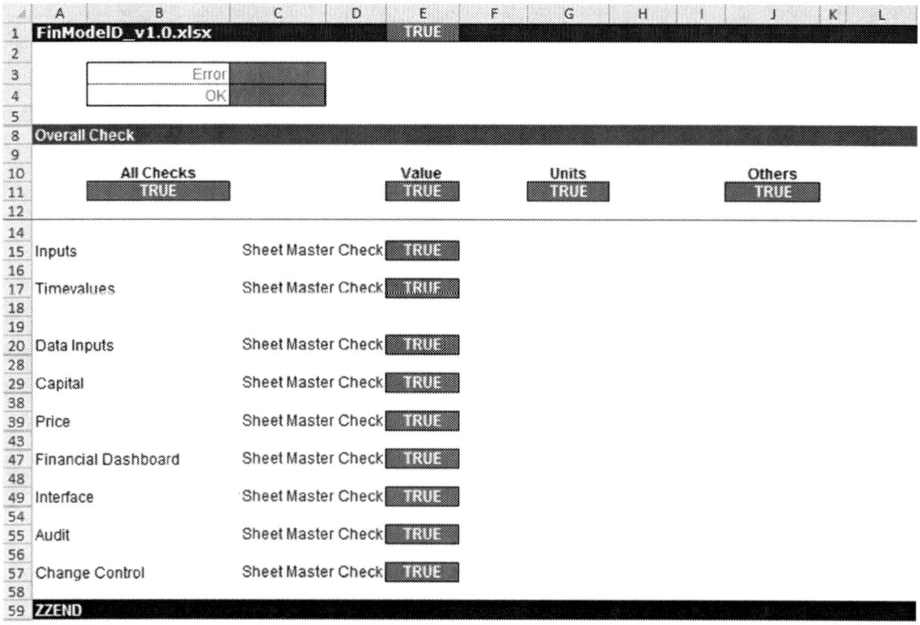

Figure 2-13. The error checking worksheet is used to consolidate all the error checks in the model into one master worksheet

Errors Explained

Errors in spreadsheets are inevitable and therefore should be expected in financial models, rather than dismissed. This section will be devoted to errors, because they are the single most damaging aspect of financial modeling and are so intrinsic to modeling. A modeler who can model without a single error is as rare; in fact I have yet to come across such a modeler. The foremost expert in spreadsheet errors is Professor Ray Panko from the University of Hawaii. He states the following about errors in a paper published in 1988:

> All in all, the research done to date in spreadsheet development presents a very disturbing picture. Every study that has attempted to measure errors, without exception, has found them at rates that would be unacceptable in any organization. These error rates, furthermore, are completely consistent with error rates found in other human activities. With such high cell error rates, most large spreadsheets will have multiple errors, and even relatively small 'scratch pad' spreadsheets will have a significant probability of error.
>
> Despite the evidence, individual developers and organizations appear to be in a state of denial. They do not regularly implement even fairly simple controls to reduce errors, much less such bitter pills

> as comprehensive code inspection. One corporate officer probably summarized the situation by saying that he agreed with the error rate numbers but felt that comprehensive code inspection is simply impractical. In other words, he was saying that the company should continue to base critical decisions on bad numbers.
>
> A major impediment to implementing adequate disciplines, of course, is that few spreadsheet developers have spreadsheeting in their job descriptions at all, and very few do spreadsheet development as their main task. In addition, because spreadsheet development is so dispersed, the implementation of policies has to be left to individual department managers. While organizations might identify critical spreadsheets and only impose hard disciplines on them, this would still mean that many corporate decisions would continue to be made based on questionable analyses.[1]

You may think that because Ray Panko wrote about errors way back in 1988 things have moved on. While this may be partially right in that we now understand errors, but there has been little change in the number of errors that have entered into models. In fact, this situation has increased as more people rely on Excel spreadsheets.

So, how does all this apply to the financial modeler? Well, we have established that errors will occur. The issue, however, is not that errors occurring, but how they are then treated. Dealing with errors is a fundamental part of financial modeling. The more complex and larger the model, the more likely it is that some of those errors will not be caught. But in order to effectively work with errors, you need to better understand them. This next section will provide you with a more in-depth understanding of errors and why they occur.

The Reasons for Errors

Errors in Excel are seldom a cause for concern in organizations, largely because very few organizations have adequate controls and model review processes. This means that the first instance of an error being caught is when the damage has already been done, which is too late. The reasons why errors occur are numerous, but there are some that are easily identifiable, such as unskilled users, lack of planning, and data and recycling.

---

[1]Panko, 1988, `http://panko.shidler.hawaii.edu/ssr/Mypapers/whatknow.htm`

Unskilled Users

Spreadsheet training is not just for new modelers. In fact, lack of adequate training will result in poor or mediocre modeling, such as improper referencing, linking to other workbooks and files, or using inaccurate formulas to master complex calculations.

Focused training in the use of modeling tools that include Excel is one way to help achieve internal control. For instance, long-term learning plans that incorporate spreadsheet training will help ensure that users are up-to-date with the latest version of the spreadsheet in use.

Lack of Planning

If the policies and procedures to mitigate spreadsheet risks are inadequate, errors will become more common and lack of consistency will be a major contributor toward errors not being handled. Therefore, the style, content, and accountability for spreadsheets should be documented in the organization's policies and procedures or in the spreadsheet used.

To this end, documentation is a best practice to explain how spreadsheets are used. Organizations need to explain in common language the purpose of the spreadsheet and intended functions within the workbook file, on the worksheet (for example, at the top of the page), or in written policies and procedures. This way, other users can read the instructions before using it. If documentation is kept separately (such as in a policies and procedures document), it should identify the style and organization-wide requirements for using spreadsheets.

Furthermore, an inventory of spreadsheets used to prepare complex tasks or financial statements will help ensure where adequate documentation is needed. In addition, documentation needs to be kept up-to-date and include who was responsible for preparing or updating the spreadsheet or policy.

Data and Recycling

People are creatures of habit, which is one reason why spreadsheets are reused from year to year. Unfortunately, after cutting and pasting information, the spreadsheet might not work the way it did previously because the formula has been overwritten or a link has been broken.

To help mitigate spreadsheet recycling risks, modelers need to make sure the information added to the spreadsheet is as good as the expected. The following tasks are from a paper by Larry Metz published by the Royal Institute of Auditors in 2008[2]:

- Saving input data separately from the active spreadsheet used for calculations
- Using a control total (that is, a result obtained by subjecting a set of data to an algorithm to check the data at the time the algorithm is applied) to prevent errors in formulas totaling columns of data, numbers, or dollars
- Using self-checks, like a hash or batch total, to verify that formula results are accurate
- Utilizing automated tools to isolate where errors have occurred and could occur
- Making verifications that spreadsheet templates are not changed accidentally by using password protection

Intrusions

Intrusions are the precursors to an error emerging in a spreadsheet. Intrusions include phone calls, chatty coworkers, unscheduled office breaks, or changing work demands. Typical studies, including one by PriceWaterhouseCoopers in early 2000, shows that up to 91% of sophisticated spreadsheets contain errors. The issue is what constitutes an error. In modeling, errors are far more stringent than simple spreadsheet errors. For instance, is a circular reference an error? The answer is that some modelers would consider them to be errors and some don't, and therefore it depends on which camp you want to take. I sit in the camp that circular references are errors because they reflect a procedure that will produce unpredictable and potentially incorrect results.

Who Will Review or Check for Errors?

The obvious answer of who will review or check for errors is the auditor. An auditor's duty is to take reasonable steps to detect situations that may lead to fraud. The landscape has changed dramatically since the days of Enron and will move even further as regulators tackle the case of fraud head-on. For instance, several laws and regulations in Europe and North America (such as the USA Patriot Act of 2001, the Foreign Corrupt Practices Act of 1977,

---

[2] http://www.theiia.org/gap/index.cfm?act=GAP.printa&aid=2808

the Sarbanes-Oxley Act of 2002, Statement on Auditing Standard No. 99, and Auditing Standard No. 5) have developed an array of regulatory compliance mechanisms, which are meant to deter persons from criminal activities. These laws and regulations have emphasized the importance for the auditor—internal or external—to continually be on the lookout for misstatements that could have been intentional.

There are any numbers of ways to reduce errors in models, but there are positions that should be taken if one is serious about reducing or eliminating errors, such as the following:

- Models of a serious nature should always be accompanied with a model plan. This step gives direction and allows the modeler to create adequate checks while modeling.
- The act of modeling should be left to experienced and trained persons. While it may cost less to use someone with spreadsheets skills and therefore suffice as a modeler, when issues start to arise a modeler is irreplaceable.
- Create a culture where models are reviewed. This can be in the form of peer reviews, model audits, and model testing. Reviews are by far the most potent method of reducing errors in models, as it's unlikely that two people will make the same error in exactly the same place in exactly the same manner. Also there are a number of third party software (Operis OAK, Spreadsheet Detective, or Rainbow Analyst) that can make the act of finding errors a lot slicker.

Real-Life Errors

Whether an organization was large or small, spreadsheets were an overlooked risk by many people until Sarbanes-Oxley mandated spreadsheet controls compliance in Section 404. Flexibility, ease of use, and transferability are a few of the advantages of spreadsheets. However, the same features that make spreadsheets useful can also make them risky.

There are clear examples of where issues with errors in spreadsheets have had an indirect economic impact. Consider the DTF (Department for Transport) in the UK, whose bungled bid of the West Coast train line in 2012 caused a major public sector outsourcing project to make a complete U-turn of the tender process because the financial modeler made an error by failing to add inflation into the ten-year model. The compensation by the UK government to all the potential bidders ran into several tens of millions of pounds.

The experience of the French bank Societe Generale with a rogue trader who lost approximately seven billion dollars through a series of fraudulent transactions should be a warning for anyone who uses spreadsheets to make key decisions about money. This rogue trader managed to conceal his fraud by creating losing trades in European stock index futures with the intention of offsetting his previous gains.

It is unlikely that we'll ever know exactly how and what happened. However, a credible theory indicates that inadequate, spreadsheet-based internal controls may have played a part in allowing the trader to build up his positions, which eventually resulted in the tremendous loss for the bank. Some also speculate that, in addition to disguising his trades through a fictitious company and a colleague's accounts, the trader was able to circumvent the bank's internal warning systems by opening and manipulating Excel spreadsheet reports used by managers to monitor traders' activities.

You may wonder how we have moved from looking at errors into fraud. But when you are dealing with very large financial numbers, you will likely be working with financial models and you are never far from the question of fraud arising. As the modeler, you will always be one step away from the model being used maliciously or yourself being connected to misdoings. It is imperative that you always make sure you understand why errors occur, which will allow you to mitigate for when they can occur.

A Tip on Errors

There is a term by Ray Panko that says "keep it simple, stupid," which makes an excellent point: the less complex, the less errors. We need to reduce modeler overload as much as possible. Keeping things simple should also help with reviews and audits. Surprisingly, Panko found that errors were detected much more frequently in short formulas than in long formulas, which may seem at odds.[3]

But note that Panko was looking purely at frequency; the likelihood is that there is a higher prevalence of short formulas over the lengthy ones in most models and hence the frequency will be higher. I maintain, however, that the longer the formula, and hence more complex, the higher the probability of undetected errors creeping into the model.

There is a perception among spreadsheets users that a great number of errors are from mistyping, which does occur. But mistyping is not the dominant cause

[3]Dr. Raymond R. Panko, " Spreadsheet Errors: What We Know. What We Think We Can Do, July 2000, `http://panko.shidler.hawaii.edu/SSR/Mypapers/EUSPRIG_2000.htm`

of errors. Logical errors (such as using the wrong formula) and omissions (such as leaving tax out of the calculation) are also common culprits. We humans can be very inventive when it comes to mistakes.

Catching and Trapping Errors

So errors are going to happen, even to experts, and checking is only partly effective. Should we just give up? Not just yet. We can create methods to either mitigate or trap errors and also create pre-release models (alpha and beta). In my opinion, this is the direction in which financial modeling should be heading, which is going toward a more software development-like process with some sort of product life cycle methodology.

For a glimpse of how error checking will develop for financial models, take a look at the software development life cycle. In particular, consider software and systems that are built but just have no room for failure, such as the critical aircraft system management. One example would be the NASA space shuttle. The space shuttle had its share of fatal quality problems, but its software development passed review. How? Because the shuttle program had put in place so many checks and balances, even with failures or errors occurring, the shuttle engineers were always able to isolate the issue problem and fix it.

On this topic, I would recommend the book *Code Complete* (second edition) by Steve McConnell (Microsoft Press, 2004). While the book is quite technical, it nevertheless will give you a very strong feel of where building financial models could be heading.

Note Industries that depend on absolutely accurate software have very stringent and thorough processes for building, testing, and retesting the software. This method is usually too expensive for most businesses and too much to expect of a humble spreadsheet builder. One thing these industries do well is to build models in small chunks and test each chunk thoroughly. In this way, testing is always manageable. In contrast, when NASA built the space shuttle, they built the main engine all at once because it was at the cutting edge of technology and had nightmares testing it.

The airline industry has to get it right all the time or people die. One key approach is to build in layers. In other words, if one thing goes wrong, another system will cover for it. This is sometimes known as a Swiss cheese security because although there may be many holes, no hole goes all the way through.

The challenge for financial modelers is to develop models that have sufficient error checking built-in that will not just alert the user to the error, but in certain circumstances will revert to a default in order to make sure the model doesn't fail.

Caution Be wary of creating models that automatically apply defaults in the event of an error. It then becomes difficult to ascertain where the actual problem stems from unless you design very robust in-model user and system logs.

How to Work with Errors in Models

At the end of the day, we are human and we need to decide how we can work with errors. Even if the errors in the model are totally eradicated, others could easily creep into the model at a later stage. The best way is to create error checking within the model. For example, I build some sort of checks that will alert the user that an error has occurred if it has and will also alert the user that no errors have occurred if they haven't.

Figure 2-14 is an example of a structural error. It is referred to as structural because it breaks the consistency and hence destroys the structure within the model. The sum formula looks innocuous; however, notice the "$" signs. These are called absolute references, and they anchor the formula.

SYD fx =SUM($C$4:$G$4)

	A	B	C	D	E	F	G	H	I
1	FinModelD_v1.0.xlsx								
2									
3		Sales Rep	Jan	Feb	Mar	Apr	May	Total	
4		John Doe	2,300	1,940	1,866			=SUM(C	
5		Maggie Avery	1,840	-	674				
6		Tom Watts	1,920	2,300	2,005				
7		Agatha May	1,850	2,560	2,211				
8		Tori Smith	1,544	1,520	1,470				
9		Ceri Tuvali	4,020	3,890	3,763				
10		Karina Johns	3,111	-	5,890				
11		Anton Silver	210	370	302				
12		Michela Qunitech	1,153	1,203	1,440				
13		Todd Brown	845	980	744				
14		**Total Month**	**18,793**	**14,763**	**20,365**	-	-	**6,106**	
15									
16	END								
17									

Figure 2-14. The totals formula has an absolute reference, which will create a structural error

The problem is if the formula is simply copied down, it will be anchored onto row 4 and will not give the correct totals. In fact, the totals will look just like Figure 2-15.

SYD =SUM($C$4:$G$4)

	A	B	C	D	E	F	G	H	I
1	FinModelD_v1.0.xlsx								
2									
3		Sales Rep	Jan	Feb	Mar	Apr	May	Total	
4		John Doe	2,300	1,940	1,866			6,106	
5		Maggie Avery	1,840	-	674			6,106	
6		Tom Watts	1,920	2,300	2,005			6,106	
7		Agatha May	1,850	2,560	2,211			=SUM(C	
8		Tori Smith	1,544	1,520	1,470			6,106	
9		Ceri Tuvali	4,020	3,890	3,763			6,106	
10		Karina Johns	3,111	-	5,890			6,106	
11		Anton Silver	210	370	302			6,106	
12		Michela Qunitech	1,153	1,203	1,440			6,106	
13		Todd Brown	845	980	744			6,106	
14		**Total Month**	**18,793**	**14,763**	**20,365**	-	-	**61,060**	
15									
16	END								
17									

Figure 2-15. The formula in column H is copied down but has calculated on row 4

This is a very common issue because initially it does not appear to be an error. However, this is an example of an error being introduced only once data populates the model. For this type of error where totals are being calculated in a column, it is best to keep the formula as it is and avoid any absolute or relative references as in Figure 2-16. (Absolute and relative cell references will be described in Chapter 3.)

SYD =SUM(C7:G7)

	A	B	C	D	E	F	G	H
1	FinModelD_v1.0.xlsx							
2								
3		Sales Rep	Jan	Feb	Mar	Apr	May	Total
4		John Doe	2,300	1,940	1,866			6,106
5		Maggie Avery	1,840	-	674			2,514
6		Tom Watts	1,920	2,300	2,005			6,225
7		Agatha May	1,850	2,560	2,211			=SUM(C7:
8		Tori Smith	1,544	1,520	1,470			4,534
9		Ceri Tuvali	4,020	3,890	3,763			11,673
10		Karina Johns	3,111	-	5,890			9,001
11		Anton Silver	210	370	302			882
12		Michela Qunitech	1,153	1,203	1,440			3,796
13		Todd Brown	845	980	744			2,569
14		**Total Month**	**18,793**	**14,763**	**20,365**	-	-	**53,921**
15								
16	END							
17								

Figure 2-16. Totals appear as they are with no absolute or relative cell referencing

Adding Error Checks

While having errors in the model is somewhat expected and we have discussed why, there is absolutely no reason why a modeler should omit building error checking in their models. When I am asked to give assurance on a model by auditing and certifying, it will not matter how well-structured the model is or whether it was designed following best practice if there are no error checking mechanisms. If I don't see any, then that is a model I will not certify.

Figures 2-17a and Figure 2-17b contain a visual error check for the totals by assessing the sum of the total in column H against the sum of the months in row 14, which should always be same. Also in this case, the check shows "TRUE" to signify that the check is correct.

A18

	A	B	C	D	E	F	G	H	I	J	K
1	FinModelD_v1.0.xlsx										
2											
3		Sales Rep	Jan	Feb	Mar	Apr	May	Total		error	
4		John Doe	2,300	1,940	1,866			6,106			
5		Maggie Avery	1,840	-	674			2,514			
6		Tom Watts	1,920	2,300	2,005			6,225			
7		Agatha May	1,850	2,560	2,211			6,621			
8		Tori Smith	1,544	1,520	1,470			4,534			
9		Ceri Tuvali	4,020	3,890	3,763			11,673			
10		Karina Johns	3,111	-	5,890			9,001			
11		Anton Silver	210	370	302			882			
12		Michela Qunitech	1,153	1,203	1,440			3,796			
13		Todd Brown	845	980	744			2,569			
14		**Total Month**	**18,793**	**14,763**	**20,365**	-	-	**53,921**		TRUE	
15											
16	END										
17											

Figure 2-17a. In this figure, error checking is performed on the totals

SYD =IF(SUM($H$4:$H$13)<>SUM($C$14:$G$14),1,0)

	A	B	C	D	E	F	G	H
1	FinModelD_v1.0.xlsx							
2								
3		Sales Rep	Jan	Feb	Mar	Apr	May	Total
4		John Doe	2,300	1,940	1,866			6,106
5		Maggie Avery	1,840	-	674			2,514
6		Tom Watts	1,920	2,300	2,005			6,225
7		Agatha May	1,850	2,560	2,211			6,621
8		Tori Smith	1,544	1,520	1,470			4,534
9		Ceri Tuvali	4,020	3,890	3,763			11,673
10		Karina Johns	3,111	-	5,890			9,001
11		Anton Silver	210	370	302			882
12		Michela Qunitech	1,153	1,203	1,440			3,796
13		Todd Brown	845	980	744			2,569
14		**Total Month**	**18,793**	**14,763**	**20,365**	-	-	**53,921**
15								
16	END							

Figure 2-17b. A formula has been created using a combination of an IF() and a SUM() statement to create an error check

The modeler can use a creative formula like the one in Figure 2-17b to provide error checks. The model has a built-in mechanism that can then alert the user to problems as in Figure 2-18, where the check has shown that an error has occurred, and will then allow the user to assess the validity of the model outputs. In Figure 2-19 is an alternative method of showing the error check that uses the statement "OK" to show there are no errors. ("Error" would show when an error has occurred.)

A18

FinModelD_v1.0.xlsx

Sales Rep	Jan	Feb	Mar	Apr	May	Total	error
John Doe	2,300	1,940	1,866			6,106	
Maggie Avery	1,840	-	674			1,840	
Tom Watts	1,920	2,300	2,005			6,225	
Agatha May	1,850	2,560	2,211			6,621	
Tori Smith	1,544	1,520	1,470			4,534	
Ceri Tuvali	4,020	3,890	3,763			11,673	
Karina Johns	3,111	-	5,890			9,001	
Anton Silver	210	370	302			882	
Michela Qunitech	1,153	1,203	1,440			3,796	
Todd Brown	845	980	744			2,569	
Total Month	**18,793**	**14,763**	**20,365**	-	-	**53,247**	FALSE

END

Figure 2-18. In this figure, there is problem in the totals formula, and the error check has highlighted the error

A18

FinModelD_v1.0.xlsx

Sales Rep	Jan	Feb	Mar	Apr	May	Total	error
John Doe	2,300	1,940	1,866			6,106	
Maggie Avery	1,840	-	674			2,514	
Tom Watts	1,920	2,300	2,005			6,225	
Agatha May	1,850	2,560	2,211			6,621	
Tori Smith	1,544	1,520	1,470			4,534	
Ceri Tuvali	4,020	3,890	3,763			11,673	
Karina Johns	3,111	-	5,890			9,001	
Anton Silver	210	370	302			882	
Michela Qunitech	1,153	1,203	1,440			3,796	
Todd Brown	845	980	744			2,569	
Total Month	**18,793**	**14,763**	**20,365**	-	-	**53,921**	ok

END

Figure 2-19. A more popular method of showing the error check is by using common language messages

Note Error checks are shown in different ways in financial models and much depends on the preference of the modeler. The popular method is to show an actual message which states "ok" when there is no error and "error" when there is an error, as in Figure 2-19. There is no right or wrong, although I would recommend the visual method that uses RED for error, AMBER for warning, and GREEN for no errors. I use this convention in all the models that I design and build because it has major benefits for the end user. By giving a visual cue using the three colors, the modeler will be treading on well-worn ground. This color system is how financial dashboards and project plans are represented, and most senior executives are familiar with the red, amber, and green system. It is also a universal language called "traffic lights."

Secondly, my preference is always to assume that future users of the model may not necessarily have English as their first language. Therefore, I try as much as possible to avoid using English common language messages in favor of something generic.

Best Practices in a Nutshell

Financial modeling best practice is about doing things that make the model simpler and easier to use and also to audit. Here are the essential aspects:

- Keep the inputs, calculations, and outputs in separate sections. In larger and more complex models, keep them in separate worksheets.
- Use consistent formulas across a row.
- Make the formula as simple and small as possible.
- Use styles to guide the user.
- Model timescales at the smallest levels and then work up.
- Do not hard-code numbers into formulas cells.
- Make your layout and formats clear and consistent.
- Deal with errors.
- Always document the model.
- Make sure that you make your assumptions clear and provide references.

Take a look at Figure 2-20. This is an excerpt from an actual model that includes several aspects based on best practice. Can you spot them?

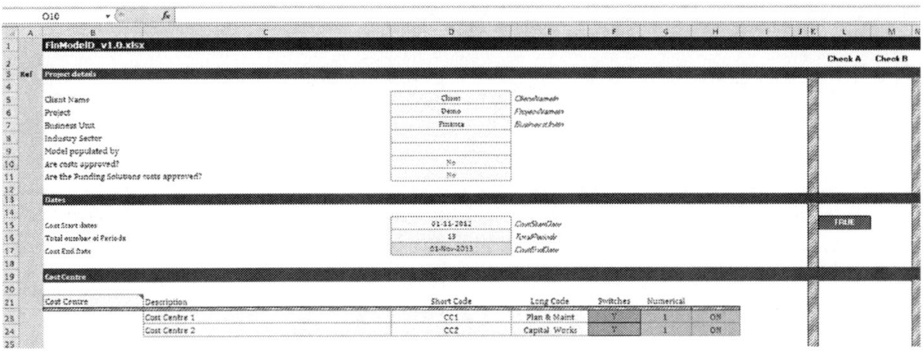

Figure 2-20. This excerpt features some best practice elements

Case Study: Financial Model Gone Awry

In this case study, the brief is as follows:

> *"Deliver a simple financial model that will provide a cash forecast over a period of two years. The model should allow for the user to flex 'what if' scenarios."*

This is quite typical of the information that would be provided for a financial model. Note that as the brief is loose, there is no guidance as to the format or size of the model, nor does it indicate how the output (the cash forecast) should be laid out. The following assumptions will need to be made as well:

- We can assume we know the output formats based on previous models we have built for this customer.
- We know what the key financial drivers are, which we will use when we create "What If" scenarios. The model planning and specification has previously been completed.

This case study will highlight where a model has not achieved the appropriate best practice and then demonstrate how this could have been achieved. Using the brief provided, we will create two scenarios: the first is with a model that has truly gone awry and the second is a best practice version. This case study is from an actual modeling brief, and it is based on a customer who had developed an in-house model that was later rebuilt by a financial modeler. Why the financial modeler had to rebuild the model will hopefully become clear as we work through this case study.

The Non-best Practice Model

The forecast cash flow in Figure 2-21 gives us the output from the model, which we can evaluate.

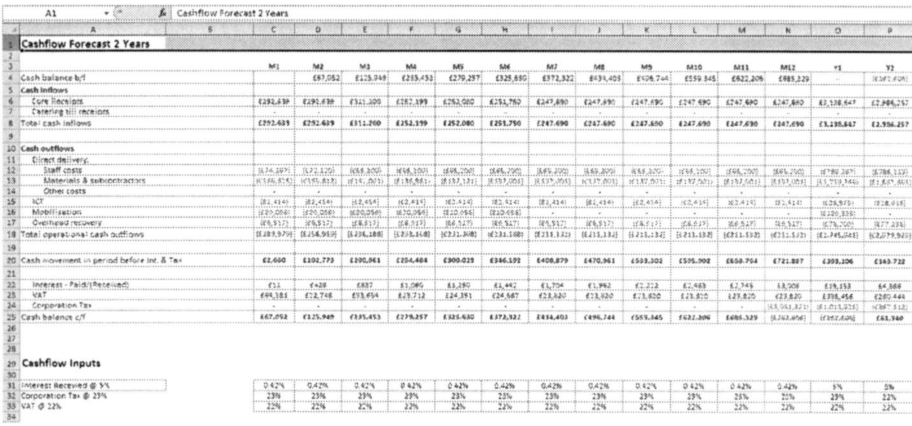

Figure 2-21. The forecast cash flow output has been determined without any best practice modeling

Outwardly, the forecast output in Figure 2-21 would seem to be intact. In fact, this may suffice as it does provide all that is required under the brief:

- The timescales are correct with the two-year forecast. Additionally, Year 1 has been broken down into the lowest constituent months.
- It would appear that the inputs can be flexed to create "what ifs" by altering the interest, tax, and vat rates.
- We can quickly see where the cash will be at a given time.
- The format is clear, and it is a simple model as required by the brief.

Don't worry too much about the actual calculation methodology. We can just assume this is a given and that all calculations are performing correctly.

The Best Practice Model

Let's turn our attention now to an alternative model in Figures 2-22a–2-22d, which address some known best practice modeling.

	A / B	C	D	E	F	G	H	I	J	K	L
1	ForecastCashflow_v1.0.xlsm				TRUE						
2	No Such Company										
3		Yr1	Yr1	Yr1	Yr1	Yr1	Yr1	Yr1	Yr1	Yr1	Yr1
4		M1	M2	M3	M4	M5	M6	M7	M8	M9	M10
5		Yr1M1	Yr1M2	Yr1M3	Yr1M4	Yr1M5	Yr1M6	Yr1M7	Yr1M8	Yr1M9	Yr1M10
6		Currency	Currency	Currency	Currency	Currency	Currency	Currency	Currency	Currency	Currency
7	Inputs										
8	Inflows (Positive Values)										
9	Core Receipts	292,639	292,639	311,200	252,199	252,080	251,750	247,690	247,690	247,690	247,690
10	Catering till receipts	-	-	-	-	-	-	-	-	-	-
11											
12	Outflows (Negative values))										
13	Staff costs	(74,167)	(72,120)	(65,200)	(65,200)	(65,200)	(65,200)	(65,200)	(65,200)	(65,200)	(65,200)
14	Materials & subcontractors	(186,825)	(155,812)	(142,001)	(138,981)	(137,121)	(137,001)	(137,001)	(137,001)	(137,001)	(137,001)
15	Other costs	-	-	-	-	-	-	-	-	-	-
16	ICT	(2,414)	(2,414)	(2,414)	(2,414)	(2,414)	(2,414)	(2,414)	(2,414)	(2,414)	(2,414)
17	Mobilisation	(20,056)	(20,056)	(20,056)	(20,056)	(20,056)	(20,056)				
18	Overhead recovery	(6,517)	(6,517)	(6,517)	(6,517)	(6,517)	(6,517)	(6,517)	(6,517)	(6,517)	(6,517)
20	Interest & Tax (As %)										
21	Interest Received Per Month	0.42%	0.42%	0.42%	0.42%	0.42%	0.42%	0.42%	0.42%	0.42%	0.42%
22	VAT %	22%	22%	22%	22%	22%	22%	22%	22%	22%	22%
23	Corporation Tax %	23%	22%	22%	22%	22%	22%	22%	22%	22%	22%

Figure 2-22a. This figure shows the results of the inputs

	A / B	C	D	E	F	G	H	I	J	K	L
1	ForecastCashflow_v1.0.xlsm				TRUE						
2	No Such Company										
3		Yr1	Yr1	Yr1	Yr1	Yr1	Yr1	Yr1	Yr1	Yr1	Yr1
4		M1	M2	M3	M4	M5	M6	M7	M8	M9	M10
5		Yr1M1	Yr1M2	Yr1M3	Yr1M4	Yr1M5	Yr1M6	Yr1M7	Yr1M8	Yr1M9	Yr1M10
6		Currency	Currency	Currency	Currency	Currency	Currency	Currency	Currency	Currency	Currency
25	Calculations										
26	**Caculations to Cashflow Inputs**										
27	Cash balance b/f	-	67,052	125,949	235,453	279,257	325,630	372,322	434,403	496,744	559,345
28	**Cash inflows**										
29	Core Receipts	292,639	292,639	311,200	252,199	252,080	251,750	247,690	247,690	247,690	247,690
30	Catering till receipts	-	-	-	-	-	-	-	-	-	-
31	Total cash inflows	**292,639**	**292,639**	**311,200**	**252,199**	**252,080**	**251,750**	**247,690**	**247,690**	**247,690**	**247,690**
32											
33	**Cash outflows**										
34	Staff costs	(74,167)	(72,120)	(65,200)	(65,200)	(65,200)	(65,200)	(65,200)	(65,200)	(65,200)	(65,200)
35	Materials & subcontractors	(186,825)	(155,812)	(142,001)	(138,981)	(137,121)	(137,001)	(137,001)	(137,001)	(137,001)	(137,001)
36	Other costs	-	-	-	-	-	-	-	-	-	-
37	ICT	(2,414)	(2,414)	(2,414)	(2,414)	(2,414)	(2,414)	(2,414)	(2,414)	(2,414)	(2,414)
38	Mobilisation	(20,056)	(20,056)	(20,056)	(20,056)	(20,056)	(20,056)	-	-	-	-
39	Overhead recovery	(6,517)	(6,517)	(6,517)	(6,517)	(6,517)	(6,517)	(6,517)	(6,517)	(6,517)	(6,517)
40	Total operational cash outflows	(289,979)	(256,919)	(236,188)	(233,168)	(231,308)	(231,188)	(211,132)	(211,132)	(211,132)	(211,132)
41											
42	Cash movement in period before Int. & Tax	**2,660**	**102,773**	**200,961**	**254,484**	**300,029**	**346,192**	**408,879**	**470,961**	**533,302**	**595,902**
43											
44	Interest - Paid/(Received)	11	428	837	1,060	1,250	1,442	1,704	1,962	2,222	2,483
45	VAT	64,381	22,748	33,654	23,712	24,351	24,687	23,820	23,820	23,820	23,820
46	Corporate Tax paid	-	-	-	-	-	-	-	-	-	-
47	**Cash balance c/f**	**67,052**	**125,949**	**235,453**	**279,257**	**325,630**	**372,322**	**434,403**	**496,744**	**559,345**	**622,206**
48											
49	Calculate Tax Paid	(612)	(22,610)	(44,211)	(55,986)	(66,006)	(76,162)	(89,953)	(103,612)	(117,326)	(131,099)
50	VAT owing	-	(41,633)	(34,810)	(31,771)	(31,107)	(30,698)	(30,671)	(30,671)	(30,671)	(30,671)

Figure 2-22b. In this figure, the calculations are below the inputs in the same layout

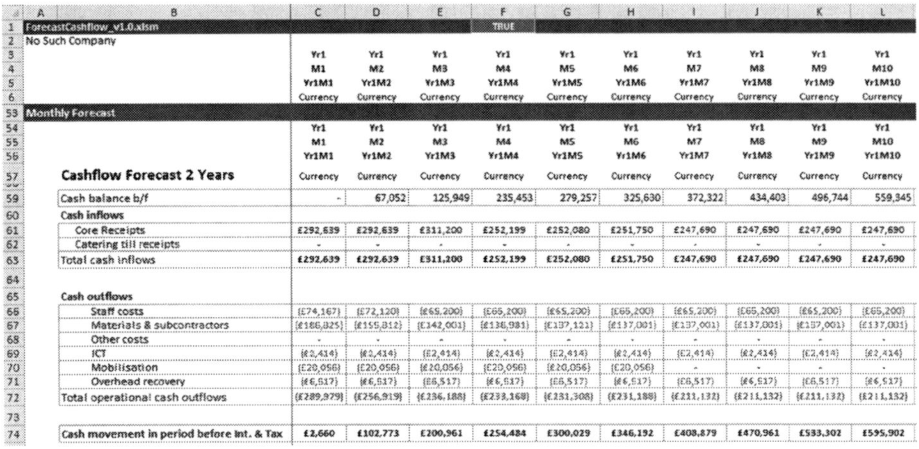

	A / B	C	D	E	F	G	H	I	J	K	L
1	ForecastCashflow_v1.0.xlsm				TRUE						
2	No Such Company										
3		Yr1	Yr1	Yr1	Yr1	Yr1	Yr1	Yr1	Yr1	Yr1	Yr1
4		M1	M2	M3	M4	M5	M6	M7	M8	M9	M10
5		Yr1M1	Yr1M2	Yr1M3	Yr1M4	Yr1M5	Yr1M6	Yr1M7	Yr1M8	Yr1M9	Yr1M10
6		Currency	Currency	Currency	Currency	Currency	Currency	Currency	Currency	Currency	Currency
53	Monthly Forecast										
54		Yr1	Yr1	Yr1	Yr1	Yr1	Yr1	Yr1	Yr1	Yr1	Yr1
55		M1	M2	M3	M4	M5	M6	M7	M8	M9	M10
56		Yr1M1	Yr1M2	Yr1M3	Yr1M4	Yr1M5	Yr1M6	Yr1M7	Yr1M8	Yr1M9	Yr1M10
57	**Cashflow Forecast 2 Years**	Currency	Currency	Currency	Currency	Currency	Currency	Currency	Currency	Currency	Currency
59	Cash balance b/f	-	67,052	125,949	235,453	279,257	325,630	372,322	434,403	496,744	559,345
60	**Cash inflows**										
61	Core Receipts	£292,639	£292,639	£311,200	£252,199	£252,080	£251,750	£247,690	£247,690	£247,690	£247,690
62	Catering till receipts	-	-	-	-	-	-	-	-	-	-
63	Total cash inflows	£292,639	£292,639	£311,200	£252,199	£252,080	£251,750	£247,690	£247,690	£247,690	£247,690
64											
65	**Cash outflows**										
66	Staff costs	(£74,167)	(£72,120)	(£65,200)	(£65,200)	(£65,200)	(£65,200)	(£65,200)	(£65,200)	(£65,200)	(£65,200)
67	Materials & subcontractors	(£186,825)	(£155,812)	(£142,001)	(£138,981)	(£137,121)	(£137,001)	(£137,001)	(£137,001)	(£137,001)	(£137,001)
68	Other costs	-	-	-	-	-	-	-	-	-	-
69	ICT	(£2,414)	(£2,414)	(£2,414)	(£2,414)	(£2,414)	(£2,414)	(£2,414)	(£2,414)	(£2,414)	(£2,414)
70	Mobilisation	(£20,056)	(£20,056)	(£20,056)	(£20,056)	(£20,056)	(£20,056)	-	-	-	-
71	Overhead recovery	(£6,517)	(£6,517)	(£6,517)	(£6,517)	(£6,517)	(£6,517)	(£6,517)	(£6,517)	(£6,517)	(£6,517)
72	Total operational cash outflows	(£289,979)	(£256,919)	(£236,188)	(£233,168)	(£231,308)	(£231,188)	(£211,132)	(£211,132)	(£211,132)	(£211,132)
73											
74	**Cash movement in period before Int. & Tax**	£2,660	£102,773	£200,961	£254,484	£300,029	£346,192	£408,879	£470,961	£533,302	£595,902

Figure 2-22c. In this figure, the monthly outputs are below the calculations

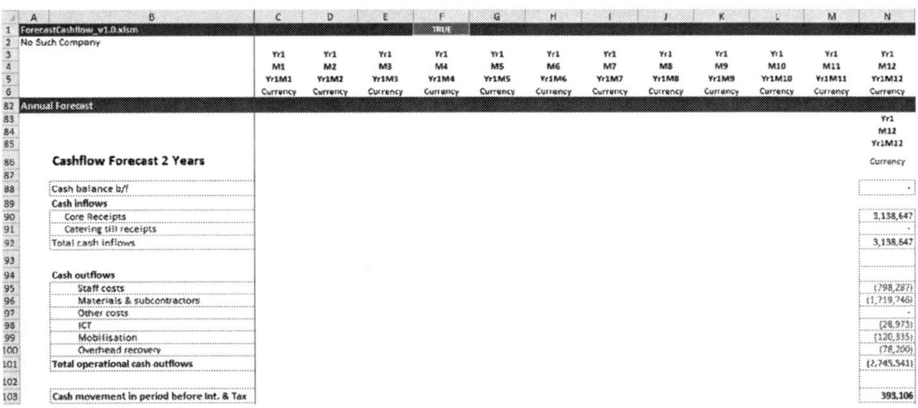

	A / B	C	D	E	F	G	H	I	J	K	L	M	N
1	ForecastCashflow_v1.0.xlsm				TRUE								
2	No Such Company												
3		Yr1	Yr1	Yr1	Yr1	Yr1	Yr1	Yr1	Yr1	Yr1	Yr1	Yr1	Yr1
4		M1	M2	M3	M4	M5	M6	M7	M8	M9	M10	M11	M12
5		Yr1M1	Yr1M2	Yr1M3	Yr1M4	Yr1M5	Yr1M6	Yr1M7	Yr1M8	Yr1M9	Yr1M10	Yr1M11	Yr1M12
6		Currency	Currency	Currency	Currency	Currency	Currency	Currency	Currency	Currency	Currency	Currency	Currency
82	Annual Forecast												
83													Yr1
84													M12
85													Yr1M12
86	**Cashflow Forecast 2 Years**												Currency
87													
88	Cash balance b/f												-
89	**Cash inflows**												
90	Core Receipts												3,138,647
91	Catering till receipts												-
92	Total cash inflows												3,138,647
93													
94	**Cash outflows**												
95	Staff costs												(798,287)
96	Materials & subcontractors												(1,719,746)
97	Other costs												-
98	ICT												(28,973)
99	Mobilisation												(120,335)
100	Overhead recovery												(78,200)
101	**Total operational cash outflows**												(2,745,541)
102													
103	Cash movement in period before Int. & Tax												393,106

Figure 2-22d. In this figure, the annual outputs follow the monthly, but are in single columns

The inputs are placed at the top of the worksheet, followed by the calculations and then the cash flows. It's important to follow a set rule of how the model will show inputs, calculations, and outputs. Some modelers prefer to have the outputs at the top.

It should be immediately clear from looking at this sequence of figures that there are some differences between the two models, and some are quite glaring. Here is a summary of these differences between the two examples:

- The outputs have been split into inputs, calculations, and outputs, even though they are all on one worksheet.
- The inputs are at the top, and the calculations and outputs run down the worksheet top to bottom as in reading a book.

- There is an error check at the top of the worksheet, which incorporates several error checks within the calculations to give an overall check on the model.
- The inputs are visually marked using styles (yellow cells), and the calculations are marked using green and gray cells.
- The units are clear, in this case shown as currency.
- The calculations follow a consistency. When this consistency is not possible, the color style has been used to signify the change to the user. For example, green cells indicate a primary formula, and gray cells indicate the formula is copied from the cell immediately to the left.

In addition, examine closely Figure 2-23, which features a style sheet to guide the user as to the formats and cell colors.

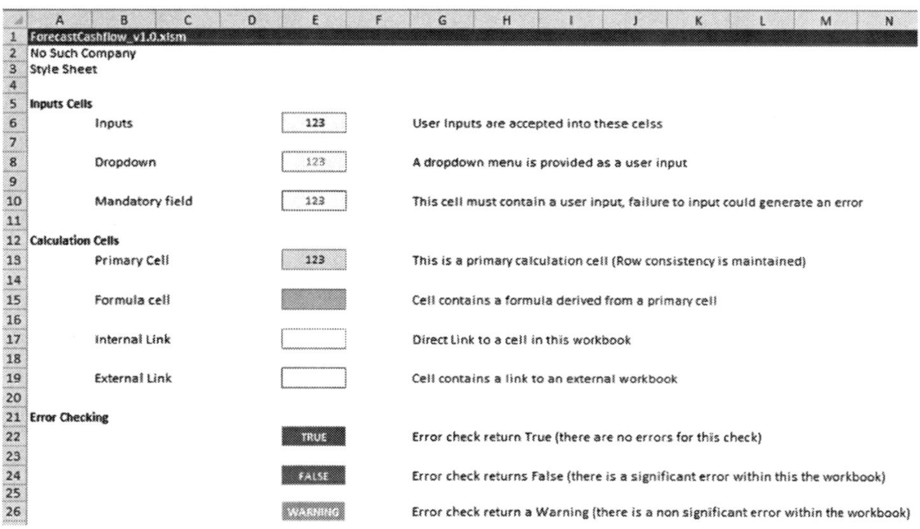

Figure 2-23. This figure is a forecast cash model style sheet

While these models are not the defacto in best practice, they highlight some very simple differences that can be observed from a model that is planned and designed with some best practice with one that is not. Keep in mind that using a best practice approach is not just about looking pretty. There are some major advantages with adopting this method to modeling, and many of the pitfalls that can beset any modeler can be avoided or worked around by choosing to take this approach.

CHAPTER

3

Modeling Functions and Tools

I have been asked often if there is a certain group of Excel functions, routines, and tools that are essential for financial modelers. It's a tricky question because on the one hand, there are certain functions that are a must. But on the other, modeling is a strange beast and very often situations arise that require some thinking outside of the box. When these situations occur, modelers may need to ditch the must-have functions and either create their own or use a totally new function. This versatility is something that separates the good modeler from the exceptional modeler.

In this chapter, I will cover the functions that are of immediate value to modeling. These functions are indispensable and as you build more and more models, the frequency of using these functions will increase. After you become familiar with these must-have functions, you will have confidence to begin experimenting and creating different solutions.

This is a long and technical chapter. You will be introduced to many concepts and skills for modeling. Don't expect to understand these concepts immediately. I recommend that you have a copy of Excel open and work through the examples, take your time, and really become familiar with the functions. You will be using many of these functions and concepts later in the book, so it's important that you begin to develop your skills with using them. Don't be tempted to skip this chapter.

Excel Formulas and Functions for Modelers

This section will include several important functions that are not just useful but in most instances essential for modeling. The notation "Function Name()" refers to an actual function, in addition, where possible there is also a description of the function syntax. I have also provided descriptions on how some of these functions work, which are shown with the syntax. Here is an example: *=SUMIF(C3:C9,E12,D3:D9)* (text will be in italics). Then I have included a description of what each part of the formula is doing.

Most Used Functions

Following are descriptions of some of the functions you will be using most often.

IF()

The IF() function is perhaps the most versatile of functions for Excel. This is the workhorse of functions, and I can't stress its importance enough. When you encounter unusual modeling situations, your knowledge and experience with the IF() function will be a great asset when you need to think out of the box. Those unusual situations will become simpler to tackle.

The IF() function tests to see whether a given condition is true or false. Depending upon the result, different outcomes for the function can be specified.

Note The IF() function has also been combined with other Excel functions to create such functions as SUMIF(), COUNTIF(), and AVERAGEIF().

If the condition is true, the function will carry out one action. If the condition is false, it will carry out a different action.

The function allows you to specify the actions it should carry out depending on whether the condition is true or not. These actions can include executing a formula, inserting a text statement, or leaving the target cell blank. In Figure 3-1, the objective is to assess the amount of commission on the salary that salespeople will earn once they have reached the threshold of 30,000. This is a classic IF statement situation.

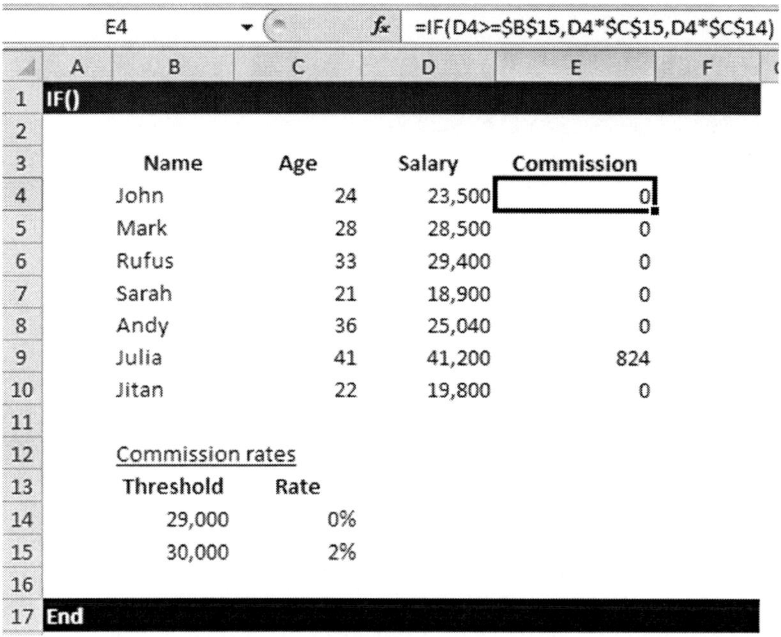

E4 =IF(D4>=$B$15,D4*$C$15,D4*$C$14)

	A	B	C	D	E
1	IF()				
2					
3		Name	Age	Salary	Commission
4		John	24	23,500	0
5		Mark	28	28,500	0
6		Rufus	33	29,400	0
7		Sarah	21	18,900	0
8		Andy	36	25,040	0
9		Julia	41	41,200	824
10		Jitan	22	19,800	0
11					
12		Commission rates			
13		Threshold	Rate		
14		29,000	0%		
15		30,000	2%		
16					
17	End				

Figure 3-1. In this figure, the IF() statement is used to calculate the commission

Let's take a closer look at the formula:

=IF(D4>=$B$15,D4*$C$15,D4*$C$14)

If the salary is greater than or equal to 30,000:

**=IF(D4>=$B$15,D4**C15D4*$C$14)

Note There are two types of cell references: relative and absolute, which behave differently when copied and filled to other cells. By default, all cell references are relative references and change when a formula is copied to another cell. Absolute references, on the other hand, remain constant no matter where they are copied and have a $ character before the column portion of the reference and/or the row portion of the reference, such as $A$5 or $A5 or A$5. The $ anchors the row or column.

Then

The salary × 2%

=IF(D4>=$B$15,**D4*$C$15**,D4*$C$14)

Else

The salary × 0%

*=IF(D4>=$B$15,D4*$C$15,***D4*$C$14***)*

The IF() function is notoriously difficult to describe because it is specific to each situation.

Tip When you have a situation with more than one outcome, this is where you should use the IF() function.

Use the IF() function with care and sparingly. It's possible to have a situation with more than two potential outcomes, and hence you can have an IF statement with a number of outcomes. These are called nested IFs, which will place many IF statements in one formula. To do this is to show your hand as lazy modeling. Why? This method is untidy and very difficult to track and resolve if there later becomes a problem with the formula. In Figure 3-2, a nested IF statement has been created to find out how members of the sales team are over 40 years old.

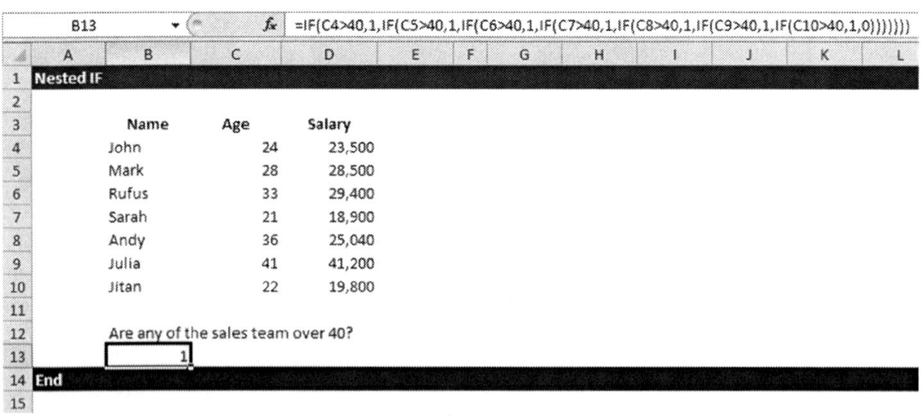

B13 =IF(C4>40,1,IF(C5>40,1,IF(C6>40,1,IF(C7>40,1,IF(C8>40,1,IF(C9>40,1,IF(C10>40,1,0)))))))

Nested IF

Name	Age	Salary
John	24	23,500
Mark	28	28,500
Rufus	33	29,400
Sarah	21	18,900
Andy	36	25,040
Julia	41	41,200
Jitan	22	19,800

Are any of the sales team over 40?

1

End

Figure 3-2. In this figure, a nested IF() statement is used to determine how many of the sales team is over 40

This is a very poor use of the IF() formula, and frankly, this type of formula usage shows a certain failure by the modeler to apply due care and a real lack of imagination. You may be wondering why this is so bad. One reason is that this kind of IF() formula is very prone to referential errors, which can be caused by simple things such as users having deleted a row somewhere they should not have. This type of referential error will wreak havoc in a model because it leaves a trail of broken links through the model. It's almost like having a computer virus; you will need to find the source to correct the problem. Generally, you will find that when presented with several outcomes, it is best to use a table with the criteria and possible outcomes rather than making a lengthy IF statement, as in Figure 3-3.

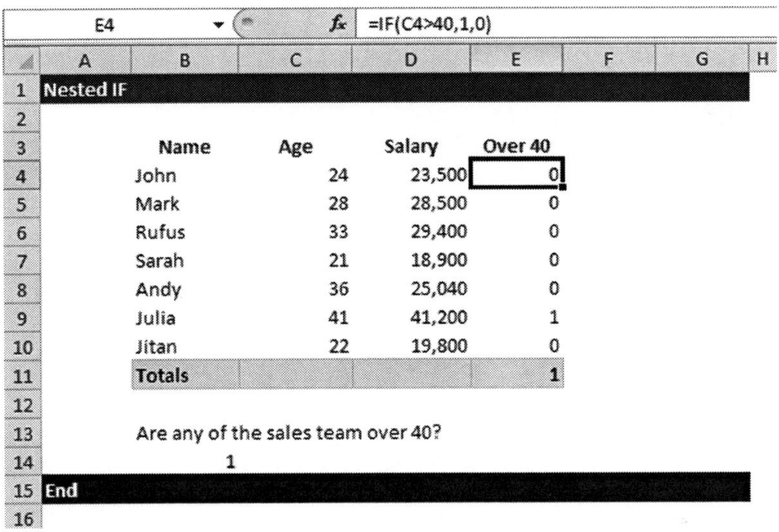

Figure 3-3. A table is used instead of a lengthy nested IF() statement

SUMIF(), COUNTIF(), AVERAGEIF()

There are a group of functions that apply a range of data such as SUMIF(), COUNTIF(), or AVERAGEIF() that meet a specific condition. These are very useful functions, and it is vitally important that you understand how they work and when you would use them. Take a look at Figure 3-4 to see the SUMIF() function in use. Notice how the function will isolate all the data that meets the criteria in cell E13 and will then total that up (cell E16).

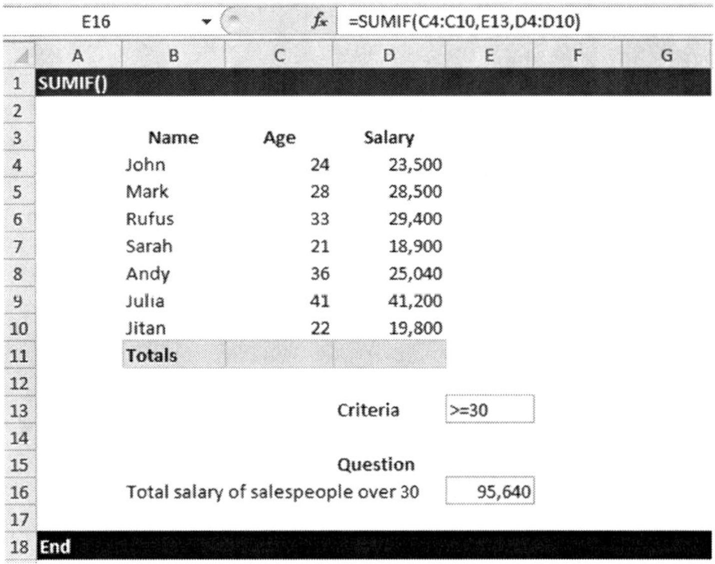

E16 | f_x =SUMIF(C4:C10,E13,D4:D10)

	A	B	C	D	E	F	G
1	SUMIF()						
2							
3		Name	Age	Salary			
4		John	24	23,500			
5		Mark	28	28,500			
6		Rufus	33	29,400			
7		Sarah	21	18,900			
8		Andy	36	25,040			
9		Julia	41	41,200			
10		Jitan	22	19,800			
11		Totals					
12							
13				Criteria	>=30		
14							
15				Question			
16		Total salary of salespeople over 30			95,640		
17							
18	End						

Figure 3-4. In this figure, the SUMIF() statement is in use

Note In this chapter, I am assuming that you have used Excel previously to using this book and that you are no stranger to the SUM(), COUNT(), and AVERAGE() formulas. If this is not the case, I would suggest that you invest in a good book on understanding Excel immediately. I would recommend this book for beginners: *Excel Formula and Functions for Dummies*, by Ken Bluttman (3rd edition, John Wiley & Sons, 2013).

Let's break this down and take a closer look at this formula:

=SUMIF(C4:C10,E13,D4:D10)

First, establish the base range that we are testing.

*=SUMIF(***C4:C10***,E13,D4:D10)*

Then

Establish the criteria we are basing our sum calculation on.

*=SUMIF(C4:10,***E13***,D4:D10)*

Then

The full range of data to sum

*=SUMIF(C4:10,E13,***D4:D10***)*

There are many rules with SUMIF() functions. For example, always make sure the base range and the sum range are aligned (that is, they are looking at a similar range). If you don't, you will end up with unpredictable results, as in Figure 3-5.

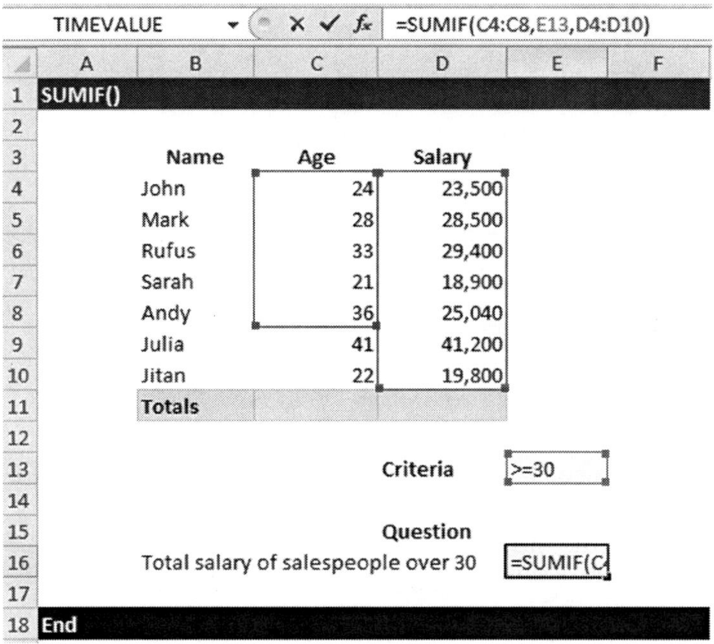

Figure 3-5. The SUMIF() formula does not have aligned ranges

Take note that the base range only runs to row eight (C4:C8) but the sum range runs to row ten (D4:D10). This will cause the result to be unpredictable. The problem usually occurs when you use range naming, which was defined before the full data was available, and subsequently more data has been added but the range name has not adjusted accordingly.

The COUNTIF() function works in a similar way to the SUMIF() function. Instead of totaling all the items that match the criteria, this function counts the number of instances in which the criteria is met. In this case, three employees meet the criteria (see Figure 3-6).

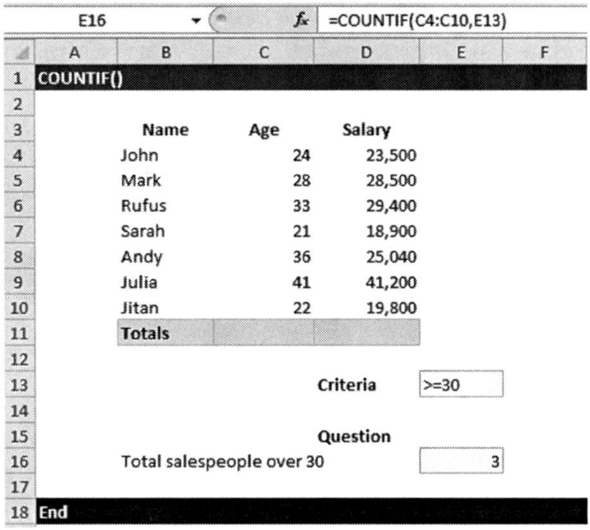

E16 =COUNTIF(C4:C10,E13)

	A	B	C	D	E	F
1	COUNTIF()					
2						
3		Name	Age	Salary		
4		John	24	23,500		
5		Mark	28	28,500		
6		Rufus	33	29,400		
7		Sarah	21	18,900		
8		Andy	36	25,040		
9		Julia	41	41,200		
10		Jitan	22	19,800		
11		Totals				
12						
13				Criteria	>=30	
14						
15				Question		
16		Total salespeople over 30			3	
17						
18	End					

Figure 3-6. Using the COUNTIF() statement, three people meet the criteria

The AVERAGEIF() function works by totaling the items that match the criteria and then dividing that total by the number of instances. In Figure 3-7, there are three employees who match the criteria of being over 30 years old. Their total salary is 95,640, and so the average is 95,640 divided by 3, which is 31,880.

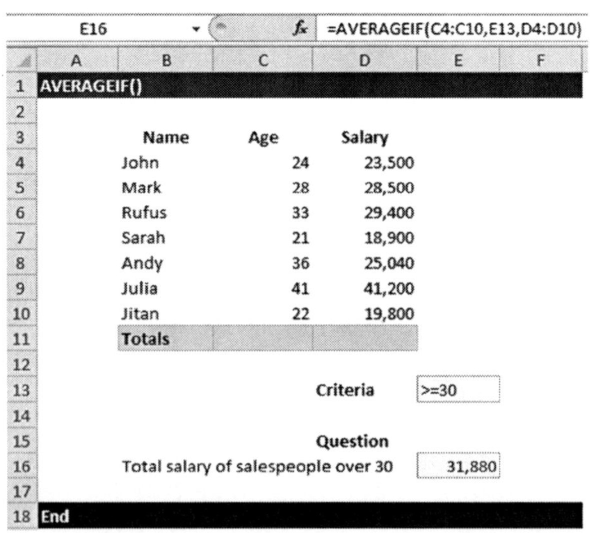

E16 =AVERAGEIF(C4:C10,E13,D4:D10)

	A	B	C	D	E	F
1	AVERAGEIF()					
2						
3		Name	Age	Salary		
4		John	24	23,500		
5		Mark	28	28,500		
6		Rufus	33	29,400		
7		Sarah	21	18,900		
8		Andy	36	25,040		
9		Julia	41	41,200		
10		Jitan	22	19,800		
11		Totals				
12						
13				Criteria	>=30	
14						
15				Question		
16		Total salary of salespeople over 30			31,880	
17						
18	End					

Figure 3-7. The "Total salary of salespeople over 30" in cell E16 is based on the criteria in cell E13

SUMIFS()

The SUMIFS() function came into existence with Excel version 2007, and it's an extension of the SUMIF in that while the SUMIF() only allows for one criterion to be tested, the SUMIFS() function can extend to multiple criteria:

=SUMIFS(sum_range,criteria_range_1,criteria_1,criteria_range_2,criteria_2 and so on).

By giving the ability to work on multiple criteria, the SUMIFS() function allows modelers to create very detailed and flexible outputs, as in Figure 3-8.

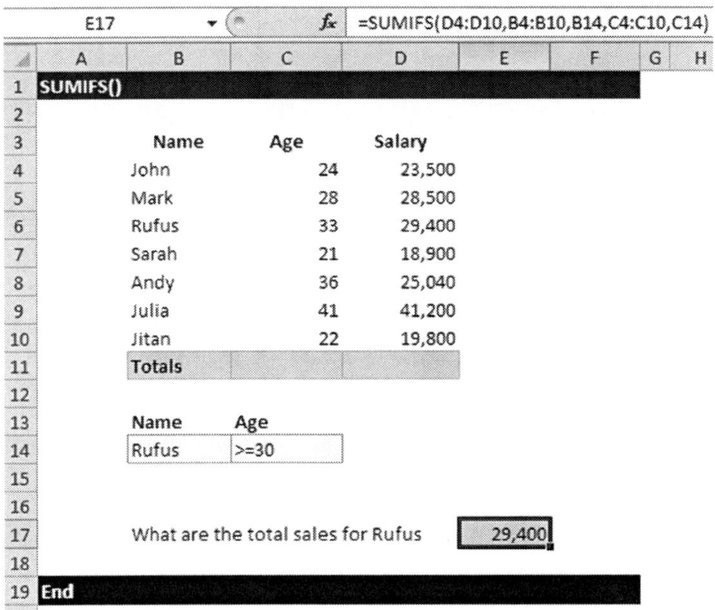

Figure 3-8. The SUMIFS() function is using two criteria—the name and the age—to produce the result

Lookup Functions

Excel lookups know-how is a must-have for the financial modeler. Lookup functions make up a suite of very powerful formulas that can interrogate data tables to isolate items that conform to specific criteria. There are a number of lookup functions, and it's quite common to see two or more of these functions combined into one formula to extend the power of Excel. While I do not advocate creating extended and complex lookup functions because they are difficult to audit, it is still important that a modeler be capable of building lookup formulas that can provide solutions during modeling.

VLOOKUP()

Once you have mastered the VLOOKUP(), your opinion on how useful Excel can be will be enhanced because nothing beats seeing an effective VLOOKUP() at work. VLOOKUPs are a legacy of Lotus 1-2-3, which was the defacto spreadsheet during the 1980s. Here is the syntax:

=VLOOKUP(value, table_array, index_number, [not_exact_match])

- *Value* is the value to search for in the first column of the table_array.
- *Table_array* is two or more columns of data that are sorted in ascending order.
- *Index_number* is the column number in table_array from which the matching value must be returned. The first column is 1.
- *Not_exact_match* is optional. It determines if you are looking for an exact match based on value. Enter FALSE to find an exact match. Enter TRUE to find an approximate match, which means that if an exact match if not found, then the VLOOKUP() function will look for the next largest value that is less than value. If this parameter is omitted, the VLOOKUP() function returns an approximate match.

Note For this book, an array is considered a collection of items. In Excel, those items can be a single row (called a one-dimensional horizontal array), a column (a one-dimensional vertical array), or multiple rows and columns (a two-dimensional array). Excel is not yet capable of allowing three-dimensional array tables.

Excel's VLOOKUP() function, which stands for vertical lookup, can help you find specific information in large data tables or table arrays, such as an inventory list of parts or a sizeable membership contact list. VLOOKUP() will take the lookup value (the item that you are trying to find from the table or list), check the leftmost column of the data that is being referenced, and then work a certain number of columns forward to get the details, as in Figure 3-9a.

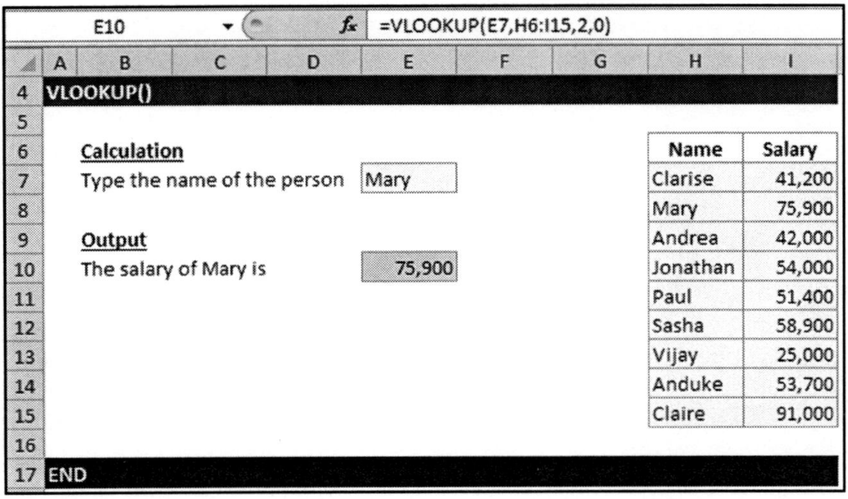

Figure 3-9a. The VLOOKUP() function uses the name to determine the salary, which starts at cell H6

Here is an example of a way to use the VLOOKUP() function. Your objective is to find the salary of the person whose name is in cell E7, which in Figure 3-9a is Mary.

The formula is VLOOKUP(E7,H6:I15,2,0), and it works in the following way:

Look at the name in cell E7, which is Mary.

If the name in E7 is an exact match to any of the names within the range H6:H15, then use the second column in the range H6:I15 to return the salary, which for the name Mary is 75,900.

If the name in E7 has no match within the range H16:I15, then return that it is not applicable (#N/A), which means a formula or a function inside a formula cannot find the referenced data. In essence, there is some data that is missing. If you were to type the name Paul into E7, the result would be 51,400, as in Figure 3-9b.

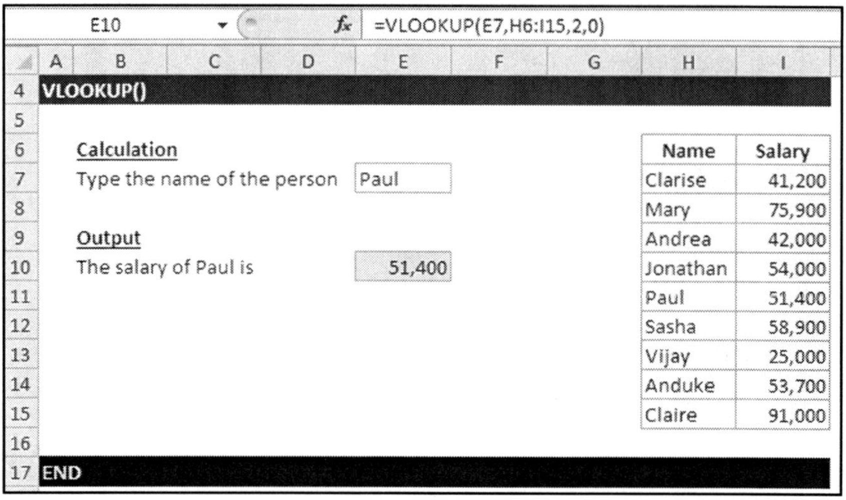

Figure 3-9b. The VLOOKUP() function has reflected the result based on the name Paul

There are several ways in which to use VLOOKUPs by combining them with other functions, which can make them that much more dynamic and versatile. The example in Figure 3-10 is a situation that you will come across in modeling, where dates are used and need to be translated into days of the week. Here I have combined the VLOOKUP() function with the WEEKDAY() function, which gives us the day of the week on which a particular date will fall.

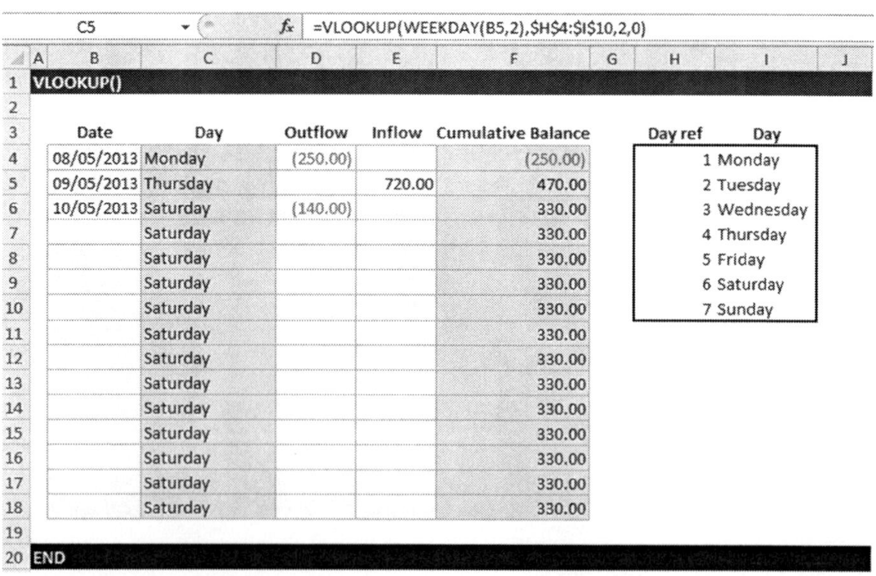

Figure 3-10. The VLOOKUP() function is used with the WEEKDAY() function to give the day of the week

The VLOOKUP() structure is basically the same, except this time instead of referencing a particular cell, I have used the WEEKDAY() function. This function checks the date in column B to produce a number between 1 and 7, matches that number against the table in column H, and then performs a lookup to see which day is linked to that number.

This is an example of expanding VLOOKUP() with functions, and it is a skill you need to become very comfortable with performing. This is the creative element of modeling that you will use to find solutions to problems.

Note that when using VLOOKUPs, moderation is imperative. VLOOKUPs are processor-intensive, and while they are not volatile, they can affect the performance of your computer. Creating several VLOOKUPs that work from large tables (that is, more than 1,000 rows) is just asking for trouble.

Caution Volatile functions are a type of function that will always recalculate. As a result, when Excel needs to calculate any part of the worksheet, cells containing volatile functions will also calculate, irrespective of whether any changes have occurred.

There is some discussion as to which functions are actually volatile and which are nonvolatile, but much depends on which version of Excel you are using. And not surprisingly, there are also degrees of volatility. The most volatile are the RAND( ), NOW( ), and TODAY( ) functions. Try to avoid having several of these in your models. Others that are also considered volatile are OFFSET( ), CELL( ), INDIRECT( ), and INFO( ), though not to the same degree as the first three. Often the way to get around using volatile is to create your own functions called user-defined functions (UDFs), which are discussed later in the chapter.

VLOOKUPs unfortunately have a built-in weakness—they rely on using the leftmost column for the lookup reference and then counting from that column to find the return data. Look at Figures 3-11 and 3-12.

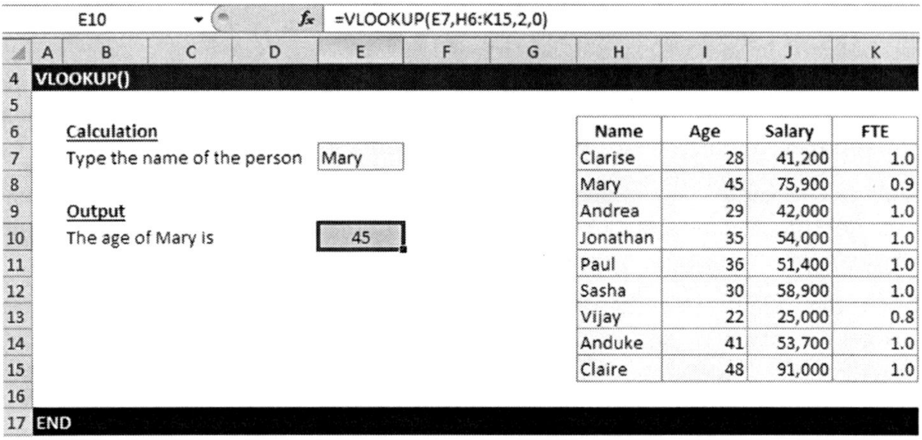

Name	Age	Salary	FTE
Clarise	28	41,200	1.0
Mary	45	75,900	0.9
Andrea	29	42,000	1.0
Jonathan	35	54,000	1.0
Paul	36	51,400	1.0
Sasha	30	58,900	1.0
Vijay	22	25,000	0.8
Anduke	41	53,700	1.0
Claire	48	91,000	1.0

Figure 3-11. The VLOOKUP() function is looking up the age on the correct column

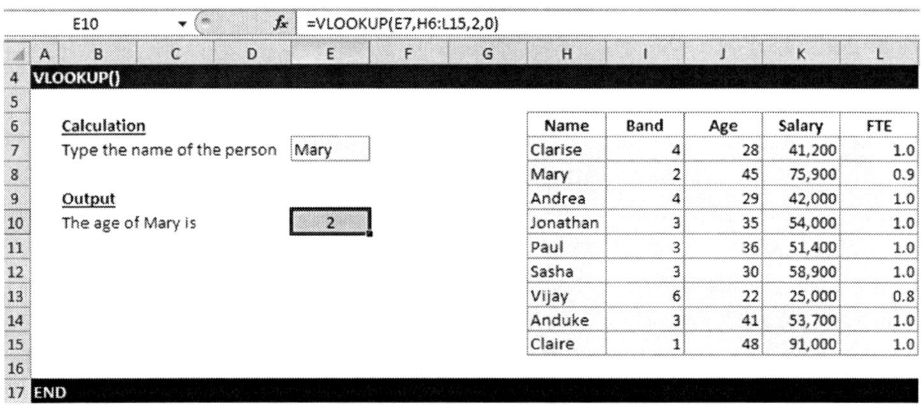

Name	Band	Age	Salary	FTE
Clarise	4	28	41,200	1.0
Mary	2	45	75,900	0.9
Andrea	4	29	42,000	1.0
Jonathan	3	35	54,000	1.0
Paul	3	36	51,400	1.0
Sasha	3	30	58,900	1.0
Vijay	6	22	25,000	0.8
Anduke	3	41	53,700	1.0
Claire	1	48	91,000	1.0

Figure 3-12. The VLOOKUP() function has remained, but a new column in column I has been introduced

From these two examples with Figures 3-11 and 3-12, the only change is that a new column called "Band" was inserted into the table with Figure 3-12. We still require the person's age, but we haven't changed the formula to look at the third column in the table. Therefore, the output is returning the band and not the age. Inserting columns into data is one of the weaknesses of VLOOKUPs. Unless you create some dynamism into the lookup to count off the return column, the model will always be vulnerable should anyone insert or delete columns from tables that are using VLOOKUPs. The alternative to insulating the model against this type of problem is to use the MATCH() function combined with the INDEX() function, which I will discuss shortly.

MATCH()

The MATCH() function can be used to find the position of specified data in a list or a selected range of cells. Here is the syntax for the MATCH() function:

= *MATCH (Lookup_value, Lookup_array, Match_type)*

- *Lookup_value* (required) is the value that you want to find in the list of data. This argument can be a number, text, logical value, or a cell reference.
- *Lookup_array* (required) is the range of cells being searched.
- *Match_type* includes these three choices: 1, 0, or -1.
- *If the match_type* = 1 or is omitted, MATCH() finds the largest value that is less than or equal to the Lookup_value. The Lookup_array data must be sorted in ascending order.
- *If the match_type* = 0, MATCH() finds the first value that is exactly equal to the Lookup_value. The Lookup_array data can be sorted in any order.
- *If the match_type* = -1, MATCH() finds the smallest value that is greater than or equal to the Lookup_value. The Lookup_array data must be sorted in descending order.

The MATCH() function does exactly as its name implies—it looks to match the data in one range with the data in another. When it finds a match, it provides the position of the matched data.

In Figure 3-13, the objective is to find the relative position of the name in cell E7 (Mary) to the table of names in the range H6:H15.

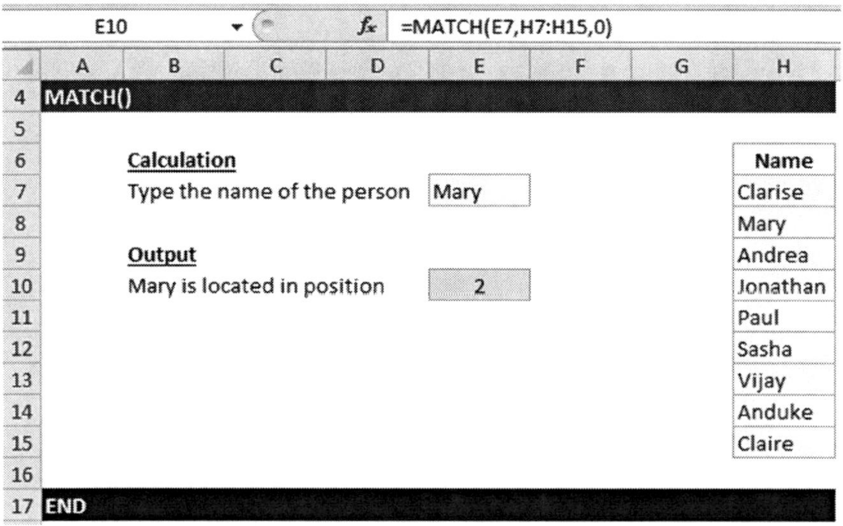

Figure 3-13. This figure shows the MATCH() function in use

The formula that has been constructed is =MATCH(E7,H7:H15,0) (Notice the starting range is at cell H7, not H6 as in the VLOOKUP(). When using a match its advisable to omit the heading row to avoid confusing the data from the headings.) It works like this:

Hold the name in cell E7 (Mary) and look for an exact match of that name in the range H7:H15.

If an exact match of the name Mary is found in the range H7:H15, then return the position where the match lies in the range and Mary appears at the second position on the list.

If the name in E7 has no match within the range H7:H15, then return that it is not applicable (#N/A!, which means a formula or a function inside a formula cannot find the referenced data).

The MATCH() function is a particular favorite of mine. By just giving the row location of the lookup match, it can be used as part of a dynamic formula that is so critical to most financial models. If you have the ability to reference data in your model by using locations instead, it is then possible to create formulas that can interact with the model user. Look at the example in Figure 3-14. I mentioned earlier some of the weaknesses of the VLOOKUP() function, but in this example I have not only eradicated that weakness, but I have also created a situation where the user can quickly alter the return data. I use this formula construct in several of my user inputs to give the users control over which information they want to view in the outputs.

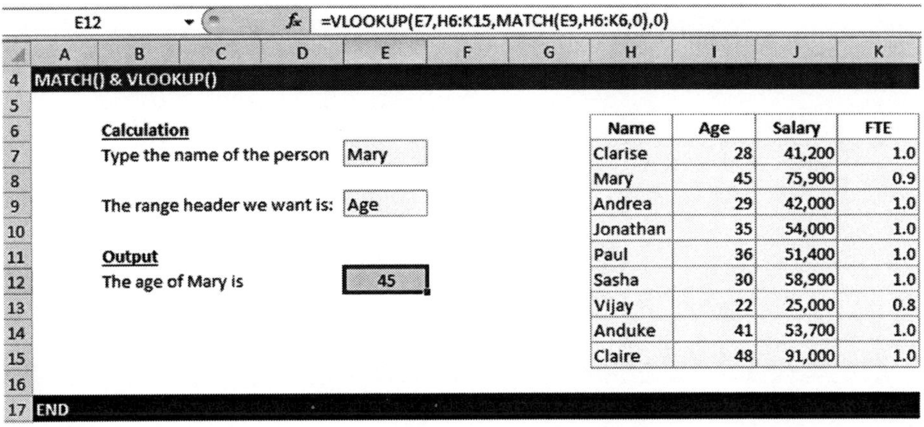

Figure 3-14. The MATCH() and VLOOKUP() functions are combined to add flexibility to the return of the formula

In Figure 3-14, the objective is to match the name in cell E7 to the range in H6:K15 using a VLOOKUP(), but the information we want to be returned could be the age, salary, or the FTE. Flexibility is a must.

For this situation, I used a combination of a VLOOKUP() and a MATCH() function because no single function is able to give the flexibility around the data. The formula construction is: =VLOOKUP(E7,H6:K15,MATCH(E9,H6:K6,0),0). This is how it works:

Hold the name in cell E7 (Mary) and look for an exact match of that name within the range H6:K15.

The second half of the formula uses the MATCH() function to find the relative column location of "Age" in the table, which is column 2.

The whole formula is then looking up the name Mary in the table, and then finding the heading column two which is the age, and then returning the value of Mary's age.

If the name Mary in E7 and/or the range header in E9 have no match within the range H6:K15, return that it is not applicable (#N/A!).

One of the benefits of using this formula construction is that there is stability with data because the matching is using references in the range. Notice that in Figure 3-15a I have inserted a new column called "Band" into column I; this has altered the range structure as it has changed from a four-column range to a five-column range. A common problem with lookups is creating a formula that uses a number as the column reference that will provide the return information. If we look at Figure 3-15b, the MATCH() function has been exchanged for a numerical reference to the return column and the result is the same. However, in Figure 3-15c, the result has become unpredictable because the range structure has been changed and a new column inserted.

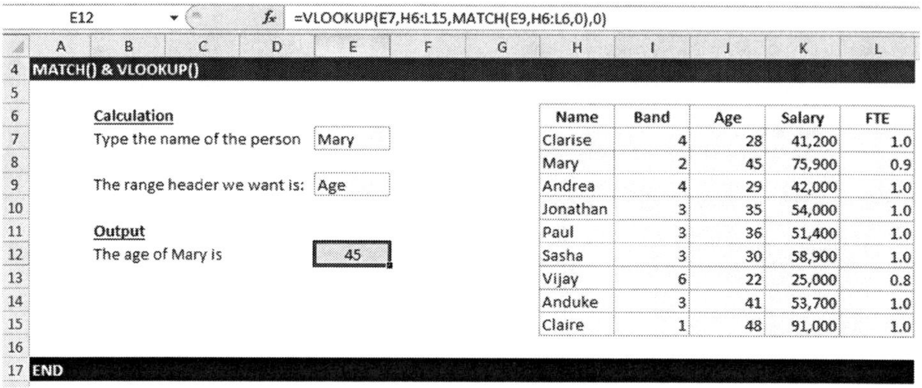

E12 =VLOOKUP(E7,H6:L15,MATCH(E9,H6:L6,0),0)

MATCH() & VLOOKUP()

Calculation

Type the name of the person: Mary

The range header we want is: Age

Output

The age of Mary is: 45

Name	Band	Age	Salary	FTE
Clarise	4	28	41,200	1.0
Mary	2	45	75,900	0.9
Andrea	4	29	42,000	1.0
Jonathan	3	35	54,000	1.0
Paul	3	36	51,400	1.0
Sasha	3	30	58,900	1.0
Vijay	6	22	25,000	0.8
Anduke	3	41	53,700	1.0
Claire	1	48	91,000	1.0

END

Figure 3-15a. The formula still remains the same and returns the same results even with a new column inserted called "Band"

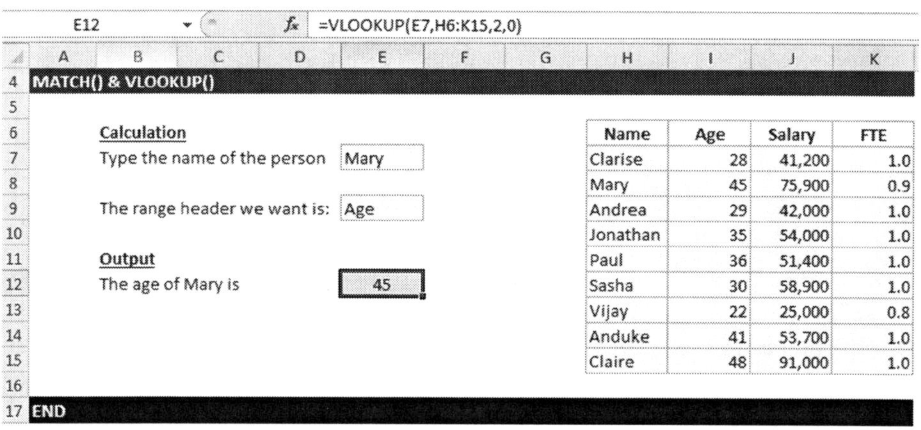

E12 =VLOOKUP(E7,H6:K15,2,0)

MATCH() & VLOOKUP()

Calculation

Type the name of the person: Mary

The range header we want is: Age

Output

The age of Mary is: 45

Name	Age	Salary	FTE
Clarise	28	41,200	1.0
Mary	45	75,900	0.9
Andrea	29	42,000	1.0
Jonathan	35	54,000	1.0
Paul	36	51,400	1.0
Sasha	30	58,900	1.0
Vijay	22	25,000	0.8
Anduke	41	53,700	1.0
Claire	48	91,000	1.0

END

Figure 3-15b. The MATCH() function has been replaced with a numerical reference to the column (2) in the formula, and Mary's age is matched correctly

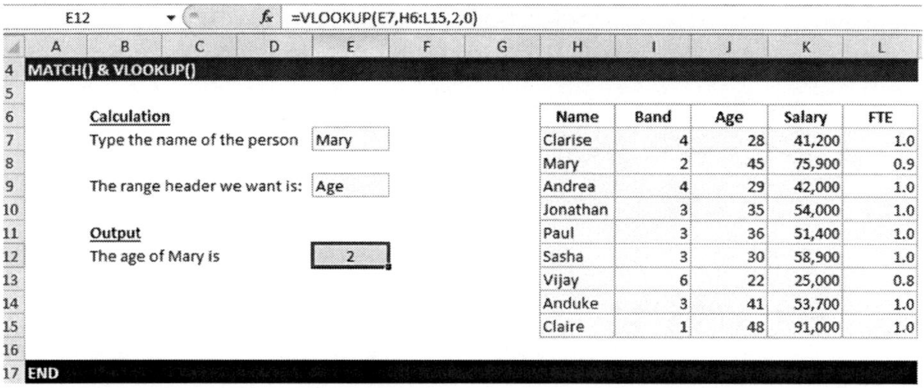

Name	Band	Age	Salary	FTE
Clarise	4	28	41,200	1.0
Mary	2	45	75,900	0.9
Andrea	4	29	42,000	1.0
Jonathan	3	35	54,000	1.0
Paul	3	36	51,400	1.0
Sasha	3	30	58,900	1.0
Vijay	6	22	25,000	0.8
Anduke	3	41	53,700	1.0
Claire	1	48	91,000	1.0

Figure 3-15c. The range structure has been changed and a new column has been added. As a result, the use of a numerical column reference has caused the results to become unpredictable

INDEX()

The INDEX() function is a two-horse cart; it can either return the value from a table or return the location reference within a table. Here is the syntax for when a value needs to be returned:

INDEX(array, row_number, [column_number])

- *Array* is a range of cells or table.
- *Row_number* is the row number in the array to use to return the value. If this value is omitted, then the Column_ number is required.
- *Column_number* is optional. It is the column number in the array to use to return the value. If this number is omitted, then the Row_number is required.

Figure 3-16 demonstrates using the INDEX() function to return a value. The objective is to see which value is returned based on a specified location within a table.

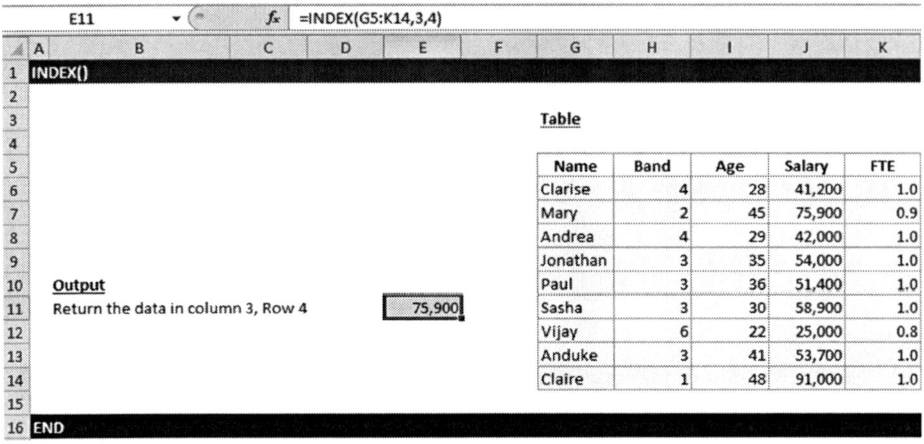

Name	Band	Age	Salary	FTE
Clarise	4	28	41,200	1.0
Mary	2	45	75,900	0.9
Andrea	4	29	42,000	1.0
Jonathan	3	35	54,000	1.0
Paul	3	36	51,400	1.0
Sasha	3	30	58,900	1.0
Vijay	6	22	25,000	0.8
Anduke	3	41	53,700	1.0
Claire	1	48	91,000	1.0

Figure 3-16. The INDEX() function is used to return the value found by referencing the rows and columns

For this situation, I used the INDEX() function with the formula =INDEX(G5:K14,3,4). Here is how it works:

Take the range of cells from G5:K14 Starting from the first cell (G5), move down three cell rows (including G5), and then move across four cell columns (including G5), which returns 75,900.

If the locations of rows and columns are not within the table, then return #REF!, which means the reference is invalid.

This is quite a simple formula to construct using the table and stating the row and column numbers. The INDEX() function together with the MATCH() function is also an effective alternative to using VLOOKUPs, and there are numerous reasons why. The main one is that such a formula does not rely on the leftmost column to read the data. Therefore, the formula can be used to work backward from a table as well as forward. The combination also has benefits by using it dynamically, as in Figure 3-17.

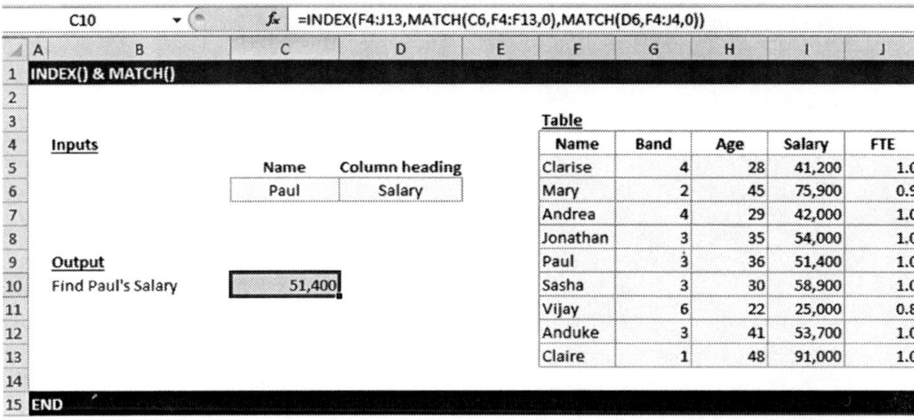

Figure 3-17. In this figure, the INDEX() and MATCH() functions are used in cell C10

In Figure 3-17, the objective is to find the value that satisfies two criteria—the name and a flexible column heading (in this case it is the salary).

For this situation, I used a combination of the INDEX() and MATCH() functions with the formula:

=INDEX(F4:J13,MATCH(C6,F4:F13,0),MATCH(D6,F4:J4,0))

Here is how it works:

Take the range of cells from F4:J13 and then find the name in cell C6 within the table F4:J13. Then using the same row of the name in C6, move across the columns until you get to the heading in cell D6 (Salary) and return the value that is in that cell.

If neither the name or column headings match the table, then return #N/A!

Using the combination of the INDEX() and MATCH() functions is also a way of giving the user inputs flexibility. When designing financial models, it is critical to give as much flexibility as you can afford to the model user. These types of formula constructs will aid you in offering this flexibility.

OFFSET()

The syntax for the OFFSET() function is as follows:

=OFFSET(starting_point, rows to move, columns to move, height, width)

The OFFSET() function returns a cell or range of cells that is a specified number of rows and columns from the original cell or range of cells (see Figure 3-18a).

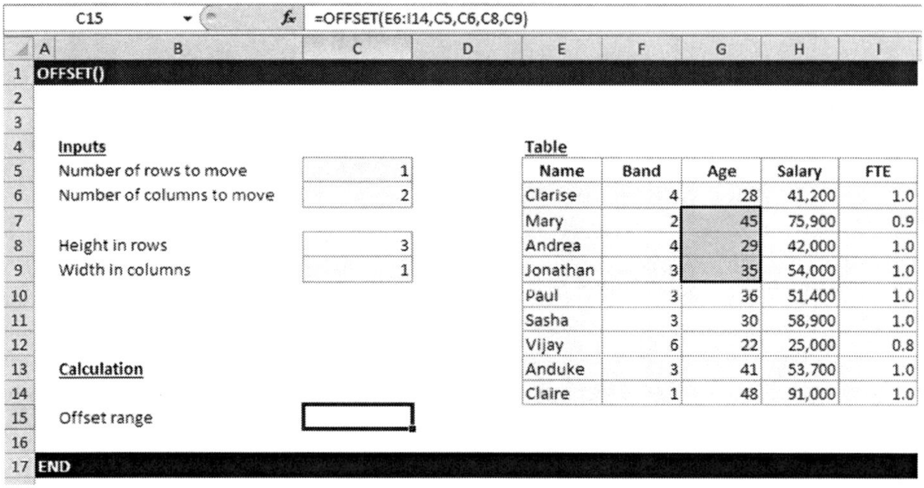
C15 =OFFSET(E6:I14,C5,C6,C8,C9)

	A	B	C	D	E	F	G	H	I
1	OFFSET()								
2									
3									
4		Inputs			Table				
5		Number of rows to move	1		Name	Band	Age	Salary	FTE
6		Number of columns to move	2		Clarise	4	28	41,200	1.0
7					Mary	2	45	75,900	0.9
8		Height in rows	3		Andrea	4	29	42,000	1.0
9		Width in columns	1		Jonathan	3	35	54,000	1.0
10					Paul	3	36	51,400	1.0
11					Sasha	3	30	58,900	1.0
12					Vijay	6	22	25,000	0.8
13		Calculation			Anduke	3	41	53,700	1.0
14					Claire	1	48	91,000	1.0
15		Offset range							
16									
17	END								

Figure 3-18a. This figure shows the OFFSET() function acting on a set of data

Let's break this formula down in order to examine it more closely:

=OFFSET(E6:I14,C5,C6,C8,C9)

Take the range from cells E6 to I14 as the reference.

=OFFSET(E6:I14,*C5,C6,C8,C9)*

Then move the specified number of rows across starting from cell E6 as input in cell C5 (in this case one row).

*=OFFSET(***E6***:I14,***C5***,C6,C8,C9)*

Then move the specified number of columns across starting from cell E6 as input in cell C6 (in this case two columns).

*=OFFSET(***E6***:I14,C5,***C6***,C8,C9)*

The range to cover is now based on cell C8 in rows (in this case three) and cell C9 in columns (in this case one).

*=OFFSET(E6:I14,C5,C6,***C8,C9***)*

The range that is the offset range is marked in blue in Figure 3-18a. The OFFSET() function is not used frequently in modeling, because it is not immediately clear what to use it for, and also because it is one of the few functions that, when used on its own, does not give a valid return. In fact the OFFESET() is almost always used with in conjunction with the SUM() function, COUNT()

function, and sometimes with the MATCH() function. However, the OFFSET() function should not be overlooked because there are situations where it is useful. For example, it would be needed if the model is expecting to have some data inputs from the model user into a table. In Figure 3-18b, I have shown a simple example of using the SUM() function to total the cells from the OFFSET() function.

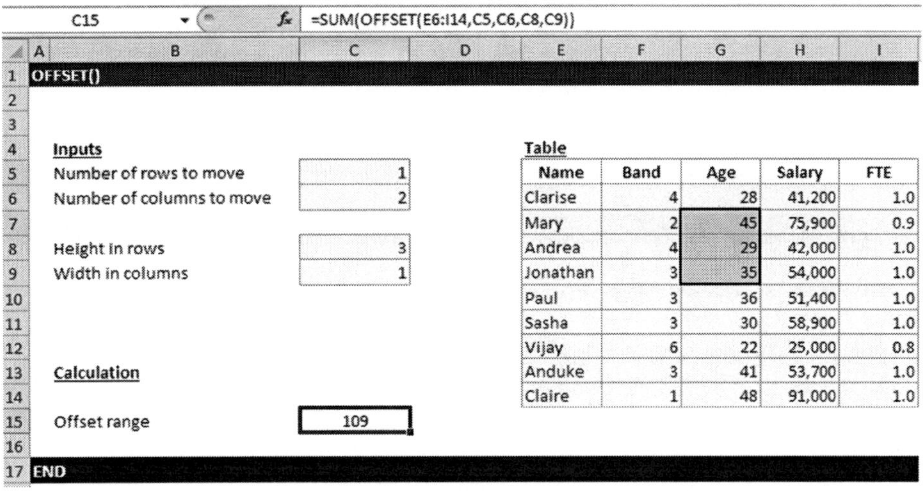

C15 =SUM(OFFSET(E6:I14,C5,C6,C8,C9))

	A	B	C	D	E	F	G	H	I
1	OFFSET()								
2									
3									
4		Inputs			Table				
5		Number of rows to move	1		Name	Band	Age	Salary	FTE
6		Number of columns to move	2		Clarise	4	28	41,200	1.0
7					Mary	2	45	75,900	0.9
8		Height in rows	3		Andrea	4	29	42,000	1.0
9		Width in columns	1		Jonathan	3	35	54,000	1.0
10					Paul	3	36	51,400	1.0
11					Sasha	3	30	58,900	1.0
12					Vijay	6	22	25,000	0.8
13		Calculation			Anduke	3	41	53,700	1.0
14					Claire	1	48	91,000	1.0
15		Offset range	109						
16									
17	END								

Figure 3-18b. The OFFSET() function has highlighted the data based on the inputs. These inputs are then totaled by using the SUM() function

---

Caution The OFFSET() function is often volatile, which I explained earlier in this chapter. Therefore you should limit the number of times that it is used in your model. As a general rule, have no more than one OFFSET() function on any given worksheet.

CHOOSE()

The CHOOSE() function is used when there is a need to choose between a number of options. Even though it is not often used in modeling, it is a simple and very useful function that I would advise you to put into your modeling tools armory. The syntax is as follows:

=CHOOSE(index_num, value1, value2, value3 . . . up to 254 values)

The example in Figure 3-19 shows the practical use of the CHOOSE() function when choosing from a set of options.

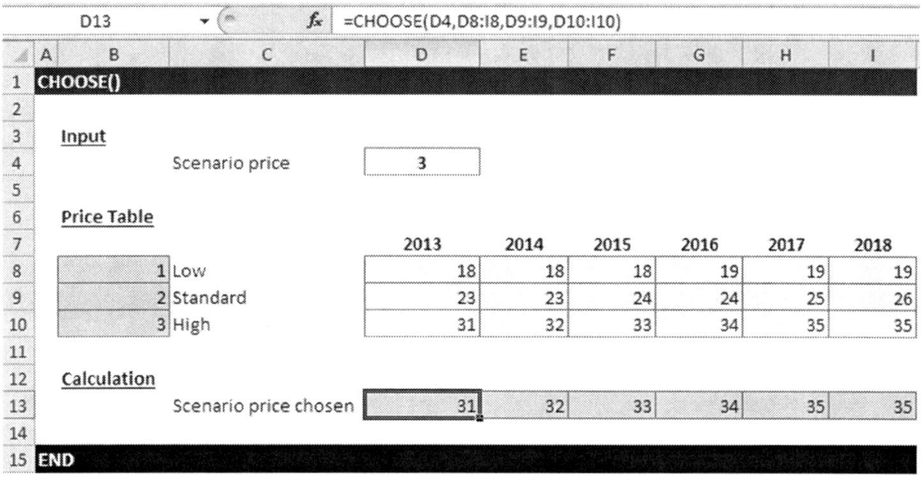

Figure 3-19. In this figure, the CHOOSE() function is used when picking out one option

In Figure 3-19, there is a table with three pricing options (low, standard, and high), numbered 1, 2, 3 respectively. There is a scenario price option in cell D4, which allows the model user to choose one of the three numbers (1, 2, or 3).

Once the user has selected one of the numbers, a CHOOSE() function will then return the data that corresponds to that number. Let's take a closer look at this function.

First use the index number in cell D4.

=CHOOSE(D4,*D8:I8:D9:I9:D10:I10).*

Then use reference number 1 from cell D8 to I8, reference number 2 from cell D9 to I9, and reference number 3 from cell D10 to I10. Then match the reference number to the index number chosen and display the relevant price.

*=CHOOSE(C6,D9:***K9,D10:K10,D1:K11***)*

The example in Figure 3-19 is a very common occurrence in models where you need to show distinct viewpoints or when you need to reflect many unlike scenarios from a set of data. Becoming familiar with the working of the CHOOSE() function will provide you with a relatively easy solution to modeling scenarios.

Date and Time Functions

Dates are very important in financial modeling because they just crop up time and time again. Almost all the information that is produced as outputs have a time impact; therefore, at some juncture in every model dates have to be dealt with. My advice to you is to come to grips with working with dates. Many users of Excel find dates tricky because dates do not conform to the binary formats. But with a little perseverance, you will overcome any inhibitions you have concerning dates, and it will be worth it to you.

NETWORKDAYS.INTL()

The NETWORKDAYS.INTL() function is used to calculate the number of whole business or working days between the start date and end date that is specified in the formula. You may have come across the NETWORKDAYS() function previously, but the NETWORKDAYS.INTL() function is different. This function allows you to specify which days and how many are considered weekend days rather than automatically removing two days per week (such as removing Saturday and Sunday from the total number of days), which is more practical.

With this function, days specified as weekend days are automatically removed from the total. In addition, specific days, such as statutory holidays, can be omitted as well, all within the formula in contrast to making adjustments if you use NETWORKDAYS().

The syntax for the NETWORKDAYS.INTL() function is as follows:

= *NETWORKDAYS.INTL(Start_date, End_date, Weekend, Holidays)*

- *Start_date* (required) is the start date of the chosen time period. This function does not have real time date validation (avoid entering dates directly into the formula), and so you should always use a cell reference that is expecting a date to avoid issues related to date syntax.
- *End_date* (required) is the end date of the chosen time period. As with the Start_date, use a cell reference that is expecting a date.
- *Weekend* (optional) is the number of days and which days of the week with 1 = Saturday and Sunday, 6 = Thursday and Friday, and 7 = Friday and Saturday. If this weekend option is left blank, then the function will revert to the default, which is number 1 (Saturday and Sunday).

- *Holidays* (optional) are more additional dates (sometimes it is just one date) that are excluded from the full number of working days. Although it is possible to enter the series of holidays as dates, I advise that you use a reference to a range that contains the holiday dates. If you don't, the formula construction becomes cumbersome (see Figure 3-20).

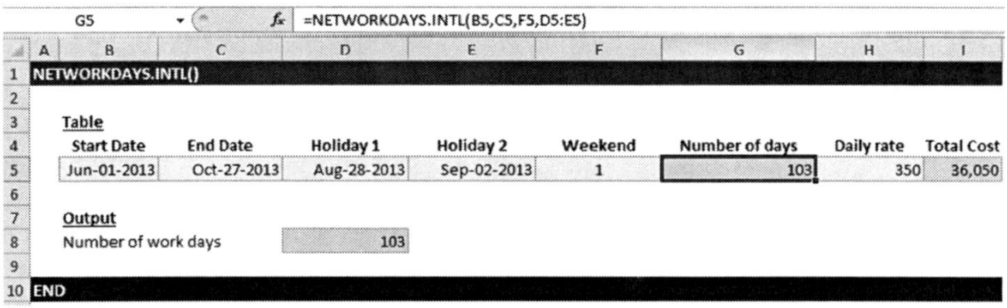

Figure 3-20. Calculating the number of working days is served by using the NETWORKDAYS.INTL() function

DATEDIF()

The DATEDIF() function is used to calculate the time period or difference between two dates. This time period can be calculated as the number of days, months, or years between the two dates. You will often find that you will need to make some modeling calculation based on a time lapse. The function is very useful when a certain passage of time has elapsed that will trigger some mechanism.

An interesting point about DATEDIF() is that it is an "undocumented" function. This means that it is not listed with other date functions under the Formula tab in Excel, so you won't find it if you try to look for it in the Formula dialog. Therefore, you will need to type it in manually and not rely on the formula defaults.

The syntax for the DATEDIF() function is as follows:

=DATEDIF(start_date,end_date,"interval")

The function has three arguments that need to be entered as part of the function:

- *Start_date* (required) is the start date of the chosen time period. This function does not have real time date validation, and so you should always use a cell reference to the start date to avoid date syntax issues.
- *End_date* (required) is the end date of the chosen time period. As with the Start_date, use a cell reference for the end_date.
- *"Interval"* (required) tells the function to find the number of days ("D"), complete months ("M"), or complete years ("Y") between the two dates.

Caution When entering the interval argument, you must include the quotation marks such as "YD." Always remember there is a space before the quotation marks.

The interval argument can also contain a combination of days, months, and years in order to increase the variety of answers returned by the function.

- "YM" calculates the number of months between two dates as if the dates were in the same year.
- "YD" calculates the number of days between two dates as if the dates were in the same year.
- "MD" calculates the number of days between two dates as if the dates were in the same month and year.

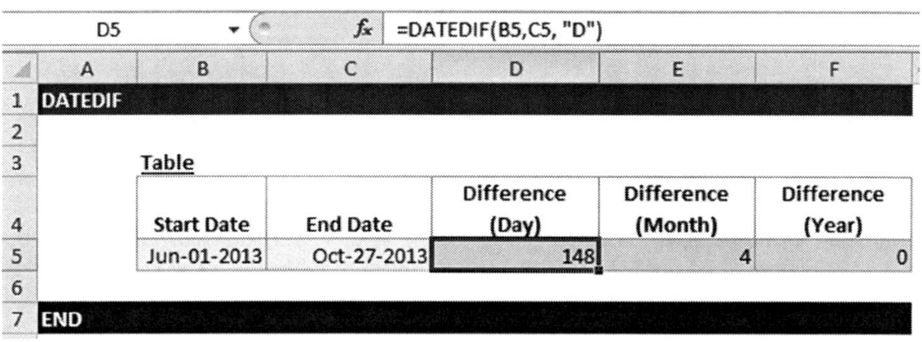
D5 =DATEDIF(B5,C5, "D")

	A	B	C	D	E	F
1	DATEDIF					
2						
3		Table				
4		Start Date	End Date	Difference (Day)	Difference (Month)	Difference (Year)
5		Jun-01-2013	Oct-27-2013	148	4	0
6						
7	END					

Figure 3-21a. This figure shows the DATEDIF() function using the day ("D")

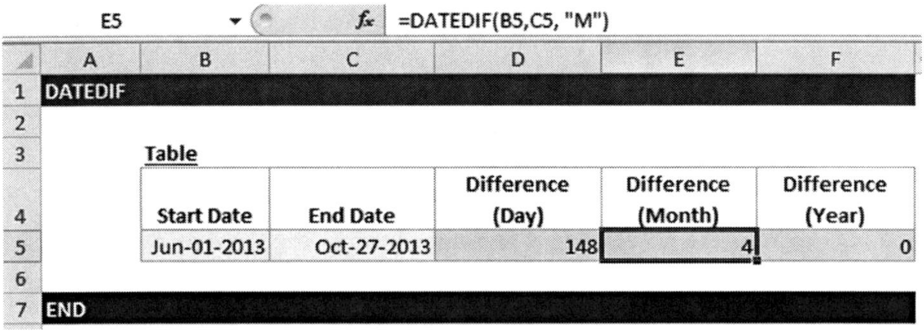

Figure 3-21b. This figure shows the DATEDIF() function using the month ("M")

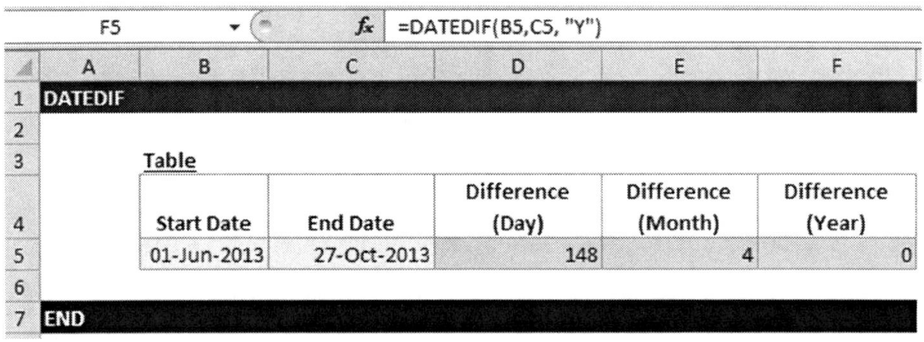

Figure 3-21c. This figure shows the DATEDIF() function using the year ("Y")

As the DATEDIF() function has to be typed manually, it is very easy to mistype it as DATEIF() and then receive a naming error. This can be quite frustrating, but just remember there is a "D" after the "DATE."

WORKDAY()

The WORKDAY() function finds the start or end date of a project or assignment. This is another workhorse function—you will use it time and time again. One of the real benefits of this function is that it can be used to check the user inputs and then calculate number of days thereafter. I use this function in tax calculations and also where there are schedules, such as amortization and depreciation calculations.

The number of workdays automatically excludes weekends and any dates that are identified as holidays.

Uses for the WORKDAY( ) function include calculating the following:

- The end date for a project with a set number of workdays following a given start date
- The start date for a project with a set number of workdays before a given end date
- The due date for an invoice
- The expected delivery date for goods or materials

The syntax for the WORKDAY( ) function is as follows:

=WORKDAY(Start_date, Days, Holidays)

- *Start_date* (required) is the start date of the chosen time period. The actual start date can be entered for this argument or the cell reference to the location of this data in the worksheet can be entered instead.
- *Days* (required) is the length of the project. This is an integer showing the number of days of work that were performed on the project. For this argument, enter the number of days of work or the cell reference to the location of this data in the worksheet.
- *Holidays* (optional) is one or more additional dates that are not counted as part of the total number of working days. Use the cell reference to the location of the data in the worksheet for this argument.

Note To find a date that occurs after the Start_date argument, use a positive integer for Days. To find a date that occurs before the Start_date argument, use a negative integer for Days. In this second situation, the Start_date argument could be identified as the end date of a project.

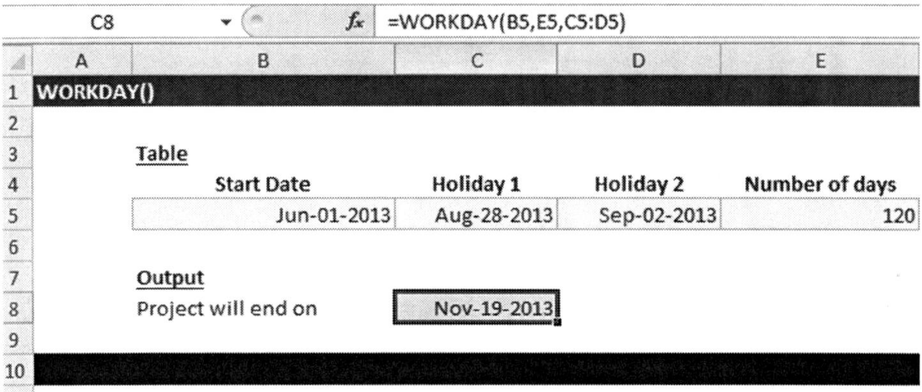

Figure 3-22. The WORKDAY() function also using the optional holidays and the start date to produce an end date

Let's look at this formula more closely:

First get the start date.

=WORKDAY(B5,E5,C5:D5)

Then get the number of days projected.

=*WORKDAY(B4,***E5***,C5:D5)*

Next, add the start date and end date of the holidays (optional).

=*WORKDAY(B5,E5,***C5:D5***)*

Caution Be wary of how you use the holiday options. If you do use them, the formula actually adds the holidays to the total number of days. In reality, most projects or work processes do not work in this way. Holidays are incidental and do not get added onto projects because they are already built around the number of days. As a result, you could be double-counting. If you are not sure, just reduce the number of days by the number of holidays.

EOMONTH()

The EOMONTH() function (or End of Month function) defaults to the end-of-month date for any start date and the number of months before or after that date between -12 to 12.

Here is the syntax for the EOMONTH() function:

= *EOMONTH(Start_date, Months)*

- *Start_date* is the start date of the project or time period in question.
- *Months* is the number of months before or after the Start_date.

It may seem curious looking at this function as to when you would ever use it. Surprisingly, the EOMONTH() is a very commonly used function in financial models. It is most useful when you need to set time scales based on a flexible date. For instance, I use this function in outsourcing bid models to check when the model user's project start date begins. I would then set a preproject bid preparation period that is based on this start date, as in Figure 3-23.

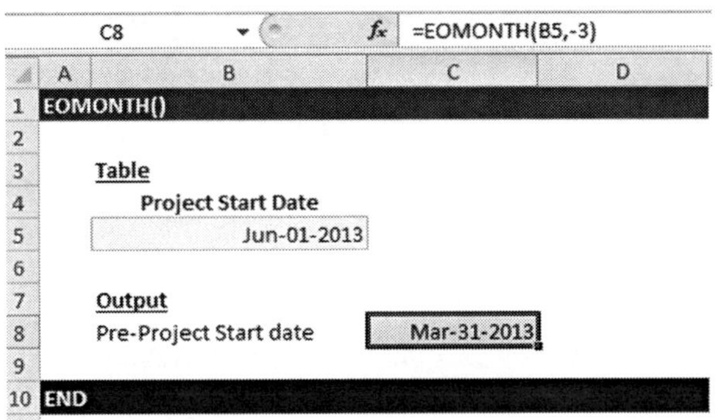

Figure 3-23. The EOMONTH() function is used to set the preproject date

---

Note Keep in mind that the EOMONTH() function will always give the end of the month irrespective of the start date.

DAYS360()

The DAYS360 function gives the number of days between two dates, but it is based on a 360 days per annum in contrast to the full calendar year. I am not sure why this function is based on a 360-day year, but it just means the modeler should be aware that the function is out of synchronization with the calendar year. However, this is an important function when trying to create payment terms or creditor and debtor terms in your models as every month is 30 days (it's quite common for organizations to have payment terms that are built on 30 days, 60 days, or even 90 days).

Here is the syntax for the DAYS360( ) function:

= *DAYS360(Start_date, End_date, Method)*

- *Start_date* is the start date of the chosen time period.
- *End_date* is the end date of the chosen time period.
- *Method* is a Boolean value (TRUE or FALSE).
- *If FALSE* uses the US method of calculating start and end dates.
- *If TRUE* uses the European method of calculating start and end dates.

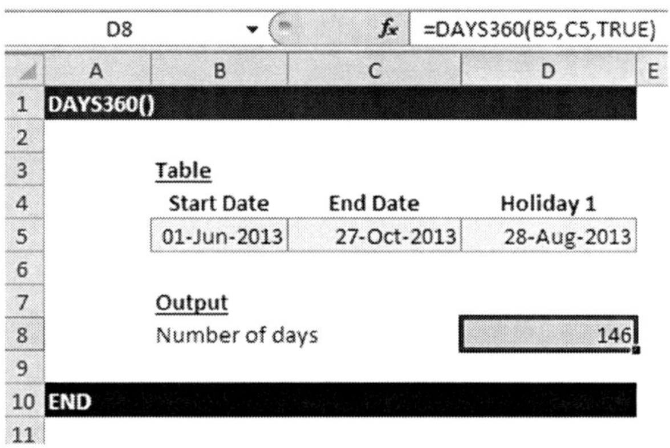

Figure 3-24. The DAYS360( ) function is shown in this figure

DATE( )

I have previously mentioned that dates are often one of the key drivers in financial models. Excel treats dates as numbers and, although these numbers can be formatted to represent months, days, and years, they are still essentially a number. Excel generally recognizes dates when they are simply typed in, such as 06/21/2013. However, depending on how the cell has been formatted, that date could actually be a text (as opposed to a numeric), in which case it will not be recognized.

When working with these functions, I recommend that you use the DATE( ) function rather than simply typing dates as in Figure 3-25. This function will clarify the numeric date irrespective of the cell format.

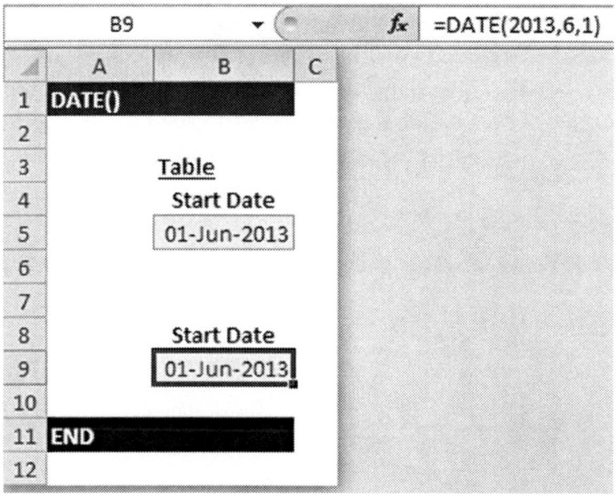

Figure 3-25. The date in row 5 is manually typed, and the date in row 9 is using the DATE() function

The syntax for the DATE() function is as follows:

= *DATE(Year,Month,Day)*

- *Year:* Enter the year as a four-digit number or the cell reference where it is located.
- *Month:* Enter the year as a two-digit number or the cell reference where it is located.
- *Day:* Enter the day as a two-digit number or the cell reference where it is located.

Math Functions

Math functions are a used to calculate particular mathematical problems and, while these functions are in common use, such as the SUM() function, they need to be treated with care because they give specific returns.

MOD()

The MOD() function is used to divide numbers. But unlike a regular division, it returns the remainder as the answer.

The syntax for the MOD() function is as follows:

= *MOD(Number, Divisor)*

This function is particularly useful when trying to set events or triggers within a model that occur at regular and irregular time intervals and could also then trigger some action. In Figure 3-26, the objective is to set a trigger that will allow us to identify when a bill should be sent based on the month. The formula is =MOD(E10,$D$5). Let's see how it works.

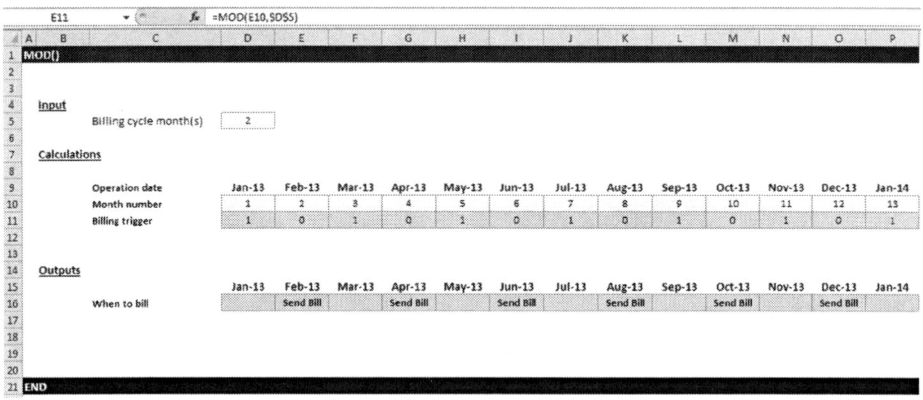

Figure 3-26. The MOD() function is used to return the divisor set by the billing

- Take the month number starting from cell D10 to P10 and divide that by the billing cycle months in every column and return the value in cell D11 to P11.
- If the formula returns a number greater than zero, then the billing is not required. If the formula returns a zero, then it's time to bill.
- In cells D16 to P16, a simple message can be created to flag when to bill.

PRODUCT()

The PRODUCT() function is used to multiply data together. This function is an alternative to writing a lengthy formula summing several numbers.

The syntax for the PRODUCT() function is as follows:

=PRODUCT(Number1,Number2,... Number255)

In Figure 3-27, I have shown how you can simply set up a table and multiply the numbers consecutively.

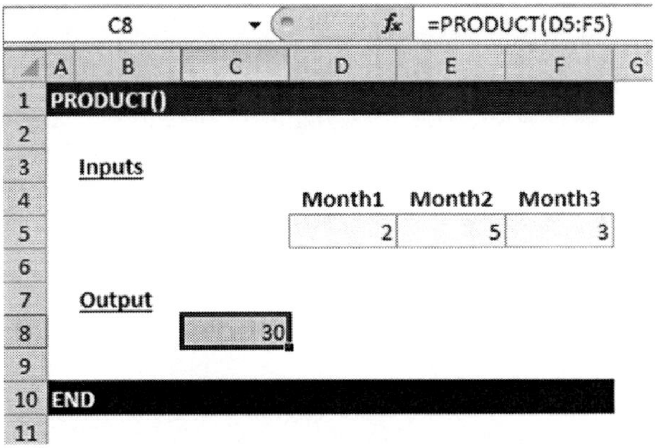

Figure 3-27. This figure shows the PRODUCT( ) function in use

Figure 3-28 shows the alternative to using the PRODUCT( ) function.

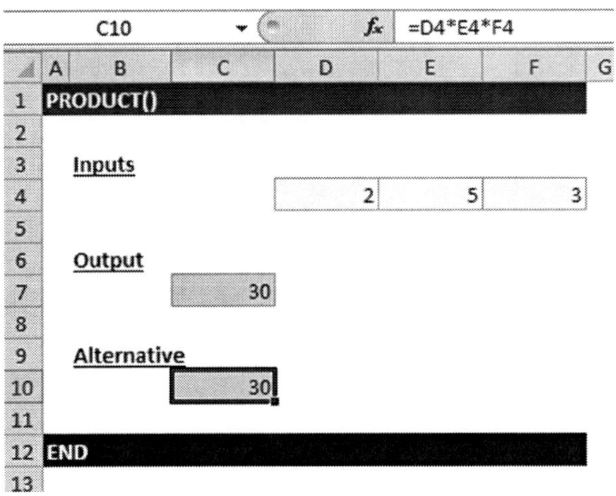

Figure 3-28. The alternative to the PRODUCT( ) function is to multiply each number individually

You can probably see already that the formula in Figure 3-27 can be clumsy. If you have a large set of numbers, it will very quickly become a lengthy and quite ugly formula.

SUM()

The SUM() function provides a quick way to total columns or rows of numbers in an Excel worksheet, thus creating a total as in Figure 3-29. For modeling purposes, this is a must function—there is no possible way that any model can be without a number of SUM() functions. It is the most widely used Excel function. If you have not yet come across it, then this is where you need to make sure you understand how to use it.

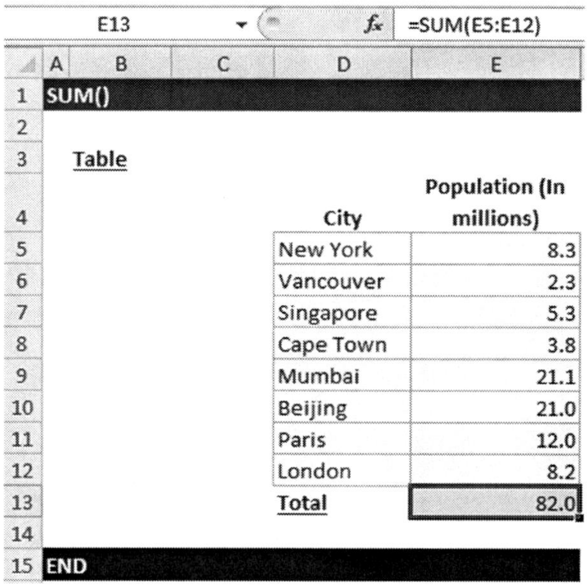

Figure 3-29. This figure shows the SUM() function in use

The syntax for the SUM() function is as follows:

=SUM(Number1,Number2,... Number255)

The SUM() function is very versatile and quite simple. It's just a matter of highlighting all the cells or numbers that you want to total.

Logical Functions

These functions return only a true or false variety. They can be used individually or combined with one or more other functions, such as the IF function.

Note Excel has seven built-in logical functions; these are AND( ), FALSE( ), IF( ), IFERROR( ), NOT( ), OR( ), and TRUE( ). These functions appear on the drop-down menu with the Logical command button. The Logical command button is found on the Formula tab of the ribbon. All the logical functions return either the logical TRUE or logical FALSE when their functions are evaluated.

AND( )

To determine whether the output will be TRUE or FALSE, the AND( ) function evaluates at least one other mathematical expression located in another cell in the spreadsheet. The AND( ) function on its own is not very useful and is generally used in combination with the IF statement.

Generally, the syntax you would use is as follows:

=AND(logical-statement.)

- *Logical* refers to the cell reference that is being checked. Up to 255 logical values can be entered into the function.
- *Statement* is an expression of a condition that should be met by the logical.

In the example in Figure 3-30, the AND( ) function is combined with the IF( ) function for evaluating the final answer. Notice the formula construction and the use of the brackets.

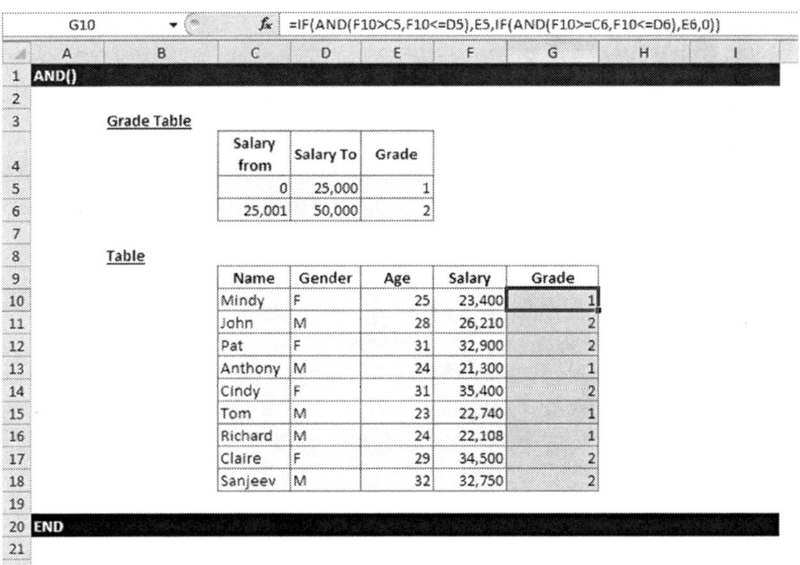

G10 =IF(AND(F10>C5,F10<=D5),E5,IF(AND(F10>=C6,F10<=D6),E6,0))

AND()

Grade Table

Salary from	Salary To	Grade
0	25,000	1
25,001	50,000	2

Table

Name	Gender	Age	Salary	Grade
Mindy	F	25	23,400	1
John	M	28	26,210	2
Pat	F	31	32,900	2
Anthony	M	24	21,300	1
Cindy	F	31	35,400	2
Tom	M	23	22,740	1
Richard	M	24	22,108	1
Claire	F	29	34,500	2
Sanjeev	M	32	32,750	2

END

Figure 3-30. Using the AND( ) function with the IF( ) function is shown here

The formula in Figure 3-30 is already starting to look complex, and it's best to avoid embedding any more levels of IFs and ANDs. The objective is to find at which grade employees should be placed based on their salary. This is a classic IF( ) and AND( ) situation. Let's take a closer look at the formula:

=IF(AND(F10>C5,F10<=D5),E5,IF(AND(F10>=C6,F10<=D6),E6,0))

If the value in cell C5 is less than the value in cell F10

And

If the value in cell D5 is greater than or equal to the value in cell F10

Then

The solution can be found cell E5.

=IF(AND(F10>C5,F10<=D5),E5,*IF(AND(F10>=C6,F10<=D6),E6,0))*

Or else

If the value in cell C6 is less than or equal to the value in cell F10

And

If the value in cell D6 is greater than or equal to the value in cell F10

Then

The solution can be found in cell E6.

*=IF(AND(F10>C5,F10<=D5),E5,***IF(AND(F10>=C6,F10<=D6),E6**,*0))*

Otherwise, the solution is zero.

*=IF(AND(F10>C5,F10<=D5),E5,IF(AND(F10>=C6,F10<=D6),E6,***0***))*

The formula will look through all the permutations, select the one that matches exactly with the two statements, and then find the solution cell. If none of the statements match, then it will make the solution zero.

I have mentioned about making sure the IF statements do not become too embedded and hence too long, but I will mention it again because it's such an important principle. Do not be tempted to make long IF statements even if you can. It's not a sign of cleverness—it's a sign of weakness for a modeler. Take a look at the formula in Figure 3-31. Imagine that you have hundreds of these to audit and correct. How much fun would that be?

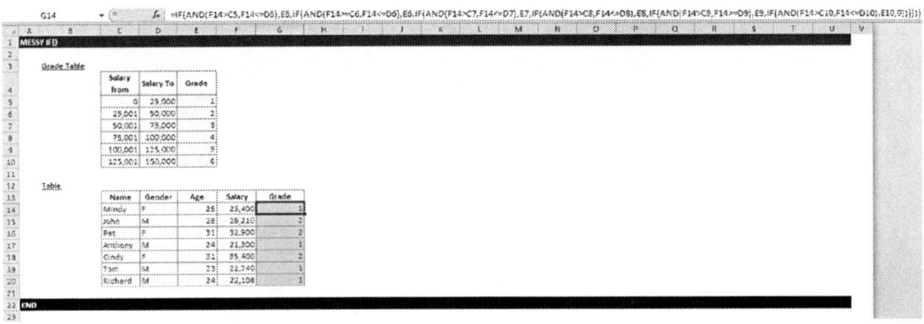

Figure 3-31. This is an example of an embedded IF() statement with the AND() function. It's so complex that it's unreadable

OR()

The OR() function is similar in every way to the AND() function except for the logic of what it is looking at. While the AND() function checks that two points (cells) both satisfy the criteria, the OR() function will check two points but is satisfied if just one of the points matches the criteria.

The syntax for the OR() function is as follows:

= *OR(logical-1, logical-2,... logical-255)*

Figure 3-32 is exactly like the AND() function from Figure 3-30, with just the change of the AND() to an OR(). While the AND() is looking to fulfill two conditions, the OR() looks for just one condition to be fulfilled.

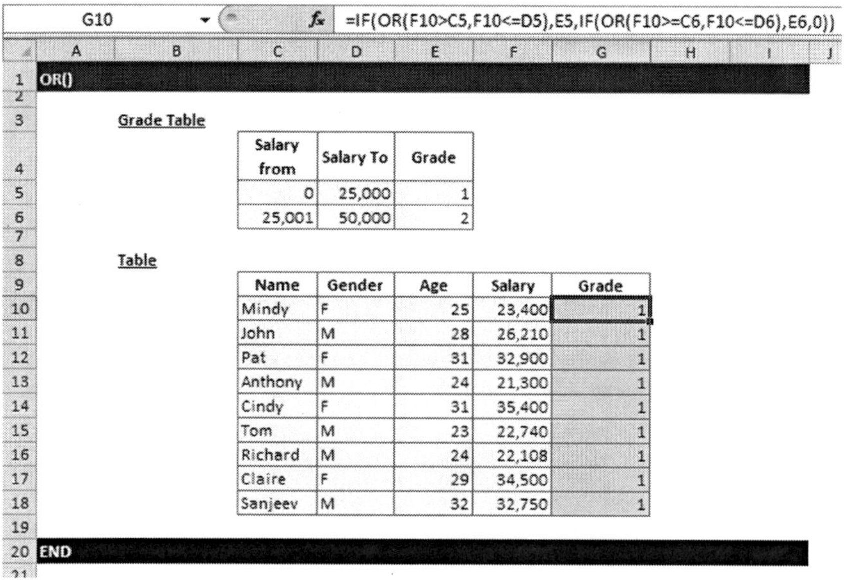

Figure 3-32. The IF() function is used with the OR() function to find the grade but not so successfully

ISERROR()

Prior to wrapping up logical functions, there is one other function that really should be part of the modeler's armory and that is the ISERROR() function. In essence, this function checks a cell or range to see if there is some sort of error. In other words, the values that are expected to be in that location are somehow not coming through as they should.

The syntax you would use is as follows:

=ISERROR(value)

The most effective way to use this function is with the IF statement. This way, you can check to see if there is an error in a specific cell and then return a specific message if an error is found. A different message could be returned if there is no error. In the following example, Excel will check to see if there is an error in cell G6. If there is, it will return the text "Problem." If not, it will return "OK."

=IF(ISERROR(G6,"Problem","OK")

Functions That Use Arrays

There are some functions in excel that are designed to work with a list of data, called an array. These functions have the advantage in that one formula can read a whole list of data and perform a calculation on the whole list if required.

SUMPRODUCT( )

The SUMPRODUCT( ) function is one of the most powerful summing formulas in Excel, but it does require some getting used to in order to use it effectively. At the outset, the SUMPRODUCT( ) formula may not seem like all that useful. However, once you understand how Excel works with lists (or arrays) of data, the relevance of this function becomes clear.

Note In Excel, the term "array" signifies a range, a list, or even a group of related data values. The crucial word is "related."

The syntax is as follows:

=SUMPRODUCT (list 1, list 2,...)

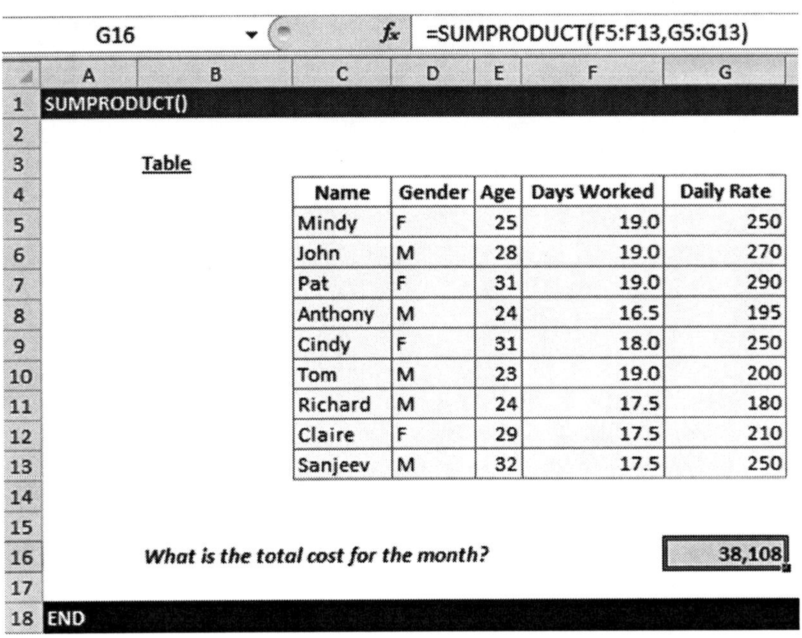

G16 =SUMPRODUCT(F5:F13,G5:G13)

SUMPRODUCT()

Table

Name	Gender	Age	Days Worked	Daily Rate
Mindy	F	25	19.0	250
John	M	28	19.0	270
Pat	F	31	19.0	290
Anthony	M	24	16.5	195
Cindy	F	31	18.0	250
Tom	M	23	19.0	200
Richard	M	24	17.5	180
Claire	F	29	17.5	210
Sanjeev	M	32	17.5	250

What is the total cost for the month? 38,108

END

Figure 3-33. This figure shows the use of the SUMPRODUCT( ) function

Let's take a closer look at the formula:

=SUMPRODUCT(F5:F13,G5:G13)

Take the range (array) starting from cell F5 and ending at cell F13.

=SUMPRODUCT(F5:F13,*G5:G13)*

Then take the range starting from cell G5 and ending at cell G13.

*=SUMPRODUCT(F5:F13,***G5:G13***)*

And

Match the corresponding cells in the two ranges and multiply each of the days worked by its corresponding rate. Then produce the total for all the cells.

=SUMPRODUCT(F5:F13,G5:G13).

The alternative is to multiply out each row's days worked × daily rate individually and then add the results together using a SUM() function as in Figure 3-34.

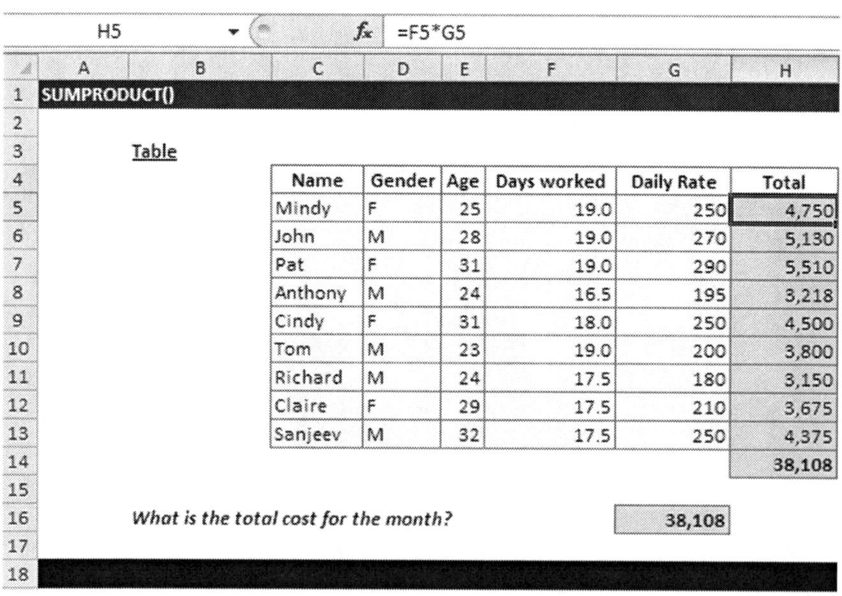

H5 =F5*G5

SUMPRODUCT()

Table

Name	Gender	Age	Days worked	Daily Rate	Total
Mindy	F	25	19.0	250	4,750
John	M	28	19.0	270	5,130
Pat	F	31	19.0	290	5,510
Anthony	M	24	16.5	195	3,218
Cindy	F	31	18.0	250	4,500
Tom	M	23	19.0	200	3,800
Richard	M	24	17.5	180	3,150
Claire	F	29	17.5	210	3,675
Sanjeev	M	32	17.5	250	4,375
					38,108

What is the total cost for the month? 38,108

Figure 3-34. An alternative to the SUMPRODUCT would to multiply the days worked x daily rate for each row and then get the total 38,108

From the examples in Figures 3-32 and 3-33, it should be clear that although it's possible to achieve the same results using other means, the SUMPRODUCT() is a powerful and efficient function and requires fewer computing resources. In this example, I would be using ten SUM() functions to get the same results as one SUMPRODUCT() function.

The SUMPRODUCT() is reliant on matching arrays or matching lists, just make sure that the arrays are the same sizes. For instance, in Figure 3-34, they start at row 5 and end at row 13. If any of these is a different size, you will receive a result but it will be incorrect. This is called a "pointing error." Pointing errors are incredibly easy to make, particularly if you are in a rush. The best way to avoid such a mistake is to make sure you visibly mark out the array so that you can see it on your screen and avoid manually typing the row number and column letter.

Working with Custom Functions or UDFs

In this section, I will take you through using user-defined functions (UDFs). These are functions that the modeler creates using the VBA editor within Excel and can then use in the model alongside the built-in functions.

What Are UDFs?

Excel typically has over 300 built-in functions, some of which we have already covered in this chapter. But as you build up your experience of financial modeling and also with using Excel, you will come across situations where these built-in functions will not provide a satisfactory solution to a modeling problem. As a modeler, it is beneficial at this point if you are able to turn your hand to creating custom functions, known as user-defined functions (UDFs).

UDFs can be used the same way you would use the SUM() function or some other built-in Excel function. They are not complex; however, to create them you must have some level of VBA coding experience. Even if you are familiar with the Excel macro recorder, you will find that the recorder is not suitable for recording UDFs. Therefore, you have to create the UDF yourself. (If you are unfamiliar with VBA, Chapter 12 contains a primer that can get you started.) Nevertheless, this is not to say that you cannot copy and paste bits of a recorded macro into your UDF. UDFs do not have the same flexibility as a standard procedure (VBA) and have many limitations including the following:

- A UDF cannot alter the structure of a worksheet, such as changing the worksheet name, turning off gridlines, protecting the worksheet, and so forth.

- A UDF cannot change a physical characteristic of a cell, including the one that houses the UDF. You cannot use a UDF to change the font color, background color, and so forth of any cell.
- A UDF cannot be used to try and change any part of another cell in any way. This means a UDF cannot place a value into any other cell except the cell housing the UDF.
- A UDF cannot use many of Excel's built-in features, such as auto filters, advanced filters, find, and replace. You can use a UDF to call (run) another standard procedure, but if you do the standard procedure will then be under the same restrictions as the UDF itself.
- When a UDF has a run-time error (that is, it cannot be executed), there are no messages produced. This means you will not know that something has gone wrong, except that there will be an error in your model such as #VALUE. You need to be aware of this issue and either develop a mechanism that will react to any errors or have some documentation in the model that instructs users what they should do if an error occurs.
- UDFs are less efficient than the 300 or so built-in Excel functions because the built-in functions are written using C++, which is a faster language than visual basic.

All this negativity may leave you thinking, "What is the use of UDFs then?" But let me assure you that they can and do come in very handy, as long as you are aware of the restrictions imposed upon them.

When used in the correct context, you can build your own library of functions that are on hand to accompany your models that just aren't available to other users of Excel. The next part of the chapter will include examples of UDFs that I have used previously and continue to use in model building.

Tip Your UDF can be found using the paste function wizard (Shift+F3). Select "User Defined" which is near the bottom of the left-hand window and your UDF will appear on the right-hand window.

When Would You Design and Use UDFs?

When modeling, there will come a time when a UDF is really the only way to get past a particular issue. UDFs will need to be designed and created in the following situations:

- When you need a complex or custom math function that is not available, for instance, a tax calculation based on regional locations.
- When you need to simplify formulas that would otherwise be extremely long "mega formulas," such as to get around using a nested IF statement.
- When you need to use diagnostics such as checking cell formats.
- When you need to use custom text manipulation.
- When you need to include advanced array formulas and matrix functions.

Caution Be careful about using custom functions in spreadsheets that you need to share with others. If the recipients do not have your add-in, the functions will not work when they use the spreadsheet. In such a situation, you will need to send additional details to the recipients to install the add-in.

LINKADDRESS()

The LinkAddress() function is used to show the address details to a cell that has been hyperlinked. In other words, it will show which location the hyperlink is pointing to. Often a model will have hyperlinks to various source references and to other files and documents as a way of providing background information about the model to the user. The fact that Excel has no native function to replicate this link address means that this function is very practical when you need to alert the model user that certain cells include a hyperlink and the details. Another reason is that the place where the hyperlink was originally pointing to may have been deleted or has moved, in which case the hyperlink will not work. However, by giving the details to the user, the user can use that information to follow up. This function is also very useful for auditing. For example, I use this as a tool to check the status of all the hyperlinks when I perform model audits as in Figure 3-35.

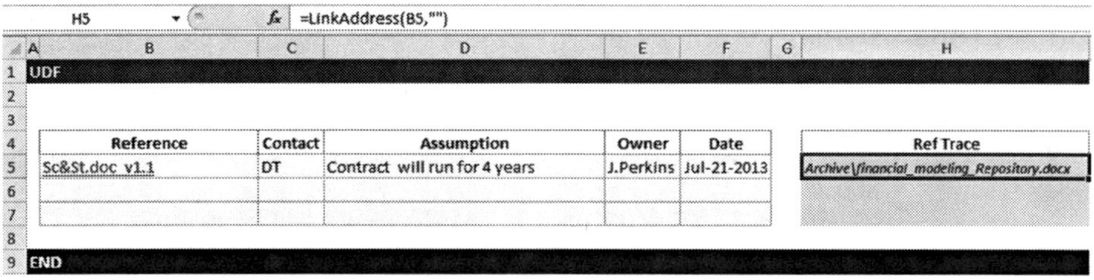

Figure 3-35. A custom function is included to give details of where the hyperlink is pointing

The syntax for this function is as follows:

=Linkaddress(Cell, [Default Value])

- *Cell* is the cell that contains the hyperlink.
- *Default value* is the value that you want returned if the function finds no hyperlink. This can be anything of your choice. But keep in mind if it is not a numerical value, then place it in quotation marks (" ").

The quickest and most efficient method of learning how to create UDFs is to look at the code to an actual working function. In this section, I have included the actual code for the UDFs, which you should examine and try out, and get an understanding of how they work. In time, you could expand the code or even make it more efficient.

The Code

```
Function LinkAddress(cell As range, _
                     Optional default_value As Variant)
  'Lists the Hyperlink Address for a Given Cell
  'If cell does not contain a hyperlink, return default_value
  If (cell.range("A1").Hyperlinks.Count <> 1) Then
      LinkAddress = default_value
  Else
      LinkAddress = cell.range("A1").Hyperlinks(1).Address
  End If
End Function
```

You can use the code directly from this book and paste it into your VBA editor. In your Excel model, press ALT+F11 to open the VBA editor, in the menu choose Insert then menu, then add a module and paste this code directly into the windowpane.

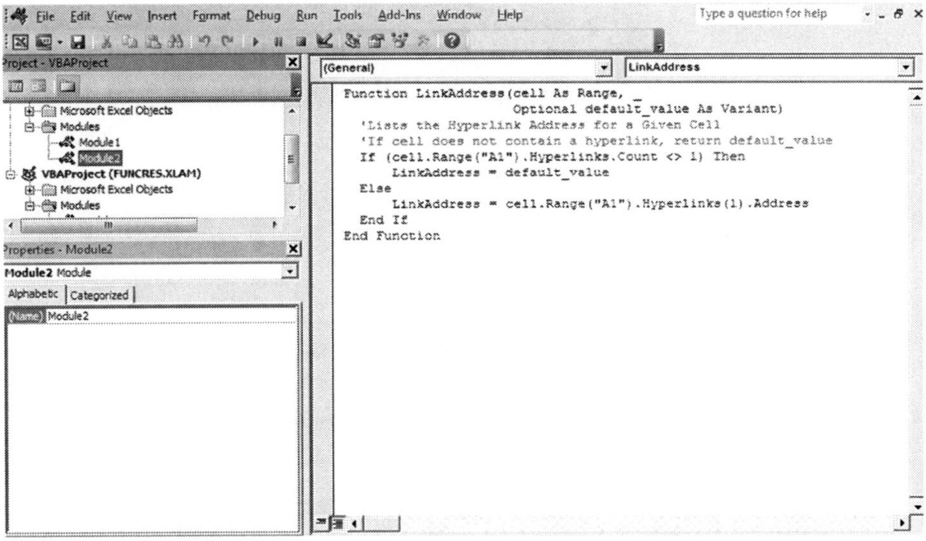

Figure 3-36. The VBA editor is where the UDFs are created by inserting a module and typing code into the editing screen

EFFINDEX()

I have used the EFFINDEX() function to demonstrate how a simple function can be created and can make such a difference. This function takes two values, the demand and the supply, which can both be any value. The demand will then be divided by the supply to give an index. The real power from the EFFINDEX() function is how it treats the values should one of them be a zero. In Excel, when you create a formula that uses divisors, you need to consider what will happen if the divisor has met a zero. Excel will always give an error in this circumstance, placing the #VALUE error where your result should have been. The problem will become exacerbated if that cell with the error has any other cells that are dependent on its value. If so, your model will quickly become strewn with error.

The way to avoid such a situation is to create a formula with an IF() statement and an Error function together. Take a look at Figures 3-37a and 3-37b.

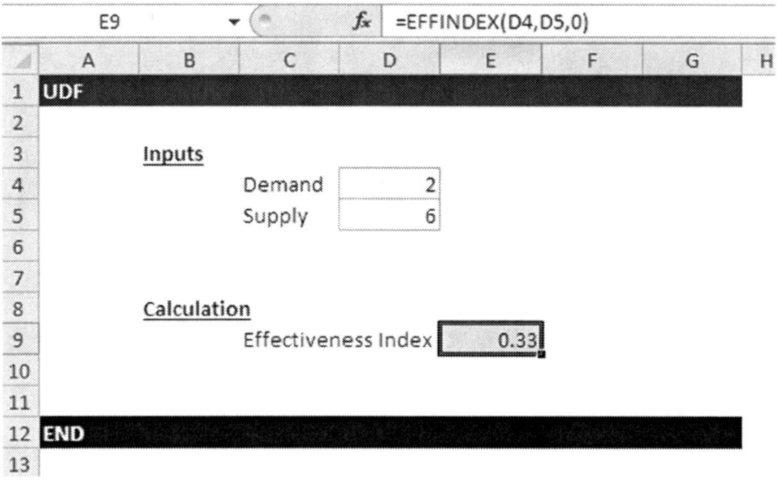

Figure 3-37a. The EFFINDEX() function with a standard divisor is shown here

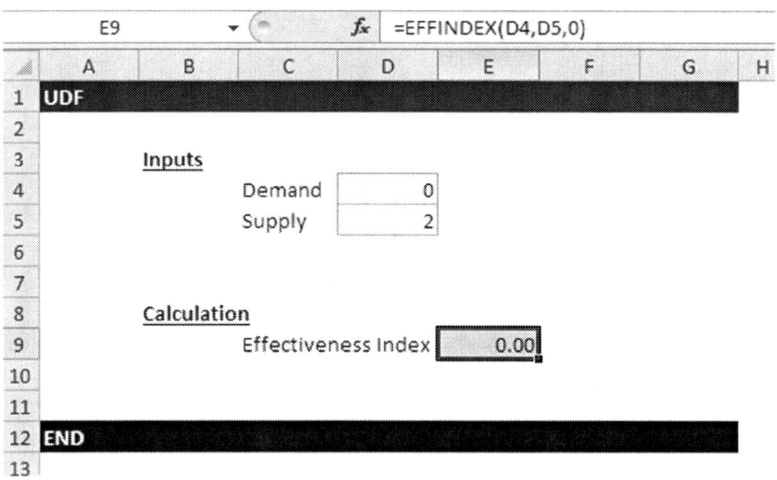

Figure 3-37b. The EFFINDEX() function with a zero divisor, but it shows the default_value and not an error

The syntax for the custom UDF is as follows:

=EFFINDEX(demand,supply,[default_value])

- *Demand* is any value that gives the total demand.
- *Supply* is any value that gives the total supply.
- *Default_value* chooses the default should the answer be an error.

In Figure 3-37a, the demand is simply divided by the supply to give an index of 0.33 or 33%. Notice the default_value is a zero. In Figure 3-37b, we can see how that default_value comes into play, because ordinarily the effectiveness index would have shown a #VALUE error.

I have included the code you will need to create the EFFINDEX() custom function.

The Code

```
Function EFFINDEX(demand As Variant, supply As Variant, _
            Optional default_value As Variant) As Variant
'Effectiveness Index (EFFINDEX)
    If IsMissing(default_value) Then
        default_value = "n/a"
    End If
    If IsNumeric(demand) And IsNumeric(supply) Then
        If supply = 0 Then
            EFFINDEX = demand
            Exit Function
        Else
            EFFINDEX = demand / supply
            Exit Function
        End If
    End If
    EFFINDEX = default_value
End Function
```

SUMCOLOR()

This SUMCOLOR() function can sum data based on the color. Although I have included this function to demonstrate custom functions, I would not recommend using it in models as standard sum for colors. Why? It is vulnerable to some serious problems based on changes to the Excel color palette. However, this function is very useful for auditing financial models. It allows the auditor to color-code specific data and then make checks on that data. Therefore, this is also an example of a function that should be used outside of the model but remains useful to the modeler.

Caution The colors that you will see in your Excel environment are not necessarily the same for all Excel users. This is called the color palette, which can be changed by users and sometimes will change itself depending on your desktop profile. If you sum by colors, just be aware that you are reliant on their colors being exactly the same on their computer as they were on yours.

The syntax for this function is as follows:

=*SumColor(ColorRange,SumRange)*

- *ColorRange* is the list or range of cells that has been colored.
- *SumRange* is the list or range of cells you need to get the sum value.

The example in Figure 3-38 demonstrates how the formula works. This function is also useful because you can tailor it to your specifics for modeling. It doesn't need to be about colors. Once you gain experience creating these functions, you can use such a function to sum on any manner of criteria like names, locations, formula types, dates, and so forth. It can even be changed to do a count rather than a sum.

The Code

```
Function SumColor(rColor As Range, rSumRange As Range)
'Sums cells based on a specified fill Color.
Dim rCell As Range
Dim iCol As Integer
Dim vResultiCol = rColor.Interior.ColorIndex
For Each rCell In rSumRange
If rCell.Interior.ColorIndex = iCol Then
vResult = WorksheetFunction.Sum(rCell) + vResult
End If
Next rCell
        SumColor = vResult
End Function
```

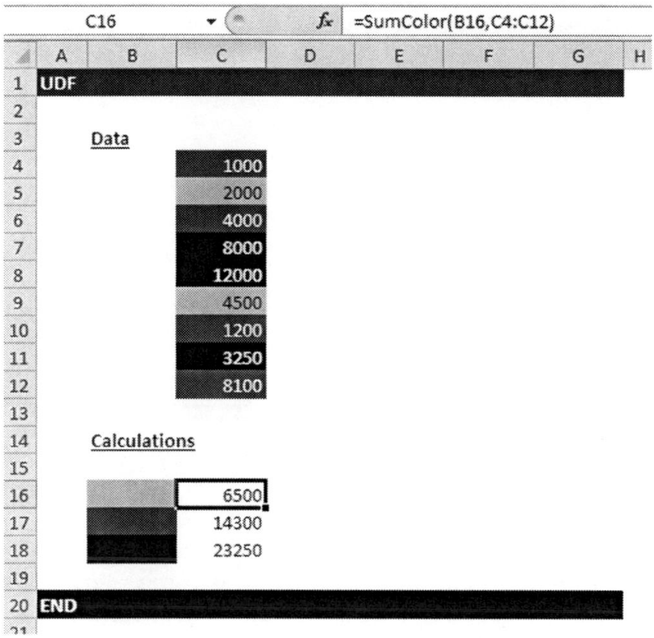

Figure 3-38. The SUMCOLOR() function in use is shown here

Caution As this function stands, it won't be much use for summing text; you will need to make some considerable adaptations should you wish to go that route. Summing on text is something I would not choose to do as it's a sure way of rubbishing a model. However, that is my opinion and I do know some modelers who have used text summing successfully. Good luck!

SUMTB()

I have included the SUMTB() function (SumTopBottom) because it's so useful for financial dashboards. For some reason, users of financial models really like to see results that show the top performing and the bottom performing results, that is, the top 5 or bottom 10. Trying to produce this using Excel's advanced filters is awkward. The SUMTB() function also has a more complex deeper VBA coding, which I will explain more in chapter 12.

The syntax is as follows:

=SumTB($A$2:$A$100,10) For top 10

=SumTB($A$2:$A$100,10,TRUE) For bottom 10

I have included the code for the SUMTB()

The Code

```
Function SUMTB(rRange As Range, N As Long, Optional bBottomN As Boolean) As
Single
Dim strAddress As String
On Error Resume Next
strAddress = rRange.Address
    If bBottomN = False Then
        SUMTB = Evaluate("=SUMPRODUCT((" _
& strAddress & ">=LARGE(" & strAddress & "," & X & "))*(" & strAddress & "))")
    Else
      SUMTB = Evaluate("=SUMPRODUCT((" _
& strAddress & "<=SMALL(" & strAddress & "," & X & "))*(" & strAddress & "))")
    End If
End Function
```

ISDATE()

One real gap in Excel is that it has nothing to check the date cell format. You will find that it is very useful in models to have some method of checking if an input cell that is expecting a date has actually received a date from the user. Dates are a cause of errors in models due to problems with syntax and also typing mistakes. I use the ISDATE() function as an error check to give the users a warning if there is a problem with the date that they have inputted. The ISDATE() function is also used to check if a cell contains a date, as in Figure 3-39a, and if not then the function will return a FALSE. Figure 3-39b shows that it will return TRUE if it has a date.

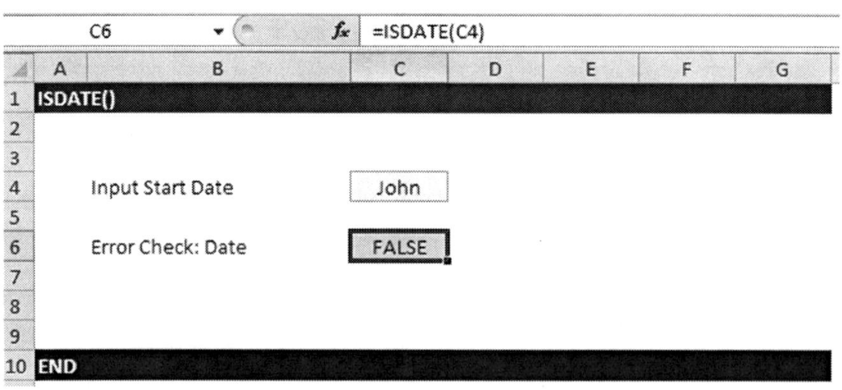

Figure 3-39a. The ISDATE() function has verified that cell C4 is not a date

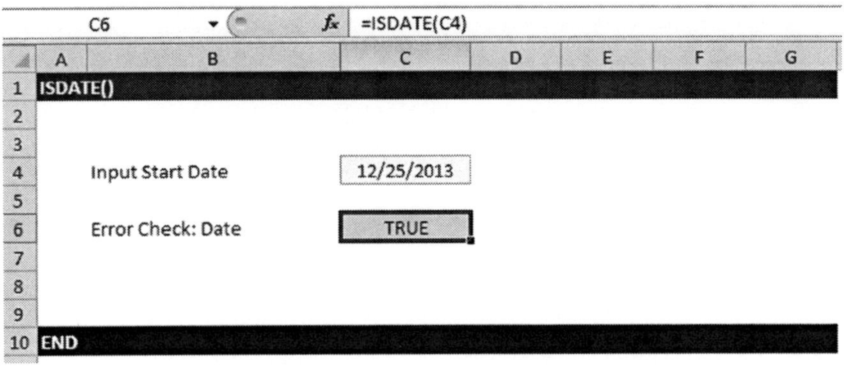

Figure 3-39b. The ISDATE() function has verified that cell C4 is a date

The syntax for the ISDATE() function is as follows:

=ISDATE(Cell)

The Code

```
Function ISDATE(cell) As Boolean
ISDATE = VBA.ISDATE(cell)
End Function
```

Caution Changing the format between text and number (or between number and text) will have no effect on data already entered. If the cell was already formatted as a number and that format was in effect, then you can change to another number format and it will be immediately effective.

WORKSHEETSTATS()

This formula is very useful for producing stats on the data in a worksheet. I use this as part of the documentation in each worksheet as it keeps a record of any changes and the contents of the worksheet and gives valuable feedback to the model user. The results can be seen in Figure 3-40. This is a relatively long function, and my main purpose for including it is to provide some achievement goal. Keep in mind that if you use this function on a blank worksheet, the results will not be accurate. Only use it when there is actual data in the worksheet.

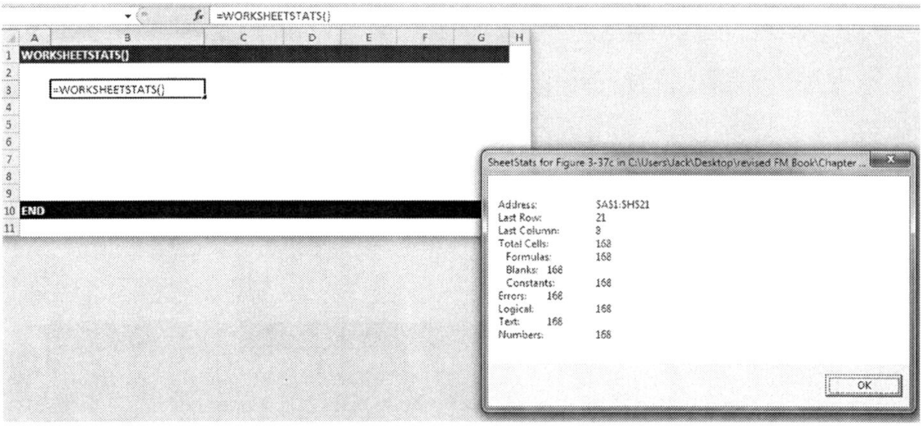

Figure 3-40. The WORKSHEETSTATS() function includes a pop-up message box with information on the worksheet

The syntax for the WORKSHEETSTATS() function is as follows:

=WORKSHEETSTATS()

The Code

```
Function WORKSHEETSTATS()
Set rng1 = ActiveSheet.UsedRange
On Error Resume Next
numConstants = rng1.SpecialCells(xlCellTypeConstants).Count
If Err <> 0 Then numConstants = 0: Err = 0
numerrors = rng1.SpecialCells(xlCellTypeConstants, xlErrors).Count
If Err <> 0 Then numerrors = 0: Err = 0
numLogical = rng1.SpecialCells(xlCellTypeConstants, xlLogical).Count
If Err <> 0 Then numLogical = 0: Err = 0
numText = rng1.SpecialCells(xlCellTypeConstants, xlTextValues).Count
If Err <> 0 Then numText = 0: Err = 0
numNumbers = rng1.SpecialCells(xlCellTypeConstants, xlNumbers).Count
If Err <> 0 Then numNumbers = 0: Err = 0
numformulas = rng1.SpecialCells(xlCellTypeFormulas).Count
If Err <> 0 Then numformulas = 0: Err = 0
numBlanks = rng1.SpecialCells(xlBlanks).Count
If Err <> 0 Then numBlanks = 0: Err = 0

Msg = "Address:      " & Chr(9) & rng1.Address & Chr(10) & _
      "Last Row:     " & Chr(9) & rng1.Rows(rng1.Rows.Count).Row & Chr(10) & _
      "Last Column: " & Chr(9) & rng1.Columns(rng1.Columns.Count).Column &
Chr(10) & _
      "Total Cells: " & Chr(9) & rng1.Count & Chr(10) & _
      "   Formulas: " & Chr(9) & numformulas & Chr(10) & _
      "   Blanks:   " & Chr(9) & numBlanks & Chr(10) & _
      "   Constants:" & Chr(9) & numConstants & Chr(10)
```

```
Mg2 = "Errors:      " & Chr(9) & numerrors & Chr(10) & _
      "Logical:     " & Chr(9) & numLogical & Chr(10) & _
      "Text:        " & Chr(9) & numText & Chr(10) & _
      "Numbers:     " & Chr(9) & numNumbers

 title1 = "SheetStats for " & Application.ActiveSheet.Name & _
" in " & Application.ActiveWorkbook.FullName

iANS = MsgBox(Msg & Mg2, , title1)

End Function
```

Typical Modeling Issues and How to Address Them with Functions

There are any number of issues that arise with modeling. In fact, a large part of how to model is based on dealing with potential issues, predicting their likelihood and severity, and modeling for these occurrences. In this chapter, we have looked at functions, which in general will cover the vast majority of issues that will arise. There is one that I will cover now, specifically because it is perhaps the single most destructive problem that can occur, and unfortunately it is very common.

Dealing with Text When You Need Values

One of the most common issues in any model is predicting how the user will respond to the inputs. Will they follow the protocol or deviate? For instance, if a user input cell requires a number (value) and the user places text, how should we deal with this as the model calculation will have corrupted data? Are there any functions we can use to mitigate? To explore this issue more and learn how to mitigate, I have included a series of examples from Figures 3-41 to 3-46.

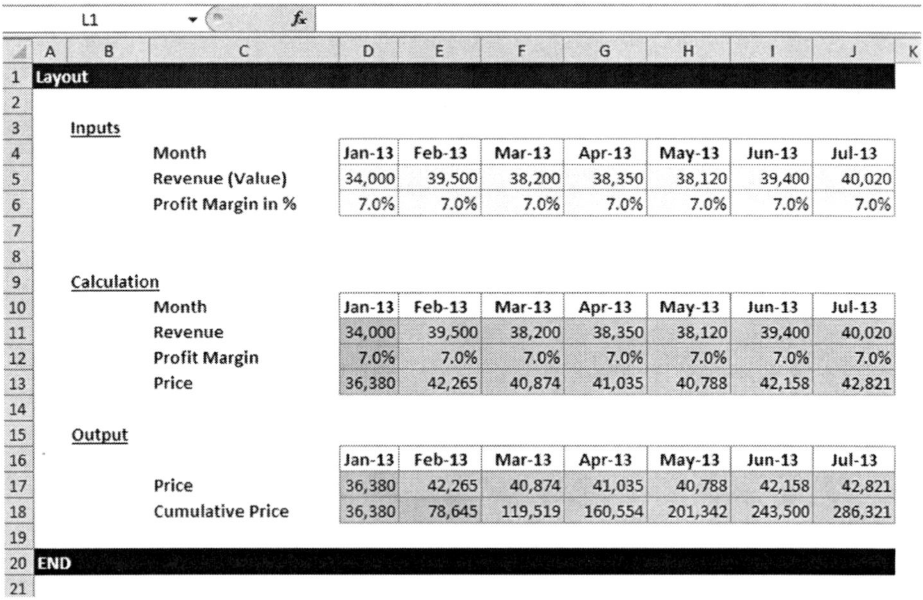

L1

	A	B	C	D	E	F	G	H	I	J	K
1	Layout										
2											
3		Inputs									
4			Month	Jan-13	Feb-13	Mar-13	Apr-13	May-13	Jun-13	Jul-13	
5			Revenue (Value)	34,000	39,500	38,200	38,350	38,120	39,400	40,020	
6			Profit Margin in %	7.0%	7.0%	7.0%	7.0%	7.0%	7.0%	7.0%	
7											
8											
9		Calculation									
10			Month	Jan-13	Feb-13	Mar-13	Apr-13	May-13	Jun-13	Jul-13	
11			Revenue	34,000	39,500	38,200	38,350	38,120	39,400	40,020	
12			Profit Margin	7.0%	7.0%	7.0%	7.0%	7.0%	7.0%	7.0%	
13			Price	36,380	42,265	40,874	41,035	40,788	42,158	42,821	
14											
15		Output									
16				Jan-13	Feb-13	Mar-13	Apr-13	May-13	Jun-13	Jul-13	
17			Price	36,380	42,265	40,874	41,035	40,788	42,158	42,821	
18			Cumulative Price	36,380	78,645	119,519	160,554	201,342	243,500	286,321	
19											
20	END										
21											

Figure 3-41. The inputs, calculations, and outputs are shown in this figure

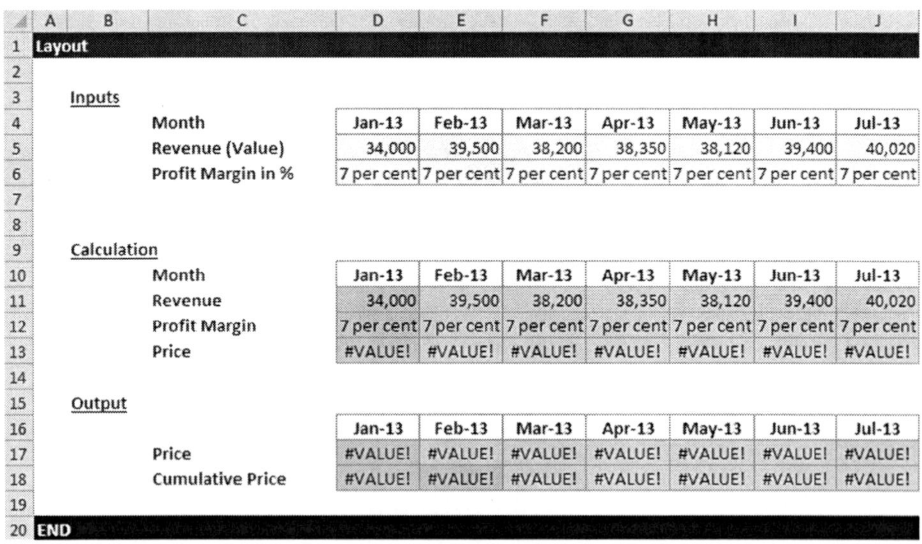

	A	B	C	D	E	F	G	H	I	J
1	Layout									
2										
3		Inputs								
4			Month	Jan-13	Feb-13	Mar-13	Apr-13	May-13	Jun-13	Jul-13
5			Revenue (Value)	34,000	39,500	38,200	38,350	38,120	39,400	40,020
6			Profit Margin in %	7 per cent	7 per cent	7 per cent	7 per cent	7 per cent	7 per cent	7 per cent
7										
8										
9		Calculation								
10			Month	Jan-13	Feb-13	Mar-13	Apr-13	May-13	Jun-13	Jul-13
11			Revenue	34,000	39,500	38,200	38,350	38,120	39,400	40,020
12			Profit Margin	7 per cent	7 per cent	7 per cent	7 per cent	7 per cent	7 per cent	7 per cent
13			Price	#VALUE!	#VALUE!	#VALUE!	#VALUE!	#VALUE!	#VALUE!	#VALUE!
14										
15		Output								
16				Jan-13	Feb-13	Mar-13	Apr-13	May-13	Jun-13	Jul-13
17			Price	#VALUE!	#VALUE!	#VALUE!	#VALUE!	#VALUE!	#VALUE!	#VALUE!
18			Cumulative Price	#VALUE!	#VALUE!	#VALUE!	#VALUE!	#VALUE!	#VALUE!	#VALUE!
19										
20	END									

Figure 3-42. The inputs have text entered in value cells

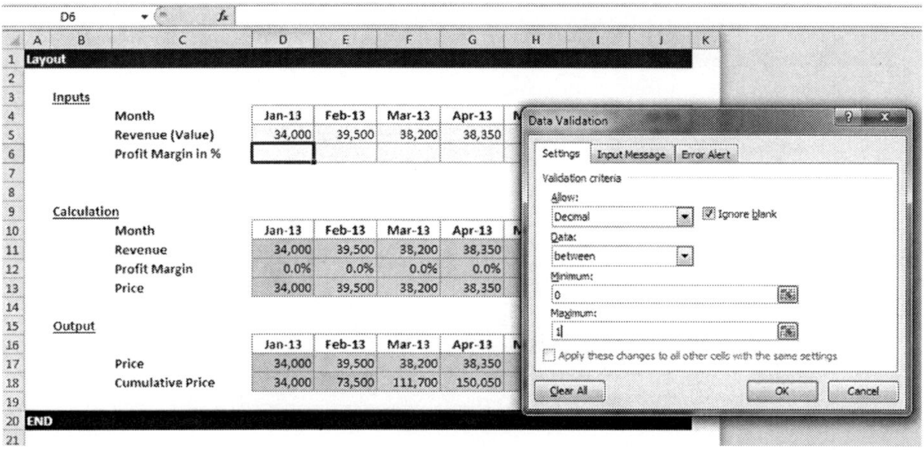

Figure 3-43. Data validation has been introduced into the model in this figure

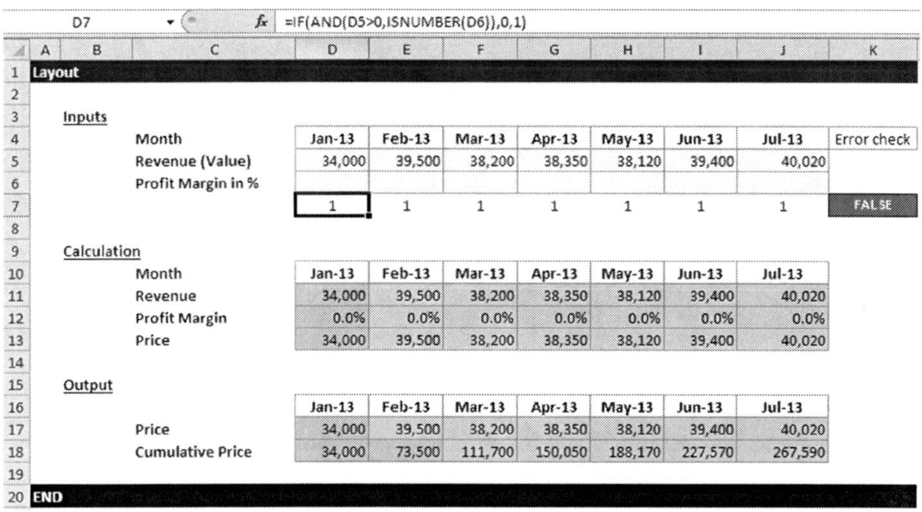

Figure 3-44. Error checks have been added into the model in this figure

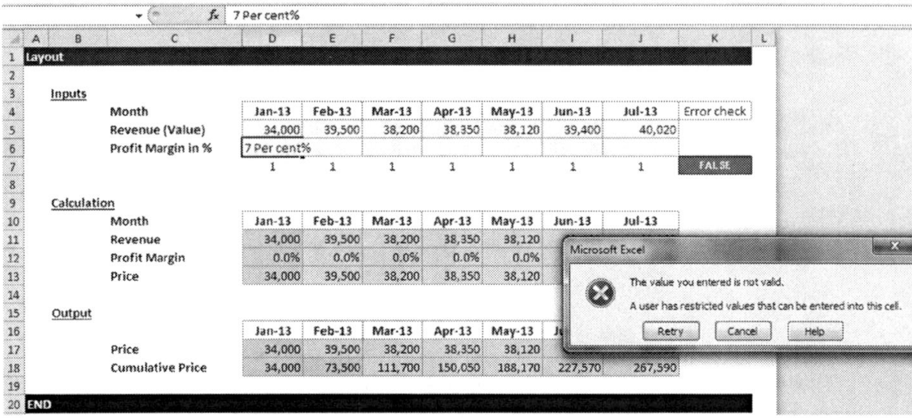

7 Per cent%

	A	B	C	D	E	F	G	H	I	J	K
1	Layout										
2											
3		Inputs									
4			Month	Jan-13	Feb-13	Mar-13	Apr-13	May-13	Jun-13	Jul-13	Error check
5			Revenue (Value)	34,000	39,500	38,200	38,350	38,120	39,400	40,020	
6			Profit Margin in %	7 Per cent%							
7				1	1	1	1	1	1	1	FALSE
8											
9		Calculation									
10			Month	Jan-13	Feb-13	Mar-13	Apr-13	May-13	Jun-13	Jul-13	
11			Revenue	34,000	39,500	38,200	38,350	38,120			
12			Profit Margin	0.0%	0.0%	0.0%	0.0%	0.0%			
13			Price	34,000	39,500	38,200	38,350	38,120			
14											
15		Output									
16				Jan-13	Feb-13	Mar-13	Apr-13	May-13			
17			Price	34,000	39,500	38,200	38,350	38,120			
18			Cumulative Price	34,000	73,500	111,700	150,050	188,170	227,570	267,590	
19											
20	END										

Figure 3-45. The error check and data validation are used in combination to give maximum feedback

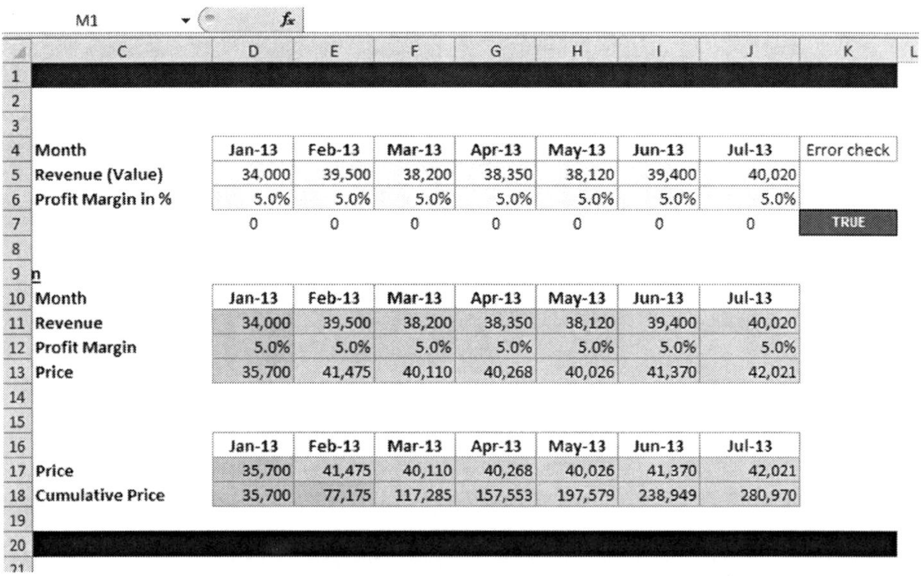

M1

	C	D	E	F	G	H	I	J	K
1									
2									
3									
4	Month	Jan-13	Feb-13	Mar-13	Apr-13	May-13	Jun-13	Jul-13	Error check
5	Revenue (Value)	34,000	39,500	38,200	38,350	38,120	39,400	40,020	
6	Profit Margin in %	5.0%	5.0%	5.0%	5.0%	5.0%	5.0%	5.0%	
7		0	0	0	0	0	0	0	TRUE
8									
9	n								
10	Month	Jan-13	Feb-13	Mar-13	Apr-13	May-13	Jun-13	Jul-13	
11	Revenue	34,000	39,500	38,200	38,350	38,120	39,400	40,020	
12	Profit Margin	5.0%	5.0%	5.0%	5.0%	5.0%	5.0%	5.0%	
13	Price	35,700	41,475	40,110	40,268	40,026	41,370	42,021	
14									
15									
16		Jan-13	Feb-13	Mar-13	Apr-13	May-13	Jun-13	Jul-13	
17	Price	35,700	41,475	40,110	40,268	40,026	41,370	42,021	
18	Cumulative Price	35,700	77,175	117,285	157,553	197,579	238,949	280,970	
19									
20									

Figure 3-46. The inputs now have error checking and validations

Figure 3-41 is a small model, and the objective is to derive the price. I am asking the user to input the revenue and profit margin for each of the months. The price is a simple calculation: revenue × margin. Notice that I have used a color style, just as we discussed in Chapter 2 about best practice.

In Figure 3-41, the profit margin expects a value that should be a percentage. Instead of a number, the user has used a text and has actually written "7 percent." The effect of this text entry can be seen in the calculations in rows 11 and 12 with an error now creeping into the model. When we reach the outputs, the error is now firmly entrenched into the model. This is not acceptable modeling, but unfortunately this is a very common occurrence. If the user is not fully versed with all the inputs in the model, this issue will occur. Fortunately for this situation, there are some options we can take to minimize the effect this issue can have on the model.

In Figure 3-43, in order to help the user input the correct type of data, I have created a data validation, which can be found in the data menu. With the data validation, you can stipulate the data type that can be entered in each cell and only that data type will be allowed. In this case, I have created a validation for a decimal between 0 and 1, which will be a percentage (0% to 100%).

The next step after creating a data validation is to have some visual error check to alert the model user that there is an issue with the data, as in Figure 3-44. In this case, I have created an IF statement with the ISNUMBER() function. This function checks that the cells in row 5 are numbers. If so, the formula returns a 0; if not, it returns a 1. By using this type of error check, I can provide a visual guide to the user that something in the inputs is incorrect. Now that I have two solutions to the issue—the data validation (Figure 3-43) and the error check (Figure 3-44)—it would be reasonable to assume I have done what I can to mitigate the value/text problem.

The combination of the data validation and the error check will result in a message pop-up as in Figure 3-44, which will need some feedback from the user in order to continue with using the model.

To continue with no issues, users would need to make sure all possible errors are eradicated, whereby they would receive a TRUE check with no validation pop-up messages as in Figure 3-46.

This example was illustrative, but I should add that most issues in financial models can be solved in this manner with the use of some functions and error checking.

Case Study: Using Modeling Functions and Tools

This last part of the chapter is a case study to examine a specific situation that is very likely to occur in financial models and particularly in valuation models.

Here is the brief:

Create a model template that will demonstrate how the capital budgeting can be performed in a model.

Let's begin by going over some of the terminology that will be used:

- Capital flow is the amount of set-up money injected into a project.
- Cash flow frequency is the time periods that money inflowing is measured.
- Discount rate is the rate of interest that investors demand from the project.
- Monthly income is the cash flows that occur from a project (not profit).
- Net Present Value (NPV) compares the value of money today to the value of that same money in the future.

Don't worry if you don't understand the financial aspects at this stage. An introduction to finance and accounting for modelers is included in Chapter 8. For this case study, just concentrate on the formula usage and the layout. Figures 3-47 and 3-48 will be used as examples.

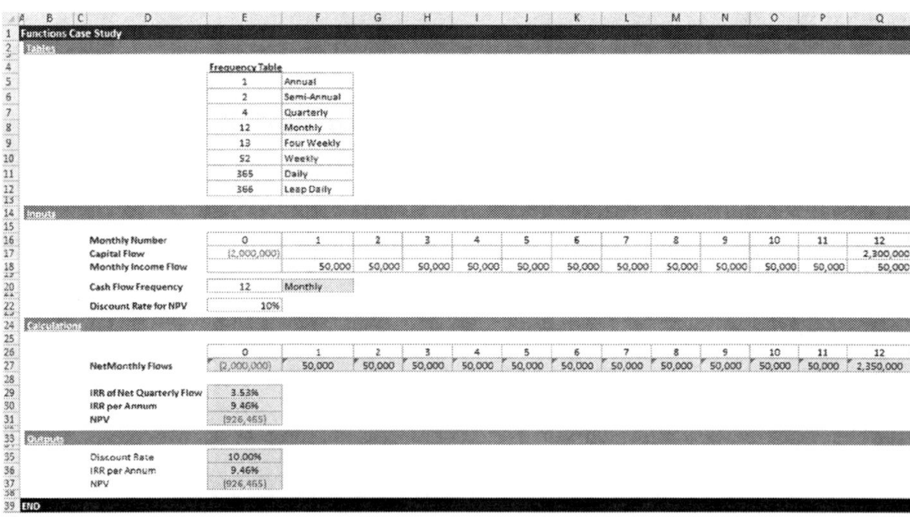

Figure 3-47. This figure shows the capital budgeting model layout

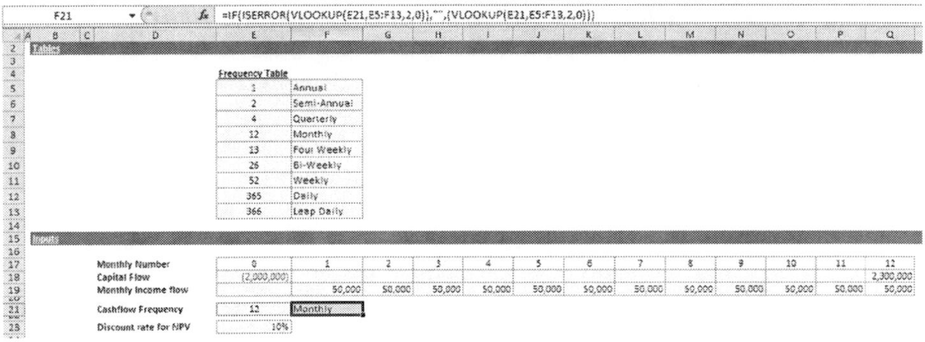

Figure 3-48. The VLOOKUP() function is encased within an IF() statement together with an ISERROR() function in order to catch errors in cell E21

The layout has been sectioned into inputs (user inputs), calculations (workings), and outputs. Inputs are presented in the yellow cells, and calculations are in the gray cells. Notice that cell E21 has yellow shading and a green border; this is a drop-down menu and is signified as such by the green border. Looking at Figure 3-48, you will note that a VLOOKUP() function has been used, but it has been encapsulated in the ISERROR() function to catch any errors.

- VLOOKUP() is referencing cell E21 to the frequency table. It's possible that the user could enter a frequency in cell E21 that is not recognized in the frequency table, which would result in an error. Therefore, the ISERROR function is used to return a space should that happen.

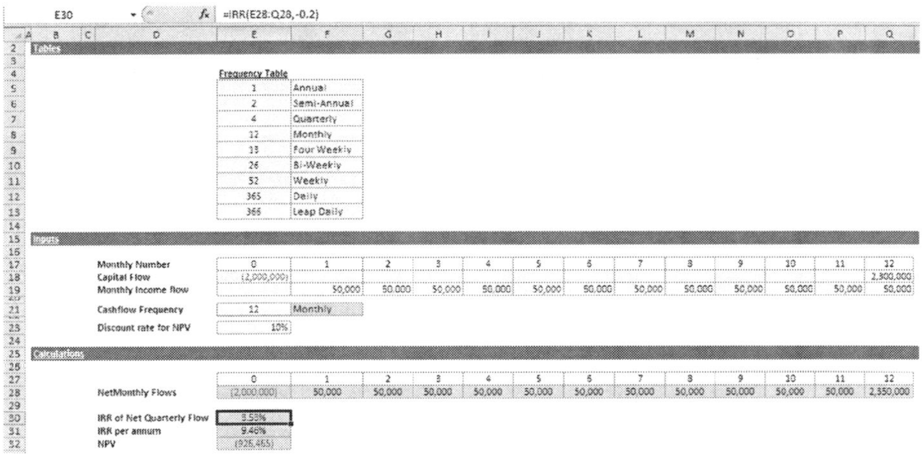

Figure 3-49. The IRR() (internal rate of return) function is shown here in this figure

- The IRR() function has been used to get the internal rate of return. Fortunately Excel has a built-in formula construct so when you need to get the internal rate of return (IRR), the only modeling concern is to make the layout of the cash flows fit the formula construct. There is one feature of the IRR function that does confuse people, and that is the "guess" that is required. In effect, the function is asking you to guess at what rate the IRR will be (before it gives you the result). When using this function, don't become too concerned about this guess as it won't alter the result significantly unless you have somehow constructed the formula incorrectly.
- The IRR per annum (Figure 3-50) uses the FV math function(the FV() function gives the future value of an investment using the interest that would have accrued) and is derived from the IRR function. This means you will first get the IRR for the frequency and then convert this to per annum using the FV function.

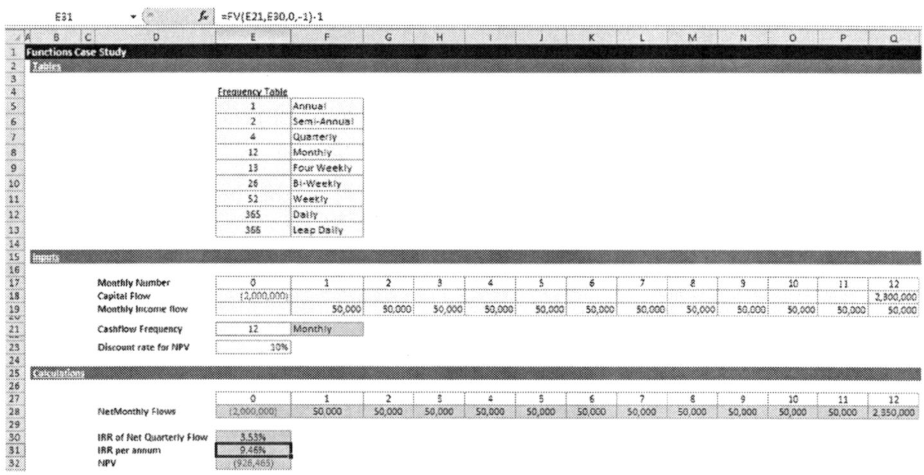

Figure 3-50. The IRR is turned into an annual rate in this model

Generally the IRR( ) function is used together with the NPV( ) function, as the NPV (net present value) gives you an indication of how much the investment or project will be worth in the future based on today's money. It is a relatively simple function except for one flaw that you should always be aware of. If you look at Figure 3-51 in the formula construct, you will notice that I have added the capital cash flow to the formula (Year 0, +E28). When using NPV, remember to add back the initial capital, which will always be a negative value even after the discounted cash flow, or you will get a significantly flawed NPV. When making calculations using the NPV( ) function, you should always remember to add the capital in year 0 to the formula. I have come across numerous models that have omitted this capital addition. Why should this be a problem? Let's just say NPV is used quite widely for financial metrics and comparisons about investments, and the last thing you want to do as a modeler is to give an incorrect result for the NPV. Trust me on that.

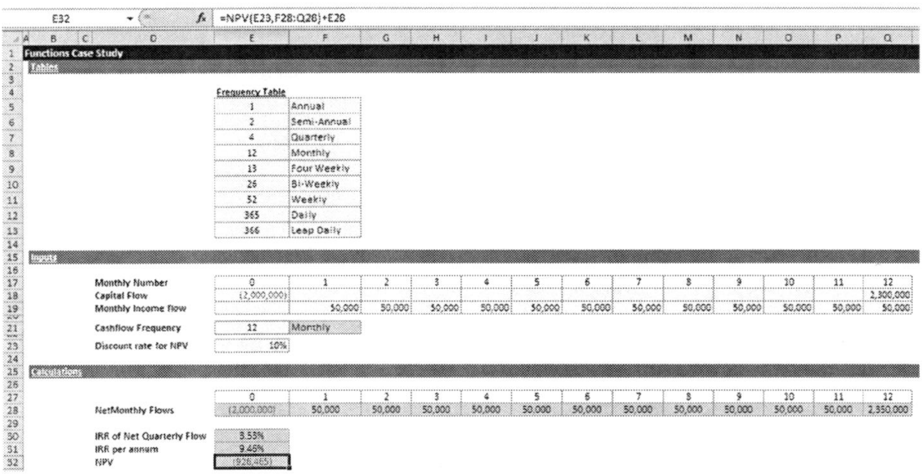

Figure 3-51. This figure illustrates using the NPV( ) function

This was a long chapter that introduced many technical parts to financial modeling, but it is essential that you meet these functions early. You will hopefully have reached this point having tried some of the functions and are now more familiar with them. Many of these functions will be appearing again and again throughout the book, which is why it's important that you have familiarized yourself with them early on.

CHAPTER

4

Planning Your Model

Based on my fieldwork in financial modeling, my opinion is that the majority of models built have little or no planning involved. There are some cases where there really is no need. But as a financial modeler, at some point, you will need to have some coherent plan for your models, particularly when working on a project where the modeling is only one aspect, such as being on a bid or in a transformation program. It is critical to understand not just how to build models but also how to fulfill all the aspects of planning. This way, you will provide a final model that meets and exceeds user expectations. This chapter introduces the modeling life cycle and will take you through the process of how to manage and take ownership of the entire modeling space.

Introduction to the Financial Modeling Life Cycle

What exactly do I mean by financial modeling life cycle? First, let's take a look at the term "life cycle." It was born from biology, and although there are several definitions, it essentially is about the stages of change during the development of an organism from inception to maturity. Biologists aside, the description would be too literal for financial modeling. However, it does have the hallmarks that we need to create a suitable definition. The key aspects are stages of change during the development, inception, and maturity. Therefore, we can define a financial modeling life cycle as the following:

> The key developmental stages of a financial model that will ensue with the beginning of the initial feasibility and ending with a final living and working functional model.

Take notice of the use of the word "key." There can be a number of development stages to any financial model, but not all of them are necessary and therefore not "key" in every single model. Some stages if omitted would result in a modeling process that is flawed and a final model with key weaknesses. In other words, a substandard model would be the final product.

Here is a list of the ten key development stages:

- Feasibility
- Scope
- Specification & Strategy
- Design
- Build
- Test
- Final Version & Protection
- Document
- Handover & Implementation
- Maintain

While no two financial models are exactly alike, the planning from the beginning to the end resulting in a fully operational model should be the same. The brevity and depth with which each stage is approached will be entirely up to the modeler. As I mentioned before, some may feel they can actually go through the feasibility and scoping stages mentally and even believe the specification stage does not require any formal document. What is important is that these stages are considered, assessed for their usefulness, and then acted upon.

If you are very familiar with financial modeling, you may be wondering why a model audit has not been included in the life cycle. The answer is that it could be, but I have chosen not to since the model audit is not an essential or critical part of the modeling. Obviously it is good to have an audit, but all models do not need to be audited, particularly if they undergo a period of testing. Only the most stringent model audit will actually provide assurance beyond the logical model. In other words, an audit will pinpoint where the model's structure has issues and the problems in the logic, but it will not give assurance as to the materiality of the information about the model, unless the sponsor is willing to pay a considerable fee.

For models that will have an external facing element and will be used to provide information that is sensitive and will be acted upon, I would recommend that the model audit be added to provide assurance above and beyond the testing. But in general, the testing will be sufficient. Figure 4-1 shows the stages in the modeling life cycle.

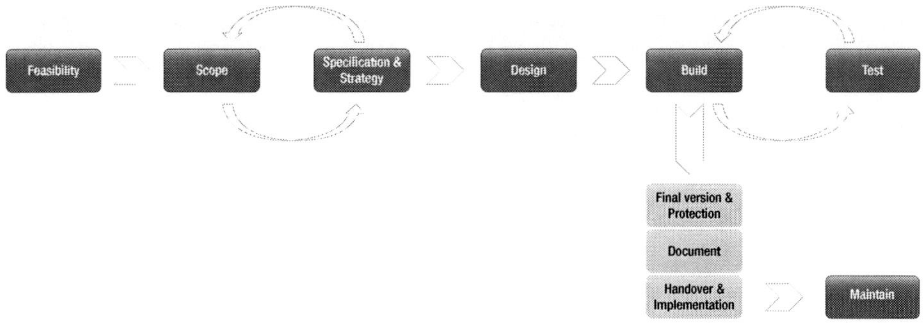

Figure 4-1. This figure is a typical financial modeling life cycle showing the different stages

---

Note I am aware that there is a large group of organizations who actively use financial models but have no formal review process, which means no one is checking the models. This is not necessarily wrong, as those organizations may not place so much importance on making decisions from models. In that case, any errors would have little magnitude. The concern though is once any of these key development stages are missed, the model process becomes flawed and eventual users of the model will be at the mercy of that planning.

Planning to Build a Model

The planning of the project is actually essential to model building because it helps to eliminate and also mitigate against surprises and issues. There is no worse feeling as a modeler than to find yourself going in circles with no end in sight—either because of problems that have not been resolved, or because the scope of the project has started to creep into something far larger than originally expected with a result that the model becomes large and more complex. The start of planning is marked by a feasibility evaluation of the project, followed by scoping, and then creating the modeling specifications.

To give you just a flavor of the issues modelers are likely to face from the outset of a modeling project, I have described a few in the next few sections. These issues seem to crop up irrespective of where you build the model or what type of model it is, which should be highlighted in the feasibility evaluation.

Is There a Clear Understanding of Cash?

A common mistake in financial models is not having a solid understanding of what cash is and what cash is not. Ask yourself these questions:

- Are revenues cash?
- Are gross margins cash?
- Are profits cash?

The answer to all three of these questions is a resounding "no." If you didn't know this, don't panic. Not everyone in the business world is clear about this either. Then what is cash?

There is no satisfactory answer to the cash question without creating a cash flow statement. Financial models should always makes sure there is a cash flow statement because it's a fundamental requirement of modeling. Without this statement, the user will have difficulty with even performing rudimentary tasks like balancing the balance sheet, estimating availability of funds, or even understanding when the bank account will be in deficit or overdraft. Read through the following example:

Suppose you sell something this month for $100, and the cost of making it was $50 in total. You have to pay your suppliers within 30 days, while the buyer probably won't pay you for at least 60 days. In this case, your revenue for the month was $100, your profit for the month was $50, and your cash flow for the month was zero. Your cash flow for the transaction will be negative $50 next month when you pay your suppliers. Although this example may seem trivial, slight changes to the timing between cash receipt and disbursement, even just a couple of weeks, can bankrupt a business. Therefore, a good model will reflect not only cash flows generated by the organization but also their timing.

How Much Detail Is Required?

When planning, take a look at the financial information that has been requested by the model owner and model users and work out how much detail will be required. For instance, the requirement might be to have a summary level profit and loss (income) statement that just shows revenue, costs of sales and services, expenses, and net profit. Don't be fooled into believing this is really all you will need. My advice is to always plan to build at the detail level; the financials should be constructed from the bottom-up and then validated from the top-down.

A bottom-up model starts with details, such as the types of revenues and when they are invoiced and received, or the different types of expenses and again when to expect to pay them. The top-down validation means that you examine your overall summary and compare it with the bottom-up details to be sure they match.

Note When I audit a financial model, there are some threads that I look at that will tell me if the model financials have been built with detail or not. One of them is to look at the outputs and see how they have been rounded. Numbers that show neat rounding, for example, staff costs are two million in Year 1 and three million in Year 2, is a sign that the bottom-up approach is missing.

Create Scenario Analysis and Sensitivity Analysis

One of the purposes of good financial models is that they include some scenario and sensitivity analyses showing how your projected results will change if your assumptions turn out to be incorrect. If planned properly, the building of these scenarios and sensitivities will subsequently help the user identify and track the assumptions that can have a material effect on future performance. These can then be validated further during the testing.

Note Scenario analysis is the process of creating a basic model or base case and then changing all the variables to extremes. One extreme creates the best case while the other develops the worst case, allowing you to see the full range of possible outcomes. If the range between the best and worst case is too large for comfort, more research may be warranted before proceeding.

Performed after a scenario analysis, the sensitivity analysis is similar with one significant difference. Instead of changing all the variables simultaneously, you change one variable at a time to its own best and worst case value and rerun the model. Then reset the assumptions to the base case and go on to the next individual variable, and so on. The result from this series of iterations shows which of the assumptions drives the greatest variation in the results or outputs. These specific variables are the ones the user must control to optimize future results.

Assumptions: How Realistic Are They?

During the planning, it's important to set the tone of how the assumptions for the model are going to be validated. The validation is important from the modeler's perspective, because once that is finalized, the modelers will input the assumptions into the model and will be responsible for how those assumptions are interpreted. The question of ownership of assumptions is critical. While the assumptions will be given to the modelers and therefore will have an owner and contact, once they enter the model the modeler is responsible for having them in there. If you don't understand an assumption that is sitting within your model, it's imperative that you do. Why? Because you will have to validate every assumption in order for the users and owner of the model to have assurance that the model is fit for purpose.

Ironically, validating the assumptions can be time-consuming and requires effort in people management. As a result, it is somewhat common to find good working models where the modeler has not fully validated the assumptions. As a result, the assumptions remain in the model, but there is no rational link with reality. I warn against this practice because it leads to the modeler's integrity being questioned. The assumption validation is a two-way process. First, the modeler collects and organizes the assumptions and then sends them back to the original provider of the information. The provider should then confirm that the information now in the assumptions is valid and can be used in the model. By acquiring this information from the assumption owner, the modeler can subsequently make a more informed opinion on the assumption and start to validate. The validation should be based on getting a second or even a third opinion from different sources. If this is not possible, try to throw the assumptions back to the original owner after some elapsed time to see if the assumptions remain the same.

Modelers need to have a firm grip on the assumptions and be willing to push the owner of the assumptions to move as close to reality as possible. For example, few companies achieve huge growth in revenues, profits, and cash flow after a slower period. Projecting numbers that an organization cannot support is never a good idea. It not only wastes your time but assists people in making ill-informed and hence bad decisions that will have long-term negative perceptions on your modeling ability.

Something to keep in mind is that the majority of people who will be viewing and making decisions based on the outputs will be looking for some input from the modeler as to the profile of the assumptions. For example, they may ask if the assumptions are practical and if so how pragmatic, or are they based on empirical evidence and so forth. While it is valid practice to provide some feedback into the assumptions, stop short of making overall assessments, such as that the assumptions are "aggressive" or "conservative" or even "pessimistic" (even if you truly believe they are.) Why is this restraint needed? By giving a general assessment such as "conservative," you will be creating a message that somehow the assumptions have been massaged to suit the audience, which brings the credibility of the model and the modeler into question.

Furthermore, with these types of assessments, modelers open up themselves to someone in the audience wanting to take a different angle. For example, if you decree that the assumptions are conservative, you may be directed to make them more pessimistic. This does happen and more often than not the modeler is left with trying to shape the results from the model to suit another's views. The solution is to use the scenarios that have been built into the model and create a scenario that shows the pessimistic view without altering the base model assumptions.

Tip The best way to achieve these realistic assumptions is to make sure that you have challenged the assumption owner to give you as much background as possible. Also try and support this feedback with something solid (like past results). In essence, always create a relationship with assumption owners that allows them to help you to substantiate everything they give you.

Missing Key Elements in Financial Statements

Make sure that all the financial statements and outputs conform to generally accepted accounting principles. For instance, if the organization's financials are caught under IFRS (International Financial Reporting Standards) and the model is reporting revenues, then be sure that they conform with the IFRS standards on revenue recognition.

Plan how far the model will project. Will it be three years, five years, or even ten years? Is it possible to project the years? If not, then how credible is the model? With most models, it is common to project out three to five years into the future. And while nobody can see five years into the future, having this projection in the model gives some assurance to the model users and anyone else reading the model that you have thought through the process and validated your initial assumptions.

As much as possible, the financial model should provide benchmark comparisons to past performance or leaders and other competitor analysis. Showing key indicators—liquidity ratio, return on capital employed or revenues per employee, gross margin per employee, gross margin as a percentage of revenues, and various expense ratios—can be very helpful and show that there has been a concerted planning and thought process behind the model build.

Developing a Feasibility Assessment

The modeler should commence a model project with a feasibility assessment of the entire model project. More directly, the modeler must assess the relative merits of building the model with reference to physical constraints, such as resourcing, monetary constraints, and skills availability. This assessment will encapsulate aspects like the following:

- Determine the knowledge and size of the team (it could be just yourself) and the adequacy of the resources.
- Establish the timescales from start to delivery and if they are realistic. You will need to cite examples of other similar projects.
- Evaluate the risks and potential pitfalls of developing such a model.
- Assess the relative importance of the model, such as whether it will be used to make key decisions. Is this a one-time-only model to help in a process? Or is this an ongoing model? You will also need to clarify the key personnel, such as the users, owners, stakeholder(s), sponsors, and those who have a vested interest in providing information for the model.

- Consider the readiness of the project, organization and resources, equipment, and software. In other words, determine how rapidly all of these elements can be mobilized.
- Review the appropriateness of the locations or which will be the ideal location. If there is a lot of in-person communications required, the project will benefit from being close to key personnel.
- Know the cost impact of having or not having the model.
- Determine the skill level of the financial modeler with relation to the project requirements (notice this may need to be performed after the requirements gathering).
- Establish if the deliverables are clearly understood. If not, they will need to be developed and stated manifestly at this stage.
- Consider if this exercise is going to be a team effort. If so, the roles within the team should be very clear at this stage. In addition, the resources and time commitment that will be available during the course of the project should be planned.

Scoping the Modeling Project

The scope is a very critical aspect of the planning. As a modeler, you should insist that you are given a clear and unambiguous communication of the full scope for the model. I reiterate the word "full." This means that not only do you gain understanding of what is in scope, but also crucially what is out of scope. For instance, a scope may state that the model "will be used to support the finance teams to identify the key cost drivers." This statement is short and vague, so it will be your responsibility to tie it down. For instance, in this situation, you could start by addressing these questions:

- Who are the finance teams? They need to be stated either by the team name or the chief contact.
- Are the finance teams responsible for providing the information and data to the model? If not, who will? Does the modeler need to build this information?
- Can we define support? Is this a one-time model for a precise purpose and limited time, or is this an ongoing model that will need to be maintained and refreshed with data?
- Do the cost drivers include resources (staff) time?

Once you have covered just about every conceivable aspect, write a scope document, which will need to be approved by the model sponsor. The document should not be more than two pages and should clearly state what is in scope and what is out of scope. In this document, avoid using vague language. You do not want to open the scope to misinterpretation and cause confusion between the modeler and model sponsor as to what should be delivered.

Note When thinking about what is in scope and what is out of scope, I am reminded of a photographer taking a group photo for a football team. When composing the photo, once the photographer looks through the camera lens, what he sees is in scope. Anything outside of the lens is out of scope. However, the photographer still needs to be aware of what is out of scope because it could affect the photo (for example, a bird moving into view at the last second).

I recommend that as the modeler, even though you may be given the scope, be proactive in the scope document creation. Take responsibility for writing the scope document in order to understand exactly what the full project entails. You will also be able to get some control over scope creep, which is very common during model builds. The scope document is the critical element that you would use to control scope creep with the model sponsor, the stakeholders, and the model users.

Note Scope creep is the continuing growth of the size of a project in an uncontrolled manner and usually occurs when the scope is not accurately defined and communicated. Scope creep should be considered as one of the key risks in the feasibility stage and can have an impact on costs by creating cost overruns. The best place to be as the modeler is to have your scope documented, communicated, and be explicit about the change control, such as creating procedures on how to change the scope.

Keep a copy of the approved document and circulate copies to the sponsor and stakeholders. Also place a summary of the scope in the model where it will be visible, such as a part of the documentation or in the assumptions.

The Specification & Strategy

The specification should be a detailed document with a series of requirements for the model that have been gathered from the eventual model users, model owner, sponsor, and stakeholders.

In this stage, the modeler should identify the output parameters (generally the financial statements) of the model. The modeler should also have a design for the types of calculations that will be used in the model and should assess whether there will be a need for VBA programming. The question of the VBA is important for the reason that not all modelers are competent at coding in VBA. What if VBA coding is required and the modeler does not have the skills to deliver such a model? There answer is to alert the project sponsors about the situation. At the same time, the sponsors should be advised either to bring in a VBA programmer to assist the modeler, or secure a modeler who has the VBA skills. It is also important to identify the inputs required for the financial model. Finally, the model parameter should be identified, and all options should be highlighted.

The specification will be quite detailed and will be the reference template that the modeler will use during the design and build of a financial model. The specification is crucial to the model design and therefore should not be produced to reflect the modeler's point of view. It should instead reflect to a large extent the specification of the stakeholders and the users.

The sponsor of the model who may be a stakeholder should sign off on the specifications before you begin any design and build. This is a critical point because many model designs commence before the specification sign-off, for several reasons such as the sponsor is too busy but wants results immediately. My advice is do not be compromised—this is your design plan and also your checklist when the model is complete. In many ways, this is your insurance against scope creep. If you were a constructor, would you start building someone's dream house without the architect's plans? Be strong; do it right!

The specification should address the following requirements:

- What is this model for?
- Whom is this model for?
- What should the model do?
- What are the inputs required?
- Where will the data and assumptions come from?
- What business logic is required?
- What level of detail is required for the model?
- What flexibility is required? In other words, what needs to be able to change?
- Who will use it and how? What are their skills?
- How often will it be used, for how long, and how?
- How soon is the model required to be live?

These are the requirements that should be gathered in the early stages of the project. In fact, begin working through these as soon as the scope to the project has been produced. (Always entertain the idea that there is a scope document. This is not the modeler's responsibility to create, but it will be the modeler's responsibility to communicate.) You should be as detailed as possible and remember not to make any of your own assumptions as this impartiality will really help when you design and build.

These requirements should always originate from the people who want the model. The modeler can fill in technical, economic, and resource implications as well as any constraints once base specifications have all been put together.

In the beginning, clearly identify the stakeholders and the sponsor (usually the same person who has asked for the model) and their roles and responsibilities within the project. The sponsor should be able to provide a set of high-level requirements that you can use for the specification, which will be your initial template.

The sponsor's requirements are a key component. Therefore, should the sponsor fail to provide the document, insist that you are given access to someone who can give a clear view of the scope. Under no circumstances should you, the modeler, be pushed to a position of creating an initial specification. If you do, you will then run the risk of a project failure due to unclear specifications and miscommunications from feedback. This aspect will ultimately decide the success of the modeling project.

For all modeling projects (irrespective of size), develop the habit of documenting the specifications and model design because it provides a visible and relatively easy checklist during the testing period. I liken this to a presentation. How can you be sure the presentation has gone to plan without an agenda to refer to?

It is extremely important for the modeler to fully understand the business logic, such as all the business rules that need to go through the model. For instance, many business models involve some type of taxation or accounting for inflation (usually termed "indexation") so that you would expect some rules on how the model will be affected by implementing such rules.

Also be sure to heed the warnings surrounding errors in logic and especially omissions as they are among the hardest to find in any model. Don't underestimate the damage that errors can do to the model and how quickly a modeler's work can be undermined if errors are left unchecked.

In the specification stage, keeping all source documents, files, notes, and discussions is imperative for reference, as these should guide the modeler as to the business logic and model. Keep in mind that ultimately the closing working model will reflect this understanding by the modeler and any weaknesses in the modeler will affect the concluding model. However, it seems obvious that the modeler should maintain a healthy respect for referencing information regularly throughout the project. For example, if you are modeling capital investments, you would need documentation on the actual item's lists, depreciation schedules and valuations, assets conditions, and so forth.

My advice is to keep all documents, review, read, understand, always question, and get confirmations. Never in any circumstance leave yourself in a position where you cannot explain the business or project due to a lack of understanding. If you do, you will eventually be found out. If this occurs very late in the project, the modeler would be expected to take full responsibility for any mistakes in the model that reflect this lack of business understanding. Suffice it to say, every modeler should be covered by professional indemnity insurance.

Caution Any modeler who is involved in undertaking projects on behalf of clients and customers should always have professional indemnity (liability) insurance. This should not be an option but a requirement, and it should be at a level well above $1 million in today's money. Once all the matters of compensation and legal fees are totted up, that is the kind of money that you will need to have.

The Benefits of Model Specification

The discipline of performing a model specification will ensure that you produce a definitive statement of what the model should do and how it will do it. It allows the modeler to take on the most difficult problems associated with the model from the very start of the planning. The specification is the only method that allows model users, the model sponsor, and the modeler to collectively agree what the model will be and how it will be delivered. A successful specification establishes a common understanding of what the model will do.

A model specification will make the testing of the model easier and will also provide an effective means of preaching solutions to any defects detected. It is a clear statement of what the model is doing. The model tester then has to check whether the finished model agrees with the written specification.

Failure to write a model specification will lead to difficulties later in the planning because it won't be clear to the modeler exactly what is required by the model sponsor. The following types of problems can occur:

- More time is needed to build the model because the issues that could have been identified in the specification were not resolved and keep coming back.
- Continual late changes keep occurring in the model logic, not all by the model sponsor or users, but also by the modeler who has failed to come to terms with some of the more difficult issues of the model early enough. This is potentially the greatest single cause of errors in completed models.

- Vague objectives characterize the model. It is easy to start with a small model that aims to solve one problem but ends up with a large model that solves all sorts of other problems, but solves them badly.

Defining Model Outputs

The first stage during the model specification process is to refine the broad output requirements that were defined from the scope stage into defined outputs that the model will produce. Do not underestimate how much time and effort this step can take. On a large project plan, this can be a matter of days and possibly weeks to get a final specification. Note this difference: the scope is about "where do we want to be?" and the defined specifications are about "what do we need to get to where we want to be?"

The simplest method of presenting the model outputs is to produce templates or outline reports using Excel. Outline reports will look like the final output without the data. These outline reports will give everyone involved the best possible idea of what the last outputs will look like early and can also be approved or modified by the model owner. Whenever possible, try to get the model sponsor to produce the outline reports, as this will add to the sign-off of the specification.

This is a stage in which the model sponsor needs to be involved to agree on what information is required in the model reports. Here is a list of typical questions that need to be answered:

- Who is going to use the model reports?
- What purpose is each model report going to serve?
- What is the appropriate level of detail to include on each report?

When you have established an outline for the model reports, you can consider the calculations needed to give you the required outputs.

Defining Calculations: Techniques for the Model Specifications

Developing the calculation rules that define the workings of a model can be difficult, especially when your understanding about the problem to be modeled is vague. That is why the process of defining the model specification will most likely be iterative, as more than one attempt is required before you get it right. In order to develop the calculations, you will need to address the type of information organization you will use. For instance, will the model consist of several tables with data? Will there be user inputs to affect these tables? By thinking through the data, it will become clear about the types of calculations and hence functions and formula that will be required.

For instance, if there will be numerous tables holding data, it is certain that the lookup functions such as MATCH() and INDEX() will be required. Also, if totals are required from these tables, you will not be able to ignore the SUMIF() or COUNTIF() functions.

When defining the calculations, start by listing the functions that will definitely be required. Then list those that will be useful and finally those that will have very minimal usage. In this way, you will have a record later for documenting the calculations used in the model.

Defining the Inputs

Once you have defined the model calculations, the inputs required for the model should be implicit (based on intuition and specification but have not yet been formalized). It is frequently worth considering in more detail what inputs are required and how they are to be sourced. It is never easy defining inputs because by their nature, they rely upon the final user's vision of which sensitivities they will need, which may not be available during the planning. My advice is to look at the outputs, which should have been defined previously. It should be clear from these outputs exactly what types of inputs and sensitivities will be required, although this is also a matter of what level of experience the modeler has of such projects. For instance, if the outputs (reports) have an income statement showing five years of revenues and financials, it is certain that inputs of the selling price for five years will be required.

One method is to list the various inputs and types in a data sheet; you can then map these input items to actual outputs. A data input list of this form is useful for the following reasons:

- Establishes the level of detail required in the input assumptions at an early stage in a form that is easy to communicate.
- Highlights where special effort will be required in data collection and assigns responsibility for producing the data.
- Lists the type of estimate that will be used for each input assumption in the status column. This can help identify the inputs that will be candidates for sensitivity analysis.

Creating specification of a model can be challenging, which would explain why very few models have a specification. With small models, there is little need for these specifications; these types of models are generally not complex. For large models that will have a complexity, forgoing the specification increases the risk that the final model will not fulfill the needs of the model user and the model sponsor. The best way to view the specification is as blueprint for the model building.

CHAPTER

5

Testing and Documenting Your Model

In this chapter, I will examine the process of testing models and providing user documentation for models. Without question, one of the most neglected stages of building models are the testing and documentation, because they are often performed toward the end of the modeling project and are subject to time constraints. I want to make sure that you have a firm understanding of why the testing and documentation should be considered just as important as any other stage in modeling.

Testing the Financial Model

You will notice that I have jumped into model testing before model building. Rest assured that this is deliberate, because the testing is planned around the model. There are no standard tests for financial models, but there are a series of test types that are used. Not all of these are appropriate for each model, and in order for the tester to understand which test types will be right for the model, the tester must first understand the model. The testing is never incidental; it doesn't just happen because the model has been built. It is a carefully planned and organized activity that has a significant part to play in the delivery of the model. Therefore, it is a critical part of the model design.

Why Test?

A best practice spreadsheet model should be reliable because decisions are likely to be made based upon the results and outputs that come from the model. This is only possible if the user has complete confidence in the model. It is impossible to guarantee that even a moderately complex model is an error-free model. Testing can, however, substantially reduce the risk of significant errors in a model.

Caution If testing is skipped or poorly handled, errors are likely to be discovered after the model has been put into use. There is nothing more damning than a model that has supposedly been tested but appears to be rife with errors. Errors at this stage can undermine the credibility of the model, the modeler, and the organization behind the model. Also keep in mind that the value of testing can be measured against the potential cost of a wrong decision. If a model is being used for an important and expensive business decision, the time and resources spent testing the model is time and money well spent. We have not yet discussed model audit, but it is important to know this distinction with testing. The model audit gives assurance that the model is what it says it is. In other words, if the requirement is ten-year cash flow model only, the model audit will sign off that the model is suitable for purpose. Testing, on the other hand, is about catching and minimizing the errors and verifying that the model works.

Who Should Test?

When testing a model, the objective is to demonstrate that the model does not work as it was intended. From this standpoint, the testing can focus on catching all the aspects in the model that are causing it to fail. It is impossible for modelers to be sufficiently critical of their own work; therefore, testing should always be carried out by an independent third party.

It is best for testing to be done by a team member who has been involved in other aspects of the overall project or aspects of the modeling other than the build stage. There are obvious benefits to using someone who is familiar with some of the issues that the model reflects. However, the technical skills required for a good tester are similar to those required for building the model. The tester should be able to understand and critique the detail of the formula and any code within the model.

When to Test?

When should testing commence? This is entirely based upon the program schedule. Testing, however, can only take place between the build and handover stages of the modeling life cycle. Under more pressing circumstances, it can be more difficult to identify the most appropriate time to test. Here are two examples:

- When there is great pressure for immediate results from the model, there is a trade-off to be made between gaining confidence in the model's results and trying to produce some reasonable answers quickly.
- When the model develops in a number of incremental stages, it is difficult to know when the time is right to first test the model, or when further changes are significant enough to require retesting.

There is no single correct answer for these questions, but there are points in time when testing should be considered. Generally, the testing period would commence just after the first version of the model is completed and run until all the errors are fixed and recommendations are implemented into the final model version. With very complex modeling projects, however, the modeler should consider implementing testing into the change control process. This way, testing will take place at regular intervals and after every major change in the model. This will be surplus to requirements for smaller models and can be costly. But with this approach, the model will always take into consideration any errors that are highlighted from testing.

Types of Tests

One of the unfortunate aspects of model testing is that there is no standard test. Instead, there are different types of tests that can be used, but not all of them are appropriate for every model. This dilemma of test choices is one reason why it is best for the tester to have spent some time with the modeler in order to gain an understanding of the model's structure and objectives. The next sections will provide brief summaries of the main model tests.

Numeric Tests

Numeric tests are used to determine if the outcome of an equation is in accordance with expected results by using an independent verification as a check. There are various ways to subject the results from a model to independent verification, including the following:

- It may be possible to reproduce some of the model results by hand or in a "quick and dirty" independent model.

- When the model is developed to replace a precursor model, any similarities or differences in common results can be explained by differing assumptions.
- When you know that there will not be time to test the model, ask two modelers to independently do the analysis and then compare their results.

A well-designed model will contain some internal numerical tests. A balanced balance sheet and consistency between calculated totals and subtotals are both necessary signs of a reliable model, but they are not proof that no errors still remain in the model. You will only get sensible results out of a model if you put realistic input assumptions in. While it is often outside the scope of the independent tester's work, the validity of the input assumptions will obviously affect the appropriateness of the answers.

Robustness Tests

The longer the expected life span of the model and the more different users of the model there will be, the more difficult the model test becomes. Instead of testing the validity of the model just under current circumstances, the tester needs to consider all the feasible circumstances that the model may be used for in the future. The two categories for robustness testing look at the environment that the model will operate in and the boundaries at which the model will potentially fail.

Environment Tests

Environment tests evaluate the operation of the model through several different computer configurations. Points to check include the hardware specification of the computer to be used, network and printer operations, and the specific versions of software being used. These tests will confirm that technical specification has not been exceeded, in particular the model size and calculation speed.

Boundary Tests

Boundary tests assess the behavior from the model when inputs reach sensible limits. For example, these tests would answer the following questions:

- How does the model cope with extremely large or extremely small inputs?
- Does typing in a zero produce division by zero errors?

If you type junk into a model, you expect to get junk out. But for many models, some form of data validation may be appropriate. Nevertheless, extreme cases of using particularly good or bad input assumptions are often important sets of model results, so the model should be able to cope with these.

Macro Tests

If the model contains macros, testing these can be extraordinarily time-consuming. Macros often only cause errors in a particular circumstance, which the tester will need to replicate to get an idea of how the error happens. The following issues are typical of the checks:

- Do the buttons, dialog boxes, and menus work appropriately?
- How does the macro cope with inappropriate data? How elegantly does it crash?
- If the macro involves file handling, what happens with duplicate or nonexistent files?
- Does the macro assume any default settings for the spreadsheet, such as sheet names, which a user may change?
- What happens when the user presses Escape during the macro execution?

When enough changes have been made in the model since the previous test, it makes material changes to the results possible. You need to consider how big a change to the results constitutes a material change and should then fall into the change control process.

Specification Tests

One of the objectives of the specification stage is to establish a common understanding of how the model should work. To achieve this objective, it is necessary to test that the specification agrees with the model sponsor's understanding of what the model will do. Clearly, this process does not require the model build to have been completed or even started.

Unique Formulas Tests

To test that the formulas in the model have been written correctly, check the model itself against the logical assumptions described in the model specification or in a similar document. A review of every unique formula in the model is an essential part of any thorough model test. Even so, the number of formulas in a reasonably large model makes this a daunting task.

I recommend resolving this problem by using the formula maps produced by a spreadsheet auditor package, such as OAK (by Operis) and Spreadsheet Professional (by Spreadsheet Innovations).

Common Types of Errors to Test

Fortunately, there are some errors in models that are very likely to occur, and an experienced tester will be able to quickly target those errors in the model. Once these errors have been corrected, the more unique errors can then be tackled. The next few sections will describe the more common errors.

Formulas Not Copied

With this error, a formula needs to be reflected either across a row or down a column, but it has somehow been missed and is not copied into all the required cells. There are several reasons how this would happen. In Chapter 2, the reasons why specific types of errors occur were discussed, such as the modeler talking on the phone while modeling. This type of error is quite difficult to locate, particularly if you have an erratic design for the model because a tester will be unable to be definite if the error is actually an error or if it is intended.

Wrong Reference

Nearly every formula in a spreadsheet refers back to another input or calculation. With the quantity of references in any large spreadsheet, it is inevitable that you will make mistakes and refer to the wrong cell (a pointing error). Sometimes, the resulting formula will produce a meaningless result, making it easy to spot with some simple numerical testing. If you are unlucky, the error in the result will be more subtle. While these types of errors are common, the testing should catch these quite easily. One way to alleviate these errors is to get into the habit of actually pointing to the cell that is being referenced rather than just naming it. Although this is a slower modeling process, it is more precise and mitigates the potential risk of using incorrect figures.

Sum Over the Wrong Range

A similar mistake is to include the wrong cell reference in a SUM formula. It is particularly easy to introduce this error when you insert an additional row in a block of cells that are being summed. If you insert a row in the middle of the block, the formula will automatically adjust to include the additional row. But if you insert a row immediately above or below the block, the new row will be omitted from the formula. This type of error should be picked up in the error checks built into the model.

Relative and Absolute References

Another commonly found error is caused by confusion between relative and absolute references. Remember that a cell reference in a formula of the form =D4 will change if you copy the formula across the row to E4, F4, and so on. Copied down a column, it will change to D5, D6, and so on. If you use the reference =$D$4, it will not change when copied across or down. You can also use semi-absolute references of the form $D4 or D$4.

The most common mistake is probably to use a relative reference instead of an absolute one. This is easy to spot numerically, but if you use an absolute reference in place of a relative one, it can be much more difficult to detect. The only way to find this mistake reliably is to use a formula map to go through all the unique formulas in the spreadsheet.

Unit Errors

Mixing up the appropriate unit for the elements in a calculation is another frequently occurring problem. Especially common is confusion between the order of magnitude for inputs, such as $s vs. $000s. This error should always be caught in testing. The modeler should be able to avoid making this type of error purely by making sure the units are clear and constant throughout the model.

Commonly Misused Functions

Certain functions are frequently used incorrectly. For instance, the most commonly misunderstood is the NPV function, used to calculate net present values.

The NPV function takes the form =NPV (rate, value1, value2, . . .) where a rate is an appropriate discount rate and value1, value2, and so on are a stream of cash flows to be discounted. One common error in the NPV function is using an inappropriate discount rate, especially when the model contains calculations in a mixture of real and nominal prices.

A second common mistake concerns the timing of cash flows. By default, the NPV function assumes that all cash flows occur at the end of the time period you are considering. For an ongoing business, it is usually more appropriate to assume that cash flows occur in the middle of each time period.

For a model based on annual time periods, using a discount rate of 10% and an end year rather than a midyear assumption decreases the present value calculated by 5%.

You can work through these problems by making an appropriate adjustment to the NPV function. Alternatively, it is often easier to calculate present values from first principle or use the Excel add-in function XNPV, which allows you to explicitly state the dates on which cash flows occur.

Other Functions That Often Cause Errors

Lookup and reference functions, such as VLOOKUP, HLOOKUP, INDEX, and MATCH, are susceptible to misuse, particularly when they return what may seem like an appropriate lookup instead of an error. This generally occurs when the range of the lookup reference is smaller than the true range, which means the lookup is working on a subset of the data. To avoid such mishaps, it is simpler to use a defined name (range name) to the data being referenced. That way, all the modeler needs to make sure is that they call the correct range name.

Using complex IF statements is a common issue for testing. The problem is magnified if there are embedded IF statements, which are notoriously difficult to decipher. Even when they have been detected, simplifying the formula is time consuming. Therefore, always test IF statements while they are being created. Even though there is a limit to how many IF statements (seven) can be embedded, still be sure to work well below this limit. If you are finding that you are using all seven IF statements in one formula, carefully consider your modeling technique as this is a clear sign of excessive complicated formula use.

Although these functions are often very useful, make sure that you understand exactly how they work before using them in your model. By making the formulas in your model easy to understand, you reduce the risk of introducing errors and increase the chances that a tester will find your mistakes.

The Test File

Testing is concerned with increasing confidence about the reliability of the model's results, so it is important that the testing process itself inspires confidence. A well-documented testing process will do just that. A test file is a useful document to illustrate how the model was tested and demonstrates that reasonable steps were taken to establish the accuracy of the model.

A test file should contain a record of the different tests that were carried out, such as annotated printouts of the model output and formula maps. The test file should also include an auditable trail of the errors found and corrections made and any other supporting documentation, such as the results of independent numerical tests.

Change Requests

An important part of the test documentation is a record of the changes recommended in the model and how they were implemented.

The tester completes the first section, which includes a description of the error found and, if appropriate, a suggested correction. The description should contain sufficient information for the modeler to correct most errors without having to spend time redoing the original test. The model builder takes the completed forms and makes the required changes, completing the second part of the form. I do not recommend that the tester make the changes to the model for the following reasons:

- The model builder usually understands the detail to the model better than anyone else. Change requests are sometimes the result from a misunderstanding by the tester rather than an actual error.
- When more than one person is working with the model at one time, it is important that a single copy is kept as the master version. The model builder can continue to work on the master version while testing is underway.

The third part of the form should be completed by the tester to check that the change has been made appropriately. Retesting changes is important because changes to a model, incorrectly made, can have knock-on effects in other parts of the model.

When going through the testing process, using a different version number for each batch of model changes will allow you to keep track of the effect of each correction. It will also make the test file clearer and the process easier to understand.

It can also be useful to classify requests on the change request form depending upon their importance:

- High priority for errors that materially change the results produced by the model
- Medium priority for errors that have a very small effect or may affect the results in the future
- Low priority for changes that are recommended to make the model easier to understand, but will not affect the results quoted

When time is limited, the builder can concentrate on high and medium priority changes and turn to low priority changes when time permits.

Points to Keep in Mind When Testing

The role of testing in modeling is not always appreciated, and it is important to ensure that models do get tested. The following points should be on your mind when building models.

- Testing can reduce the risk of significant errors appearing in your model results and build up the credibility and influence of the finished model.
- Errors discovered after the model has been put into use undermine the credibility of the modeler.
- Testing should always be done by someone other than the model builder, someone who is motivated to find mistakes in the model.
- If the model builder uses only one unique formula per row or column, it is much easier to test all the formulas in the model.
- Documenting the test process will help to build confidence in the finished model's results.

Providing Documentation in Models

The financial modeler should keep a log of all amendments made to the model to ensure a proper audit trail and documentation of changes made. A guide to using the financial model should also be developed to make certain that future users are able to become familiar with and use the model with ease.

Just as writing the specification often seems like a mission in complete boredom, writing the documentation can be very mundane. The unfortunate truth is there are far too few examples of documentation in financial modeling, possibly due to this boredom factor. Another reason why documentation is not completed or even commenced is due to timetables. For example, sometimes the point from beginning to handing over or implementing a model is very short, and there is barely enough time to even test the model. Finding the time to document a model under such circumstances may seem impossible.

Documentation, however, almost always needs to be done. The model that you develop could be responsible for helping to form decisions that have a significant financial impact on a project or an organization. Therefore, it is imperative that some details of how and why the model works accompany the model. Documentation is like the contents section in a study book; it puts into place where everything is located and how it all works together. Without it, you are blindly a trusting that the book will actually take you to where you want to go.

Good documentation is needed to ensure that the model is handled properly, even by users who were not involved throughout the development process. Ideally, your specification will serve as the basis for the user documentation. Remember that the better your specification, the more of it you can "recycle" in the final user guide.

The secret to documenting is to start as early as possible and keep on top of it each day. Avoid procrastinating because the longer it is left undone, the harder it will become to finish. During my model builds, I make sure the documentation is always performed at the end of each day and reviewed the following morning before carrying on with the model development. Another tip is to employ what I call "spot checks," whereby I choose a particular part of the model and check that there is documentation. I won't move on until that part is in place. Often I will nominate an independent party who will check through parts of the model and through the documentation to test if everything makes sense (not someone with the immediate modeling team but someone who is totally removed from the model build).

Documentation Structures

Consider that not all users of the model will be Excel "power users." If you know this will be the case, then it is imperative that there is some additional care placed on the documentation. For example, you will need to explain what a macro is before you explain what your macros does, and do the same for model checks before you explain how a user can go error-hunting.

Here is one way to organize the structure of your documentation:

Introduction

The first section of your documentation should explain the scope and the goal of the model. The user should understand what to use the model for and what to expect from it.

Assumptions and Inputs

Following the introduction, explain the structural assumptions and the relevant inputs. The user also needs to understand the interaction between the assumptions and the inputs. For instance, if any of the assumptions are subsequently changed during the modeling process, will the inputs automatically adjust to reflect this change, or will someone have to manually adjust the inputs?

Macro Handling

If the macros in the model are complex and require some user proficiency, include a section on handling macros. Depending on the client, this may even become technical with some code explanations. In simpler models with no (or automatic) macros, you may drop this section.

Outputs

One chapter should be dedicated to the output sheets. In this section, explain what the sheets show and how they should be read. This is also the section where you should include the definitions of the KPIs (key performance indicators).

Known Issues

Obviously, there should not be any issues with your model when it is final. Nonetheless, there may be points you will want to highlight to make sure that "user expectation" does not diverge too far from reality. Typical issues may include the following:

- Extreme elasticity effects: Your model may be accurate for certain input values, like a planned equity ratio anywhere from 5% to 95%, but may deliver wrong results for ratios of 0% or 100%. Known effects like that should be documented. Ideally, you should also explain the reason, for example, if this is due to a calculation simplification in order to increase usability of the model.
- Performance issues: Complex models may require a lot of processor power and memory, and recalculations and macros may take their time. Let the user know if this is the case. If applicable, give advice on how to improve the model's performance.
- Compatibility issues: It happens rarely but include in your documentation if you know your model has problems with certain versions of Excel (or Office), Windows, locale settings, and so forth.

Documentation Standards

Documentation is crucial to models. Irrespective of whether a model has it or not, every model should be documented. How that documentation occurs can be wrapped up by a generally accepted documentation standard.

Using Cell Comments

Cell comments are a way of communicating tips and instructions to users. When a user's cursor hovers over a commented cell, a text box appears displaying the message. To add a cell comment, right-click the cell you want to attach the comment to and choose Insert Comment. A yellow text box will appear with an arrow pointing to the activated cell. Type in your comment. When you are finished, click on any other cell. The comment will be saved, attached to its anchor cell. The anchor cell will show a red triangle, indicating that a cell note is attached. (Note: The red triangle can be turned off by the Options dialog box, by choosing the Advanced option and scrolling down to Display.)

Tip When cell comments are shown, they sometimes hide the data behind them. You can move and resize the comment box by clicking directly on the box to activate it, then dragging the comment box to a new location. The comment's pointing arrow will stretch and remain attached to the comment's anchor.

If you have many comments in your worksheet, you might use the Reviewing toolbar to manage them. The toolbar appears when you choose Comments from the Review menu (to display all comments in Excel 2007/10/13, on the REVIEW tab, in the Comments group, click Show All Comments). Different buttons on the toolbar allow you to add comments, delete them, show all comments on the sheet, and tab from comment to comment.

By default, cell comments do not print when you print a worksheet. If you want comments to print, change the Comments setting in Page Setup. You have the choice of printing no comments, all comments at the bottom of the sheet, or as the comments appear directly on the sheet.

Note The comments must be displayed in the worksheet for them to print correctly. To display your comments on the sheet, choose the Show All Comments in the Comments group on the REVIEW tab.

Documentation Worksheets

Should you find that the instructions and explanations for a particular workbook are too unwieldy for cell comments, consider adding a separate worksheet in the workbook that contains only instructions and explanations. Give this worksheet tab a descriptive name, such as "InstructionsToUser" or "ModelnameDocumentation."

Note Notice that the suggested names for worksheets include no spaces between the words. This is a naming convention. If you are using hyperlinks and VBA, you will benefit by using this type of naming convention.

Excel's word processing capabilities are very limited, making editing of long text entries tedious. People often try to use Excel as a word processing tool, but that is just not in its bag of tricks. Don't fall into this habit as well. If you need to create considerable text documents in Excel, consider using MS Word and object linking the document to Excel. If you must use Excel, however, take these steps to make entering and editing long text passages easier:

- Format cells with the Wrap Text feature turned on. To activate this feature, on the HOME tab, in the Alignment group, click Wrap Text.
- Consider widening column A and using it for all entries.
- Always segment instruction topics into separate rows to minimize alignment problems when text is changed.

Thoughts About the Application to be Used

At some stage, the specifications will be locked down, and you will be in a position to begin developing the model. But first, put some thought into the application in which the model will be designed. Although you may already know you will be using Excel for modeling, consider that even with Excel there are different versions that can alter how you build the model. It is a safe assumption that your model will be developed in Excel 2003, Excel 2007/10, or Excel 2013. The essential modeling is the same throughout; however, the ease of development becomes more apparent in the later versions.

Spreadsheet packages are good at numerical manipulation and have a wide range of financial and mathematical functions. It is easy to present calculations in a readable form and to mix text and graphical display. Spreadsheets are enormously popular, widely available, and easy to use.

The flexibility of spreadsheets makes it possible to use them to tackle problems that would be more appropriately modeled with different software. Their availability and ease of use makes this an extremely common mistake. Therefore, before you design a spreadsheet, make sure that a spreadsheet is the most appropriate tool for the job.

Excel 2010/13 has a wide range of add-in functions that allows you to do numerous unusual calculations. Many of these can be very useful, but if you find that you are using them often, you would probably be better off using a specialist package. For example, if you are using a lot of the database functions, a database application such as Microsoft Access may be the better option.

This chapter is an augmentation to the planning of the modeling process. When working on medium to large models, there is so much that can be gained from having a plan with all the stages clearly established. I have come across completed large commercial models where there has been no documentation whatsoever. In my opinion, these models are not complete if they lack documentation. In the case of testing, although it irks me to say it, it is possible to complete a model without going through testing. Much depends on how that model will be used. For instance, testing may not be necessary if the model will be used to calculate the break-even point of an investment.

On the other hand, if a model is calculating how much funding from financial institutions and investors will be required to push a company through some turbulent times, then clearly a tested model is a must.

CHAPTER

6

Designing and Building Your Model

The design of the model is all about ensuring that the physical model will work once it is built and will actually function in the manner that is expected in the planning.

How the model is designed will be influenced by the ability of the modeler to translate requirements of the model sponsor into a methodical modeling project. This means prior to designing the model, the modeler must look at aspects such as:

- The impact of the requirements on the three key modeling concepts: inputs, calculations, and outputs.
- The intended use of the model. This will determine if it will be a deterministic-type model (a deterministic model is one that, given a fixed set of inputs, always produces the outputs), or a stochastic model, which means the modeler must consider the effects of probabilities on the outputs.
- The time scales of the model. Is this a time-value model or one that represents a specific moment only?
- The dependency of the model on external data such as databases and ERP (Enterprise Resource Management) systems.

- The potential size of the model, which is usually based on how much data the model is expected to hold.
- The project time scale, which will allow the modeler to assess whether building the model is realistic.
- The complexity of the modeling project. The model will generally reflect the environment that it is built in; a complex environment is likely to require a complex model.

Don't be tempted to start building the model too soon, especially when you are under pressure to produce results from the model quickly. Taking time to complete the design is well worth it, because it will allow the modeler to manage any complexities all during the design rather than when building. You will also enjoy the following results:

- The model is quicker and easier to build because you have a model specification that describes what the model will do rather than having to work it out as you go along.
- The model is less prone to errors if you have a written description of how the model works.
- The model is less likely to have to be reworked if you have taken some time to build a common understanding of the requirement of the model. To have such an understanding will mean the design should be preceded by a project scope document that has been jointly agreed upon by the model sponsor and the modeler.

Managing Complexity

There are several books that cover writing error-free software, none better than *Code Complete* (second edition) by Steve McConnell (Microsoft Press, 2004). McConnell states that the most important problem is managing complexity, which is a problem with financial modeling simply because Excel's versatility comes at price. Excel models tend to become complex quickly and easily. One of the reasons why so many Excel models become far too complex is that there are literally so many facets to Excel. With so many functions, codes, and utilities, there are just too many that are not matched by a user's knowledge.

If asked to rate their ability, many Excel users would claim to be far higher than an independent experienced Excel practitioner would. In other words, most believe that their skills in Excel are more than adequate, and why? One reason may be because Excel does not impose any intrinsic methodologies and structures on the user. For example, if you look at a complex model, you would only see one formula at a time and it may refer to cells and sheets you cannot see. What you can see is (often) a sea of numbers, which creates visual clutter. What this means is that users are not always aware of what is really going on outside of the cell they are working in. And because there are few alerts given by the application, users will actually believe that once a formula has been created everything is okay. Herein lies the problem—this is not necessarily the case.

As a result, it is possible to use some of the functions erroneously without really understanding their full impact until quite late in the modeling process when those errors start to appear. Most modelers at this stage would plough on regardless, firefighting any problems as they arise. Unfortunately, the result would be a finished model that is really a hodgepodge of functions, hard-coded adjustments, and dead links that has gone some way off the original route.

To put it bluntly, the reality is that of the 120 models I have reviewed in a four-year period, there were less than 12 that I would class as models that show any sense of planning and design to warrant being called financial models. This may be just a coincidence, but clearly there is a problem that needs to be addressed with the way models are being built.

Figure 6-1 presents a high-level design model of medium complexity in a flow diagram. You can clearly see that the model will be made up of several items or modules, such as the time-related inputs, the workings (calculations), and the reports. These modules have been classed into categories, for instance, inputs, calculations, or outputs. Notice the addition of the category called "Admin." This topic will be covered later in Chapter 14 when I discuss modeling in a way that gives the users transparency.

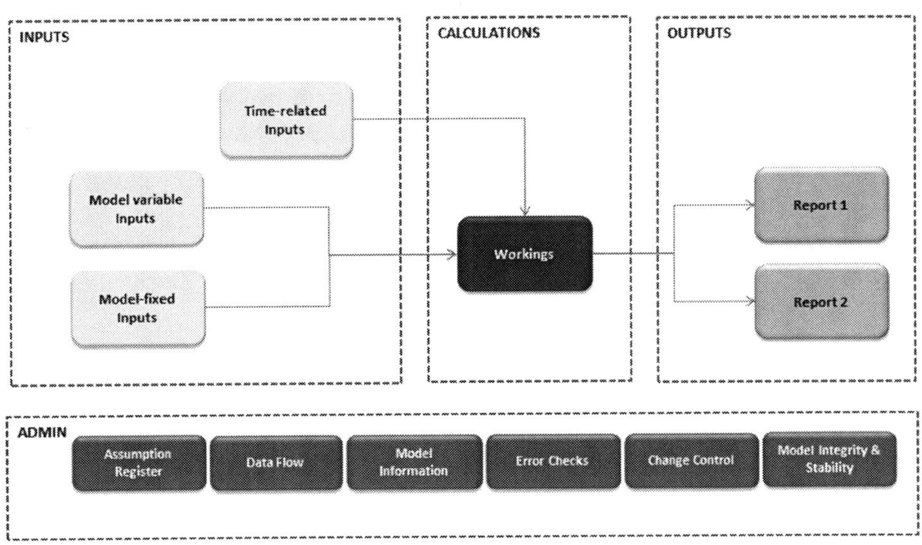

Figure 6-1. A high-level diagram of the model components is shown here

By creating such a diagram, you can start to see how these modules (which are essentially worksheets) will link to each other, and you can begin to make a map of the entire model.

You can consider the data flow and links between the modules in the high-level diagram by creating a data-flow table. The data-flow table is useful as a control mechanism for the data and links, and it also serves as a checklist of the data during the model building. A sample of a data-flow table can be seen in Figure 6-2.

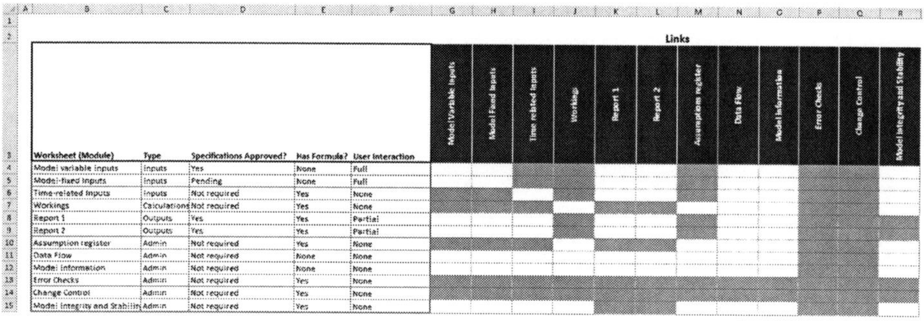

Worksheet (Module)	Type	Specifications Approved?	Has Formula?	User Interaction
Model variable inputs	Inputs	Yes	None	Full
Model-fixed inputs	Inputs	Pending	None	Full
Time-related inputs	Inputs	Not required	Yes	None
Workings	Calculations	Not required	Yes	None
Report 1	Outputs	Yes	Yes	Partial
Report 2	Outputs	Yes	Yes	Partial
Assumption register	Admin	Not required	Yes	None
Data Flow	Admin	Not required	None	None
Model information	Admin	Not required	None	None
Error Checks	Admin	Not required	Yes	None
Change Control	Admin	Not required	Yes	None
Model Integrity and Stabilit	Admin	Not required	Yes	None

Figure 6-2. A table with the data flows in the impending model serves as useful control for the modeler

The next part to the design is to explore each of these modules and decide the layouts, the look and feel, and the information that they will hold. This may mean you will start by developing a template that will be the standard template for all the modules in the model.

Figure 6-3 is a snapshot of the model-fixed inputs template. Notice that each individual section is clearly labeled; also there is an unused column in column A. This column will be used to provide references to the assumptions.

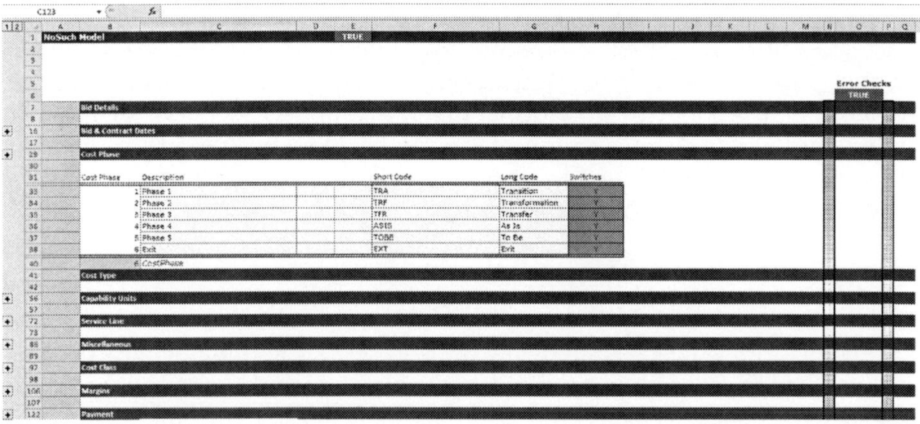

Figure 6-3. This is a sample of the model-fixed inputs template which contains the non-variable inputs to the model

During the design of all the worksheets, it will be important that the physical file size of the full model is considered. In addition, make sure that the specifications clearly indicate who will be the model owner and describe what exactly the model will be and which application it will be built in. Even though it may be clear to the modeler that the application will be Excel, this should still be stated in the specification to establish a clear understanding between the model sponsor and the modeler. There should also be some mention of the acceptable speed of processing.. In the design, the modeler must be careful to keep these specifications in sight. With numerous worksheets in a model, each with numerous calculations, more computer processing power is required. Remember that it is simply not good enough to deliver a model to the model user. Even though the model may function, it may be so large and so processor-intensive that it takes minutes rather than seconds to perform any calculations.

Tip What is the optimum Excel file size? The answer is that "it depends." No two workstations have uniform performance compared to one another. Another point to consider is what the model user will tolerate. Excel version 2007 and later versions have a more efficient file system; therefore, models developed with these versions are considerably smaller and more compact than those developed in older versions. I have my own hard-and-fast rules that I use to discipline myself when developing client models. I never exceed 0.5 megabytes per worksheet within the model. If I have a model with ten worksheets, it will be less than five megabytes. Again, this is my rule and it works for me, but it's a good idea to come up with your own working rule to the file size.

Building Your Model

At this stage, you should be clear about the model's design; have an understanding of the inputs, calculations and the outputs; and have in hand an approved scope and specification of the model. Now it is time to begin actually building the model. In this section, I will discuss the intricacies of the model build and how to best approach it.

Define the Modeling Tool(s) for the Job

When performing financial modeling using Excel, it is first important to establish whether Excel as your only tool of choice. In such situations where there is a heavy reliance on data, I do use Microsoft Access in combination with Excel. In these cases, Access handles all the data and becomes the back end of the model and Excel handles the calculations and outputs and becomes the front end. However, handing over such a model can be fraught with problems. Some quirks with Access and how it works with Excel that are not problematic on your computer may crop up on the user's computer. One way to avoid this problem is to create an application so that the entire model becomes an executable program, irrespective of whether it is part of Access or Excel. That is, however, beyond this book. I bring it up because occasionally as a modeler you may need to consider using Access. However, for the purposes of this book, the tool of choice will only be Excel.

Have a Clear Approach

There are two approaches to building models: the top-down method (see Figure 6-4) and the bottom-up method (see Figure 6-5). I endorse the top-down approach because the other method can cause even the most seasoned modeler to make errors.

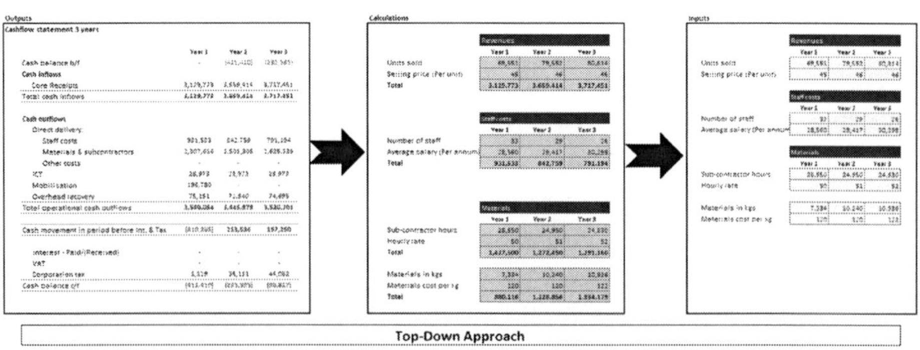

Figure 6-4. The top-down approach starts with the outputs

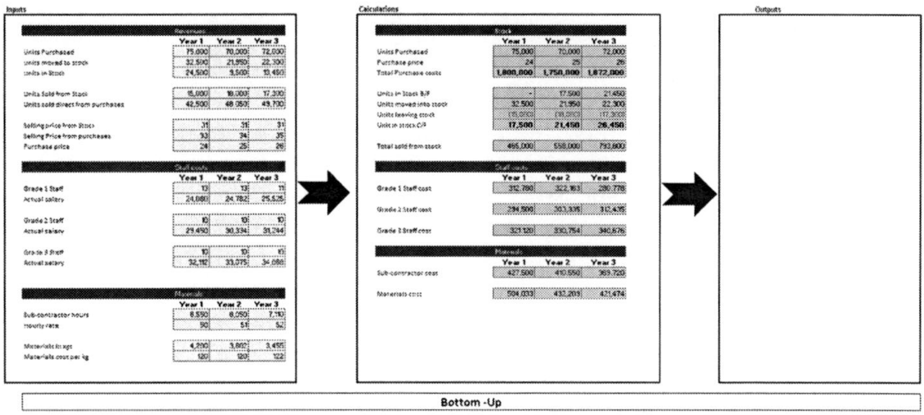

Figure 6-5. The bottom-up approach starts from the detail inputs and calculations, but the outputs are not used as the target

With the bottom-up method, the real problem is that this approach is focused on collecting data and how that data can be manipulated with calculations. This is the main priority and therefore this approach ignores the overall structure of the model. In other words, it works at the detail end of modeling first and puts the comprehensive presentation last. The problems start to appear once the modeler is in the development stage, because inevitably issues begin to emerge that weren't foreseen and planned. As a result, the modeler now has some major reworking to do. Due to this unstructured approach, the modeler is most likely going to create errors along the way because the modeling is based on "as you see it" type thinking.

Telltale signs of models built in this manner can be observed in the way that parts in the model just don't seem to relate together. For example, often it is unclear exactly what each part from the model is doing and even if some of the parts are really necessary. The model then becomes more a showcase of the individual modeler's changeable thought processes in each stage of the model and so lacks any real coherence or consistency.

Let's contrast this approach with the top-down approach by going through this example:

A model that will have a cash flow forecast for the next three years and should also have actual cash for the previous year.

How would you go about building this model? First, take a look at what you need to produce, which is a cash flow statement. Even though it was not required, you will need to create a profit and loss statement in order to look at revenues and costs. It's also clear that the model will need to accommodate some data inputs from users of the model, so they can punch in the previous year's actuals. Again, even though it hasn't been asked for, you will also need to build in some sensitivity, which means including a separate area for the user to flex the model inputs.

This top-down approach means that you are looking at the wider model and beginning to think about how the components will fit together. You are also defining the boundaries and subsequently working at the bottom in contrast to having no boundaries and working at the top. My advice is to work from top to the bottom by starting the model build with the outputs. Think in terms of the reports the sponsor and model users require and then work back into the inputs. That way, you will fit the inputs and calculations to the outputs, in contrast to a bottom-up method, where the outputs will not be known until the end of the model build. In this case, you will end up with far too many inputs and calculations.

Get Approval of the Outputs

The outputs that will be the reports and statements should always be the modeler's primary goal because they are the reason for the model build. Within the specification, you should have established the exact outputs. In most instances, the sponsor will have a clear idea of what is needed, such as financial statements (profit and loss, balance sheets, or cash flow statements) or budgets. It could even be a mix of these outputs and also include a number of financial valuations and financial metrics.

Crucially the modeler will need to make sure these outputs are not only clear but are approved and signed off by the sponsor. The best way to achieve this is to create physical samples of these outputs without any financial data that can be presented to the sponsor. Then the sponsor can make any adjustments and amendments and give final approval of the samples. Once the outputs are locked down, the process of building the model becomes defined and the final goals are clear and set. Often organizations will have standard templates or may require that any outputs have a particular layout and feel to them, so the modeler should also make sure that the model outputs are in line with the model user's requirements.

Time Scales

When building the model, it's inevitable that you will need to establish some method of working with time periods, which can be years, quarters, months, weeks, and even days. The trick is how to get the model to relate to moving periods, for instance, a change from reporting in years to reporting in quarters and then annually after the first year. In addition, the model needs to also have the ability to handle variations in dates, such as changes in specific dates like project milestone dates, project start dates, or even changes in payment terms for different suppliers. This aspect of modeling presents major problems for modelers and as a result leads to shortcuts being taken, which later will prove to be counterproductive.

The key is to build the model with the smallest time periods that could be effectively used. Don't get concerned if the specification asks for reports to be in years. The actuality is that to get to those years you need to have the months, so build the model based on months. If you happen to ignore this facet, you will eventually end up regretting it.

Here is an example. You have been asked by the sponsor to build a model that gives cash flow forecasts for three years. You happily build a model that is based in years ignoring the months. Further down the line, you discover that, in fact, the model users will require the ability to process sensitivity analysis that allows them to see what would happen if they change their creditor payment terms from 30 days, 45 days, 60 days, or 90 days. This small adjustment will have a big impact on your model, and you will be forced to rebuild it because the effect of these period changes will affect all the date-reliant calculations on the model.

The solution to this time issue is to create a template in the model that has the smallest time periods (such as months) to the largest (such as years) and subsequently be synchronized as in Figure 6-6. This allows the modeler to refer to this template for any dates and time periods and then use lookups to see when that date occurs within the time periods.

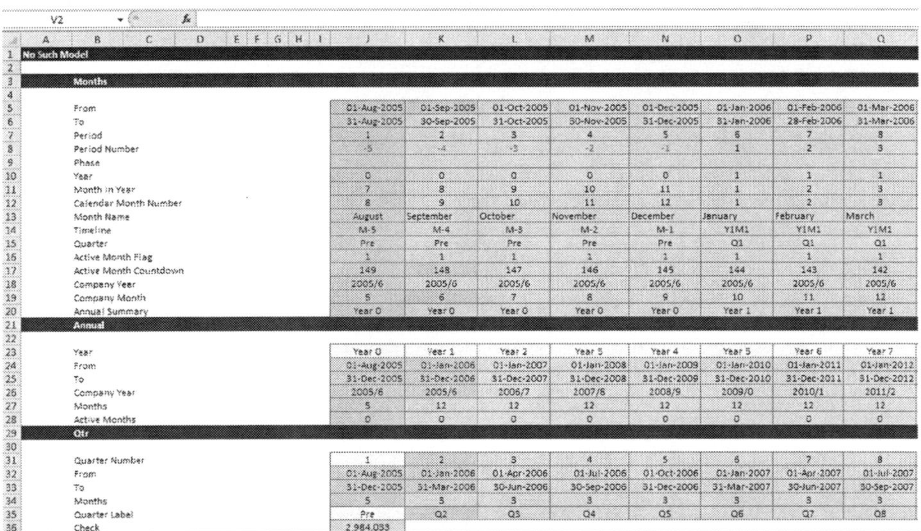

	A / B	J	K	L	M	N	O	P	Q
1	No Such Model								
2									
3	Months								
4									
5	From	01-Aug-2005	01-Sep-2005	01-Oct-2005	01-Nov-2005	01-Dec-2005	01-Jan-2006	01-Feb-2006	01-Mar-2006
6	To	31-Aug-2005	30-Sep-2005	31-Oct-2005	30-Nov-2005	31-Dec-2005	31-Jan-2006	28-Feb-2006	31-Mar-2006
7	Period	1	2	3	4	5	6	7	8
8	Period Number	-5	-4	-3	-2	-1	1	2	3
9	Phase								
10	Year	0	0	0	0	0	1	1	1
11	Month in Year	7	8	9	10	11	1	2	3
12	Calendar Month Number	8	9	10	11	12	1	2	3
13	Month Name	August	September	October	November	December	January	February	March
14	Timeline	M-5	M-4	M-3	M-2	M-1	Y1M1	Y1M1	Y1M1
15	Quarter	Pre	Pre	Pre	Pre	Pre	Q1	Q1	Q1
16	Active Month Flag	1	1	1	1	1	1	1	1
17	Active Month Countdown	149	148	147	146	145	144	143	142
18	Company Year	2005/6	2005/6	2005/6	2005/6	2005/6	2005/6	2005/6	2005/6
19	Company Month	5	6	7	8	9	10	11	12
20	Annual Summary	Year 0	Year 0	Year 0	Year 0	Year 0	Year 1	Year 1	Year 1
21	Annual								
22									
23	Year	Year 0	Year 1	Year 2	Year 3	Year 4	Year 5	Year 6	Year 7
24	From	01-Aug-2005	01-Jan-2006	01-Jan-2007	01-Jan-2008	01-Jan-2009	01-Jan-2010	01-Jan-2011	01-Jan-2012
25	To	31-Dec-2005	31-Dec-2006	31-Dec-2007	31-Dec-2008	31-Dec-2009	31-Dec-2010	31-Dec-2011	31-Dec-2012
26	Company Year	2005/6	2005/6	2006/7	2007/8	2008/9	2009/0	2010/1	2011/2
27	Months	5	12	12	12	12	12	12	12
28	Active Months	0	0	0	0	0	0	0	0
29	Qtr								
30									
31	Quarter Number	1	2	3	4	5	6	7	8
32	From	01-Aug-2005	01-Jan-2006	01-Apr-2006	01-Jul-2006	01-Oct-2006	01-Jan-2007	01-Apr-2007	01-Jul-2007
33	To	31-Dec-2005	31-Mar-2006	30-Jun-2006	30-Sep-2006	31-Dec-2006	31-Mar-2007	30-Jun-2007	30-Sep-2007
34	Months	5	3	3	3	3	3	3	3
35	Quarter Label	Pre	Q2	Q3	Q4	Q5	Q6	Q7	Q8
36	Check	2,984,033							
37	END								

Figure 6-6. The time-scale template is used to control the model time values by calculating all the different time periods that could be used in the model

For instance, using our example about the cash flow and change in creditor payment date, we could still produce a yearly cash flow for the users. However, when they made their change request, we could use the time-scale template in Figure 6-6 to state the number of days. This time scale would then work out when in the year 30 days, 45 days, or 60 days occur in the cash flow.

Developing Styles and Templates

Using colors in a model can be very helpful for the users. There is a general idiom that you should avoid creating worksheets with several colors for a number of reasons, one being that it's distracting. However, I firmly endorse the use of colors in financial modeling so long as they are consistent and practical. By creating a model style using colors, you can distinguish between the types of information and also alert the user to how the model is processing the information. For instance, you could use a pale yellow to alert the user that this is an input field and use a grey color to signify that a cell has a function or link. This way, the user will not be required to do anything but observe.

Choose your own color styles but make them distinctive and also themed. For example, if you use a pale yellow to designate an input cell, you could also use a pale yellow with a green border to designate an input cell that has a drop-down list. This way, the users will know that inputs are always a pale yellow but you still have the option of distinguishing between types of inputs.

Figure 6-7 gives a sample of a style sheet. This should be provided within the model to act as a legend and to inform the user of the color conventions being used. Look closely at the top of the worksheet in Figure 6-7. Notice that this style sheet is also incorporating the template format that will be used throughout the model as in Figure 6-8.

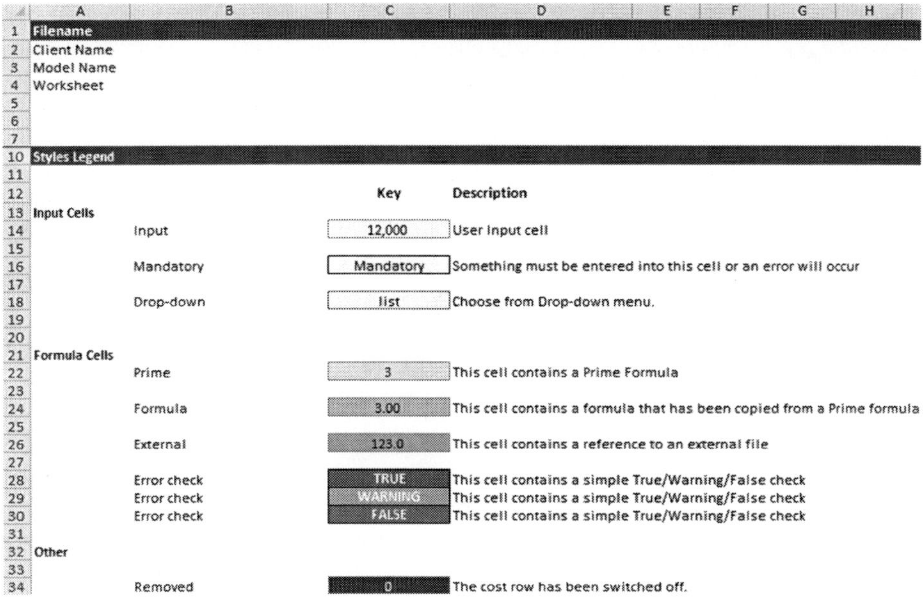

Figure 6-7. This is a sample of a style sheet

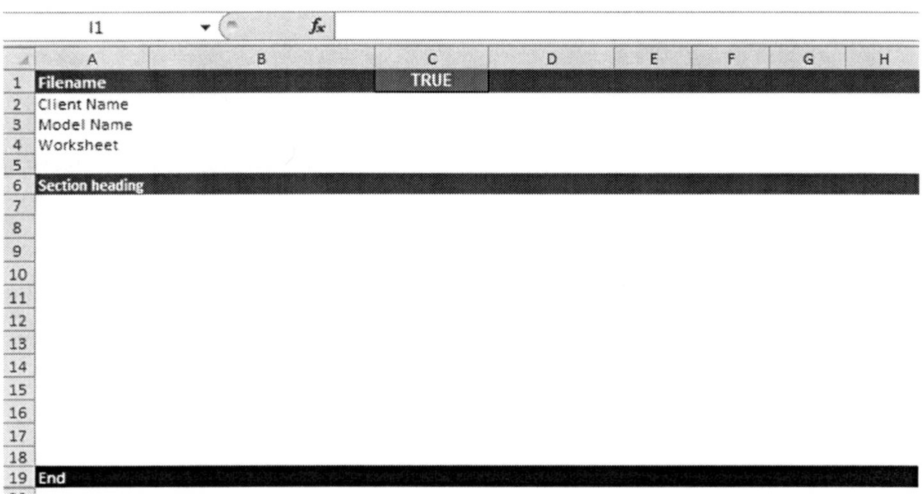

Figure 6-8. This shows the worksheet template format

Define the Structure of the Workbook

Each workbook should have a broad set of rules that are consistent across all the worksheets in the model. The modeler should establish these rules at the start of the model build and maintain them throughout the model. For instance, column A could be left blank on all worksheets. (I leave this blank as I can then use it for documentation and assumption references before closing the model.) The other most important feature is to keep all data within the same structure of columns. For example, if Year 1 starts in column D and Year 2 in column E, this should be replicated across the entire model in the inputs, calculations, and outputs. By using a consistent structure, there are definite benefits for reducing the risk of errors, such as pointing errors.

Working with the Inputs

The inputs should be kept distinct from any other model information. I choose to always keep the inputs on a different worksheet, and if there are unlike data types for inputs also separate these onto different worksheets. A sample input worksheet is presented in Figure 6-9. Notice that the format and style are consistent through each model and that the inputs are distinguished from the calculations by using colors.

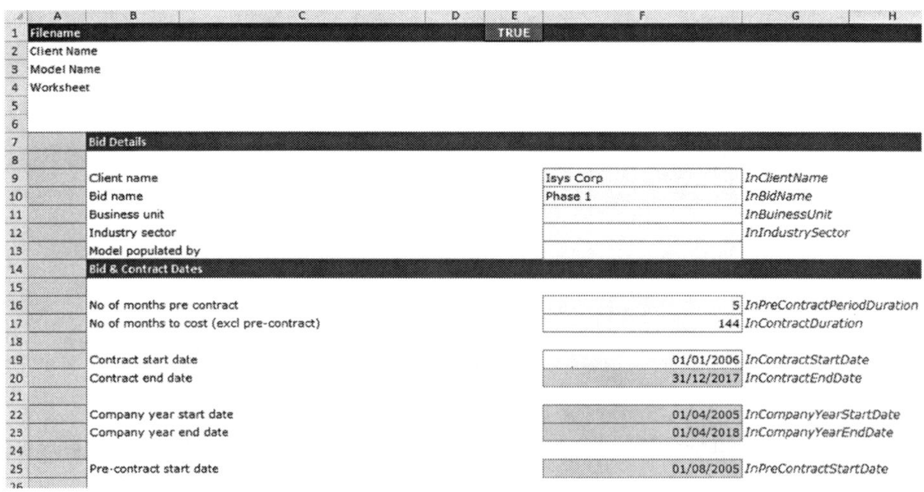

Figure 6-9. With this inputs worksheet, notice that the format and styles are now consistent

Figure 6-10 is different because the data is time-based. Therefore, a separate worksheet has been used, but the style still remains the same.

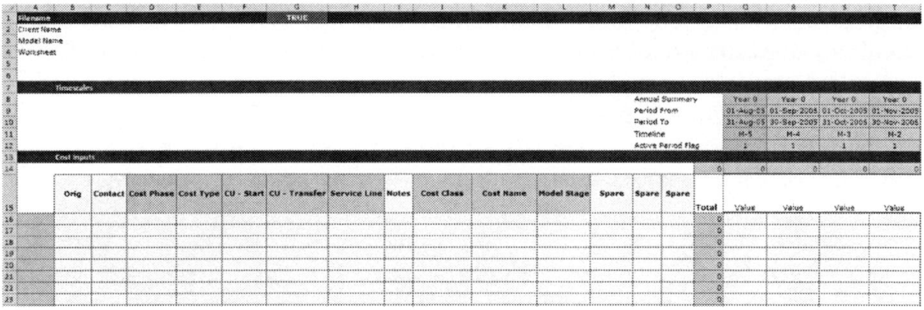

Figure 6-10. This figure shows a time-based inputs worksheet

Working with the Calculations

What do I mean by the term "calculations"? Well, in their simplest form, calculations are the formulas that are used on the inputs to create the outputs. They are also the methods that are used to bring functionality into the model and make up the process of translating information into something tangible for the model owner or sponsor. I want to get these points across because the calculations are often seen as just a set of formulas. From my experience, little attention is given to them from anyone but the modeler.

The calculations performed on the model are without a doubt the most critical element to any model. It is here where the modeler's interpretation and understanding about the process, or business, is clearly demonstrated. Frankly, anyone who is looking at a model will gain some valuable insight into the inner workings of the model by taking a look at the calculations. The reason so many users of models are put off by the calculations is more due to the aesthetics of the calculations rather than the actual calculations themselves. There can be nothing more frustrating than having a jumble of formulas staring at you with numerous levels of links all throughout the model.

Therefore, it is vitally important that calculations have these characteristics: structured with a consistent layout, follows best practice by not having a long or too complex formula, and maintains row consistency.

First, consistently try to put your calculations into one worksheet as much as possible. Even if it means that it will be a long worksheet, you can invariably create categories and keep a neat structure. There is a good reason behind having just one worksheet. Calculations that are developed on several worksheets will lead the modeler into creating a myriad of links from one worksheet to another, which will be terribly difficult to follow. It's very easy to then lose control and introduce duplication errors as another formula or link is created to do exactly the same job simply because you have lost track of what all the links are doing. By employing just one calculation worksheet, any issues with links and errors will clearly be coming from just that one worksheet.

Something else to keep in mind is that there should never be any hard-coded numbers or static hard-coded numbers within the calculations. After all, they are calculations. It really does dismay me when I find a modeler has placed a static hard-coded number right in the middle of a row of formula. It just brings in a suspicion about the credibility of the modeler and if there is a possible fudge factor coming to play.

Note Fudge factor is a term used to describe a random or ad hoc number that has been introduced into an otherwise logical model in order to induce a specific result.

If you have to use some fudge factor, my advice is to not place it into the calculations as a hard-coding. Instead, add it to the assumptions and create an input in the input worksheet and document the reasoning for this factor. Now you can introduce this input into the calculations, but at least there is some reference as to why it's being used.

In Figure 6-11, although I have not used any type of expansive functions, the calculations are in one worksheet shown in their categories. You can clearly see the link to the input and the subsequent calculation. The modeler should be aiming to maintain a structure that follows the inputs so that it's easy to keep up with where the link comes from and how the calculation has been put together. It is also good practice to bring the actual input into the calculation worksheet as a link and then make the calculation from that worksheet and not directly from the inputs.

Calculations

Revenues	Year 1	Year 2	Year 3
Units sold	69,550	79,552	80,814
Selling price (per unit)	45	46	46
Total	3,129,750	3,659,392	3,717,444

Staff costs	Year 1	Year 2	Year 3
Number of staff	32	28	26
Average salary (per annum)	28,560	29,417	30,299
Total	913,920	823,670	787,782

Materials	Year 1	Year 2	Year 3
Subcontractor hours	8,550	8,050	7,110
Hourly rate	50	51	52
Total	427,500	410,550	369,720
Materials in kgs	4,200	3,601	3,454
Materials cost per kg	120	120	122
Total	504,000	432,120	421,388

Inputs

Revenues	Year 1	Year 2	Year 3
Units sold	69,550	79,552	80,814
Selling price (per unit)	45	46	46

Staff costs	Year 1	Year 2	Year 3
Number of staff	32	28	26
Average Salary (per annum)	28,560	29,417	30,299

Materials	Year 1	Year 2	Year 3
Sub-contractor hours	8,550	8,050	7,110
Hourly rate	50	51	52
Materials in kgs	4,200	3,601	3,454
Materials cost per kg	120	120	122

Figure 6-11. The calculations worksheet follows the same logic as the inputs worksheet

In Figure 6-12, the calculations are made directly from the inputs (sometimes referred to as a three-dimensional formula). Although this is still a viable way to model, it is clearly a lot more difficult to trace the calculations. Imagine that there are hundreds of inputs and calculations, and there are some errors that need to be corrected. The method of finding them will now require switching between the inputs and the calculations; a switch that could be compounded if there are also numerous calculation worksheets. Although it seems like duplication bringing the inputs into the calculation worksheet and making the calculations in that worksheet, it is cleaner and more sensible modeling. Once you develop this method of working, it will become second nature.

Calculations

	Year 1	Year 2	Year 3
Revenues			
Total	3,129,750	3,659,392	3,717,444
Staff costs			
Total	913,920	823,670	787,782
Materials			
Total	427,500	410,550	369,720
Total	504,000	432,120	421,388

Inputs

	Year 1	Year 2	Year 3
Revenues			
Units sold	69,550	79,552	80,814
selling Price (per Unit)	45	46	46
Staff costs			
Number of staff	32	28	26
Average salary (per annum)	28,560	29,417	30,299
Materials			
Sub-contractor hours	8,550	8,050	7,110
Hourly rate	50	51	52
Materials in kgs	4,200	3,601	3,454
Materials cost per kg	120	120	122

Figure 6-12. There are no links to the inputs; the calculations are made on the inputs directly

Working with the Outputs

The outputs will be governed by the approval from the sponsor and model users; therefore, it is likely they will need to conform to a specific layout and format. Even with this in mind, there should still be consistency. For instance, no matter what type of outputs (reports) are required, these should link to the calculations worksheet. In other words, do not make the mistake of linking the outputs to inputs—this a characteristic of a model that has not been well thought out. By linking to the calculation worksheet, the flow of information will run from the inputs to the calculation to the outputs; therefore, any problems in the outputs can be traced to the calculations, then to the inputs and corrected.

If the modeler breaks this flow and makes some direct links to the inputs, thus bypassing the calculations, there is a strong likelihood that the following will happen:

- Any changes that are made in the outputs that require some conversion with calculation before they can be presented will be circumvented. The output will now be different than the calculation worksheet (see Figure 6-13).

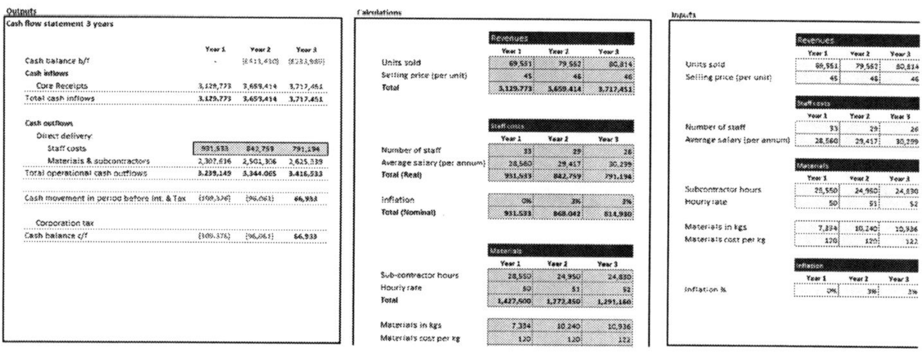

Figure 6-13. The staff costs in the outputs do not match the staff costs in the calculations worksheet because they have come from the inputs worksheet

- There is a strong likelihood of having split variables. For instance, the cost of sales in the profit and loss output could be coming from the inputs, and the cost of sales in the cash flow output could be coming from the calculations.

- It will be difficult to create adequate error checks that can signify a problem because the checks will have two sources. How will you determine which one is correct?

Recap

The model build will consist of a number of principles and actions. Here is what has been discussed so far in this chapter:

- Think about which tools you will be using or require for the project.

- Set yourself up for a top-down approach as opposed to a bottom-up approach.

- Make sure the outputs have been approved by the sponsor and model user and then close off.

- Develop a time scale template with the lowest time periods to the highest.
- Develop a consistent worksheet template for the entire model.
- Create a modeling style and format and put these into a legend template.
- Work according to a defined structure for all the workbooks.
- Create the inputs in one workbook but make a separate workbook for calculations and outputs.
- Use the calculations and bring all inputs into the calculations. Do not use hard-coded numbers or fudge factors in the calculations.
- Worksheets should have a flowing link. Calculations are linked to inputs and outputs are linked to calculations. Avoid hopping from outputs to inputs.

Planning for Errors

In Chapter 2, the theory and the reality of errors was covered thoroughly, so in this section I will discuss how to deal with the knowledge that errors are a symptom of financial modeling. Planning for errors means dealing with them, and this is more about the modeler's mindset. The modeler needs to think about "what is it that made this error?" and then think further about what can actually happen. In other words, the modeler needs to be a couple of steps ahead of the model user in order to foresee the potential errors that can occur.

For instance, an error may occur within a cell that has totals in it because the users may choose to overwrite the formula and put in place a different function that they feel is more suitable. Whether the model user has the right to do this is beside the point; the simple fact is that an error occurs because a calculation cell has been tampered with. The crucial aspect here is this: has the modeler foreseen this possibility and added some sort of error checking?

Creating the Error Template

The modeler should create an error worksheet that collects all the errors in the models on a worksheet-by-worksheet basis. What this means is that each worksheet can contain its own error checks, which are subsequently collected as a group check on the worksheet. After that, the group check is collected by the error checking template.

In Figure 6-14, the error check is shown, and it shows the group check from seven worksheets. The error check template then shows the status of all seven worksheets. Notice the time inputs worksheet has returned an error. By looking at this template, the user will know that there is a problem in that one worksheet.

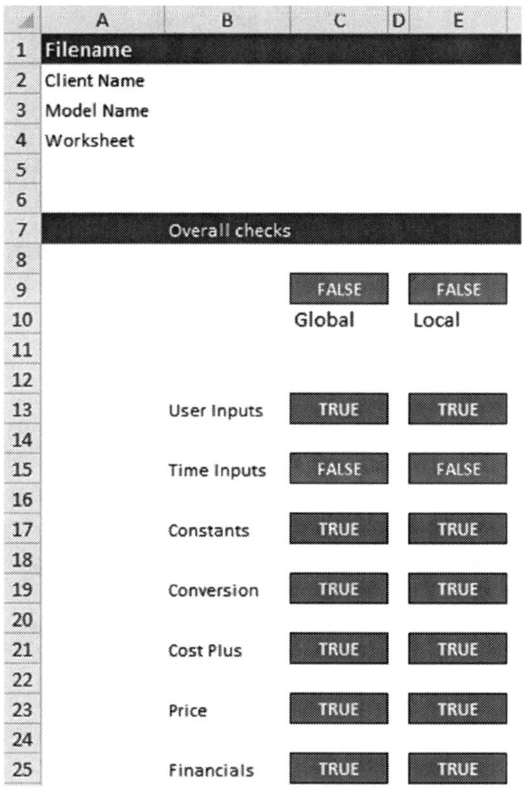

Figure 6-14. An error check template is shown here

In Figure 6-15, the time inputs worksheet has an error in one of the staff cost lines. The modeler has anticipated that if any of the detail columns are blank, then an error will occur; this is the error that is collected in the error template. The top of the worksheet shows the group error taken from column U, which now signifies that this entire worksheet is in error and will need fixing. The error cell in E1 is then linked to the worksheet named error check.

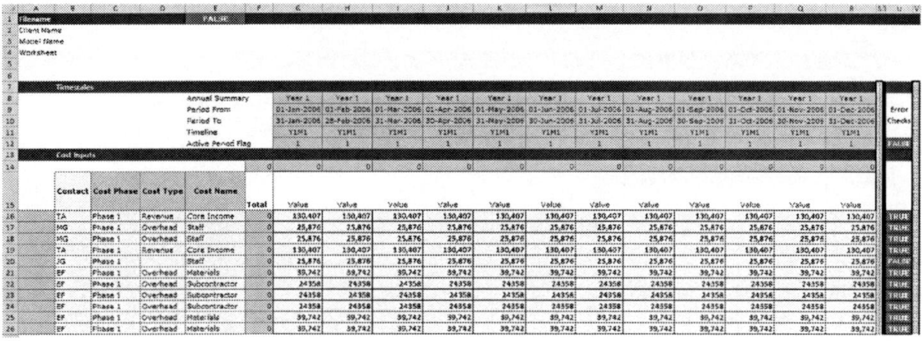

Figure 6-15. The time inputs worksheet with data is shown here. Notice that there is an error because something is missing

Displaying the Errors

There is no standard method of displaying errors. The method I use is visual as well as providing a message—either "False," "Warning," or "True." The message "False" means that a significant issue is apparent and needs to be rectified as it has an effect on the model. The "Warning" message is little used, but I use it to signal that there is an issue although it will not have any detrimental effect on the model. For example, "Warning" would appear where the user has input a number that is exactly the same as another number that has already been inputted. This would just be a warning to check that this is intentional. "True" signifies there are no issues and therefore no error has occurred. However, do not feel that you should use the same messages as I use, for instance, you could use "OK," "Investigate," and "Error" instead.

Creating and formatting the error message is a two-stage process. First, select a cell and on the Home tab and in the Number group, click the Dialog Box Launcher. Use the Custom Number format and in the Type textbox type "FALSE";"WARNING";"ERROR" or any combination that you wish to use (see Figure 6-16).

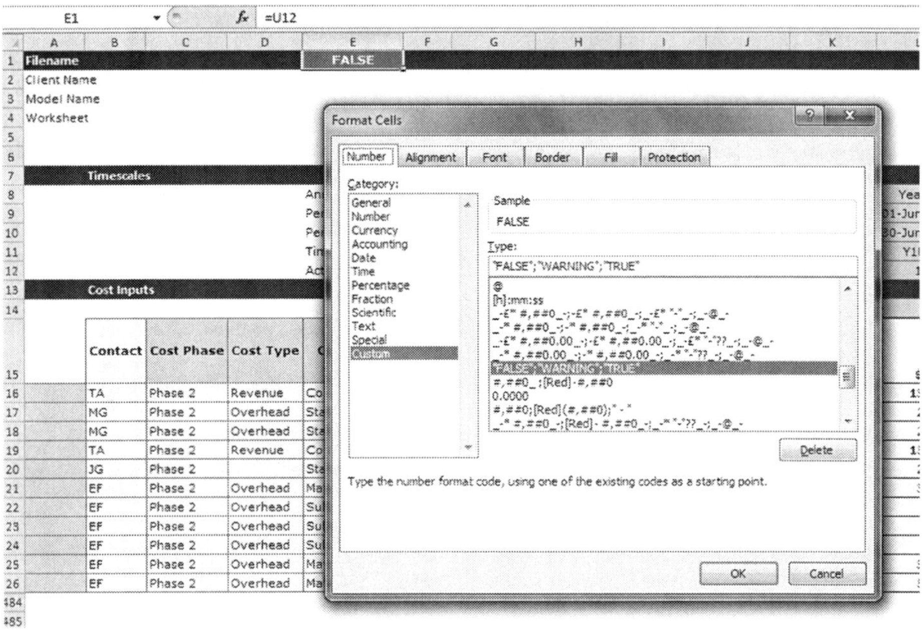

Figure 6-16. The error checks can be created through the format menu

Next, apply conditional formatting for each of the three conditions to the same cell, starting with ERROR. On the Home tab, in the Styles group, click Conditional Formatting and then click New Rule. Choose Format only cells that contain, as shown in Figure 6-17.

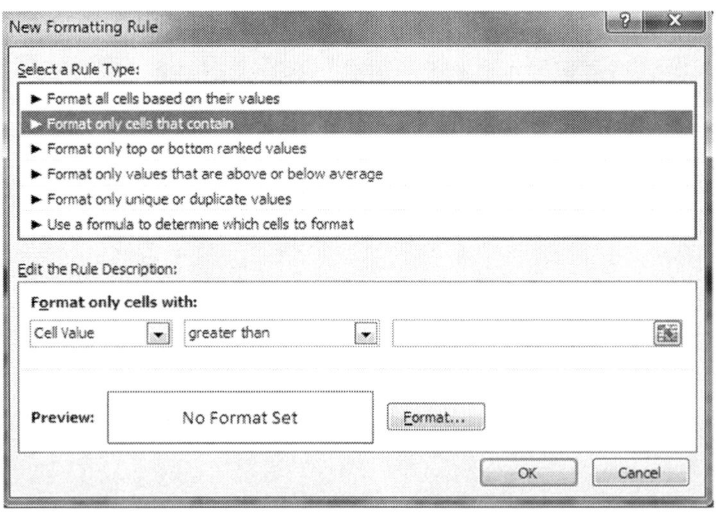

Figure 6-17. The conditional formatting with a new rule is shown here

There are three conditions that must be set. First, ensure that Cell Value is displayed in the first drop-down under Edit the Rule Description. Click the next drop-down arrow and select greater than. Click in the last box on the right and enter the number 1. Now format the condition with a red fill. Click the Format button, then the Fill tab, then the Color arrow, and then click Red (see Figure 6-18).

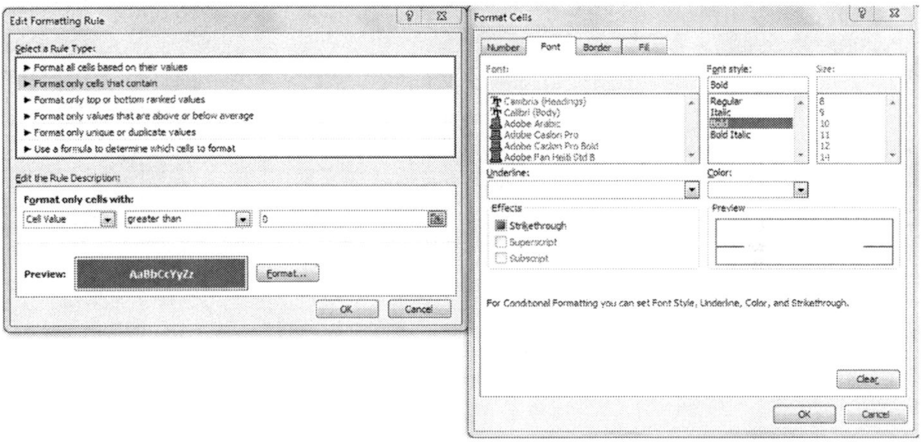

Figure 6-18. Use the fill color to set the condition

Make sure you also set the font and font style (on the Font tab) to the preference that you require. Click OK when you are finished. Now, apply two more conditions: one for WARNING and one for TRUE. For WARNING, use the less than 0 condition with a fill color of orange. For the last condition, TRUE, set the rule description to equal to 0 and use the green fill color.

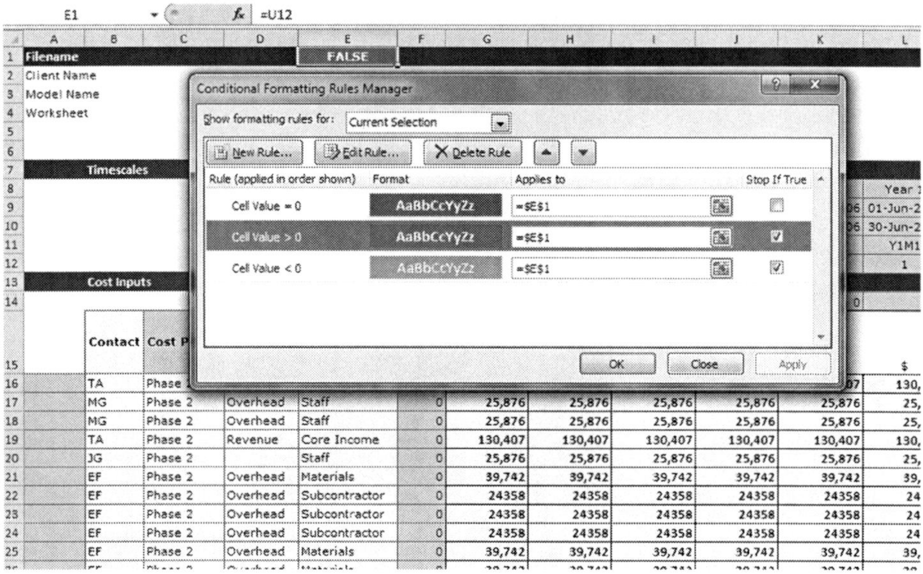

Figure 6-19. Establishing the conditional formatting for all three error conditions is shown here

Now, there are only two steps left for the modeler: determine which parts to the model require error checks and what exactly the checks should be testing.

Case Study: Planning a Financial Model

In this case study, we will be planning an actual model from the feasibility to scoping and then getting the specification, putting together the model design, and finally creating a testing specification. We are not going to go through the model build, so the assumption will be that the model is built. This case study is focused on how to mount a feasibility study for a model build. The reason I have used this example is that the feasibility is the start of any modeling. It is a crucial piece for financial modeling because it will dictate whether the model build will continue or not. It is imperative that you understand the basics of building a good feasibility study to present to the sponsor or customer.

The Brief

The newly appointed vice president of financial analysis and metrics for Nonsuch Corporation is dissatisfied with the level of financial information available to the organization. The organization is going through a two-year transformation program to change the way it delivers services to clients, and the availability of up-to-the-minute and accurate financial information is critical to the VP's decision-making.

The VP has brought in a financial modeling firm to produce a feasibility study for the company on the strength of their financial information and provide any options on how to improve on the weaknesses.

About the Feasibility Study

The process of conducting a feasibility study can be quite lengthy, although the document or findings will be reasonably short and concise. A feasibility study is a document that identifies each of the solution options available and rates the likelihood of each option achieving the desired result. It should include the following parts:

- A description of the business problem (the modeling project)
- A list of the requirements for a solution to fix the problem (or realize the opportunity)
- Available options for delivering a solution
- An assessment of the feasibility of each option
- A list of the risks and/or issues associated with each option
- A preferred option to be approved for implementation

This feasibility assessment will be undertaken by the financial modeler and presented to the model sponsor.

For our case study, the assumption is that the business case for the project will have been completed previously, and therefore completion of this feasibility will add more rigor to the solution options presented in the business case.

The main purpose of the feasibility study is to ascertain the likelihood of each solution option identified for meeting the stated business requirements. Although the risks, issues, and constraints are important, the project is less likely to be a success if the solution option chosen is unlikely to be feasibly implemented.

To determine the likely feasibility of an option, a range of "assessment" methods are undertaken. As there are a myriad of potential methods attainable to assess feasibility, I suggest you take time to consider the most appropriate method available in your project. The outcome of the feasibility study is the confirmed solution option for inclusion within the business case. The next stage, after the solution option has been approved, is to define the project scope and structure within the project's terms of reference document (a statement of the objectives and purpose of the project).

The Assessment

As we work through this case study, let's call this project the financial tool feasibility (FTF). Now let's break down the feasibility study into its components to be presented to the VP of financial analysis and metrics.

Problem Statement

When conducting a feasibility assessment or study, it is very likely that some issues will arise during the assessment. These issues should be collected during the study and then listed in priority from the most to the least severe.

Business Environment

Any successful organization requires timely and up-to-the-minute financial information to support decision-making and to forecast the future. Nonsuch Corporation has either lost or has not had the mechanism in place to deliver financial information that can be quickly and easily outputted to senior staff. Due to the demand of the transformation program, there is now a serious requirement that this financial information be available to the VP of financial analysis and metrics.

Business Vision

The corporation is looking to redefine how it interacts with its customers and clients in the next two years as a step toward achieving higher growth and profit maximization for the future.

Business Units

The current business unit relevant for this project is the financial analysis and metrics departments, which are part of the wider finance department.

Business Location

This is a global business with locations across several countries and regions. This feasibility study is for the group vice president and is therefore relevant for every location.

Business Information

There is a need to understand the repositories, databases, and enterprise resource systems (ERPs) available in the organization, which once the due diligence has commenced will result in a data flow diagram.

Business Technologies

The list of the existing business technologies that are relevant for this project (like network attached storage or data servers) is not available until the completion of the due diligence. Once the details are provided, a description for each major technology together with a technology architecture diagram to highlight the interfaces between current business technologies will be placed in this section.

Business Problem

The business problem is a lack of visibility of the key financials of the business and therefore no transparency.

The reasons why this problem exists are currently unknown but could be due to the lack of historical investment in the financial systems and infrastructure. This problem is having a major negative impact on the organization's response to its market. It is envisaged that the problem will need to be resolved quite rapidly as the transformation of the entire organization (not just the finance department) will be two years from start to delivery.

This problem is likely to have an impact on the following areas:

- The finance business process including efficiency, timeliness, clarity, accuracy, and relevancy.
- The financial analysis and metrics business unit:
  - Definition (lack of financial vision, scope, and objectives)
  - Direction (misalignment with corporate vision)
  - Financial structure of the organization (currently no feasible method to measure the inefficient or inappropriateness of the current structure)
  - Financial performance (the product and service quality cannot be immediately measured in financial terms)
  - Financial data (validity and quality)

- Business location
  - Security of financial data (exposure and risks)
  - Relevancy of the current financial information
  - Finances (too expensive and these finances may not be able to be measured)

Business Opportunity

The following opportunities have been identified in this project:

- The availability and timeliness of key financial information
- The possibility that the business unit can respond rapidly to the changing environment by having up-to-the-minute information
- The ability to measure the cost and relevancy of the finance department and make further efficiencies
- The ability to support the transformation by adding financial information to operations

Requirements Statement

The requirements statement is a document that contains information about the needs and goals of an organization or project. This statement can be quite detailed, but often it is written at a summary level so as to be communicable to a broad range of people.

Business Drivers

The key business drivers for this project are as follows:

- An organizational transformation that must be achieved within two years
- A limited timeframe for competitive advantage
- Timing of other related changes to the business or external marketplace

Business Requirements

For each business problem (or opportunity) identified previously, document the detailed business requirements using the format shown in Figure 6-20.

Opportunities & Problems	Requirement
A lack of visibility of the key financials of the business and therefore no transparency.	Identify the key personal, the system, the data sources, and the technologies.
The availability and timeliness of key financial information.	Explore and evaluate all the current constraints and enablers and implement a process that will improve financial information efficiency by at least 50%.
The possibility that the business unit can respond rapidly to the changing environment by having up-to-the minute information.	Develop a tool that will enable the VP to analyze forecasts and predict future financial trends with 95% accuracy.
The ability to measure the cost and relevancy of the finance department and make further efficiencies.	Create a financial management suite (MIS) that will provide measurement metrics for all key financial drivers.
The ability to support the transformation by adding financial information to operations.	Develop a stable tool that will constantly achieve 99.9% availability.

Figure 6-20. A list of opportunities and problems is shown here

Feasibility Assessment

A number of assumptions need to be made as we cannot adequately take on a full feasibility assessment in this case study. So we should assume that we have now assessed and identified each of the solution's options available and the feasibility (or likelihood) of each option meeting the requirements defined in Figure 6-20.

In addition, we should assume that we have reviewed risks, issues, and assumptions associated with the feasibility of each option. The process for assessing the feasibility of an individual solution is shown in Figure 6-21.

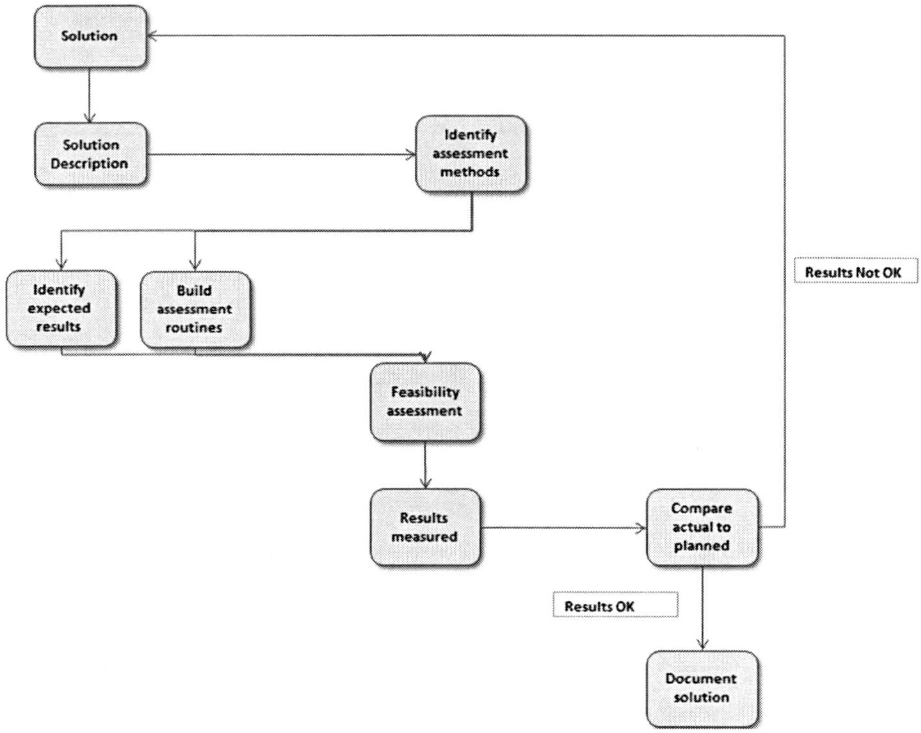

Figure 6-21. This figure shows the feasibility assessment process

Option One: Implementing Off-the-Shelf Software

This section gives a summary of the description of the option, the assessment, and the result.

Description

The option is to purchase a renowned software package such as one of the following:

- Quantrix Modeler
- IBM Cognos
- Oracle Hyperion
- Statistical Analysis Suite (SAS)

All the software mentioned will integrate with relational databases and provide a front-end interface that can be tailored to produce custom metrics and financial analysis.

Assessment

Here are the methods that have been used to assess the feasibility of this solution:

- Prototyping: This involved the construction of a demo software (called a prototype) to prove that at least a part of the full solution is achievable. In our example, the prototype was tested so that we could prove that the highest risk areas of the solution are feasible and to test that the package can be integrated into other application systems used for the business.
- Staff survey: This survey involved presenting the finance staff with a series of questions that had optional answers to assess their readiness and also their acceptance toward learning and using a new system.

Results

The expected result from the assessment for this solution is that there would not be any significant issues in the implementation. The actual results that were born from the prototyping support that assumption.

However, from the results from the staff survey, there would be a considerable cultural shift that would be required in order to use the software effectively.

Risks

There are some risks associated in the software implementation solution. These risks are defined as any event that may adversely affect the ability of the solution to produce the required deliverables. Risks may be strategic, environmental, financial, operational, technical, industrial, competitive, or customer-related. A list of the likely risks for our example is shown in Figure 6-22.

Description	Likelihood	Impact	Mitigating Actions
Inability to fully implement the software into Nonsuch systems.	Low	Very High	Outsource project to a company with proven industry experience and appropriately skilled implementation staff.
Technology solution is unable to deliver required results.	Medium	High	Complete a pilot project to prove the full technology solution.
Additional capital expenditure may be required in addition to that approved.	Medium	Medium	Maintain strict capital expenditure processes during the project.
Scope creep.	High	Medium	Get scope document approved and put in place change control process.
Additional training and cost for staff.	High	Medium	Make sure software vendor can assist with on-going training suited toward Nonsuch Corp.

Figure 6-22. A list of likely risks is shown here

When identifying the risks, I recommend that a formal risk assessment be undertaken and documented in a *risk management plan* to improve the likelihood and impact of each risk eventuating. Furthermore, a clear risk-management process (including risk forms and registers) should be used from the outset.

Issues

A list of current issues that adversely affect the ability of the solution to produce the required deliverables is included with Figure 6-23.

Description	Priority	Resolution Actions
Required capital expenditure funds have not been budgeted.	High	Request funding approval as part of this proposal.
Some of the required software is only at 'beta' phase and has not yet been released live.	Medium	Design a solution based on current software version and adapt changes to the solution once the final version of the software has been released.
There is a question as to the state of the data in the database.	High	A data audit and subsequent validation must ensue immediately.

Figure 6-23. A list of issues is shown here

Assumptions

This is a list of the assumptions associated with the adoption of this solution:

- There will be no legislative, business strategy, or policy changes during this project.
- Additional human resources will be available from the business to support the project.
- The organization as a whole will support the project.

Option Two: Developing a Financial Model Tool

This section gives a summary of the description of the option, the assessment, and the result.

Description

This option is to develop a dedicated financial model tool from a recognized financial modeling firm.

The model will be expected to integrate with existing relational databases and provide a front end that encapsulates all the outputs based upon the user requirements.

Assessment

Here are the methods that have been used to assess the feasibility of this solution:

- Prototyping: This involved the construction of a prototype financial model to test the validity of implementing the current databases and also running with the incumbent ERP system. In our example, the prototype was tested so that we could prove that the highest risk areas of the solution are feasible and to test that the package can be integrated into other application systems used for the business.
- Staff Survey: The survey involved presenting the finance staff with a series of question that had optional answers to assess their readiness and also their acceptance toward learning and using a new system.

Results

The expected result for this solution would be that there would not be any issues to implementing a financial modeling tool. The actual results born from the prototyping support this assumption.

The staff survey showed that while there would need to be a cultural shift, the negative effects of this shift could be minimized by making sure the staff members were involved throughout the development of the financial model tool.

Risks

There are some risks associated with the financial modeling tool solution. These risks are defined as any event that may adversely affect the ability of the solution to produce the required deliverables. Risks may be strategic, environmental, financial, operational, technical, industrial, competitive, or customer related. A list of the likely risks for our example is shown in Figure 6-24.

Description	Likelihood	Impact	Mitigating Actions
Inability to fully implement the modeling tool	Low	Very High	The financial modeling firm and modeler should be vetted and past results, successes, and failures considered.
Technology solution is unable to deliver required results	Medium	High	Complete a pilot project to prove the full technology solution.
Additional capital expenditure may be required in addition to that approved	Low	Medium	Maintain strict capital expenditure processes during the project.
Scope creep	High	Medium	A well-structured change control and a well-communicated scope will help to mitigate.
Additional training and cost for staff	Medium	Medium	Make sure the modeling firm can assist with ongoing training suited toward Nonsuch Corp.

Figure 6-24. This is a list of risks for Option Two

When identifying the risks, I recommend that a formal risk assessment be undertaken and documented in a risk-management plan to improve the likelihood and impact of each risk eventuating. Furthermore, a clear risk management process (including risk forms and registers) should be used from the outset.

Issues

A list of current issues that adversely affect the ability of the solution to produce the required deliverables is included with Figure 6-25.

Description	Priority	Resolution Actions
Required capital expenditure funds have not been budgeted.	High	Request funding approval as part of this proposal.
There is a question as to the state of the data in the database.	High	A data audit and subsequent validation must ensue immediately.

Figure 6-25. A list of issues for Option Two is shown here

Assumptions

This is a list the assumptions associated with the adoption of this solution:

- There will be no legislative, business strategy, or policy changes during this project.
- Additional human resources will be available from the business to support the project.
- The organization as a whole will support the project.

Feasibility Ranking

The ranking is a part of the feasibility assessment that compares the options, and then creates criteria and scores these against each option.

Ranking Criteria

The ranking criteria is provided in Figure 6-26.

Ranking Scores

Score each option using the format shown in Figure 6-26.

	Option 1			Option 2		
Criteria	Score	Weight	Total	Score	Weight	Total
Cost	7	1.0	7.0	6	1.0	6.0
Benefit	9	1.5	13.5	9	1.5	13.5
Development/Implementation overrun	6	1.3	7.8	4	1.3	5.2
Business disruption	5	1.0	5	3	1.0	3
Flexibility to change specification	2	1.0	2	8	1.0	8
Cost of maintenance	7	0.7	4.9	5	0.7	3.5
Relative ease of staff adoption	6	1.4	8.4	8	1.4	11.2
Deliver precise outputs	6	1.5	9	9	1.5	13.5
Total Score	48.0		57.6	52.0		63.9

Figure 6-26. The criteria and ranking scores for both options are shown here

Note The score is typically a number from 1 (low feasibility) to 10 (high feasibility), and the weight is a number from 0.5 (criterion is unimportant) to 1.5 (criterion is very important). The total is calculated as score x weight.

Feasibility Result

Option Two has achieved a higher total score and would therefore be the most feasible option for the solution. The key reason is down to its flexibility during the development. Therefore, the project can adapt to changes in the overall transformation program. Staff adaption would also be relatively easy because the staff would be actively involved in the development and implementation on an ongoing basis.

This chapter has covered several aspects of the model planning, and I would not expect anyone to understand all that has been mentioned in one reading. However, this chapter is one that must be understood because it's at the heart of the model design. Many of these concepts will also be featured again later in this book. If you have found any of the concepts unclear, I would advise that you read through this chapter again, focusing on a section at a time, and only move on once you have a clear understanding of that section.

CHAPTER

7

The Model User: Inputs

This chapter focuses on the inputs to the model and the interaction of the model end users with these inputs. This chapter is one of the softer ones in this book but should not be underestimated in terms of the importance to financial modeling. I have found that there are few examples in the public domain of how the model end user interacts with the modeler and shapes the inputs to the model. This is a very critical juncture for the modeler and hence my reason for adding this chapter.

Thinking About the Financial Model End User

One of the first aspirations for a modeler entering into a financial modeling project will be to understand the key influences on shaping the model inputs: the model end users.

In this chapter I want to introduce you to a different way of thinking of the model end users, rather than thinking about the physical users. The term "model end user" will be used to signify those individuals who will use the model physically and also those who will use it conceptually. The key model end users include the following:

- Key stakeholder(s)
- Project sponsor(s)
- Model owner(s)
- Model user(s)

Key Stakeholders

The stakeholder (see Figure 7-1) will be an individual (or a group) who has a vested interest in the model project being a success. This person or group can have an influence either positively or negatively but will not be part of the modeling team or part of the project as a whole. I will warn you that trying to uncover who the stakeholders are may not be as straightforward as you might think. Stakeholders are not necessarily nominated or appointed to that role. In other words, they can be stakeholders purely because of who they are in the scheme of the organization. In fact, they may not even know that they are stakeholders on your particular modeling project.

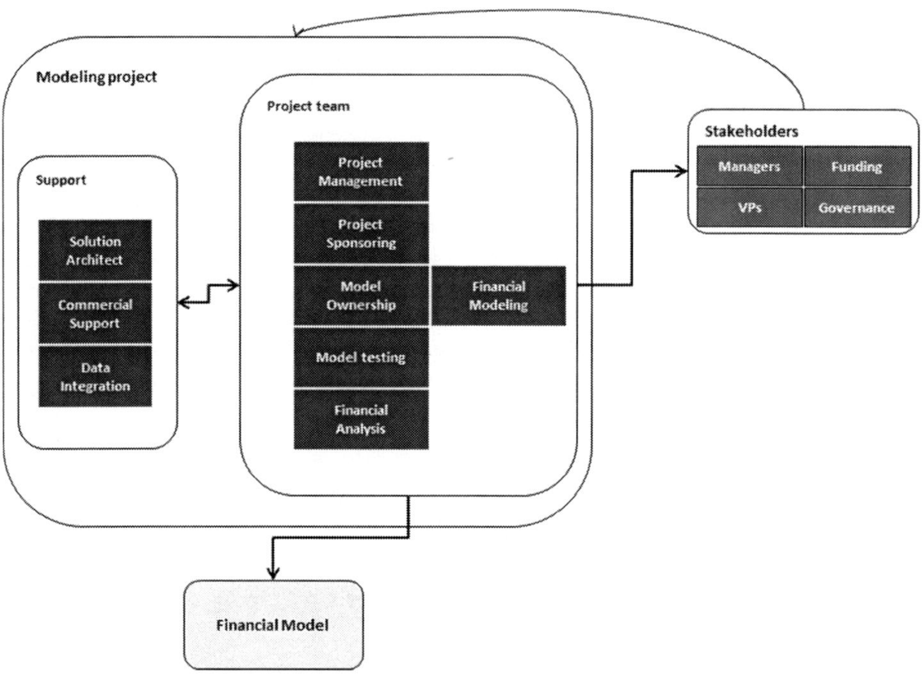

Figure 7-1. This figure is an example of the functions within a modeling project

Although it may take some investigating and digging, my advice is to take time to identify the stakeholders. Again, the stakeholders themselves may not be aware of their influence within the modeling project. Ask this question while investigating, "Who will gain by having the model completed and implemented successfully?" The answer to this question will lead you to the stakeholders.

For the modeler, it is always a good policy to build a positive relationship and rapport with the stakeholders. But at the same time, manage them and their expectations of the model in such a way that they don't end up taking control of the project. You would be well-advised to make sure that you not ignore that last point. Managing stakeholders is a real and much prized skill, and one that if poorly performed will ruin a modeling project completely.

In order to manage stakeholders effectively, the modeler should be prepared to chair frequent briefings with them. The objective is to give them a high-level view of how the project is progressing, share any prospective issues that have emerged, and communicate how the issues are being handled. Allow the stakeholders to make comments and give their opinions. Try and put them in a position where they can be useful in unblocking probable blockages or easing the path through the project. But stay clear of giving the stakeholders a hand in making policy or the direction for the model project.

In the event where there is a question concerning control over the project, remember that the stakeholder is never in control. This is the hallmark of healthy stakeholder management. The actual control will lie somewhere between the sponsor and the modeler and will largely depend on the experience of the modeler. I have seen modeling projects that are fully controlled by the modeler, and others where the sponsors take an active role, but essentially the modeler has the responsibility for making sure the model is built to the requirements of sponsor.

The Project Sponsor

The project sponsor is the individual or body that has requested or commissioned the model and is therefore instrumental in setting the course that the model project will take. It is the sponsor who must outline the scope of the project and who is accountable for effectively communicating to the modeler the model's purpose and the outputs and reports that must be provided. The sponsor is also responsible for selecting (or if not selecting, then vetting) the modeling team. The overall role of the sponsor is to deliver the model to the organization. In many cases, the sponsor will be the direct recipient and ultimate user of the model; however, this is not always the case. For instance, a senior director or vice president may be the sponsor of the model, but the end user may be members of his or her staff.

If you have project management experience, you will note that I have put some distance between the sponsor and stakeholders. It is possible for the sponsor to also be a key stakeholder, although the responsibilities of the two positions will be different. For our purposes, I am separating them. With a modeling project, the sponsor will have more day-to-day influence on the model.

Modelers should work closely with the sponsor and be responsible for providing details about the model build and any issues, risks, and potential delays to the timescales. From Chapter 4, it's also clear that they should provide a feasibility assessment to the sponsor. For modelers, it is critical to instill a sense of confidence about their modeling ability and skills to the sponsor because invariably the sponsor is often the person who will approve payments for work completed. It is also the sponsor who has ultimate responsibility for assigning the modeler and thus has responsibility for firing the modeler.

The Model Owner

The model owner will always be the individual or group that will have responsibility for running the model—maintaining and providing the outputs that the model generates. In many cases, the project sponsor is also the model owner; however, do not make this assumption. When confronted with a model project, ask the sponsor who the model owner is during the project and who will be the owner once the model is completed.

The model owner is responsible for the validity of the information that goes into the model and its integrity. I will warn you that the model owner must have full confidence in the model project and the financial modeler because, in effect, the owner is taking over the responsibility after the model is built. Don't be surprised if there are no model owners put forward during the project; this is not your responsibility. However, once there is someone who is in this role, include them in as much of the model build process as possible without hindering the project. For example, the model user guide should be vetted by the model owner, and the documentation of the model must also be prepared with a view to the model owner.

The Model User

In many respects, the model user will seem like the model end user. But keep this in mind: the model user is the operator of the model, the person who will physically play with the model, type in the inputs, make changes to the sensitivities, and generate the output reports. The modeler should invariably assume that this person is not nor will they be a modeler. From my experience, a model user tends to be someone who has a financial background, some knowledge of Excel, and relatively junior in the organization pecking order. Therefore, the modeler should consistently build in terms of that profile. This means that the modeler should be thinking about all the facets of best practice modeling that was covered in Chapter 2 in order to make the model user-friendly.

The Role of the Model End User

In the modeling project, the end user is a mix of roles, which can be the operator of the model, the maintainer of the model, and also the recipient of the model outputs. On large modeling projects, these roles can be taken up by several individuals. That means that the modeler has access to a number of people who are able to give feedback and information that will be useful for the model. In particular, the modeler should be looking for the end users to supply guidance about which outputs, particularly the format and organizational governance, need to be adhered to. Furthermore, and something that will be discussed later in this chapter, is the role the model end user will have in shaping the inputs. In an ideal situation, the modeler will utilize all the individuals who make up the model end user to elicit the information to create the model inputs.

Defining Inputs and Understanding Their Importance

The model inputs should be seen as the conduit that allows the user to interact with the model. It is through the inputs that the outputs can be made flexible and sensitivity analysis can be incorporated within the model.

What Exactly Are the Inputs?

The inputs make up a section of a model where the users are able to interact directly with the model. They are the means by which the reports (the outputs) can be adjusted. Consider this example. Let's suppose we are looking to buy some land that we will to some extent develop and partly hold as an investment. The money we will use to buy the land will come from funds from various shareholders who will be given a share of the land based on their commitment. That same amount of the money will also come from a bank loan, with the liability being shared among the investors. There is ample land to distribute, but it's just dependent on how much the group can afford. We need to provide some information, such as the following:

- How much shareholding will investors have based on their commitment?
- For each shareholding, exactly how much would each investor hold?

- What will be the liability for the bank at each shareholding?
- How much interest annually does each investor need to pay?

These are the assumptions:

- There are five potential shareholding investors.
- There are 1,000 acres of land available.
- The price for land is $75 per square meter.
- The annual interest of the loan is 10%.

Quite clearly it would be very difficult to try to produce any outputs without creating some kind of a working calculation with inputs based upon the assumptions as a guide. This scenario that I have presented is hypothetical, but typically it is about the inputs. It is important to identify the key inputs and work out what exactly should be done to them to determine answers (outputs).

To decipher which assumptions are inputs, you can perform the variable test, which asks these questions: "Is this assumption variable? Does it have more than one possible outcome?" If the assumption elicits a "yes," it is always an input, which means that the element should be modeled so that it can be changed. For our example, see Figure 7-2 and review the assumptions. They have been laid out as discrete variables, which means each assumption can be manipulated. Therefore, the modeler no longer has to be concerned as to what the mix of variables will be. As long as the structure is in place, the calculations can then be created to give the answers as in Figure 7-3.

	A	B	C	D	E	F	G	H
5	About the Land							
6								
7								
8						Yr1	Yr2	Yr3
9		Land Price per Meter Square				75.00	82.00	91.00
10								
11		Available Land (In Acres)				1,000		
12								
13								
14	Shareholders							
15								
16						Yr1	Yr2	Yr3
17								
18		Shareholder 1 Commitment				80,000	0	0
19		Shareholder 2 Commitment				75,000	45,000	0
20		Shareholder 3 Commitment				75,000	25,000	0
21		Shareholder 4 Commitment				75,000	0	25,000
22		Shareholder 5 Commitment				130,000	22,000	25,000
23								
24	Calculation conversions							
25								
26		Square Meters in Acres				4,046.86		
27		Acre to Square Meter				0.00247105		

Figure 7-2. The assumptions from the example have been collected and laid out as inputs

Shareholder Land Holding

	Yr1	Yr2	Yr3
Shareholder 1 Sqm	1,067	-	-
Shareholder 2 Sqm	1,000	549	-
Shareholder 3 Sqm	1,000	305	-
Shareholder 4 Sqm	1,000	-	275
Shareholder 5 Sqm	1,733	268	275
Total Square Meters	**5,800**	**1,122**	**549**

	Yr1	Yr2	Yr3
Shareholder 1 Acres	2.64	-	-
Shareholder 2 Acres	2.47	1.36	-
Shareholder 3 Acres	2.47	0.75	-
Shareholder 4 Acres	2.47	-	0.68
Shareholder 5 Acres	4.28	0.66	0.68
Total Acres	**14.33**	**2.77**	**1.36**

	Shareholding	Loan Liability	Yr1	Yr2	Yr3
Shareholder 1 Investment	14.3%	13.9%	80,000	0	0
Shareholder 2 Investment	20.7%	20.8%	75,000	45,000	0
Shareholder 3 Investment	17.5%	17.3%	75,000	25,000	0
Shareholder 4 Investment	17.1%	17.3%	75,000	0	25,000
Shareholder 5 Investment	30.5%	30.7%	130,000	22,000	25,000
	100.0%	100.0%	435,000	92,000	50,000

Available Land

	Yr1	Yr2	Yr3
Acres Available	1,000	986	983

Figure 7-3. This figure shows the calculations from the inputs

Note that in Figure 7-2, the conversation factor between acres and meters is clearly stated and is placed as an input cell. Although the conversion factor is a fixed number, and it can never change, you should still insist on placing any such variables into input cells where they can clearly be seen and not use them directly in a calculation as a hard-coded number. By modeling in this manner, the model calculations will be auditable and relatively easy to track.

The inputs must have a consistent format type and, as the modeler, you should make sure that all possible assumptions and variables that will have an effect on the outputs have been taken into account in the inputs. From an organization perspective, I tend to prefer to keep all inputs in one worksheet broken up by section headings going down the worksheet. The inputs that have the most significant impact on the model are nearest the top of the worksheet. For example, interest rates, revenue prices, and cost details would be called key drivers.

Types of Inputs

In the previous section, I briefly touched on the types of inputs, but I would like to explore these types more. Gathering and creating the inputs is not as clear as other parts of modeling, such as creating the calculations or outputs.

I tend to categorize inputs into four types: fixed inputs, time period–based inputs, model control inputs, and user inputs. The next few sections will explore inputs that would be organized in these categories in order to provide you with the information to categorize inputs going forward.

Fixed Inputs

Fixed inputs are those items that are important to working on the model but have only one value. In other words, they have no variability in what they could be—they are fixed. So what is the point of having a fixed input that has just one value? These types of inputs potentially cause models to have hard-coded or static numbers. Let's take a look at the typical instances of fixed inputs in models.

Number Multiplier

When you have a number that has been applied to a calculation, the answer will most likely need to be rounded either up or down as in Figure 7-4. In this figure, the calculation has produced numbers with decimals. This is very common when creating calculations for the model; therefore, it is good modeling to treat all numbers in a consistent manner. Note that this treatment is transparent, documented, and potentially can be changed easily throughout the model.

	A	B	C	D	E
1					
2	Input				
3			Yr1	Yr2	Yr3
4		Units	20,311	22,742	22,747
5					
6		Price per unit	15.22	16.13	17.14
7					
8		Discount	2.02%	2.02%	2.02%
9					
10		Multiplier	1,000		
11					
12	Calculation				
13					
14		Total revenue	309,133.42	366,828.46	389,883.58
15					
16		Discounts given	6,244.50	7,409.93	7,875.65
17					

Figure 7-4. The calculations need to be rounded in this model

A method that I employ is based on using a multiplier that can be in tens, hundreds, thousands, or even in tens of thousands. The modeler would set the input purposely with a mathematical rounding which is then multiplied to any calculation so that the resulting number has been smoothed and rounded. If this happens consistently, then the result would be a model where all the calculated numbers have had the same multiple effect applied as in Figure 7-5. In the figure, a multiplier (1,000) has been added; you divide this multiplier into all the numbers to get the rounding.

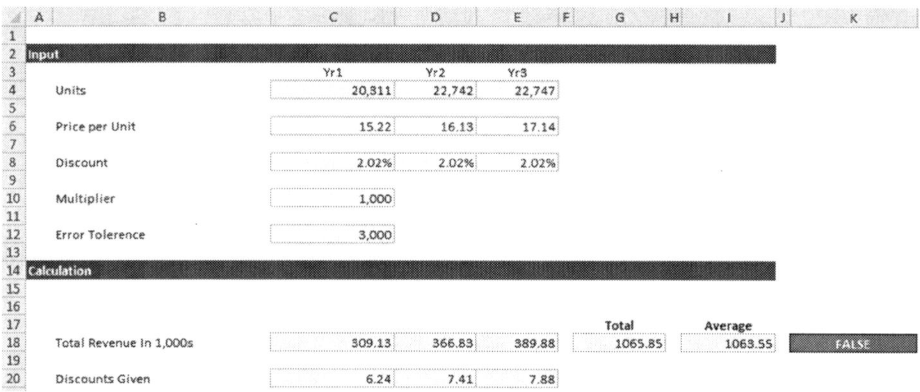

Figure 7-5. The numbers have been rounded by using a multiplier in the inputs

Error Checked Tolerance

Error checks can present problems of their own when dealing with precise numbers. For instance, you may create an error check to compare two numbers, which should be the same, by taking one number from the other. With this method, if there is no error, the result will be zero; if there is an error, it will be a nonzero. However, when dealing in large numbers and several calculations, there could be differences in two error checking numbers due to cell roundings. While this is not an error, it will be flagged as such.

Modelers can alleviate this problem by creating a tolerance level that they are comfortable with. Setting this tolerance level to anything that is more than a three-decimal difference would be acceptable. In Figure 7-6, the total revenue has been compared with the average revenue (average price × total units). When dealing with averages and the real total, there will be differences from roundings, but by applying the tolerance, the differences will not cause an error as they are known and therefore produce a "TRUE" on the error check.

Also in Figure 7-6, an error tolerance has been included so that any difference less than 3,000 is accepted in the error checks. Modelers need to apply common sense and not abuse the tolerances in order to get a clear error check. It is preferable, however, to have a tolerance number running through the model as an input because it can easily be changed. For instance, in this situation, if you decide that there will be no tolerances, you would simply clear the 3,000. This way, any error checks that were using this tolerance would immediately become errors.

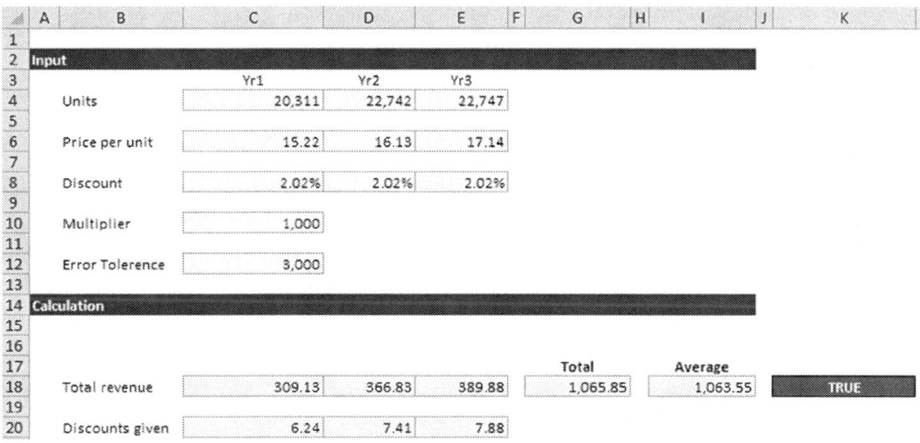

Figure 7-6. The numbers with totals are applied against a tolerance

Other Fixed Inputs

There is a number of other fixed inputs that deserve attention, including these next three that I have described:

Currency

Including the currency as part of the model allows the modeler to state the obvious currency. This is useful because by stating the currency and then applying a conversion rate of one, the model will be in the local currency. But if a requirement is later introduced to change the currency for the entire model, the modeler can simply change the conversion rate to the applicable forex rate for the new currency, and the model will now be in another currency.

Number of Months in a Year

Although it may seem obvious, the number of months in a year should be in the inputs. At some point in the model, it is likely that an annual number will be broken down into its equivalent in months. Rather than placing a static hard-coded number 12 in the formula, best practice would be to use inputs to hold the number 12 and then refer to that input in the formula. You may wonder why go to such lengths for something so obvious, but the benefit of modeling in this manner, should a change be required and we no longer want to use the number 12, is that we can simply change the input to the new number. The alternative would require finding every formula that has a 12 in it and changing it. But keep in mind that I have created models for organizations that have 13 financial months a year. This scenario does happen with public sector and some government agencies. Therefore, using the inputs for months in a year is the best way to handle these potential disparities.

Modeling Days per Month

This critical input states the average number of days per month that the model will use for calculations. The days in the month may seem obvious, but if it is not stated in the inputs, will the model work out to 30 days, 30.44 days, or 31 days per month? By setting these days, it is far simpler to set debtor and creditor payment days that can run concurrently with the dates in the model.

There are several fixed inputs to consider. The three that were discussed are not immediately obvious because they *are* so obvious. Modelers should also keep in mind accounting codes (a general ledger chart of accounts), supplier codes, supplier payment terms, and organization locations and sites.

Time Period–Based Inputs

Time period–based inputs are those inputs that occur at specific intervals and times and are variable. These inputs will not be consistent across every time period. For instance, an organization may collect its sales receipts from the credit card merchant every 30 days, but the amount will be based on sales, which will vary from month to month. The key feature of these inputs is that when organized consistently, they allow for a good degree of manipulation of data and are crucial for scenario analysis. They also alleviate the need to create a complex date formula. Figures 7-7 and 7-8 demonstrate the potential problems of not using time period–based inputs and resorting to a complex formula.

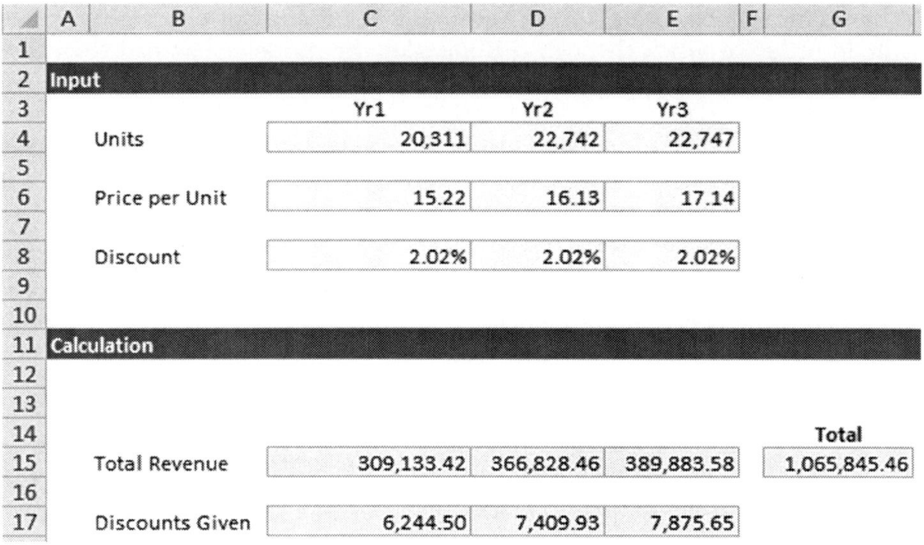

Figure 7-7. The revenue is calculated from the units and price time periods in the inputs

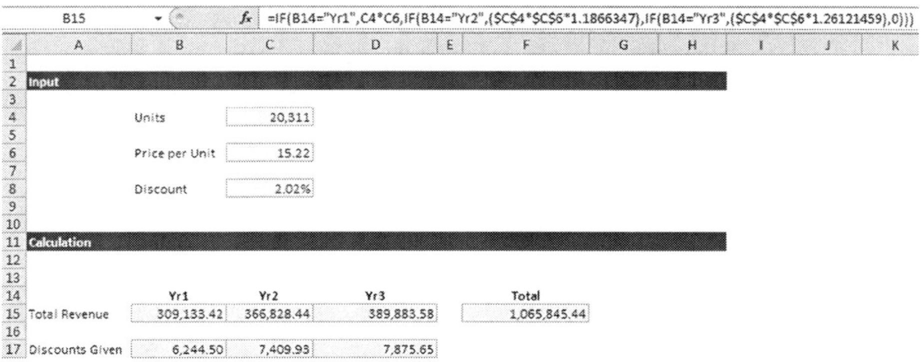

Figure 7-8. The revenue is calculated by using a combination of IF functions and hard-coded numbers

Both methods produce the same results. However, in Figure 7-8, notice that it was necessary to go to the additional expense of creating some IF functions and including hard-coded numbers. This formula is already looking ugly. If you were to expand the tables from three to ten years, the result would be a completely unworkable formula. Such a situation where a complicated formula is required is typical of using the wrong type of input.

When critically appraising financial models, I find that many models show this fault. In order to work through this mistake, the modeler has had to create some seriously complex formula construction. While the modeler may be proud that the potential issue has been resolved, there is nothing impressive with that sort of modeling. I am far more impressed with seeing models where the modeler has recognized which types of inputs to use and has simplified the calculation. The motto should be to spare a moment for the auditor or the reviewer.

Any inputs that appear to be connected to a date or cannot be utilized immediately are time period–based inputs.

Model Control

The model controls are inputs that are relatively fixed and are related to the change control in the model. These inputs are more about the status, ownership, and naming of the model.

Note Change control is a systematic approach to managing all changes made for a system. The purpose is to ensure that no unnecessary changes are made, all changes are documented, services are not unnecessarily disrupted, and resources are used efficiently. The change control process is usually conducted as a sequence of steps proceeding from the submission of a change request that is recorded.

Figure 7-9 shows the inputs that would typically be associated with the model control, which includes all aspects of the model ownership and contacts and the development path through the model. By having the development path with the version number, it is then just a matter of naming the model file name according to the version number. Notice in the figure the authorized user list. Typically all aspects of who uses the model and how they use it would be controlled with this list by tying the username to the computer login name. As a result, anyone whose username is not recognized will trigger a response from the model, for instance, the model could close down, provide a warning message, or lock all the worksheets.

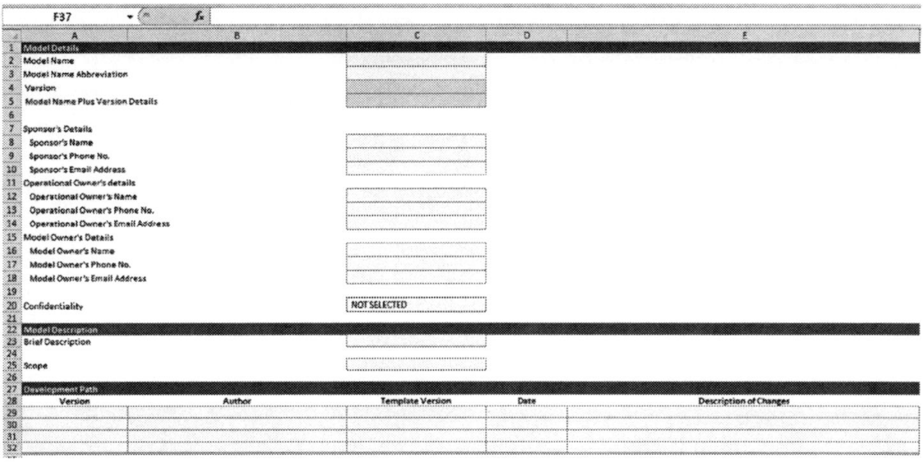

Figure 7-9. This figure shows the model control inputs

User Inputs

User inputs are those inputs that do not fall into any of the categories previously discussed. These are all the inputs that will be directly interacting with the model user and will have a significant effect on the model workings. They are typified by how they are almost always generated by the outputs and the assumptions that would be built from the requirements gathering to the model. As a result, these inputs are very user-centric.

Figure 7-10 is a typical user inputs worksheet from a modeling project, which has inputs based on the user community, the project sponsor, and from the assumption register.

	A	B	C	D
1	**Financial Model User Inputs**			
7	***Project/Model Dates***			
9	Model Start Date			01/04/2005
10	Commercial/Financial Close			31/12/2005
11	First Annual Balance Date			31/03/2006
12				
13	***Project Phasing Dates - Services Go-Live***			
15	Financial Application Services			31/12/2007
16	Information Services			31/12/2006
17	Implementation Services			31/12/2006
20	***Project Suppliers***			
22	Supplier 1			Supplier1
23	Supplier 2			Supplier2
24	Supplier 3			Supplier3
25				
27	Modelling Periods During Implementation			Monthly
28	Months Per Period During Implementation			1
29	Base Project Length (Years)			12
31	Project End			31/12/2017
33	Number of Additional Periods			24
35	Modelling Periods Post Implementation			Annual
37	Months Per Period Post Implementation			12
39	Number of Project Periods			144
41	Reporting Periods Project Authority	Report Option1		Apr - Mar
43	Reporting Periods Project Concessionaire	Report Option2		Jan - Dec
45	Reporting option in Use			Report Option1
47	Financial Report Price Parameter			Nominal Prices

Figure 7-10. A typical user's inputs are included in this model

It is not unusual for the user inputs to span many rows in the input sheet, as this directly relates to the size and complexity of the model and also the number and types of outputs requested. The essence of a good user input worksheet is one that has sections and is formatted consistently. Often when the user inputs become very large, it is helpful to use the first column (column A) to include reference codes, which will show where the input is being used in the model.

How to Build Inputs

Building assumptions depends on the modeler understanding the aims and goals of the model. This is one reason why I advocate that the model inputs be built around the outputs, which would then make the building of inputs more a process of intuition. What follows next is an example of how to build a set of inputs by using the outputs and working back to the inputs.

Figure 7-11 is from the outputs of a financial model. In this case, it is the income statement that was mandated by the project sponsor.

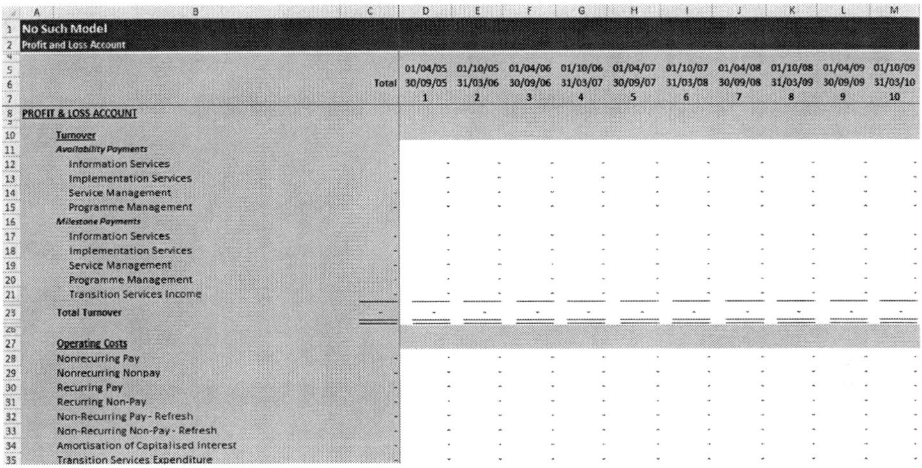

		Total	01/04/05 30/09/05 1	01/10/05 31/03/06 2	01/04/06 30/09/06 3	01/10/06 31/03/07 4	01/04/07 30/09/07 5	01/10/07 31/03/08 6	01/04/08 30/09/08 7	01/10/08 31/03/09 8	01/04/09 30/09/09 9	01/10/09 31/03/10 10
1	**No Such Model**											
2	Profit and Loss Account											
8	PROFIT & LOSS ACCOUNT											
10	Turnover											
11	*Availability Payments*											
12	Information Services	-	-	-	-	-	-	-	-	-	-	-
13	Implementation Services	-	-	-	-	-	-	-	-	-	-	-
14	Service Management	-	-	-	-	-	-	-	-	-	-	-
15	Programme Management	-	-	-	-	-	-	-	-	-	-	-
16	*Milestone Payments*											
17	Information Services	-	-	-	-	-	-	-	-	-	-	-
18	Implementation Services	-	-	-	-	-	-	-	-	-	-	-
19	Service Management	-	-	-	-	-	-	-	-	-	-	-
20	Programme Management	-	-	-	-	-	-	-	-	-	-	-
21	Transition Services Income	-	-	-	-	-	-	-	-	-	-	-
25	**Total Turnover**	-	-	-	-	-	-	-	-	-	-	-
27	Operating Costs											
28	Nonrecurring Pay	-	-	-	-	-	-	-	-	-	-	-
29	Nonrecurring Nonpay	-	-	-	-	-	-	-	-	-	-	-
30	Recurring Pay	-	-	-	-	-	-	-	-	-	-	-
31	Recurring Non-Pay	-	-	-	-	-	-	-	-	-	-	-
32	Non-Recurring Pay - Refresh	-	-	-	-	-	-	-	-	-	-	-
33	Non-Recurring Non-Pay - Refresh	-	-	-	-	-	-	-	-	-	-	-
34	Amortisation of Capitalised Interest	-	-	-	-	-	-	-	-	-	-	-
35	Transition Services Expenditure	-	-	-	-	-	-	-	-	-	-	-

Figure 7-11. This is an income statement from commercial financial model

In the figure, the turnover is broken down into detail based on the service's availability payments and milestone payments. If you concentrate on the turnover, notice that you can immediately establish that it will be broken down into two categories: availability and milestone. Under each category, there will be a number of services. Therefore, inputs are needed for each of the services.

Figure 7-12 is an input worksheet, and inputs have been incorporated that directly affect the income statement by creating the ability to post milestone dates, implementation percentage, and actual payments of those milestones within the payment assumptions. Don't be concerned with the functionality aspects of this stage. In building the inputs, you are primarily looking forward to capturing all the elements that will fulfill the output requirement.

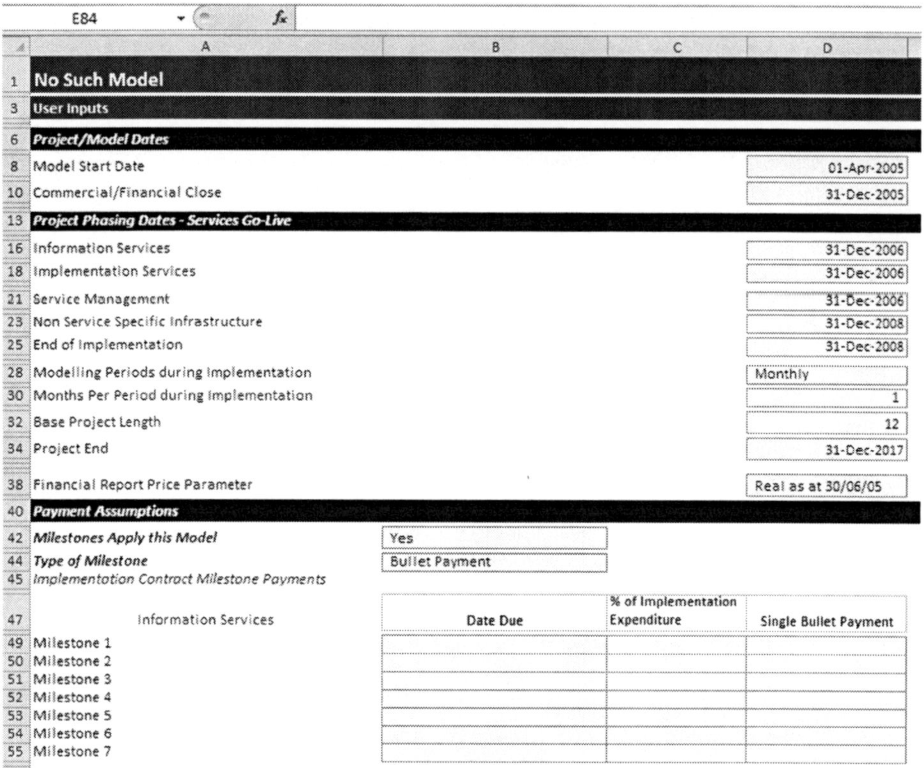

Figure 7-12. The inputs incorporate every variable that is required to create the outputs

In Figure 7-13, the availability payments for the income statement have been further incorporated. The model has also started to build the operating costs split between recurring and nonrecurring costs.

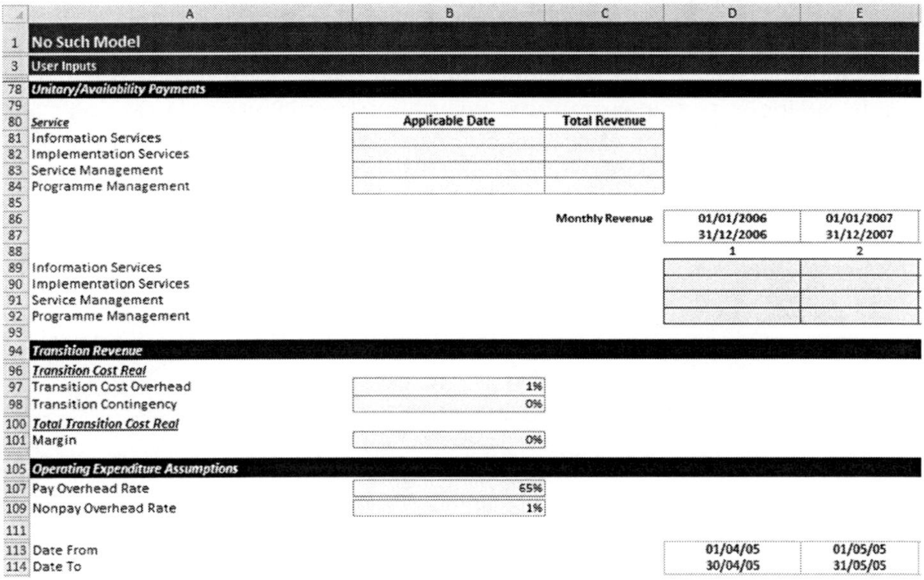

Figure 7-13. This model is creating inputs for availability payments

Although it sounds counterintuitive, as stated previously, the starting point is the outputs, followed by the inputs, and the calculations are the last element. Building the inputs is very much about understanding the goals and expectations—do not be tempted to start building inputs until you have understood the outputs.

Case Study: The Real-World Impact of Inputs

In this section, I will provide some samples of inputs from commercial models that have been used successfully in one capacity or another in the real world. The inputs you will see represent business projects whose total value is in excess of a billion dollars, and thus these are tried and tested inputs and not theoretical. One cautionary note: there are precious few examples of real-world inputs available anywhere in the public domain for a reason. Financial modelers have to abide by a code of confidentiality. Whether this is stated or not, it is almost always implied. Therefore, pushing anything into the public domain that will affect an organization in any way should not be encouraged. The samples that I am presenting in this book are carefully selected from models for which I have the ultimate copyright and unequivocal use of the model. The data has been scrubbed and filled with dummy information that has no connection to anyone or any organization, but demonstrates the use of inputs.

Inputs to Count the Cost of Redundancy

The inputs in Figure 7-14 are from a financial model for a takeover bid. This particular input examines staff that will be converted after the takeover and applies some statutory requirements for pensions and redundancy payments. The total cost to cover redundancy and pension commitments was just over $15 million.

Calculation Date 31-Dec-2013

Staff ID	Job Title	Grade	Locations	Start Date	Length of Service (In Years)	Age at Calculation Date	No of weeks Service	Weeks over 104 weeks	Enhanced Pension (1=Yes, 0=No)	Date of Birth	Full time equivalent	Salary	One Month Salary	Redundancy Pay	Pension	Enhanced Pension
940459-D	Junior administrator	1	1	11-Oct-1999	14.23	50.6	742.1	638.1	1	16-Jun-1963	0.27	18,200	1,517	21,387	0	0
940462-G	Junior administrator	1	1	16-Nov-2008	5.12	59.8	267.0	163.0	1	19-Mar-1954	0.43	18,200	1,517	7,756	51,454	860
940458-D	Junior administrator	1	1	24-Mar-2003	10.78	35.3	562.1	458.1	1	21-Sep-1978	0.41	18,200	1,517	16,351	0	910
940492-G	Junior administrator	1	2	01-Dec-2008	5.08	44.3	265.1	161.1	1	15-Sep-1969	0.56	18,200	1,517	7,712	0	213
940470-G	Administrator	2	1	10-Dec-1990	23.07	56.0	1,203.1	1,099.1	1	29-Jan-1958	0.45	23,350	1,946	44,898	114,649	2,049
940468-G	Administrator	1	1	17-Oct-1988	25.22	45.2	1,315.1	1,211.1	1	07-Nov-1968	0.50	18,200	1,517	38,253	0	2,272
940456-D	Administrator	2	1	23-Sep-1999	14.28	51.6	744.7	640.7	1	20-Jun-1962	0.61	23,350	1,946	27,791	74,083	1,437
940464-G	Administrator	2	1	21-Oct-1993	20.21	40.4	1,053.7	949.7	1	15-Aug-1973	0.59	23,350	1,946	33,322	0	1,547
940457-D	Administrator	2	2	06-Dec-2010	3.07	26.3	160.1	56.1	1	14-Sep-1987	1.00	23,350	1,946	5,976	0	213
940461-G	Administrator	2	2	29-Nov-2010	3.09	26.6	161.1	57.1	1	10-Jun-1987	1.00	23,350	1,946	6,013	0	213
940460-D	Personal Assistant Grade1	2	2	01-Jun-2009	4.59	33.3	239.1	135.1	1	19-Sep-1980	1.00	23,350	1,946	8,934	0	1,955
940469-G	Personal Assistant Grade1	2	2	08-Jun-2004	9.57	54.4	499.0	395.0	1	12-Aug-1959	0.81	23,350	1,946	18,621	71,886	1,321
940475-T	Personal Assistant Grade1	2	1	21-Mar-1994	19.78	47.4	1,032.1	928.1	1	05-Sep-1966	0.50	23,350	1,946	38,517	0	2,214
940482-T	Personal Assistant Grade1	2	1	03-Nov-1997	16.17	47.2	843.1	739.1	1	25-Nov-1966	0.50	23,350	1,946	31,464	0	1,300
940487-T	Personal Assistant Grade2	2	1	14-Jul-2003	10.47	45.9	546.1	442.1	1	05-Feb-1968	0.60	23,350	1,946	20,381	0	3,284
940483-T	Personal Assistant Grade2	2	1	22-Mar-1995	18.79	52.0	979.9	875.9	1	04-Jan-1962	0.53	23,350	1,946	36,566	175,450	3,372
940472-G	Personal Assistant Grade2	3	1	01-Sep-2001	12.34	32.1	643.4	539.4	1	15-Nov-1981	0.60	28,500	2,375	29,307	0	3,299
940467-G	Engineer	4	1	24-Nov-2008	5.10	27.7	266.1	162.1	1	12-Apr-1986	1.00	36,800	3,067	15,653	0	2,601
940490-G	Engineer	4	1	19-Mar-1996	17.80	50.8	928.0	824.0	1	23-Sep-1963	1.00	36,800	3,067	54,578	126,478	2,514
940498-G	Engineer	4	1	14-Jul-1987	26.48	61.3	1,381.0	1,277.0	1	25-Sep-1952	1.00	36,800	3,067	81,220	71,658	1,169
940474-G	Engineer	4	1	01-Nov-1999	14.18	36.5	739.1	635.1	1	28-Jun-1977	0.61	36,800	3,067	43,471	0	1,923
940471-G	Engineer	4	1	04-Feb-2008	5.91	51.3	308.1	204.1	1	28-Sep-1962	1.00	36,800	3,067	18,123	58,608	1,148
940485-T	Technical Engineers	3	2	07-Mar-1979	34.84	68.9	1,816.9	1,712.9	1	11-Feb-1945	0.65	28,500	2,375	82,754	148,951	2,161
940490-T	Technical Engineers	3	2	01-Jul-2000	13.51	40.2	704.4	600.4	1	21-Oct-1973	0.60	28,500	2,375	32,085	0	2,357
940479-T	Technical Engineers	3	2	14-Nov-1977	36.15	54.7	1,885.1	1,781.1	1	08-May-1959	0.78	28,500	2,375	85,864	255,149	4,866
940484-T	Technical Engineers	3	1	26-Jan-1998	15.94	52.4	831.1	727.1	1	03-Aug-1961	0.78	28,500	2,375	37,857	196,672	3,750
940477-G	Technical Engineers	3	1	01-Jul-2000	13.51	37.8	704.4	600.4	1	08-Mar-1976	1.00	28,500	2,375	32,085	0	2,585

Figure 7-14. This model shows the staff redundancy and pension costs inputs for a takeover bid

Examining the Cost of Software

In Figure 7-15, the inputs were used in a model that provided information about the cost of implementing software for clients. These inputs give the total cost for the year, but in addition, the user can use drop-down lists to get more detail on the cost of individual applications.

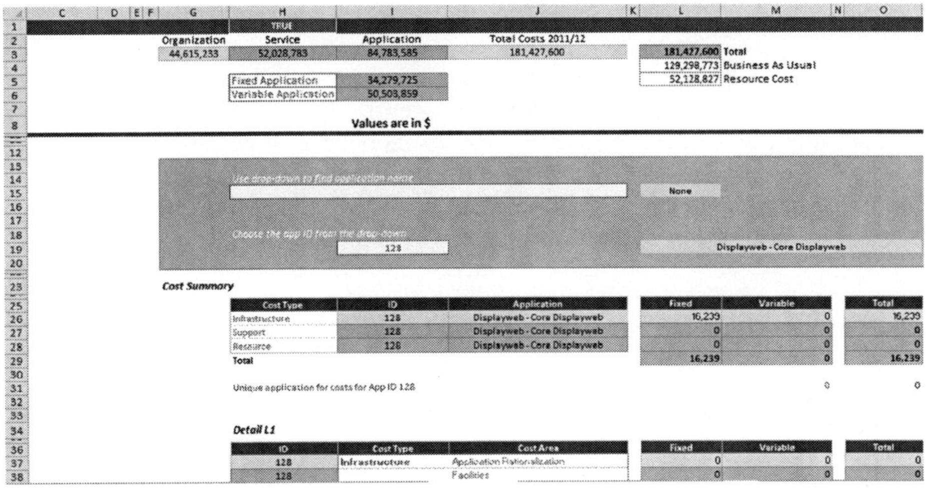

Figure 7-15. This model shows the inputs for the cost of software applications

Inputs to Control the Model User

Inputs can be used not just to collect information that will be calculated in the model, but also for administration and security. Figure 7-16 demonstrates that with the use of a little VBA code, the username of the person who has opened the model is collected (in this case, John). This username is matched against a prepopulated list of names that have authorization to use the model. In this manner, anyone whose username is not on the list will cause the model to produce an warning.

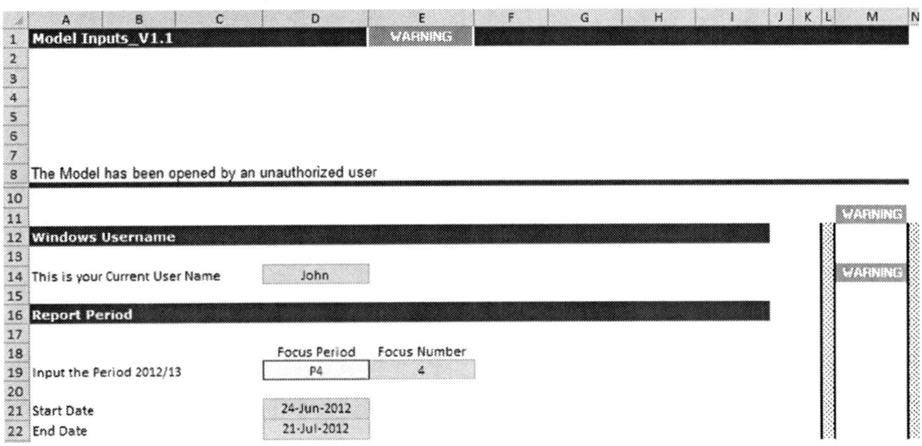

Figure 7-16. In this figure, the model has detected a username. In this case, the one who accessed the model is not authorized to use the model

Airline Model

The next four diagrams are taken from a financial model for a joint venture (JV) startup to develop an international airline. The model has inputs relating to staff and roster hours, aircraft capacity, and cost of routes. You will note that the inputs from this airline model look very different from the types of inputs discussed earlier. This is an example of where the client sponsor was heavily involved in the design and format of the model.

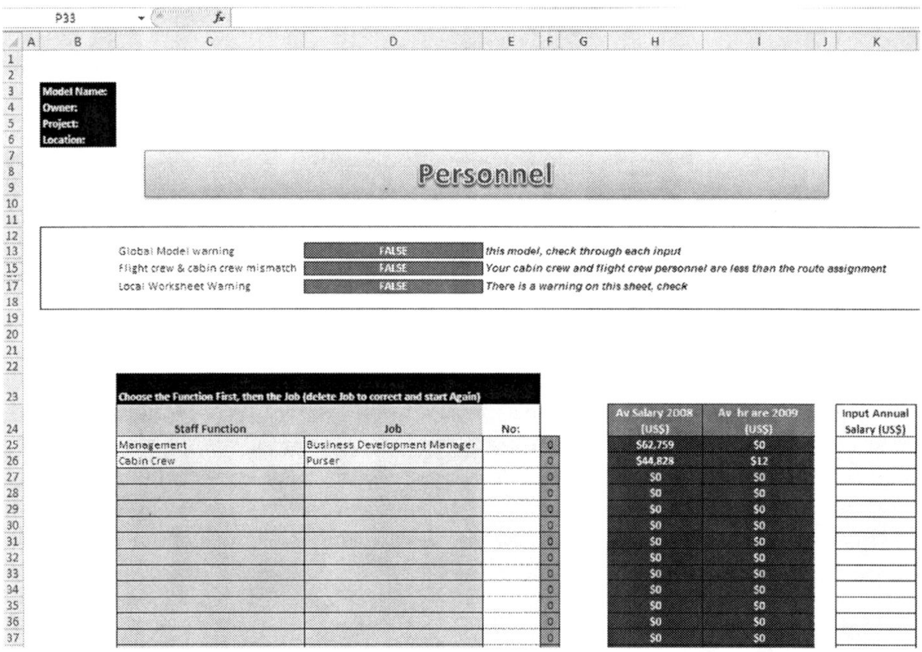

Figure 7-17. This figure depicts the cost of staffing inputs

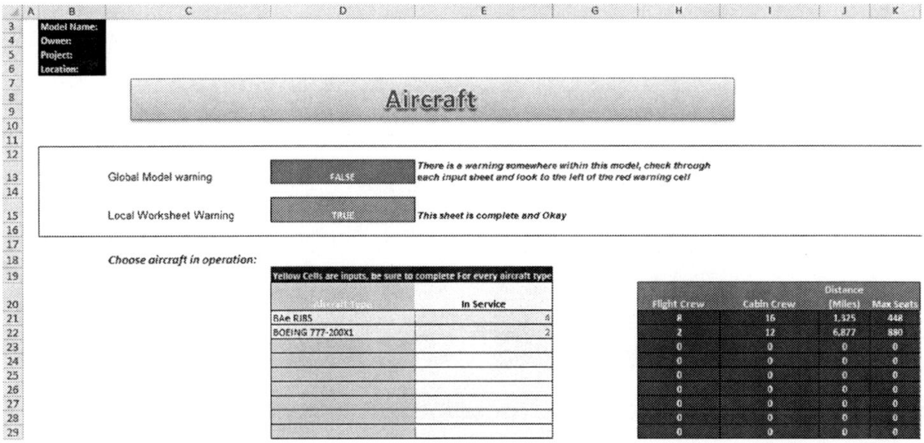

Figure 7-18. This figure shows the aircraft capacity inputs

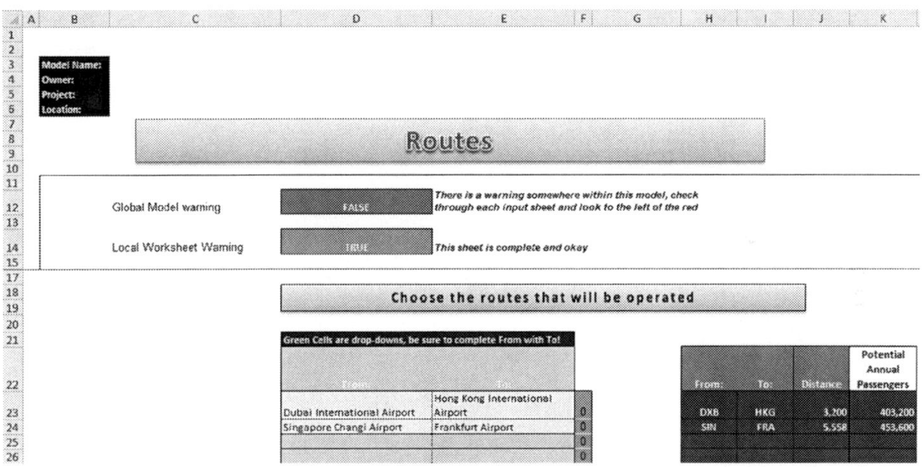

Figure 7-19. This figure depicts the route distances and total number of passenger inputs

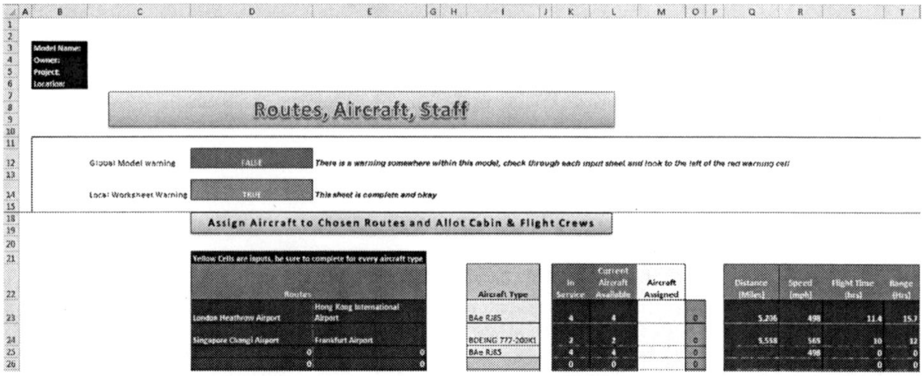

Figure 7-20. Aircraft routing and staff assignments are shown in this figure

The inputs discussed in this chapter should provide you with a varied view of the types of inputs that are likely to be used in models. It will always be difficult to try and balance the client's expectations and the modeler's best practice methodology. But the prime requirement when creating inputs is to make them clear, practical, and logical. In the next chapter, I will introduce some basic accounting and financial concepts that will be useful to understanding where the inputs end up.

CHAPTER

8

Finance and Accounting for Modelers

In financial modeling, all roads lead to the outputs, which are almost always financial. At the end of the day, modeling is really about putting together a clutch financial analysis and statements that have had an acute level of rigor applied to them. This way, they offer the best possible representation of the real world as you can get.

Simply put, all financial models have financial outputs, of which the majority should be familiar to modelers. Figure 8-1 shows many of the financial statement and ratios that are typical in financial models. One of the required skills of a financial modeler is the ability to distinguish and select the most useful and fitting statements and then use them in a way that will give an accurate story about the project.

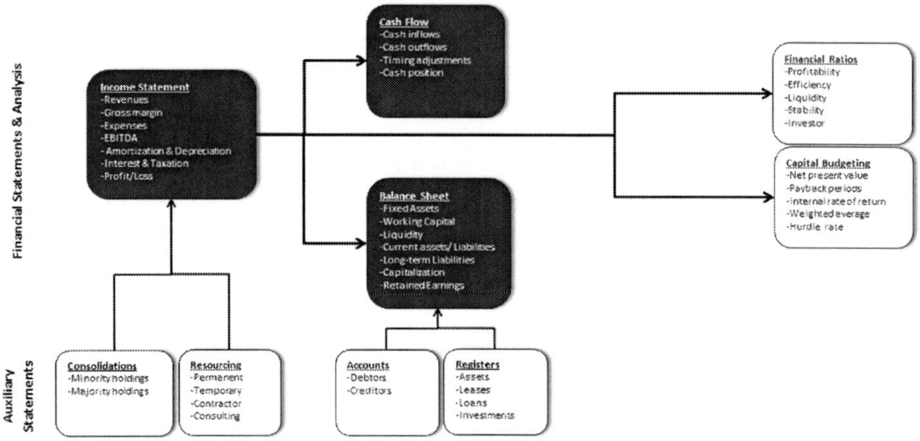

Figure 8-1. This figure shows financial statements and analysis that could be used in financial models

Experience suggests that in the majority of financial models, there are three core financial statements: the income statement (also called the profit and loss or revenue statement), the cash flow statement, and the balance sheet (see Figure 8-1). Typically, all financial modelers will be very conversant with the main financial statements to the extent they are able to create them from scratch, and then communicate them effectively to interested parties. These three statements also make up the foundation to most of the financial ratios; therefore, they cannot be ignored. In the next chapter, I will go into more detail about financial ratios.

Financial statements and their analysis are very powerful tools in the hands of someone who understands them. This is a key point to understand because they offer insights into an organization or project that would otherwise be unclear. This point is one that all modelers need to understand. Financial modelers have a responsibility to produce the outputs and to ensure they are in accordance with any statutory requirements. They should be confident and assured that the outputs give as best a representation of the financial health of whatever is being modeled. There should be no question about artificially altering or fudging these statements to give an alternative representation.

On occasion, I have been subtly asked to change the financial statements, to slant them toward a given goal. My answer to this is always, unequivocally, "no." My advice to any modeler is that you do the same. If you slant the financial statement, that path will invariably lead at best to loss of credibility and at worse to loss of livelihood and possible litigation.

But if you should find yourself backed into a corner and have no alternative but to fudge the numbers, my advice would be to reflect the changes or fudges on the assumption register and include the detail of who required these changes. Follow this step by creating a second set of outputs, identical to the first in everything but the fudged numbers, which should be clearly labeled with the owner of the adjustment. Although this is more work and could delay completing the model, constantly use this procedure when you have outputs that have external influences. By having two sets of outputs, there will be one set of the base outputs that have not been adjusted and another set of the alternative outputs that have been altered.

Accounting Primer

This section will cover a great deal of basic accounting. If you have no formal accounting background, it is an essential foundation for understanding financial statements. Even if you are familiar with basic accounting principles, it will be useful for you to look through this section and reacquaint yourself with some of the accounting fundamentals.

The Need for Accounting

Every organization should maintain sound records to keep track of such questions as the following:

- How much money does the organization currently have?
- How much did the organization used to have?
- Where does the money come from?
- How is the money being spent?
- Where is the money being spent?

Keeping track of these questions will provide answers that will then be used to assess the strengths and weaknesses of the organization. Answering another set of questions like the following will help identify the strengths and weaknesses:

- Is the business making or losing money?
- How much is the business worth?
- Does more money need to be put into the business?
- How much money is owed to the business?
- How can the business change the way it operates so that it can make a profit or even more profit?

As the financial modeler or accountant, you will be required to provide the valuable information needed to assist management in the decision of tackling these questions.

Accounting and Business

Accounting is a system used in business and commerce to measure financial performance by noting and classifying all the transactions, such as sales, purchases, assets, and liabilities in a manner that adheres to accepted standard formats. It allows the audience to evaluate a company's past performance, present condition, and future prospects.

By far, the main exponents of accounting and creating financial statements are business organizations. Although the detail structure of organizations may vary from country to country, most of the world still works under these three structures:[1]

- Sole proprietorships
- Partnerships
- Corporations

Sole Proprietorships

A sole proprietorship is a business that is wholly owned by a single individual. It is the easiest and the least expensive way to start a business, often associated with small "one-person" type businesses. The advantage of the sole proprietorship is that it is relatively free from red tape and legalities that restrict other forms of business. Its major disadvantage is that it comes with unlimited liability. The owner and the business are regarded as the same from a legal standpoint, which means a legal issue from business will also have a detrimental effect on the individual's personal status as well. Very few large organizations are sole proprietors because aside from the legal constraints, structurally it is virtually impossible to expand and still operate efficiently.

Partnerships

A partnership is a legal association of two or more individuals called partners who are co-owners of a business for profit. Like proprietorships, they are easy to form. This type of business organization is based upon a written

[1]Because definitions and regulations regarding business formation vary from country to country, consult a book or local attorney or accountant to understand the particular rules governing your situation.

agreement that details the various interests and rights of the partners. It is always advisable to seek legal advice and document each person's rights and responsibilities.

There are three main kinds of partnerships:

- General partnership
- Limited partnership
- Master limited partnership

General Partnership

A general partnership is a business that is owned and operated by two or more persons where everyone has a right as a co-owner and is liable for the business's debts. All partners report their share from the partnership profits or losses on their individual tax returns. The partnership itself is not responsible for any tax liabilities. The partners also report their share of partnership profits or losses on their individual tax returns and pay the tax on those profits. The partnership itself does not pay any taxes on its tax return.

Limited Partnership

In a limited partnership, one or more partners run the business as general partners. The remaining partners are passive investors who become limited partners and are personally liable only for the amount of their investments. They are called limited partners because they cannot be sued for more money than they have invested into the business.

Master Limited Partnership

Master limited partnerships are related to corporations in that they can trade partnership units on listed stock exchanges. They have many advantages that are similar to corporations, such as limited liability, unlimited life, and transferable ownership. In addition, these partnerships have another rewarding advantage if 90% of their income is from passive sources (for example, rental income). If this is the case, then they pay no corporate taxes since the profits are paid to the stockholders, who are taxed at individual rates.

This type of partnership has several of the same benefits of sole proprietorship, particularly with new investment. If more capital is required, it's quite possible to attract a new partner who is required to put up the required capital investment. One of the concerns of this partnership is how long the business runs. It is dependent on the partners and therefore disputes, ill health, and death can all dissolve the partnership.

Corporation

Corporation is the general term for legally chartered enterprises with legal rights rather like a person. Therefore, a corporation is able to buy and sell goods and services, engage in contracts, sue and be sued, and pay taxes. A corporation can have different names depending upon the country but they all essentially have the same basic structure.

The corporation is the most dominant form of business organization worldwide. Since the corporation exists as a separate entity apart from an individual, it is legally responsible for its actions and debts.

The strength of a corporation is that its ownership and management are separate. In theory, the owners may get rid of the managers if they vote to do so. Conversely, because the shares of the corporation, known as stock, can be sold to someone else, the corporation's ownership can change drastically, while the management stays the same. The corporation's unlimited life span coupled with its ability to raise money gives it the potential for significant growth.

A company does not have to be large to incorporate. In fact, most corporations, like most businesses, are relatively tiny. The majority of small corporations are privately held.

One disadvantage of corporations is that they suffer from higher taxes than unincorporated businesses. In addition, shareholders must pay income tax on their share of the company's profit that they receive as dividends. This means that corporation profits are taxed twice.

There are several different types of corporations based on various distinctions, such as how they raise capital. Private corporations, while having shares, are limited in how those shares in the company can be bought and sold. The non-private companies, which are called public corporations, can sell and buy shares on the open market. Their shares are listed in public indices with the price per share.

Professional corporations are set up by businesses whose shareholders offer professional services (legal, medical, engineering, and so forth). This allows them to set up beneficial pension and insurance packages.

Note A corporation is an entity that has been created by law or by charter and hence is a legal body with rights and liabilities which are distinct from the parties engaged in the formation.

Limited liability companies (LLCs) combine the advantages of S corporations (corporations in the U.S. that pass profits and losses through to owners) and limited partnerships without having to abide by the restrictions of either. LLCs allow companies to pay taxes like partnerships and be protected from liabilities beyond their investments.

Types of Accounting

There are two methods of tracking accounting records:

- Cash-based accounting
- Accrual accounting

Cash-Based Accounting

Most of us use this cash method to keep track of our personal financial activities. The cash method recognizes revenue when payment is received and recognizes expenses when cash is paid out. For example, your personal checkbook record is based upon the cash method. Expenses are recorded when cash is paid out, and revenue is recorded when cash or check deposits are received.

Accrual Accounting

The accrual method of accounting requires that revenue be recognized and assigned to the accounting period in which it is earned. Similarly, expenses must be recognized and assigned to the accounting period in which they are incurred.

A company tracks the summary of the accounting activity in time intervals called accounting periods. These periods are usually a month long. It is also common for a company to create a yearly statement of records. This annual period is also called a fiscal or an accounting year.

The accrual method relies upon the principle of matching revenues and expenses. This principle states that the expenses for a period, which are the costs of doing business to earn income, should be compared with the revenues during the period, which is the income earned as the result of those expenses. In other words, the expenses for the period should accurately match up with the costs of producing revenue for the period.

In general, there are two types of adjustments that need to be made at the end of the accounting period. The first type of adjustment arises when more expense or revenue has been recorded than was actually incurred or earned during the accounting period. An example of this might be the prepayment of a two-year insurance premium for $2,000. The actual insurance expense during the year would be only $1,000. Therefore, an adjusting entry at the end of the accounting period is necessary to show the correct amount of insurance expense for that period.

Similarly, there may be revenue that was received but was not in fact earned during the accounting period. For example, the business may have been paid for services that will not actually be provided or earned until the next year. In this case, an adjusting entry at the end of the accounting period is made to defer, or postpone, the recognition of revenue to the period when it is actually earned.

Although many companies use the accrual method of accounting, some small businesses prefer the cash basis. The accrual method generates tax obligations before the cash has been collected. This benefits the government because the IRS gets its tax money sooner.

Cash vs. Accrual Accounting

Let's look at these accounting methods in more depth.

When a business bills a client or customer, that business will experience an increase in its income on paper. This will be reflected in the financial statements, such as the income statement. The increase will also trigger an increase in the accounts receivable. When the business is paid by the client, the paper asset now turns into money, which is placed into the business bank account and becomes a tangible asset. Through a process of recording the payment and the deposit, accounts receivable decreases and the bank balance increases. This system is based on an accrual such that the accounts receivable is an asset that is owed to the business. However, the business does not have money in the bank or property to show that it has any ownership other than an invoice, which is shown in Figure 8-2. It only exists on paper. It grows or accumulates as The business issues invoices; consequently, accounts receivable is part of an accrual accounting system.

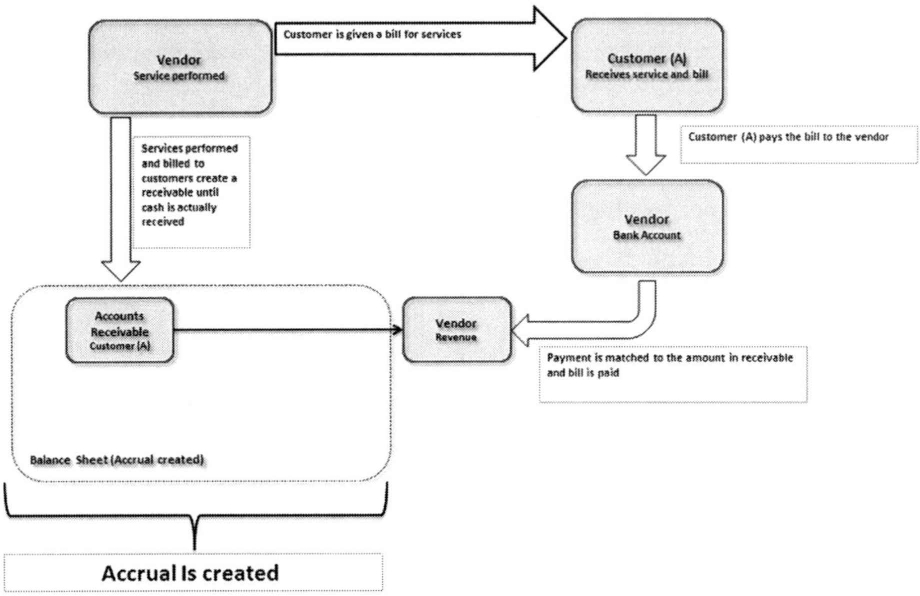

Figure 8-2. This figure shows the creation of the accrual and the bill payment

A cash accounting method only counts income when money is received. It does not keep track of accounts receivable, which means there is a direct compensation between the customer and vendor, as in Figure 8-3.

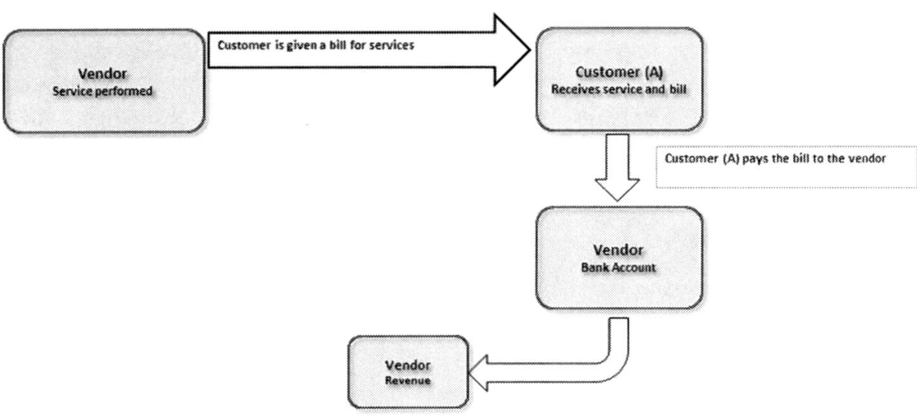

Figure 8-3. The cash accounting takes the cash directly with no accounts receivable

However, in real life, small businesses tend to use both methods without realizing the difference until income tax time when they use an accounting general ledger item to manage their finances. This general ledger system (GL) can handle both accrual and cash-based accounting. Almost all GL systems will allow users to create a setup where they can choose which type of accounting method to use. By and large, most businesses today use some kind of GL system for their accounting.

Accounts

The accounting system uses accounts to keep track of information. Consider this simple way to understanding accounts. In your office, you usually keep a filing cabinet. In this filing cabinet, you have multiple file folders, and each file folder gives information for a specific topic only. For example, you may have a file for utility bills, phone bills, employee wages, bank deposits, bank loans, and so forth.

A chart of accounts is like a filing cabinet. Each account in this chart is similar to a file folder. Accounts keep track of money spent, earned, owned, or owed. Each account keeps track of a specific topic only. For example, the money in your bank or the checking account would be recorded in an account called "Cash in Bank." The value of your office furniture would be stored in another account. Likewise, the amount you borrowed from a bank would be stored in a separate account.

Each account has a balance representing the value of the item as an amount of money. Accounts are divided into several categories, such as assets, liabilities, income, and expense accounts. A successful business will generally have more assets than liabilities. Income and expense accounts keep track of where your money comes from and how it is spent. This helps make sure you always have more assets than liabilities.

Account Types

In order to track money within an organization, different types of accounting categories exist. These categories are used to denote if the money is owned or owed by the organization. In these next sections, I will discuss the three main categories: assets, liabilities, and capital.

Assets

An asset is a property of value owned by a business. Physical objects and intangible rights—money, accounts receivable, merchandise, machinery, buildings, and inventories for sale—are common examples of business assets because they have economic value for the owner. Accounts receivable is an unwritten promise by a client to pay later for goods sold or services rendered.

Assets are mostly listed on a balance sheet according to the ease with which they can be converted to cash. They are usually divided into three main groups:

- Current
- Fixed
- Intangible

Current Assets

A current asset is an asset that is either

- Cash including funds in checking and savings accounts
- Marketable securities such as stocks, bonds, and similar investments
- Accounts receivables, which are amounts due from customers
- Notes receivables, which are promissory notes by customers to pay a definite sum plus interest on a definite date at a certain place
- Inventories such as raw materials or merchandise on hand
- Prepaid expenses like supplies on hand and services paid for but not yet used (e.g., prepaid insurance)

In other words, cash and other items that can be turned back into cash within a year are considered a current asset.

Fixed Assets

Fixed assets refer to tangible assets that are used for the business. Commonly, fixed assets are long-lived resources that are used during the production of finished goods. Examples include buildings, land, equipment, furniture, and fixtures. These assets are often included among the title property, plant, and equipment that are used in running a business. The following four qualities are usually required for an item to be classified as a fixed asset:

- Tangible
- Long-lived
- Used in the business
- Not available for sale

Certain long-lived assets such as machinery, cars, or equipment slowly wear out or become obsolete. The cost of such assets is systematically spread over its estimated useful life. This process is called depreciation if the asset involved is a tangible object (such as a building) or amortization if the asset involved is an intangible asset (such as a patent). Of the different kinds of fixed assets, only land does not depreciate.

Intangible Assets

Intangible assets are assets that are not physical assets like equipment and machinery but are valuable because they can be licensed or sold outright to others. They include the cost of organizing a business, obtaining copyrights, registering trademarks, securing patents on an invention or process, and valuing goodwill. Goodwill is not entered as an asset unless the business has been purchased. It is the least tangible of all the assets because it is the price a purchaser is willing to pay for a company's reputation, especially in its relations with customers.

Liabilities

A liability is a legal obligation of a business to pay a debt. Debts can be paid with money, goods, or services, but they are usually paid in cash. The most common liabilities are notes payable and accounts payable. Accounts payable is an unwritten promise to pay suppliers or lenders specified sums of money at a definite future date.

Current Liabilities

These are liabilities that are due within a relatively short period of time. The term "current liability" is used to designate obligations where the payment is expected within the next 12 months.

Current liabilities include, accounts payable, notes payable, and accrued expenses. Current liabilities reflect money that is owed to people or organizations by the company, and that must be paid shortly.

Accounts Payable

Accounts payable is are a general liability resulting from buying goods and services on credit. The goods are received and the money for them is paid to the supplier at later date, creating the payable item.

Suppose a business borrows $28,000 from the bank for a 120-day period. The instant the money is lent by the bank, the business incurs a liability of $28,000 plus interest. This is a note payable (must be paid back). The bank may require a written promise to pay before lending any amount, although there are many credit plans such as revolving credit where the promise to pay back is not in note form.

On the other hand, suppose the business purchases supplies from the ABC Company for $15,000 and agrees to pay within 30 days. Upon acquiring title to the goods, the business has an accounts payable liability (owes the money and must make good the amount) to the ABC Company.

In both cases, the business has become a debtor and owes money to a creditor. Other current liabilities commonly found on the balance sheet include salaries payable, interest payable, and taxes payable, which are all accrued expenses. These are expenses that have been incurred, but for which the bills have not yet been received.

Long-term Liabilities

Long-term liabilities are obligations that will not become due for a comparatively long period of time. The usual rule of thumb is that long-term liabilities are not due within one year. These include such things as bonds payable, mortgage notes payable, and any other debts that do not have to be paid within one year.

You should note that as the long-term obligations come within the one-year range, they become current liabilities. For example, mortgage is a long-term debt, and payment is spread over a number of years. However, the monthly mortgage payments that are due within one year of the date of the balance sheet are classified as a current liability.

Capital

Capital, also called net worth, is essentially what would be left over if you paid off everyone the company owes money to. If there are no business liabilities, the capital, net worth, or owner's equity is equal to the total amount of the assets of the business.

Key Accounting Concepts

There are two fundamental accounting concepts that were developed centuries ago but remain central in the accounting process:

- The accounting equation
- Double entry system

The Accounting Equation

To put it simply, the accounting equation keeps all the business accounts in balance. In this section, this equation will be explained in steps to clarify your understanding of this concept.

In order to start a business, the owner usually has to put some money down to finance the business operations. Since the owner provides this money, it is called owner's equity. In addition, this money is an asset for the company. This can be represented by the following equation:

Assets = Owner's Equity

If the owner of the business was to close down this business, he would receive all its assets. Let's say that the owner decides to accept a loan from the bank. When the business decides to accept the loan, the assets would increase by the amount of the loan. In addition, this loan is also a liability for the company. This transaction can be represented by the following equation:

Assets = Liabilities + Owner's Equity

Now the assets of the company consist of the money invested by the owner (the owner's equity) and the loan taken from the bank (a liability). The company's liabilities are placed before the owner's equity because creditors have first claim on assets.

If the business was to close down, after the liabilities are paid off, anything left over (assets) would belong to the owner.

The Double-Entry System

As mentioned earlier in this chapter, today's accounting principles are based upon a system created more than 500 years ago by an Italian monk named Fra Luca Pacioli. Pacioli devised this method of keeping books, which is today known as the double-entry system of accounting. He explained that every time a transaction took place—whether it was a sale or a collection—there were two offsetting sides. The entry required a two-part "give-and-get" entry for each transaction.

Here is a simple explanation of the double-entry system. Continuing with the earlier example, let's say that you took a loan from the bank for $5,000. Remember that the following equation was used in our earlier discussion:

Assets = Liabilities + Owner's Equity

Because the company borrowed money from the bank, the $5,000 is a liability against the company. In addition, now that the company has the extra $5,000, this money is an asset for the company. If you were to record this information in your accounts, you would put $5,000 in an account called "Loan Taken from the Bank," and $5,000 in an account called "Cash Saved in the Bank." The former account will be a liability, and the second account would be an asset. As you can see, two entries were created. The first one is to show from where the money was received (the source of the money). The second entry is to show where the money was sent (the destination of the money received).

In a double-entry accounting system, every transaction is recorded in the form of debits and credits. Even for the simplest double-entry transaction, there will be a debit and a credit. In simpler terms, a debit is the application of money, and a credit is the source of money.

Here are some examples to help you understand the concept of debits and credits:

Example One

You write a check for $100 to purchase some stationery. This transaction would be recorded as a credit of $100 to the Cash in the Bank account, and a debit of $100 to the Stationery account. In this case, you made a credit to the Cash in the Bank account, as it was the source of the money. The stationery account was debited, as it was the application of the money.

Example Two

You receive $200 cash for services rendered to a client. This transaction would be recorded as a credit of $200 to the Income from Services account, and a debit of $200 to the Cash in the Bank account. In this case, you made a credit to the Income from Services account, as it was the source of the money. The Cash in the Bank account was debited, as it was the application of the money.

Example Three

You receive a $10,000 loan from a bank. This transaction would be recorded as a credit of $10,000 to the Loan Payable account, and a debit of $10,000 to the Cash in the Bank account. In this case, you made a credit to the Loan Payable account, as it was the source of the money. The Cash in the Bank account was debited, as it was the application of the money.

Example Four

You made out a payroll check to an employee for $300. This transaction would be recorded as a credit of $300 to the Cash in the Bank account, and a debit of $300 to the Payroll Expense account. In this case, you made a credit to the Cash in the Bank account, as it was the source of the money. The Payroll Expense account was debited, as it was the application of the money.

The previous examples illustrated some of the transactions that are recorded in a double-entry accounting system. These transactions are also referred to as journal entries. Your accounting application automatically creates the journal entries for you. In Example One, you would create a check in the system, and on the check, you would give the expense account number for stationery. The checkbook program would then automatically credit the cash account and debit the stationery expense account.

Journals

Looking at the ledger account alone, it is difficult to trace back all the accounts that were affected by a transaction. For this reason, another book is used to record each transaction as it takes place and to show all the accounts affected by the transaction. This book is called the general journal, or journal.

Each transaction is first recorded in the journal, and then the applicable entries are made to the accounts in the GL. Because the journal is the first place a transaction is recorded, it is called the book of original entry. The advantage of the journal is that it shows all the accounts that are affected by a transaction and the amounts the proper accounts are debited and credited—all in one place. Furthermore, included with each transaction is an explanation of what the transaction is for. Transactions are recorded in the journal as they take place, so the journal is a chronological record of all transactions conducted by the business.

There is a standard format for recording transactions in the journal. A journal transaction usually consists of the following:

- Journal transaction number
- Transaction date
- Journal type (general journal, sales journal, and so forth)
- Actual journal entries adjusting the account balances

In addition to the general journal, other specialized journals contain entries from other accounting modules to track sales, purchases, and the disbursement of cash. Some of the important journals include the following:

- Invoice journal report
- Cash receipts report
- Purchases journal
- A/P journal (transactions and payments) report

The GL system comes with sample chart of accounts already installed. If you prefer, you can modify these accounts or create your own chart of accounts. In addition, all the debits, credits, and journals are automatically maintained for you. When you create invoices, checks, and other transactions through the system, all the journal entries are created for you automatically.

In this chapter, I have touched on some of the more important aspects of accounting to give you just an introduction to accounting. At some point in modeling, you will need to have an appreciation of at the very least the basics of accounting. The further you develop your modeling, the more likely that you will need to also further develop your appreciation for accounting. Many modelers are not accountants, but all modelers should have at least a basic understanding of accounting principles. My advice is that you go through the concepts in this chapter again until you feel familiar with them.

CHAPTER

9

Managing and Evaluating a Business for Modelers

In order to control an organization, the finance person must manage key areas. These areas include cash, sales, income, expenses, assets, inventory, and payroll. These areas are so intrinsic to an organization's financial wellbeing that most models will encompass one or more of them.

The landscape of financial modeling has moved greatly in recent years to the extent that a modeler is very often required to demonstrate a depth of awareness and understanding in several areas of finance. This chapter covers these areas.

Managing Cash

Managing cash is about managing the cash flow of an organization. That means keeping abreast of incoming and outgoing cash. Simply put, failure to manage cash will cause the organization to grind to a halt. At the grass roots level, it is impossible to manage cash unless you know where and when your money is being spent, and that means coming to grips with bank accounts and physical cash in the organization. I will discuss aspects of managing bank accounts, as well as bank reconciliations and petty cash.

These topics may seem too removed from the modeler, as they are performed by finance people, but I would urge you spend some time to understand them. At some point, every modeler will be required to create a cash flow forecast, and it's always helpful to have an understanding of the bank accounts and cash, because almost every transaction in the cash flow affects them.

Bank Reconciliation

Typically, a business will use a bank checking account to help control the flow of cash. Cash received during the day is deposited periodically in the bank account, and checks are written from the account whenever cash is paid out.

When the bank account is opened, each authorized person signs a signature card. The bank can use the signature card at any time to make sure that the signature on the check is authentic and that money can be paid out of the account.

When cash is deposited into the account, a deposit ticket is filled out listing the check number and the amount of each check and any additional currency.

As the business makes payments, it will write checks on the bank account and record each check payment in the checkbook or on the check stub. Every month, the bank will send the business a bank statement, along with the canceled checks paid that month. The bank statement shows the balance at the beginning of the month, each check paid, any deposits, other charges or credits to the account, and the balance at the end of the month.

Usually the ending balance on the bank statement will not match the current cash account balance shown in the checkbook. This is because there may be checks that have been written and recorded in the checkbook but have not yet been processed and paid by the bank. The bank may also have deducted from the bank statement balance a service charge or other charges that have not yet been recorded and deducted from the checkbook balance.

For this reason, it is necessary at the end of each month to reconcile your bank statement. This is simply the process of making the proper adjustments to both the bank statement balance and to the checkbook balance to prove that they do in fact balance.

There are three steps to reconciling your bank statement:

- Step 1: Compare the deposits shown in the checkbook with those shown on the bank statement. Any deposits not yet shown on the bank statement are deposits in transit. In other words, they are not yet received and recorded by the bank. Subtract the total of the deposits in transit from the final balance in your checkbook.
- Step 2: Compare the canceled checks as shown on the bank statement with those recorded as written in the checkbook. Checks that have been written but not yet processed and paid by the banks are called outstanding checks. Add the total of the outstanding checks to the final balance in your checkbook.
- Step 3: Now look at the bank statement and see if there are any service charges or credits that have not yet been recorded in the checkbook. Add the credits and subtract the charges from the final balance of your checkbook. The adjusted balance of your checkbook will now be equal to the ending balance on the bank statement.

All the checks and deposits were once entered in a specific accounting system element, called a cash book, which checked all the transactions. The term *cash book* relates to physical book that was used to record all the cash transactions of an organization on a daily basis. At the end of each day, those transactions were totaled and the date was then registered with that total. Nowadays, the cash books are automated and they are part of larger, computerized accounting system called the general ledger (GL). The GL handles just about all aspects of an organization's accounting needs.

Petty Cash

As we discussed earlier, the principal method for maintaining internal control of cash is by using a checking account. However, a business usually has insignificant expenses, such as postage or minor purchases of supplies that are easier to pay for with currency rather than with a check.

To handle these minor expenses, a petty cash fund is set up. A small amount of money, say $100, is placed in a petty cashbox or drawer, and an individual is given responsibility for the funds. This individual is the petty cashier. When money is needed for an expense, the cashier prepares a petty cash ticket, which shows the date, amount, and purpose of the expense and includes the signature of the person receiving the money. This ticket is then placed in the petty cashbox. At any time, the total amount of cash in the box plus the complete amount of all tickets should equal the original fixed amount of cash originally placed inside the box.

As expenditures are made, the petty cash fund will eventually need to be replenished. This is usually done by writing a check to bring the amount in the fund back to the original amount of $100.

Managing Sales

The sales of an organization constitute the income earned and are the main driver for the existence of the business. Sales reflect the products and services sold to customers. The customers will typically pay for them either by paying in cash or check, or on account (credit terms).

Cash Sales

Some businesses sell merchandise for cash only, while others sell merchandise either for cash or on account. A variety of practices are followed in the handling of cash sales. If such transactions are numerous, it is probable that one or more types of cash registers will be used. In this instance, the original record of the sales is made in the register.

Often, registers have the capability of accumulating more than one total. This means that by using the proper key, each amount that is punched in the register can be classified by type of merchandise, department, or salesperson. Where sales tax is involved, the amount of the tax may be separately recorded. In accounting terms, a cash sale means that the asset cash is increased by a debit, while sales and the liability account sales tax payable are credited.

In many retail establishments, the procedure in handling cash sales is for the salesclerks to prepare sales tickets in triplicate. Sometimes the preparation of the sales tickets involves the use of a cash register that prints the amount of the sale directly on the ticket. Modern electronic cash registers serve as input terminals that are online with computers and in direct communication with the central processor. At the end of each day, the cash received is compared with the record that the register provides. The receipts may also be compared with the total of the cash sales tickets, if the system makes use of the latter.

Sales on Account

Sales on account are often referred to as charge sales because the seller exchanges merchandise for the buyer's promise to pay. In accounting terms, this means that the asset accounts receivable of the seller is increased by a debit or charge, and the income account "Sales" is increased by a credit.

Selling goods on account is a common practice at the retail level of the distribution process. Firms that sell goods on account, however, should investigate the financial reliability of their clients. A business of some size may have a separate credit department whose major function is to establish credit policies and decide upon requests for credit from persons and firms who wish to buy goods on account.

Seasoned judgment is needed to avoid a credit policy that is so stringent that profitable businesses may be refused, or a credit policy that is so liberal that uncollectable account losses may become excessive.

Generally, no goods are delivered until the salesclerk is assured that the buyer has established credit. The client must have an established account with the company. In the case of many retail businesses, clients with established credit are provided with credit cards or charge plates, which provide evidence that the buyer has an account. These are used in mechanical or electronic devices to print the client's name and other identification on the sales tickets. In the case of merchants who commonly receive a large portion of their orders by mail or by phone, this confirmation of the buyer's status can be handled as a matter of routine before the goods are delivered.

Managing Income

The income of an organization is derived from its business activities and also from other activities that are incidental to the organization's existence such as selling old assets or receiving interest from the bank for money held in deposit accounts. The simple fact is that without income, an organization will ultimately have to close. Therefore, income management is not just important, it's a critical discipline.

The activities that are part of income management are:

- Performance of the business activity which will earn income.
- Creating the invoice or bill of sale of the activity performed.
- Sending the invoice and getting acceptance from the customer.
- Collecting the money from the customer for the invoice.
- Depositing the money received from the customer into a bank account.
- Recording the transaction into the organization's accounting system

- Monitoring the full history of every business activity
- Applying the correct regulatory and financial rules to the income.

These steps are managed by finance and accounting people and, while all these steps are fairly standard and generally understood by accountants, the final step (applying the correct regulatory and financial rules) is one that presents the most difficulties because it is about revenue recognition. Revenue recognition is a complicated mechanism and would take far too long to fully explore in this book, but in essence it is an accounting principle that defines when (in the organization's financial calendar) income can be booked or realized as revenue. Income can generally only be recognized as revenue when the organization has completed the performance of a service or delivered its product to customer and has received payment for that performance or product.

There are major tax implications connected to revenue recognition, which again I won't explore. However this principle can have an effect on how a modeler designs the income calculations in models, particularly when building models that have long-range income projected to span several financial years. I would advise you to familiarize yourself with the IASB (International Accounting Standards Board) and FASB (The US Financial Accounting Standards Board) IAS18 standard on *revenue* and also the IFRS (International Financial Reporting Standards) standard IFRIC 18 *transfer of assets from customers.*

Managing Expenses

The expense authorization system is a commonly used method to keep track of and control expenses. It is based on the use of tickets. These tickets are written authorizations prepared for each expense.

With this system, before a check is written, a ticket is prepared authorizing payment. This system provides control over expenses. It does this by making sure that each expense is justified and requiring more than one person to be responsible for preparing and authorizing the payment. A ticket is prepared for every transaction that results in an expense.

When an invoice for a purchase is received, it is attached to a ticket, which is then filled out and signed. The information that goes on the front side of the ticket verifies the information from the invoice. Once the information is verified, an approval signature is required to authorize the expense. Once the ticket is approved, it is recorded in an expense register.

Tickets are recorded in the register in date order. Once recorded, the ticket is put into an unpaid tickets file where it remains until it is paid. The tickets are filed according to the date they should be paid in order to take advantage of discounts.

When it comes time to pay a ticket, it is removed from the unpaid tickets file, and a check is issued. The check number and payment date are recorded on the ticket and in the ticket register next to that ticket entry. Each ticket is paid by check. As each ticket is paid, the payment is recorded in the check register. With the ticket system, the check register is the book of original entry for recording payments, and it takes the place of a cash payments journal.

In a computerized accounting system, the function for controlling expenses is controlled by the accounts payable program. You would enter, track, and pay your invoices with accounts payable.

Managing Assets

The assets of an organization are split into *tangible*, which are broadly physical assets such as computer equipment, vehicles, property, or machinery, and *intangibles*, which are assets that are more conceptual, such as goodwill, patents, or intellectual property.

Assets can also further be split between fixed assets (tangible and intangible) and current assets, which are those items that are available to the organization a relatively short time such as money in the bank account or accounts receivable.

Managing these assets involves addressing a number of specific disciplines such as:

- Asset tracking
- Amortization and depreciation policies
- Asset valuation principles
- Asset replacement and refresh policies
- Asset management (handling investments)
- Leasing arrangements
- Capital allowances and taxation rules for assets

For modelers, the ability to create models that can provide for the items above is very challenging. For instance, creating an asset tracking model almost certainly requires the modeler to have skills in developing models that can be integrated into live database systems in order to download data.

Managing Inventory

Inventory management is the process of controlling the constant flow of items into and out of some domain called an inventory. The aim of inventory management is to prevent the inventory from becoming too large, which means the organization is spending money on items that are not generating any income, or becoming too low, which could then interrupt the organization's operations.

Merchandise Inventory

Merchandise inventories are the goods that are on hand for the production process or available for sale to final customers. There are two basic methods for determining inventory:

- Perpetual inventory method
- Periodic inventory method

With the perpetual inventory method, the cost of each item in the inventory is recorded when purchased. When an item is sold, its cost is deducted from the inventory. This results in a perpetual record of exactly what is in inventory.

This method is best suited for businesses that have a relatively low number of sales each day and whose merchandise has a high unit value. For example, a car dealer might use the perpetual inventory method to keep track of inventory because it's easy to keep track of each item as it is purchased by the business and then resold.

For businesses that manually track inventory value, it would be impractical to adjust the cost of inventory each time an item is sold. Instead, these types of businesses use the periodic inventory method, which involves periodically taking a physical count of the merchandise on hand. This is usually done once a year at the end of the accounting period.

Once the physical count is done, the exact quantity of merchandise immediately available is known. The different costs of all the available items are then totaled to give a total cost of the inventory on hand at the end of the year.

Calculating Inventory Value

A company can raise or lower its earnings by changing the way it calculates the cost of goods sold. As inventory items are purchased during the accounting period, their unit cost may vary. A costing method is a way of calculating the cost of goods sold. The first time you purchase a product, the value is whatever you paid. Once you receive more stock at a different price, it is necessary to use one of three standard methods to determine the value of what you sell:

- First in, first out (FIFO)
- Last in, first out (LIFO)
- Average cost

First in, First out (FIFO)

This method assumes that the first items to come into the inventory are the initial items sold, so the most recent unit cost is used to determine the inventory's value. FIFO assumes that the oldest stock you have is sold first. At a time when your cost is constantly increasing, the first items sold are the least expensive ones; therefore, your cost of goods sold is low and your income is greater.

Last in, First out (LIFO)

This method assumes that the last items to come into the inventory are the first items sold, so the oldest unit cost is used to determine the inventory's value. With LIFO, the newest stock is sold first. An inventory value should generally reflect the replacement cost of your stock, and that is what LIFO does. When prices are increasing, The inventory management system will calculate cost of goods sold at the most recent price, resulting in a higher cost of goods and lower income.

Average Cost

This method uses the average unit cost for all items that were available for sale during the accounting period. The average method is the total cost of all goods divided by the number in stock. This has the effect of leveling out price fluctuations, providing a constant cost of goods and income.

Managing Payroll

Payroll is about the welfare of the human resources in organizations. As well as managing the payments of salaries and wages, payroll is also about managing employee benefits, insurances, taxes, and pensions. As a result, payroll management is quite a specialist field and requires skills that are very particular.

It is not uncommon to build models that have to consider staffing implications such as salaries, pensions, insurance, and taxes, particularly when building an outsourcing model that requires staff to be transferred between organizations.

It is vitally important, when modeling payroll, that the modeler can utilize a specialist in human resources, because there are always complex statutory and regulatory issues relating to staff. It is unlikely that the modeler has the requisite background to model effectively.

Break-Even Point

One of the first steps in evaluating a business is determining the break-even point. This is the number of units that must be sold for income to equal all expenses incurred in producing the merchandise.

The concept of breakeven is very important for any business as it provides a view of the level of sales required for the business to survive and ultimately make profit. In modeling terms, understanding the concept of breakeven is crucial for the modeler to understand how to calculate.

Break-even analysis is the calculation process that is used to find the break-even point of a business. Again, that is the point where the sales are enough to cover the costs.

Let's take a step back and look at costs. In business, costs can be categorized in two types. The first is fixed costs, which are the costs that are always present irrespective of the level of business-generated costs such as rent, insurance, lease equipment charges, some federal and government taxes, and some types of wages and salaries.

The second type is variable costs, which are costs that change in relation to business activity such as materials, suppliers, freight charges, or billable staff.

The key to calculating how many sales will be needed to cover costs and thus breakeven is to find the contribution. The contribution is a term used to describe the difference between the variable costs per unit and the selling price per unit. In Figure 9-1a, the variable cost per unit is $11 and the selling price is $15 per unit. The contribution is therefore the selling price subtracted from the less variable cost, which is $4.

G10 =G9-G5

	A	B	C	D	E	F	G
1							
2		Non Such corporation					
3		Breakeven					
4					Per month	Units	Per unit
5				Total variable cost	$55,000	5,000	11
6				Total fixed cost	$25,000		
7					$80,000		
8							
9				Selling price per unit			15
10				Contribution			4
11							

Figure 9-1a. The difference between the variable cost per unit and the selling price per unit is the contribution

Now that we have the contribution of $4 per unit, the question is how many units do we need to sell to make sure that we can cover the fixed cost, which is $25,000?

In Figure 9-1b, the calculation to find the number of units that constitute the break-even point is included: the total fixed cost of $25,000 divided by the contribution of $4 per unit, which is E6/G10.

F12 =E6/G10

	A	B	C	D	E	F	G
1							
2		Non Such corporation					
3		Breakeven					
4					Per month	Units	Per unit
5				Total variable cost	$55,000	5,000	11
6				Total fixed cost	$25,000		
7					$80,000		
8							
9				Selling price per unit			15
10				Contribution			4
11							
12				Units required to Breakeven		6,250	

Figure 9-1b. The break-even point is the fixed cost divided by the contribution, which is calculated in cell F12 at 6,250 units

The break-even point is represented in number of units that are required to be sold, which is the 6,250 units shown in cell F12.

It is important for a business to understand its break-even point because the contribution from every unit sold above this point adds to profit. Not only does the break-even point provide a focus for the business, it also helps the business work out whether the forecast sales will be enough to produce a profit and whether further investment in the product is worthwhile.

Financial Statements

In order to manage a business or project effectively, you need to have reports that can provide clarity on business performance. For example, you may want to know the value of your assets like cash you have on hand, cash in bank, and inventory in stock. In addition, you would want to know the value of your liabilities, loans, income earned, and expenses incurred. Two of the most important reports for managing your business are thus the income statement and the balance sheet.

Be careful not to underestimate the importance of producing sound financial statements. One of the most damaging impacts of the financial model is when a modeling project fails to deliver operationally in the real world, and it simply fails. Many times this happens because the modeler lacks understanding and knowledge of financial statements.

Financial statements are the principal means of reporting financial information to people within an organization. To have a functional understanding of finance, it is essential to thoroughly understand income statements, cash flow statements, and balance sheets.

The Income Statement

The income statement is an integral component of any business's financial statements. It shows how revenue is converted into net income by displaying the revenues recognized for a specific period, and then by subtracting the costs and expenses from these revenues (including depreciation, interest, and taxes).

The income statement shows internal and external stakeholders whether the business made or lost money during the reporting period. A fundamental requirement of any modeler is to have a very good understanding of the income statement; it's unlikely that you will avoid having to create one. Another reason why you should be totally conversant with the income statement is that you will likely be required to communicate this statement to an audience and describe the meaning of the results. Figure 9-2 is an example of a typical income statement.

Income Statement for the Year Ending December 2013
(In 1,000s)

Sales Revenue		40,521
Less: Returns and Allowance		340
Net Sales Revenue		**40,181**
Direct Costs		
Supplies & Services		30,250
Direct Labor		6,035
Insurance		125
Risk		360
		36,770
Gross Profit		**3,411**
Operating Expenses		
Selling Expenses		290
Salaries		644
Admin Expenses		540
Overheads		890
		2,364
EBITDA		**1,047**
Depreciation		195
EBIT		**852**
Interest - Paid/(Received)		78
Profit Before Taxation		**774**
Corporation Tax		73
Profit After Taxation		**701**

Figure 9-2. This figure is a sample income statement

Often called the profit and loss statement (P&L), or statement of operations, the income statement shows the performance of a business over a period of time (a month, quarter, or year). Here is the basic formula for determining performance:

Revenues – Expenses = Income

This report summarizes all income (or sales), the amounts that have been or will be received from customers for goods delivered or services rendered to them, and all expenses (the costs that have arisen in generating revenues).

To show the actual profit or loss of a company, the expenses are subtracted from the revenues to determine the net income, which can also be reported as EBITDA (earnings before interest, taxation, depreciation, and taxation).

Income accounts are accounts that are used to track income earned during the process of operating the business. The income of a business comes from sales to customers or fees for services or both.

The income statement always begins with revenues. This is how $25,000 in revenue would look on the income statement:

Revenues *$25,000*

The next item is direct costs or cost of goods sold, which is normally the manufacturing cost or purchase price of the goods, freight from the supplier, royalties, and so forth. Direct cost is subtracted from revenue to show gross profit. If we assume the direct cost is $20,000 and we subtract this from the revenue of $25,000, the gross profit is $5,000. Gross profit, sometimes called gross margin, is the amount left over before deducting operating expenses and taxes. The added items would appear on the income statement as follows:

Revenues	*$25,000*
Direct cost	*$20,000*
Gross profit	*$ 5,000*

The next entries that go on an income statement are the expenses connected with running the business. These are usually referred to as operating expenses, and they include such items as rent, utilities, office supplies, and overhead. Operating expenses can be both cash and accrued. When they are subtracted from gross profit, you are left with operating income.

Sometimes businesses have sources of income that are not part of the principal business, such as interest income from a bank account. When this is the case, it is considered as "other incomes" and is listed individually after operating income. Income taxes are normally listed separately on the income statement. The words "income," "profit" and "earnings" are often used synonymously on income statements.

In the following example, expenses totaling $184,200 are identified.

Salaries	*$125,900*
Utilities	*$4,500*
Rent	*$23,000*
Office supplies	*$1,900*
General overhead	*$28,900*

Note A glossary of income statement terminology is included in Appendix B.

Cash Flow Statement

With the accrual method of accounting, sales are recorded on the income statement when the goods and/or services associated with those sales are delivered or shipped to a customer. The direct costs are recorded on the income statement at the same time the revenues are recorded. Revenues and direct costs are recorded regardless of when the business receives cash for the goods delivered or when the business had to pay cash for the expense associated with the cost of the goods sold.

Here is an example. A hardware store owner orders two electric lawn mowers in order to resell them. The lawn mowers are delivered in March, and the owner must pay for them ($100, plus $10 delivery, for each mower) in April. He sells one mower to Mr. Jones in March for $180; Mr. Jones pays by check. The other mower doesn't sell until June to a credit customer who does not have to pay until July. What is the effect of these transactions on the hardware store's cash and income?

Even though total cash taken in equals total sales and the total cash paid out equals cost of goods sold, there is a difference in the timing of when cash and income are recognized. It is not just important for the modeler to know this timing difference but to also make sure that the models that are built reflect these timings in such a way that the model users will also understand it. Even though a business may show a profit on the income statement, it cannot continue as a business unless it has the cash flow necessary to pay its bills. Cash is the lifeblood of every business.

The cash flow statement is the most popular method of calculating and showing the cash situation of a business or project, although there are several formats that can be used. Figure 9-3 shows a typical monthly cash flow statement.

Sample Cash Flow Statement

	Annual Budget	Month 1 Forecast	Month 2 Forecast	Month 3 Forecast
Cash In (Sources)				
Beginning Cash Balance	-	-	2,850	203,750
Cash Sales	1,500,000	-	175,000	185,000
Interest Received	15,000	-	2,300	4,600
Contributions from Owners	540,000	170,000	300,000	-
Loans/Borrowed Money	423,000	25,000	-	-
Total Receipts	**2,478,000**	**195,000**	**480,150**	**393,350**
Cash Out (Uses)				
Inventory	(70,000)	-	-	
Operating Expenses	(818,000)	(67,000)	(74,500)	(78,100)
Furniture and Fixtures	(200,000)	(79,000)	(91,000)	-
Equipment	(95,000)	(25,000)	(60,500)	-
Interest Paid		(21,150)	(22,400)	(22,400)
Income Taxes	(100,000)	-	(28,000)	(30,000)
Distributions to Owners	-	-	-	
Total Disbursements	(1,283,000)	(192,150)	(276,400)	(130,500)
Ending Balance	**1,195,000**	**2,850**	**203,750**	**262,850**

Figure 9-3. This figure shows a sample cash flow statement

In any business, a lack of cash, even for a short time, can force a business to close. A cash shortage is very difficult for a business to overcome. To foresee and hopefully avoid cash flow problems, it is a good practice to maintain a cash flow statement.

The balance sheet shows the health of a business as of a specific date. An income statement tells how a business performed over a period of time. Instead of looking back, you can use the cash flow statement as a planning tool to help you in the future. This statement will help you target when cash will be needed to pay bills and help managers to make business decisions, such as when to expand a business or take on a new product line. The cash flow statement only deals with cash activity: cash paid out and cash taken in. It also helps identify those periods when borrowing should be considered and allows you to make arrangements before cash is actually needed. Preplanning is very helpful when working with bankers.

An estimated cash flow statement should be made during the budgeting process for the year of operations. The year can be broken down by quarter or month to provide greater control. The cash flow statement should include as much detail as possible without making it too cluttered. Importantly, get as many line item details in the statement as you can; that will provide greater transparency than a summarized version.

The Balance Sheet

The balance sheet (Figure 9-4) is also called the statement of condition or statement of financial position. It is a snapshot that gives you the overall picture of the monetary health of a company at one moment in time. This report lists the assets, liabilities, and owner's equity in the business. Unlike the income statement, this report is always created to show the financial status as of a certain date. Balance sheet are usually created at two ending periods: the end of a month and the end of the year. Again, the balance sheet is a snapshot in time and will only reflect the accounts as of that time. When creating outputs of the balance sheet, be careful that the date of the balance sheet is always clearly shown and understood. Balance sheets change, often daily, and for that reason can very quickly become obsolete.

Balance sheet as at: 13-Oct-2013	
Fixed Assets	
Buildings	305,000
Leasehold Improvements (Less Depreciation)	28,400
Vehicles (Less Depreciation)	30,000
Total Fixed Assets	**363,400**
Current Assets	
Cash/Deposits	26,600
Bank	95,000
Receivables	48,300
Prepayments	16,400
Inventory	155,500
	341,800
Total Assets	**705,200**
Current Liabilities	
Payables	(58,400)
Tax Payable	(14,300)
Short-term Loans	(35,000)
	(107,700)
Long-term Liabilities	
Bank Loans Payable	(39,300)
Notes Payable to Shareholders	(15,000)
Total long-term Liabilities	**(54,300)**
Total Liabilities	**(162,000)**
Owner's Equity	
Capital Invested	(200,000)
Retained Earnings	(343,200)
Total Owner's Equity	**(543,200)**
Total Liabilities & Equity	**(705,200)**

Figure 9-4. A sample balance sheet

Why Is It Called a Balance Sheet?

The key word is balance. The total assets must equal the total liabilities plus the net worth. This is true even if the liabilities exceed the assets. In this case, net worth becomes negative, and it must be subtracted from the liabilities instead of being added.

A balance sheet uses the principle of double-entry accounting. It is called double-entry (this was introduced in chapter 8) because each business action affects two or more accounts. For example, a sale will increase cash or accounts receivable but decrease inventory. An account can include the following: cash, inventory, money you owe (accounts payable) and money owed to you (accounts receivable). Accounts payable and accounts receivable are called accrual accounts. The balances in these accounts represent cash that must be paid to suppliers or will be received from customers at some future time.

The balance sheet has two sections. The first section lists all the asset accounts and their balances. At the end of the list, the totals of all assets are listed. In the second section, the liability and owner's equity accounts are listed. There are two subtotals for the liability and the equity accounts. At the end, there is a combined total of the liabilities and owner's equity. The profit or loss that comes from the income statement feeds into the retained earnings.

It is crucial to check on the balance sheet that the total assets and the total liabilities and owner's equity are in balance. If this is not the case, there are issues somewhere either with the income statement or cash flow statement.

Getting the balance sheet to balance seems to present problems for many modelers. From experience, the reason for this is generally somewhere in the calculation of cash there is an item which has an impact on the cash that has been omitted. If you recall during the discussion on cash flow statements, I mentioned that you should include as much detail as possible and use as many line item as you can. It's common to find that the reason the balance sheet won't balance is one of these line items in the cash flow statement has been excluded, and by doing that a vital number has also been omitted.

Some of the more important accounts in a balance sheet include the following:

- Current assets: These include cash and other items that can be converted into cash within the following year, such as funds in checking and savings accounts.
- Accounts receivable: This account represents money owed to the business. The accounts receivable are customer accounts that usually result from the sale of merchandise or performance of services for a client on account. The phrase "on account" indicates that on the

date the goods were sold to the client or the service performed for the client, the business did not receive full payment. However, it did obtain an asset—the right to collect payment for merchandise sold or services performed. The claim a business has against a credit client is referred to as an account receivable. It is an asset because it represents a legal claim to cash.

- Inventory: This account may represent merchandise purchased for resale as well as the raw materials acquired by a manufacturing firm to put into the product. In the case of a manufacturer, the term "inventories" also includes manufacturing supplies, purchased parts, the work that is in process, and finished goods. Inventory is also an asset account.
- Accounts payable: When you purchase goods or services on account, you are usually required to pay within a fixed period of time. These amounts you owe for the goods or services purchased are called accounts payable. The payment of these purchases is as a rule due within a relatively short period of time. Usually this period is one year or less. Typical periods are 30 to 60 days. The payment for these short-term liabilities requires the use of existing resources like the cash or checking account.

Why Net Worth Is Not Always the Same as Market Value

A fundamental principle of finance is that all business transactions are recorded on the balance sheet at the dollar value actually agreed upon at the time of the transaction. For example, in the balance sheet shows that the business purchased a building for $100,000. That is the dollar amount that appears on the company's balance sheet under the buildings account regardless of how the building was financed (all cash vs. long-term debt) and regardless of what the building is appraised at or worth today.

Recording all business transactions at their historic costing method used on all transactions. For this reason, the net worth of a company shown on the balance sheet should not be confused with the sales or appraised value. Net worth or stockholders' equity on the balance sheet merely reflects the difference between assets and liabilities.

Introduction to Ratios

In this section, I will cover several common ratios that can be used to measure and control a business. These ratios are not prescriptive, hence not all of them will be of use to every organization. It's a matter of the modeler and the customer being able to select the ratios that are suitable. I have let this section on ratios come after the financial statements, in particular the balance sheet, because with many ratios you will need to have details from the financial statements to complete the ratio.

The simplest and most auditable method of calculating ratios is to first make all the calculations for the financial statements in the calculations worksheet, and then create the ratio calculations (in the worksheet) by referring to the statement item. The ratio outputs will then be links to the ratio calculations. It is not necessary to memorize the ratios or their meanings presented because you can always return to this part of the book for reference.

The first set of ratios is called liquidity ratios, which measure the amount of cash available to cover expenses both current and long-term. These ratios are especially important in keeping a business alive. Not paying your bills due to a shortage of cash is the fastest way to go out of business. Lending institutions often don't want to loan money when it is actually needed the most. Make arrangements ahead of time for a line of credit. The best time to do this is when your business liquidity looks very good. (Make sure your line-of-credit agreement is always in writing!)

The second set of ratios is called profitability ratios. These ratios measure and help control income. This is done through higher sales, larger margins, getting more from your expenses, and/or a combination of these methods.

The third set of ratios is called efficiency ratios, which measure and help control the operation of the business. They add another dimension to help you increase income by assessing such important transactions as the use of credit, control of inventory, and/or management of assets.

The fourth set of ratios is called market ratios. Market ratios are primarily used by investors to determine whether or not to purchase stock in a company. Several market ratios are reported on the stock pages of most daily newspapers. Although these ratios may not be prominent to many small businesses, it is important to know what they are and how to calculate them.

Why Ratio Analysis?

Ratios are common—you use them every day. They are important because they provide a better understanding of a wide range of situations. For instance, the miles you get per gallon of gasoline and the unemployment rate presented as ratios are easier to grasp than the whole number of gallons of gas used and the total number of unemployed people. Ratios are used when we look for the best price per ounce for food, compare batting averages of baseball players, or measure the cost of building in dollars per square foot.

In businesses, ratios are critically important because they measure the progress of a business and can be used to compare a business with its competitors.

How Ratios Are Developed

Ratios are expressed by placing one number over another number. For example, 50:100 is a ratio. It means that 50 is to be divided by 100. The answer will be a percentage. In this case, the answer is .50 or 50% because 50 is half of 100.

The number on top of a formula represents the figure you are comparing with the bottom figure (the base). For instance, if 50 in the previous ratio represents $50 in sales, and 100 represents $100 of fixed assets (such as a piece of equipment or fixture), you are then able to compare the amount of sales generated by the fixed assets, or 50%.

Another way to express the calculation is to use proportions. This means that sales to fixed assets is in the proportion of 1 to 2. If the numbers were reversed, the ratio would be 100:50. Then the sales would become $100 and the fixed assets would be $50. In this case, the fixed assets generated 200% or two times their value. In other words, 50 can go into 100 twice. The proportion of fixed assets to sales is now 1 to 2.

Ratios are used to indicate how a business is doing. They do not make decisions for you in themselves, but they do provide information to help you make sound decisions. When I build a model which includes financial ratios, I will always make sure the model has three or four ratios together and there is some documentation explaining the ratio and what the result means for the project or business. Right now, let's dig deeper into percentages and ratios.

What Ratios Measure

Ratios measure proportions. In the previous example, we could determine what proportion one figure is of another. Ratios also measure relationships. How? They can translate assets (tools and inventory) and liabilities (payables and loans) into common dollar figures. By doing this, it is easy to see valuable relationships between two seemingly unrelated items. Ratios also allow you to make comparisons between time periods. For example, a ratio lets you measure your inventory turnover from one month to another, or year to year.

Trend Analysis

By calculating the same percentages or ratios at the same time each month or year, you can look for trends in the business. Trends illustrate the extent and direction of change over time. Generally, trend analysis is performed at the end of each month. For instance, a common analysis is to calculate the net profit or EDITDA for a business or project at the end of each quarter of the financial year. The change between the same time period in the previous year and the current year is represented as movement in the growth of the business.

Points to Remember About Using Ratios

I have included three points that will be useful to keep in mind when creating ratios.

- Maintain an objective attitude: Don't use ratios to support predetermined conclusions. Use them to help you better understand the business.
- Don't use the wrong figures: For instance, when looking at a percent change between two dollar figures, such as a rise in price from \$2 to \$3, the number you want to compare is the difference between the two dollar figures. With this example, the answer would be \$1. This difference figure (\$1) is then divided by \$2 for a percent raise of 50%. Don't divide \$2 by \$3 or vice versa.
- Don't compare meaningless numbers: For example, don't compare expenses to fixed assets. This number is easy to calculate but has no meaning in the operation of a business.

Liquidity Ratios

Liquidity ratios are those rations that focus on the short term cash abilities of the organization to meet current liabilities.

Current Ratio

The current ratio is an indication of the organization's ability to meet its short-term liabilities. Banks and other bodies who are providing credit to the organization will use the ratio to ascertain the risk of lending to that organization. The calculation is:

Current ratio = Current assets/Current liabilities

What does low ratio mean? A low ratio (below 1) is not necessarily a negative. However, it shows that the organization has more short liabilities than it has readily available cash to cover those liabilities. In essence, if the creditors all demanded their money back the organization could not meet that demand.

What does a high ratio mean? A high ratio points to an organization that does have more-than-sufficient cash to meet liabilities. But the cash may not be well utilized in the organization. Again this is not a negative point, because the cash could be invested securities or interest-bearing deposit accounts and would be earning interest income for the organization.

Modeler's Tip

The proper ratio for a business depends on the type of business, the time in the business cycle, and the age of the business. You need to inquire about what is customary in the industry of the organization being modeled.

For an organization that is both efficient and worthy of credit, the current assets should be two times, or 200%, of current liabilities.

The variation to the current ratio is the quick ratio. The quick ratio has one major difference to the current ratio in that it does not include inventory in the current assets, because inventory cannot be turned into cash rapidly. The calculation is therefore:

Quick ratio = Cash and cash equivalents + Accounts receivable + Short-term investments/Current liabilities

Turnover of Cash Ratio

The turnover cash, or the working capital, of the organization is to show how efficient the organization can be in using its cash to generate revenue. The calculation is:

Turnover of cash ratio = Net sales/Cash + cash equivalents.

What does a low ratio mean? A low ratio is an indication that the organization is able to generate cash through its operations efficiently and is therefore unlikely to risk having a shortfall when its short-term obligations come due.

What does a high ratio mean? A high ratio indicates that the organization has a low cash level and high sales, which could put the organization in situation known as "overtrading." That's where the sales revenue might not be high enough to cover cost of goods, and there may not be enough cash available to meet short-term liabilities, including indirect costs such as salaries.

Modeler's Tip

When creating models, there is a quick test that can be applied: look at the current ratio and, if it is low, then the turnover of cash should be high. That's because this is showing that a low level of working capital is generating high sales.

Ideally an organization should be aiming for a turnover of cash ratio of around five or six times the working capital to signify an efficient operation.

Profitability Ratios

Profitability is why most of us are in business. We want a better return on our money and time than we can get from a bank or other low-risk, interest-paying opportunity. This, by the way, is one of the most commonly used methods to evaluate whether you are doing well with your business. For example, if the savings accounts or money-market accounts are paying a higher percent than you are earning on the money you have invested in a business, you will probably want to consider selling your business investment and reinvesting your money elsewhere (unless you particularly like your business investment better than making more money).

Profitability ratios provide you with the means to measure your earnings in several ways. They measure your return on sales, return on assets, and return on investment. As a general rule, profitability (or income), will emerge from changes in price or volume or both. Therefore, changes in your ratios will always move over time due to changes in selling price and volumes.

Rate of Return on Sales Ratio (ROS)

The ROS gives an indication how much profit is being produced per dollar of sales and is a regularly used in industry to evaluate the growth of profits for an organization of a time period. The calculation is:

Rate of return on sales ratio = Net income (before interest and taxes)/sales.

This ratio is a comparative measure and is very dependent on the industry. There is no universally accepted high or low ratio. For instance, a business that has a high turnover of inventory or one that uses low margin to attract business (such as a grocery store) might show a low ROS but still be healthy. However, the best use of this ratio comes when comparing it with other organizations in the industry or to its own previous annual ratios. The latter will highlight the changes in the efficiency of the organization.

Modeler's Tip

The modeler can test to see if this ratio has been calculated correctly in models by changing the price or volumes of the services or product, which should result in an immediate effect on the ratio. One point to be very careful with in models is to make sure this ratio is used in conjunction with others. For example, it's simply not right to show a ratio of 5% without some other financial indicators to show why this is low.

Rate of Return on Assets Ratio (ROA)

The ROA is an indicator of how well the organization is utilizing its assets to generate profits. The calculation is:

ROA = Net income/Total assets

The ROA is a comparative measure used in industry to compare the performance of an organization over a number of time periods, and to analyze the trends. It is also industry sensitive and should really be only used to compare organizations within the same industry. For example, an oil company must have refineries, which require an enormous amount of fixed assets, while a men's clothing store would have minimal fixed asset requirements.

Modeler's Tip

Modelers need to be aware of the types of anomalies that can greatly affect the results of this ratio when making comparisons to past years or to other organizations in the same industry. You need to be particularly careful of any changes in the organization's depreciation policy from one year to the next, or any assets that have been fully depreciated but are still used within the organization. Also pay attention to changes in the balance sheet assets of any intangible assets such as goodwill, or any unusual expense or income in one time period. Such anomalies will need to be explained in order to alleviate any alarm in the sudden changes to the trend.

To avoid anomalies caused by assets, often it is useful look at the fixed and current assets individually and look at the changes in their value over the same period. This will alert you to issues and remind you to document any changes.

Rate of Return on Investment Ratio (ROI)

ROI is used mainly for comparisons to assess the merits of two or more investments against each other, or to look at the return possibilities on an investment. The calculation is

ROI = (Gain from investment – Cost of investment)/Cost of investment

The power of the ROI is not in whether it gives a high ratio. Admittedly, any ratio that is above 15% should signify that the project is showing a good return. But the real strength is in identifying what a good return level is for the type of investment. For instance, say we are comparing two investments for the same amount of money. One is for an acquisition of some equity shares in another organization, and the other is for an infrastructure project to build roads. We would need to be looking at very different time scales and ultimately different investment rates. The rate for the roads may be quite low, for example 10%, as opposed to the equity investment, which could be 15%.

You'd need to take care with these investments, because the ROI rate is compounded over the number of years. If the road project were for 30 years at 8% compounded, and the equity were for 10 years at 15% compounded, the road project would bring close to twice the money over the 30 years than the equity. This may seem obvious, but often it's not clearly understood.

Modeler's Tip

You should plan on having a calculation for ROI in every valuation model that you build. It is that important. Even if you have not been required to create the ROI, you should still include it, because it is the best measure of the investment return rate. The modeler should, when using the ROI, make some assessment in relation to risk, because you just cannot have a ROI comparison or assessment while ignoring the impact of risk. For instance, in the example, some documentation would need to highlight that the equity investment has a higher risk of the stock price falling over the period.

Efficiency Ratios

Efficiency ratios measure how well you are conducting your business. These ratios indicate, for example, how fast you are collecting your money for credit sales, and how many times you are turning over your inventory in a given period of time. They measure the amount of sales generated by your assets and the return you are earning on them.

Efficiency ratios are an important benchmark to keeping your business in balance. For instance, if you become too loose in offering credit to generate sales, this will show up as an increase in the average number of days it takes to collect your accounts receivable. If you overbuy, even with well-meaning intentions of not passing up a real bargain, this will be reflected in a decrease in the turnover of your inventory. Similarly, if you acquire too many fixed assets without a corresponding increase in sales, your fixed asset turnover ratio will quickly decline.

Of course, other ratios will also play a part in maintaining a balance in your business that will aid you in maintaining healthy growth, but the efficiency ratios will usually note it sooner. You will notice that some efficiency ratios are in days and not percentages or proportions. There are many efficiency ratios, but I'll cover just one as an example.

Fixed Asset Turnover Ratio (Also Called Net Sales to Fixed Assets Ratio)

The fixed asset turnover ratio is a calculation between a company's sales revenue to its fixed assets. This ratio indicates the efficiency of an organization in using its fixed assets to generate revenues and thus is about asset productivity. If a company has a high fixed asset turnover ratio, it shows that the company is efficient at managing its fixed assets well. The calculation is:

Fixed Asset Turnover = Sales revenue/ Total fixed assets

This is also a comparison ratio, best used to examine the trend of the organization over a time period. A low ratio is usually an indication that assets are not being fully utilized, but again this is industry specific. For instance, in organizations where the assets are very expensive, as in healthcare, the ratios are low. But this is not a negative sign because the revenue per transaction is high.

High ratios may indicate that assets are fully employed and lead to greater profitability, but it will largely depend on the industry's norms.

Modeler's Tips

With any use of the ratio to create trends or comparisons, you should be careful to also highlight the value of the assets in the same time periods. This ratio is underpowered without a view on the underlying assets.

To summarize, this chapter covered a number of concepts on evaluating a business. On the surface, this may appear to be outside the remit of the financial modeler and more for the business owner. The expectations of customers toward financial modelers has begun to change from that of being someone who purely builds models to someone who can also apply commercial business acumen and advise the business owners and stakeholders, which is even more acute to financial modelers who are consultants. I can testify to this fact because without exception all my customers require for me as a modeler to treat their business as if it were my own. Having a perspective from the business owner is a very valuable asset in the skills armory of a financial modeler.

CHAPTER

10

The Implications and Rules of Accounting for Modelers

In this chapter, I will discuss an aspect of financial modeling that should never be overlooked, and that is the implications to the financial modeler of presenting financial statements. I mentioned earlier in this book that financial statements are heavily relied upon by various audiences and can have a significant influence on decision-making. While there are rules and regulations anywhere that are specifically aimed at the financial modeler, there are some implied responsibilities that if breached can have serious implications for whoever builds the model.

The Modeler's Financial Statement Responsibilities

The financial modeler who has produced the financial statements has the following responsibilities:

- Understands the substance, gravity, and uses of the financial statements. While this may seem obvious, what it means is that modelers are not in a position to deny that they were unaware of the content of the financial statements.

- Provides due care. Accountants are always aware of this responsibility; therefore, it is important that financial modelers, who are also deemed to be in a position of responsibility, should exercise their superior knowledge with some care. Failure to provide duty and care is viewed as very serious.
- Validates and maintains the accuracy of the statements. This is the most important responsibility and goes to the heart of the modeler's competency.
- Discloses any information that has a substantial bearing on the statements. Keeping back information that can directly or indirectly affect the interpretation of the financial statement is a serious breach and not just for the modeler who produced the model. Anyone who is involved with providing financial statements has an obligation to disclose information that is material.
- Provide comments, notes, and supplementary information that will help to make the financials more transparent.
- Present justification and evidence to back up and prove the information that is in the statements has substance.

The implications of glossing over or eluding these responsibilities depend on how those who have been affected decide to proceed with matters.

However, the implications can lead to an accusation of professional negligence. The effects of professional negligence will vary. At the very least, you will lose the ability to continue to build models commercially. At the worst, you will lose your living, and you may have to make repatriation and compensation to the damaged party, which could be a corporation or an organization that has lost several million dollars.

Linking Inputs to Financials

A crucial part of the overall end model is how the modeler has aligned the financial statements to the inputs. In a well-designed model, the link between the outputs and the inputs is transparent, which means any adjustments to the inputs are observable in the results of the outputs. To achieve this transparency, the modeler should employ a consistent approach to building the inputs and the outputs and avoid placing anything that breaks that consistency in the model.

The key to linking the inputs and outputs is to use a top-down approach and start with the outputs and work back to the inputs. By using this approach, we already know what the outputs template should be, and we can then design the inputs to fit into that template. In Figure 10-1, our output is the an income statement.

Income Statement for the Year Ending December 2013
(In 1,000s)

Sales Revenue	40,521
Less: Returns and Allowance	340
Net Sales Revenue	**40,181**
Direct Costs	
Supplies & Services	30,250
Direct Labor	6,035
Insurance	125
Risk	360
	36,770
Gross Profit	**3,411**
Operating Expenses	
Selling Expenses	290
Salaries	644
Admin Expenses	540
Overheads	890
	2,364
EBITDA	**1,047**
Depreciation	195
EBIT	**852**
Interest - Paid/(Received)	78
Profit Before Taxation	**774**
Corporation Tax	73
Profit After Taxation	**701**

Figure 10-1. This figure is a sample income statement

The best approach to creating inputs is top-down, that is starting with the outputs working to the inputs and then developing the calculations. In the income statement, each of the revenue items (income) and each of the costs (direct costs and expenses) will have a specific input section. The inputs have been put together working back from the outputs as in Figure 10-2.

	A	B–D	E	F	G	H	J–K
1		**NonSuch Financial Model**					
2		*Model Inputs*					
3							
4							
5		Financial year	Dec-13	Dec-14	Dec-15	Jan-16	
6		**1.00 Income**					
7	1.01	Sales price	14.22	14.22	15.00	15.00	*Affects revenue*
8							
9	1.02	Sales units (in 1,000s)	2,850	2,900	2,740	2,695	*Affects revenue and returns*
10							
11	1.03	Number of units returned	9	15	9	6	*Affects returns*
12							
13	1.04	% discounts given	0.52%	0.50%	0.50%	0.50%	*Affects allowances*
14							
15		**2.00 Direct costs**					
16		Suppliers & Supplies (in units)					
17	2.01	Units purchased from supplier A	605	420	500	500	*Affects supplies and services*
18	2.02	Units purchased from supplier B	500	500	100	200	*Affects supplies and services*
19	2.03	Units purchased from supplier C	2,000	2,000	2,000	2,000	*Affects supplies and services*
20							
21		Suppliers & Cost (per unit)					
22	2.04	Purchase cost from supplier A	10.00	10.00	10.00	10.00	*Affects supplies and services*
23	2.05	Purchase cost from supplier B	12.00	12.00	12.00	12.00	*Affects supplies and services*
24	2.06	Purchase cost from supplier C	9.10	9.10	9.10	9.10	*Affects supplies and services*
25							
26	2.07	Direct labor					
27	2.08	Average labor rate (per hour)	8.50	8.76	9.02	9.29	*Affects direct labor*
28	2.09	No of hours worked	710	740	650	641	*Affects direct labor*

Figure 10-2. This figure shows part of the inputs for the income statement

By using the outputs to create the inputs, it becomes a matter of intuition and investigation to break down all the aspects of the output. For instance, for the sales revenue, you could simply have an input called sales revenue and input the total revenue per annum. However, you need to have flexibility; therefore, it is best to split the detail of the revenue into sales price × sales units. That gives you flexibility about whether the price or the number of units derive the sales revenue.

In column A of Figure 10-2, reference codes have been included. These originate in the inputs, and they are also used in the assumption register and to a lesser extent in the financial statements themselves. By employing a reference system such as this, the assumptions and the inputs can be tracked, in effect giving an audit trail. This referencing does mean the modeler has to spend considerable time documenting, but it is well worth it, particularly for when the model goes into testing. Additionally, it helps the modeler to keep abreast of how each part of the model is functioning.

The next step is to create the calculations, which should be based upon the information in the inputs as in Figure 10-3.

R40

	A	B/C/D	E	F	G	H	
1		**NonSuch Financial Model**					
2		***Model Calculations***					
5		**Financial year**	**Dec-13**	**Dec-14**	**Dec-15**	**Jan-16**	
6		**Input Links**					
7	1.01	Sales price	14.22	14.22	15.00	15.00	
8	1.02	Sales units (in1, 000s)	2,850	2,900	2,740	2,695	
9	1.03	Number of units returned	9	15	9	6	
10	1.04	% discounts given	0.52%	0.50%	0.50%	0.50%	
12	2.01	Units purchased from supplier A	605	420	500	500	
13	2.02	Units purchased from supplier B	500	500	100	200	
14	2.03	Units purchased from supplier C	2,000	2,000	2,000	2,000	
16	2.04	Purchase cost from supplier A	10.00	10.00	10.00	10.00	
17	2.05	Purchase cost from supplier B	12.00	12.00	12.00	12.00	
18	2.06	Purchase cost from supplier C	9.10	9.10	9.10	9.10	
20	2.08	Average labor rate (per hour)	8.50	8.76	9.02	9.29	
21	2.09	No of hours worked	710	740	650	641	
23		**1.00 Income**					
24	1.01, 1.02	Sales price	40,518	41,229	41,100	40,425	*Sales price x Sales Units*
26	1.01, 1.03	Returned units	128	213	135	90	*Sales price x Number of units returned*
28	1.01, 1.02, 1.04	Discounts Given	212	206	206	202	*Sales price x Sales Units x % discounts given*
30		**2.00 Direct costs**					
31		Purchase costs					
32	2.01, 2.04	Supplier A	6,050	4,200	5,000	5,000	*Unit Purchase price from Supplier A x Purchase cost from Supplier A*
33	2.02, 2.05	Supplier B	6,000	6,000	1,200	2,400	*Unit Purchase price from Supplier B x Purchase cost from Supplier B*
34	2.03, 2.06	Supplier C	18,200	18,200	18,200	18,200	*Unit Purchase price from Supplier C x Purchase cost from Supplier C*
35		**Total**	30,250	28,400	24,400	25,600	
37		Direct labor					
38	2.08, 2.09	Labor cost	6,035	6,479	5,861	5,954	*Average labor rate x No of hours worked*

Figure 10-3. The inputs are shown at the top of the worksheets and the calculations refer to them

The calculations are linked to the inputs, and you will notice in Figure 10-3 at the top of the worksheet that all the inputs were brought in by simply creating a link. This may seem odd as I am duplicating the work that is already in the inputs, but it is to make sure that all the calculations that follow have a formula coming from the same worksheet, as in Figure 10-4.

SYD =E7*E8

	A	B/C/D	E	F	G	H	
1		**NonSuch Financial Model**					
2		***Model Calculations***					
5		**Financial year**	**Dec-13**	**Dec-14**	**Dec-15**	**Jan-16**	
6		**Input Links**					
7	1.01	Sales price	14.22	14.22	15.00	15.00	
8	1.02	Sales units (in1, 000s)	2,850	2,900	2,740	2,695	
9	1.03	Number of units returned	9	15	9	6	
10	1.04	% discounts given	0.52%	0.50%	0.50%	0.50%	
12	2.01	Units purchased from supplier A	605	420	500	500	
13	2.02	Units purchased from supplier B	500	500	100	200	
14	2.03	Units purchased from supplier C	2,000	2,000	2,000	2,000	
16	2.04	Purchase cost from supplier A	10.00	10.00	10.00	10.00	
17	2.05	Purchase cost from supplier B	12.00	12.00	12.00	12.00	
18	2.06	Purchase cost from supplier C	9.10	9.10	9.10	9.10	
20	2.08	Average labor rate (per hour)	8.50	8.76	9.02	9.29	
21	2.09	No of hours worked	710	740	650	641	
23		**1.00 Income**					
24	1.01, 1.02	Sales price	=E7*E8	41,229	41,100	40,425	*Sales price x Sales Units*

Figure 10-4. The calculations are generated from within the calculation's worksheet

What this means is that when trying to track a particular item in the financial statements, you can locate that item in the calculations and then also analyze how the formula works—all within one worksheet. In Figure 10-5, all the references are shown on this income statement, which means anyone looking at this statement would be able to track the information. The use of these references also allows you to assess quickly how to remedy any errors. You will be able to either correct the formula in the calculations or look back at the inputs worksheet and alter the input.

K34 *fx*

	A	C	F	H
1		NonSuch Financial Model		
2		Income Statement for Year Ending December 2013		
3		(In 1,000s)		
4				
5	Input ref:			Notes & Comments
6	1.01, 1.02	Sales Revenue	40,518	
7	1.01, 1.03	Less: Returns and Allowance	340	
8		Net Sales Revenue	40,179	
9		Direct Costs		
10	2.01, 2.04, 2.02, 2.05, 2.03, 2.06	Supplies & Services	30,250	
11	2.08, 2.09	Direct Labor	6,035	
12		Insurance	125	
13		Risk	360	
14			36,770	
16		Gross Profit	3,409	
18		Operating Expenses		
19		Selling Expenses	290	
20		Salaries	644	
21		Admin Expenses	540	
22		Overheads	890	
23			2,364	
25		EBITDA	1,045	
26		Depreciation	195	
27		EBIT	850	
28		Interest - Paid/(Received)	78	
29		Profit Before Taxation	772	
30		Corporation Tax	73	
31		Profit After Taxation	699	

Figure 10-5. This figure shows a linked income statement

Once the calculations have been created, it is then a matter of linking the relevant items in the financial statement back to the calculations. Thus, the statement is linked to the calculations, and the calculations are linked to the inputs. This may take some getting used, going through such a process, but a process it is for very good reasons. If the statements in the model are consistently following this linking, then any time there is a problem with statements, the process is always going to be the same. You will be able to check through the references and links.

In Figure 10-5 take a look at column A, and you will see "Input ref:" This is a reference column where, row by row, a code is supplied that references the input in the input worksheet. By creating this type of reference, it is then possible for whoever is using the model to track to the source of the information. I have also added a Notes & Comments section, which while not necessary is a good accompaniment to the financial statement. These notes are eventually linked to the assumption register, and a lookup is created that will use the input reference number to locate the comments that have been used in the assumption register.

Understanding When to Use Financial Statements

The financial statements are not purely for accountants. In fact, while accountants are always interested in these statements, the main beneficiaries of the financial statements in the model are those who want to gain a better understanding of where the project or organization has been or is going. This group of people will likely include the following:

- Project owner
- Business owner
- Stakeholders
- Investors
- Lenders
- Clients or customers
- Bid tenderer
- Public at large

The question then becomes who should view which statement when. In a nutshell, which statements are the right ones to use and in which situations?

Surprisingly, the answer is fairly simple. As the modeler, you should always be prepared to have available the three core statements: the income statement, the cash flow statement, and the balance sheet, even if these have not been asked for by the sponsor. These three statements combined are the basis for interpreting financial performance and make up the foundation behind so many other financial metrics and financial ratios.

How would a modeler know which capital-budgeting metrics (net present value, payback, internal rate of rate, or weighted average cost of capital), or which financial ratios, should be used?

My advice is that you tread carefully when looking at which metrics or ratios to use because they all tell their own story. They also are very much dependent on what message you really want to put forward.

If you are in any doubt as to which metrics to present, then bear in mind that these are the messages you should be trying to give in the outputs:

- When is the payback of the project or investment going to occur?
- What type of return would the investor get for putting funds into the project?
- When will the project begin to break even? In other words, when will it will start to look after itself through generated revenues and will no longer require any investment? Again, this break-even point does not require a statement, but the modeler should be prepared to communicate when the break-even point will be achieved.

To conclude, when determining how to use the financial statements, you should always use the three core statements and be clear on the payback period and, equally important, the break-even point. With any other financial statements, metrics and ratios will be on an as-needed basis. Also it's a good point to refer to the project sponsor as to which additional statements (aside from the income statement, balance sheet, and cash flow) would be required. As I mentioned earlier, all these metrics and ratios give some financial story; it's up to you to make sure you know what is required.

The accuracy of the outputs—whether they are income statements, balance sheets, cash flow or liquidity ratios—should always be a paramount concern for any financial modeler. Let me be clear about what is meant by accuracy: you are testing the ability of the information to give whoever is looking at it as good an indication of reality as one can possibly get. When looking at historical data, expect the data to be a complete reflection of what has happened in the past.

CHAPTER

11

Financial-Based Calculations

If you recall from Chapter 2, one of the key modeling disciplines is the separation of inputs, calculations, and outputs. The outputs are linked to the calculations, and the calculations are linked to the inputs. Thus the calculations are in the middle—they are the link between the inputs and the outputs like the glue between two components.

I have purposely made sure that we only tackle the calculations once we have established both inputs and outputs because if you follow best practice, that is how the model develops. You want to start with outputs because they can be defined, follow up with the inputs because they originate from the drivers in the outputs, and afterward link the two elements with the calculations. Think of making a plastic model of an airplane. First, you need to understand what the final model should look like (the output). Then you subsequently check that all the parts to make the final model are available (the inputs). Finally, you piece it all together with the glue (the calculations), and so go financial models, hence why this chapter is the last of the three elements.

How to Lay Out Your Calculations

In my opinion, one of the worst sights in any model is where the calculations are badly laid out and resemble a jumble of functions and formula with no coherency. In other words, it's just plain ugly. In order to avoid establishing any bad habits with laying out calculations, I want to show you which formats will work best.

When I think of the layout of calculations, I am reminded of soldier ants, or worker ants. This will seem like a bizarre analogy, but you will soon understand the similarities. Ants always seem to have a purpose. There may be thousands of them in a colony, but if you watch them, you will notice that they are generally organized in a trail. They all follow the same unbroken and consistent path. Should something break that trail, they will scatter briefly. But in no time, they will establish the trail again and carry on with efficiency.

I want you to think of calculations in a similar vein. There are literally hundreds of formulas and functions, but they are all serving a single purpose: to link the inputs to the outputs. In doing so, it's more efficient if they follow an unbroken and consistent path, that no matter the complexity of the calculation, you can still recognize that it is a calculation and also where it is going.

In Figure 11-1, I have included a layout that I use in models. Notice first that once you are accustomed to the layout, it begins to look consistent. For example, all the narrative is down in a column, in this case column C. The calculations all begin from column E, and they are consistent across the row as can be seen in Figures 11-2 and 11-3.

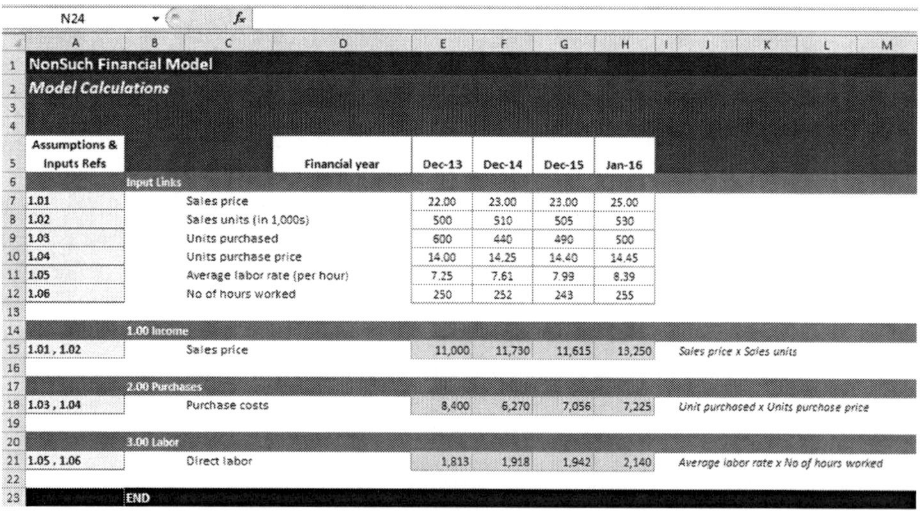

Assumptions & Inputs Refs		Financial year	Dec-13	Dec-14	Dec-15	Jan-16	
	Input Links						
1.01		Sales price	22.00	23.00	23.00	25.00	
1.02		Sales units (in 1,000s)	500	510	505	530	
1.03		Units purchased	600	440	490	500	
1.04		Units purchase price	14.00	14.25	14.40	14.45	
1.05		Average labor rate (per hour)	7.25	7.61	7.99	8.39	
1.06		No of hours worked	250	252	243	255	
	1.00 Income						
1.01 , 1.02		Sales price	11,000	11,730	11,615	13,250	Sales price x Sales units
	2.00 Purchases						
1.03 , 1.04		Purchase costs	8,400	6,270	7,056	7,225	Unit purchased x Units purchase price
	3.00 Labor						
1.05 , 1.06		Direct labor	1,813	1,918	1,942	2,140	Average labor rate x No of hours worked
	END						

Figure 11-1. This figure shows a typical layout for the inputs

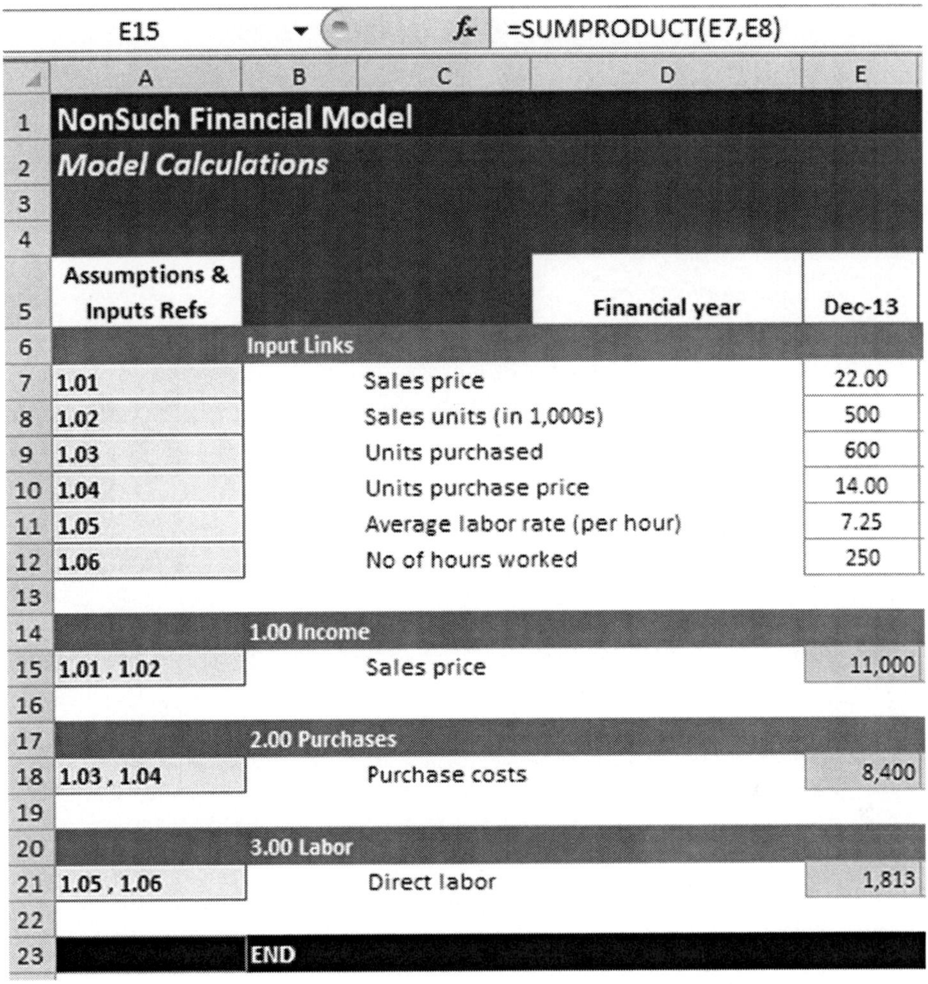

Figure 11-2. Single SUMPRODUCT() function has been used Column E

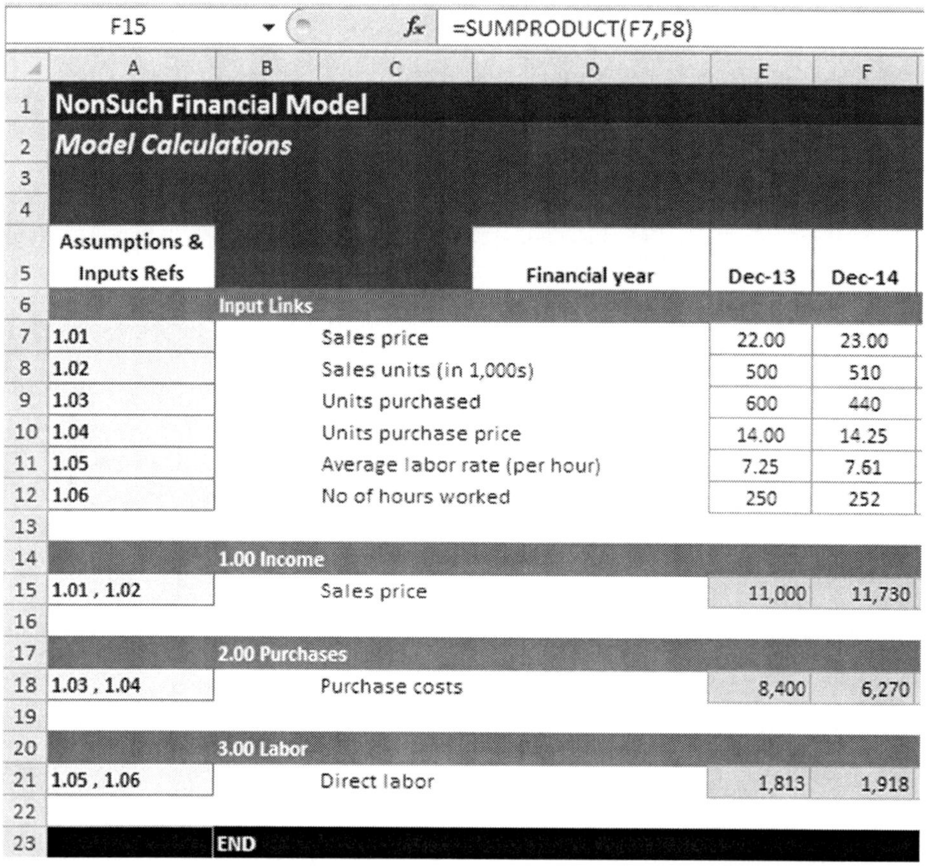

F15 | f_x =SUMPRODUCT(F7,F8)

	A	B	C	D	E	F
1	NonSuch Financial Model					
2	*Model Calculations*					
3						
4						
5	Assumptions & Inputs Refs			Financial year	Dec-13	Dec-14
6		Input Links				
7	1.01		Sales price		22.00	23.00
8	1.02		Sales units (in 1,000s)		500	510
9	1.03		Units purchased		600	440
10	1.04		Units purchase price		14.00	14.25
11	1.05		Average labor rate (per hour)		7.25	7.61
12	1.06		No of hours worked		250	252
13						
14		1.00 Income				
15	1.01 , 1.02		Sales price		11,000	11,730
16						
17		2.00 Purchases				
18	1.03 , 1.04		Purchase costs		8,400	6,270
19						
20		3.00 Labor				
21	1.05 , 1.06		Direct labor		1,813	1,918
22						
23		END				

Figure 11-3. The Same SUMPRODUCT( ) function is used in column F as in Figure 11-2 to maintain consistency

In Figure 11-1, the inputs have been included in the calculation worksheet at the top of the worksheet just by creating a link. The reason for having these inputs for the calculation is to ensure that all the calculations are based on cells within the worksheet. You want to avoid having calculations that cross multiple worksheets because it will become very difficult to manage. It also becomes an excruciating problem when there are issues that need to be corrected in the model or when the model goes through testing or auditing.

Figure 11-4 is the input sheet, which provides the inputs to the calculation worksheet in Figure 11-5. Notice in this calculation worksheet that the links with the inputs have not been brought to the top of the worksheet, and so the formula references another worksheet. This contrasts the formula in Figure 11-2, which just references data within the worksheet.

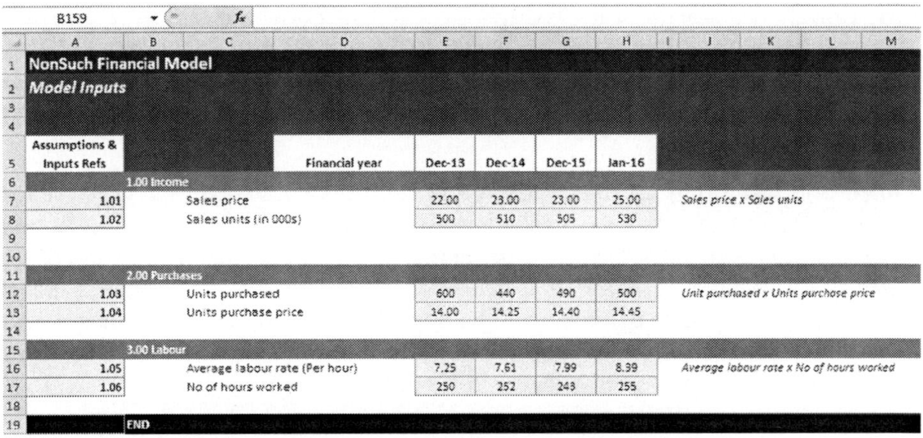

B159

	A	B	C	D	E	F	G	H	I	J	K	L	M
1	NonSuch Financial Model												
2	*Model Inputs*												
3													
4													
5	Assumptions & Inputs Refs			Financial year	Dec-13	Dec-14	Dec-15	Jan-16					
6		1.00 Income											
7	1.01		Sales price		22.00	23.00	23.00	25.00		*Sales price x Sales units*			
8	1.02		Sales units (in 000s)		500	510	505	530					
9													
10													
11		2.00 Purchases											
12	1.03		Units purchased		600	440	490	500		*Unit purchased x Units purchase price*			
13	1.04		Units purchase price		14.00	14.25	14.40	14.45					
14													
15		3.00 Labour											
16	1.05		Average labour rate (Per hour)		7.25	7.61	7.99	8.39		*Average labour rate x No of hours worked*			
17	1.06		No of hours worked		250	252	243	255					
18													
19		END											

Figure 11-4. The input worksheet supports the calculations

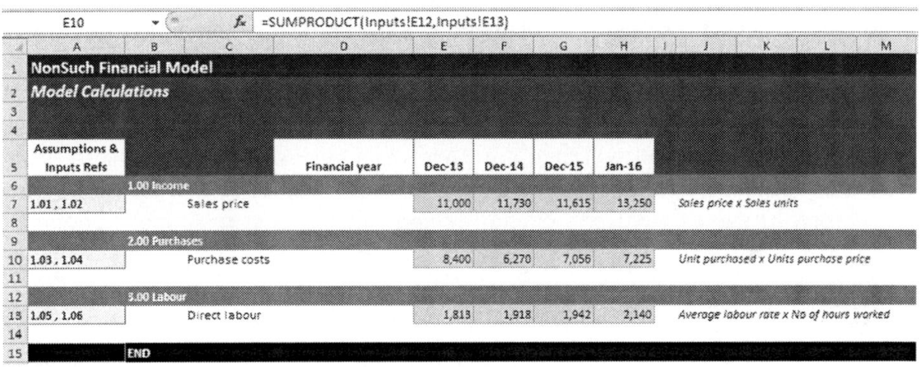

E10 =SUMPRODUCT(Inputs!E12,Inputs!E13)

	A	B	C	D	E	F	G	H	I	J	K	L	M
1	NonSuch Financial Model												
2	*Model Calculations*												
3													
4													
5	Assumptions & Inputs Refs			Financial year	Dec-13	Dec-14	Dec-15	Jan-16					
6		1.00 Income											
7	1.01 , 1.02		Sales price		11,000	11,730	11,615	13,250		*Sales price x Sales units*			
8													
9		2.00 Purchases											
10	1.03 , 1.04		Purchase costs		8,400	6,270	7,056	7,225		*Unit purchased x Units purchase price*			
11													
12		3.00 Labour											
13	1.05 , 1.06		Direct labour		1,813	1,918	1,942	2,140		*Average labour rate x No of hours worked*			
14													
15		END											

Figure 11-5. The calculations are drawing on the data in the input sheet as can be seen in the formula

These calculations may seem pedantic, but it's vital that you maintain consistency with the structure throughout the model when creating calculations. Make sure the inputs are brought into the calculation worksheet as links at the top and make all the calculations work from those links. This will make the model layout so much easier to navigate, and troubleshooting issues is then intuitive. Just be aware that often in a large and complicated model, there are a number of input worksheets. If you deviate from the practice of bringing input links into the calculations and make the formula go directly to the input sheet, you will have a function that references multiple worksheets. This will create a three-dimensional formula, like the one shown next, which makes the formula more intricate than it needs to be.

=SUMPRODUCT('Inputs1'!E7:H7,'Inputs2'!E7:H7)

Not only is this formula messy and ugly, if you continue this way, you will at some point make a pointing error (referencing the incorrect cells by mistake). Once you have trawled through a few hundred functions to locate the error, it will become apparent why you should avoid this type of formula construction.

I have one last point to make about the layout for calculations. Going back to Figure 11-1, note that each calculation is a discrete calculation, that is, one item, one calculation. Although this seems obvious, don't be tempted to cut corners by make one almighty calculation that captures, for instance, sales income and purchase cost at once. The key here is to follow the input's layout as much as possible—so for every input, there should be a single calculation. It's fine to repeat the calculation again if necessary.

Using Best Practice Calculations

You may be wondering if I am about to give a list of functions that are considered best practice modeling. If this is your expectation, I have some bad news. There just isn't such a premise. Almost all of Excel's functions are ready for use by anyone, and they all have their own advantages and disadvantages. What makes them particularly effective is how they are applied and used. With that in mind, in this section, I will take you through a series of calculations (a situation that requires a calculation to be performed) and offer a solution of how to perform these calculations efficiently and follows best practice modeling.

Whole Range Calculations

The whole range calculation is an efficient calculation method with several benefits, particularly on large models. If you can invest some time setting up a range, I can assure it's well worth the effort. It involves giving a name to a series or a range of cells, and once that range has been named, it can then be used simply by referring to the name in the formula.

In Figures 11-6 and 11-7, take a look at the inputs at the top and the calculations below the inputs. At the top of the calculations, the input links have been brought into the calculations; however, instead of linking each cell across the eight years individually, I have referenced the name "Inp_Income" (input income). By using this name, I now only need to use the same name across the income row, and the link will give me the corresponding income amount. This method does away with having potential pointing areas because the modeler just needs to know the range name of each input row, which I have added in column L as a reference.

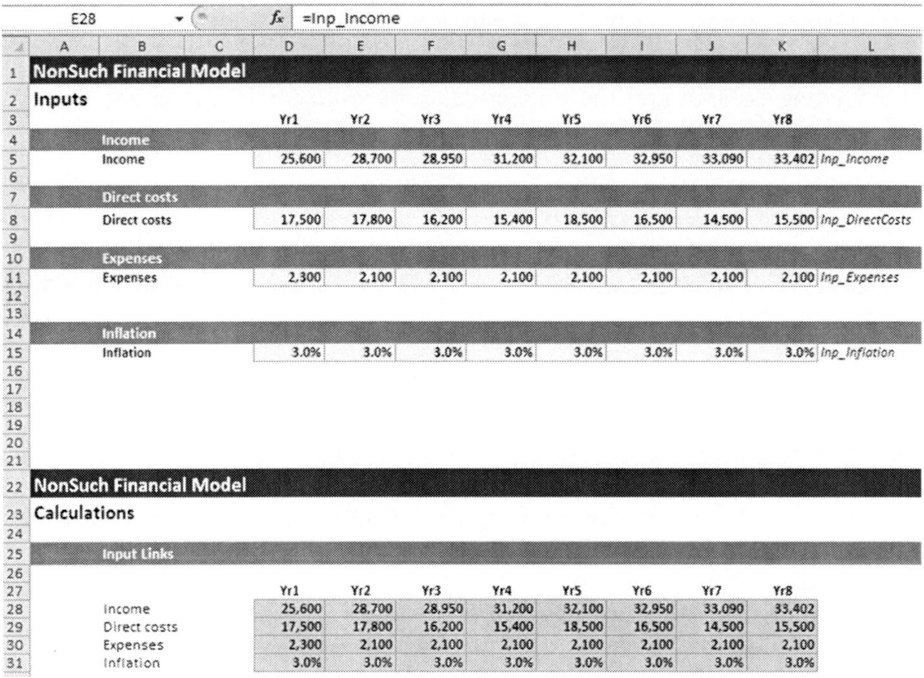

E28 =Inp_Income

	A	B	C	D	E	F	G	H	I	J	K	L
1	NonSuch Financial Model											
2	Inputs											
3				Yr1	Yr2	Yr3	Yr4	Yr5	Yr6	Yr7	Yr8	
4		Income										
5		Income		25,600	28,700	28,950	31,200	32,100	32,950	33,090	33,402	*Inp_Income*
6												
7		Direct costs										
8		Direct costs		17,500	17,800	16,200	15,400	18,500	16,500	14,500	15,500	*Inp_DirectCosts*
9												
10		Expenses										
11		Expenses		2,300	2,100	2,100	2,100	2,100	2,100	2,100	2,100	*Inp_Expenses*
12												
13												
14		Inflation										
15		Inflation		3.0%	3.0%	3.0%	3.0%	3.0%	3.0%	3.0%	3.0%	*Inp_Inflation*
16												
17												
18												
19												
20												
21												
22	NonSuch Financial Model											
23	Calculations											
24												
25		Input Links										
26												
27				Yr1	Yr2	Yr3	Yr4	Yr5	Yr6	Yr7	Yr8	
28		Income		25,600	28,700	28,950	31,200	32,100	32,950	33,090	33,402	
29		Direct costs		17,500	17,800	16,200	15,400	18,500	16,500	14,500	15,500	
30		Expenses		2,300	2,100	2,100	2,100	2,100	2,100	2,100	2,100	
31		Inflation		3.0%	3.0%	3.0%	3.0%	3.0%	3.0%	3.0%	3.0%	

Figure 11-6. The cell in E28 has been linked to the range name Inp_Income

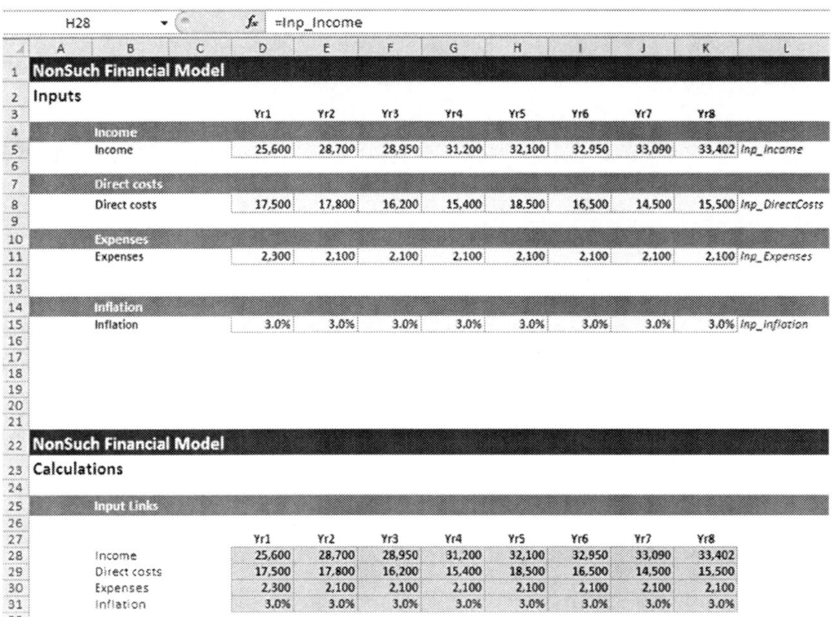

H28 =Inp_Income

	A	B	C	D	E	F	G	H	I	J	K	L
1	NonSuch Financial Model											
2	Inputs											
3				Yr1	Yr2	Yr3	Yr4	Yr5	Yr6	Yr7	Yr8	
4		Income										
5		Income		25,600	28,700	28,950	31,200	32,100	32,950	33,090	33,402	*Inp_Income*
6												
7		Direct costs										
8		Direct costs		17,500	17,800	16,200	15,400	18,500	16,500	14,500	15,500	*Inp_DirectCosts*
9												
10		Expenses										
11		Expenses		2,300	2,100	2,100	2,100	2,100	2,100	2,100	2,100	*Inp_Expenses*
12												
13												
14		Inflation										
15		Inflation		3.0%	3.0%	3.0%	3.0%	3.0%	3.0%	3.0%	3.0%	*Inp_Inflation*
16												
17												
18												
19												
20												
21												
22	NonSuch Financial Model											
23	Calculations											
24												
25		Input Links										
26												
27				Yr1	Yr2	Yr3	Yr4	Yr5	Yr6	Yr7	Yr8	
28		Income		25,600	28,700	28,950	31,200	32,100	32,950	33,090	33,402	
29		Direct costs		17,500	17,800	16,200	15,400	18,500	16,500	14,500	15,500	
30		Expenses		2,300	2,100	2,100	2,100	2,100	2,100	2,100	2,100	
31		Inflation		3.0%	3.0%	3.0%	3.0%	3.0%	3.0%	3.0%	3.0%	

Figure 11-7. In this financial model, the whole range of cells from E28 to K28 references a single rage name called Inp_Income

Let's take a look now at how to create a whole range name:

Begin first by highlighting the whole range that will be named and make sure the starting column and the ending columns will remain consistent through the model. In Figure 11-8, columns D and K are the starting and ending columns, respectively.

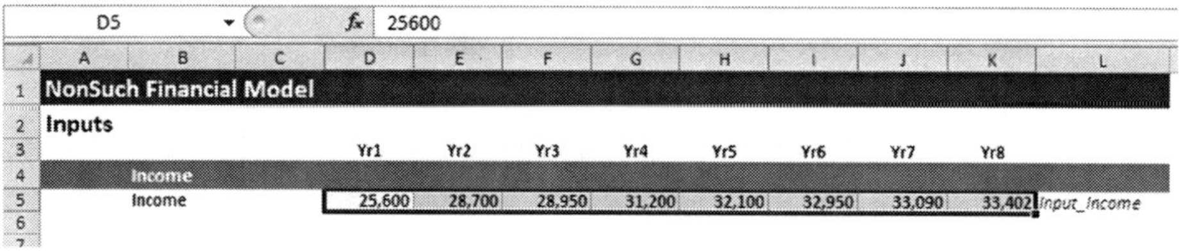

Figure 11-8. The first step is to highlight the full range that will be named

The range can then be named using the name box, which is located in the upper left of the worksheet just above the A and B column headings. Give the range an appropriate name (see Figure 11-9). By creating these range names, you can make calculations that are based on names. For example, to determine the gross income, you could write the following calculation:

*Input_Income *(1+Inputs_SalesTax)*

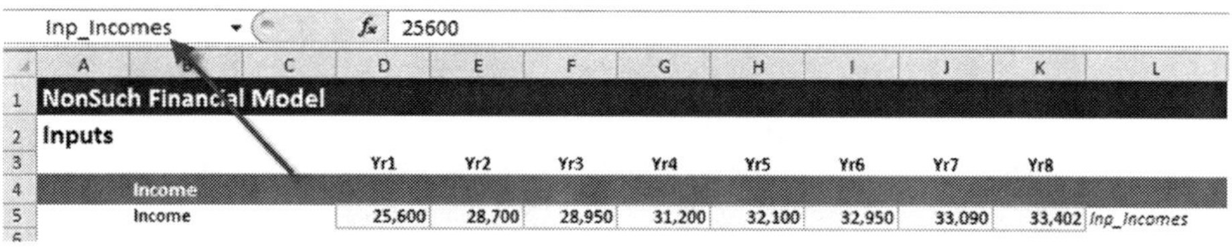

Figure 11-9. The whole range has been named "Inp_Income"

By using the whole range names, you can start to make calculations that when viewed become more meaningful. However, always make sure the columns are consistent, as any calculations that are made on inconsistent columns will mean that the results are unreliable (see Figure 11-10).

E18 =E15*(1+E16)

	A	B	C	D	E	F	G	H	I	J	K	L
1	NonSuch Financial Model											
2	Inputs											
3				Yr1	Yr2	Yr3	Yr4	Yr5	Yr6	Yr7	Yr8	
4		Income										
5		Income		25,600	28,700	28,950	31,200	32,100	32,950	33,090	33,402	*Input_Income*
6												
7		Sales Tax										
8		Sales Tax		20.0%	20.0%	20.0%	20.0%	20.0%	20.0%	20.0%	20.0%	*Input_SalesTax*
9												
10												
11												
12												
13	Calculations											
14		Actual Income										
15		Income			28,700	28,950	31,200	32,100	32,950	33,090	33,402	#VALUE!
16		Sales Tax			20.0%	20.0%	20.0%	20.0%	20.0%	20.0%	20.0%	#VALUE!
17												
18		Income with Sales Tax			34,440	34,740	37,440	38,520	39,540	39,708	40,082	#VALUE!

Figure 11-10. The columns between the inputs and calculations are misaligned, and therefore the calculations are unreliable

Calculating Time Periods

Making calculations that are based on time periods and time intervals can be very frustrating because of the conflict between what is pleasing and intuitive to the eye and what is practical and sensible modeling. To explain, see Figure 11-11. This is an all-too-typical situation. The modeler needs to produce some outputs, which are likely to be in a standard format based upon the client's requirements. The results do not look very appealing.

	A	B	C	D	E	F	G	H	I	J	K	L
1	NonSuch Financial Model											
2												
3	Outputs											
4												
5												
6			Quarter 1	Quarter 2	Quarter 3	Quarter 4	Year 1 Total	Quarter 1	Quarter 2	Quarter 3	Quarter 4	Year 2 Total
7		Income	5,800	5,950	5,004	5,101	21,855	5,740	5,703	5,649	5,830	22,922
8		Direct costs	2,700	2,710	3,920	2,700	12,030	2,750	2,755	2,790	2,700	10,995
9		Gross profit/(Loss)	3,100	3,240	1,084	2,700	10,124	2,990	2,948	2,859	3,130	11,927
10		Expenses	2,220	2,700	2,640	2,655	10,215	2,620	2,530	2,500	2,490	10,140
11		Net profit/(Loss)	880	540	(1,556)	45	(91)	370	418	359	640	1,787
12												
13		END										

Figure 11-11. The outputs are reported in quarters and years

In this model, the outputs are reporting in quarters and then totaled into years. Although there may appear to be nothing particularly harmful about such an output, it couldn't be further from the truth. This output is a disaster, and it really is the antithesis for any financial modeler. There is a lack of consistency across the columns as some are showing quarters and others are showing years; they should all the same timescale. In each row, there are four calculations for the quarters and then a different calculation on the total. One of the problems with this output is if you needed to reference it from another worksheet, you would be required to always check which cells are being used because some are in quarters and others are in years. The importance for modeling is to break this type into an output with quarters and an output with annual numbers in your calculations. By creating two separate calculations, you can then create outputs that give both quarterly and yearly numbers without breaking best practice consistency.

Different ways are available; one of the solutions is to use a tool called pivot tables. These pivot tables are very popular in financial circles, but there is just no room for them in financial modeling, such that I am not going to discuss them. In short, they are cumbersome and present major problems if you want to create calculation links from them. A better way is to use a calculation mask. A mask is a simple function that is created specifically to signal whether certain cells are included or excluded. Figure 11-12 is an example of a mask that has been created to accept time period quarters but nothing else.

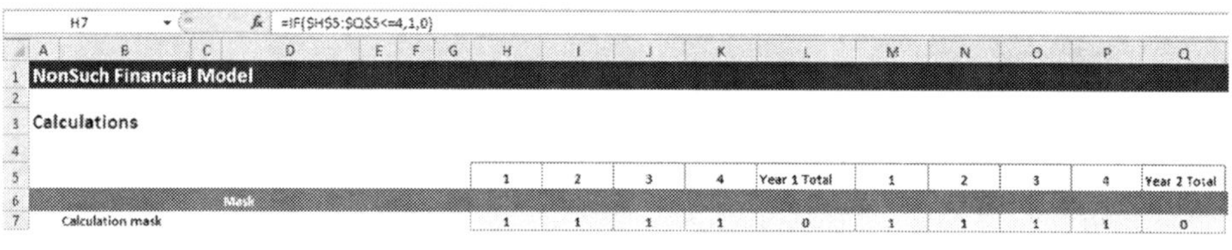
H7 =IF($H$5:$Q$5<=4,1,0)

	1	2	3	4	Year 1 Total	1	2	3	4	Year 2 Total
NonSuch Financial Model										
Calculations										
Mask										
Calculation mask	1	1	1	1	0	1	1	1	1	0

Figure 11-12. In this model, the calculation mask is being used on the time periods

You can see that the quarters are simply labeled 1, 2, 3, and 4. It's generally easier to perform calculations on labels if they are numbers and not text. I have named the table with the time periods "TableHeadings," which makes it simpler for referencing. The formula in the mask simply states that if a number is less than or equal to 4 (there are 4 quarters for a year), then return a number one. Otherwise, return a zero. This mask can now be used to include or exclude quarters and annual amounts as in Figure 11-13.

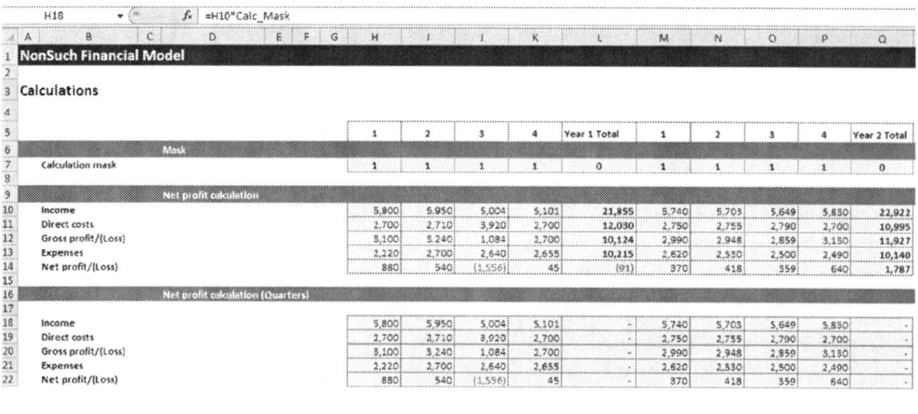
H18 =H10*Calc_Mask

	1	2	3	4	Year 1 Total	1	2	3	4	Year 2 Total
NonSuch Financial Model										
Calculations										
Mask										
Calculation mask	1	1	1	1	0	1	1	1	1	0
Net profit calculation										
Income	5,800	5,950	5,004	5,101	21,855	5,740	5,703	5,649	5,850	22,922
Direct costs	2,700	2,710	3,920	2,700	12,030	2,750	2,755	2,790	2,700	10,995
Gross profit/(Loss)	3,100	3,240	1,084	2,700	10,124	2,990	2,948	2,859	3,150	11,927
Expenses	2,220	2,700	2,640	2,655	10,215	2,620	2,530	2,500	2,490	10,140
Net profit/(Loss)	880	540	(1,556)	45	(91)	370	418	359	640	1,787
Net profit calculation (Quarters)										
Income	5,800	5,950	5,004	5,101	-	5,740	5,703	5,649	5,850	-
Direct costs	2,700	2,710	3,920	2,700	-	2,750	2,755	2,790	2,700	-
Gross profit/(Loss)	3,100	3,240	1,084	2,700	-	2,990	2,948	2,859	3,130	-
Expenses	2,220	2,700	2,640	2,655	-	2,620	2,530	2,500	2,490	-
Net profit/(Loss)	880	540	(1,556)	45	-	370	418	359	640	-

Figure 11-13. The calculation mask is used to include quarters but not years

The process is to multiply the quarterly numbers with the calculation mask, and anything that is multiplied by zero produces a zero. This way you can completely eradicate the annual amounts. The next part is to produce a table that just takes the yearly amounts and excludes the quarters; this step is slightly harder because you are now reversing the use of the zero and the one, as in Figure 11-14.

H25 =IF(Calc_Mask=1,0,SUMPRODUCT($H$7:H$7,$H10:H10))-C25

	A–D	H	I	J	K	L	M	N	O	P	Q
1	NonSuch Financial Model										
2											
3	Calculations										
4											
5		1	2	3	4	Year 1 Total	1	2	3	4	Year 2 Total
6	Mask										
7	Calculation mask	1	1	1	1	0	1	1	1	1	0
8											
9	Net profit calculation										
10	Income	5,800	5,950	5,004	5,101	21,855	5,740	5,703	5,649	5,830	22,922
11	Direct costs	2,700	2,710	3,920	2,700	12,030	2,750	2,755	2,790	2,700	10,995
12	Gross profit/(Loss)	3,100	3,240	1,084	2,700	10,124	2,990	2,948	2,859	3,130	11,927
13	Expenses	2,220	2,700	2,640	2,655	10,215	2,620	2,530	2,500	2,490	10,140
14	Net profit/(Loss)	880	540	(1,556)	45	(91)	370	418	359	640	1,787
15											
16	Net profit calculation (Quarters)										
17											
18	Income	5,800	5,950	5,004	5,101	-	5,740	5,703	5,649	5,830	-
19	Direct costs	2,700	2,710	3,920	2,700	-	2,750	2,755	2,790	2,700	-
20	Gross profit/(Loss)	3,100	3,240	1,084	2,700	-	2,990	2,948	2,859	3,130	-
21	Expenses	2,220	2,700	2,640	2,655	-	2,620	2,530	2,500	2,490	-
22	Net profit/(Loss)	880	540	(1,556)	45	-	370	418	359	640	-
23											
24	Net profit calculation (Annual)										
25	Income	-	-	-	-	21,855	-	-	-	-	22,922
26	Direct costs	-	-	-	-	12,030	-	-	-	-	10,995
27	Gross profit/(Loss)	-	-	-	-	10,124	-	-	-	-	11,927
28	Expenses	-	-	-	-	10,215	-	-	-	-	10,140
29	Net profit/(Loss)	-	-	-	-	(91)	-	-	-	-	1,787

Figure 11-14. In this model, the calculation mask is used to include the years and exclude the quarters

The calculation now will exclude anything that has a one in the mask and will include anything with zero.

Calculating Depreciation

Calculating asset depreciation used to be a major problem because Excel didn't have a dedicated function to handle the different depreciation methods. I have included this calculation not because it is best practice, but because few modelers or Excel users realize that Microsoft actually included a few depreciation calculations in Excel 2007 (and later versions) that have now simplified the entire depreciation calculation.

When I create depreciation calculations in financial models, I aim to make them clear and clean. I also make one set of calculations for every asset as in Figure 11-15. This is the only real hassle with depreciation calculations; I have seen models where the assets have been grouped in order to save time. Be very careful with grouping—much will depend upon the classification of the assets and the type of allowances that are allowed by the tax authorities.

Simply grouping them together could get you into major trouble if you haven't taken authoritative tax advice. Therefore, it is better to make individual calculations that can be altered very quickly should any changes be required.

	A	B	C	D	E
1	NonSuch Financial Model				
2	Calculations				
3					
4		Input Links			
5		Asset:	Original Cost:	Life (Years):	Salvage Value:
6		Printer	$35,000	7	$500

Figure 11-15. The inputs for the depreciation calculation are referenced from the calculation worksheet

For all the depreciation methods, there are four requirements or details that will be required. Don't worry if you are unable to get these details from the inputs. The prominent part is that the calculations are set up correctly as in Figure 11-16. This way, the inputs can just be assumptions, and again this is where it is important that each asset be calculated separately to avoid mixing different asset life of each asset and depreciation rates. The asset life, which is the predicted number of years that an asset is expected to be useful, is very important because it will govern the rate at which that asset should be depreciated. In Figure 11-16, there is an expected seven-year asset life.

G30 *fx*

	A	B	C	D	E	F
1	NonSuch Financial Model					
2	Calculations					
3						
4		Input Links				
5		Asset:	Original Cost:	Life (years):	Salvage Value:	
6		Printer	$35,000	7	$500	
7						
8						
9		Depreciation Calculation				
10						
11		*Depreciation Amount*				
12		Year	SLN	DB	DDB	SYD
13		1	$4,928.57	$15,925.00	$10,000.00	$8,625.00
14		2	$4,928.57	$8,679.13	$7,142.86	$7,392.86
15		3	$4,928.57	$4,730.12	$5,102.04	$6,160.71
16		4	$4,928.57	$2,577.92	$3,644.31	$4,928.57
17		5	$4,928.57	$1,404.96	$2,603.08	$3,696.43
18		6	$4,928.57	$765.71	$1,859.34	$2,464.29
19		7	$4,928.57	$417.31	$1,328.10	$1,232.14

Figure 11-16. This model displays the depreciation calculations

The calculations are then relatively straightforward. I find it simpler to create a calculation table of the number in columns rather than rows because it is much easier to create a lookup from a column in a table if needed. There are four widely practiced depreciation methods:

- Straight-line method
- Declining balance method
- Double-declining balance method
- Sum of the year's digits method

I will not be describing depreciation strategies or methods in this book, as it is an extensive topic. If you want to gain a solid understanding of depreciation, the best way is to find a tax accountant who is willing to explain it to you. Firsthand knowledge when discussing depreciation is invaluable. The other alternative would be to purchase a good accounting book.

However, for this book, based upon my experience the majority of modeling projects will use the straight-line method. If you create a table like in Figure 11-16, you will have all the methods calculated. Notice in Figure 7-16 how each of the methods produces different depreciation rates, which is why it is important that the method used can be justified accordingly. Here are the functions that represent the methods:

- =SLN() Straight-line method
- =DB() Declining balance method
- =DDB() Double-declining balance method
- =SYD() Sum of the years digits' method

Each of these functions uses the mix of the four inputs elements. For instance, the straight-line method requires the original cost, asset life, and salvage value, while the declining balance also requires the year, as in Figure 11-17.

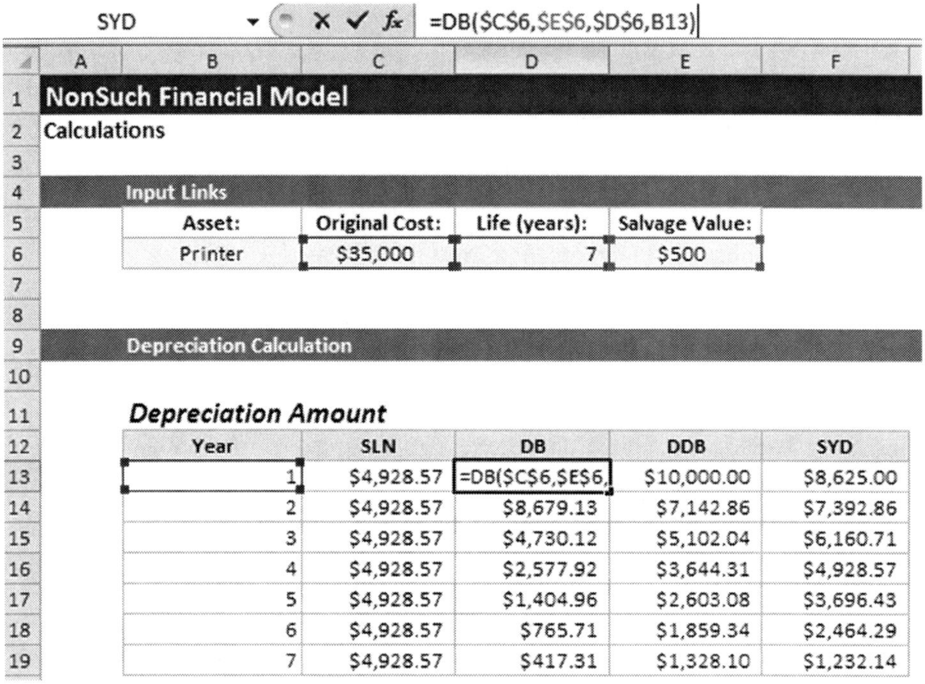
SYD =DB($C$6,$E$6,$D$6,B13)

NonSuch Financial Model

Calculations

Input Links

Asset:	Original Cost:	Life (years):	Salvage Value:
Printer	$35,000	7	$500

Depreciation Calculation

Depreciation Amount

Year	SLN	DB	DDB	SYD
1	$4,928.57	=DB($C$6,$E$6,	$10,000.00	$8,625.00
2	$4,928.57	$8,679.13	$7,142.86	$7,392.86
3	$4,928.57	$4,730.12	$5,102.04	$6,160.71
4	$4,928.57	$2,577.92	$3,644.31	$4,928.57
5	$4,928.57	$1,404.96	$2,603.08	$3,696.43
6	$4,928.57	$765.71	$1,859.34	$2,464.29
7	$4,928.57	$417.31	$1,328.10	$1,232.14

Figure 11-17. These elements make up the declining balance method

In addition to creating a deprecation calculation, you should also create a table that shows the value of the asset in each year after it has been depreciated, as in Figure 11-18. This information will be needed for the balance sheet in the fixed assets. The formula is calculated by taking the starting value of the asset and taking off the depreciation amount based upon the depreciation calculation each year. Then use the balance again to deduct the depreciation the following year.

SYD | =C25-C13

NonSuch Financial Model

Calculations

Input Links

Asset:	Original Cost:	Life (years):	Salvage Value:
Printer	$35,000	7	$500

Depreciation Calculation

Depreciation Amount

Year	SLN	DB	DDB	SYD
1	$4,928.57	$15,925.00	$10,000.00	$8,625.00
2	$4,928.57	$8,679.13	$7,142.86	$7,392.86
3	$4,928.57	$4,730.12	$5,102.04	$6,160.71
4	$4,928.57	$2,577.92	$3,644.31	$4,928.57
5	$4,928.57	$1,404.96	$2,603.08	$3,696.43
6	$4,928.57	$765.71	$1,859.34	$2,464.29
7	$4,928.57	$417.31	$1,328.10	$1,232.14

Value of Asset

Value of Asset

Year	SLN	DB	DDB	SYD
0	$35,000.00	$35,000.00	$35,000.00	$35,000.00
1	=C25-C13	$19,075.00	$25,000.00	$26,375.00
2	$25,142.86	$10,395.88	$17,857.14	$18,982.14
3	$20,214.29	$5,665.75	$12,755.10	$12,821.43
4	$15,285.71	$3,087.83	$9,110.79	$7,892.86
5	$10,357.14	$1,682.87	$6,507.71	$4,196.43
6	$5,428.57	$917.16	$4,648.36	$1,732.14
7	$500.00	$499.85	$3,320.26	$500.00

END

Figure 11-18. This model shows the value of the assets after depreciation

Database Calculations

At some point, it is very likely that the modeler will need to work with data tables. Data tables are sets of data, which consist of headings and several rows of data under these headings like in Figure 11-19.

7	NonSuch Financial Model				
8	Inputs (Data)				
9					
10	Month	Employee	Region	Age	Annual Earnings
11	Jan	Susan	Northern	42	283,800
12	Jan	Chris	Western	40	507,200
13	Jan	Jamie	Eastern	38	107,600
14	Jan	Randy	Southern	46	391,600
15	Jan	Anil	Northern	36	226,700
16	Feb	Yasmin	Northern	48	411,800
17	Feb	Vladimir	Northern	29	154,200
18	Feb	Jason	Southern	33	258,000
19	Feb	Coreen	Southern	34	233,800

Figure 11-19. A data table is a set of data consisting of headings and rows of data

These databases are formed when the modeler has to collect and collate much information from various sources, which then need to be grouped. They are also needed when importing information such as when a comma-separated values (CSV) file from an external data source is required. Fortunately, there are a number of functions in Excel that can ease the burden of calculation from large data tables, and they are collectively known as the database function. There are 12 database functions, which provide help with counting the data, determining totals, or getting the average.

I am often surprised at how seldom modelers use these functions when in fact they are quite simple to use and, when used effectively, are powerful and not processor-intensive. Every financial modeler should be comfortable with knowing when and how to use these database functions.

To demonstrate, look again at Figure 11-19, which is a database that consists of names with their locations, age, and annual earnings. Typically, these would be the data inputs in the model, and normally a number of calculations would be created with this data. When dealing with data like this in a table, the modeler should assume that the user of the model is going to want to see the effects on the model outputs based on different views of the data. For instance, the user may want to see the total of all salaries in the northern regions or the total high test salary in the southern region. The use of data tables allows for greater flexibility, because any changes in the content of the model is applied by changing the data in the table and not the structure of the model.

All the database functions have similar requirements—they all need to have a table of data, a column that will be referenced, and a criterion. In Figure 11-20a, I have provided a criterion that consists of a cut-down version of the table in Figure 11-19. The column headings will be used as the criteria. In the example, the criteria is for the month of Jan (January), but you could just as easily select a region and an age as well that would then make the criteria multifaceted. Note that there is only one row of criteria available; however, this is only because I have chosen to construct the inputs that way. In fact, I could just as easily add a second or third row to the criteria, as in Figure 11-20b.

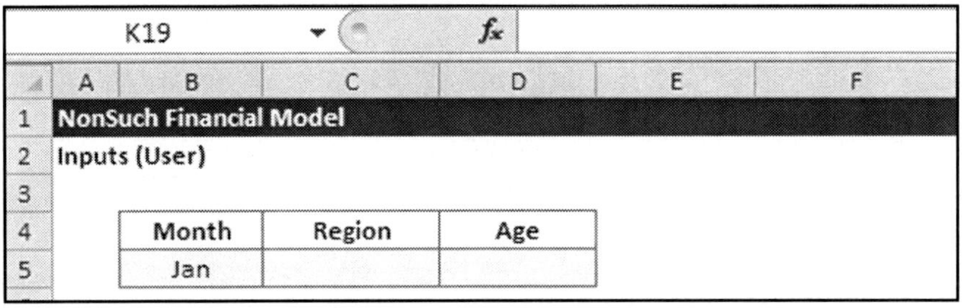

Figure 11-20a. This figure shows the inputs criteria

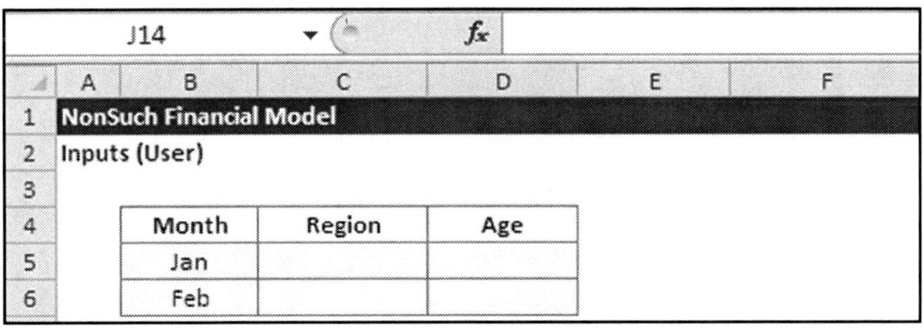

Figure 11-20b. This figure shows a multirow criteria input

When dealing with large data sets, it is useful to be able to provide a criteria selection that can handle more than one parameter for each heading, However, for our example, we only need the one row as in Figure 11-20a.

In Figure 11-21a, the inputs from the criteria have been brought into the inputs links. Four database calculations have now been created by using four functions: DSUM, DAVERAGE, DMAX, and DMIN The syntax for each of these functions is as follows:

=DFUNCTIONNAME(Full table, Reference column, Full criteria).

23	NonSuch Financial Model	
24	Calculations	
25		
26	Input Links	
27		
28	Month	Jan
29	Region	0
30	Age	0
31	Database Calculations	
32		
33	Total for input selection	1,516,900
34	Average for input selection	303,380
35	Maximum for input selection	507,200
36	Minimum for input selection	107,600

Figure 11-21a. This figure shows the database functions' calculations

In Figure 11-21b, the formula for the DSUM can show that it is accessing the table in the range B11:F20, the reference column is the annual earning in column F row 11, and the criteria are the inputs in B4:D5.

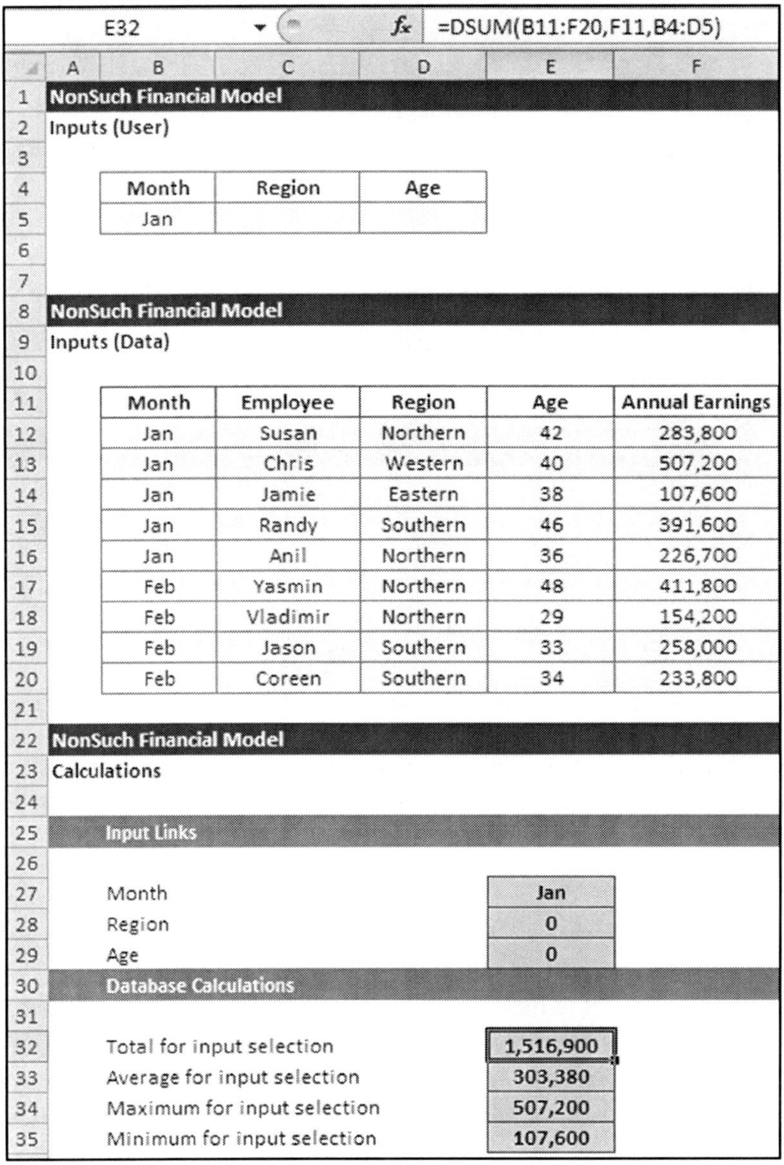

E32 | =DSUM(B11:F20,F11,B4:D5)

	A	B	C	D	E	F
1	NonSuch Financial Model					
2	Inputs (User)					
3						
4		Month	Region	Age		
5		Jan				
6						
7						
8	NonSuch Financial Model					
9	Inputs (Data)					
10						
11		Month	Employee	Region	Age	Annual Earnings
12		Jan	Susan	Northern	42	283,800
13		Jan	Chris	Western	40	507,200
14		Jan	Jamie	Eastern	38	107,600
15		Jan	Randy	Southern	46	391,600
16		Jan	Anil	Northern	36	226,700
17		Feb	Yasmin	Northern	48	411,800
18		Feb	Vladimir	Northern	29	154,200
19		Feb	Jason	Southern	33	258,000
20		Feb	Coreen	Southern	34	233,800
21						
22	NonSuch Financial Model					
23	Calculations					
24						
25		Input Links				
26						
27		Month			Jan	
28		Region			0	
29		Age			0	
30		Database Calculations				
31						
32		Total for input selection			1,516,900	
33		Average for input selection			303,380	
34		Maximum for input selection			507,200	
35		Minimum for input selection			107,600	

Figure 11-21b. The DSUM() database function is used to define the table

The database calculations have a number of uses because they are reliant on the criteria. They are also very versatile and can be used to engage the model user to create "what if?" scenarios. Another use for the calculations is to provide dashboard information for the model. I often use the database functions to provide feedback to the model user about the status of the data based upon the user selection (see Figure 11-22).

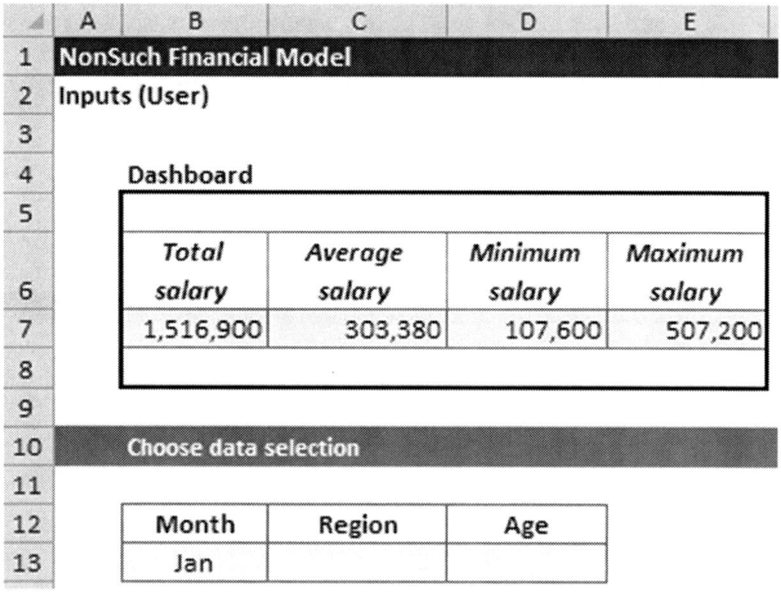

Figure 11-22. The database calculations are used in a dashboard

Another use for the functions is for internal admin for the model. These functions can be used to check for changes in the model that have occurred after the model has been opened and to report on those changes. This information can then be placed in a user log with a date and timestamp, which provides admin information of when changes to the model were made.

Calculating Net Present Value (NPV)

The net present value (NPV) is one of those calculations that is a must for modelers. Whether it is being used on the model that you have built or not, every modeler should be able to calculate the NPV and be aware of the shortcomings of using the NPV function in Excel.

In Figure 11-23, I have used four time periods, 0 to 3. These can be months or years, but with this example they will be called time periods. The NPV function has the following syntax:

=NPV(Discount NPV (Discount rate, cash flows), rate, cash flows).

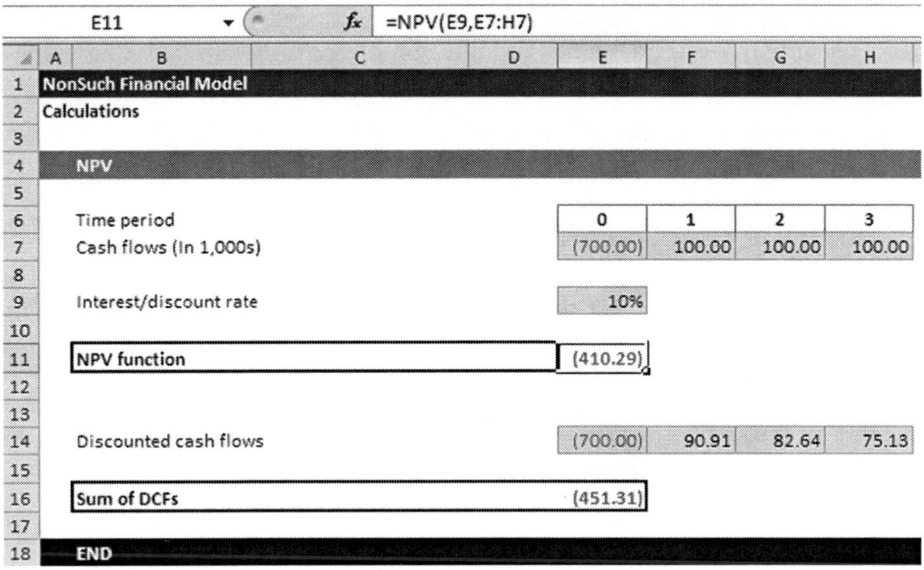

Figure 11-23. The NPV calculation of the sum of the discounted cash flows is shown here

In the example, the discount rate is 10%, and the cash flows are in row 7.

In addition to the NPV, there is also a calculation for the discounted cash flows in row 14, which uses the cash flows, discount rate, and time periods. I have provided the sum of the discounted cash flows (DCFs) to give a check on the NPV.

The sum of the discounted cash flows should always equal the NPV value, but as can be seen in Figure 11-23, that is not the case. This means there must be an issue with either how the function has been used or the calculation itself. Fortunately, I am aware that the Excel NPV calculation is flawed because it doesn't actually give the NPV. What it does give is a present value (PV), and unless an adjustment is made the NPV will be incorrect.

To understand the flaw in the NPV function, think about what happens when a project starts. You can assume that the investment for the project is made up front, and so you would call this time period "zero" (Day 0). The cash flows for the project will start to flow from the time period 1 onwards, but as the investment is made on time period 0, it should not be included in the discounted cash flows.

Unfortunately, the Excel NPV function has a built-in assumption that even the first cash flow, which is the investment, happens at the end of the year. Although in reality, the initial investment is almost always made up front as there are likely to be up-front costs, such as deposits and capital that must be secured prior to the project commencing. With this understanding, you would need to adjust the NPV calculation to reflect this reality, which means adding the investment without discounting and then using the NPV function to discount the rest of the cash flows.

A further issue with the NPV function is that it assumes that the cash flows are at the end of time period. So, for instance, if the time periods are annual (years), it assumes that the cash received for the investment is in the very last month, and is therefore not realistic. The modeler should be aware of this feature of the function and be prepared to explain this to model users.

In Figure 11-24, the correct version of the NPV function has been used. The cash flow has been shortened to reflect period 1 to period 3 as the cash flows to be discounted by using the discount rate 10%. The initial investment has subsequently been added back undiscounted. To see of the calculation is correct, it can be checked by testing it against the total of the discounted cash flows in Figure 11-24 to make sure the NPV and the DCFs are the same, which now works.

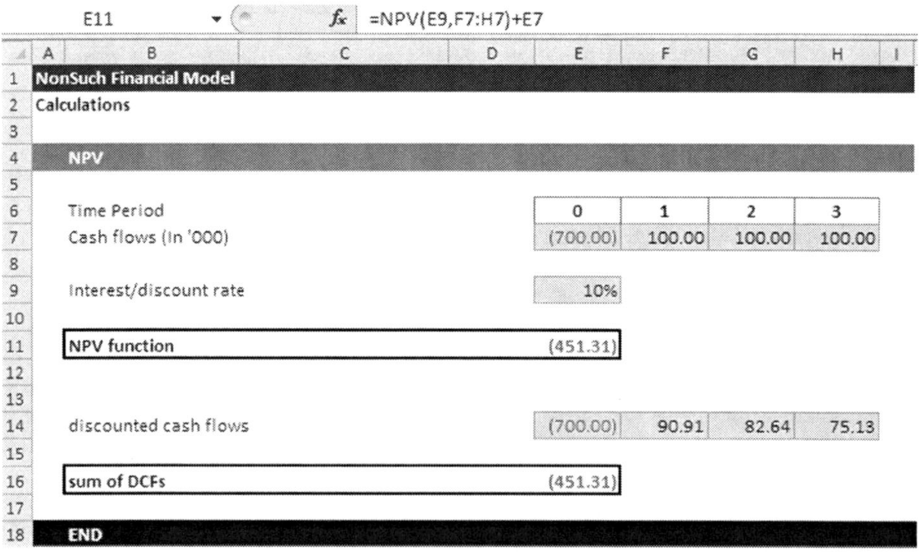

Figure 11-24. This figure shows a corrected version of the NPV function

It is imperative that modelers have a solid understanding of how to make the NPV calculation correctly. This understanding will ensure that mistakes are not made during the NPV calculation. This is a key financial calculation, so be sure you really understand how to make NPV calculations correctly.

Indices Calculations

A very frequent calculation, particularly in models where there is historical data or forecast data, is creating indices. Indices are useful because they give a view of trends quickly and also provide a method of comparing two or more items against each other. They also make very good visual representations for graphs. While they are simple to create, it is surprising how often I have seen indices created incorrectly inside models. The basic tenet of the calculation is to create a growth data based on this calculation:

(The period that is being measured minus the previous period) divided by the period being measured.

The result from the growth data should be applied to the base year (the year that will be used to measure differences in growth):

Base Year times (1 plus Growth Data)

Figure 11-25a features data about the price of a Big Mac converted into US dollars across a series of nations (taken from the Big Mac Index published by *The Economist*).

J22 fx

	A	B	C	D
1				
2	The Price of a Big Mac (In US$)			
3		2008	2009	2010
4	Australia	3.36	3.37	3.84
5	Brazil	4.73	4.02	4.91
6	Britain	4.57	3.69	3.48
7	Canada	4.08	3.35	4.00
8	China	1.83	1.83	1.95
9	Hong Kong	1.71	1.72	1.90
10	Norway	7.88	6.15	7.20
11	Russia	2.54	2.04	2.33
12	South Africa	2.24	2.17	2.45
13	United States	3.57	3.57	3.73

Figure 11-25a. The table shows the price of a Big Mac in US dollars across different nations

You need to apply the calculation to each of these time periods, as in Figure 11-25b.

C17 f_x =(C4-B4)/C4

	A	B	C	D	E
1					
2	**The Price of a Big Mac (In US$)**				
3		**2008**	**2009**	**2010**	
4	Australia	3.36	3.37	3.84	
5	Brazil	4.73	4.02	4.91	
6	Britain	4.57	3.69	3.48	
7	Canada	4.08	3.35	4.00	
8	China	1.83	1.83	1.95	
9	Hong Kong	1.71	1.72	1.90	
10	Norway	7.88	6.15	7.20	
11	Russia	2.54	2.04	2.33	
12	South Africa	2.24	2.17	2.45	
13	United States	3.57	3.57	3.73	
14					
15	**Growth Data**				
16		**2008**	**2009**	**2010**	
17	Australia		0.3%	12.2%	
18	Brazil		(17.7%)	18.1%	
19	Britain		(23.8%)	(6.0%)	

Figure 11-25b. The growth data is calculated by comparing the change from the previous year

Note the calculation in Figure 11-25b. This is the root of the index calculation. While it is simple, just be careful to use the parentheses in the right place. You should be aware that indices can also be shown as proportion of 100, as in Figure 11-25c.

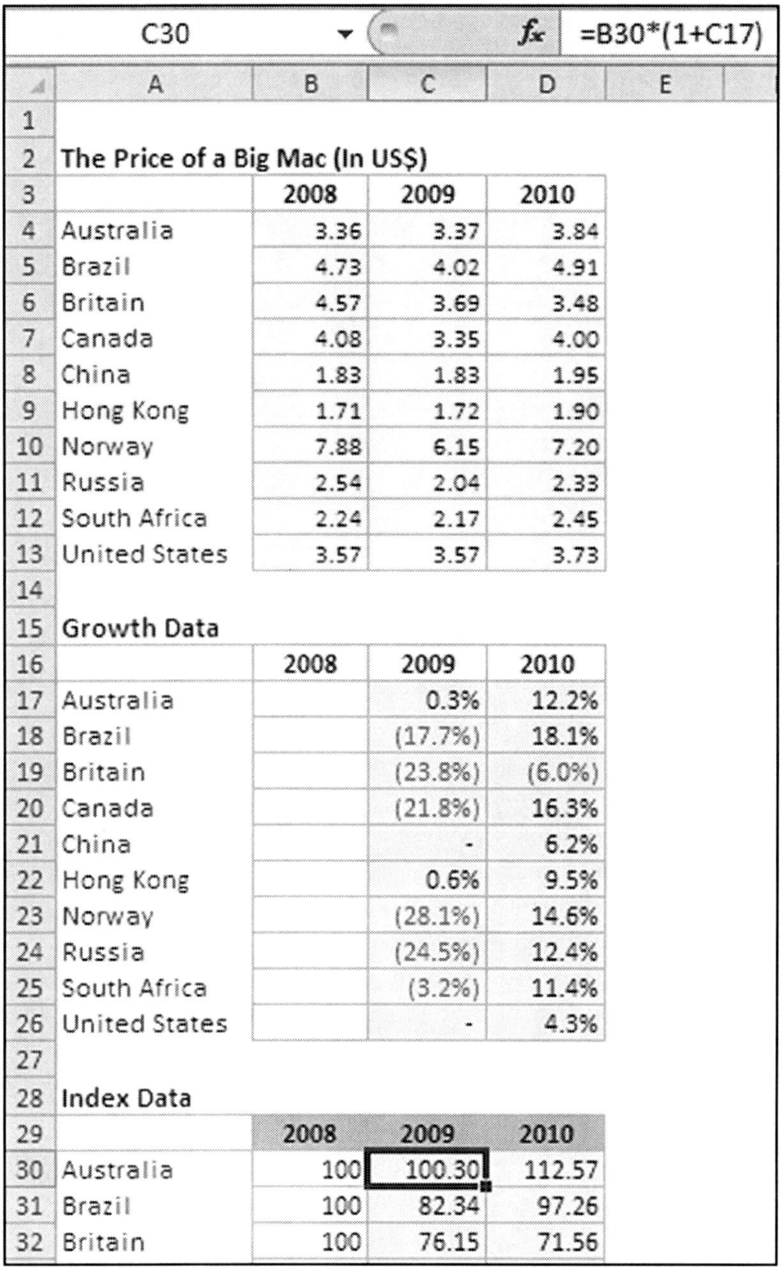

C30 | f_x =B30*(1+C17)

	A	B	C	D	E
1					
2	The Price of a Big Mac (In US$)				
3		2008	2009	2010	
4	Australia	3.36	3.37	3.84	
5	Brazil	4.73	4.02	4.91	
6	Britain	4.57	3.69	3.48	
7	Canada	4.08	3.35	4.00	
8	China	1.83	1.83	1.95	
9	Hong Kong	1.71	1.72	1.90	
10	Norway	7.88	6.15	7.20	
11	Russia	2.54	2.04	2.33	
12	South Africa	2.24	2.17	2.45	
13	United States	3.57	3.57	3.73	
14					
15	Growth Data				
16		2008	2009	2010	
17	Australia		0.3%	12.2%	
18	Brazil		(17.7%)	18.1%	
19	Britain		(23.8%)	(6.0%)	
20	Canada		(21.8%)	16.3%	
21	China		-	6.2%	
22	Hong Kong		0.6%	9.5%	
23	Norway		(28.1%)	14.6%	
24	Russia		(24.5%)	12.4%	
25	South Africa		(3.2%)	11.4%	
26	United States		-	4.3%	
27					
28	Index Data				
29		2008	2009	2010	
30	Australia	100	100.30	112.57	
31	Brazil	100	82.34	97.26	
32	Britain	100	76.15	71.56	

Figure 11-25c. The growth data is applied to the base year to give an index

The index is now created and can be used to reflect changes in growth against the base year as in Figure 11-25d.

D41 *fx*

	A	B	C	D
2	**The Price of a Big Mac (In US$)**			
3		**2008**	**2009**	**2010**
4	Australia	3.36	3.37	3.84
5	Brazil	4.73	4.02	4.91
6	Britain	4.57	3.69	3.48
7	Canada	4.08	3.35	4.00
8	China	1.83	1.83	1.95
9	Hong Kong	1.71	1.72	1.90
10	Norway	7.88	6.15	7.20
11	Russia	2.54	2.04	2.33
12	South Africa	2.24	2.17	2.45
13	United States	3.57	3.57	3.73
14				
15	**Growth Data**			
16		**2008**	**2009**	**2010**
17	Australia		0.3%	12.2%
18	Brazil		(17.7%)	18.1%
19	Britain		(23.8%)	(6.0%)
20	Canada		(21.8%)	16.3%
21	China		-	6.2%
22	Hong Kong		0.6%	9.5%
23	Norway		(28.1%)	14.6%
24	Russia		(24.5%)	12.4%
25	South Africa		(3.2%)	11.4%
26	United States		-	4.3%
27				
28	**Index Data**			
29		**2008**	**2009**	**2010**
30	Australia	100	100.30	112.57
31	Brazil	100	82.34	97.26
32	Britain	100	76.15	71.56
33	Canada	100	78.21	90.92
34	China	100	100.00	106.15
35	Hong Kong	100	100.58	110.11
36	Norway	100	71.87	82.35
37	Russia	100	75.49	84.89
38	South Africa	100	96.77	107.83
39	United States	100	100.00	104.29

Figure 11-25d. The is a layout for the full index table, which would be placed in the outputs of the model

This chapter has discussed the difficult concept of financial-based calculations. They are difficult because there can be several different methods of performing the calculations, and each has its own foibles. A big fear for modelers is making mistakes when performing calculations in models. Unfortunately, I cannot tell that you won't make mistakes. However, even if you do make mistakes, understanding how and why those mistakes were made is the key better modeling.

CHAPTER

12

Logical and Structural-Based Calculations

In this chapter, I want to take a look at functions that fit into a specific part of modeling. I will be discussing functions that work with dates, lookup functions, mathematical functions, and also some functions that are specific to particular situations. I will also outline the functions that fit into various modeling structures and point out functions that modelers should be learning to use. In financial modeling, there are no defined methods of using functions; in fact, there are no prescribed functions for any given modeling situation. The functions that are used in models are instead a reflection of the modeler's skills, experience, and understanding of best practice modeling.

Array Calculations for Single Values

In this section, I want to show you how to use array functions to solve calculation problems. Array calculations have their uses in modeling because they allow the modeler to create calculations that are tailored toward the results that are required. An array formula is a formula that works with an array, or series, of data values rather than an individual data value. There are two types of array formulas. The first type returns a singular value to a single cell and works with a series of data and aggregates it, typically using SUM, AVERAGE, or COUNT. The second type returns an array of values as their result into two or more cells. This section will demonstrate the use of a number of array calculations that are very practical for modeling, and in doing so will offer the premise for using the array formula while still maintaining a best practice model.

The first example is how to force a calculation on a series of data even when there is an error. Keep in mind that Excel is a very logical application. If it encounters an error for a series of data, then it's impossible to make any calculations on the data series without picking that error. In other words, it won't calculate just using traditional functions (see Figure 12-1).

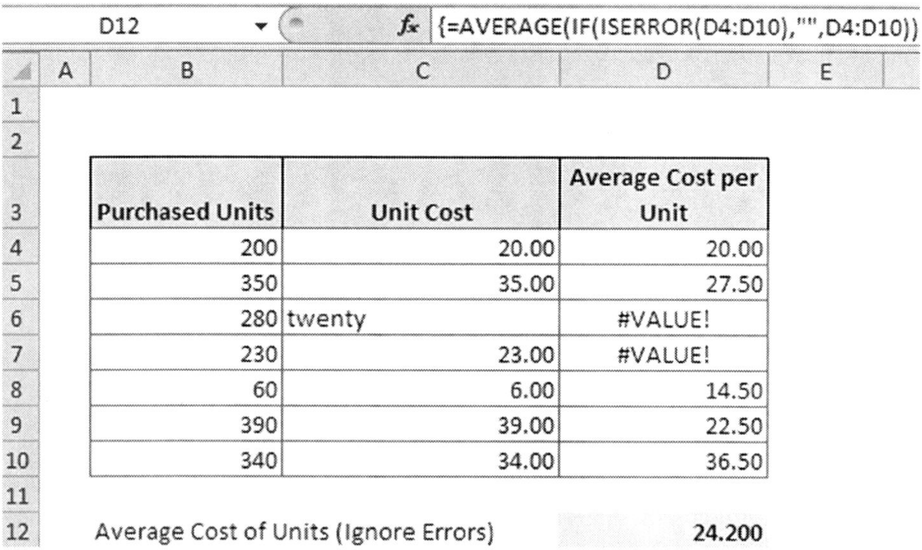

D12 fx {=AVERAGE(IF(ISERROR(D4:D10),"",D4:D10))}

	A	B	C	D	E
1					
2					
3		Purchased Units	Unit Cost	Average Cost per Unit	
4		200	20.00	20.00	
5		350	35.00	27.50	
6		280	twenty	#VALUE!	
7		230	23.00	#VALUE!	
8		60	6.00	14.50	
9		390	39.00	22.50	
10		340	34.00	36.50	
11					
12		Average Cost of Units (Ignore Errors)		24.200	

Figure 12-1. This model is using the average function as an array to calculate over errors

In the calculation, the formula is calculating an average cost per unit. But I have added in an extra dimension so that if an error occurs in the column where I am reading data (column D), then I can just substitute the error with blank data (" ") and calculate the average. Otherwise, calculate the average as usual. (The syntax of the formula is not explained for the reason that it will be explained in the next section.)

This array function is extremely useful because it can be used to check the inputs, and even if the inputs are in error, the calculation is still made. However, always be aware that when using such a calculation with averages, the result will be skewed because there is some missing data. Notice the curly braces around the formula. Do not be tempted to place these yourself as they are automatically created when you type Ctrl, Shift, and Enter, which is how to create arrays.

Formulas That Are Based on Condition

This next array calculation is based on creating a formula that will give results based upon a condition. Again, this is another classic example of a situation that comes up repeatedly in financial models. The SUMIF function, while extremely useful, is not capable of handling conditions beyond two dimensions without having to make a highly complex formula. I know of several modelers who are very uncomfortable with using arrays, but there is nothing to fear. Yes, it's not good practice to have hundreds of arrays strewn through the model. But at the same time, you should be capable of using them when required to do so. In Figure 12-2, I have created a simple conditional calculation that illustrates the use of COUNT, but this can be expanded to take on several more conditions or used with SUM, AVERAGE, or even SUMPRODUCT.

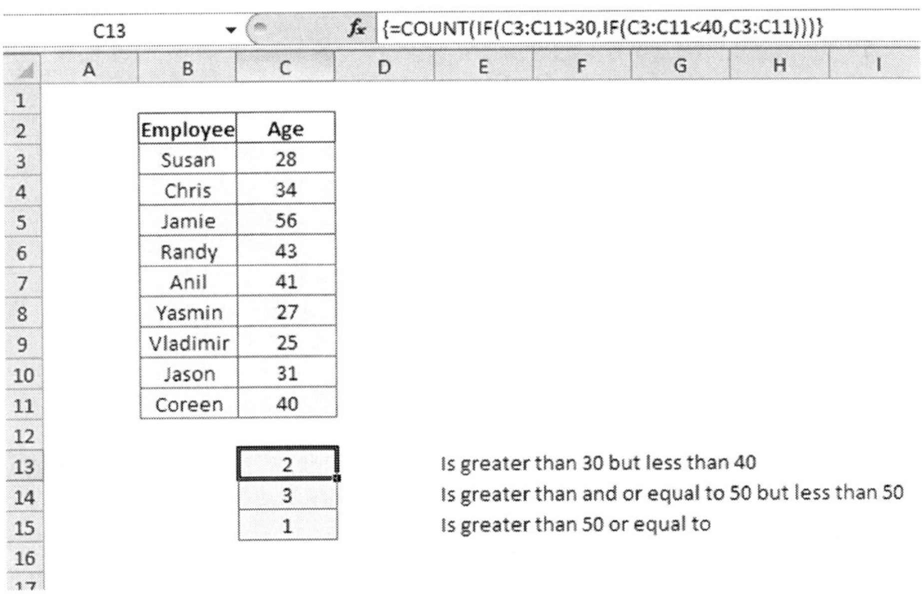

Figure 12-2. This model uses the array calculation with conditions

Notice the syntax. The IF statement in Figure 12-2 is looking for two conditions in the table. The first condition is finding where the age is greater than 30, and the second condition is to find where the age is less than 40. The return is to show how many occurrences happen with these conditions. There is an IF placed for each condition. It is possible to have several more conditions (up to seven), but I would argue that anything beyond three conditions is excessive. At that stage, you would start to verge on using online analytical processing (OLAP) cubes, which will not be covered in this book.

OLAP cubes would be used on tables of data and information where one row of data can have several columns of information because the formula is able to accommodate several conditions.

Getting the Closest Match to an Input Target

This next array calculation is one that I have used in order to test the data for a specific target. Put simply, the formula allows the user to input a target, which can be text or a numeric value depending on which part of the data the calculation is referencing. By then entering the target inputs, the formula checks through the data range and picks out the item that comes closest to matching the target.

This array formula is very useful for checking the tolerance in a date, for instance. When I create models that are required to receive a download of a CSV file from an external data store of personal data, I will often have this target input in place. This way, I can check to see any of the ages, for example in Figure 12-3, are near zero or 100, as that will provide me with highest and lowest tolerances. If the closest match falls below or above this range, then I can be reasonably sure that the data is lacking integrity.

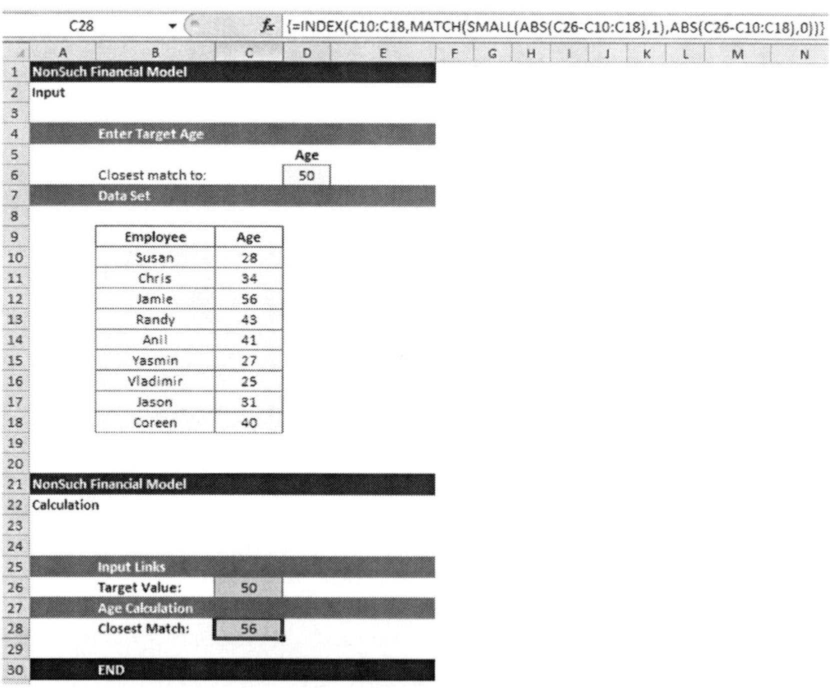

Figure 12-3. The input is used to set the target age, and the closest match is identified

Using Crosstab Calculations

For those who have used relational databases such as Microsoft Access, you should already be aware of the crosstab. This is a method of summarizing categorical data by using an algorithm that searches between those categories. Crosstab calculations are far from essential to modeling, but they are useful, particularly for representing data in a logical manner. I use crosstab calculations mainly for presenting dashboards by creating tables that can easily be digested. Figure 12-4 shows how a cross table can be created with an array calculation.

C24 fx {=SUM(($B24=$B$4:$B$20)*(C$23=$C$4:$C$20)*$D$4:$D$20)}

Date	Category	Amount
11/08/2014	Expense	23,500
11/08/2014	Expense	15,000
11/08/2014	Expense	9,120
11/08/2014	Revenue	16,950
11/08/2014	Direct cost	145,500
16/02/2014	Revenue	65,950
16/02/2014	Revenue	20,000
16/02/2014	Revenue	7,800
03/03/2014	Revenue	20,000
03/03/2014	Direct cost	89,000
03/03/2014	Direct cost	9,000
03/03/2014	Direct cost	3,500
06/01/2014	Direct cost	11,020
06/01/2014	Direct cost	78,440
06/01/2014	Direct cost	75,300
23/12/2014	Taxation	11,500
23/12/2014	Expense	15,500

	Expense	Revenue	Direct cost	Lodging	Taxation
11-Aug	47,620	16,950	145,500	-	-
16-Feb	-	93,750	-	-	-
06-Jan	-	-	164,760	-	-
03-Mar	-	20,000	101,500	-	-
23-Dec	15,500	-	-	-	11,500

Figure 12-4. A crosstab calculation is useful when presenting dashboards

Applying the Right Function to Your Calculations

I am often asked if I can give some advice on which functions are best to use when modeling and which ones should be avoided. This then leads to conversations on which functions are best for specific calculations.

You may be surprised by my response to these questions. I believe that there really are no answers because, unfortunately, not every calculation is identical. This is one reason why Excel has so many functions capable of achieving solutions for the equivalent calculation. Numerous functions are needed, because there are subtle differences that can have a significant effect on the result. With so many functions available, hopefully there should always be one that meets the modeler's needs.

Now that I have burst that bubble, let's look at the positive. While I cannot give definitive answers as to which are the right functions to apply to calculations, I can tell why certain functions work better than others for specific calculations.

Functions That Look Up Information

The majority of calculations that are used in models are based on the lookup; that is, by using a key or reference you can unlock further details that can then be substitutes and used through the calculation. There are several lookup functions, and some are more specialized for specific types of calculations. For instance, the function =GETPIVOTDATA is designed purely for getting information from a pivot table and will not work properly unless it's applied to a pivot table.

There following three lookup functions are ones that all modelers should be familiar with:

- =VLOOKUP()
- =MATCH()
- =INDEX()

In addition, the VLOOKUP() is also partnered by the HLOOKUP() function, and the MATCH function is generally combined with INDEX() to for an INDEX() MATCH() formula. In Chapter 3, these functions were covered. If you are unclear on how to use them, turn back to that chapter and refresh your memory. The best way to learn these functions is to actually practice them. Get a worksheet and carefully go through writing the syntax, even with minimal data, just to begin to understand how the functions work and to start becoming comfortable with using them.

I have one final note about these three functions. I always prefer to use the INDEX() MATCH() combination in contrast to VLOOKUPS, although this is a matter of preference. There are a number of potential issues in relation to computer processing capability with VLOOKUPS that steer me away from using it.

Functions That Require a Condition

For calculations where a specific condition must be reached in order to get the correct result, the majority of go-to functions include the following:

- =IF()
- =SUMIF()
- =COUNTIF()
- =SUMIFS()
- =AVERAGEIF()

Do not allow yourself to go through this book without knowing how to use the =IF() and =SUMIF() functions They are the most important condition-driven functions you will ever get to use. In order to build a serious model, these will be your most useful functions for calculations reliant on the data held in another cell or when you require input from the model user. (Again, these functions were covered in Chapter 3.)

Functions That Are Driven by Dates

Dates and times are always tricky because they just don't work on a typical denary level, and so require some conversions. In other words, if you try to add two dates together, the result will not be as you expect unless they are converted. In almost every model you create, you will need at least one of the following functions when working with dates:

- =DATEVALUE()
- =EOMONTH()
- =WORKDAY()
- =WEEKDAY()
- =TODAY()
- =DAYS360()
- =YEAR()
- =MONTH()

All of these functions are crucial in one way or another. You will seriously limit your ability to creating efficient, fast, and clear calculations if you neglect to use any of these functions.

Functions for Precise Situations

Excel is seen as a financial application in many quarters and is really the most widely used application in finance circles today. One ironic aspect of Excel is that many of the popular financial functions have some odd quirks or just don't feel complete. In other words, you generally need to have strong financial background in order to use them. This brings us to our next point—many of these functions can be created in other ways, which means they have alternatives. There are a clutch of functions that have no alternatives and are used in precise situations that should be understood by modelers. The functions that you should always be able to use:

- =DB()
- =DDB()
- =IRR()
- =XIRR()
- =NPV()
- =XNPV()
- =SLN()
- =SYD()
- =FV()

For instance, the DB(), DDB(), SYD(), and SLN() functions are all about calculating depreciation, while the NPV(), XNPV(), IRR(), and XIRR() are for capital budgeting. However, you should still be familiar with how they work and be capable of applying them to calculations that demand that particular situation.

Mathematical Functions

All calculations are mathematical in one way or another, so why are some calculations described as specifically being mathematical? The reason why some of the functions are called mathematical is that they are designed to simulate a specific mathematical problem or solution. For instance, the SUM() function is mathematical because it is designed to calculate the total of a range of cells. When discussing mathematical functions in Excel, I am referring to functions that are built around particular math problems and their solutions. These functions are often too limited for general modeling, but there are some that have some major uses in modeling. Yes, you could get by without them, but you will find that having them greatly enhances your ability to create good calculations. Here is a list of the most commonly used mathematical functions in models:

- =MOD()
- =ABS()
- =CEILING()
- =INT()
- =RANDBETWEEN()
- =ROUND()
- =ROUNDUP()
- =ROUNDDOWN()
- =SUM()
- =SUMIF()
- =SUMPRODUCT()
- =SUMIFS()
- =SUBTOTAL()

You will immediately spot that a number of the functions appeared previously in other sections of this chapter, such as the SUMIF function. These functions operate on calculations in several ways, and so there are some that can be considered conditional or mathematical. Aside from the massive importance of SUM(), which cannot be understated; SUMPRODUCT() is another must-know function because it saves an enormous amount of time and effort when used correctly. All of these functions mentioned in this and the previous sections should be part of the modeler's armory, and not one should be neglected.

Functions Dependent on Text

In an ideal world, you wouldn't need text functions in Excel because after all Excel is not a word or text tool. However, the reality is text is part of the data and information that modelers routinely work with. Being able to do even relatively simple calculations like extracting the last name from a lump of text is very important. This list of text functions is critical to know because you will always need them in a model and they will save you time:

- =FIND()
- =LEFT()
- =MID()
- =RIGHT()
- =LEN()
- =REPLACE()
- =TEXT()
- =TRIM()
- =VALUE()

Without exception, all of the listed functions are critical to know because they help you deal with the more common problems that afflict modelers. For example, these functions can correct the data that is inconsistent from row to row, or when you need to extract first names and last names and some of the names have middle names and others do not.

Calculations Involving Logical and Information Functions

Logical functions are about adding functionality rather than making pure calculations, and so they are not always critical. However, being capable of building error checking and being competent to work with unknown issues is what differentiates good modeling from standard modeling. These functions should also be part of the modeler's kit:

- =IF()
- =AND()
- =FALSE()
- =TRUE()
- =NOT()
- =OR()
- =ISERROR()
- =ISBLANK()

- =ISTEXT()
- =ISNUMBER()
- =CELL()

Linking Your Calculations to Inputs and Outputs

I have previously discussed the Inputs (Chapter 7) and the Outputs (Chapter 10), and we looked at how the calculations link the inputs to the outputs by bringing into the calculation worksheet the input links. Then the calculations were created, which are then picked up by the outputs as links.

All that can be said is that the outputs should not have any calculations. They should be purely linkages to the calculation.

Case Study: Math in Modeling

How much of financial modeling is about math? Or to put it another way, does the modeler need to have an above average grasp of math to succeed? These questions are valid and also have a lot of gravity, mainly since modeling has yet to be defined. Does it fall into the category of science, business, IT, mathematics, engineering, or commerce? Because so many modelers have accounting backgrounds, it does seem as if modeling falls somewhere between business and math, but I am not convinced on that score.

In this case study, I will discuss math—specifically how much math is involved in modeling and what aspects of math should the modeler be ready to apply. In order to investigate this topic, a few examples of calculations and solutions that are commonplace in modeling will be discussed. Before launching into the examples, I want to first explain one aspect about modeling and math: BODMAS.

BODMAS

BODMAS stands for BRACKETS,ORDER (Power), DIVISION, MULTIPLICATION, ADDITION, SUBTRACTION. This is the foundation of how to perform calculation orders in mathematics, and this is how Excel will always interpret calculations. Therefore, it makes sense that modeling would use the same order. So with BODMAS, how would you order a calculation?

In the United States, this can also be referred to as PEMDAS: PARENTHESIS, EXPONENTS, MULTIPLICATION and DIVISION, ADDITION, and SUBTRACTION.

4 + 8 x 2 -10 x 6/2

The simplest way to solve this equation is to look for the order of BODMAS in relation to the calculation.

BRACKETS	None
ORDER	None
DIVISION	6/2 = 3
MULTIPLICATION	8 x 2, 10 x 3
ADDITION	4 + 16
SUBTRACTION	20 – 30

Because this may still feel complicated, let's go a step further. The BRACKETS part is very important because it is the first operation that will be executed. As long as you use brackets, you can force the order to execute how you want. When creating calculations that have a mix of operators, always use the brackets to control the order. From a modeling standpoint, this is good practice because it then becomes clearer exactly which operations are executed first to last. For the previous equation, rewrite it this way:

(4 + 8 x 2) – (10 x 6/2)

This will give us this equation:

8 x 2 = 16 + 4 =20 - 6/2 = 3 x 10 = 30

20 – 30 = -10

Understanding BODMAS and correctly applying this order is so critical to modeling calculations. If this subject is difficult for you to understand, purchase a math book and make the effort to gain a solid understanding of it. Excel will always use the BODMAS order to evaluate calculations. If you are unclear on this order, the results from your formula calculations will not match expectations. And because your understanding of the orders is unclear, you will be unaware that the calculation is wrong.

The Math in Modeling

Fortunately, there is not a lot of math that the modeler needs to apply because most of it is already captured in the functions. It may surprise you that I know many modelers who do not have a mathematical background and actually consider themselves weak in math, but nonetheless they are modelers. The main difference is that they are comfortable around numbers and are not overawed by them. The math that comes in modeling is the ability to perform calculations and recognize the functions that are most appropriate like the those in Figures 12-5a and 12-5b.

Cells that sum totals

SUMIF()	Gives the total for a range cell with one condition		
SUMIFS()	Gives the total for a range of cells with more than one condition		
SUMPRODUCT()	Multiplies the elements of one or more arrays		
SUM()	Gives the total for a range of cells an the sums or adds the products together.		
SUBTOTAL()	Gives the sub total of a range of cells using anyone of the eleven pre-set calculations.		
	Function Number	Pre-set calculations	
	1	AVERAGE	
	2	COUNT	
	3	COUNTA	
	4	MAX	
	5	MIN	
	6	PRODUCT	
	7	STDEV	
	8	STDEVP	
	9	SUM	
	10	VAR	
	11	VARP	
AVERAGE()	Gives the arithmetic mean for a set of numbers in a range of cells.		
AVERAGEIF()	Gives the arithmetic mean for a set of numbers in a range of cells that match a given		

Figure 12-5a. There are number of functions that sum cell ranges, and each should be applied against structure of the model calculations

Cells that count ranges

COUNT()	Counts the cells in range that contain numbers only.
COUNTA()	Counts the cells in range that contain data.
COUNTIF()	Counts the cells in range that fulfil given condition

Arithmetic

+
-
/
*

Figure 12-5b. This figure shows the count functions and arithmetic that will be required in the majority of models

Making Checks in Models

The making of checks shows that the numbers in the model add up properly and with integrity. The checks should also be used to alert the model user to issues with the model when numbers are not matching the checksum. Creating the checks is where modelers will need to apply as much of their own math knowledge as possible. This part is about testing that the calculations and formula are working accurately and relies on the modeler interpreting what constitutes an adequate check as can be seen in Figure 12-6.

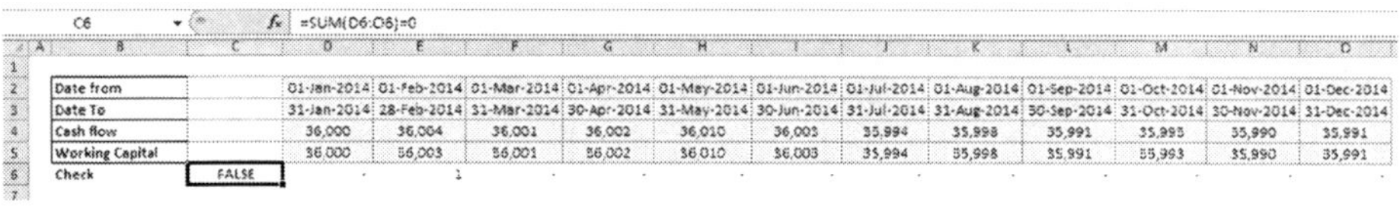

C6 =SUM(D6:O6)=0

	C	D	E	F	G	H	I	J	K	L	M	N	O
Date from		01-Jan-2014	01-Feb-2014	01-Mar-2014	01-Apr-2014	01-May-2014	01-Jun-2014	01-Jul-2014	01-Aug-2014	01-Sep-2014	01-Oct-2014	01-Nov-2014	01-Dec-2014
Date To		31-Jan-2014	28-Feb-2014	31-Mar-2014	30-Apr-2014	31-May-2014	30-Jun-2014	31-Jul-2014	31-Aug-2014	30-Sep-2014	31-Oct-2014	30-Nov-2014	31-Dec-2014
Cash flow		36,000	36,004	36,001	36,002	36,010	36,003	35,994	35,998	35,991	35,993	35,990	35,991
Working Capital		36,000	36,003	36,001	36,002	36,010	36,003	35,994	35,998	35,991	35,993	35,990	35,991
Check	FALSE	-	1	-	-	-	-	-	-	-	-	-	-

Figure 12-6. Simple financial checks are about math

Adapting Math Functions

There are two math-based functions that I find extremely useful. The first is the ABS( ) function, which stands for Absolute. This function turns any number to a positive and allows the modeler to continue to use a number irrespective of whether it's a positive or negative. This function becomes useful when creating outputs that have to be in a standard format, although that format may not conform the way the model has been built. For instance, in an income statement, the revenue is credit and so is a negative, and the expenses are debits and are positive. These may be modeled in this way, but the outputs might need to show all the numbers as positive. This is when the ABS( ) function becomes useful (see Figure 12-7.)

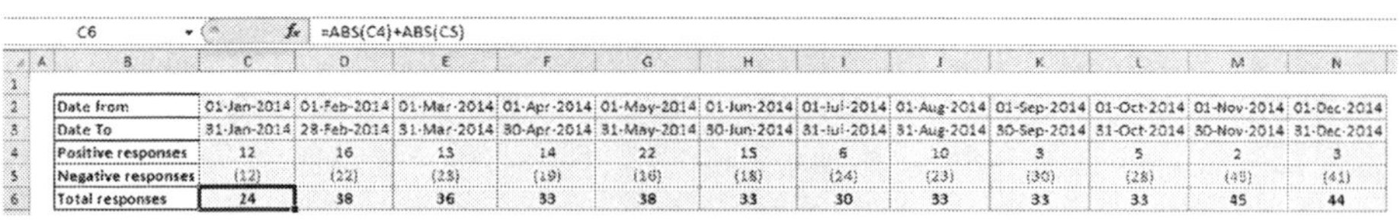

C6 =ABS(C4)+ABS(C5)

	C	D	E	F	G	H	I	J	K	L	M	N
Date from	01-Jan-2014	01-Feb-2014	01-Mar-2014	01-Apr-2014	01-May-2014	01-Jun-2014	01-Jul-2014	01-Aug-2014	01-Sep-2014	01-Oct-2014	01-Nov-2014	01-Dec-2014
Date To	31-Jan-2014	28-Feb-2014	31-Mar-2014	30-Apr-2014	31-May-2014	30-Jun-2014	31-Jul-2014	31-Aug-2014	30-Sep-2014	31-Oct-2014	30-Nov-2014	31-Dec-2014
Positive responses	12	16	13	14	22	15	6	10	3	5	2	3
Negative responses	(12)	(22)	(23)	(19)	(16)	(18)	(24)	(23)	(30)	(28)	(43)	(41)
Total responses	24	38	36	33	38	33	30	33	33	33	45	44

Figure 12-7. The ABS( ) function is used to provide a total response

The other math function is MOD( ); this function gives the result of the remainder when a number is divided by a divisor. For instance, if you have a number five and the divisor is two, you divide the five by the two.

5/2 = 2 remainders 1

The MOD() function in this case will return a one. This innocuous function may seem of little use, but it has real value when you need a mechanism that can activate and deactivate a calculation based on a result. I use MOD() mainly for creating timelines and time period—which are activated by a specific user input. In Figure 12-8, the formula is looking for the remainder after dividing the period with the number 12.

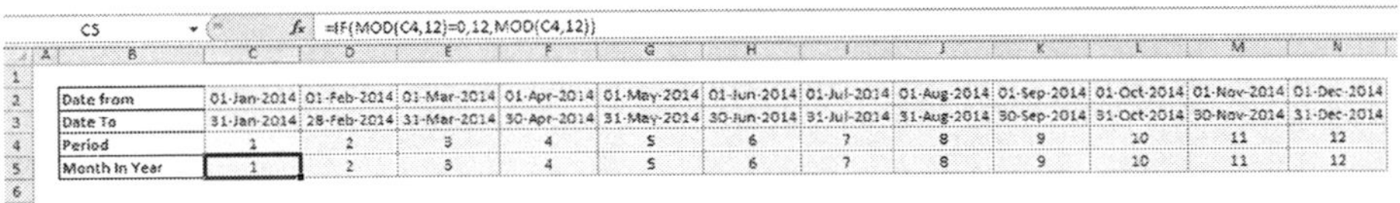
C5 =IF(MOD(C4,12)=0,12,MOD(C4,12))

Date from	01-Jan-2014	01-Feb-2014	01-Mar-2014	01-Apr-2014	01-May-2014	01-Jun-2014	01-Jul-2014	01-Aug-2014	01-Sep-2014	01-Oct-2014	01-Nov-2014	01-Dec-2014
Date To	31-Jan-2014	28-Feb-2014	31-Mar-2014	30-Apr-2014	31-May-2014	30-Jun-2014	31-Jul-2014	31-Aug-2014	30-Sep-2014	31-Oct-2014	30-Nov-2014	31-Dec-2014
Period	1	2	3	4	5	6	7	8	9	10	11	12
Month In Year	1	2	3	4	5	6	7	8	9	10	11	12

Figure 12-8. This model uses the MOD() function to calculate the month in the year

While financial modeling requires an understanding and healthy respect for math, there is no reason why a modeler who does not have a math background should not prevail. The math that is used in modeling is applicable to the models that are being built and so can be learned. However, having said that, there is no reason for not having a sound grasp of basic arithmetic and understanding arithmetic ordering. There are definite advantages to having a more mathematical grasp when building quantitative models such as Monte Carlo or Black-Scholes, but even with those models most of the math can be learned while modeling.

CHAPTER

13

How to Capture, Document, and Track Assumptions in Your Model

In this chapter, the administrative side of financial modeling will be discussed. These are the aspects of modeling that are quite often forgotten or not considered in so many models. Yet it is the administration that will tell you if what you are looking at is a true financial model or just a set of worksheets.

As you go through this chapter, don't be tempted to skip over any of the sections. Some may not appear to be about creating formulas or calculations or building outputs and inputs. However, the information provided in this chapter is every bit about modeling as doing calculations.

Incorporating the Model Assumption Register

The model assumption register is a document that the modeler uses to capture, document, and track assumptions prior to the initiation of the modeling project throughout the life cycle. These assumptions require some validation in order to determine whether or not they will impact the model project. It is very possible that some of the assumptions may be project risks or may become risks during the modeling. Therefore, the register can and should be used to augment the risk register.

Throughout this book, I have mentioned assumptions to the model and the assumption register. So what are model assumptions? They are conclusions that are made based on partial or unclear information, and they can also serve as guides toward achieving specific goals and ends. However, I would prefer to create a definition that is more suitable to financial modeling:

> Model assumptions are documented comments on the shape and direction of a project or assignment that are used when real facts either do not exist or are unclear.

The important message here is that the assumptions are documented. Often the assumptions are in someone's head and not written down, but that they still need to be written down and documented. From here on, I will view documented as being the physical act of recording the assumptions. In other words, the assumptions should be written down or placed on some kind of register.

The assumption register should be updated as items are closed or more information is obtained. The project team should also review the assumption register regularly to ensure that all project team members are informed and that any additional actions or information is captured.

Standard Assumption Register Template

There are two thoughts on where the assumptions should be kept: in the model or in a self-contained document. In my opinion, placing assumptions anywhere but in the model is not a good idea. I just don't have any good experiences to draw on for assumptions that have been placed in a text document or in an external Excel worksheet, and I will tell you why.

Almost all commercial models will go through a development process that will have version control or version history; the big changes to each model version will require a version number. The assumptions are intrinsic to the model version history and are therefore closely aligned. By holding the assumptions anywhere but in the model, it now creates a two-process version control, such that every time the model version is changed, the modeler needs to get the assumptions wherever they are stored. The modeler would then need to reflect the necessary changes to make sure the versions are coordinated. By doing so, the possibilities of getting out of synchronization are high, and unless the modeler is an experienced change control practitioner or is extremely diligent, misalignment between the model version and the assumptions' versions is going to happen.

My preference is very clear: keep the assumptions in the model. Any changes in the model will affect the assumptions of that version of the model and will be updated at the same time as the changes. This is just a matter of working through an update process. Or if the modeler has suitable VBA skills, a log file can be created that can be used to update the assumptions. Furthermore, by keeping the assumptions within the model, referencing can be more dynamic and hyperlinks can be used to navigate through the model with ease.

Creating the Assumption Register

The assumption register should reflect the type of information that is going to be required, such that the detail and the depth are suitable. The assumption register is important because there should be a record and reference that anyone who is using the model can use to gain an understanding about the model and the premise and the conditions under which it was built. For instance, if the model uses an inflation rate of 5% per annum over the ten years after the model, the model user may need to understand why 5% has been applied when the real inflation rate is only 2%. By referring to the assumption register, it should become clear how this happened. It's not about whether the users agree or not—it's more about understanding the modeler's thinking.

Every item in the assumption register should have a minimum set of detail, which should include the following: the assumption originator, assumption validator, the assumption owner, the assumption ID, the input reference, assumption name, assumption description, entry date, due date, status, closure date, and any actions which might be required as part of the validation (see Figure 13-1).

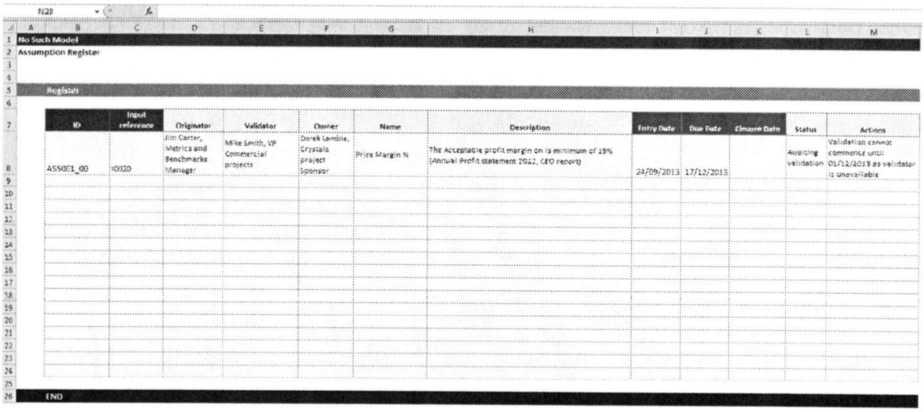

Figure 13-1. This figure shows the assumption register in a model

Assumption Originator

The assumption originator could either be a person or a reference in a document, file, or online reference that pinpoints the evolution of the assumption. However, do not confuse the originator with the owner. The assumption owner will often provide details of where the assumption originates. For example, the modeler may be advised which corporate tax rate to use throughout the model and be referred to a government web site to get the details. This web site would be the originator, and the adviser would be the owner.

Assumption Validator

The validator is the person who will review the assumptions and give assurance that the conditions relating to the assumptions are tolerable for the current model project. This is not an admission of an assumption being true or false—it is about relevancy and reasonableness. Are the assumptions prudent, reasonable, and acceptable to this project and this model?

For instance, if you have an assumption that the project must give an IRR (internal rate of return) of more than 20%, the validator will follow up and check where the 20% threshold came from. Then the validator will verify if this is a reasonable estimate under the current conditions (with the reason) and will assess what is in fact a good rate to use in the absence of any decent advice (prudence). Often the validator is actually the project sponsor, but it could be anyone who has a vested interest in the project. However, the validator is not the modeler or someone involved in building the model.

Assumption Owner

The owner of the assumption is the person who will have his name placed into the register as responsible for that assumption. The owner will make sure the assumption has a solid basis and makes sense commercially, legally, financially, and socially. The assumption owner will also make sure the assumption has been implemented into the model. Generally, the assumption owner will wait for the validation before officially assuming the responsibility, although it's likely that the validator could be the same person. The assumption owner is often one of the project stakeholders, the project sponsor, or a person who has specific or specialist knowledge about that assumption topic.

Being an assumption owner does carry some major risk. In the event that the finished model has serious issues that result in bad decisions that were made using the faulty model, one of the areas to investigate will be the assumption register. Subsequently, the owner of the assumptions that may have influenced the model's design may also be investigated. In my experience, I have yet to come across a situation where an assumption owner has punitive action for being the owner; however, I have witnessed a few assumption owners who have left their jobs under a cloud so to speak.

Assumption ID

The assumption ID should be a sequential reference code or number that is used for every assumption. The importance of such a reference cannot be understated because it will be used throughout the model in the outputs, inputs documentation, and with the notes for the model tester. This reference number should also be incorporated with the version control history by employing a referencing system that uses subnumbers to show version changes.

Input Reference

The input reference is a reference that will link directly to the inputs that are relevant to the assumption. Don't be surprised if each assumption has more than one input reference. You will find that the input reference is one of the last elements that is typed into the register because there is often a continual circularity involving inputs and assumptions. In other words, you can't have an input without an assumption, but the assumption needs the input reference. Avoid omitting this step and always make sure assumptions can be tracked through inputs. This step will make the tester's job that much easier, will ensure that the assumption validation and ownership can quickly be identified, and the implementation into the model will be able to be verified.

Assumption Name

The assumption name is a short name for the assumption. It should be no more than 20 words and should be direct and to the point where it identifies the assumption. For instance, there may be an assumption behind the depreciation policy to be used in the model; therefore, the assumption name would just be "Depreciation Policy."

Assumption Description

The description is a concise note that adequately describes the background and the action to be used on the assumption. In this element, it's possible to add tags that give references to other materials such as emails or papers.

Entry Date

The entry date is the date on which the assumption receives an ID reference. This is quite an important distinction because it's plausible that there will be several listed items in the assumption register, especially when a project is first initiated. Some of these items will be filtered and discarded because of the overlap with other items or because they are just not relevant. Following this cleansing, what will remain is the start of the assumption register, which can then be given an assumption ID. It is at this point that the entry date is used.

Due Date

The due date is invariably based on the final date the assumption needs to be implemented into the model. Make sure the due date is stated early in the creation of the assumption register. This date once its confirmed and inputted should also be closed and should never move. Should you find that the date has changed, you should create another assumption with a fresh ID and the adjusted date. The reason for this brand-new ID is that the assumption register should regularly be tracked, so any change after an ID is issued must be a new ID. This way, you will be able to track how the assumption has developed over time. If there are any changes, there will need to be another validation and the owner will need to be identified, as it may be a new owner.

Status

This status should be based on the validation of the assumption. It is better to create a consistent and clear labeling to use a status, something like "awaiting validation," "in progress," "in issue," or "completed" for instance.

Closure Date

The closure date is the date that the assumption has been implemented into the model. You may think this will be the same as the due date, but it may be an earlier date. The closure date cannot be after the due date. Why? If the due date is the last potential date that an assumption can be assimilated into a model, then it would not be possible to have a later assimilated date. Should the assumption not make the due date, then leave the closure date blank.

Actions

The actions are those associated with the assumption or validating the detail in the assumptions.

Referencing the Assumption Register

The register should be within easy reach at all times to whomever is using the model. The ideal situation is that it is within a two-step reach. This is important because at any point the model user will need to have access to the background and assumptions that are pertinent. But how is it possible to know at exactly the point the user requires the assumption register and also to know where the user's location is at that point in time?

The way through this is to effectively use the reference numbers and codes and the hyperlinks within Excel. If you look at Figure 13-2, the reference number in the ID column has a six-digit code, followed by an underscore and two digits with zeros.

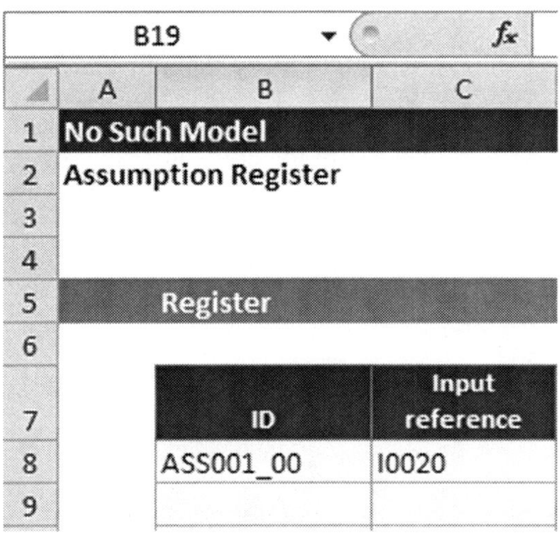

Figure 13-2. The assumption reference is in the ID column

The six-digit code is the reference number and can be whatever referencing is chosen; the two numbers after the underscore are the version numbers.

Every assumption will start with a reference number with six digits, and the version number will be two zeros. However, if for any reason an assumption has to be adapted or changed, the register should not be altered. Instead, the same reference should be issued but the version number is incremented.

In Figure 13-3, the assumption reference ASS001_00 has been altered because the expected margin is 17.5% in contrast to 15%. But instead of altering the row with this assumption, I have inserted a new assumption with the same reference ASS001, but the version has incremented to 01, forming an assumption reference of ASS001_01.

No Such Model

Assumption Register

Register

ID	Input reference	Originator	Validator	Owner	Name	Description	Entry Date	Due Date	Closure Date	Status	Actions
ASS001_00	1.02	Jim Carter, Metrics and Benchmarks Manager	Mike Smith, VP Commercial projects	Derek Lambie, Crystals project Sponsor	Price Margin %	The acceptable profit margin on is minimum of 15% (Annual Profit statement 2012, CEO report)	09/24/2013	12/17/2013		Awaiting validation	Validation cannot commence until 01/12/2013 as validator is unavailable
ASS001_01	1.02	Jim Carter, Metrics and Benchmarks Manager	Mike Smith, VP Commercial projects	Derek Lambie, Crystals project Sponsor	Price Margin %	The acceptable profit margin on is minimum of 17.5%	09/30/2013	12/17/2013		Awaiting validation	Validator must be allocated
ASS002_00	1.08	Melanie Smith	Mike Smith, VP Commercial projects	Derek Lambie, Crystals project Sponsor	Corporate Tax Rate	Tax rates are based on the online site at the Inland Revenue	09/26/2013	10/28/2013		Validated	

END

Figure 13-3. The assumption ASS001 has been altered, and a new row has been inserted

Once the referencing coding is established, it now becomes a matter of making sure that the said reference is included into all the model worksheets that are based on the assumption. One method is to make sure that on every worksheet, the first two columns are always blank. This way, the first column can be allotted the assumption reference, and the second column can be allotted the input reference, as in Figure 13-4.

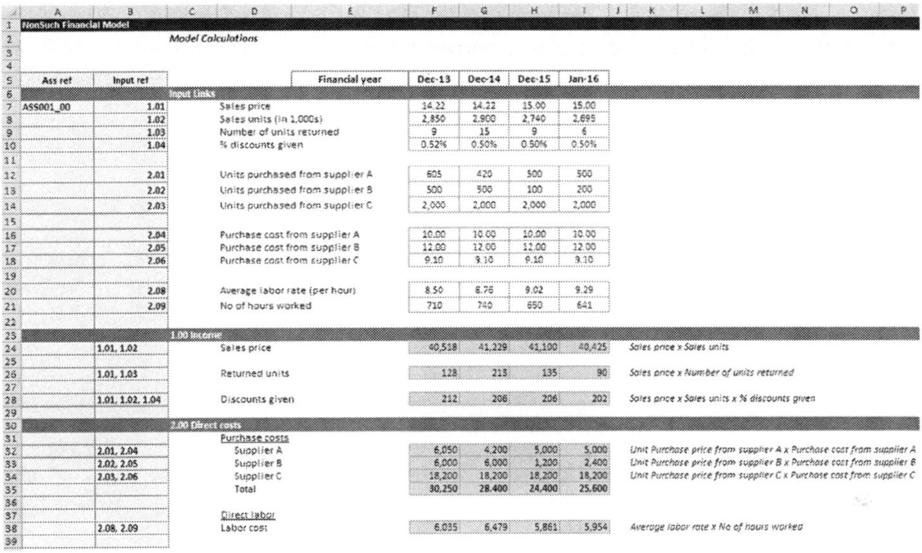

Figure 13-4. The assumption reference is provided in the calculations

The final task is to make all the worksheets that refer to the assumption reference hyperlinked to the assumption using the Insert tab (found in Excel 2007 and later versions) as in Figure 13-5.

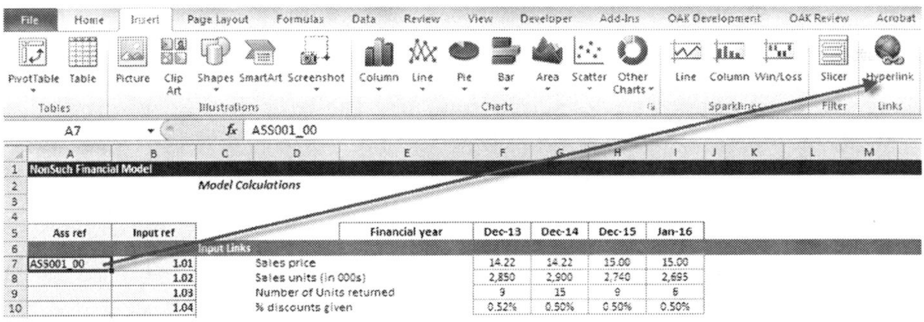

Figure 13-5. Use the hyperlink to direct link to the assumption worksheet

Documenting the Model

Providing documentation to the model is one of the most neglected aspects of financial modeling, but ironically it is the most appreciated facets from a user point of view. Doubtless, a well-documented model will gain far more user acceptance than one which has spare documentation. So what is meant by documenting the model?

Unfortunately, there is no recognized format or standard when it comes to documenting models. It very much comes down to how the modeler chooses to provide it. However, the key elements discussed in these next sections should always be present in any good documentation.

Relevant Comments and Information

Each item of the documentation should serve a purpose, which means it should give the user some information that would otherwise not be known and is helpful to using the model.

Context-Specific Information

The goal with the documentation is to make it relevant to the part of the model being described. For instance when documenting the drop-down lists in the inputs, it's better to refer to the actual content of that list.

Consistent, Clear, and Carefully Thought-Out Details

Use a format and create a standard that will be consistent throughout the model, such as using the same fonts and colors.

Make the Documentation Intuitive

There really is nothing to be gained in putting the user through a complexity in order to understand the model documentation. Therefore, the documentation should be simple, and above all, intuitive. There should be no need for the user to look through a user guide on how to activate the documentation.

Where to Begin?

When thinking about how and where to document the model, put yourself in the user's situation. In what ways will users need to understand the model, its history and developments, its status, and its features?

As a starter, never assume that the users are aware of the project or the model just because they have the model itself. Excel files are very prevalent in organizations, and without exception, most people will come across several Excel workbooks on any given day, week, or month. Because these workbooks are not applications but files, it can take some time for users to understand if they have the correct file or proper version open. This needs to be clear from the outset.

The modeler should ensure there is always a cover sheet (worksheet) that includes basic details of the model. These details should include information about the project, model, model version and its status (is it final?), a brief summary of the scope and the model's objective, and also contact information. A sample is shown in Figure 13-6.

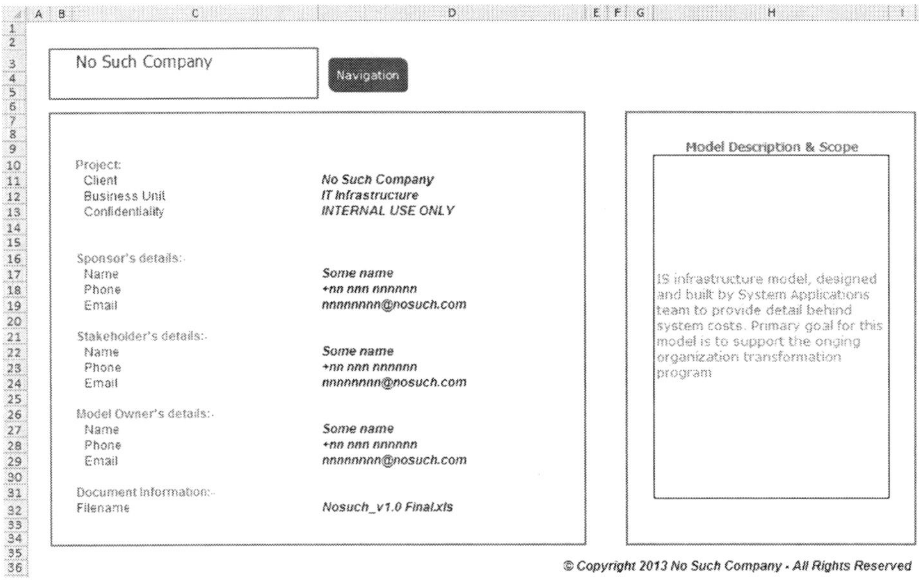

Figure 13-6. This figure is a sample cover sheet

The cover does not need to be very detailed, but it must give direct information about what the user is viewing. There is an option here to make this cover sheet the opening worksheet of the model. Excel does not contain any state management, which means it does not naturally recognize where the file should be when a new user requires it. A good example of state management is a web site. Every new user who visits the web site will always land on the home page (provided the root URL is being used), regardless of where other users of the site have visited.

In Excel, the opposite is true. When a new user opens a workbook, whatever part of the model the previous user was in and saved will be where the model will open next time. This can be somewhat disorientating, and often I find it a good idea to make sure that the model always opens at one specific worksheet, irrespective of how it was last shut down. This step can be easily done simply by creating some VBA, which can be accomplished by opening the VBA editor (ALT_F11). Then locate and double-click "ThisWorkbook" in the VBA project window and add the following code:

Private Sub Workbook_Open()

Worksheets("Worksheet name").Activate

End Sub

Incidentally, while I am mentioning VBA coding, I will often place some message to the users when they open the model that will flash across the screen for a few seconds with a disclaimer or confidentiality warning as in Figure 13-7.

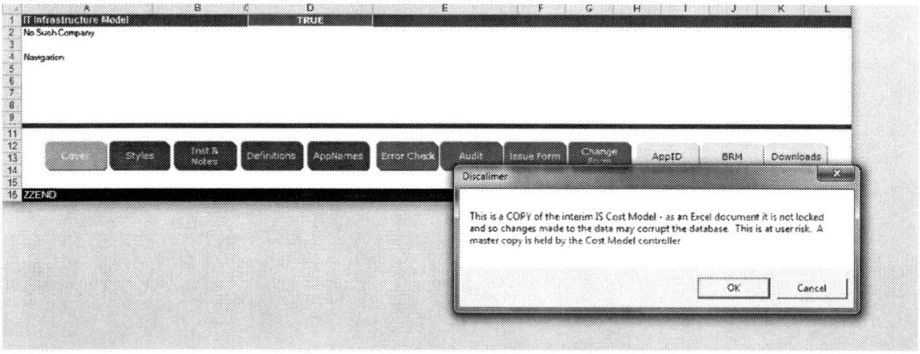

Figure 13-7. This message appears when the model is opened

Audit Summary

At some point in the model, it's useful to have an audit worksheet as in Figure 13-8. This worksheet would include information that relates to the status, issues, and model development. Generally, the health of the model can be assessed from reviewing it. I also tend to include some visual evidence that shows the status of the outputs when the model was last used. While this is by no means standard modeling, it is a nice bonus to have. The audit summary will include the following parts:

Model Name

- The model version number
- The model file name
- The model usage history (dates when the model has been previously opened)
- The modeler's name and contact
- The model features record: This is a list of the main features of the model with dates of when they were completed

or are expected to be implemented. This information can be incorporated into the future version numbers. Also record any features that were in previous versions of the model but have subsequently been deleted.

- Model features that still need to be included, with dates of when these are to be completed
- A review history that will give the number of times the model has been reviewed, the type of review (such a financial review or peer review), the name of the reviewer, and the number of model audits and model tests

	A	B	C	D	E
1	No Such Model				
2	Audit				
3					
4					
5		Model detail			
6					
7		Model name	Nosuch		
8		Version number	3.01		
9		File name	nosuchmodel.xls		
10		Modeler name	John Smith		
11		Email	js@models.net		
12		Usage history			
13					
14		Model Name	Model version	Date	User
15		Nosuch	1.00	04/04/2013	JS
16		Nosuch	1.25	04/17/2013	JS
17		Nosuch	2.00	04/28/2013	JS
18		Nosuch	3.01	07/07/2013	JS
19		Nosuch	3.01	08/07/2013	TM
20					
21					
22					
23		Model feature			
24					
25		Feature	Model version	Completion date	
26		Outputs date stamping	1.00	03/31/2013	
27		No SaveAs feature	3.01	07/07/2013	
28		Disclaimer message	3.20	08/29/2013	

Figure 13-8. A sample of an audit worksheet is shown

One of the dilemmas of the audit worksheet is whether it should be automated. For example, should the dates of when the model was last opened be automatic or hand-coded? This is a matter of preference and also depends on the skills of the modeler. My preference is to make the audit worksheet hand-coded. That way, there are very few possibilities for errors associated with weak VBA coding. Getting dates right in VBA is not for the fainthearted, and I doubt if there are many modelers who can code confidently on dates. Furthermore, by hand-coding, it ensures that the model auditing has been tracked and been through some validation.

Notes or Instructions

I regularly come across modelers who it appears are reluctant to provide any sort of user guide within the model. Their reasons may be because it's just another work overhead or to protect some intellectual rights to the model. Whatever the reason, there is no excuse for not providing even a basic amount of instructions or notes within the model, even if there is a healthy user guide produced off the model.

Model users are always grateful to have a model that includes notes and instructions.

Be sure to provide this information in a dedicated worksheet. This worksheet should contain a summary of the scope or mission, elemental data flow to show how information is moving through the model, a data dictionary on each worksheet and each part of the model, and some essential information on how to operate the features in the model. Figure 13-9 is just a small section of the instruction and notes, but there can be several hundreds of rows.

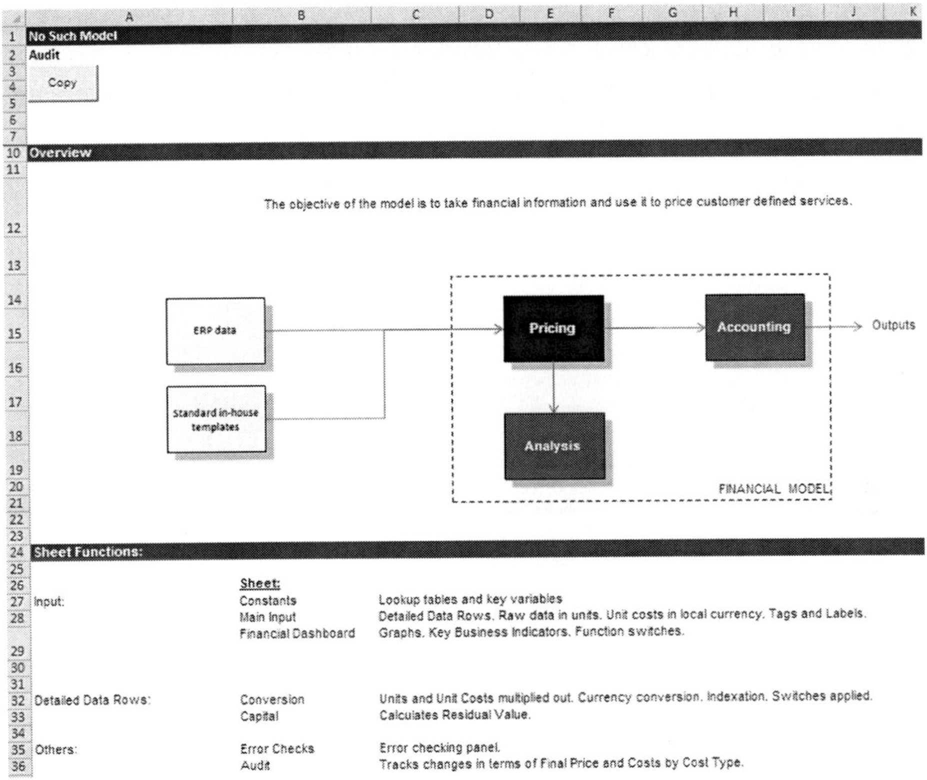

Figure 13-9. This figure is a sample of the notes and instructions

Model Styles

During the development of a financial model, there will be a number of formats that will be used in cells, rows, and columns, which will give the user additional information on the data. For instance, it's preferable to differentiate between a cell requiring user inputs and one that contains a formula. The most applied method is to use different visual aids to make these distinctions, and this can be by using colors, comments, borders, or font types.

By far, the best approach is to use colors, which are called model styles or styles. It is imperative to make sure that somewhere in the model is a worksheet that gives a description of the styles that can be found throughout the entire model. Think of it as a key—it gives the users a ready referenced area where they can become familiar with the visuals used in the model. In Figure 13-10, a sample of the style sheet shows the types of cells that are in the model and also their style (color).

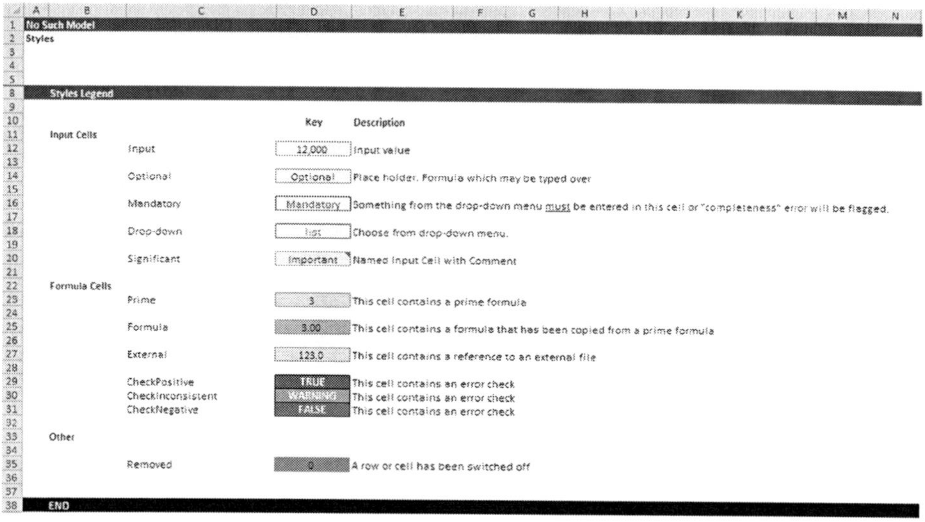

Figure 13-10. A sample style worksheet is shown

You should always have a style sheet in any model—no matter how small or complex. It is the height of decadence for a modeler to build a model that incorporates styling but then fail to provide a style worksheet in the documentation. The descriptions in the style sheet should be short and concise. The key goal is to make sure the model user completely understands what each cell is being used for.

Modeling Logic

Although not strictly essential, I always like to provide a worksheet that has a detailed view of the logic in the model. What do I mean by the logic? This is a worksheet where modelers can be free to showcase their input into the model. In other words, the logic worksheet would contain a detailed flow of the data and the worksheets within the model and comments that describe how and why it was designed in this manner. There would also be some indication as to what each worksheet does and how it does it.

Think of the logic worksheet as being for modelers. The intention is to supply the sort of information and at a level of detail that will allow another modeler to understand and work with the model (see Figures 13-11 and Figure 13-12.)

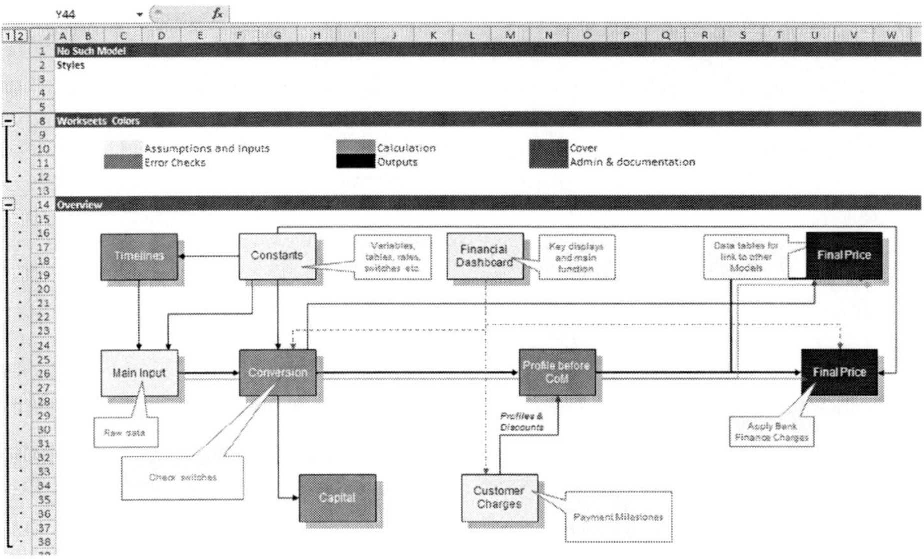

Figure 13-11. The logic worksheet contains a detailed overview of the model for modelers

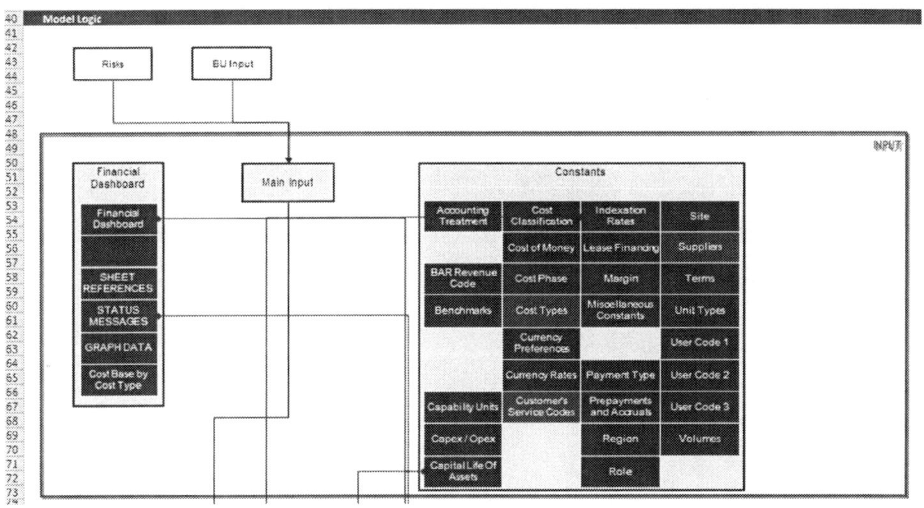

Figure 13-12. Detailed hyperlinks are included in the model logic

The examples in Figures 13-11 and 13-12 show various details about every aspect of the model. These diagrams are all linked to a detailed worksheet that provides information; therefore, all the model user would need to do is locate the desired information and then click on it to link to the detail.

This model logic may appear to be surplus to the other requirements. After all, who would need to have such an understanding of the model? This may be true, and modelers should use their best judgment to decide if this level of detail is required. I have provided information on just how to document your models, but not all models will need such a heavy documentation. However, all models should have a basic level of documentation.

Using Comments

Excel has a great feature called Comments, which are text boxes that can be used at the cell level to provide additional information about the content of the cells to which they are applied. To insert a comment, right-click a cell and click Insert Comment.

Cells that contain comments display a small red triangle at the top-right of the cell to alert users that a comment is present (see Figure 13-13). Comments can either be displayed by default or hidden. When a comment is hidden, it will appear when the user positions the pointer in the vicinity of the cell (see Figure 13-14). By using comments, it's very possible to provide a context-sensitive help within the model. Be sure to use comments judicially and add a key in the style sheet, even if it may seem obvious.

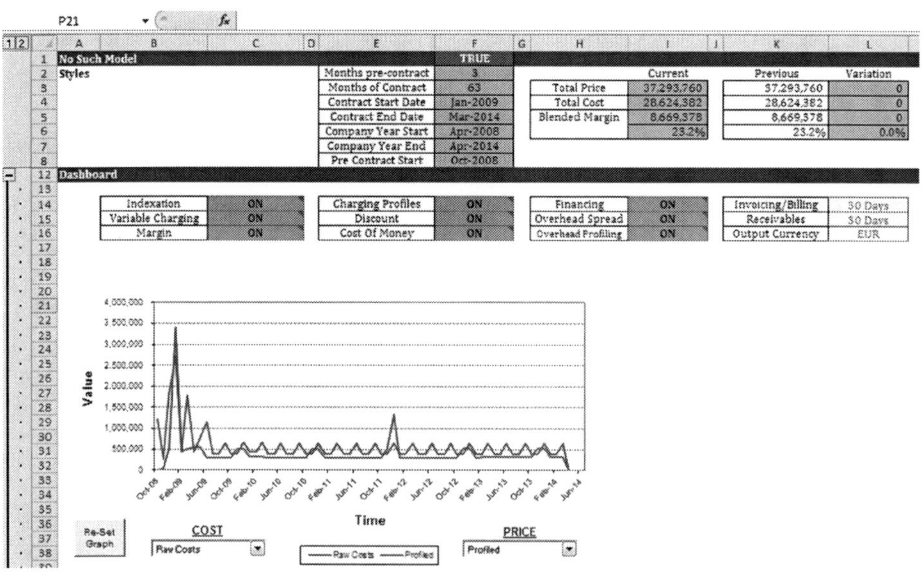

Figure 13-13. The dashboard can always benefit from comments. Notice the mark in the top-right of the cells under the dashboard

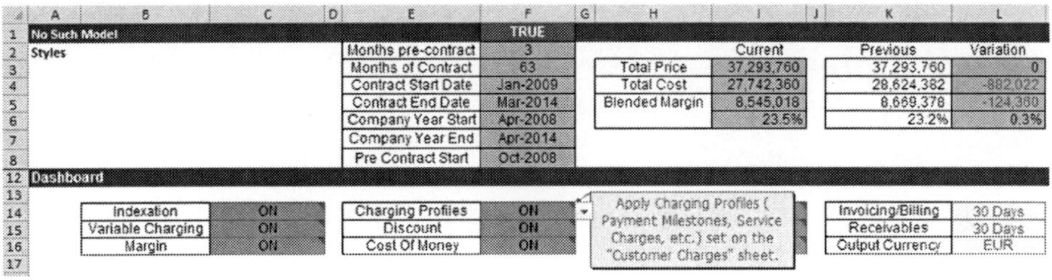

Figure 13-14. The comment has now been activated by hovering over the cell

With comments, try to make them short and clear. If possible, use a color for the text that does not coincide with the cell styles (right-click in the comment and click Format Comment). I usually use a medium green or a medium purple, but choose yours and stay with it for consistency. While comments are a good thing, do not go overboard and apply comments for cells that clearly are not enhanced by them. My rule is to create the comments when you are reviewing the model, which as a modeler you should do regularly. Don't be tempted to add comments as you go along, as it is very easy to get the cross referencing wrong. Comments are like a story: choose a particular aspect to the model to review and then add comments until it aligns and informs from start to finish.

CHAPTER

14

Modeling to Give the User Transparency

In this chapter, I will be describing modeling elements that will allow the user of the model better visibility of the model's functions and also provide some feedback as to expectations of inputs.

User Functionality

When working with models, the role of the user should be paramount in shaping the way the model works. User functionality is all about creating an environment that coerces the user to interact with the model, in the way it was intended by the modeler, with simplicity. Keep in mind that user functionality is not about adding "bells and whistles" that enhance the model's function—that is model functionality.

In this section, I will discuss methods to enhance user functionality that are useful and often essential. This functionality is not mandatory modeling or a part of best practice, but everything here is tried and tested in commerce and industry.

Using Drop-down

Drop-downs are in their basic form lists of information with possible options. Adding drop-downs into models is a very useful method of getting the user to select one of a number of options. If crafted thoughtfully by using data validations, it can be a means of restricting the user to just those options. In Figure 14-1, a drop-down is provided in column D row 10 (D10). The user can select any of the options that are listed.

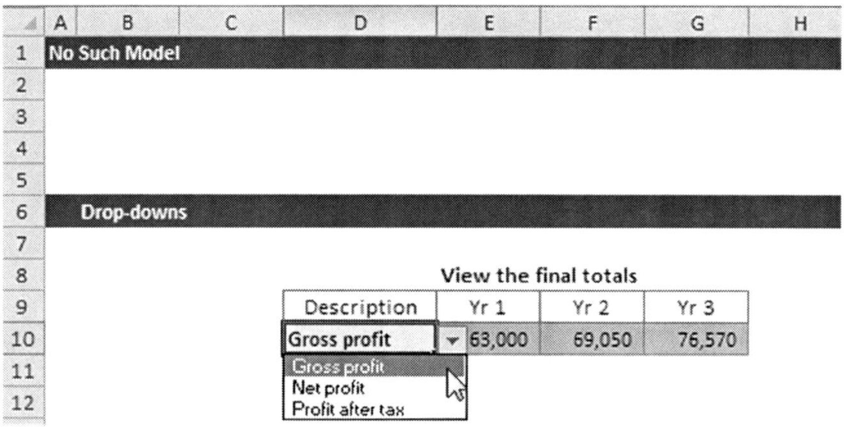

Figure 14-1. The drop-down menu list options are displayed here

To make sure that anyone using the drop-down cannot insert, unvetted, items into the drop-down list, you can add a data validation that will lock the list and prevent any insertions and changes. Figure 14-2 shows what happens when the user attempts to circumvent the drop-down list.

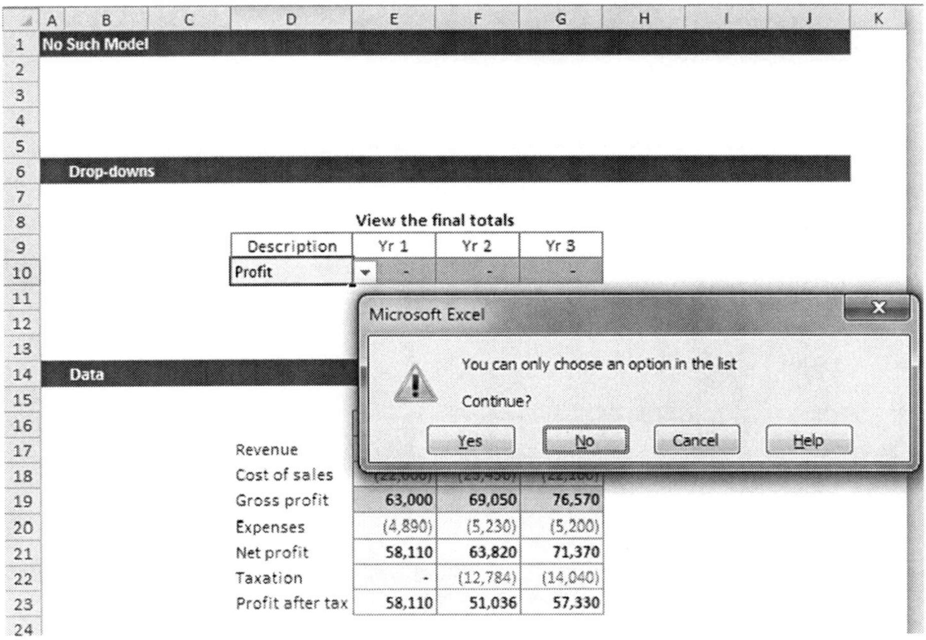

Figure 14-2. The drop-down list options have not been circumvented

By using a drop-down, you can then create a certain amount of predictability about what the user is going to select and make appropriate reactions to that choice.

Creating a Drop-down

The best method of creating a drop-down is through the data validation, which is found on the Data tab (see Figure 14-3). Clicking Data Validation on the tab opens the Data Validation dialog box (see Figure 14-4).

Figure 14-3. The Data Validation tool is highlighted here

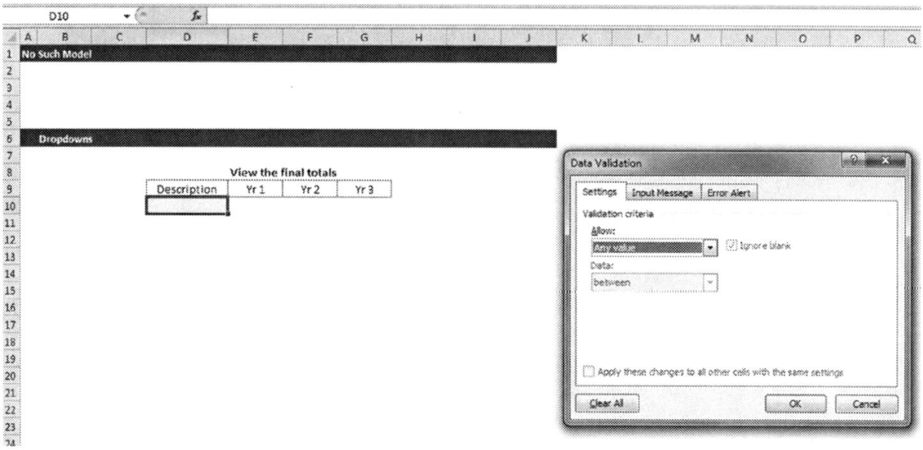

Figure 14-4. The Data Validation selection is shown here

The validation selection can be used to validate all manner of data, including dates, numbers, times, and so forth. For this section, the focus will be on the lists (see Figure 14-5).

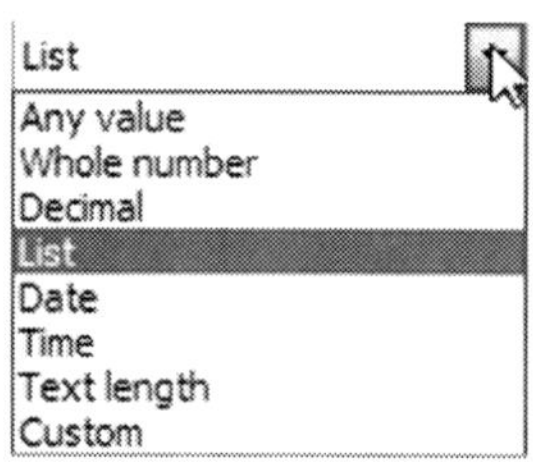

Figure 14-5. The types of data that are allowed are shown here

The next part is to create the option list. There are many ways to create this list, but the easiest is to input your options directly into the source box and place a comma (,) at the end of each option, as in Figure 14-6.

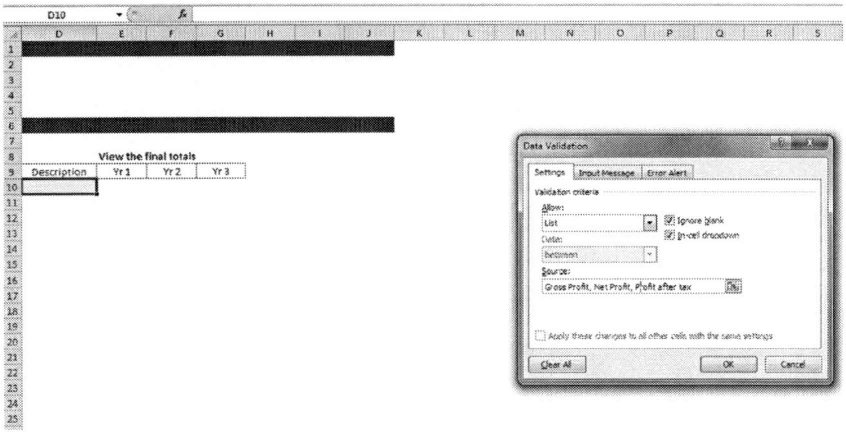

Figure 14-6. This figure displays how to fill in the list options into the source box

Another method of filling in the list options is to have a list of the options already created in the table range (see Figure 14-7). Then in the source box, simply highlight the list. Or if you have given the list a range name, then type in the range name.

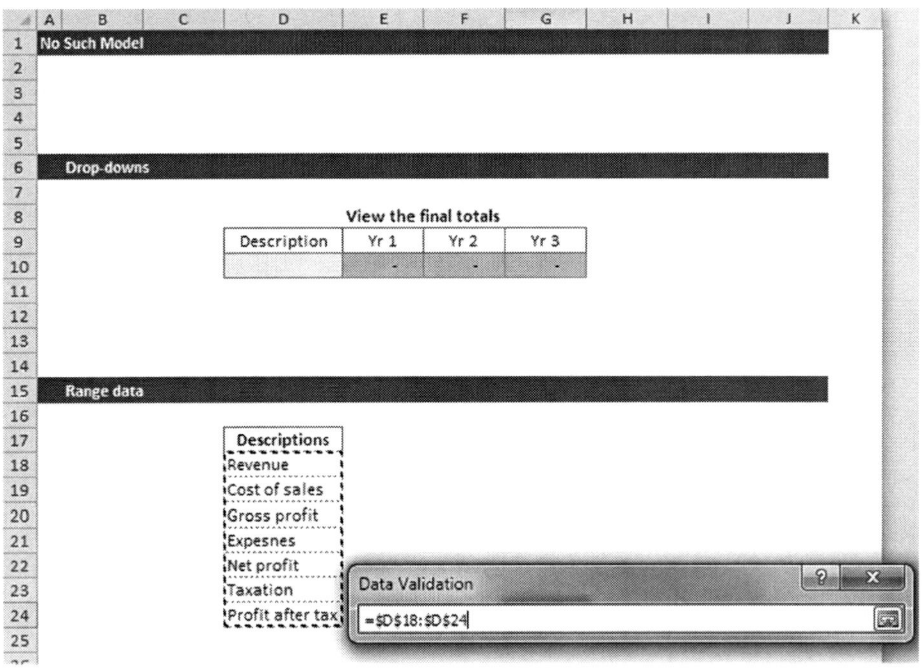

Figure 14-7. The source of the validation list is the table with the range data

To add a restriction so that the user can only use the options that you have provided, keep the cursor over the cell on the drop-down list and return to the Data Validation dialog box. This time instead of going to the Default tab, select the Error Alert tab instead (see Figure 14-8). Then choose a style warning and type in an error message in the message box. Make sure the "Show error alert after invalid data is entered" check box is selected or the message will be ignored. You have now created a validated list that will restrict the user to the list options.

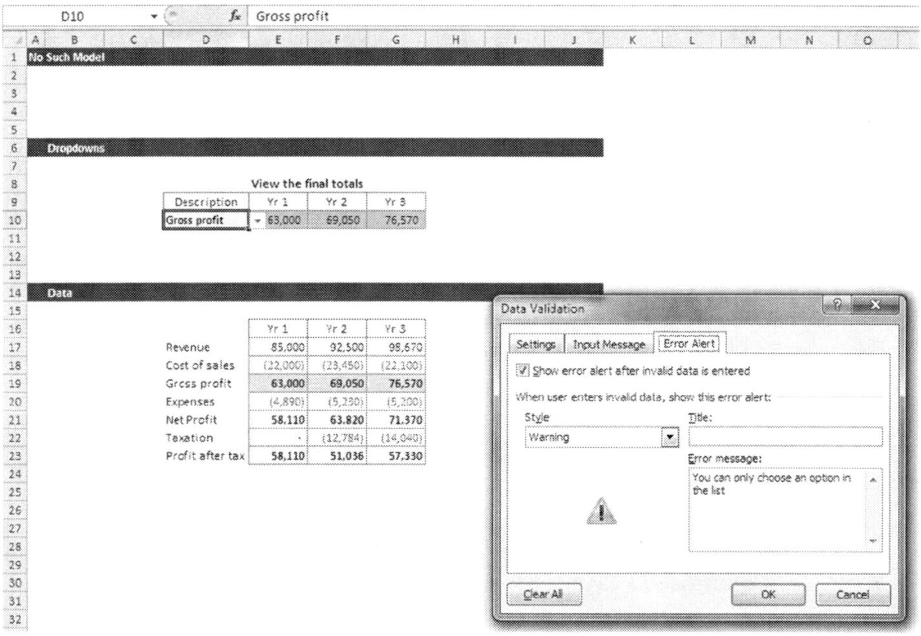

Figure 14-8. Make sure the "Show error alert after invalid data is entered" check box is selected

Switches

Switches involve a method of using drop-down lists that allow the user to turn on or turn off calculations for the model. You can create a switch in exactly the same manner as the drop-down list is created. The only difference is that the source will just have two values ("on" and off") in the data validation list. By having this option, the user can then make "What If" decisions about the outcomes. For instance, you can design a model that will provide outputs that give real values (or today's values) and nominal values (have inflation in them). This way, the user can switch been these two values merely by turning on or off a switch. In Figure 14-9, the switches are placed in the inputs worksheet. The user simply clicks on the selected topic and turns the switch to off or on, as in Figure 14-10a.

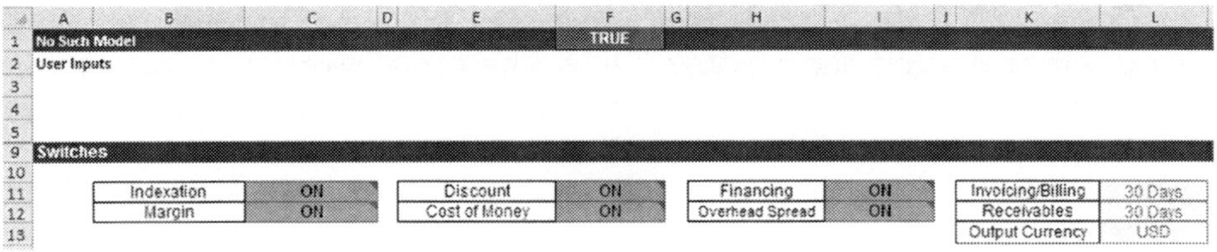

Figure 14-9. Numerous switches are available in this model

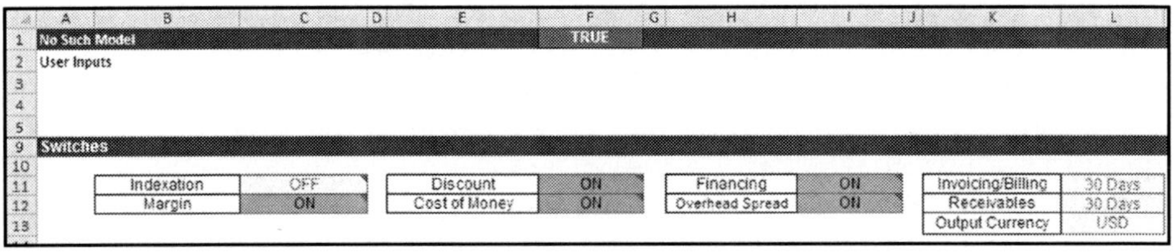

Figure 14-10a. The indexation switch has now been turned off

You should note that by turning the switch to off in Figure 14-10a, the styles have changed to a pale color. These styles can be created by using conditional formatting, as shown in Figure 14-10b.

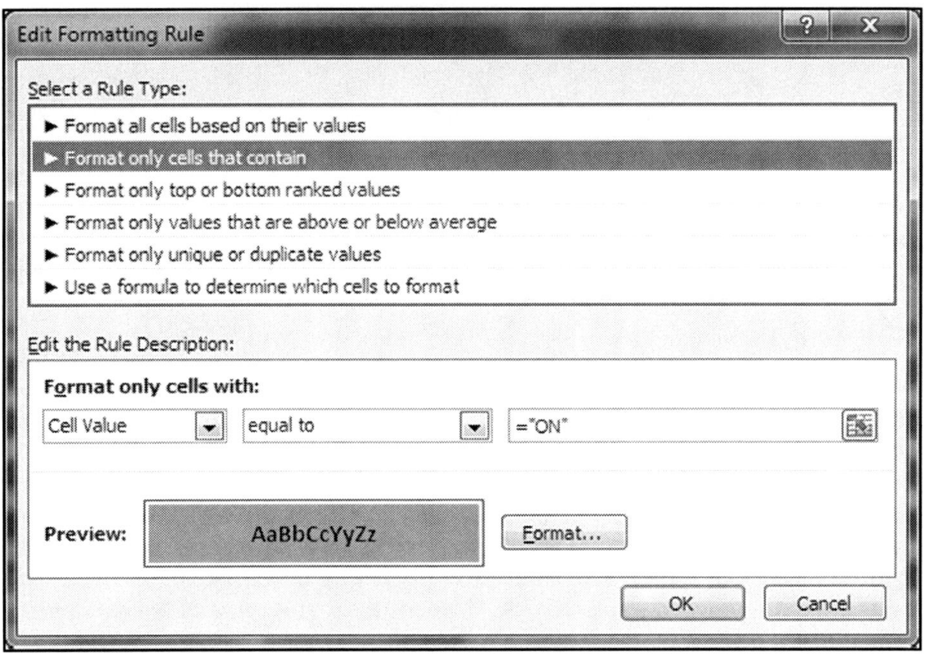

Figure 14-10b. To create the switches, use conditional formatting and create a color style for the "ON" position

The ON and OFF are switches that, when used, will either include some variable (ON) or exclude the variable (OFF). The use of switches is common in models and it is an effective method of allowing the user to interact with the model data. If you employ these types of switches in your models, you must make sure that the user is aware at all times exactly what the calculations are now giving.

In addition to using different styles to signal on and off, I would advise that other signals be provided throughout the model irrespective of location that will alert the user to the switch changes. Figure 14-11 is an example of a calculation worksheet. It is visible at the top that the indexation has been turned off because status buttons have been added across the entire model. Also the color band in row 1 of the worksheet has changed to the color red from the default blue, which provides a warning that the model has changed its calculation method. These are typically the kinds of messages the model should provide when using switches.

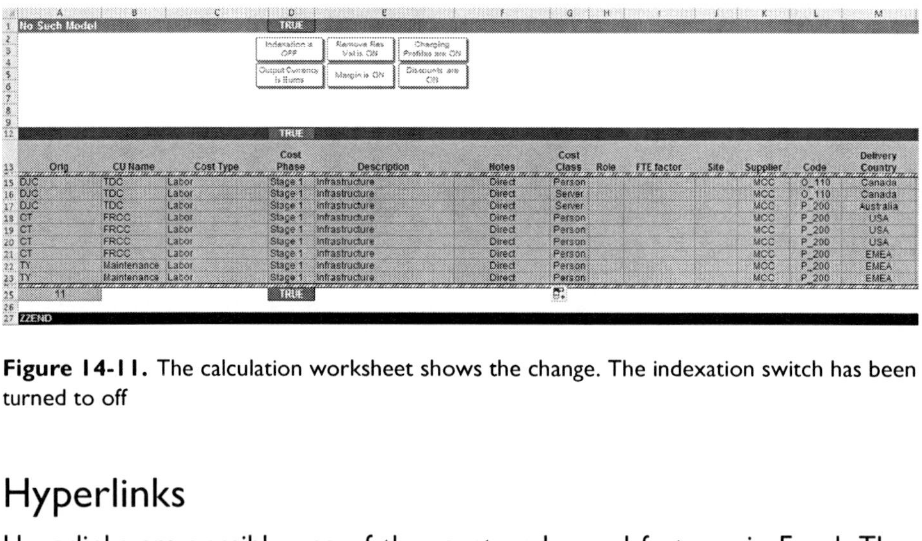

Figure 14-11. The calculation worksheet shows the change. The indexation switch has been turned to off

Hyperlinks

Hyperlinks are possibly one of the most underused features in Excel. They do not demand any knowledge of coding or formula, but when used constructively, they can be a tremendous help to modeling. Hyperlinks can be created on just about any object in Excel, and they are used to direct or link to a particular location either in the model itself, on the web or intranet, or to any other file. I advise that you never use hyperlinks to link to an exterior location. There is a clear risk of eventually getting dead links unless you have total control over the external link. This is also a sure way of frustrating the model users if they are unable to hit the link.

The hyperlink can be found on the Insert tab (see Figure 14-12) or by right-clicking an object or cell.

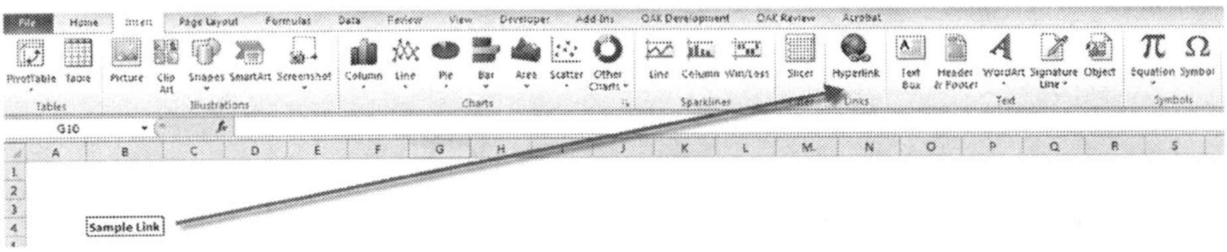

Figure 14-12. The hyperlink button is highlighted here

The question then is to decide where the link will land and in which cell, as is Figure 14-13.

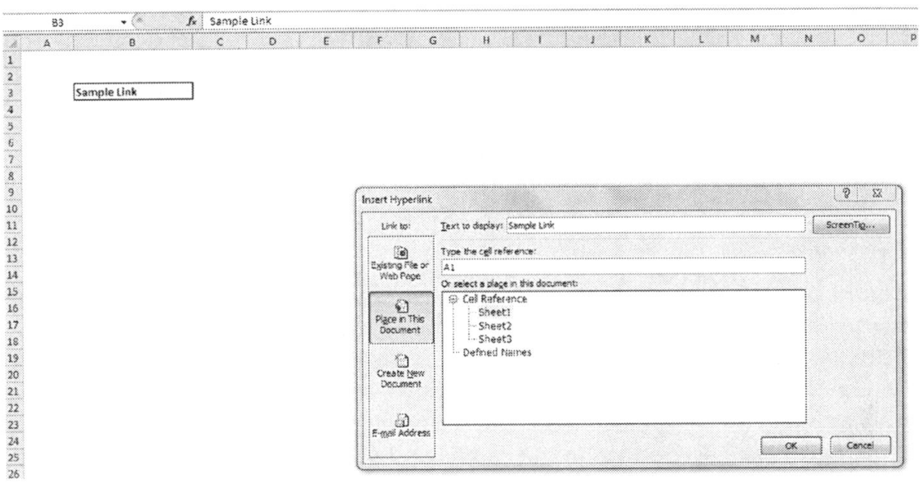

Figure 14-13. The next step is to select where in the model the link will land

How will a user know if a hyperlink is present on an object or cell? When the user hovers the cursor over the item, the cursor will change to a figure with a hand. To activate the hyperlink, the user will just click it, as in Figure 14-14a.

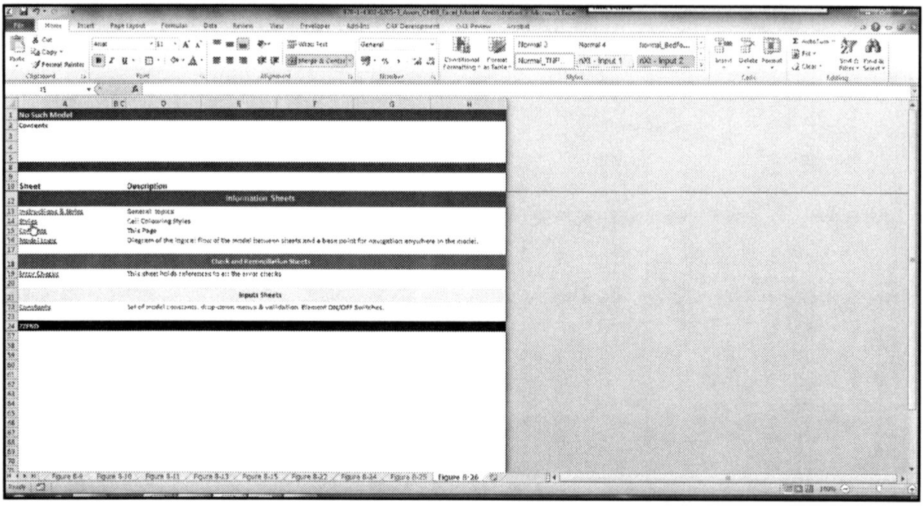

Figure 14-14a. The hand icon signifies that a hyperlink is present

Buttons

Buttons are three-dimensional objects that have either a link to a particular location or another object, or they are tied to some VBA code and when clicked will run a computer code. These buttons can be created by accessing the Developer tab and clicking on the insert icon to bring up the developer tools as in Figure 14-14b. Choose the button icon, which will bring up a menu of the existing VBA routines in the model and select the one that will be linked to the button.

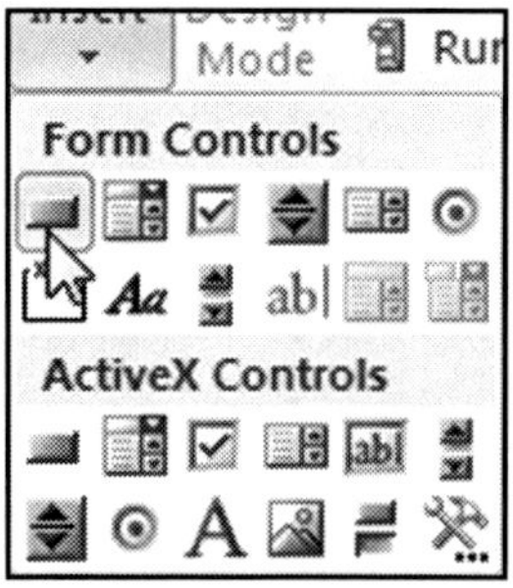

Figure 14-14b. The button icon is in the Developer tab under the insert icon

The next step is to left-click on the button icon and then left-click in the worksheet where you want to place the button. This action will bring up a menu box that will list all the macros available in the model as in Figure 14-14c. You will then select the one that should be linked to the button. A button will then be created, as in Figure 14-14d.

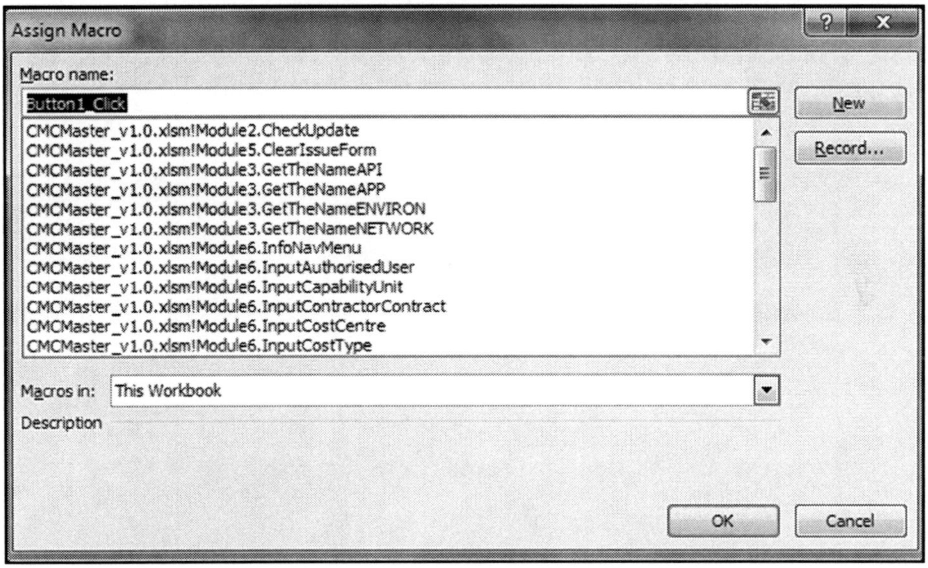

Figure 14-14c. The insert icon allows you to choose any of the macros available in the model to link to the button

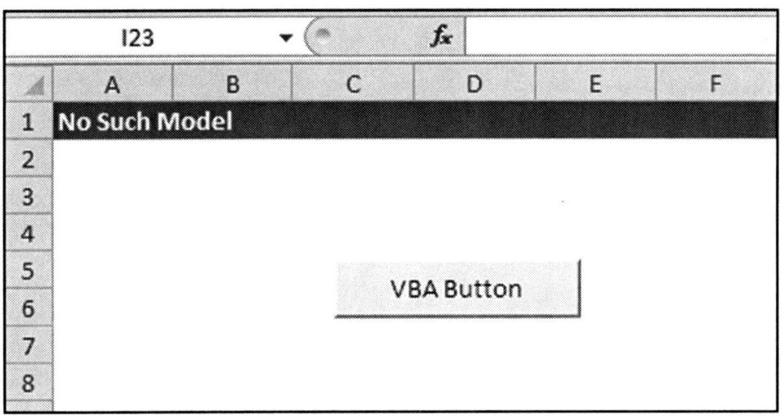

Figure 14-14d. The button will be created and ready to use after the macro is assigned

Adding User Flexibility to Accounting and Financial Statements

Now that user functionality has been discussed, we can start to use that functionality to bring flexibility to the financial statements. In essence, making the financial statements more flexible is not about changing or altering the underlying information—it's about changing the view and perspective. This functionality gives the user a choice of how to see the information. I can demonstrate this functionality by using the financial dashboard in Figure 14-15.

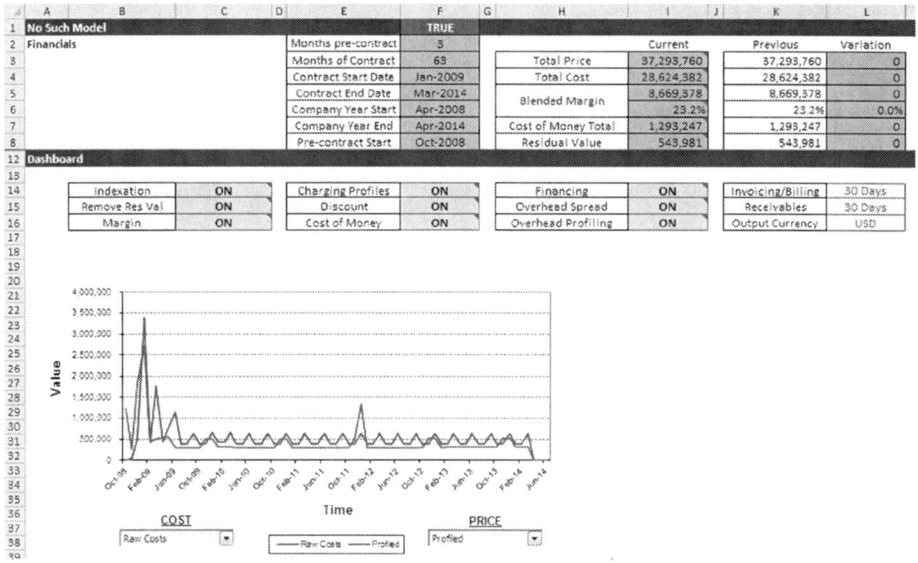

Figure 14-15. The financial dashboard can be used as a method of giving model users extra functionality on the outputs

From the dashboard, there are a number of switches that can alter the outputs in the financial dashboard. By using drop-downs and switches, you can effectively add flexibility to any financial statement and financial dashboard without altering the base data.

For example, a number of switches are turned off in Figure 14-16. Look at the change in total price and total cost as a result of the currency being changed to dirhams (AED), which is the United Arab Emirates currency.

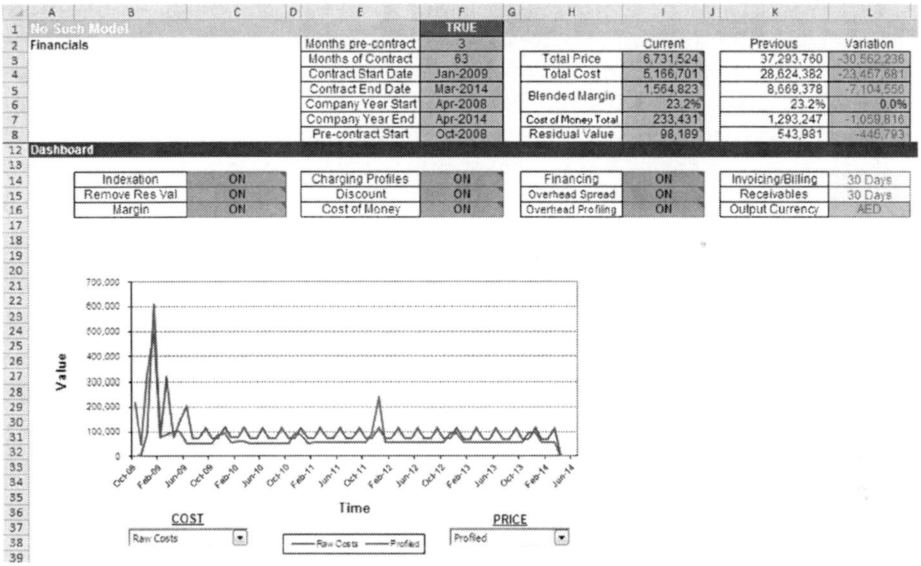

Figure 14-16. The currency in cell L16 has been changed to AED

In Figure 14-17, some of the switches, including indexation and overhead spread, have been switched to off. This switch has changed the base numbers.

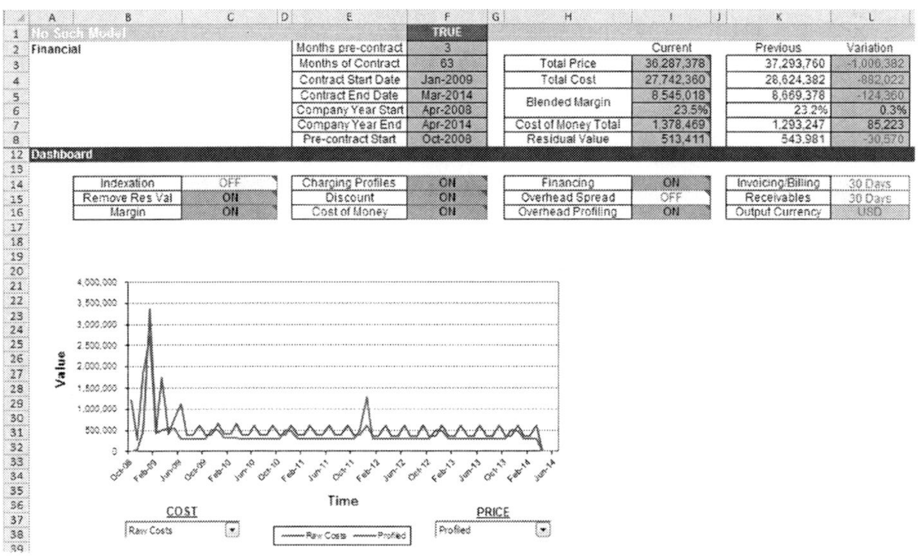

Figure 14-17. Changes in the indexation (cell C14) and overhead spread (cell I15) have affected the base totals

Flexibility of the financial statements is not always a good thing. As the modeler, you need to consider whether by providing that flexibility it will enhance the user's experience of the model. I do urge caution because giving that flexibility could confuse the users. This would result in erroneous reporting, for instance, if the users do not understand the difference between nominal and real values. If they turn off the indexation switch, what do the financials now mean? Are they nominal or real?

Error Checking

In Chapter 2, the importance of error checks and how to build them was discussed. In this section, how these error checks help with model administration will be explained.

The significance of errors in financial models has been emphasized throughout this book, and modelers must plan for them because they are invariably going to occur. As the modeler, you should consistently be thinking ahead about how the users of the model will likely react to all facets of the model. For instance, will they put text into an input cell that needs dates, insert rows and columns in a calculation worksheet, or change the descriptions in the financial outputs? There are literally hundreds of things a user can do.

Some of these actions can be mitigated by making simple adjustments to the model, such as creating data validations to block any data that doesn't conform to a specific type. But there will always be actions that cannot be foreseen, and this is where error checking is so important.

The modeler should always be thinking ahead and considering these questions:

- Will the user understand how to use the model?
- Will the user try to circumvent some model calculations?
- Is the model going to function correctly in another computer environment?
- How will the model function if the user deactivates various options, such as auto calculations or iterations for circularities?

As the list of possible actions builds, it's time to think of error checks that can be placed in the model to alert the user that the model may not function correctly as a result of some errors. The sign of a truly good model is one where the error checking is so pervasive it just cannot be ignored by the user.

In the past, I have created models that are mission critical and developed error checks where if the model has more than five crucial errors it will automatically shut down and produce an error log. This type of error check is surplus to the requirements with most models; however, it illustrates that as the modeler, you are in command of how that model will function. Therefore, anything that goes wrong should be quickly highlighted so that the users are aware of the mistakes. This will allow the users the chance to decide how to proceed. They may need to change the inputs or request that a modeler check that the model is functioning correctly.

The model should be littered with error checking all through its worksheets. Figure 14-18 is one example of a worksheet with time value inputs. Notice that there are numerous checks occurring on this worksheet. These checks provide feedback on whether the user has used valid inputs.

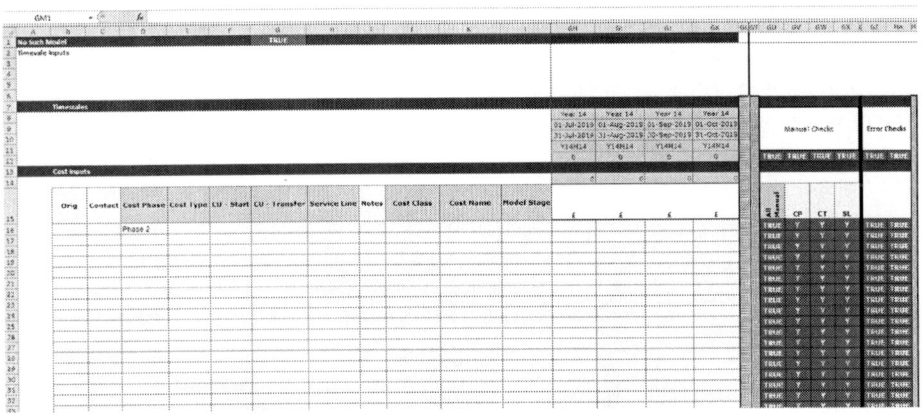

Figure 14-18. There are a number of error checks going on in this worksheet

I am asked often what error checks a modeler should employ. The answer to this question is dependent upon the model and the modeler's design. Error checks that look for the data type should always be included. (Is this the right type of data type for this input?) There should also be error checks to look at the integrity of the worksheet. (Has its structure changed? And if so, will that affect its functions?) Therefore, error checks should also test consistency. (If the cost center has previously been entered as belonging to the IT department, has it somehow changed in a later entry?) In general, the modeler must predict where potential errors can occur. After all, it is your model. If you know where the errors may occur, you can create the type of check that is required.

When checking for errors, make sure that the user of the model not only receives indications of errors but also an indication of the materiality or brevity.

Take for instance the previous examples of the financial dashboard. When the user switched off the indexation (inflation), what if the company's policy was to always have indexation in cost calculations? Because the model user turned it off, the model is strictly speaking in error. But does this error make the model unusable? Not by any means. So how would users start to understand that there are logical errors and their artificial error was caused by the business environment the model is working in?

The way forward is to provide three possible states of the error check: State 1 = Not in error, State 2 = Warning, State 3 = Is in error. These distinctions are important. If you can start to develop your models along this line, your models will always have that extra dimension of assurance often lacking in financial models.

In Figure 14-19, the indexation has been turned off. Note that this does not constitute an error in itself; however, how the model requirements state reported values should be nominal. In other words, inflation must be accounted for and hence should have indexation. This state does make reporting the financials without indexation a serious issue. Therefore, it is best to give the user a warning. In Figure 14-19, the blue band at the top is now orange (blue signifies the model is okay, orange signifies the model has a warning(s), and red signifies the model is in error).

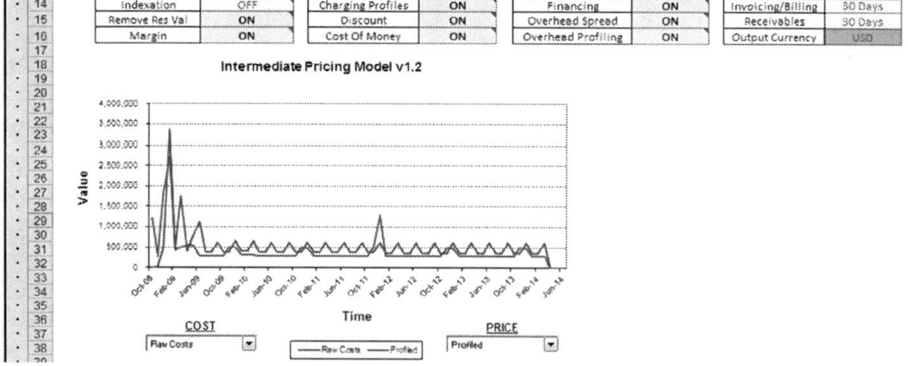

Figure 14-19. By turning off the indexation in cell C14, a warning is now produced with the orange band

The error in each worksheet should be collected and reflected at the top of the worksheet with a single error message. If you look in Figure 14-19, while the model overall has a warning and the band at the top of the worksheet is now orange, the error check in column F row 1 is still green and shows TRUE. This indicates that this worksheet has an error (orange band), but the model as a whole has no errors. By developing each worksheet along these lines where the complete model can be reflected as well as the individual worksheet, it is possible to give a number of different messages to the user. It also means that each worksheet collects its errors, which can then be reported back into a central error worksheet for administration, as in Figure 14-20.

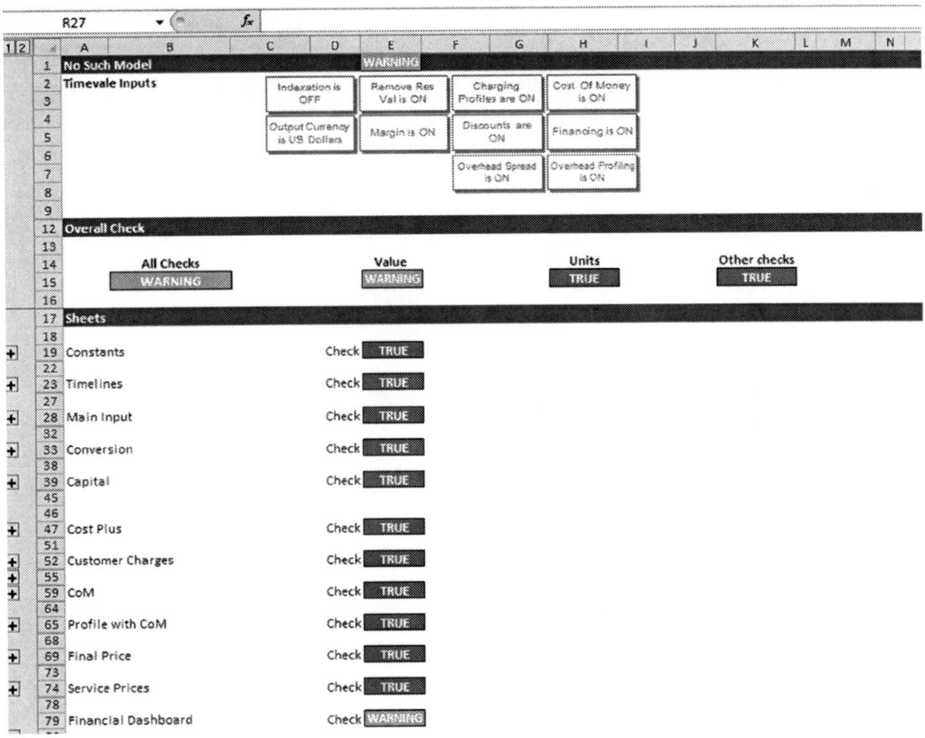

Figure 14-20. The error check central worksheet is shown here

In Figure 14-20, the warning generated in the dashboard is collected in the central error worksheet. From this worksheet, it is then possible to view the status of all parts of the model, which can even be broken down into more detail at a cell level if required. However, all the user needs to do is to check the error sheet to monitor the model errors.

User Interface Options

Excel is a strange beast in that it allows the user to take on various activities within a worksheet—both the development and the output interface. In many ways, there is no reason to create further interfaces because the Excel interface is quite clear and reasonably intuitive. I am not a major advocate for creating additional or artificial user interfaces in Excel because it's just another element that can create problems or errors.

There are instances though when the requirements are such that it is imperative to create some user interface to simplify the model. The more complex the model becomes, the more need for a user interface. Even when an interface is called for, my advice is to avoid overcomplicating it and provide the minimum required to satisfy the user requirements. Unless you are a VBA expert, Excel does not lend itself to good interface creation. It is very easy for a user to break the interface simply by accidentally moving an object or deleting one, which would cause significant problems for the model functionality.

Figure 14-21 is a simple interface that is used as the primary navigation through the model. In such a situation, the model would be locked down so that the worksheets are no longer visible, which means the user would not be able to navigate through the model by clicking on worksheet tabs.

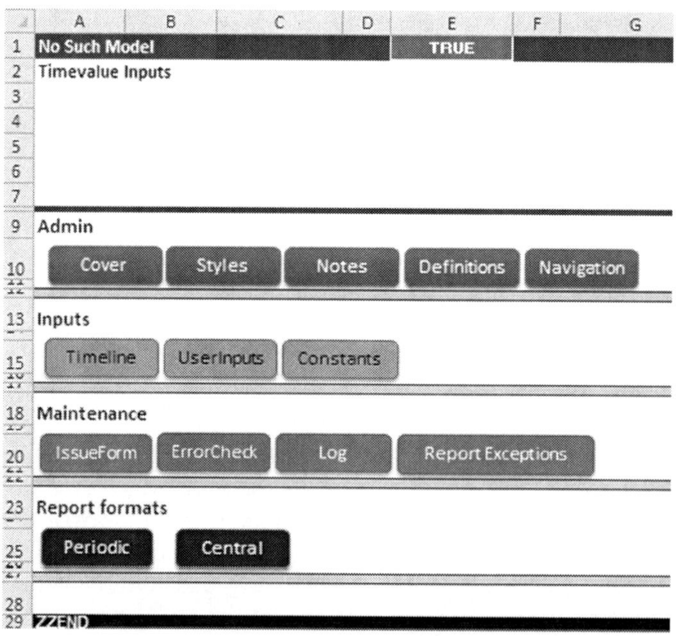

Figure 14-21. Adding a user interface for navigation will enhance the user's experience of the model

The only method of traversing the model would be through this navigation interface. The colored objects are, in fact, hyperlinks that are linked to the worksheet. Notice the arrow pointing upward at the top of the worksheet. This is a return object, and each worksheet has a similar arrow. When it is clicked, it returns the user back to the original navigation worksheet. This way, the user can subsequently choose to link to another worksheet. Navigating through the model is a two-hit situation—the user clicks to link to a worksheet, later clicks the arrow to return to the navigation, clicks to link to another worksheet, and so on.

It is possible to enhance the interface by creating custom menus and icons in the Excel ribbon, but I believe this is completely unnecessary and just adds more complications. The only exception would be if the model is so large and complex that it warrants an extensively engineered user interface.

Locking Down the Model

One of the unfortunate side effects of Excel's innate flexibility is that it is not a total secure environment. Excel worksheets are vulnerable to exploitation because even if password security is applied, that said password can be broken with a little persistence.

One of the difficult aspects of modeling is locking down the model so that it remains as the modeler built it and does not become altered. For instance, the final version of the model would look the same albeit the data would be changed, and the structure would not alter even after many years of use. The fact is that it's never really like that—the models are cannibalized or rebuilt or even thrown away after a relatively short period. Lockdown is not invariably 100% proof against changes and tampering; however, there is a procedure that I consistently use as part of the model lockdown that will be described next. (Incidentally, the lockdown should only occur after the final testing and after the reviews have been completed and cleared.)

Lockdown Procedure

1. Go through every worksheet and every cell in that worksheet and look at the protection, making sure the all cells with calculations are locked. (The locked check box should be selected.) All cells that require an input are unlocked. (The locked check box should be unselected.) All cells that are clear should also be locked. By taking these steps, users will be prevented from accidentally writing over a formula.

2. Go through every object such as shapes or arrows and check the properties to make sure the object positioning is "Don't move object or resize." This step will prevent anyone from changing the position and size of the object accidentally. Furthermore, check in the Protection tab and make sure the object and the text are locked.

3. Go through each worksheet and protect the entire worksheet.

There is a final option about the lockdown that involves copyright and potential patent. Depending on the terms of the contract between the client and the modeling entity, the model will likely be owned by the client, or in some rare circumstances belong to the modeler or modeling entity. There is a genuine conflict of who has intellectual rights of the model, and I have yet to get a standard definitive legally from a lawyer.

In models where the modeler has the rights, I would strongly recommend that you protect your intellectual rights, particularly if the model contains some original VBA coding and formula. If you don't, someone else will take it and claim it as theirs. I would also recommend that you invest in an EXE. compiler, such as LockXLS. This program turns the Excel file into an executable application (by compiling it), which means it can then be treated like any other application and have a host of security features. For instance, you can create authorizations for the model based on the network or the computer MAC code. If someone takes it off the network or opens it on a computer you haven't stipulated, the model just won't open. There are several aspects to LockXLS. I use it extensively to provide protection to intellectual rights. It is also a very good tool for providing assurance of payment. In the handover, you can stipulate how long the model will function and which features will be available or locked. If that period is breached, the model will cease to function.

Case Study: Every Model Needs a Good Manager

One of the problems associated with financial models is that they rarely survive being in use for any real length of time. The oldest working model I have come across has been two years, and even that one had been substantially reworked. This is somewhat disheartening until it is understood that the majority of models are the one-time types; that is, they are built to fulfill a specific mission and therefore should not be expected to last much beyond that.

This leads to one sticking point. Assuming an ongoing working model has been built to requirements and has been approved for use, why would that model not be in use over several years? In other words, why do financial models generally have a poor shelf life? From my experience, I believe it is because the business environment around which the model was originally built is ever changing. As a result, the model either needs to be adapted to that change or cease to be used.

Managing the Models

One of the critical aspects of dealing with financial models is how well they are understood. This is not from the perspective of the modeler, but from the perspective of the user and ultimately the owner or manager of the model. The next few sections will cover some very important management tasks that are required with managing models.

Understand What the Model Does and What It Doesn't Do

Typically, my opening question to model managers is always for them to tell me what the model is and what it does. In short, almost all the responses I have received to date fall short of the true model. In reality, it is not always the model that is failing; it's the perception of the model by management that needs to be adjusted toward understanding the intention of the model.

For example, during the mid-2000s, I was commissioned to look at a cost model that had been built for a global utility's corporation. This model was intended to provide analysis of the costs and isolate the key cost drivers in the entire business. Then it was supposed to spew out multitudes of reports to various senior managers informing them of the status of their costs.

Within hours of investigating, I noted that the prevailing view and attitude of the model was one of cynicism and lack of confidence. In fact, there was so much negativity surrounding this model that none of the managers were using it anymore and some had never used it. I even came across comments of a derogatory nature toward the modeler. Soon it became very clear to how these problems had arisen:

- The modeler had been commissioned to create a one-time model, specifically a model that would provide an analysis of costs. The model was intended for just one of the senior management teams in the finance department who would be the model owner.
- The manager who owned the model and was the gatekeeper had made several promises to other department managers about the model and its capabilities. This manager ultimately sowed the seed of its demise by providing these other managers with access to a model that was never intended for their use.
- Finally, as the model was a one-time type, the data was up to a time period. Therefore, the model was not designed to work in real time, and unfortunately this was not communicated by the gatekeeper to the other managers.
- The catalog of miscommunication meant that the model never saw much use and was scrapped.

Develop a Model Maintenance Strategy

All models without exception require maintenance at some point in their lifetime; it would be asking too much to expect anything less. The reasons why such maintenance is required are numerous. For instance, the online location of the model has moved or the address has changed, due to a restructuring in the organization, or the governance such as the organization's reporting structures and standards have changed. Therefore, the outputs of the model would be out of date.

Nevertheless, any good model manager will understand that maintenance is a must and will prepare some plan on how this can be achieved.

Keep Communicating with the Modeler

It concerns me how there seems to be a lack of continuity with models in corporations today. I come across models that are in use, but little is known about who developed the model and no contact information is available. This may be okay with a one-time, noncritical model, but when dealing with high stakes decisions made from a financial model, it is like opening and replying to an email when you don't know who the sender is. Inevitably, it's going to come back to bite the manager.

Keeping the communication lines open with the original modeler may have some cost impact. But it is invaluable for the manager to keep these lines open because the modeler can provide insight and advise on how to develop the model further. The modeler will also understand more fully the model's capabilities, weaknesses, and strengths.

In the early 2000s, I developed an employee's pay evaluation model for a medium-sized corporation. This was just a one-time use model to evaluate how the organization was treating equal pay across its employees. To my complete shock, I received an email some years later that led me to think this model was still in use. I contacted the manager who was responsible and discovered that the model had not been maintained, and so effectively the company was using the exact same model and data from several years ago. My immediate response was to offer my services to update the model and expand it to an ongoing working model, or else I advised that the company shut down the model because there was no assurance surrounding its outputs.

The manager chose to update the model, but here is the real lesson. If the company had kept a line of communication with me during the intervening years, the model would not have required such drastic actions to update it. The eventual cost impact to the organization would have been a lot less too because a huge update would not have been needed.

Managers Should Not Try to be Modelers

The model manager is there to be the keeper and the user and to understand how the model best serves the organization. But the one thing a manager should not be is the modeler. This point is clear: model managers should not involve themselves in physical building, maintenance, or updating of models. Why? It comes down to the potential skills of the model managers. If they are not modelers, then it's unlikely they will be in a position to understand the mechanics of modeling. Good financial models are built by modelers, and you can see already from this book that there are many facets to being a modeler. Dabbling in commercial use models is dangerous unless you really understand what you are doing. The manager would need to understand the thinking and the style of the previous modeler in order to make any changes. The other aspect involves detachment. The manager should not be the same person as the modeler because this is a fundamental financial practice of segregation of duties.

Note Separation of duties is also known as "segregation of duties" and "separation of powers." It is a fundamental principle that ensures that a single person does not have the ability to abuse his or her powers or make significant errors. The general principle is that collusion/error between a number of people is required to abuse the process. Segregation of duties in an accounting department serves as the primary defense against internal fraud. Therefore, no single person should have the authority to cause damage acting on his or her own. Even when separation of duty controls have been included in an information system, users are often trying to find ways around them because of business pressure. In large companies, it is the role of the internal auditor to identify these lapses of control, but very often this is an impossible task.

We can clearly see that every model needs a good manager, as this is ultimately about the survival of the model and potentially the reputation of the modeler. The modeler should take an active interest in finding out who will be manager and understanding the manager's management style. It is the modeler's responsibility to also brief the manager about the model so that the manager has a thorough understanding of it.

CHAPTER

15

Model Testing and Auditing

This chapter examines some essentials to modeling that are actually not in the hands of the modeler, namely the testing and model audits. Both model testing and model audits are broadly referred to as model reviews or peer reviews. Ironically, model reviews are not performed by the modeler who has created the model. They are instead the domain of an independent person or body. Although it may seem odd that I am including this chapter, I would urge anyone who is serious about modeling to give attention to it. As a modeler, you should have a basic knowledge and appreciation of how testing and auditing are conducted. Not only will it have a positive influence on how you model by allowing you to look from the external perspective of the model, it's also quite conceivable that at some time you may be asked to be a reviewer.

I would hasten to mention that model auditing has become a well-recognized business activity, and there are numerous organizations worldwide that provide model audits, the "big four" professional service firms—KPMG, Ernst & Young, PwC, and Deloitte—among them. Model testing is far from being an established business practice, so the options are not as clear although there are a few software applications that work well.

Few commentators recommend or even mention model testing, as the model audit is the established method of providing model assurance. However, both testing and model audit are complementary; they need not go head-to-head because they are based on differing ethos.

The following is a summary of the standards of model testing:

> Models are developed by humans: the very same humans who make errors that can have a significant effect on a model's behavior. Model testing is about discovering those errors and measuring their relationship with the behavior of the model. Thus, testing is about the quality of the model.

To put it simply, testing is quality control and model audit is assurance. If we look at it on this level, then these two processes augment each other. In my view, testing should be performed during the model building so that the errors can be caught and mitigated as part of the development and checked. Testing should look at those errors and how they affect the overall quality of the model.

In some industry sectors, model audits are not an option. In fact, there is clearly a move to make audits mandatory at some level. In the United Kingdom, for instance, private-public projects are required to have their models audited as part of the tendering process. With aspects like bank risk management, approaches such as Basel III model audit is a fundamental part of the approach.

In summary, a model that has not been audited is a potential liability, and a model that has been audited but not tested lacks guarantees.

Why You Should Always Test Financial Models

If I had to estimate the number of commercial use financial models that go through testing, I am quite sure the number would be low for the following reasons:

- Model testing has yet to be established as a stable and bona fide business practice. Therefore, there are very few model testing practitioners.
- Most organizations that use financial models are satisfied with a model audit, which in the main has a proven track record for delivering value for money.
- Little is understood of what is required to test a model, so there are few instances of in-house testing.
- More often than not, the timescale involved when developing financial models is very tight, and as a result, model testing is seen as a "nice to have" option that will be included only if time permits.

Model testing is an important part of best practice modeling. Although it may be currently not included in mainstream modeling, it is nonetheless critical. Testing is the only way to provide any guarantee that the model not only works, but it also stresses the conditions in which the model will continue to work and when it fails to work.

As an analogy, can you imagine buying a cell phone, understanding that the phone will allow you to make and receive calls, but not knowing under which conditions the phone would not work? For instance, most of us know that our phones will not work if exposed to extreme temperatures or moisture, when there is no cell mast in close proximity, or if the battery is continually being undercharged. These examples of when cells phones do not work are based on testing. We only know this information because the cell phone has undergone numerous tests. Model audits will give some assurance, but they cannot tell us under which conditions the model will degrade or cease to function, mostly that becomes a matter of intuition.

I believe that financial modeling will at some point have to embrace model testing wholeheartedly, just as the software industry has done. As models have now become more vital to everyday business, they will need some amount of stress testing in order to become a business mainstay.

Types of Model Tests

There are no standard financial model test methodologies; however, over the years I have developed my own testing procedures. These procedures are based on software testing using the software development life cycle (SDLC) because these tests are most appropriate to modeling.

The key to testing is the methodology behind the test results. For instance a test report represented by a percentage such as 60% could mean 60% of all errors in the testing type will be caught in the first round of tests, or 60% could be caught after two round of tests, and so on. Clearly, the lower the percentage, the more critical that several test rounds are pursued as the percentage of errors not caught will decrease. In each of the tests, the detected errors are identified and then fixed by the modeler before the model continues on to development.

The Test Plan

Prior to commencing any testing, one vitally important task is to create a test plan. The test plan is a document describing the scope, approach, resources, and schedule of intended testing activities. It identifies test items, the features to be tested, the testing tasks, and who will do each task. An example of a test plan is shown in Figure 15-1. It should also identify any risks involved with planning the tests and contingencies for those risks. If the entire idea of a test plan just seems far too formal, then you should keep in mind that the testing phase can be detailed and complex. It's very easy to lose track of which tests yielded which results and any issues and corrections that were made.

Test Plan

1 Introduction

Document Description
Related Documents
Schedule and Milestones

2 Resource Requirements

Hardware
Software
Test Tools
Staffing
Responsibilities
Training

3 Features To Be Tested / Test Approach

4 Features Not To Be Tested

5 Test Deliverables

6 Dependencies/Risks/Contingencies

7 Entrance/Exit Criteria

Figure 15-1. The headings with a typical test plan document are shown here

The test plan allows for the planning; without the plan it is unlikely that the tests will yield any success. Crucially the test plan should never be created by the modeler; this is the domain of the chief tester. There should be as little interference from the modeler or modeling team as possible. When I have performed tests on models, I will allow the modeling team to review the test plan once it has been finalized, but no one from the team is given the chance to change or make any amendments. Nor does the modeling team get the chance to provide any additional material that may interfere with the test. If this were to happen, I would reject the said material and report it as an issue in the test report.

The Tests

In the next few sections, I have provided descriptions of different tests, each of which are designed to examine specific aspects of a model and can be used in the test plan. Not all these tests are relevant all the time for every model. The chief tester will first need to discuss with the modeler about the model's purpose and design ethic. Then the model tester should evaluate, based on the type of model, which types of tests would be most appropriate and effective.

Static Testing

During static testing, you have a checklist to check whether the work you are doing is going as per the set standards of the organization. These standards can be for coding, integrating and deployment, reviews, inspections, and walkthroughs.

Dynamic Testing

Dynamic testing involves working with the model, giving input values, and checking to see if the output is as expected. Validation activities include unit tests, integration tests, system tests, and acceptance tests.

Black Box Testing

Black box testing takes an external perspective of the test object in order to derive test cases. These tests can be practical or nonfunctional, though they are usually functional. The test designer selects valid and invalid input and determines the correct output.

This method of test design is applicable to all levels of software testing: unit, integration, functional testing, system, and acceptance. The higher the level, and hence the bigger and more complex the box, the more one is forced to use black box testing to simplify. While this method can uncover unimplemented parts of the specification, the tester cannot be sure that all existent paths are tested.

White Box Testing

White box testing is a security testing method that can be used to validate whether code usage follows an intended design, to confirm implemented security functionality, and to uncover exploitable vulnerabilities.

Unit Testing

In computer programming, unit testing is a procedure used to validate that individual units of source code are working properly. A unit is the tiniest testable part of a coded application.

Requirements Testing

Requirements seem to be ephemeral. They flit in and out of projects; they are capricious, intractable, unpredictable, and sometimes invisible. When gathering requirements, the tester is searching for all the criteria for a system's success by throwing out a net and trying to capture all these criteria. The methods used with this type of testing include using blitzing, rapid application development (RAD), joint application development (JAD), quality function deployment (QFD), interviewing, apprenticing, and data analysis.

Regression Testing

Regression testing is any type of software testing that seeks to uncover regression bugs. Regression bugs occur whenever software functionality that formerly worked as desired stops operating or no longer works in the same way that was earlier planned. Typically, regression bugs occur as an unintended consequence of program changes.

Common methods of regression testing include rerunning earlier run tests and checking whether previously fixed faults have re-emerged.

Error Handling Testing

Error handling refers to the anticipation, detection, and resolution of programming, formula, and communications errors. Specific formulas are created as error handlers.

Compliance or Static Testing

Compliance testing is all about checking to what degree the model is working as per the set standards of the organization. These standards can be for the outputs (financial statements), styles, wording, macro coding, how the data is organized, confidentiality, change control or issue handling capabilities, how the model is integrated into in-house systems, and also how the model is deployed. On basic-level compliance, testing is an inspection of the model with a checklist to test the quality of conformity. Therefore, the starting point is always a list of standards that the organization requires from all models or spreadsheets and a check against them. Figure 15-2 is a typical compliance test checklist that I have used in model tests.

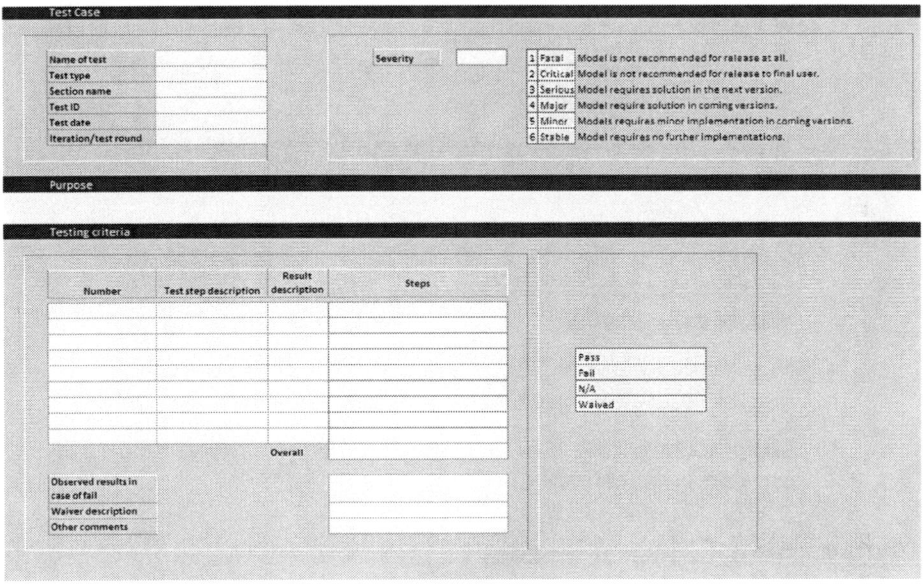

Figure 15-2. A typical compliance test checklist is shown here

The criteria that would be used during testing would be:

- Name of test: The name should reflect the type of test.
- Test type: This is the type of test conducted, which should match the test plan.
- Section name: The part of the model, for instance could be a worksheet, or input section.
- Test ID: This is a reference to the test; each test and test round should have a sequential reference.
- Test date: This is the date when the test was carried out and should be in synchronization with the iteration and test round.

- Iteration/test round: A number that shows how many tests have gone before this one.
- Severity: This is a code that summarizes the results of the test in that round.
- Number: This is a sequential number for the order of the criteria order.
- Test step description: This is a description of what is being tested.
- Result description: This is a description of the result of the test for that criterion.
- Steps: The drop-down gives four options that will reflect the result of the test: pass, fail, N/A, and waived.
- Observed results in case of fail: If the test fails, it is imperative to describe exactly what was observed as it is possible the failure was the result of an external matter and not the model.
- Waiver description: This is a description of the potential impact to the end user if the test fails.
- Other comments: This is for any further comments that are deemed necessary.

Management Control Testing

Management control testing (see Figure 15-3) is used to evaluate the level of control in the model. For example, this would look at the inputs to test if it is possible for one input to have an effect on several calculations. This differs from compliance testing because it is all about the processes and edicts from management, which are current at the time. For instance, management may stipulate that data should always be accurate and not hypothetical, that all transactions should be authorized by senior figures, or that there should be an audit trail for all assumptions.

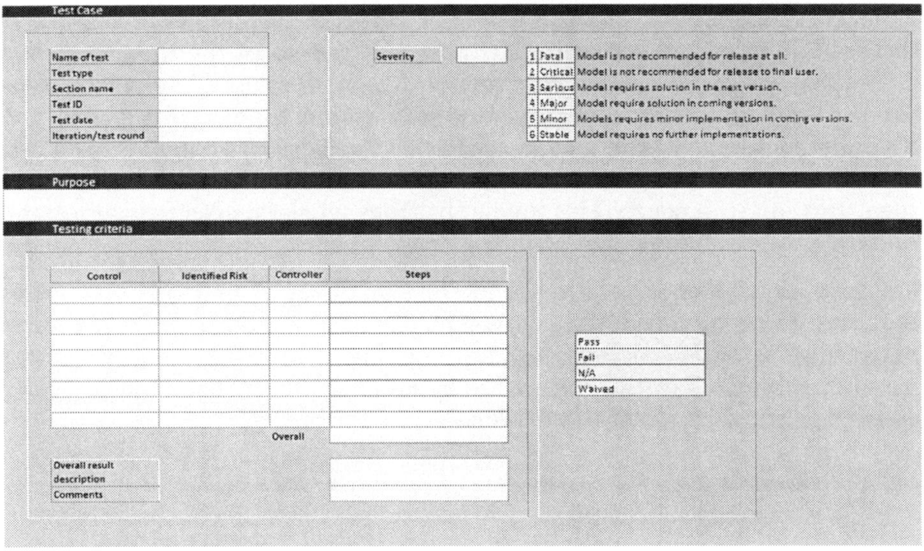

Figure 15-3. A template for a control test check is shown here

The major criteria that would be included in the test are:

- Control: This is the name of the control as prescribed by management.
- Identified risk: This is the prevailing risk associated with this control.
- Controller: This is the name or contact of who is responsible for the control.
- Overall result description: This is the test case result: pass, fail, N/A, and waived.
- Comments: These are any comments that can provide some detail behind the overall test case result.

Stress Test

Stress testing deals with the quality of the application in the environment. The idea is to create an environment more demanding of the model than the model would experience under so-called normal work use. This is the hardest and most complex category of testing as it is totally based on the model design.

Conflict conditions, for example where an input for taxation rate also affects the inflation rate, and system capacity issues are two of the most common errors that will come out of stress testing. The method used to get results for the two conditions is to run two tests in parallel one is looking for conflict and the other is examining the system capacity. The tester is looking to see if one or both tests fail either because they negate each other or create an unforeseen equation to emerge. This is what happens when inputs, calculations, and outputs have not been designed in the correct order.

In Figure 15-4, a sample is given of the test that I use. This stress test allows the tester to set up to five input parameters by using the drop-down to choose between very low, low, normal, high, and very high. By mixing and varying input parameters, the tester can review the behavior of the model under a mix of conditions and thus stress the model.

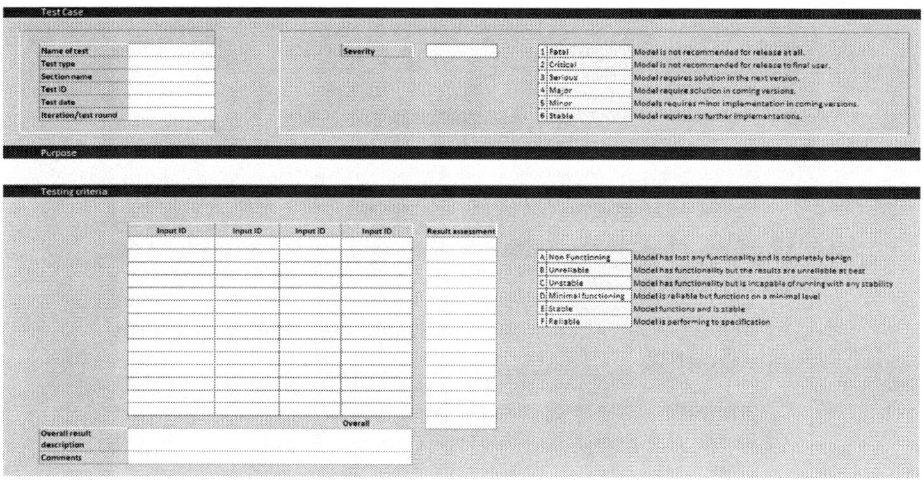

Figure 15-4. A template of a stress test is shown here

System capacity happens when a test leaves allocated memory behind and does not accurately return the memory to the memory allocation scheme. The test seems to run correctly, but after being exercised several times, available memory is reduced until the system fails.

System Performance Test

With this type of testing, the systems under which the model is working are tested and then differing configurations are also tested. The network performance is also tested under different levels of user usage. This may involve testing the model on the network during the morning, afternoon, and evening. The model is placed in a calculative state. In other words, the model is induced into processing data and subsequently a system's performance tool can then be used to compare the processor performance. There are tools available that are able to measure performance, which is generally assessed in terms of response time and throughput rates under differing processing and configuration conditions.

Functional Testing

Functional testing means testing the model against business requirements. In this type of testing, the tests are written in order to check if the model behaves as expected. Although functional testing is often done toward the end of the development cycle, it should be started much earlier. Individual components and processes can be tested early on, even before it's possible to do functional testing on the entire system. Functional testing covers how well the VBA code (if there is any) executes the functions it is supposed to execute, including user commands, data manipulation, searches and business processes, user screens, and integrations.

If there is just one test that is a must, it is this one. Functional testing always verifies that the model is fixed for release. Functional tests also define your working model in a useful manner. With this type of testing, the tester has to validate the model to see that all specified requirements of the project and customer are met.

Functional testing is always concentrating on customer requirements.

What Do You Test in Functional Testing?

These are the main areas that are tested with functional testing:

- **Mainline functions**: The main functions of an application are tested.
- **Basic Usability**: This involves fundamental usability testing of the system and checks to see whether a user can freely navigate through the screens without any difficulties.
- **Accessibility**: It checks the accessibility of the system for the user.
- **Error Conditions:** It checks for error conditions to see whether suitable error messages are displayed.

The testing process will consist of the following:

- Understand the requirements.
- Identify test input (test data).
- Compute the expected outcomes with the selected test input values.
- Execute test cases.
- Compare the actual and computed expected results.

How to Test Your Model

Model testing is very much in its infancy, and it is certainly not as highly developed as software testing. The information presented in this section is something to aim for; as mentioned before this is not in general practice today. However, it should be something that modeling will need to have as part of its life cycle. Although I use this type of methodical approach to testing models myself, this area of modeling is very much exploratory.

Testing is an important part of model development. It should always be started as early as possible and should be part of the process of deciding model requirements. You will find that it is worthwhile to provide time for the testing during model development as it will give a guarantee that the model quality is high.

Testing is part of a model life cycle. The model development life cycle is about developing a credible tool that will fulfill the requirements of the users, stakeholders, owners, and other people who have an interest in what the model does. Hopefully, their requirements can all be captured in the model in the first development cycle. However, if there is a need for additions or changes, then the cycle must continue and that would include testing.

Testing is a proxy for the customer. You could conceivably perform your testing by releasing it to the customer. Then you would wait for the complaints and compliments to come back from the customers. But you are always in a better position to try and make sure that the model will satisfy the customer before you hand it over.

Therefore, it is better to design tests based on the stakeholders' needs and run the tests before the product reaches the users. Preferably the testing should be done well before then, so as not to waste time working on something that isn't going to do the job.

In this light, two important principles become clear:

- Tests represent requirements. Whether you write user stories on sticky notes on the wall or use cases in a thick document, your tests should be derived from and linked to those requirements. Devising tests is a good vehicle for discussing the requirements.
- You are not finished with the model until the tests pass. The only useful measure of completion is when tests have been performed successfully.

These principles apply no matter how you develop your model.

The Testing Cycle

The testing cycle is as follows:

1. The modeler provides the model requirements to the tester and gives a detailed view of the model development concerning the requirements.
2. The tester creates a test script(s) based on the requirements but will have no input or interference from the modeler during this stage. The test scripts is a description of which aspects of the model will be tested and which types of test will be performed. The upshot is that each requirement will have its own test case, which will be tested.
3. When the model is in a usable version, it is made available to the tester, who will now commence with physical testing.
4. Any issues and errors that are discovered are passed on to the modeler, and a round count is concluded.
5. The tester will review the results of each round of tests with the modeler for quality and effectiveness of the implementation of the solutions. Also at this stage, the tester using the previous round of tests as the baseline will subsequently decide whether another round of testing will be required later.
6. Once the reviews of the modeler and tester have reached a level where the tester deems the results to be of sufficient quality that no more testing is required, the tester will sign off on the tests.
7. Following the tester's sign-off, the modeler will get approval from the sponsor that the testing phase can be concluded. The model has now been tested and is ready for lockdown final documentation and handover.

Note Depending on the number of issues and implementations, several rounds could be needed. The tester will decide what is sufficient to meet an acceptable level of model quality. It's possible to have anything from 1 to 20 rounds.

In view of the stages of testing, the unfortunate reality is that the time required for testing is often underestimated. There are usually concerns that the project timescales will be compromised unless the model can be completed on time, so the testing is concluded prematurely. Therefore, it is vitally important that the modeler provide beforehand a realistic and reasonable estimate of time in the project timescales for testing. This is possibly the biggest reason why testing is not always performed or performed poorly. Testers are not responsible for setting the timescales and must be placed in a position where they have the freedom to properly test and give a sign-off with no caveats or further issues that need resolving.

In the past, I have compiled a checklist (included next) that is used after the model testing and audit have been completed, approved, and signed off. Many of the items on this checklist are not always appropriate for all models, so you should use your best judgment to adapt it to suit your particular environment.

Model development	Is a project manager assigned to the project?
	Is the model development methodology divided into a reasonable number of phases?
	Are there management checkpoints at the end of each phase?
	How frequently is the progress reported to the project manager?
Model change control	Does the model have a version number?
	How many modelers have access or are developing the model?
	Does the model's Change Request form tally with the actual changes made to the model?
	Did the modeler write comments on the model?
	Were there any emergency changes made to this model? If so, when were they made and when were they checked and authorized?
	Is the user manual updated after a major change to the model?

(*continued*)

Separation of duties	Are development and testing facilities separated from operational systems?
	Have the duties been separated to ensure that no one individual performs more than one of the following operations:
	Data origination?
	Data input?
	Output distribution?
	Are the functions of the preparer and verifier adequately segregated?
Data handling	Are errors displayed or printed immediately on detection for immediate correction by the user?
	Do error messages provide clear, understandable, cross-referenced corrective actions for each type of error?
	Are error messages produced for each input containing data?
	Are transaction rejections, caused by data entry errors, corrected by the terminal operator?
	Are there checks to ensure that the correct data files are used?
	Is there a logging type facility (audit trail) in the model to assist in reconstructing data files?
	Does the model support concurrent or multiuser data inputs?
Connectivity	Is the model using connectivity such as ODBC or MDX for Oracle? What are they?
	Does the model have application program interfaces (API)?
Independency	Is this model tested independently of the modeler(s)?
	Are end users involved in independent testing?
	Does the independent testing include testing of documentation?
	Does the independent testing analyze the manual portions of the model?
	Are independent test reports prepared?
	Does independent testing validate all the support systems on the model, including user procedures and backup procedures?
	Does the independent testing analyze the adequacy of the system of internal control?
	Does the independent test group understand the business nature of the model being tested?

(*continued*)

Functional specification testing	Has the end user agreed that the defined requirement is correct?
	Did the end user participate in the development of the requirements?
	Is there a user sign-off at the end of the requirements phase?
	Do the requirements define the limits of possible changes to the data volumes during the expected life of the application system?
	Was an analysis of security requirements carried out at the requirements analysis stage of the project?
	Have the security requirements been identified and agreed upon prior to the development of the application system?
	Have appropriate security controls including audit trails been designed into the model?
	Is an audit trail part of the functional specification?
Test error conditioning	Has a brainstorming session with end users been performed to identify functional errors?
	Have functional error conditions been identified for the following cases:
	Rejection of out-of-range values?
	Rejection of invalid dates?
	All blank conditions in a numeric cell?
	Negative values in a positive cell?
	Positive values in a negative cell?
	Negative balances in a financial account?
	Test for numeric cells?
	Blanks in an alphabetic field?
	Values longer than the field permits?
	Totals that exceed the maximum size of total fields?
The model state	Has the state of empty tables been validated?
	Has the state of an insufficient quantity been validated?
	Has the state of a negative balance been validated?
	Has the state of duplicate inputs been validated?
	Has the state of entering the same transaction twice been validated?
Model implementation	Are model defects apparent before being handed over?
	Is the end user aware of model deficiencies before handover?
	Are detailed handover plans prepared before handover?

(*continued*)

Model training	Are users trained in operating the model?
	Are the training materials consistent with the updated model?
	Are the training needs assessed?
	Is the operations staff informed of how to handle all abnormal conditions of the model, such as abnormal terminations or functions that fail to yield results?
Model backup strategy	How frequent is the data backup?
	How frequent is the model backup?
	Are copies of the model and data stored offsite?
	Is the backup tested on a separate machine to confirm recovery?
	Is there a procedure for recovery and business continuity including manual work required in case of a disaster?
	How long does it take to set up the model on a new machine?
Security and access	Are VBA codes protected from unauthorized access?
	Is model documentation protected from unauthorized access?
	Has all confidential information been identified?
	Have the potential consequences of unauthorized disclosure been assessed?
	Are only those who have a "need to know" authorized to access?
	Is information transmitted over telecommunication networks encrypted?
	Is storage media containing sensitive data and programs stored in a securely locked area and protected from unauthorized removal?
	Is test data protected and controlled?
	Has the sponsor reviewed the model authority levels in the event of a purported or real security violation?

How to Perform a Model Audit

You will find that the terms "model audit" and "model review" are used interchangeably. Keep in mind that it's become more likely that large corporations will prefer the term "model review" in order to avoid the implication that a statutory audit has been performed with the same levels of due diligence and therefore possibly raise issues about liability. For the purposes of this book, I will use the term "model audit." In my opinion, this term more accurately describes what exactly what is happening, whereas a review seems to imply something with less rigor and control.

The Process

Model audits tend to be one of the last procedures of modeling, usually because there are other activities that are required, prior to an audit commencing, that just seem better left to the end. However, a model audit can commence at any time there is a physical model available and does not need to start at the final model. The general procedure of auditing a model is as follows:

- A familiarization activity of the model structure begins this process with an added focus on the worksheets and the linking of the worksheets.

Note The model is partitioned and dispatched to more than one reviewer for detailed low-level scrutiny. The model audit often takes place in parallel, where different parts of the model are reviewed simultaneously, and it is typically performed by graduates working for a formal accounting qualification.

- A cell-by-cell inspection is almost always used as it is the only sure method of systematically discovering errors. The audit will employ proprietary software that will help with this approach.
- Model errors are fed back to the modeler for correction by using a simple error management system.

Model audits can generate a considerable amount of data during inspection, and it's not unheard for the audit file to be more than 100 megabytes in size. This is the equivalent to 50,000 letter-size pages of text. The time taken to perform a model audit can range from a matter of days to weeks with few hundred man-hours. I have come across many instances where it's been claimed that model audits are an excuse for modelers to charge high fees to the client for very little work. Don't let yourself buy into this opinion. If you are given the chance to perform a model audit, you will quickly understand how much effort and painstaking time is required to audit. The fees should reflect this process because it's well worth the money.

Following the low-level review that will have established the correctness of the detailed model formulas and other model parts, a high-level review takes place. During the high-level review, wider issues such as the correct handling of accounting and financial issues (i.e., Inflation, taxation, depreciation, interest, and margins).

Once the model is correct, it can then be used to investigate sensitivities. For example, a few key model variables—interest rates, cost, and revenue assumptions—could be changed to review the characteristics of the transaction under various commercial scenarios. The performance of the model under these scenarios is checked and documented.

After numerous feedback iterations with the model developer have taken place to correct errors and with financial closure invariably pressing, a report is then issued to the client. This report will confirm that various previously agreed review procedures have been performed on the model. Any unresolved issued are documented.

The Low-Level Review

A low-level review looks at the logical and structural makeup of the model. This is a very detailed inspection and very slow process with large or complex models. Fortunately, there are a small number of model audit software tools like OAK, SPACE, and Spreadsheet Detective that are able to determine the likelihood and severity of error in client spreadsheets and the likely location of errors.

Different aspects will infer information about the relative ease or difficulty and the time needed to review a given model. These include the length of the formula, the ratio of original to repeated cells, the number of cell precedents and dependents, and the locality cell linkages. The tools also produce model maps of a worksheet where the contents of each cell are coded based on whether they have formulas or labels using colors and test labels, such as "F" when there is a formula. These maps allow the reviewer to quickly assess if the worksheet is following best practice modeling rules in relation to formula construction.

During the process of examining the formulas in a spreadsheet, the following issues should be considered:

- Cell references should be valid and not redundant, particularly to highlight any pointing issues.
- The correct use of functions and its arguments in the formula are needed.
- There should be no technical errors present, such as #ERR or #REF.
- No circularities should be present.
- No hard-coded constants should be in the formulas.
- There should be a consistent use of the units of weight and measure.

- Absolute and relative cell addresses should be understood by the modeler.
- Models with VBA code need checking. This is performed by printing out, inspecting, running, and testing all executable entities. This part of the process of reviewing a spreadsheet is directly comparable with the code review phase of traditional software.

The High-Level Review

Immediately following the low-level review, the next step would be to execute a high-level review. This review would check aspects of the overall integrity of the model that may have been missed by the low-level review. This type of review will generally address the consistency of the model with any supporting documentation. It will also include checks to ensure that finance and accounting issues have been dealt with correctly. For instance, does the revenue recognition conform with IFRS standards, or does the model adhere to GAAP (Generally Accepted Accounting Principles)? A high-level review will also check to see if the jurisdiction is catered for within the model. In some instances, the model audit will also address commercial issues relevant to the project that is being modeled. However, this will depend on the engagement agreement between the client and the model auditor.

Some of the typical steps that will be taken in a high-level review include the following:

- Make sure that the balance sheet balances, which surprisingly is quite a problem in models.
- Look at whether retained earnings flow from the profit and loss account to the balance sheet. This is particularly key to how the calculations for the outputs have been designed.
- Ensure that fixed assets do not depreciate below zero. This may sound obvious, but it does happen if the controls in the formula have been formed incorrectly.
- Examine how taxation is treated and ensure that taxes and deferred taxes are handled correctly.

High-level checks on the model and its documentation will certainly include a detailed review of the terms of any debt and other funding to ensure that the precise details of the debt provisions are reflected in the model.

The high-level review comes with its own control. Any changes to the model during this stage will cause another low-level test to be performed.

Sensitivities

Following both the low-level and high-level reviews and the finalization, the model will now be running to specification and is therefore correct. At this point, running sensitivities on the model by playing with some key cost and revenue variables, dates, rates (interest, tax, or inflation), discount rates, and debt/equity ratios. For a large model, running sensitivities can be time-consuming, particularly if the model has not been designed logically. However, in a properly built model, these sensitivities should not cause much of time hindrance. Should any errors be found at this late stage, the model auditors will request a rapid correction from the modeler and a new cleaned version will need to be produced within days.

Final Review Report

The concluding part of a model audit is a drawing together of all the work that has been performed on the model. A package of documentation will be assembled, which can be used to demonstrate that every check that was required was performed. Any final queries regarding model performance will be cleared if possible. Any areas of concern that remain will be clearly documented.

The wording of the final audit report could be stated this way: "The agreed upon procedures have been performed" or "The model is free of material error." You could also state that the audit provides assurance that all errors are no longer present in the model.

Care is taken in final reports to identify exactly which model was the subject of the audit. Typical identification data will include basic information, such as the file name, date, time, and size. The limit to the contractual liability of the firm performing the model audit work is an important issue. A liability figure is always agreed upon prior to any work taking place and is often restated in the final report. In some cases, liability is (or has to be) unlimited, placing onerous responsibilities upon firms and individuals who perform this work on large transactions.

Final Say

A model audit is a detailed, time-consuming process that is about ensuring all parties involved that they can rely upon the integrity of the model's financial outputs. Although the practice of including model audits is growing and is now considerably more widely applied than in the early 2000s, it is still not as prevalent is it could or should be. There are literally thousands of models produced each month around the world, but one can only be certain that there are nowhere near that many model audits performed. Although there are no official figures to assess how many commercial models go through a model audit annually, I would guess that it is less than 5%. If my guess is close to being correct, this issue needs some serious addressing.

Case Study: Never Assume Perfection

This case study is based on an incident involving the financial models for an outsource bid in the United Kingdom. It shows why it is important for everyone involved in building models to never assume things are perfect or correct without applying stringent testing and audit.

The Background

The West Coast mainline (WCML) is one of the busiest train lines in western Europe and runs from greater London through the Midlands area, then to the north of England and up into central Scotland with a core track length of 640 kilometers.

The WCML is one of the most highly visible and important passenger routes in the United Kingdom, connecting the major cities of London, Birmingham, Manchester, Liverpool, Glasgow, and Edinburgh. More than 23 million people use this train line (the total population of the United Kingdom in the 2011 national census was 63.2 million).

In 2011, the UK government concluded a review of the franchise for the line by opening up the competition for the track going forward. This commenced in a detailed bidding process by a number of franchisees, which included the incumbent, Virgin Trains. The corporation that eventually won the bid was called FirstGroup and narrowly outbid Virgin Trains in August 2012. FirstGroup was awarded a 15-year deal to run the line worth £13 billion (just under $20 billion in 2012 US dollars).

Unfortunately, the bid process did not go smoothly, and a legal challenge then ensued between the government and the losing bidder, Virgin Trains. Virgin Trains were successful in that legal challenge, proving that the government bid process was flawed. The ramifications of that legal challenge are still being felt in late 2013. The upshot of this process has been a loss to the UK taxpayer of around $150 million as legal compensation started to mount up because of a number of legal disputes pending during 2013. The most controversial aspect has been that FirstGroup was actually stripped of the contract, which was then given back to Virgin Trains. On all accounts, Virgin Trains, the incumbent operator before the bid, even though they lost out to FirstGroup, has continued run the rail franchise while the government considers how to proceed with a new tender process. So why should this have happened?

The Models

On August 15, 2012, the UK government announced that FirstGroup had won the bid to run the WCML and would take over running the line from Virgin Trains at the beginning of December 2012.

At £5.5 billion, FirstGroup had offered considerably more money for the 15-year contract, as well as offering to pay much more in compensation should the firm prove unable to fulfill its obligations. Soon after the announcement, Virgin Trains immediately called into question the UK government's decision, arguing that FirstGroup's bid simply did not stack up. The company argued that the franchise would be at risk as FirstGroup was never likely to achieve any of the assurances they were giving on costs, savings, and compensation. Virgin Trains was so convinced that there was something wrong that they began legal proceedings against the Department of Transport that very month to challenge its decision.

Virgin Trains' legal basis was that the revenue projections of FirstGroup were too wildly optimistic. The company pointed out that these projections were based on passenger growth on the train line of 6% per annum, which was unlikely given that Virgin Trains had seen growth of 5% a year from a much lower base passenger base. Because Virgin Trains had already been operating the line, their predictions were based on fact rather than assumptions. As a result of this 6% passenger growth, FirstGroup's revenue from the franchise would grow by more than 10% a year, which Virgin Trains found entirely unpalatable and unrealistic.

Once these issues were raised by Virgin, there appeared to be a number of commentators who agreed. Very quickly, the suspicion of wrongdoing or mistakes being made by the Department of Transport started to become the focus.

What was at issue here was that the revenue targets projected by FirstGroup could not be met. Then, as a result, the company wouldn't have the money to pay the government the promised fee for the contract, which in FirstGroup's case was backloaded toward the end of the 15-year term. That risk of non-payment by FirstGroup would result in the taxpayers having to step in and cover the shortfall of money, which on such a large deal could run into billions of cash.

FirstGroup wasn't totally unthinking about the risk, and in their bid they offered to make $400 million in compensation to the UK taxpayer should the company fail to meet revenue targets. FirstGroup's promise sounded good, but Virgin Trains pointed out another problem. Analysts with Virgin Trains could immediately see that the potential contract shortfall would be in billions. What exactly would a paltry $400 million do for taxpayers when they would be required to come up with a few billion?

A hard-hitting statement by the boss of the Virgin group, Sir Richard Branson, pretty much hit things on the nail: *"This is the fourth time that we have lost a competitive tender as the runners-up . . . on each occasion the winner went bust, or they ran into serious financial difficulties."*

That statement was to prove to be the silver bullet because within days there was an announcement that the Department of Transport had gotten its numbers wrong.

What Went Wrong?

For starters, the departments that were evaluating the bidders were using an entirely new financial model that was untried and lacked independent testing. This model was given to the bidders by the Department of Transport in order to create their bid. But because of issues in the modeling, the model took a very optimistic view to financial forecasts. In essence, the outputs from the model had no inherent error checks, or if there were error checks, they were incorrectly implemented, because the model did not register that the inflation had been excluded from the financial results.

What is not clear is if the model ever went through model audit and if so when and who conducted it? Given that no audit firm has been prosecuted or cited for erroneous auditing, it's very likely that the model was never tested and never received a model audit.

There were also several suggestions that the model was far too complex and documentation too light. Therefore, the bidders were left in a situation where they managed to input key numbers incorrectly.

It is also unclear why the revenue forecasts and the capital that would be required to compensate the taxpayer were not flagged as potential risk. It is clear the risk was not even considered, because that is why there was such a low compensation amount offered ($400 million) when in fact there was a real risk it could be billions of dollars. Hence the low calculation for the capital.

In this case study, the Department of Transport overestimated its modeling capability and failed to take on board the clear message that models have errors and those errors have to be caught and a solution provided. Again, their failure to do so implies that neither an audit nor testing was deemed to be necessary, a very expensive mistake that is costing the UK taxpayer. In addition, the senior modeler and a number of the modeling team members lost their jobs as well. This case proves that, when modeling, never assume perfection.

CHAPTER

16

Modeling Handovers Dos and Don'ts

This chapter deals with the handover of models from the modeler to the maintainer. I use the term "maintainer" quite loosely to signify anyone who is purported to own, use, or maintain the model. Model handovers are not specified affairs, and there are no standard procedures relating to the handover. In reality, they are often casual "here is the model" type situation. Therein lies the problem because modeling does not end when the model is finally built. Modeling ends when the model has been accepted by the receiving party. Until that acceptance is received, the handover is not official.

In this chapter, I want to make this distinction clear. I have come across too many situations where the modeler has physically given the model to what is expected to be the receiving party or placed the model in a location for the maintainer, only to find that on a later date the model has been altered or is not in the same condition the modeler left it in. Because of this confusion, issues start to arise about what was actually delivered.

Handing Over the Model in Theory

The model handover is a process during which the modeler passes the responsibilities for the model to the maintainer. Activities performed before transferring a model have a great impact on a successful transition. Similarly, postdelivery maintenance activities are significantly affected by the handover phase.

This is mostly a theoretical exploration of how the handover process should ensue under the ideal conditions. It's simpler to break down the process into stages.

Stage 1: Pre-Handover Preparations

During the predelivery stage (running in parallel with model development), the modeler should consider how to prepare the maintainer to accept the model. This may require holding some workshops for the maintainer to get acquainted with the model. Typically, the workshop will including the following:

- A walk-through of the functional specification for the model.
- A review and finalization of the user manual by the modeler with the maintainer.
- A review of the technical manual by the modeler with the maintainer.
- Providing the maintainer with the testing document and detailed brief on results and potential issues.
- A review of the version control and version history detail with user details.
- A review of the details of username, password, lockouts and access controls.
- Deployment diagram if applicable.
- Model configuration and build.
- Details of any support tools, databases, and applications that are required.
- A thorough walk-through of the full capability of the model, including examining the structure and any VBA coding.

Stage 2: The Model Handover

In the handover stage, the responsibilities for the model and accompanying materials are transferred from the modeler to the maintainer performing maintenance and support. Typically, these actions will be taken:

- Transfer of the model through an agreed method.
- Transfer of data, assumptions, manuals, and other documents and material reviewed in Stage 1 and also that are required to operate and maintain the model.

- Transfer of all previous builds and versions of the model.
- An acceptance from the maintainer confirming the items handed over, which should include versions and dates. (It is sometimes preferable to also have an assurance from the maintainer that the items in Stage 1 have been covered.)

Stage 3: Post-Handover

The post-handover phase involves the modeler providing support and maintenance to the model and support for the maintainer for any activities that could not be provided for during Stage 1. This phase would also involve general maintenance of the model for a limited time only. This is potentially the most contentious aspect of the handover because it involves setting time limits on the length of time of the support. In addition, any possible handover activities that are required to be performed on the model should be clearly communicated and an assessment given of their impact on the model. Another aspect that would cause potential issues is the financial remuneration connected with the support. Does the modeler charge for this maintenance or is this part of the modeling brief and project? This situation should be based on a firm agreement between the receiving entity and the provider.

Handing Over the Model in Reality

The reality of model handover is somewhat different to the theory because circumstances are usually far from ideal. So let's take a look at what does happen during the handover.

Pre-Handover Preparations

The crucial part of all model handovers is the pre-handover because the other two stages are dependent on this stage. I will focus primarily on this stage to show the types of issues and situations that can occur in reality.

Functional Requirements Are Not Transparent in the Model

A situation that often occurs during the handover is that somehow the model has not previously been checked against the functional requirements. This mistake happens mainly because time ran out or because this exercise was not seen as being the core activity. Although the handover can still proceed without requirements being demonstrated in the model, it does leave the model and the modeler wide open in terms of any changes that occur after the handover and who is was responsible for those.

The User Manual Has Not Been Completed

Another common issue is that the user manual has not been completed, does not exist, or is not synchronized to the change control. Putting together the user manual is time-consuming and requires a deep examination of the model and also a solid understanding of the level of expertise of the user. As a result, writing the user manual is quite a difficult proposition for the modeler. If left to the end of the model build, it becomes even more likely that the manual has just not been created because of time issues.

The Maintainer Does Not Have the Required Skills and Knowledge

With this situation, it is likely that there is a skill set mismatch with the maintainer. This depends on exactly what the remit of the maintainer will be. Is the maintainer going to actively maintain the model or be the user? Or is the maintainer merely going to oversee the model?

Maintainers need to possess a decent understanding of modeling fundamentals and also have a valid appreciation of VBA coding since they are responsible for modifying and correcting the model. Without the required knowledge, maintainers cannot properly make corrections and modifications. Moreover, they cannot anticipate the ripple effect of their changes. Hence, this problem has resulted in models failing to function after the modifications have been made in the initial post-handover stage.

To mitigate the skills and knowledge deficit, the maintainer should become acquainted with the model as early as possible. The modeler should identify who the key personnel will be very early in the project and begin interacting with the maintainer. For example, the maintainer should participate in the design of the model and in defining the requirements. Maintainers can also play a role in the acceptance testing. In this way, when taking over the model, they will already possess the essential knowledge required for providing support and maintenance.

The Maintainer Is Reluctant or Is Not the True Maintainer

I have found to my horror on a fair number of occasions where maintainers have been placed in a position where they are uncomfortable or unhappy with their responsibilities as maintainers. In other words, they don't want to be the maintainer—worse still they might be a temporary solution and the actual maintainer is not available. Don't let this surprise you because it's quite common. In fact, in terms of handing the model, all you need to make sure of is that you have satisfied all the handover requirements.

There Is No Time to Fulfill All Handover Requirements

In this situation, the project is running on a very tight timetable and the customer is keen on getting the model because of some impending activity or deadline. Therefore, the full handover is scrapped, and the model is just passed to a nominated person or the sponsor. I have a particular loathing for this situation because it's a no-win for both parties. Eventually the customer will need to return the model to the modeler to get a proper handover, but this becomes an added inconvenience because the modeler has likely moved on to another project. Such an occurrence can be mitigated by preparing for the handover at an earlier stage such as before the testing and auditing.

The Model Documentation Is Not Sufficient

Documentation is considered as a primary source of information and the first point of reference in case of difficulties with or misunderstandings of the model. Maintainers cannot perform their duties adequately right after the handover process if the model is not properly documented.

Version Control Is a Must

In the post-handover stage, it's quite likely that the maintainer has to make some model modifications as the needs of the business changes. A change control process should be one of the earliest processes established. This is one of the areas where handovers lose clarity between the modeler and the maintainer as to how and who will affect the change control, particularly if the modeler is going to provide support and maintenance after the physical handover.

Advice for Handing Over the Model

Here are some tips that will help the handover succeed and will assist with the transition from the project to operations:

- Treat the handover as a process with a start and an end, always making sure the end is when the acceptance is received from the receiving entity.
- Identify the model maintainer ahead of time and involve this person in as much of the model design, specifications, and testing as possible. In other words, get this person's buy-in early.

- Break up the handover into stages. It doesn't have to be done in three stages like I have presented in this chapter; you can break it up into more stages. Keep it in manageable chunks and possibly make a checklist of all activities and updates on their status.
- Do not neglect the documentation. In particular, always produce a user manual as so much can be achieved if the handover contains the manual and so much will be lost without it.
- Do not get caught up in any internal politics. The handover is just a process. Make sure you run the process through to the end while staying clear of any issues with the receiver.
- Always make sure all documents, files, model versions, and data are also handed over. Do not put yourself in a position where it can be misconstrued that material is being kept back.
- Avoid being too casual. Make as much of the handover as possible through official channels, such as emails, meetings, and workshops. If there is just the modeler and maintainer, try to always involve a third party.
- Do not undertake or offer any post-handover support without a clear communication from both parties.
- When providing all the physical materials and model, use the advice of the maintainer on how that package will be delivered. Also make sure a copy of everything given to the maintainer is also provided to the receiving organization either in email or placed on their servers.
- If any of the model is password protected, make very sure the maintainer is aware and knows the key to unlocking all passwords or eradicating them altogether.

Case Study: When Handovers Go Wrong

It's unlikely that there are any accounts of model handovers that have gone wrong anywhere in the public domain for a good reason. Why? Because this would be seen as an admission of failure, and no one is about to take such blame. Therefore, I have based this case study on a modeling project that I was asked to resurrect as there were a number of problems, including the handover. In fact, the handover was fraught with several issues and was never totally completed.

No modeler is immune to issues and failed handovers regardless of experience. Sometimes there are factors involved that are just beyond the immediate control of the modeler, such as the culture within the customer or client organization. As the modeler, you have two paths: you can choose to learn from your own mistakes or learn from others. Fortunately for you, I can describe for your benefit a real-life handover that went wrong in so many ways and why.

Handover to Whom?

In this example, the mistake occurred when the modeler assumed that the person being handed the model was the one who knew the details of the modeling project.

As a result, the model was handed over to a business manager who had been one of the stakeholders of the modeling project. This person had also been highly critical of the need to bring in a professional modeler to head the project. In his opinion, there were people in his department with ample skills that could have taken on the project.

If you are already wincing at this situation, then you may can guess what happened next. The upshot was that the model was at no time perceived to have been handed over because the maintainer did not sign off any approval of receipt. Instead, the maintainer gave the impression that he had not received a completed and final model and was only given a draft version.

The crucial factor here was that the maintainer had no interest in using this model. In fact, he was unclear as to the intentions of the model. Also at fault was the modeler because he did not take enough interest in the model's future. He was too eager to finish the project without ensuring the implementation. This may seem like a factor that is out of the control of the modeler, but the solution is very simple. The modeler should have ensured that the maintainer had been identified far earlier into the project and had a sufficient buy-in. This way, if the maintainer had been part of the model design, testing, and review, he would have been unlikely to discredit the model because he would have had a sense of ownership.

Scope of the Model Is Too Large

If the scope of the model is too large, this is a reflection of the project and how it has been managed. It's not a handover issue per say; however, it ultimately comes to bear during the handover. In this case, the model was unfortunately perceived to be the solution for a great number of problems. Scope creep ultimately changed what was a small and specific model to a large and complicated one, as the modeler struggled to fulfill the needs of several different end users.

The eventual upshot was that not one of the end users had enough confidence in the model to sign off on it, as the overriding feedback was that it was far too complex. They instead only wanted something simple for their business (the problem being that if you service too many people you need a comprehensive model). The result was that the model was canned and labeled a failure.

This situation could have been remedied relatively simply. The modeler needed to have control of the scope and a clear understanding of what it entailed. The modeler should then have made sure that the scope document was signed off by the project sponsor. Any movement from the original scope would require a change request and approval from the project sponsor; therefore, any scope creep would rest with the project sponsors and not the modeler. In addition, changes to the scope would require a review of the specifications and lead to project delays. At this point, the issues of scope creep would have been brought to light way before the handover. Although in most cases this is a project management problem, in financial modeling projects the responsibility for scope creep lies squarely with the modeler. Unless you want to have a fraught handover, the scope needs to be controlled all the way through the project.

The Focus Is on Integrating the Model into an Existing System

If the integration between a new model and existing legacy systems is not clearly understood, then it will become apparent at the handover. However, this issue should be caught during testing if there was a testing. The model unfortunately never went through testing as there were time constraints and also the customer had issues about the project costs.

The upshot was at handover the maintainer quite rightly decided to base the sign-off on the model being able to produce a sample of the reports in the specifications. These reports were reliant on an integration with the data repository system. Unfortunately, the integration had a number of issues the maintainer stumbled upon when the reports were not being generated correctly. As a result, he refused to sign off on the model handover.

The solution here is not as simple, but it does involve the maintainer again being involved with the handover at an earlier stage and also being a part of the testing environment. In this situation, the modeler did request to have the maintainer available early in the project, but the customer was for one reason or another slow to respond. As a result, the modeler continued on with the project. The modeler should have made it clear to the project sponsor that without the maintainer being available early in the project, there were going to be handover risks. Because this was also coupled with the reluctance to have any testing of a system integration model, the sponsor was inviting major risks.

In this type of situation, keep in mind that the modeler is responsible for highlighting the risks and potential problems and getting them aired. It's simply not good enough to quietly let these be hidden because they will come to haunt you later, as was the case here. The reluctance of the customer to play ball must also take some blame; however, the modeler should have identified where the problems would be and absolved himself from the blame by communicating these issues.

There Is No Clear Management Involvement

The model project needs to go through some kind of approval and possible procurement process, which would involve some senior management involvement. When there is no clear management involvement, the difficulties begin when the project ceases to be a project, moves into an operational model, and become more "business as usual" (BAU).

This is a very common situation, and unfortunately it is beyond the modeler's scope of work and influence. What I can guarantee is if you as a modeler cannot discern any type of real ownership and management of the model, all that work during the project will fail. In cases like these, catch the train while it's still in motion. In other words, at the project stage request that the project sponsor and stakeholder give clear direction as to where the model will be going, to whom it will be going to, and how it will be managed. You may find that the response is vague. But at the very least, you can make sure you are raising the issue early and getting the sponsor to think about this issue. Too often in these situations the model project, including any personnel involved with the project, become the scapegoat for a failed handover.

Handover Timelines Are Not Enforced

Of all the handovers-gone-wrong scenarios, not enforcing timelines is the worst possible situation because it is totally in the hands of the modeler and completely avoidable. In the United Kingdom, this type of mistake is referred to as a "school boy error," which means getting the basics wrong when you should know better. This is one such error.

The problem with handover timelines not being enforced is really about the handover simply taking too long. This type of situation usually starts with high handover momentum at first, but quickly starts to fizz out as key personnel become unavailable. Unfortunately, this is the start of a vicious cycle. Once timelines are pushed backward, the odds are high that this same occurrence will happen again in the following weeks. Before you know it, the pushback becomes an acceptable behavior and there goes the handover.

The way to work around this problem is to simply not change the timelines (assuming they were realistic enough in the first place). Also take the steps to engage the key stakeholders and bring them into the handover process by giving them an insight into how the model moves from the project to operational. Also be sure they understand the model's benefits and what damage can occur if the handover does not go to plan. Why should the focus be on the key stakeholders? They are more likely to have influence with others who are involved with the handover. In any organization, people are busy with their day-to-day work, but it is imperative that time is made for the handover. It is also the modeler's responsibility to use the necessary resources to make that clear and get a push.

Case Study: When the Handover Goes Right

I could just simply state that to ensure that a handover goes right, just do the reverse of what happens when a handover goes wrong. However, it's just not that easy. You can actually mitigate against all the aspects you know could be detrimental and still experience the handover going wrong.

In the next few sections, I have chosen a few common characteristics that I have observed with handovers that have gone smoothly and my reasoning why they are important.

There Is Evidence of a Handover Plan

This has been a repeated point, but I will stress it once more: there needs to be a well-thought-out plan, like just about everything in business that involves people and transactions. If it is planned out, it will work far better than if it wasn't planned out. The same is true with model handovers. A good handover always has a detailed plan with timelines, resource requirements, measurable goals, and contingencies clearly thought through before commencing. All of these details will galvanize support and will ensure that all concerned are clear about where the model is heading and what is its final handover.

Everyone's on Board

New models can be intimidating, and potential users may be positively or adversely affected by a model that is handed over and correctly implemented. It's possible to meet some reluctance during the project and handover, which can take shape in all manner of ways but ultimately will hit at the model handover. The modeler can help with this transition by getting employees involved early in the process and developing a quasi team that includes the people who will be impacted most by the model. With this team, have them discuss and potentially be involved in the approval of the handover. This option also has several other benefits including that additional information and new processes could be uncovered. In addition, team members could make known new tasks that are running in conjunction with the model handover that the modeler is unaware of but will have a bearing on how the model will be used.

The Users Have Received Training

There really is no excuse for not providing training to the end user. The best handovers by far are those where the maintainers and users of the model are not in any way insecure about using the model and clearly understand its capability and noncapabilities. I have even witnessed model projects where the stakeholders have been trained.

I always make it part of the process of the handover on any project to provide three levels of training based on the interaction with the model, which are model user, a model maintainer, and a modeler. These levels are then allocated to the employees based on how they will interact with the model. In addition, it's also worth considering with business critical models to have a "train the trainer" scheme. In other words, the modeler will have trained one or two users who have reached such a high level of skill that they are able to train others. With this option, it's very important that the trainers are identified at the outset of the project.

Clearly, there are ways to handle model handovers and also aspects to avoid. With experience, most of these will become more clearly defined for the modeler as you strive to maintain a good practice of handing over models. As a final say, I would recommend that during the model project, you should maintain a modified checklist (found in Chapter 15) in order for you to keep updates on the status of the project. In the end, you will be able to ensure that the handover becomes just another part of what is a well-managed modeling project.

CHAPTER

17

Case Study: Building a Full Life Cycle Model

This chapter is a demonstration of how you would tackle a model project from planning to the model build. The intention is to give you an appreciation of how to plan a model based upon a brief and then deliver the model. Many of the topics that have been covered throughout the book will be brought together in this chapter, so I urge you to give this chapter some attention.

The Modeling Brief

Isys Corporation is a global information technology (IT) service provider with profit centers across several countries. Its core business is IT hardware and software, and operating IT facilities in medium and large organizations generally with revenues in excess of $100m per annum. Recently, Isys was invited to bid on a contract for IT services, which includes the provision of a help desk, hardware solutions, and software solutions for a multinational corporation in 24 locations around the world. Isys Corporation will assist the commercial and business development team to come up with a price to provide this service. They have commissioned a pricing tool to be developed where they are able to flex the pricing and perform any number of "what if" scenarios. Teams are open to advice on how the tool will be developed, and the commissioned modeler is responsible for delivering the tool but not for the data. There are some very tight deadlines to adhere to for the commercial and business development team to submit a price; therefore, this tool is required as soon as possible.

The Modeling Plan

Now that we have a model brief, it's time to develop a plan of how the model will be built. Before diving into the plan, there are a number of given assumptions to address.

Some Assumptions

For this example, we will assume that the feasibility assessment has been performed previously and will not be part of the plan. The conclusion of the feasibility was positive, which makes this a viable project.

The project team consists of a project sponsor, who is a member of the executive board at Isys Corporation and is also a stakeholder. Delivering a model, particularly a complex type, will require a significant investment in time, energy, and resources, which really does require some strict planning. The model plan will consist of the following parts:

- Scope
- Specification and strategy
- Design
- Build
- Testing and audit
- Final version and protection

Scope

We have not been provided with a scope document from the project sponsor, and so we will need to come up with a document of this nature. We can use the brief as the starting point. In the scope, we should include the following:

- Decide what needs to be included within the model and what can be omitted.
- Consider the level of detail required at the input and logical assumptions.
- Understand in outline form how the model will work.
- Estimate the time and resources required for the model development and get approval from the key stakeholders.

What We Know

- Isys will be bidding to provide IT services to a customer.
- The customer is global and will therefore be located in several jurisdictions and currencies.
- The requirement is a tool, which implies it should be portable and not based on an IT system.
- The tool will need to incorporate scenario models.
- This is a model tool and does not require the data for the model.

What We Don't Know

- Is the model solely for the commercial and business development team?
- Is the model required to be reusable on other bids?
- The financial statements that are required are not provided.

With the information we have gleaned, we can now create a scope document that should be presented to the project sponsor and will require an approval.

The Scope Document

For the sake of simplicity, we will call the model that will be built the model pricing tool (MPT). We will use this term throughout the case study to refer to the model. The completed scope document is shown in Figure 17-1. We can assume the project sponsor has also approved the scope, which will now be filed and should be referred to whenever any changes are being applied to the scope.

Scope Document

Model Pricing Tool (MPT)

1. Business Requirements

The model pricing tool (MPT) will provide a means by which Isys Corporation can derive the optimum price for their services using their cost base and applying margins. The model is required to provide pricing for a bid for a single customer on a one-time basis only and is being built for the commercial and business development team.

1.1. Background

There is significant opportunity for Isys Corporation to gain substantial revenues and benefits by providing the customer with a fixed price that is both competitive and also ensures that the cost base is covered. Isys has deemed that the best way this can be achieved is by having a working tool (MPT) that can be exploited to derive the price. There is a lack of resources internally to develop the model and therefore an outside specialist has been commissioned.

1.2. Business Objectives and Success Criteria

The MPT will ensure potential revenues have a realistic chance of coming to fruition. The success criteria will be based on the model being able to provide the functionality that will allow the commercial and business development team to make informed decisions.

1.3. Customer Needs

The customers make up the commercial and business development team. The needs can be broken down into the following:

1) To provide a means by which pricing of services can be achieved.

2) To provide a transparent view of the cost underlying the price.

3) To provide a simple and easily learned method of extracting revenues.

4) To provide a tool that can perform on existing hardware (workstations and laptops) and user applications (Microsoft Office)

1.4. Business Risks

The business risks are based around the timing issues, user acceptance and technical issues (where the model will be hosted and maintenance). Risk is also involved as to whether the model is auditable and can be suitably tested.

2. Scope and Limitations

The MPT scope is to deliver a tool that will provide pricing analysis and information. The model will include scenarios, and outputs that can assist with the decision-making and will also include mapping exercises. The model will take into account the types of services that Isys offers, and will also incorporate the ability to model on several currencies. The model will be built using Microsoft Excel, will have no reliance on any systems of third-party tools and will be portable. There will be a number of outputs that will be produced by the modeler that are deemed suitable for a pricing model of this kind.

Figure 17-1. The scope document for the model pricing tool (MPT) is shown here

Specification and Strategy

The specification and strategy is a blueprint for the design and build of the model which, once completed, will ensure that the model has been built according to the requirements of the end user. In this section, we will be looking at how to develop a specification document.

The Benefits of Model Specification

The discipline of having a model specification ensures that you produce a definitive statement of what the model should do and how it will do it. It also allows you to tackle the most difficult problems associated in the model before you have started to build it.

A model specification can be understood, discussed, and challenged by all the parties involved in the model. A successful specification establishes a common understanding of what the model will do. It also makes model testing easier and much more effective because the specification provides a clear statement of what the model is doing. The model tester then just has to check whether the finished model agrees with the written specification.

Failure to write a model specification will create difficulties later. An inadequate specification will lead to the following problems:

- More time spent building the model because the issues that could have been resolved during the specification will come back to haunt you.
- Numerous late changes to the model logic—perhaps the greatest single cause of errors in completed models.
- Vague objectives in the model (it's easy to start with a small model that aims to solve one problem and end up with a large model that solves all sorts of problems but solves them badly).

Fortunately with our example, the MPT does not appear to be a very complex model, as there are a number of aspects such as the outputs that are based on how the modeler chooses to output the information. Keep in mind that the specification and strategy document that is developed will have a very significant impact upon the project because it will be used to approve the final model and will also be used during testing.

We have contacted the commercial and business development team and requested that they provide seven features to the technical specification of the tool that they will require prior to the production of the specification document (see Figure 17-2).

Ref	Feature
MPTReq001	The model should be simple to use with little or no training required.
MPTReq002	The model should cater to users with a basic knowledge of using Excel.
MPTReq003	The reports should include a cash flow statement and income statement for a total of five years with the first two years in detail.
MPTReq004	The model response times must not be restrictive.
MPTReq005	The model should be light and portable and able to be moved and sent through the e-mail system.
MPTReq006	There should be no requirement for any user to know or understand how to code with VBA.
MPTReq007	There should be no external file links in the model.

Figure 17-2. The requirements for the model by the users is a key document

The user specifications are quite vague, mainly due to them not being experienced modelers. However, this should not be a problem as the modeler will now need to turn the requirements into more technical and measurable items. The specification and strategy as a document can be very detailed and lengthy; it is important to make sure that all user specifics are captured. In essence, it is a roadmap to how the model will end up.

In our case study, I have shortened the document somewhat in Figure 17-3, but hopefully it will enhance your understanding of this part of the modeling process.

Specification and Strategy

Model Pricing Tool (MPT)

1.0 Introduction

This is a specification and strategy document for the MPT as part of the model plan. The MPT will provide a tool that will allow the commercial and business development team to effectively price the company's services for an upcoming bid

2.0 Strategic Vision and Values

The purpose of the MPTs is to give a more usable, auditable and methodical approach to forming a pricing for services. Some of the values attached to the MPT are more simplicity, accuracy, portability and flexibility

3.0 Description of the MPT

How will the MPT be built?	The MPT will utilize spreadsheets. Isys Corporation is already a major user of Microsoft Office products such as Excel, Word and Access Therefore, the MTP will not be introducing any new applications or systems.
What will the MPT be?	The MTP will be a workbook built in Excel with a number of modules (worksheets) each performing a specific task or operation A number of filters and switches will be placed in between the modules and will interact with the data and information to produce user defined outputs. The workbook will be located on a central server or SharePoint location.

4.0 Technical Requirements

Usability	MPT is a single-user environment based on worksheets, and uses internal links (hyperlinks) and switches to provide a more friendly user environment.
Size	The MTP should be less than two MB (megabytes) in total size to allow for portability.
Response Times	The average waiting time for calculations should be less than one second from a key press or mouse click.
Programming	Any VBA code within the model should not be related to the calculations or the working of the model
Documentation	All documentation, user manuals and instructions must be included within the model.
User Access & Security	The MTP is an Excel file and is inherently insecure. The users will be responsible for file security.
Outputs Range	The outputs will be primarily a cashflow, an income statement and any dashboard that the modeler chooses to include.
Structure	The MPT will employ best practice model structure.

5.0 Evaluation, Learning, and Review

How progress will be measured	There is no plan for a stakeholder on-going evaluation or review of the MPT. However, both the sponsor and the users will be given regular reviews, and it is possible on occasion that selected members could be asked to perform a review of the MPT in its current stage.

Figure 17-3. The specification and Strategy document contains details about the model

Design

Prior to any build, we need a model design, and we fortunately have a technical specification that will guide us through the best design on the model. We have been given a clear indication that the outputs will need to have at the very least an income statement and a cash flow statement. In addition, we may feel we need to add some other outputs to give the model more brevity. The difficulty for this brief is that the data and information are out of scope, which means we cannot shape the model against the data. Therefore, we will need to design a very generic model that is robust and yet also flexible to handle whatever data is used while still holding its integrity.

In this situation, there's nothing that beats a well-constructed flow diagram, as this allows the modeler to envisage how the data will move through the model and where the interaction with the inputs will take place. Before we can begin the design, a good place to start is to list all the factors that will affect the way we design the model. This step is much like a brainstorming session—you simply put down as much as you know, filter through the list, and keep the elements that will affect the model while eliminating those which will have little or no effect. For instance, we would need to keep on the list the following elements:

- Outputs
- Number of reporting years
- Users
- Model portability
- Scenarios
- Response times
- Interface

Let's go through each of these now in order to understand how they may affect the design.

Outputs

We have at least two outputs: the standard financial statement's cash flow and the income statement. We can add further outputs at our discretion. Essentially, these outputs have an effect on the type of inputs and scenarios we will build. The approach should be to have a set of outputs that is the baseline and then another set that is flexible and part of the scenarios so that users can are able to make comparison between baseline and scenarios.

Number of Reporting Years

We need five years reporting in the outputs; this is clearly an indication that we are looking at time value inputs. This requirement means that the design needs to accommodate some sort of calendar. As the first two-year reporting is detailed, we will also need to base our time scales at the lowest possible level, in this case for months. Months are generally the lowest level for modeling time; going below this into weeks or days is extremely cumbersome and very complicated. As a result, modelers rarely model at that level.

Users

The key point with the users is to create a model that is intuitive and requires minimal spreadsheet mechanics from them. Again, this is quite a challenge because we cannot design a model that is confusing for the user.

Model Portability

The model cannot be big; in fact, two megabytes is rather small for a model. This small size will present challenges because we have no visibility of the quantity of data that will eventually populate the model. Therefore, we will need to make the model smaller as two megabytes is the total.

Scenarios

The main decision with scenario options is to determine if they should be included within the model, as there are concurrency considerations (more than one scenario being calculated any one time). These concurrency issues will ultimately affect the calculation speed and processing of the model. The upshot is that the more we include the more complex the model will become and the larger it will become. But if we include too few scenario options, then it restricts the user.

Response Times

The calculations will sit between the inputs and scenarios and the outputs. We understand from the specifications that the response time is a critical measure to the model requirements, and we will need to be careful not to bog down the calculations with processor-intensive formula and VBA coding.

Interface

We know that there won't be any external links; therefore, not only will documentation be required to be robust, but we will need to have plenty of it. In designing the model, we need to keep to a system that will always allow the user to move through the model simply and intuitively with no need to understand much about spreadsheets. Taking into account the points of the design, we can now put together a design specification. Take a look at the schema for the design in Figure 17-4.

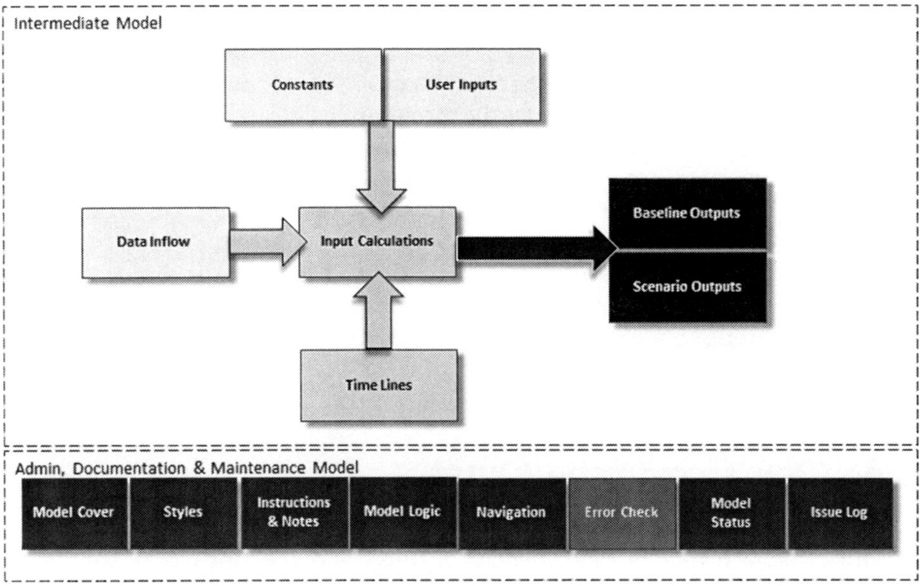

Figure 17-4. The design specification of the model is shown here

Notice that each of the blocks represents a worksheet, and while this is a high number of worksheets for one model, it is not extreme and we wouldn't want to have any additional worksheets. There are two inputs models: the user inputs that will flex the scenarios and the data input inflow. At this stage, we have no idea what it will be, so it is better to give this data a separate worksheet.

There are a number of worksheets dedicated to the admin, documentation, and maintenance. This is apparent because the users have a low tolerance for using Excel and need simplicity. You should note that there is a navigation worksheet, which will be the home page for the model and all movements through the model will emanate from the navigation.

Also consider that the model status and the issue log were also included, both of which are about maintaining the model. The model status is a procedure that will log the status of the model at its last use with the date. This means that when users open the model, they can quickly ascertain in which state the model is in and can clear out all the previous scenario inputs and start again if necessary. The issue log is a worksheet to allow the user to raise any issues with the model, which are then sent via an automated e-mail to the model maintainer.

Build

In this section, I will be putting together the aspects of the model build, which basically will follow the design in the previous section. There a number of diagrams and steps that may seem overwhelming, so I recommend you that just go through each step and when you feel you understand it, move to the next one. There are some major benefits to breaking down the model build into steps. Not all modelers work this way, as some are at different levels of skill and experience and working in steps doesn't necessarily suit their style. However, if you are starting out in building models, this approach is best. I have created this stepped approach as it will help you to put together a coherent method of building models.

Step One: Create the Outputs

Our starting point is to establish the outputs. From the outset, we have two outputs that are mandatory; therefore, these are the ones that should be built first. Let's not concern ourselves with the optional outputs, as these can be created at the end of the project if necessary. This latter point will seem confusing because on the one hand, best practice is to build the outputs first, and yet I am also going to build some last. Just remember that the key outputs are always the first step.

When creating financial statements, it's far easier if the income statement is created first because it holds so much of the financial information that is used in all three financial statements. Therefore, in Figures 17-5a and 17-5b, the template for the income statement has been created. This is a standard income statement. But because at this stage we do not have visibility of the data, there are some aspects that could potentially undergo changes, which is fine. The most important part is to get the template and format established.

	A	B	C	R	AE	AR	BE	BR
1	IsysC_CostModel_v1 2.xlsm							
2	**Income Statement**							
3								
4	Currency							
5	Profit & Loss (Annual)							
6								
7				Year 1	Year 2	Year 3	Year 4	Year 5
8	Revenue							
9	Fixed Payment			-	-	-	-	-
10	Service 1			-	-	-	-	-
11	Service 2			-	-	-	-	-
12	Service 3			-	-	-	-	-
13	Variable Payment			-	-	-	-	-
14	Service 1			-	-	-	-	-
15	Service 2			-	-	-	-	-
16	Service 3			-	-	-	-	-
17	Risk			-	-	-	-	-
18	Total Revenue			-	-	-	-	-
19								
20	Direct Costs							
21	Operational Services			-	-	-	-	-
22	Operational Services Staff Costs			-	-	-	-	-
23	Operational Services Administration			-	-	-	-	-
24	Facilities Costs			-	-	-	-	-
25	IT Costs			-	-	-	-	-

Figure 17-5a. The Profit & Loss (Annual) is shown here

	A	B	C	R	AE	AR	BE	BR
1	IsysC_CostModel_v1 2.xlsm							
2	**Income Statement**							
3								
4	Currency							
5	Profit & Loss (Annual)							
32	**Total Operating Costs**			-	-	-	-	-
34	Gross Profit			-	-	-	-	-
35	Gross Profit %			-	-	-	-	-
37	Overheads			-	-	-	-	-
39	**EBIT**			-	-	-	-	-
40	EBIT %			-	-	-	-	-
41								
42	Interest - Paid/(Received)			-	-	-	-	-
43								
44	**Profit Before Taxation**			-	-	-	-	-
45	Profit Before Taxation %			-	-	-	-	-
46								
47	Corporation Tax			-	-	-	-	-
48								
49	**Profit After Taxation**			-	-	-	-	-
50	Profit After Taxation %			-	-	-	-	-

Figure 17-5b. The Profit & Loss (Annual), Profit Before Taxation, and Profit After Taxation are shown here

There are a number of important parts of the income statement that will be discussed in the next few sections.

Currency

There is a term called "Currency" in column A, row 4. This is a placeholder, as the user may choose to view the income statement in different currency rates. By adding the currency label and placing the gray cells about the statements from Year 1 to Year 5, we have built in the ability for the model to display the symbol for the chosen currency dynamically, which means the users will not be constantly trying to deduce the currency of the financial statement.

Statement Level

This income statement will provide a report showing profit after taxation. It is not always necessary to go beyond this level; however, if you look in row 39 you should see the term "EBIT," which stands for Earnings Before Income and Taxation (see Figure 17-5b). Ideally, when creating income statements, you want to produce templates that will report down to this level. In this case, we would call this income statement "down to EBIT." It's possible to report exactly down to EBITDA (Earnings Before Interest, Taxation, Depreciation, and Amortization), and the customer may ask for just this level. But I would recommend that whenever you create income statements, always take it down to the EBIT level, as from experience this is the acceptable reporting standard in accounting.

Time Scales

If you recall during the requirements gathering, the users specified that they required financial statement with details for Year 1 and Year 2 and then yearly summaries for the remaining three years. You are probably a step ahead right now and are thinking this income statement doesn't have the detail for Year 1 and Year 2, as it is yearly summary for all five years, and you will be partially correct. But there's a twist. If you look at the column headers, you will see a plus sign (+) in columns R, AE, AR, BE, and BR. The plus sign is for grouping of columns and rows. Whenever a column has a plus sign, it signifies that there are several columns that are hidden from view that can be opened by right-clicking on the plus sign.

If we expand the grouping to reveal what is hidden, it will look like Figure 17-5c. You will notice that the plus sign has changed to a minus in column AE, which means the grouping has been unhidden from column S to AD. However, all we can see is the block of gray cells and then Year 2 at the far right, but stay with me and all will be revealed.

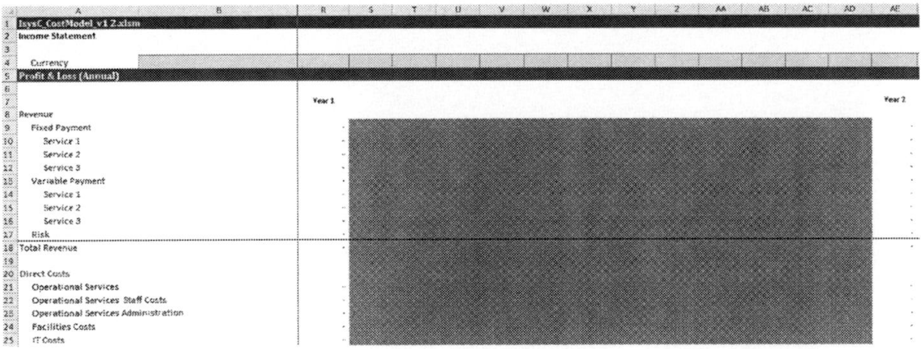

Figure 17-5c. The Profit & Loss (Annual) grouping for Year 2 has been unhidden

In row 5, note that the label that shows Profit & Loss (Annual). Further down in the worksheet, there is another label that shows Profit & Loss (Monthly) in row 53, as in Figure 17-5d.

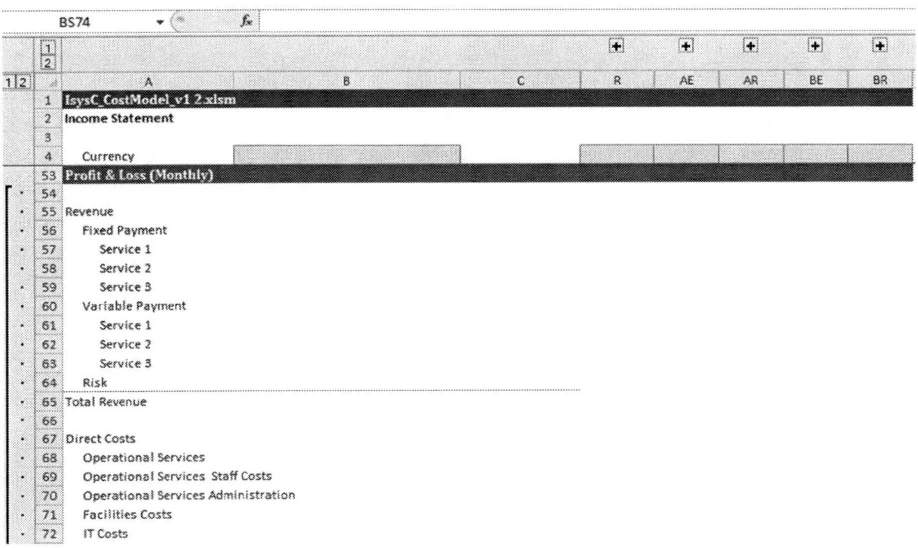

Figure 17-5d. The monthly part of the Profit & Loss (Monthly) is shown here

Looking at row 99 in Figure 17-5d, you will see the familiar plus sign again, which as we know tells us there is some further grouping. In Figure 17-5e, after unhiding the row grouping, we can now see we have monthly income statement reporting.

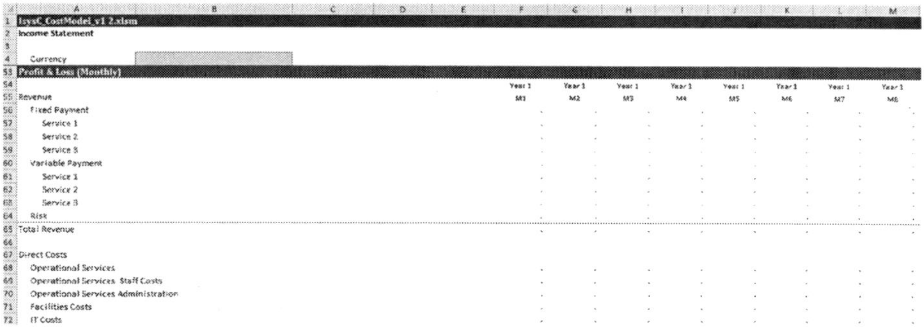

Figure 17-5e. The Profit & Loss (Monthly), Total Revenue, Facilities Costs and IT Costs t are fully exposed

Effectively, what has actually happened is that the income statement has been built from the lowest time period, which is months, and then summarized into the five years. As a result, for each year that we are able to report, there are 12 months of detail below that can be accessed simply by unhiding the columns and rows.

This is a very important modeling concept because we should always strive to make sure our calculations have row consistency, as was discussed in Chapter 2 on financial modeling best practice. When months and years are mixed into the same rows, this consistency cannot be maintained. This does mean more work for the modeler because there is so much data to consider; however, there is nothing more satisfying for the customer than to be able to view annual financial statements and then have the ability to drill further into the months at the click of two filters.

The same concept has been applied to the cash flow statement in Figure 17-6. But there is another twist to come.

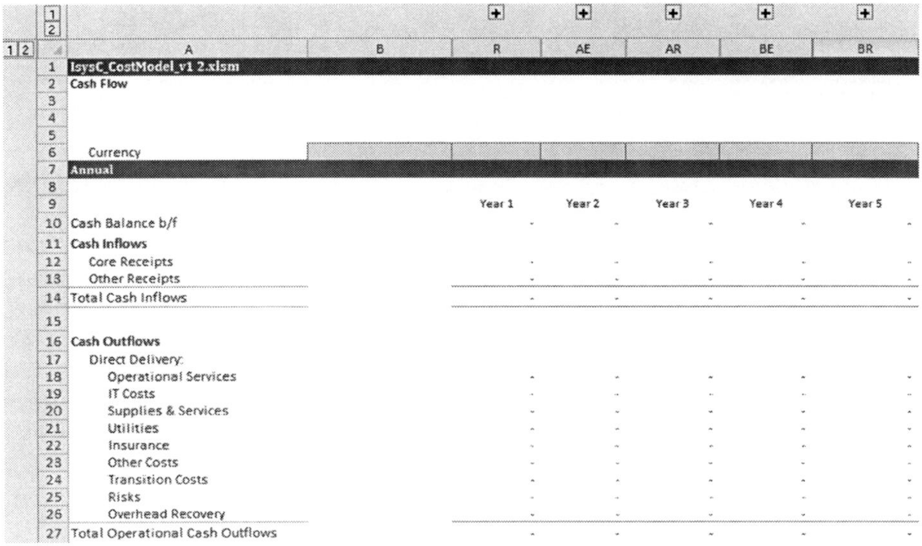

	A	B	R	AE	AR	BE	BR
1	IsysC_CostModel_v1 2.xlsm						
2	Cash Flow						
3							
4							
5							
6	Currency						
7	Annual						
8							
9			Year 1	Year 2	Year 3	Year 4	Year 5
10	Cash Balance b/f		-	-	-	-	-
11	Cash Inflows						
12	Core Receipts		-	-	-	-	-
13	Other Receipts		-	-	-	-	-
14	Total Cash Inflows		-	-	-	-	-
15							
16	Cash Outflows						
17	Direct Delivery:						
18	Operational Services		-	-	-	-	-
19	IT Costs		-	-	-	-	-
20	Supplies & Services		-	-	-	-	-
21	Utilities		-	-	-	-	-
22	Insurance		-	-	-	-	-
23	Other Costs		-	-	-	-	-
24	Transition Costs		-	-	-	-	-
25	Risks		-	-	-	-	-
26	Overhead Recovery		-	-	-	-	-
27	Total Operational Cash Outflows		-	-	-	-	-

Figure 17-6. The cash flow (Annual) statement has a similar structure to the Profit & Loss (Annual)

In this figure, the statements should calculate from the lowest time period, in our case months, and then will flow up to the annual numbers, which means all our calculations must be made in months.

Take a look at Figure 17-7. Yes, it's a balance sheet, and we were not asked by the users for this statement. However, I am going to include it anyway. Why? The income statement, cash flow statement, and the balance sheet are an act—they work together. In this situation, it's just not good practice to present reports with two statements. If you have the cash flow and income statement, you must have a balance sheet irrespective of whether it's been requested. Keep this in mind because often balance sheets are overlooked, but they are very useful. A modeler who does not include a balance sheet can be viewed as having something to hide.

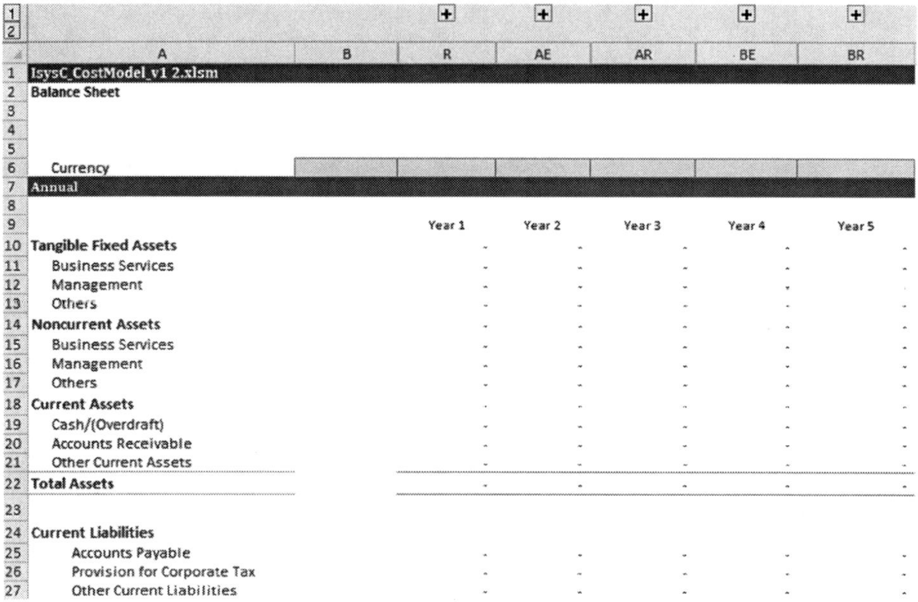

Figure 17-7. The balance sheet is shown here

There is one more item to note. Did you spot the intentional mistake in the income statement diagrams from Figure 17-5a to Figure 17-5e? Did you see that these figures also state profit & loss as well as the "income statement"? I made this planned mistake to highlight the use of terminology. An income statement, revenue statement and profit & loss statement all refer to the same thing—it's just a matter of which terminology is suitable for the customer. My advice is to work out the terminology before the building of the model and stick to it to avoid confusing the user.

Now that the statements have been designed, we need to think about the scenarios. I find it helpful when thinking about scenarios to see them as a complete copy or duplicate of the model outputs, inputs, and calculations. For instance, we have our financial statements, so now we need a finished set of these again but this time they will be linked to the scenarios. There are three options on how to design the scenarios into the financial statements:

- Build the scenario outputs in separate worksheets, which are identifiable as scenarios.
- Incorporate the scenarios into the baseline outputs and identify them.
- The baseline and scenarios are in the same statements and can be changed through a switch, which is shown in Figure 17-8.

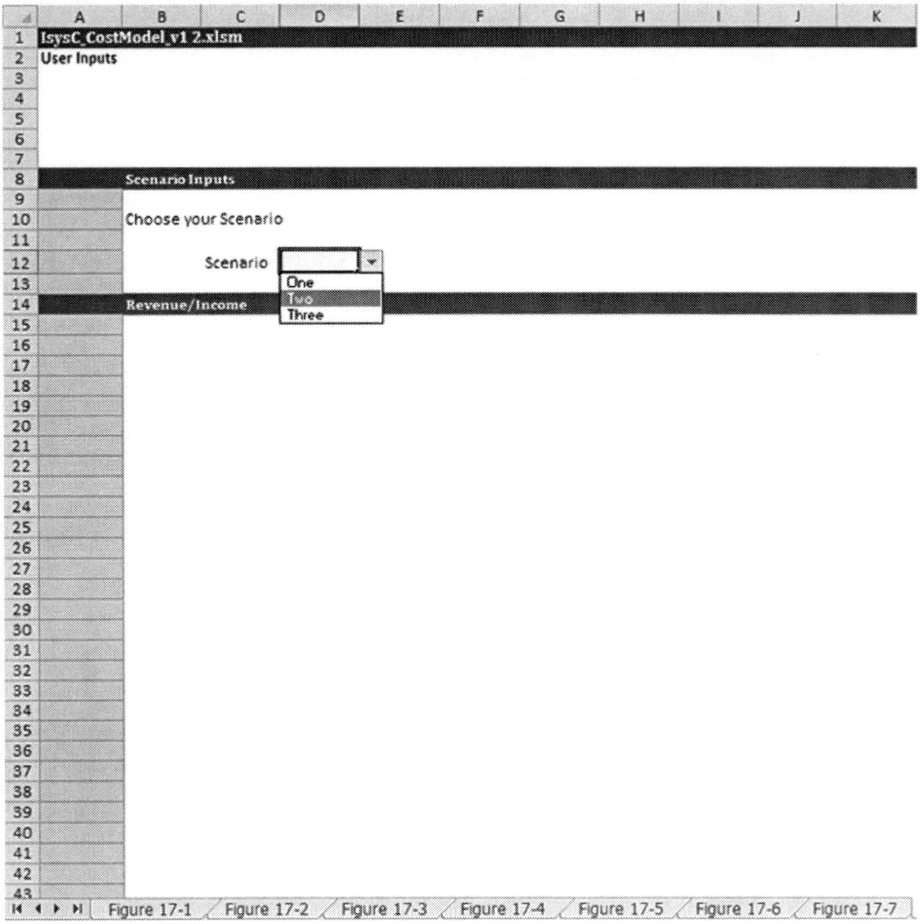

Figure 17-8. The switch to choose the scenario in the user inputs is shown here

All of these options are viable. As long as they are created clearly and consistently, none of them have any disadvantages over the other. My preference is to work from separate worksheets, just because it allows me to make changes and amendments to the scenario outputs at a later date without interfering with the baseline outputs.

I would be cautious about using the third option. With this option, there would be merely one set of outputs showing the calculations based on how the user chooses to see the reports, which could be from the viewpoint of the baseline or from a scenario. This is perhaps the most popular method of working with scenarios in modeling. While there is nothing wrong with this method, it has one risk in that care must be taken when opening the model to note the state it was left in previously. I have seen this happen on so many occasions with disastrous results. For instance, a previous user may have been looking at a partial scenario and with several hypothetical inputs and once finished did not return the model back to the baseline to save it and shut down.

The problem comes with whoever uses the model afterward and how this user reacts. It is possible for the user to think that the model outputs were at the baseline and be unaware that the model is reflecting one of the scenarios, and use these scenarios as the baseline numbers. The simplest method of creating the scenarios is to make a copy of the three financial statements and give them a suitable name, as in Figure 17-9.

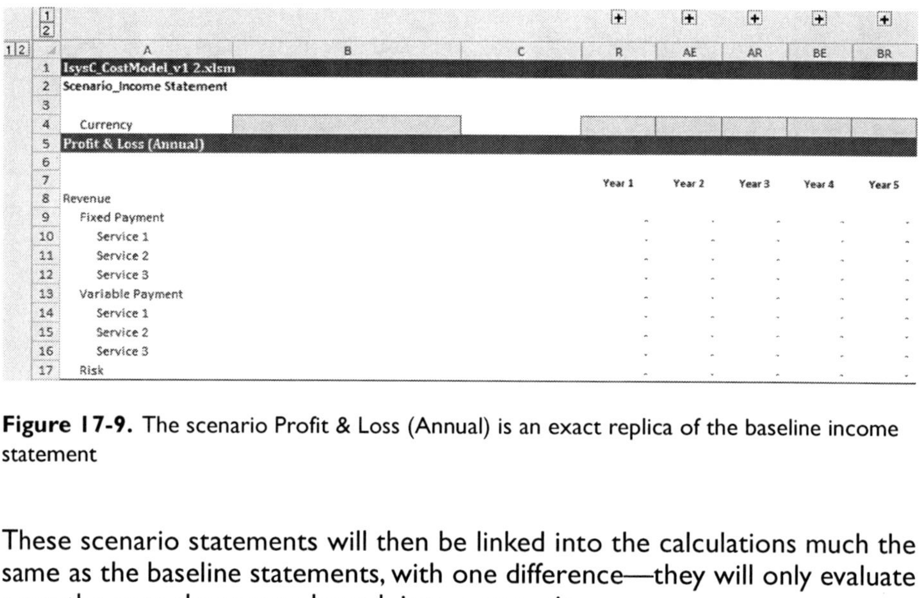

Figure 17-9. The scenario Profit & Loss (Annual) is an exact replica of the baseline income statement

These scenario statements will then be linked into the calculations much the same as the baseline statements, with one difference—they will only evaluate once the user chooses to branch into a scenario.

Step Two: Create the Time Line for the Time Periods

We have already set up the financial statements on the lowest time period, which for us is in months. What this means is that all our calculations will actually be based on this level. Then when reporting up into quarters or years, all we will need to do is total up to three months or twelve months, respectively. While working at this lower level will feel more detailed and is a longer process, this option allows the modeler extra flexibility in being able to switch into different time periods with relative ease.

The Month Periods

When creating the time line, the first part to set up will be the months from start to end. We do know that our financial statements reflect 5 years, and therefore, it's clear that we will need a minimum of 5 years × 12 months, which are 60-month periods.

In Figure 17-10, the months are now being set up with a "From" and "To" date. Later, I will cover how these dates are derived. Needless to say they should never be hard-coded in. In other words, the user will be responsible for putting in a start date, and the time line will then take its cue from there. But avoid typing in a start date even if you have been given a fixed date; you should always make dates be part of the user response.

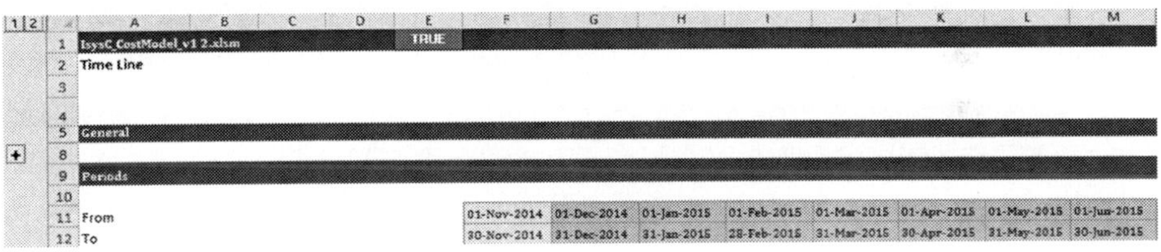

Figure 17-10. The months are created with start dates and end dates

The goal with the time periods is to make sure we have at least 60 columns of months. My advice is to always go for the greater and work from one year extra; therefore, as we know it's 60 months, we will then create 72 months. There are some practical reasons for doing this expansion of time periods. The sponsor or users may decide eventually that they need to see more years and by adopting such an approach, you will have greater flexibility. The alternative is that you are short with months and then have to adjust the time lines, a task that is time-consuming and liable to cause errors. If the time scales have some extra months built in at the start, everything is much smoother in the future when and if the specification of dates changes. And from experience, this does happen frequently.

The Other Parts of the Time Line

For our situation, the most important part of the time line is the month periods that we have just created and the additional information that can now be applied. The mark of a well-designed time line is to see how the modeler has anticipated the different forms of reporting that can occur when dealing with financial statements and also inputs. For instance, we know that we need to report in years; however, the users may also need to work in quarterly amounts. Or what happens if there are transactions of events that occur at a given interval, say every 15 months? (In IT, there is a concept called a "refresh," which is when all the IT equipment is required to be replaced or upgraded at specific time periods. This is a very important factor and these refreshes affect the capital and the depreciation calculations.) We need to have flexibility in our model and more specifically in our time lines to be able to address such situations.

With these in mind, it is always useful to add some extra factors to the time line, as in Figure 17-11a. Looking at this figure, you will notice that there are now several components that have been added to the time line, including the period number, month in the year, calendar month, quarters, year, and company year.

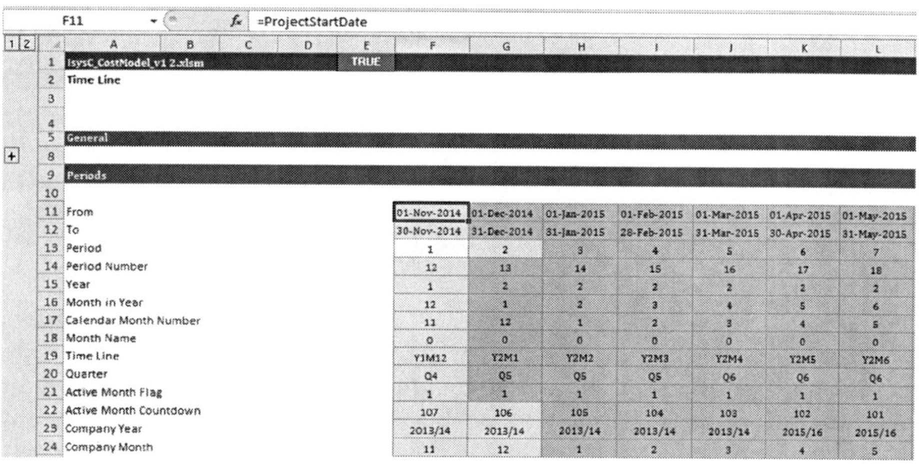

F11 =ProjectStartDate

	A	F	G	H	I	J	K	L
1	IsysC_CostModel_v1 2.xlsm							
2	Time Line							
3								
4								
5	General							
8								
9	Periods							
10								
11	From	01-Nov-2014	01-Dec-2014	01-Jan-2015	01-Feb-2015	01-Mar-2015	01-Apr-2015	01-May-2015
12	To	30-Nov-2014	31-Dec-2014	31-Jan-2015	28-Feb-2015	31-Mar-2015	30-Apr-2015	31-May-2015
13	Period	1	2	3	4	5	6	7
14	Period Number	12	13	14	15	16	17	18
15	Year	1	2	2	2	2	2	2
16	Month in Year	12	1	2	3	4	5	6
17	Calendar Month Number	11	12	1	2	3	4	5
18	Month Name	0	0	0	0	0	0	0
19	Time Line	Y1M12	Y2M1	Y2M2	Y2M3	Y2M4	Y2M5	Y2M6
20	Quarter	Q4	Q5	Q5	Q5	Q6	Q6	Q6
21	Active Month Flag	1	1	1	1	1	1	1
22	Active Month Countdown	107	106	105	104	103	102	101
23	Company Year	2013/14	2013/14	2013/14	2013/14	2013/14	2015/16	2015/16
24	Company Month	11	12	1	2	3	4	5

TRUE (cell E1)

Figure 17-11a. The time lines also contain additional information

Rather than go through the meaning of all these labels, I would recommend that at the very least you include the information I have pointed out. For instance, it's quite feasible that at some point the financial statements will need to be reconciled with actual performance financial information in order to have some forecast comparison. This comparison may need to be prepared from the company's first quarter results. The first quarter results will invariably be dependent on the company's accounting year. (Every company has an accounting year that is not always the calendar year.) In the time line, we have built in a company year's tag, which means no matter what model starting date the user chooses, the model financial statements can regularly be applied to the company's accounting year. If you don't quite follow this right now, don't worry too much. The important aspect here is that the time line should be built with an anticipation of the future, particularly for models that are not for one-time use only and are intended as ongoing business-as-usual processes.

You may be wondering where the time line fits into the structure considering your models are based on outputs, inputs, and calculations. The time line is a calculation worksheet; it reads information from the inputs and performs some calculations and passes these onto the outputs. It is possible to have more than one calculation worksheet in a model and this is so in our model, but more importantly, if there is more than one, make sure this worksheet is clearly set out.

In terms of time lines, I recommend you keep them in their own separate worksheet and not mix them with the general calculations. Time lines are crucial to the financial statement reporting periods, and any changes such as inserting a new column into the time lines will cause major synchronization problems through the entire model. So once created, lock them down and leave them. Often, after having created the time lines, I protect the worksheet.

Time Line Calculations

The time line worksheet is fundamental to any time-based model. Therefore, anytime you are confronted with a specification that mentions a time span like years or month, be prepared to build a time line. The next few sections will give you a few pointers on how the calculation to our time line was devised. Hopefully, this information will give you the foundation to create your own method in the future.

The From Date

The From date is linked with the project start date, which will be a user input. This project start date is contained in an input worksheet called "Constants." The Constants worksheet is a specific input worksheet that contains information that is needed to prime and set the fixed parameters of the model. It is distinct from the user inputs worksheet in that once these parameters are set, they rarely change. For instance, in the constants, you will have aspects such as the project sponsor's contact details or the modeler's name. You would also have aspects like the cost centers (should they be required for the model) and even credit terms for creditors, which will affect the balance creditors. In our model, the project start and end dates (60 months) are held in the constants. In Figure 7-11b, a link to the project start date is how the start date was created in the time lines.

Note You will notice that the From date does not show cell references such as C1 but a name "ProjectStartDate" (Figure 17-11a, Figure 17-11b) instead. This is a reference to a cell or group of cells, which are called ranges. In the Constants worksheet, there is a cell that holds the project start date that I have named "ProjectStartDate." Named references are useful because they offer a visual that tells you exactly what the link or formula is for. This way, when you see a name rather than a cell reference, you will know that this indicates a range.

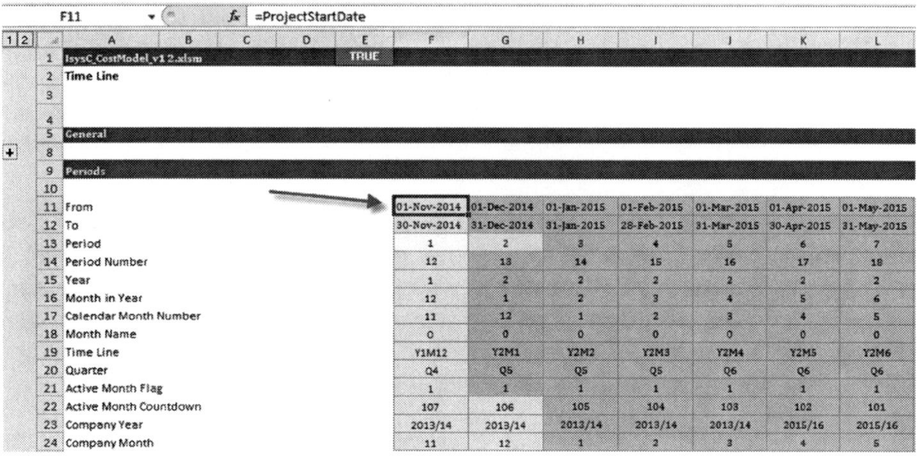

F11 =ProjectStartDate

IsysC_CostModel_v1 2.xlsm TRUE

Time Line

General

Periods

		F	G	H	I	J	K	L
11	From	01-Nov-2014	01-Dec-2014	01-Jan-2015	01-Feb-2015	01-Mar-2015	01-Apr-2015	01-May-2015
12	To	30-Nov-2014	31-Dec-2014	31-Jan-2015	28-Feb-2015	31-Mar-2015	30-Apr-2015	31-May-2015
13	Period	1	2	3	4	5	6	7
14	Period Number	12	13	14	15	16	17	18
15	Year	1	2	2	2	2	2	2
16	Month in Year	12	1	2	3	4	5	6
17	Calendar Month Number	11	12	1	2	3	4	5
18	Month Name	0	0	0	0	0	0	0
19	Time Line	Y1M12	Y2M1	Y2M2	Y2M3	Y2M4	Y2M5	Y2M6
20	Quarter	Q4	Q5	Q5	Q5	Q6	Q6	Q6
21	Active Month Flag	1	1	1	1	1	1	1
22	Active Month Countdown	107	106	105	104	103	102	101
23	Company Year	2013/14	2013/14	2013/14	2013/14	2013/14	2015/16	2015/16
24	Company Month	11	12	1	2	3	4	5

Figure 17-11b. The From date is linked to the project start date, which is in the input sheet called "Constants"

The To Date

The To date has been calculated by referring to the From date and rounding that to the end of the month by using the DATE() function in combination with the YEAR(), MONTH(), and DAY() functions (see Figure 17-c). This allows the model to pick from the From date that is the project start date and get the end of the month date through the use of the MONTH() function. The YEAR() and DAY() functions just ensure that the format of the date has some data integrity, which means if the user enters a project start date that was somehow not feasible (such as February 31), the functions would cause an error.

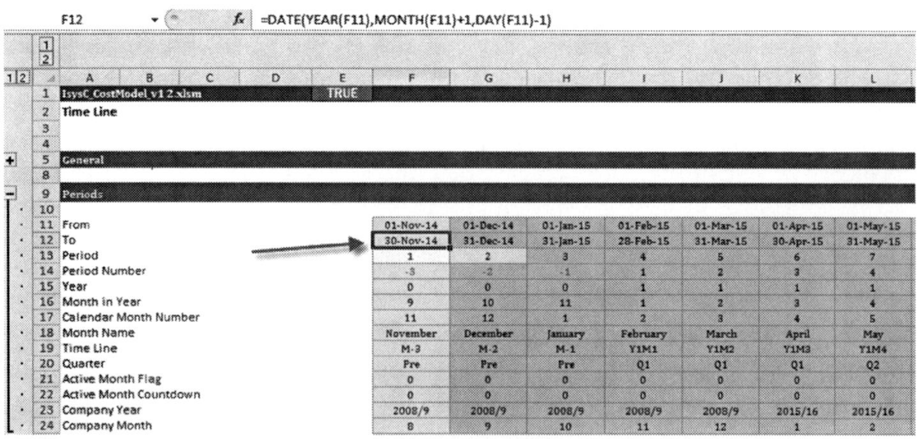

F12 =DATE(YEAR(F11),MONTH(F11)+1,DAY(F11)-1)

IsysC_CostModel_v1 2.xlsm TRUE

Time Line

General

Periods

		F	G	H	I	J	K	L
11	From	01-Nov-14	01-Dec-14	01-Jan-15	01-Feb-15	01-Mar-15	01-Apr-15	01-May-15
12	To	30-Nov-14	31-Dec-14	31-Jan-15	28-Feb-15	31-Mar-15	30-Apr-15	31-May-15
13	Period	1	2	3	4	5	6	7
14	Period Number	-3	-2	-1	1	2	3	4
15	Year	0	0	0	1	1	1	1
16	Month in Year	9	10	11	1	2	3	4
17	Calendar Month Number	11	12	1	2	3	4	5
18	Month Name	November	December	January	February	March	April	May
19	Time Line	M-3	M-2	M-1	Y1M1	Y1M2	Y1M3	Y1M4
20	Quarter	Pre	Pre	Pre	Q1	Q1	Q1	Q2
21	Active Month Flag	0	0	0	0	0	0	0
22	Active Month Countdown	0	0	0	0	0	0	0
23	Company Year	2008/9	2008/9	2008/9	2008/9	2008/9	2015/16	2015/16
24	Company Month	8	9	10	11	12	1	2

Figure 17-11c. The To date formula is shown here

Period

The period is a sequential number that always starts from 1, unless otherwise stipulated by the users. Hence the project start date is period 1, and the last month of the project will be month 36 or whatever time span is subsequently chosen by the user.

Period Number

You may be curious as to why there is a period number, when we already have the period. I have added this information purposely to demonstrate a situation of how to deal with transitions and transformations. In any project, there is a possibility that some activities may commence prior to the actual project start, such as procuring (sourcing and buying) equipment or moving and reorganizing staff and offices. This is called a transition or transformation period. Depending on the accounting present, those activities may be treated differently than the day-to-day business operations. Therefore, it's important that our model be able to reflect transitional periods. You will see in Figure 17-11d that the period begins at number 1, which is not the start date but the period number, being the preproject date starts at -3. The negative notation signifies that the period is prior to the project start date. There are three months of transition. In order to distinguish it, the period number begins its counting from a negative number counting down until it reaches 0, and then the period number starts from 1 as in Figure 17-11d.

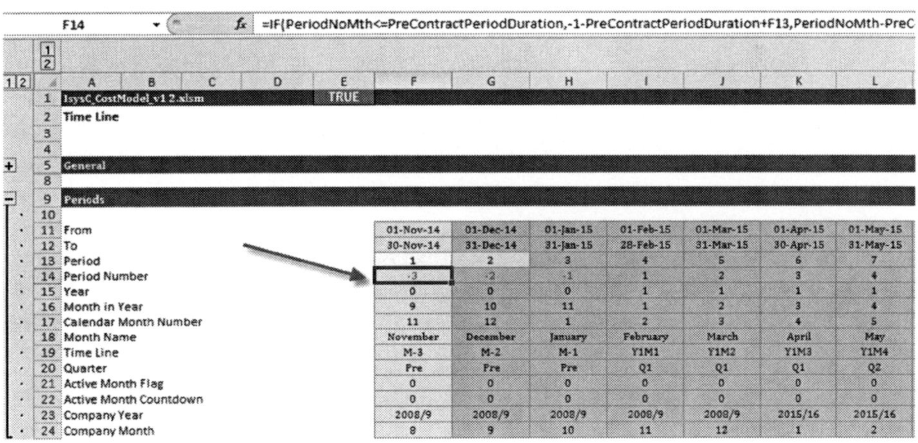
F14 =IF(PeriodNoMth<=PreContractPeriodDuration,-1-PreContractPeriodDuration+F13,PeriodNoMth-PreC

	A	E	F	G	H	I	J	K	L
1	IsysC_CostModel_v1 2.xlsm	TRUE							
2	Time Line								
3									
4									
5	General								
8									
9	Periods								
10									
11	From		01-Nov-14	01-Dec-14	01-Jan-15	01-Feb-15	01-Mar-15	01-Apr-15	01-May-15
12	To		30-Nov-14	31-Dec-14	31-Jan-15	28-Feb-15	31-Mar-15	30-Apr-15	31-May-15
13	Period		1	2	3	4	5	6	7
14	Period Number		-3	-2	-1	1	2	3	4
15	Year		0	0	0	1	1	1	1
16	Month in Year		9	10	11	1	2	3	4
17	Calendar Month Number		11	12	1	2	3	4	5
18	Month Name		November	December	January	February	March	April	May
19	Time Line		M-3	M-2	M-1	Y1M1	Y1M2	Y1M3	Y1M4
20	Quarter		Pre	Pre	Pre	Q1	Q1	Q1	Q2
21	Active Month Flag		0	0	0	0	0	0	0
22	Active Month Countdown		0	0	0	0	0	0	0
23	Company Year		2008/9	2008/9	2008/9	2008/9	2008/9	2015/16	2015/16
24	Company Month		8	9	10	11	12	1	2

Figure 17-11d. The period number is calculated by using the preproject months

In our example, we have set the number of preproject periods in the constants' inputs to three months, and therefore, we start with a −3. You should always use the period number in conjunction with the period.

Year

The year is an index based upon the project start date. If you look at Figure 7-11d, the year starts from zero, which means we must have some preproject months involved. If there were no preproject months, it would start at 1 as in Figure 17-11e.

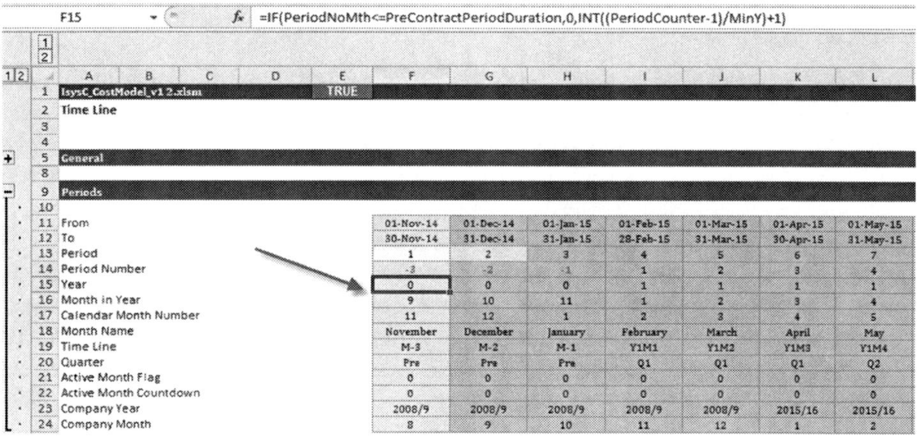

Figure 17-11e. The year now starts at 1 because we have no precontract months

Month in Year

Although useful, the month really isn't necessary. Month in Year is telling us at which month we are in based on our project start date. The project start date would start at month 1, and then it increments by 1 every month after that date. Why should we even bother to set up such a date? The reasons can be numerous. It is quite possible that we may need to view our financial statements in project months, and then synchronize that with the company's accounting months. For instance, the company's financial year ends at month 12, but the projects may begin at any time in that company year and will not necessarily be at month 1. Therefore, you could conceivably have project month 1 and company month 5 and would need to recognize where that intersection occurs.

In Figure 17-11f, you will see the calculation to derive the month uses the IF() statement and the MOD() function. The formula is looking at the value of the period number and uses this value as a count from 1 to 12. Once the period number reaches 12, the formula starts the count again from 1.

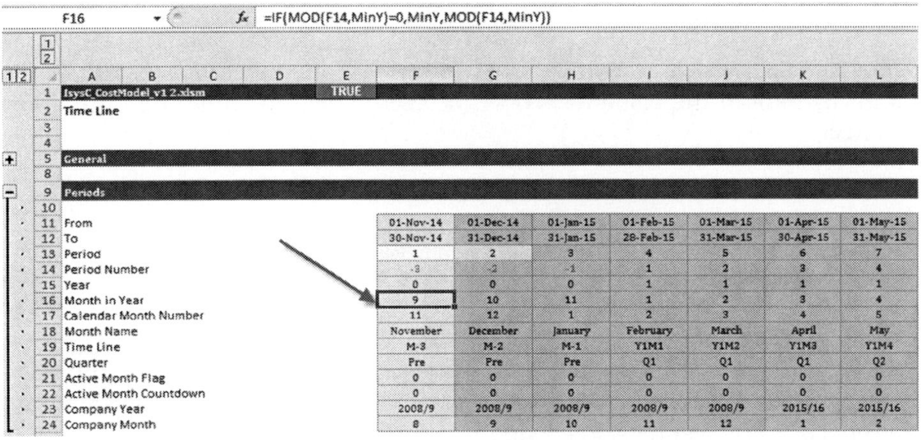

Figure 17-11f. The MOD() function is used to calculate the month in year

The MOD() function was covered in Chapter 3, and you may want to review that material before moving forward in this chapter. On the outset, this function looks long-winded. Why didn't we just use the number 12 to state the obvious that there are 12 months in a year rather than use a range name called "MinY"? As with anything with modeling, it's about adding flexibility. By using the range name MinY, we can now change the variable if we need to from 12 to another number.

Here is a problem that I have witnessed on a number of occasions. As stated, we know that there are 12 months in years. However, there are some organizations that do not work on 12 months, but rather period dates. These period dates do not start on the first day of the month (the 1st) or the end on the last day of the month (28th, 29th, 30th, or 31st). Instead, they start and end on some predefined periods, usually decided by their accounting regime. One possible reason for this is that the accounting depends on a financial IT system that is configured to work on time periods. Some civic or public bodies actually work in this manner, and it's not unusual to have 13 months in a company's financial year.

Now imagine what would happen if the model just assumed all periods were 12. When this assumption proved wrong, you can guarantee that the financial statements will be all wrong. By utilizing a variable MinY in the eventuality that the periods are different, all we will need to do is put the number of periods into the inputs and the time line will be correct. Again, the calculations are all about being flexible.

Calendar Month

The calendar month is exactly what it says—it identifies the month based upon the date in the calender. This is calculated by just using the MONTH() function.

Time Period

This time period is for labeling. It provides a detail of the year and month and therefore should be considered as the standard column label throughout the model. The usefulness of this type of calculation should not be overlooked. By using the year and month, it then becomes possible to give the user extra functionality in the model simply by creating lookups that can pinpoint an exact time period. For instance, if we need to build in some functionality to allow the user to state when dividends will be payable, we could simply add some user inputs and let the user select any dates. Then by utilizing the MATCH() and INDEX() lookups, we could enact those dividends into the model.

In Figure 17-11g, a formula has been created that uses the period number, the year and month in year, and adds the label "Y" for year and "M" for month.

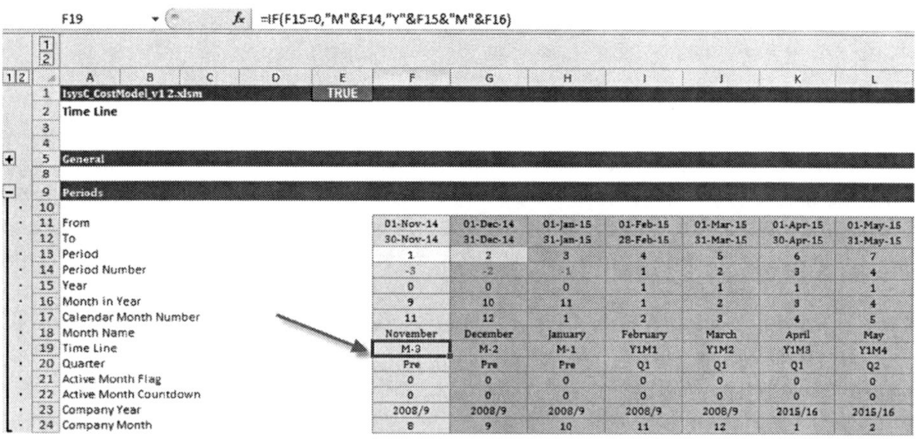

Figure 17-11g. The time period is a text formula used for labeling

Quarter

Often even when the financial statements are annual (in years), it's likely that the users will decide at a later date that they also require these statements to be broken down into quarters. Therefore, you really should not neglect having these in the time line. The formula required to create quarters may look complex, but it's actually very logical. In Figure 17-11h, the IF() statement checks the period number. If this is less than zero, it will realize this is a transition period and will insert the label "Pre" since we won't be counting quarters that fall within the transition. However, if the period number is greater than zero, it simply divides the period number (period number is between one and twelve) by three and uses the INT() function to round the number down. Then this function will apply a multiple to make sure the lowest quarter is a one.

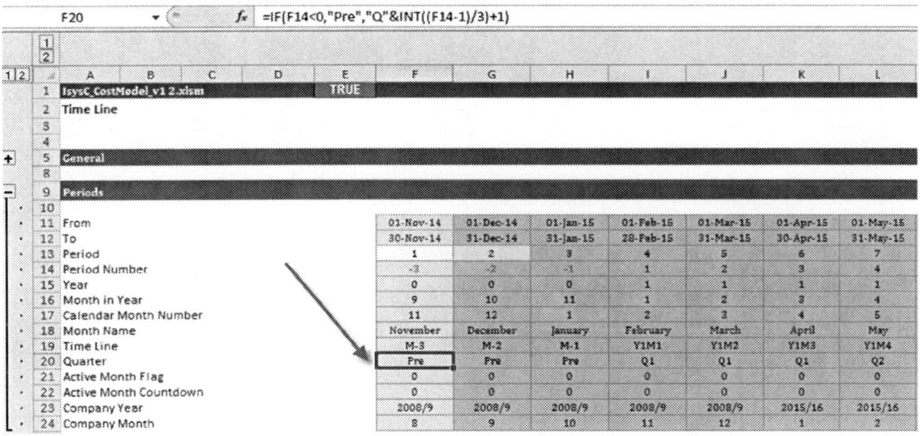

Figure 17-11h. The quarters use the IF() statement combined with the INT() (integer) function

Active Month Flag

Having some sort of flag that will produce a prescribed return if a month is active and a different return if it's not active is a useful calculation to have in the time line. This little gem can provide so many useful lookups that can be used. For example, it will show a zero if the month is not active (by not active it means that month is no longer in focus) and will show a one if it is active. One very useful routine that can be created is to use the active flag to bring particular periods into focus and ignore others. This means that aside from setting start and end dates, it's possible to shut down or activate a given number of months.

For instance, we know that in our case, we have five years of financial information. However, if for any reason we wanted to only report on year 2, we could do so easily without disrupting the model's internal calculations by just making the active months between Year 2 month 1 to Year 2 months 12 as in Figure 17-11i. This way, the model will still continue to calculate all three years, but will just report the 12 months of year 2.

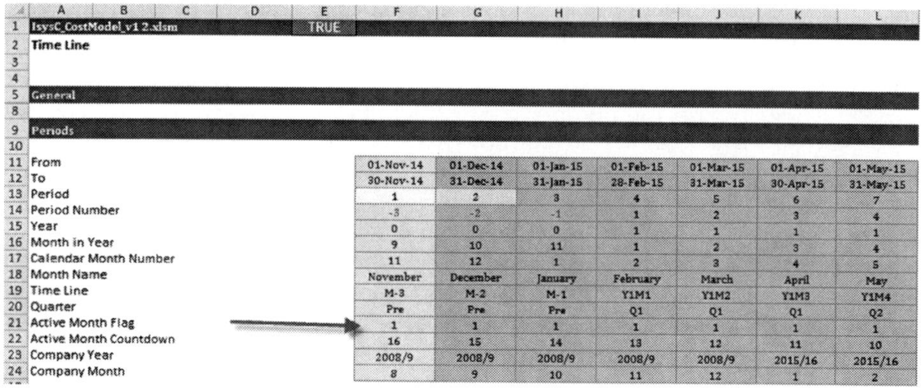

	A–E	F	G	H	I	J	K	L
1	IsysC_CostModel_v1 2.xlsm TRUE							
2	Time Line							
3								
4								
5	General							
8								
9	Periods							
10								
11	From	01-Nov-14	01-Dec-14	01-Jan-15	01-Feb-15	01-Mar-15	01-Apr-15	01-May-15
12	To	30-Nov-14	31-Dec-14	31-Jan-15	28-Feb-15	31-Mar-15	30-Apr-15	31-May-15
13	Period	1	2	3	4	5	6	7
14	Period Number	-3	-2	-1	1	2	3	4
15	Year	0	0	0	1	1	1	1
16	Month in Year	9	10	11	1	2	3	4
17	Calendar Month Number	11	12	1	2	3	4	5
18	Month Name	November	December	January	February	March	April	May
19	Time Line	M-3	M-2	M-1	Y1M1	Y1M2	Y1M3	Y1M4
20	Quarter	Pre	Pre	Pre	Q1	Q1	Q1	Q2
21	Active Month Flag	1	1	1	1	1	1	1
22	Active Month Countdown	16	15	14	13	12	11	10
23	Company Year	2008/9	2008/9	2008/9	2008/9	2008/9	2015/16	2015/16
24	Company Month	8	9	10	11	12	1	2

Figure 17-11i. The active month flag dictates the periods that need to be reported in the financial statements

There are a number of formula constructs that can be created to work out the active flag, but essentially it needs to work from the project start and end dates.

Company Year and Month

I chose not to describe the active month countdown as it's fairly obvious what it does. The company year is important, however, as it may be required that the financial statements are reported in company financial years as opposed to the project years. This is just a subtle difference in wording, but the results will be significantly different. The company year is set in the Constants worksheet. The company month is simply a MONTH function that uses the From date to give a month number.

Step Three: Build the Inputs

Now that we have established the outputs and the time line calculation, the next stage is to work backward and build the inputs that will be used to calculate the outputs. The inputs will be the user side of the model, and therefore it's important to create these with an eye toward making them intuitive and relatively simple. The best way of achieving this simplicity is to have them organized in-line with the financial statements in the outputs.

As the income statement is really the first output, we can build our inputs by using it as our starting point. In my opinion, the income statement should always be the starting point because so many of the elements in it will actually be captured in the cash flow and the balance sheet. For instance, the revenues that appear as revenue and income will affect the inflows for the cash flows and also the debtors in the balance sheet. Take a look at the example in Figure 17-12.

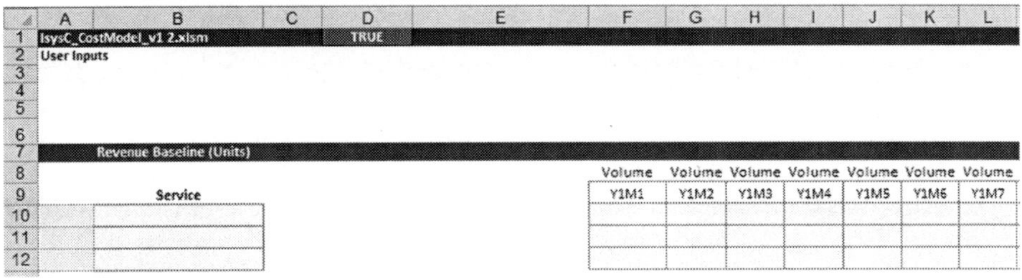

Figure 17-12. The inputs to the revenue are shown here

In the revenue input in Figure 17-12, the data required will be the volumes (units) and the price for each of the services. You will see in the figure that as we are calculating at the lowest time period, which is in months. It would be simpler to start with annual amounts, but this will become a problem as we try to convert yearly data into monthly data. It is better to just work with monthly data from the start.

In this figure, notice at which column location the inputs begin (column F). Then skip back a few pages and take a look at the figures with the time line (Figures 17-10 to 17-11i). What do you notice about the column location? They all start at column F. This is not a coincidence, and I have purposely made sure that there is a consistent location with the time line and the input. The financial statement's monthly data also starts at column F. The main reason why the column location is in sync is that it makes linking between inputs, calculations, and outputs that much easier. All that is required is to form one link at column F, and the rest will all line up correctly.

Now let's examine Figure 17-13. The column headings with the months starting at Y1M1 are taken from the time line using the timeperiod tag. All I have done is to name the range of all the time periods "timeperiod." From here on if I need to use the time periods, all I have to do is link the name. As long as the first link is in column F, all the dates and time periods will be correct. What this means is if the user changes the start and end dates of the project, you can rest assured that the dates and periods will permeate through the model correctly.

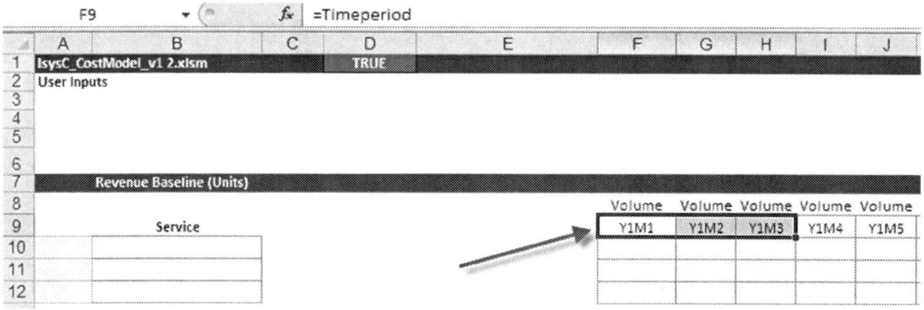

Figure 17-13. The column headings are linked to the time line by using a defined names

Creating Inputs for the Scenarios

In addition to the baseline revenue volumes, we need to duplicate these baselines with the scenarios. We are trying to achieve a situation where the user can set the inputs for the baseline, and if they so wish, they can also create some hypothetical inputs in the scenario and monitor the effect of these against the baseline by comparing them. We have given the user the opportunity to create three scenarios at a time and then revolve back and forth at their leisure.

In Figure 17-14a, the scenario revenue volume inputs have been created. You will see that there are three scenario settings, which allows the user to create "what if" types of situations.

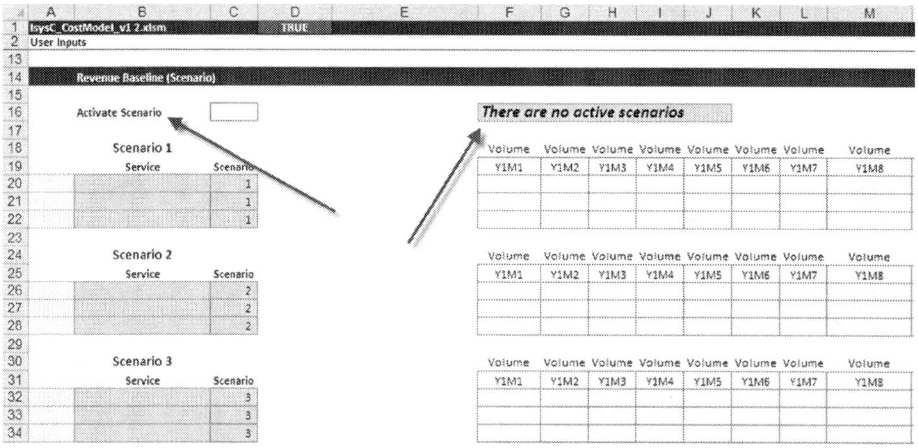

Figure 17-14a. The scenario inputs for revenue volumes are shown here

There is only one set of scenario financial statements, and as there are three possible scenarios, we need to have some mechanism to choose which scenario to make active. Notice in cell B16 the text that says "Activate scenario."

The user can choose which scenario will be active simply by selecting the required number in the drop-down list in cell C16.

Whenever we give the user the ability to select some item from a number of options, it is important that the model provide visual signs of its current status. In Figure 17-14b in cell F16, there is a signal that informs the user that currently there are no scenarios selected. However, if we select scenario 2 as in Figure 17-14c, we will see a number of signals that should leave the user in no doubt as to which is the active scenario. The message in cell F16 has now changed and informs the user that scenario 2 is active. Notice that the color style in scenario 2 inputs are now in gray to signal that this is the active scenario in use. It is not a question of using this exact visual, but it is imperative that you have some way of giving the user feedback.

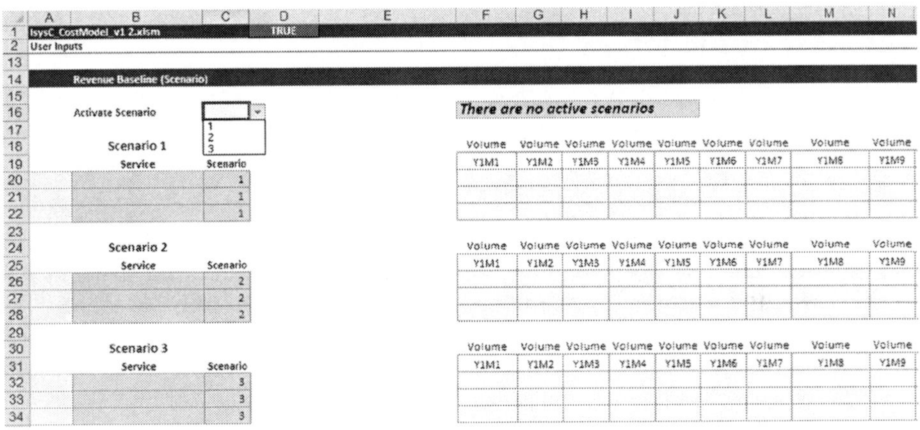

Figure 17-14b. The active scenario can be selected from the drop-down list

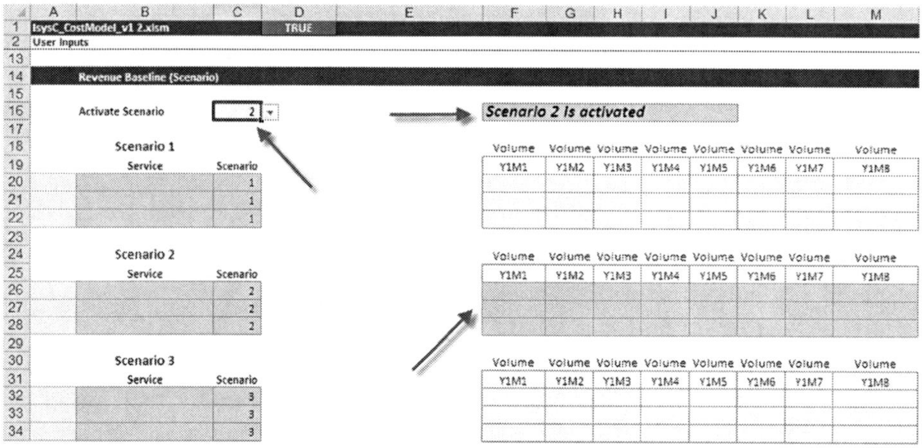

Figure 17-14c. Scenario 2 has been chosen, and a number of visual cues are available to make sure the user knows which scenario has been selected

The Rest of the Inputs

The rest of the user inputs will work according to the requirements of the financial statements. We have looked through the revenue volumes; we will also need to create a revenue price that is split between fixed and variable in much the same fashion as the volumes.

The other cost inputs for the income statement will also be created just as the revenue has. The user will need to supply the data on a monthly basis for all the costs, and a scenario with three options would need to be created. This would obviously take some time, but as with any aspect of modeling, going through each aspect in the model systematically is really the only way to avoid making serious errors.

The Calculations

The way the calculations are created that connect the inputs to the outputs really depends upon the modeler's style and use of functions. There are no standard methods of performing calculations for modeling situations. Some well-accepted guidelines do exist, such as always try to keep your formula as simple as possible, avoid lengthy formula constructs, and be consistent. This section will look at how to create these calculations between the inputs and calculations while maintaining the consistency and simplicity of the formula.

Avoid Three-Dimensional Formulas

I recommend that you make the calculation stage of the model as simple and auditable as possible by not using complex and long formulas. One technique that can really help is to avoid three-dimensional formula constructs within the calculation worksheet. Three-dimensional constructs are those where the formula relies on linking between more than worksheet. Here is an example:

=*Sheet2!C5*Sheet3!C5*,

Or, worse,

=*Sheet2!C5*Sheet3!C5+Sheet4!C5*

If this is not immediately clear to you why this should be avoided, consider if you were presented with a model to review that included several three-dimensional formulas. How would you feel about checking every single one of these formulas, following the trail through every worksheet that had hundreds of rows of data?

The surest way to avoid making these three-dimensional calculations is to bring the inputs into the calculation worksheet. These can be placed on the top of the worksheet or at the top of each section. Although this will feel like the inputs are being duplicated, by bringing the inputs into the calculation sheet, you can then make formulas that start and end in the calculation worksheet. If there are any errors, it becomes very clear where to go to fix them.

Our Calculations

In Figure 17-15, take a look at the calculations and notice that the inputs have been brought into the worksheet with an uncomplicated link to the input worksheet (Inp_User). As a result, our calculations are simple.

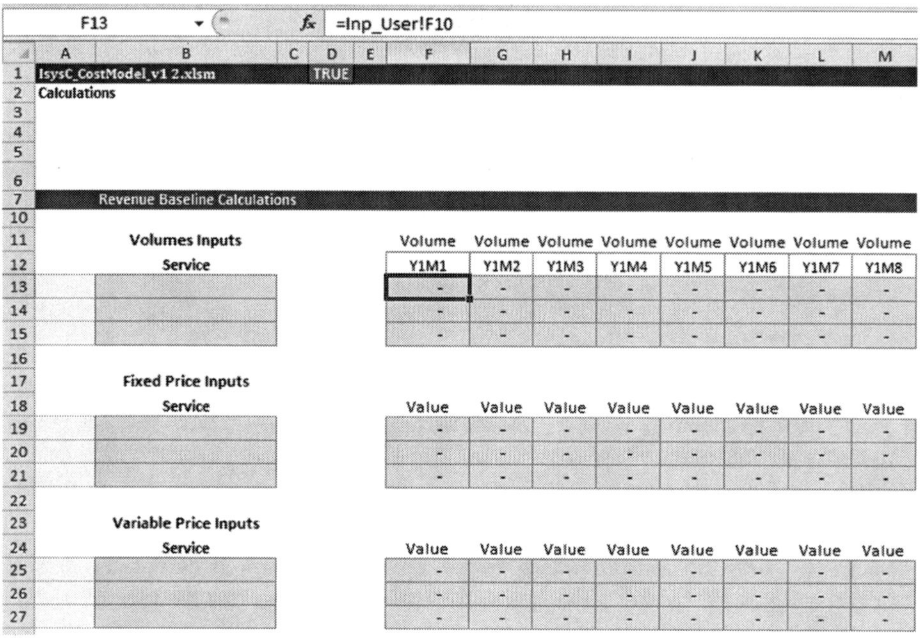

Figure 17-15. The inputs have been brought into the calculation worksheet with a simple link

The process of creating calculations is just to make sure we capture the correct cells from the input links in the calculation worksheet. Therefore, our formula looks very simple, as in Figure 17-16, where we have calculated our total fixed revenue by multiplying volumes with the fixed price.

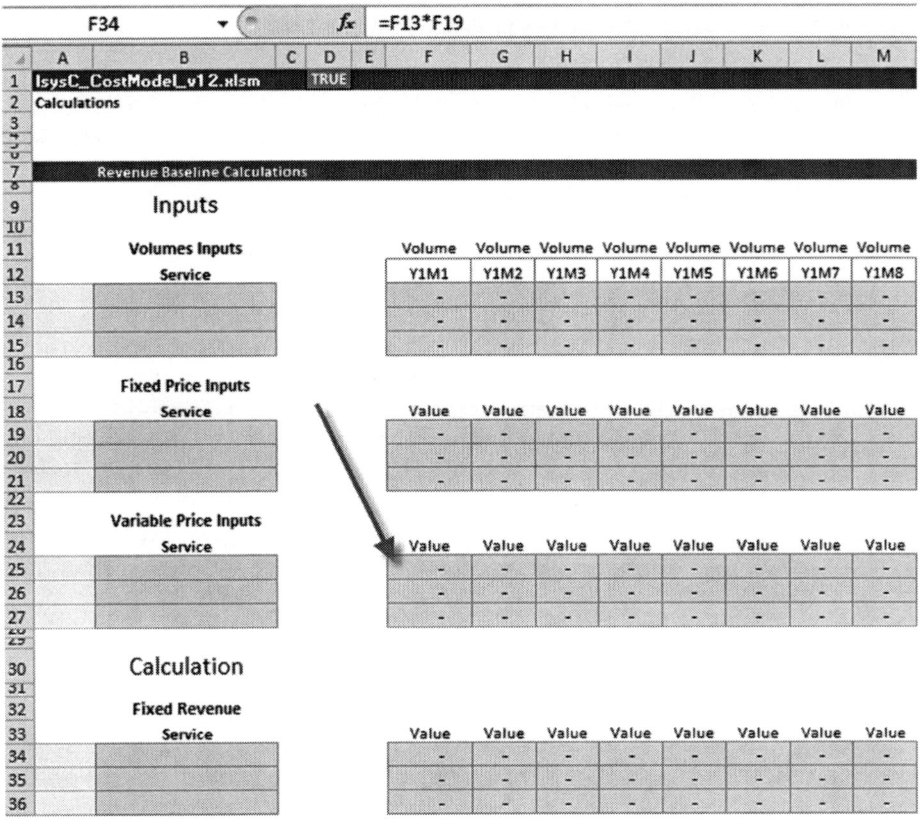

Figure 17-16. The calculation for the total fixed price is just the volume multiplied by the price

---

Caution There are plenty of people within the Excel community who will disagree on the type of construct I am advocating for a number of reasons. They will argue that it takes longer and there's some duplication, which in large models could have an impact upon the size and the speed of the model. This is a valid criticism. There are, however, some who will disagree because this is almost too simple, and their view is that modeling should be about using complex and groundbreaking formulas. Nothing could be further from the truth; a modeler's worth cannot be measured on complexity. In fact, it's exactly the reverse. A good modeler will turn a complicated situation into one of simplicity. The main point is that you should adopt what works for you, but it's important you understand why you are doing it and also the implications and potential criticisms that may come your way.

Linking the Statements to the Calculations

Unfortunately, it is not practical to use the same method of calculations in the statements as we did with the calculation worksheet because the outputs are also about presentation. If you have followed a structured build with the inputs and calculations, it's fairly likely that linking the statements to the calculations will not present much of a difficulty. In most cases, it will just be about creating a direct link into the calculations. There are some parts of the statements where that direct link will not suffice because there are a number of options that arc available.

I can give you some of my own advice as to which functions and formulas are best to use for our case study. You will have come across various lookup functions such as VLOOKUP(), and for our case study, we will need to utilize a lookup function in our calculations. Whenever there is a situation where you have an unknown choice or option that can be made by the user and there is a calculation that is reliant on that choice, you will always need a lookup function. The lookup function will pick up the choice irrespective of what it is and pass it on into the calculation.

Now that we have established that we need a lookup, which one do we choose? Remember that our model is largely looking at inputs that have a time value; then the value can then be calculated. For this type of situation with time values, it is almost always a case that the SUMIF() function will be required; place this function into the critical list of those functions that you are able to use. In Figure 17-17, the SUMIF() function uses the months on the top of the worksheet as a lookup with the time periods and then places the revenue based upon the services into the correct month.

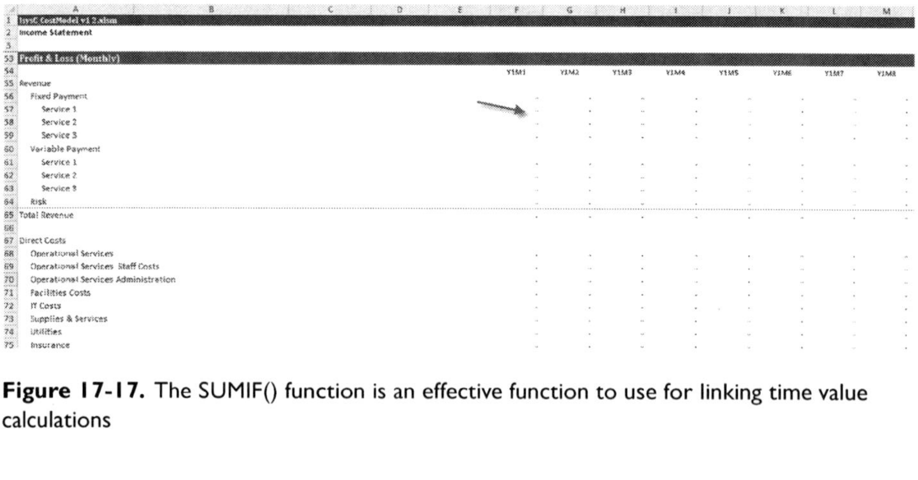

Figure 17-17. The SUMIF() function is an effective function to use for linking time value calculations

The Assumptions and Documentation

Throughout the model, we have designed the ability to add and control the assumptions by using the leftmost columns for referencing the assumption book or register. In Figure 17-18, column A has been intentionally left blank, and this column will be used to provide referencing to the inputs and assumptions.

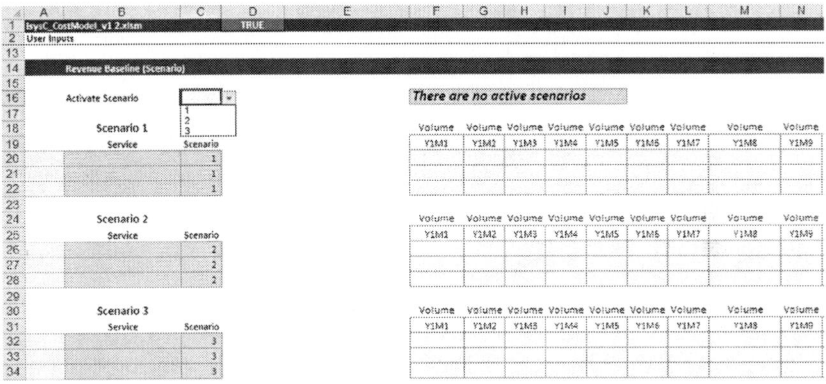

Figure 17-18. Notice that the first column is blank for use of assumption referencing

The model's internal documentation is within the admin worksheets to provide the model users with the modeling styles, as shown in Figure 17-19, and the model instructions and notes, as shown in Figure 17-20.

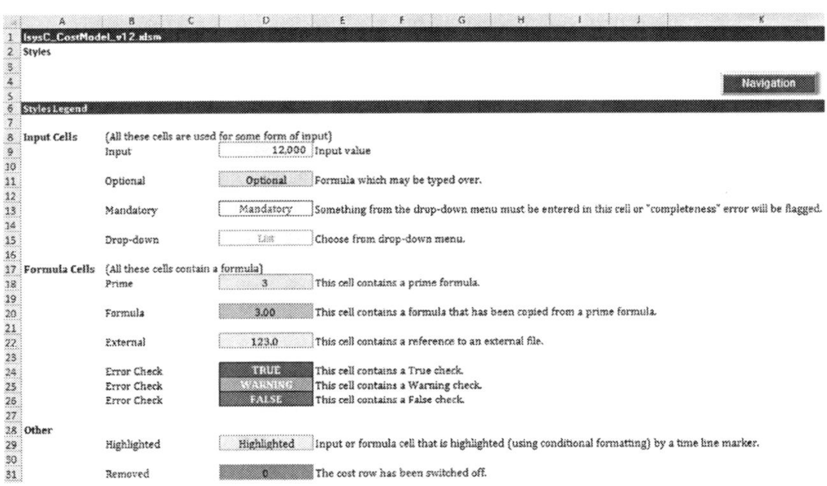

Figure 17-19. Part of the documentation is the styles of the cells in the model

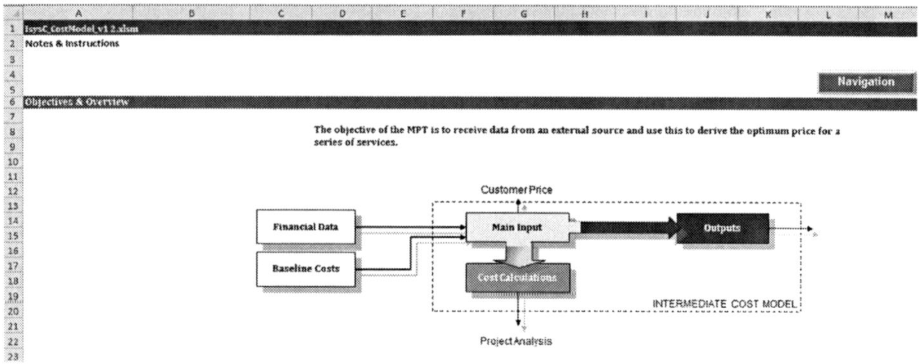

Figure 17-20. The model contains a worksheet with a detailed breakdown of the model data flow

Testing and Audit

The time constraints mean that the audit and testing have to be compressed within a short time period. There is no approval from the sponsor for an audit to be performed; therefore, it is imperative that some comment is provided giving the potential issues and implications of not putting this model into an audit. The audit would provide information on the following:

- The prevalence and identification of errors throughout the model.
- That the risks of the project are clearly stated and understood in and outside of the model.
- The model provides an audit trail from financial outputs to the most recent operating period.
- The model is designed in accordance with financial modeling best practice.
- The model is be capable of accommodating future adjustments.

The time required to check each formula depends on the readability of the spreadsheet. In terms of time scales, it would be fair to estimate that each formula would require a minute of audit time.

The best way to audit a spreadsheet is to rewrite it completely and subsequently compare the result with the original model and then focus on where and how the differences occurred. This is not, however, always a practical route. Considering the organization is unsure if the model should be placed in official audit, I would recommend a model rebuild to be conducted in-house for which some guidelines are provided.

Basic Review of the Model: Guidelines

Two things to keep in mind before commencing a review of the model:

- Make multiple backup copies.
- Make sure at every stage that your spreadsheet can reproduce the results from the original. (Be sure that the new spreadsheet is mathematically the same as the original or that you can document a clear error in the old one.)

Step One: Put everything on one sheet

- By using a backup copy of the model workbook, select the second worksheet. On the Home tab in the Editing group, click Find & Select, Go To Special, click Last cell, and then click OK. This will select the last cell for which memory has been allocated.
- Holding the Shift key, click cell A1. This will select everything active on the sheet.
- Press CTRL+X to cut everything on the sheet.
- Select Sheet 1. On the Home tab in the Editing group, click Find & Select, Go To Special, click Last cell, and then click OK. Press the down arrow once, then scroll left in the same row and click in column A.
- Press CTRL+V to paste Sheet 2 onto Sheet 1.
- Delete Sheet 2.
- Go back to Step 1 and repeat until only one sheet remains.
- Save the file under a new name.

Here, I have moved the formulas sheet to the input sheet and then deleted the blank formulas sheet.

You may overwrite blank references. If #REF errors appear, undo, then look at the instructions for finding blank references in Step Four.

What if everything doesn't fit on one spreadsheet? Come back to this step later, after further steps are completed.

Step Two: Turn off all nonnumeric formatting

- Force the display of all rows and columns by going to the File menu, then Options and Advanced. Scroll down until about halfway until you see "Display options for this worksheet" and make sure the "Show row and column headers" is checked.
- Treat every cell as an equal for now. The goal is to find the numerical structure of the spreadsheet apart from its graphical or typographical structure.
- Press CTRL+A to select the entire sheet. Right-click the selection and click Format Cells.
- In the Format Cells dialog box, change the horizontal alignment to right (indent) and be sure the orientation is set to 0 degrees. Later, you will need to align the longer labels to the left. Clear any checks in Wrap text, Shrink to fit, and Merge cells.
- Click the Font tab. Change the font to Arial, the font style to regular, the size to 10 points, and click No Underline and Automatic Color.
- Click the Border tab and then under Styles, click None.
- Click the Fill tab and ensure that the background color is set to No Color.
- Click the Protection tab and make sure Locked is checked and Hidden is unchecked. Click OK.
- On the Page Layout tab, in the Scale to Fit group, change the column width to 12 and the row height to 16.
- Save the workbook with a new name.

Step Three: Format formulas

- On the Home tab in the Editing group, click Find & Select, Go To Special, click Last cell, and then click OK. This will highlight all the formulas in the spreadsheet.
- With all the formulas highlighted, format the cells in some way. Try using a very light fill color with a medium border.
- Save the workbook with a new name.

This method of finding hard-coded data can be trickier if the writer inserts an equal sign in front of the number. Look out for this type of situation, as it does happen. If you find it, correct it by removing the equal sign.

If you find that the spreadsheet contains a lot of hard-coded data with the equal signs and few formulas, you will need to apply yet more format to the formulas to differentiate them from the hard-coded data.

Step Four: Delete unnecessary rows and columns

- Delete blank external rows and columns. An external blank row is a row between the apparent last cell (where the data looks like it ends) and the true last cell (Go To Special, Last cell).
- Delete unneeded internal rows and columns, which appear within and between tables.
- Delete blank rows and columns to condense the spreadsheet. Be aggressive with deleting unnecessary elements like useless labels and repetitive labels like the months and years.

Things Could Go Wrong If...

Some serious errors appear if the model spreadsheet is dependent on blank cells. They are most likely to appear as #REF errors at this point, when you are deleting rows and columns.

If you find #REF errors suddenly appearing after you delete a blank row or blank column, go through the blank cells with the Formula Audit group in the Formula tab to determine which blank cells are referenced. There is some VBA code that you can use to automate this step. This would also be a good point to type the code into the VBE (see Chapter 18) and begin to try to understand what the VBA routine is doing because the construction of this code is relatively simple. In addition, this code can be altered and amended to provide several different worksheet analyses.

Tip The VBA code will find all blank references and will insert a red zero in any blank cell with a dependent. You can then delete blank rows and columns with more confidence (though cells could still be hidden). Once you have made sense of the blank references, set them back to the default format.

I have provided the VBA code that you can use to find blank references; it would be useful for you to examine how this code works because it contains routines that are frequently used in during modeling.

```
Sub FindBlankReferences()
    Application.ScreenUpdating = False
    Dim c, precedentCell
    For Each c In ActiveSheet.Cells.SpecialCells(xlCellTypeFormulas)
        If NumberOfPrecedents(c) >= 1 Then
            For Each precedentCell In c.DirectPrecedents.Cells
                If IsEmpty(precedentCell) Then
                    precedentCell.Formula = 0
                    precedentCell.Font.ColorIndex = 3 ' Red
                End If
            Next precedentCell
        End If
    Next
    Application.ScreenUpdating = True
End Sub

Function NumberOfPrecedents(cell) As Integer
        NumberOfPrecedents = 0
        On Error Resume Next
        NumberOfPrecedents = cellij.DirectPrecedents.Count
End Function
```

Step Five: Delete Unnecessary Trailing Cells

By now, you will probably be getting a vague feel for the spreadsheet. Now we can start editing the numerical part.

- Find the last numeric cell (not the last cell in memory).
- Select the last numeric cell. Then on the Formulas tab, in the Formula Auditing group, repeatedly click Trace Precedents until no more blue arrows appear.
- Save the workbook with a new name.

Most likely, you will see some numerical cells with no blue arcs of precedence. These cells are dangling. Unless you have a compelling reason to keep these suspended cells (like you are solving a math model such as a linear program), delete the suspended cells. Yes, delete them—formats, labels, and all (on the Home tab in the Editing group, click Clear and then Clear All). The goal is to delete the cells that are there just for your information and retain the cells that supposedly produce the justification for the project.

The following VBA code—TrailingCells()—shown next will allow you to find all the dangling cells and turn them green. You can then choose the one dangling cell as the last numeric cell and delete all the others with their labels and formats.

```
Sub TrailingCells()
    Application.ScreenUpdating = False
    Dim c
    For Each c In ActiveSheet.Cells.SpecialCells(xlCellTypeFormulas)
        If 0 = NumberOfDependents(c) Then
            c.Font.ColorIndex = 43 ' Green
        End If
    Next c
    Application.ScreenUpdating = True
End Sub

Function NumberOfDependents(cellij) As Integer
    NumberOfDependents = 0
    On Error Resume Next
    NumberOfDependents = cellij.DirectDependents.Count
End Function
```

Step Six: Rearrange the cells in the spreadsheet to be in logical order

- Rearrange cells to flow from left to right and top to bottom and shorten the arcs of precedence. The goal is to have all cells refer only to cells above and to the left. If a cell refers to a cell to the right and/or below, work to move it.
- Keep an eye out for #REF errors. If these appear, undo the changes and try to find out what is wrong.
- Continue moving cells, putting direct precedents toward the bottom, so the logic flows from left to right and top to bottom.

Step Seven: Remove redundant cells

The goal here is to reduce the number of cells and characters in each cell. Since the model is all on one sheet, first use the Search and Replace tool to eliminate sheet names within formulas.

Look for unnecessary cells and eliminate them. Shown next is some VBA code that will find unnecessary cells and turn them green. This code turns green cells that have either definitely one precedent or precisely one dependent.

```
Sub RedundantCells()
    Application.ScreenUpdating = False
    Dim c
    For Each c In ActiveSheet.Cells.SpecialCells(xlCellTypeFormulas)
        If 1 = NumberOfPrecedents(c) Or 1 = NumberOfDependents(c) Then
            c.Font.ColorIndex = 43 ' Green
        End If
    Next c
    Application.ScreenUpdating = True
End Sub
```

Step Eight: Format Cells for Description

With this step, consistency is a powerful ally. Make sure that all cells in units of currency are formatted as currency. Also make similar numerical cells display the same number with decimal places. Take some time to make sure that every numerical cell has the proper numerical format and alignment.

Final Version and Protection

The model should be considered the concluding version only once the audit has been completed. The last version should be the version called "[Model Name]_FinalVersion_Release_v1.0." It is important on all fronts to use the text FinalVersion because it quickly pinpoints to anyone that this is the model that was intended for use and not a production version. Also by adding the word "release," we are signaling that this is a model for handover. In additional, always make sure there is a version number. The modeler's final model will invariably be version 1, and any subsequent updates and changes will increment from that number.

At this stage, remove password protections from the model, although formula cells are locked but can be quite easily unlocked by the user without the need for passwords. Check the model for spelling errors and clear any labels and data that are hard-coded into the cells. Finally, place the model in a location where it can be transferred to the client and/or sponsor.

CHAPTER

18

Additional Tools and VBA for Financial Models

Microsoft Excel is the modeler's tool of choice for building models, and fortunately for modelers, Excel has an extensive list of additional tools and services that can be attached or used in conjunction. In this chapter, I will briefly describe some of these additional tools that have a modeling impact. However, I am also going to give a more detailed view of a select group of tools that I consider not only helpful but also essential to the financial modeler.

Third-Party Tools to Enhance Financial Models

The following three tools have been chosen because of the way in which they enhance financial modeling. Several other tools are openly available to the public, and I urge you to investigate them. I have chosen to focus on these three tools because they are ones that I use or have used in the past and am recommending based on experience.

ComplyXL

Tool name: ComplyXL

Producer: Lyquidity

Modeling Uses: Spreadsheet version control and management

Website: `www.lyquidity.com`

Description

ComplyXL is a tool that helps you keep control over version history and allows you to see what has changed, who made the changes, and why those changes were made in Excel. The version history also means that all changes can be identified automatically and quickly, making it reliable and saving time in comparison to manually trying to check spreadsheets.

ComplyXL addresses the need to provide corporate managers with the ability to exert control over corporate spreadsheets and the information they contain. The objective is to allow organizations to exert that control unobtrusively so that the benefits of control can be obtained without sacrificing the essential productivity and flexibility Excel offers. These benefits include the following:

- Ensures that there are audit trails of changes to any model.
- Validates information more quickly than using a manual process.
- Reduces the time taken to analyze differences.
- Easily spots changes to large spreadsheets.
- Filters changes to focus on specific types of change.
- Does not introduce any changes to the way Excel is used.

Background

ComplyXL was developed to help create and support a compliance/assurance process that is effective. The ComplyXL Discovery service can capture all changes to spreadsheets across the organization without any need to install software on a workstation. This makes it possible to visualize the use of and changes to spreadsheets across the organization or in specific domains and find out whether controls over the use of spreadsheets are implemented, in use, and proportionate.

When using ComplyXL, all changes to all spreadsheets can be captured automatically. However, the review process supported by ComplyXL does not have to be applied equally to all spreadsheets. Spreadsheets can be categorized to reflect their inherent risk (as judged by the organization), and the central compliance function can then ensure that important, critical, or risky spreadsheets are being reviewed adequately. Other spreadsheets can be assessed if and when it becomes appropriate. However, a full audit trail of changes will be available for postmortem analysis by audit staff in the event spreadsheet(s) believed to present less risk later turn out to be implicated in a business process problem.

Sarah Hothersall, Liaison Director at Lyquidity, August 2013

Why Is This Tool Recommended for Modelers?

One of the key strengths of ComplyXL is its version control capabilities. Because Excel does not support version control, users typically resort to making occasional copies by using arbitrary file names or folders. ComplyXL enforces the recording of versions and creates a standardized trail of changes made to each spreadsheet. The version history as in Figure 18-1 is available from within Excel as a trail that records information such as the time after the change, the individual responsible for each change, the PC on which the change was made, and any comments. Of course, the cell detail such as value or formula changes and format, links, names, and all other changes are recorded as well. The version history also allows for rollbacks because not all changes are needed, and sometimes it's necessary to revert to an earlier version. Because ComplyXL maintains a version history, any spreadsheet can be rolled back.

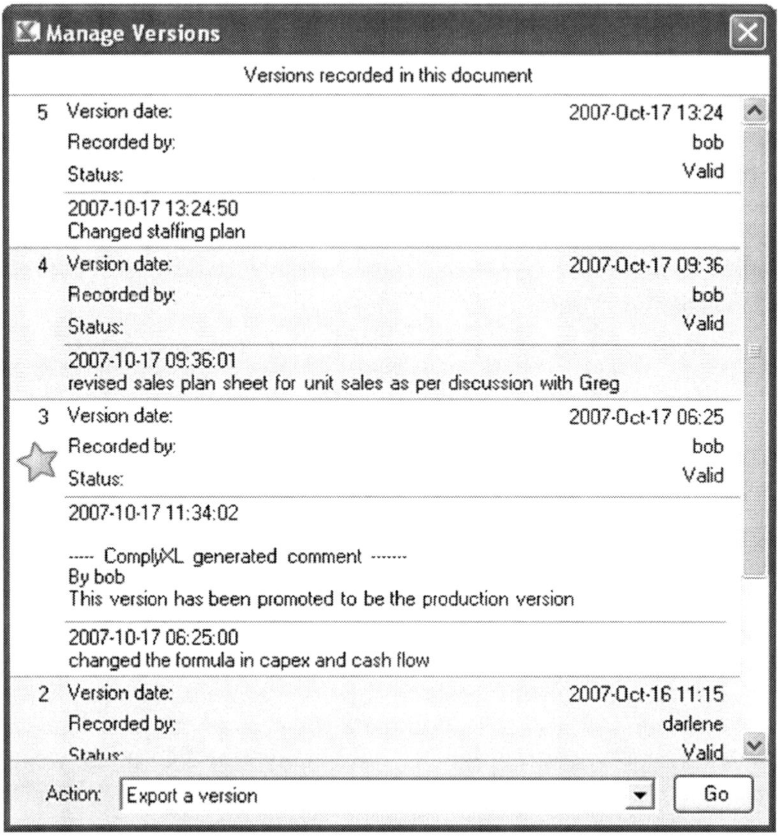

Figure 18-1. With ComplyXL, a spreadsheet version history can be accessed

One of the difficulties encountered when maintaining models is tracking changes and understanding why the changes were made, particularly when there are several modelers or maintainers of spreadsheets and models.

Because it is easy to make changes to spreadsheets and because those changes can propagate through a spreadsheet, it can be difficult to understand the set of changes applied by a user. The change tracking features make it clear to a reviewer, auditor, or compliance officer where changes have occurred, when they occurred, and who made the changes. These changes can be handled at several levels, including workbook, worksheet, and in cells.

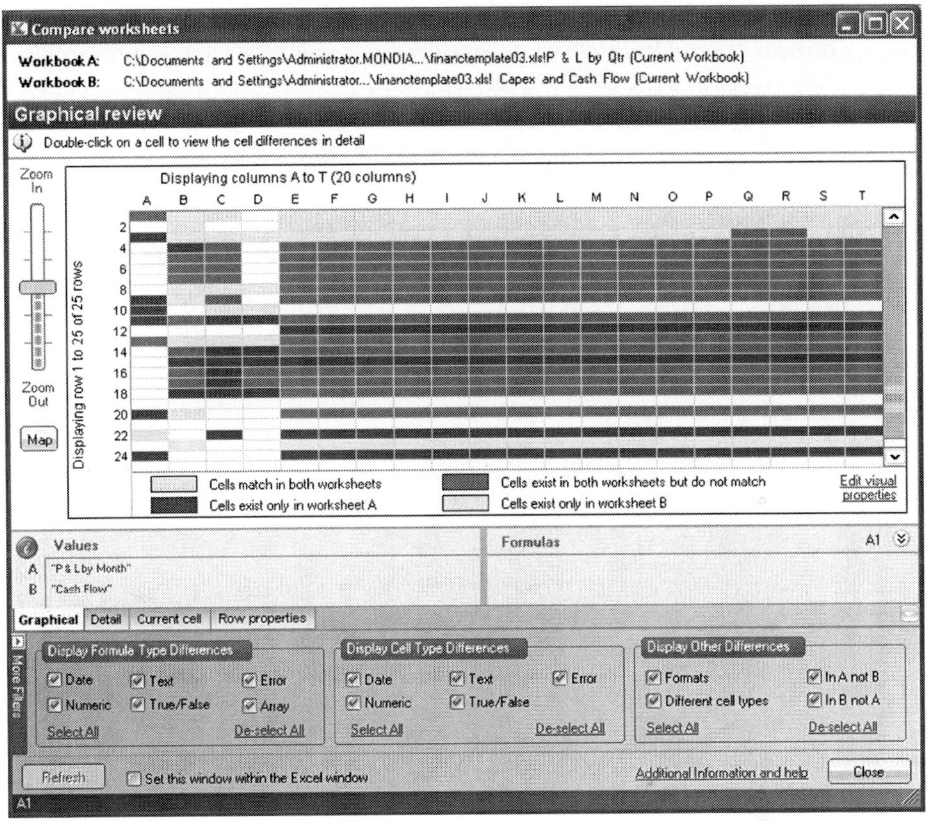

Figure 18-2. Change comparisons in ComplyXL allow a reviewer to see changes graphically or in a tabular format

LockXLS

Tool name: LockXLS

Producer: Spreadsheet Tools

Modeling Uses: Spreadsheet security tool

Website: `www.lockxls.com`

Description

LockXLS is a security tool whose primary goal is to add workbook copy protection features to Excel. It prevents workbooks from unauthorized distribution and stops anyone who has not received permission from being able to research logic in the locked workbook, formulas, and Visual Basic for Applications (VBA) code.

The current version of LockXLS is a spreadsheet compiler and also a workbook copy protector. It converts an Excel workbook to a stand-alone application totally independent of the Excel application suite. As a result, LockXLS gives access to the modeler all the copy control abilities of a fully-fledged application, for instance, to open an Excel spreadsheet or Excel model a user must enter an activation code (hardware-based) as in Figure 18-3.

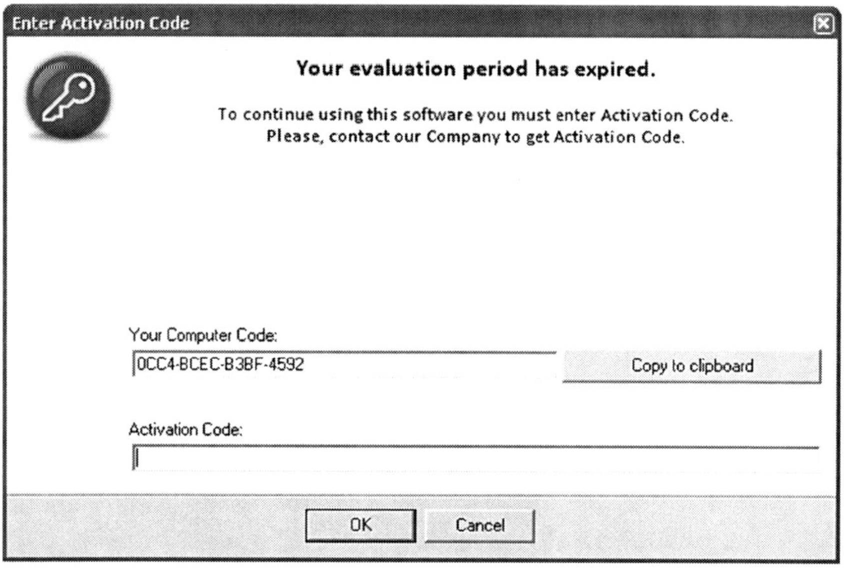

Figure 18-3. The LockXLS activation requires a code, which if not correctly applied, will not open the model

---

Note All spreadsheet compilers you can find on the market are not actually compilers but just formula interpreters that use Excel to display output. This means that the level of copy protection they can give is limited. It is widely recognized that a compiled application is the most secure method of protecting intellectual rights.

Because the model is compiled and cannot be accessed without the activation code, it is also possible to add features such as end user license agreements. Therefore, unless the users have agreed to the agreement, the model will not be available for use. This is particularly useful when incorporated into the handover, where the maintainer and sponsor must give their model approval. Importantly for the modeler is they are able to also verify that the model will be used as its build suggests and not in any other way. (You don't want your model used for other purposes.)

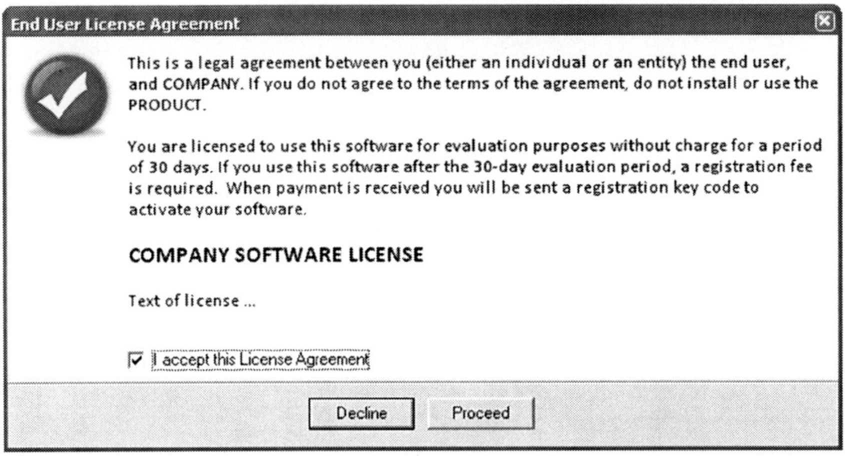

Figure 18-4. LockXLS gives you the option to include an end user license agreement, which means the model can be opened only after the customer accepts the agreement

There are a number of other very useful features to LockXLS that are all geared to protecting the modeler's intellectual property, such as the following:

- The formula construction is fully hidden from the user.
- It is impossible to create a VBA macro to get the formula in your workbook.
- Formula from a protected model cannot be used by an external VBA macro, add-in, or application.
- Formulas cannot be copied.
- Clipboard operations are blocked.
- The user is unable to see, change, or access any of the VBA code.

Why Is This Tool Recommended for Modelers?

Excel lacks any security and access rights, which means anything that is created in the Excel environment is basically insecure. There is a school of thought that believes that if you have provided all the work and efforts and time in building a model and that model reflects the creativity and skills of the modeler, it should not be possible for anyone to just take that and use it without the modeler's permission or paying for the right. As matters stand today, it is relatively easy to copy and reuse models without any reference to the builders. LockXLS has the ability to control how models are used, and in my opinion it is essential to anyone who wants to take their modeling seriously.

Operis Analysis Kit (OAK)

Tool name: OAK

Producer: Operis

Modeling Uses: Spreadsheet model audit and review

Website: www.operisanalysiskit.com

Description

The Operis Analysis Kit (OAK) adds capabilities to Microsoft Excel that are useful to those who develop substantial spreadsheet models and need to quickly understand existing models. OAK is also helpful for those who are formally auditing other people's models and may also need to enforce compliance with regimes that control spreadsheet use, including Sarbanes-Oxley Act. After installing OAK and opening Excel, there will be two additions to the menus, OAK Development and OAK Review. (See Figures 18-5 and 18-6.)

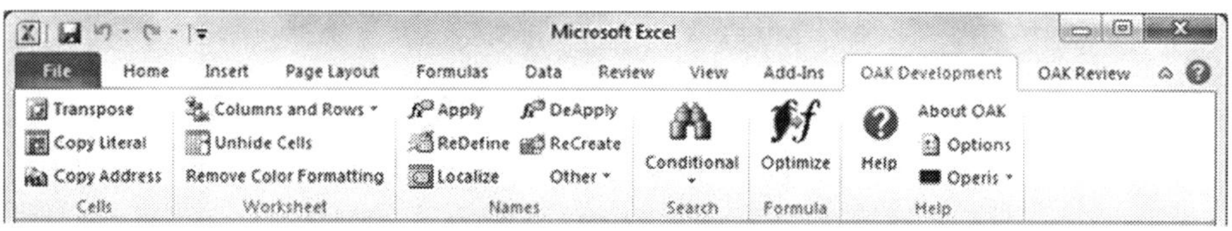

Figure 18-5. The OAK Development tab features several tools that enhance modeling

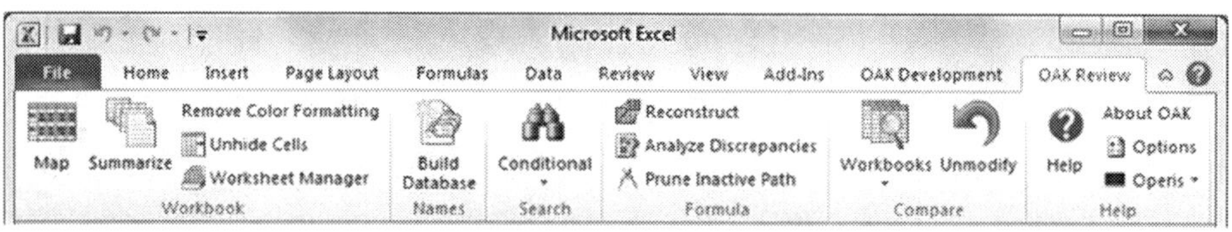

Figure 18-6. The OAK Review tab contains many more tools that that add further functionality to Excel

OAK has so many useful features and tools that not only enhance the use of spreadsheet models but also save time over manual processes. It would not be possible to go through all the capabilities of OAK, but I have included a few here:

- Inserts rows and columns even when they intersect merged cells, arrays, and data tables (which defeat the corresponding commands built into Excel).

- Gives suggestions for optimizing formulas so that they perform the calculation you are attempting more neatly.
- Offers rich options for managing Excel names.
- OAK allows changes on the choice of names, even after they've been extensively referred to in your spreadsheet. (Excel 2007 has at last added something similar, ten years after OAK provided the facility. Users of earlier versions of Excel can benefit from this feature.)
- Removes names from your formulas and turns them back to conventional coordinate notation. For example, if you like to develop spreadsheets using names but your customer doesn't understand them or doesn't like them, you can strip the names out before shipping the worksheet. Conversely, if you receive a spreadsheet that makes extensive use of names in formulas but you are more comfortable with the coordinate notation, OAK will make the necessary transformation for you.
- Provides a list of all the worksheets in a workbook, plus key statistics such as the number of formulas.
- Gives a sortable list of every formula that is distinct (not just a copy of its neighbor), along with a measure of its complexity so that the longer, more error-prone examples can be identified and prioritized.
- Supplies a list of the constants, which can then be checked against source documentation.
- Provides a diagram showing a bird's eye view of the patterns in each worksheet, showing where formulas are copied consistently and inconsistently and where named ranges are located.
- Offers a sortable list of all the names in a workbook and their locations and characteristics.
- Supplies groundbreaking facilities for deciphering the workings of individual spreadsheet calculations.
- Reconstructs formulas to receive automated reperformance of specified calculations and understands which cells they act on.
- Prunes formulas to make calculations easier to understand by showing only the elements that are actually active at the current moment.

- Provides a method of identifying the discrepancies that are preventing your attempt at a parallel reconstruction of a spreadsheet calculation from reproducing the original accurately.
- Compares spreadsheets in a way that is actually usable, distinguishing changes that are real from ones that are merely the consequence of items changing position.

Tip OAK's abilities are so extensive that I would recommend you take a look at `www.operisanalysiskit.com` and download a copy of the tool and license. This tool will become a prime asset for your modeling.

Why Is This Tool Recommended for Modelers?

As a modeler, there are always some aspects to Excel that you wish were implemented as they would make life so much easier. I used to be in that situation regularly. Once you have OAK, however, it's immediately clear how many of these issues can be tackled effectively. This is a tool built by modelers and used by everyone. In other words, OAK is the antibiotic of modeling—it is that essential.

Using Visual Basic for Applications (VBA) in Financial Models

This section is intended to take you through the basic steps of using the Visual Basic editor (VBE) window and writing a simple piece of Visual Basic for Applications (VBA) code. It will show you how to use the VBE, the project explorer, and code windows. You will learn how to write a simple macro to display a "Welcome To Modelers World" message box.

The Visual Basic Editor (VBE) in Excel

For the majority of Excel users, their first and only brush with VBA is with using the macro recording by clicking on the Developer tab and clicking the Record Macro button. It's quite possible that most of these users are unaware that aside from being a spreadsheet application, Excel happens to also be a powerful programming language development platform that is capable of even building applications. You can use VBA code to create macros that can automate tasks in models and moreover give the model a more polished feel. A macro is a procedure written in VBA code that performs definite tasks such as flashing a message on the screen for a specific number of seconds.

Excel's VBA is a complete object-oriented language hidden in VBA projects that are stored and saved within the workbook. Object-orientated programming languages such as VBA or C++ use object structures and hierarchies, and you can even create your own objects. There is a continuing debate as to whether VBA has a place in financial models or not. Some believe that models should not contain VBA and that VBA in models runs contrary to best practice. In some ways, I can understand why some would have this view. It comes from the experience that many have had with VBA, which is often that someone creates some elegant VBA macro that provides all kinds of solutions and then that person leaves the organization. In time, the spreadsheet with the fancy VBA becomes outdated, and the VBA starts to crash and go wrong. Because no one around has VBA programming experience, the file gets trashed under a cloud. To some, VBA in models has overtones of this situation.

However, I am one who does not subscribe to the notion that VBA should not be in models. In fact, I am very much for it. The question any modeler should first ask is this: can any tasks be performed efficiently without VBA? If so, then do it. But if a task is significantly better performed using VBA, why not do it? The challenge is that in order to make sure models don't contain bad VBA, the onus is on modelers to step up to the plate and become accomplished at VBA. If you are a modeler and have an aversion to VBA or are weak in it, then you must not put VBA code into your models until you have become accomplished. The opposite is also true. If you are a modeler who has good working experience of VBA, why not use it in moderation? I use VBA to automate tasks and to assist me with the model building, and then I pull the VBA out of the final model. But now and again, I will include it in the final model. Typically, I use VBA for the following tasks:

- To give a message to the user such as a confidentiality warning or a message to let the user know the status of the model when it is opened
- To perform an internal audit of the model data automatically
- To make a log of the model users with times and dates and to note any changes that were made
- To lock the model so that it cannot be saved as another file name
- To make sure the model always opens on a particular worksheet, irrespective of where it was closed
- To make issue logs for maintenance that are sent directly to the maintainer
- To make printable copies of the outputs and any other data

Basic Understanding of VBA

Let's start by finding where VBA macros are stored. Macros are kept inside hidden VBA projects that are stored and saved within the workbook, of which a typical blank worksheet can be seen in Figure 18-7.

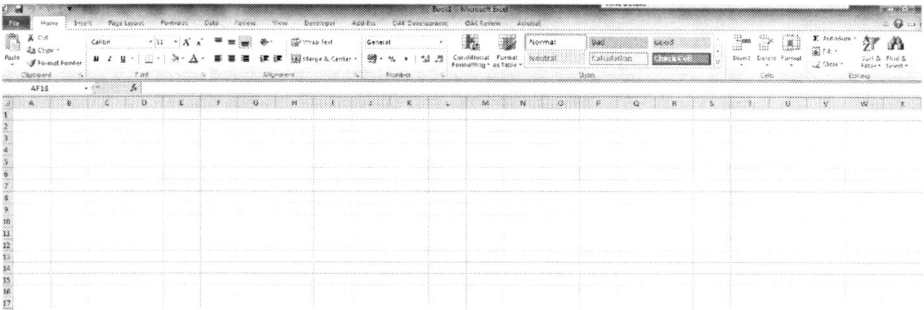

Figure 18-7. This is the typical view of a blank worksheet (Excel 2010)

VBA projects can be accessed through the VBE by pressing ALT+F11 to see the window shown in Figure 18-8.

Figure 18-8. The VBA editor in Excel is accessed by using the combination of the ALT+F11 keys

The editor window contains menus for File, Edit, View, Insert, Format, Debug, Run, Tools, Add-Ins, Window, and Help and opens in a separate window, so there should be no fear of losing any work you have done in your worksheet.

Working with the VBA editor requires a subtle change within the mindset as you need to think very logically about what you want to achieve but also at the same time what you don't want to achieve. Think of it like this: thus far, you have been working with Excel worksheets. Now imagine that each worksheet is a room in a house full of all kinds of objects. Once the VBA editor is opened, which brings up a project window explorer, we can open the doors to all those rooms to the house and each room has several objects in it. The VBA editor allows you to select the room you wish to look at and then further select an object and adjust or tune that object (called properties) according to your preferences at a detailed level.

Coding in VBA for Modelers

This section will introduce the VBA project and take you through writing some VBA code.

VBA Project Explorer and Code Windows

The VBA editor (which is sometimes referred to as the VBE) project explorer shows a project tree on the left-hand side of the screen below the menu and toolbar. If you click a branch of the tree, you'll enter that particular workbook or worksheet from the VBE.

The VBA project is the root of the tree, and the workbook and worksheet objects are the branches coming off the tree. As you add and delete worksheets or workbooks, the branches of the tree change to reflect the new worksheets or workbooks being created. Therefore, what you can now see is a list of currently loaded workbooks and the worksheets within an explorer. I mentioned earlier that VBA is an object-orientated language, which means everything in the explorer is an object including the workbook and worksheets.

There are some introductory steps to using the editor that I will go through to help you become familiar with the editor. This is by no means a tutorial on coding in VBA, and indeed I would recommend that you invest in a good introductory VBA guide such as *Definitive Guide to Excel VBA* (second edition) by Michael Kofler (Apress, 2003) or *Excel VBA Programming for Dummies* (third edition) by John Walkenbach (For Dummies, 2013).

Your first point of call is to double-click ThisWorkbook in the left project pane. The workbook object opens in the right pane, which is blank in Figure 18-9.

Figure 18-9. ThisWorkbook is now activated, and a blank editing sheet is open on the right

If you try and type something into the blank space, you will get a message box informing you that there is a compile error similar to that in Figure 18-10.

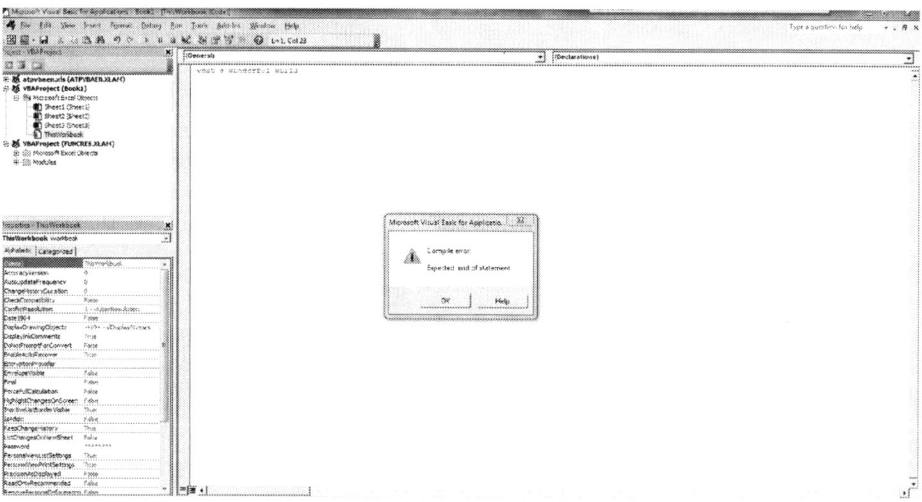

Figure 18-10. There is a compile error because the message written has been recognized and does not conform to VBA coding structures

This error is like a guide. It's likely that when you begin working with VBA, this message and others like it will become familiar because like any programming language VBA implies upon the user several strict structures. This error has occurred because you have typed in some arbitrary natural language and haven't followed the rules about how to enter VBA code. Behind this seemingly innocuous blank sheet is a system called a compiler, which you can think of as an interpreter. The compiler takes written messages that are typed into the editor and converts them into instructions that your computer can then understand and thus execute.

Note Although computing has come a long way in its relatively short history, it has yet to achieve the ability to understand everyday written and spoken language. Therefore, the compiler is required to sit in between the human interface and the machine, and as a result, we need to learn to write in a specific code.

Close the error message and delete the message that caused it to appear. Then click the drop-down list in the top left corner of the blank sheet with the word "General" as per Figure 18-11.

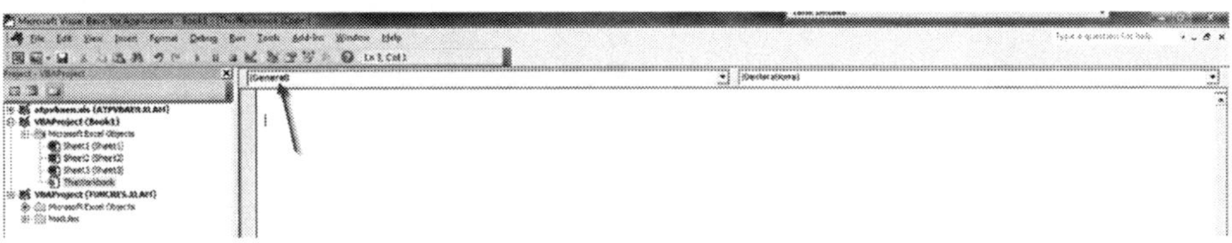

Figure 18-11. The general drop-down is the starting point for placing the VBA code

Using the drop-down, choose the option for "workbook." You will then see that there has been an automatic placement of some code into the blank sheet, as shown in Figure 18-12.

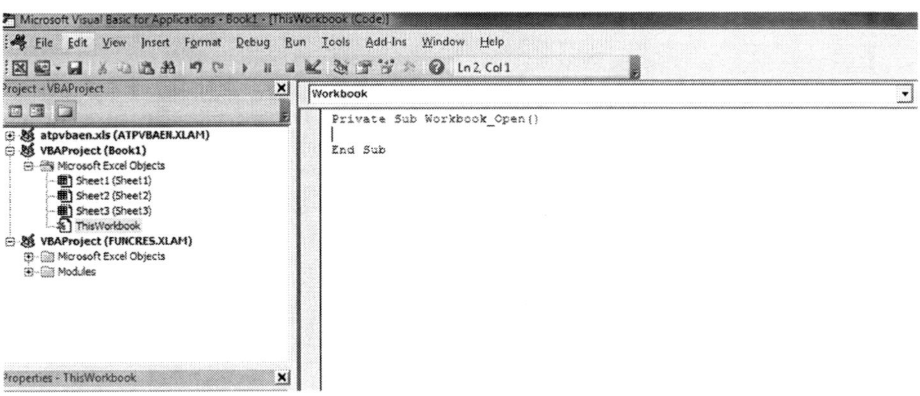

Figure 18-12. The VBE has automatically placed the workbook Open subroutine as the starting point

This is called subroutine, and specifically, it is an event. VBA has several types of events, which you should think of in exactly the same way as we use the term "event" in common language. It is an observable occurrence or a phenomenon. The event that has been automatically selected for us by clicking on workbook from the drop-down is the Open event on the workbook. Therefore, the editor is expecting some code to be placed between the starting lines and the ending lines. Once you've added the correct code, the editor will execute the subroutine when the workbook is opened. If at this point you are unclear with the process, go back over these last few paragraphs. This event is one of the most applied types of coding that is used in modeling. Here is another point to understand before I go any further. I mentioned that there are a number of events available to use. On the top right of the window, click the Open drop-down and there will be a list of many event types called declarations, as shown in Figure 18-13.

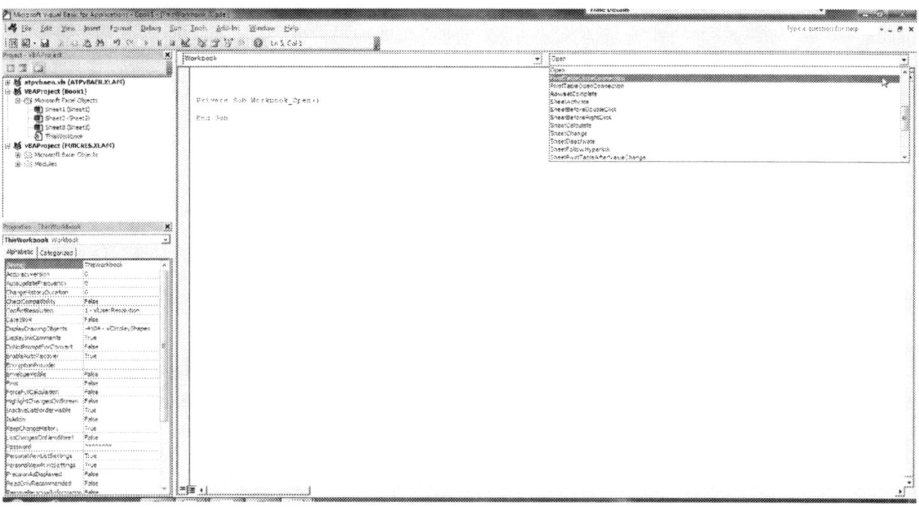

Figure 18-13. The drop down list in the VBE has a list of events

It's important to note that although the editor always places the Open event automatically, you don't have to stay with this event—you can choose any event that is on that list. In order to do so, just delete the Open event and click on the event you require in the declaration list shown in Figure 18-13.

I do have a note of caution. When you delete any events that you do not want to write code against make sure both the starting line and the last line that has End Sub are deleted. A common mistake is to leave partial code in the code window while the other part is deleted, and therefore, you end up with a subroutine that is missing its pair and becomes delinquent. This mistake will cause an error once the code is executed, and believe me, this type of error is extremely frustrating. It has to be checked manually and can be very difficult to spot, particularly when there are hundreds of lines of code. Consider yourself warned.

Now I will instruct you on how to create a simple macro with some VBA code. With the Open event displayed, click the declaration list drop-down, and directly above the Open event, click the NewSheet event. An event will be placed in the editor above the Open event, which should look like Figure 18-14.

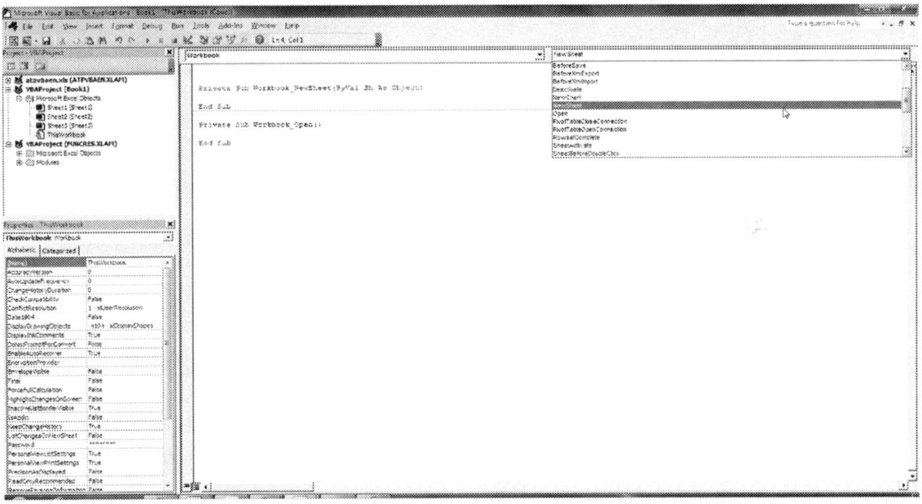

Figure 18-14. The NewSheet event has now been chosen and inserted above the Open event

Type the following into the NewSheet event between the first and last lines:

```
MsgBox "Welcome to Modelers World."
```

In this instance, I have asked you to use a defined code word called `MsgBox`, which in VBA will call up a message box (you can see how the code language is not far removed from English language but still has some way to go before it's completely intuitive). But when using a defined code word such as the `MsgBox`, you need to stick to the syntax of the language exactly. So in this instance, don't be tempted to change the case to the code, such as `MSGBOX`. It should remain as lowercase. Otherwise, it will cause a compile error. In many instances, the editor will recognize which defined word you are trying to enact and correct it by using a predictive algorithm. However, do not rely on this because often it will predict something different than what you want. Note also that once you have placed the punctuation marks after `MsgBox`, you can insert whatever you wish in between them. Figure 18-15 should resemble what you have in the editor to this point.

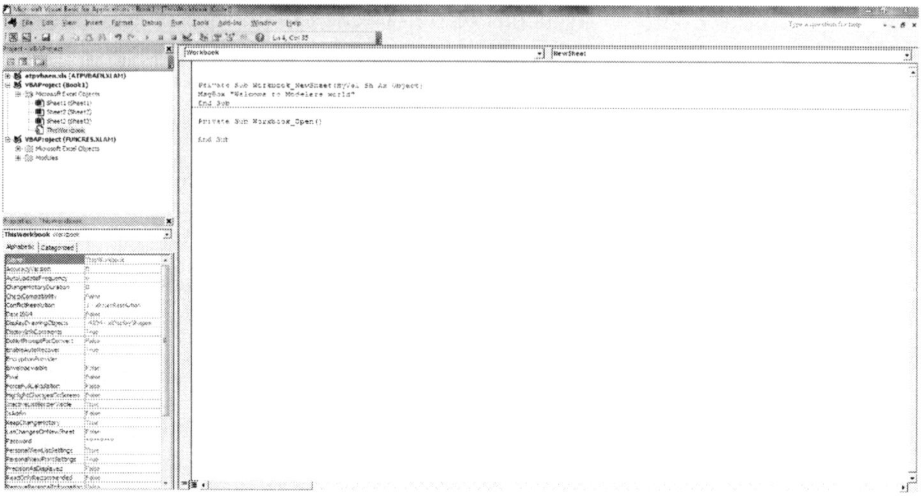

Figure 18-15. The MsgBox defined text is used to generate a message box

The `MsgBox` code is one I use in some of my models, as it's a very potent method of imparting information about the model based on a particular event occurring. For example, when a model is opened, you can provide a disclaimer message or share a warning to the user. While it's possible to make fairly sophisticated message boxes, I am not sure that plays well in models. It's always a good idea to avoid creating overly complex code when something simpler can be just as effective. I would advise that you stay with simple message boxes, which are sufficient.

You may have noticed that after you type in the word `MsgBox`, a box containing all the parameters for this defined word command is displayed. This can be useful in informing you about which parameters are required and what order is required for that function.

A concern that I have come across from modelers with VBA code is how to use it in the actual worksheets of the model. There are different ways to accomplish this task by using controls such as buttons, links, or automated functions. To see the code run, return to Excel, right-click on the sheet name (for instance, Sheet1), then click Insert, which will insert a new sheet and execute the NewSheet event you just defined (see Figure 18-16).

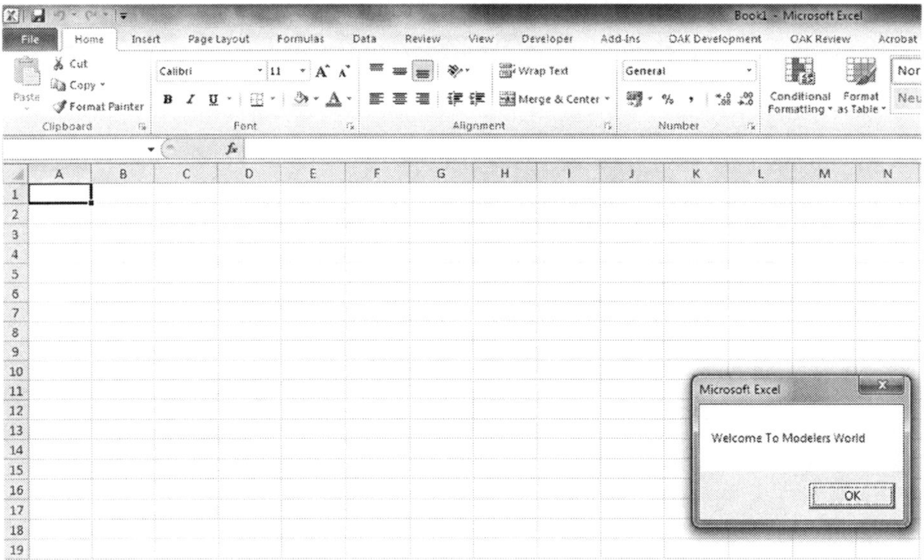

Figure 18-16. The "Modelers world" message box can be seen running from your VBA code

Again, keep in mind that this is just an introduction to VBA. You will need to develop what you have read here further, but if you found this difficult and challenging, you should take heart that as a modeler, you do not have to be a VBA expert. In fact, VBA is not the be-all and end-all of modeling. But sometimes VBA is necessary, and you need to be comfortable with using it. Your understanding of VBA should be at a level where you can write viable code. The good news is that even coming from a point of never having seen VBA before, you should be able to become reasonably accomplished within months (rather than years) for modeling. Hang in there and give it your best shot.

Case Study: How VBA Benefits Models

VBA has often been the focus of contention in financial modeling. The issue is whether financial models should incorporate VBA or not, and opinions vary depending on whom you ask. The reasons for and against can be just as varied but ultimately they all lead to the robustness of the coding.

There can be no worse situation than taking possession of a model that seems to function appropriately, only to then have an error message appear out of blue that halts the model's operations and has little or no explanation and no help as to how to rectify the problem. Unfortunately, this is an experience many users of financial models that have VBA have come across, and it has tainted their appreciation for VBA. The alternative is to build a model that has no VBA code at all.

So where do I stand? VBA is integral to modeling and by dismissing it, all that happens is that we diminish the creativity and possibilities available to the modeler.

Why Is VBA Good for Modeling?

There are a number of reasons why VBA is good for modeling and on the whole, VBA can bring more good things than bad things. These next few sections will describe the advantages with VBA.

Reduces Manual Time

With some careful thought and application, it is very possible to create VBA tools and routines that cut out much of the manual time when building models. I have created VBA routines that can analyze data and then pull out specific information I request and populate a table with it. Or the tool can check through an entire model and look for redundant formulas (formulas that lead to nowhere). Creating these routines is very quick; the hard part is just understanding what it is that you want.

Provides Quicker Processing Times

The truth is when used correctly VBA is fast. In fact, it's hundreds of times faster at processing large quantities of information than pure formulas. Often I have been shown a model by a customer that has VBA code, and unfortunately the VBA seems to have slowed down the whole functionality of the model. On closer inspection, it's obvious why. I find that modelers of Excel users who are not totally proficient at VBA will sometimes make the mistake of creating code that reads and acts on information in the worksheet cells. Then when there is a large data set, the code will run the subroutine of every single cell. As a result, this cycle will cause the VBA to run slowly, and it's not the best way to code. In fact, code should be created to work within the code itself.

Utilizes Events

This is not a well-understood point, but let me explain. When modeling, the modeler should always have an eye squarely fixed on the user's experience. Modelers should be thinking how the user can use and get the best out of the model. With this viewpoint modelers should be anticipating not only what the users are going to do, but also what they are capable of doing, and this is often not clear.

By using VBA judicially, it is possible to build code that can look for specific events that occur and provide guidance to the user. For instance, what happens if the user makes input changes to the model and closes it without saving? Believe me, this is possible. It's also possible to create VBA code that will always create a backup copy whenever there have been changes made to models. So in this case, the VBA code will execute in the event that a change is made.

Enhances the Model User's Experience

There are several aspects to modeling that could be enhanced, and often the only way is by using VBA. In some of the very large models that I have created, I have provided a context-sensitive help system. For example, when users are viewing a balance sheet, they can receive information about financial statements. There is also an automated self-audit. This means that when the model is closed, a specific VBA code will run and check the status of the model and make a record of the inputs and the results of the outputs based on those inputs and will then place this information in an archive for audit. This is useful for model maintenance because if something goes wrong with the model, it's possible to check its status before the issue happened.

There can be little doubt that VBA can benefit modeling. The question should not be how VBA can benefit modeling, but more about establishing best practice guidelines that will ensure that VBA in models adheres to a set of principles, which will benefit models and the user.

CHAPTER

19

What Is the Future of Financial Modeling?

There was a certain amount of trepidation on my part when I wrote this chapter, most notably, that I was looking into the future of financial modeling. There are several aspects of modeling for which it's possible to make pretty accurate predictions about the future, but it's always wise to use caution because financial modeling is intrinsically linked to the performance of business and finance. Drastic changes in either—as was the case with the financial crisis of 2007–2008 or the downfall of Enron in 2001—will affect its future. Nevertheless, it's still a good idea to take a look at what we can expect in financial modeling in the future.

Future Demand for Financial Modeling

The future for financial modeling is certain to be one of increasing use for modelers and models. This is clearly the case when you look at history. Before the turn of the century, financial modeling was still a relatively niche business discipline that was only adopted in certain sectors of business such as investment banking and public-private funding schemes. Today, however, financial modeling is considered in a number of sectors as crucial, and it's possible to find modeling adopted in practice in several industries such as utilities, oil and gas, telecommunications, retail banking, business process outsourcing, and so on.

Further, businesses are awake to the value that good financial modeling can enable organizations to model the effects of varying economic and environmental scenarios on an organization's performance. A decent financial model infuses confidence among financial institutions, and more often it is now a requirement to provide banks with robust models when looking forward to securing financing.

Investments in infrastructure projects such as roads, airports, and alternative power have been subjected to the need for accurate modeling, which ensures that the business case has a sound financial basis.

This means that financial modeling will continue to gain usage across business and industry for the future, and I fully expect the use of models to increase at a quicker pace than in the past, as more companies realize how useful good modeling can be for their business.

The Future Financial Modeler

All this increase in demand is bound to have an effect on the modeler, and it's certain there will be fundamental movements in the capability and certification of the modeler of the future from that of today. Nowadays, the focus is very much on building the model and less on how it's built and who has built it. But this will change because so much is at stake in so many areas of business. There are major risks involved in relying on models as a big part of a business case without ensuring the modeler is credible. There are murmurs of this weakness already happening in finance. The problem stems from the point that many people who model today are not really financial modelers. Some are spreadsheet experts because they are very accomplished at using Excel and are thus considered to be financial modelers, until something goes wrong with the thinking behind the model. The difference between a bona fide financial modeler and a modeler who dabbles then becomes apparent.

I fully expect that the financial modeler of the future will be altogether a much more rounded individual than is apparent today. There are increasing demands on modelers to go beyond being just being able to build models. There are expectations now that when an organization hires or takes on a modeler, they are getting someone with the following abilities:

- Capable of applying commercial sense to models
- Understands and can apply complex financial principles to models and can demonstrate that experience

- Understands the implications of risk and can model for this
- Able to communicate and work with people from various business functions
- Can manage a project
- Capable of interpreting the results of the models and presenting them to a wide audience that includes banks, investors, senior staff, and the public
- Bound by some code of ethics, which does not mean the modeler must have an accounting background but has followed some professional training route in the past

Don't get me wrong, there are modelers today who not only check all the boxes I have mentioned, but also have several more skills that I have not included. But there are also a great many modelers who would not be able to check even half of these. Don't be surprised to find financial modeling going through a period of establishing some worldwide accreditation, such as an association of financial modelers that has some vetting process to ensure that its members have credibility and can fulfill the requirements placed on them by companies. The increase and the profile of modeling projects in the future will necessitate that there is some rigor placed on the practitioner.

Developments, Changes, and Evolutions in Financial Modeling

Some of the big developments that must and will come for financial modeling will be in compliance. Many of the leading players who develop tools or software for spreadsheets and modeling are already hotly developing methods that will ensure that anyone using their products is compliant with rules and regulations such as Sarbanes-Oxley Act. This aspect will develop further because the repercussions of falling foul of any of these rules are great and generally falls to the officers of the organization. I do see an end to the days when modelers can freely create and build around the financial statements in their models without some review or checks.

The other evolution is around how models are built. There is best practice modeling that is now entrenched; however, there is no one prescribed methodology. Instead, there are several differing methods of building models—all with their own individual reasons why theirs is best. However, rather like software development took some time to develop its idiosyncratic life cycle methodology, I am certain modeling will evolve in this manner. In the future, there will be a financial modeling life cycle that will become the ideal and accepted process of how to develop and deliver models to a standard.

Now That You Have Read This Book

Over the course of this book, I have given many insights into financial modeling and how modelers can prepare themselves to take on a modeling project. By reading this book, my hope is that you will find that modeling can be very interesting and you can carry on to pursue modeling as a career.

There are several sources of information now available in the public domain about modeling, and you would definitely benefit by getting involved in some online discussions about modeling. I would recommend going to `www.linkedin.com` and joining groups that focus on financial modeling like the Association of Financial Modellers.

There so many challenges and new ideas that can be learned through modeling. I always find it so rewarding that by building models, I can get firsthand and in-depth experience about an industry or organization that would otherwise be unavailable to me.

With that insight comes responsibility: first, that the customer requirements are delivered exactly and on time, and second, that whatever the circumstance, always build models from an impartial position so that the models you produce reflect not the modeler, but the current conditions.

My parting advice is that no matter what types of models you are building, never be afraid to challenge the organization by asking questions. Don't just accept the status quo; seek to learn and then supplant your skills and creativity on every model. The boundaries on how to model are as yet undiscovered. Make modeling your creation.

APPENDIX

A

Keyboard Shortcuts

Provided is a table of Excel keyboard shortcuts. This is not a full list of shortcuts but is a selection based on their relevancy for modeling. The best method of learning these shortcuts is to refer to this appendix as you use Excel to tackle a situation.

Alt + =	Insert the SUM formula
Alt + F1	Insert a Chart Sheet
Alt + F11	Display the VB Editor
Alt + F8	Display the Macro dialog box
Alt + Shift + F1	Insert worksheet
F1	Open online Help or the Office Assistant
F2	Edit active cell
F5	Go to
F7	Check spelling
F9	Calculate all sheets
F11	Create chart
Shift + F2	Edit cell comment
Shift + F3	Insert a function into a formula
Shift + F5	Search

(*continued*)

Shift + F9	Calculate active worksheet
Shift + F10	Display shortcut menu
Shift + Space	Select entire row
Shift + arrow key	Extend selection by one cell
Ctrl + ; (semicolon)	Insert current date
Ctrl + 9	Hide row
Ctrl + C	Copy selected area
Ctrl + End	Move to the end of the spreadsheet
Ctrl + F1	Search
Ctrl + F12	Open
Ctrl + K	Insert hyperlink
Ctrl + N	New workbook
Ctrl + O	Open
Ctrl + P	Print
Ctrl + Arrow key	Move to the edge of the current data region
Ctrl+ R	Cells to copy cell contents from left
Ctrl + Shift + Enter	Enter a formula as an array formula
Ctrl + Shift + Space	Select all cells
Ctrl + Shift + O	Select all cells with comments
Ctrl + Shift + arrow key	Extend the selection to the last nonblank cell
Ctrl + V	Paste from Clipboard
Ctrl + Y	Repeat the last action
Ctrl + Z	Undo the last action

APPENDIX

B

Finance and Accounting Glossary

Income Statement Terms

The following is a list of terms and their definitions that are used in income statements.

Term	Detail
Cost of Goods Sold	For a retail or wholesale business, it is the total price paid for the products sold plus the cost of having them delivered to the store during the accounting period. For a manufacturing firm, it is the beginning inventory plus purchases, delivery costs, material, labor, and overhead minus the ending inventory.
Gross Profit	This is the amount before operating expenses and federal taxes have been deducted.
Income Before Taxes	This is the operating income plus other incomes.
Net Income	Before taxes minus income taxes—this is what the business earned during the period. It is added to the balance sheet and increases the net worth. This term is often called net profit or net earnings.

(*continued*)

Term	Detail
Net Sales	This is the total dollar volume of all cash or credit sales less returns, allowances, discounts, and rebates.
Operating Expenses	These are the selling expenses, administrative expenses, and overhead expenses required to run the business. It excludes cost of goods sold, interest, and income tax expense. Examples of these costs are rent, utilities, and administrative departments such as accounting, marketing, human resources, etc.
Operating Income	This is the amount left over after subtracting operating expenses from gross profit.

Cash Flow Statement Terms

The following is a list of terms and their definitions that are used in cash flow statements.

Term	Detail
Cash Sales	This is the cash received from customers for goods sold and services performed.
Equipment	This is the money spent to acquire equipment (fixed assets) required to run or expand the business.
Furniture and Fixtures	This is the money spent on procuring furniture and fixtures for the organization.
Income Taxes	This is the money paid to the authorities on profits and other income earned.
Interest Received	This is the money received from deposits, cash invested in money, and other external investments.
Inventory	This is the money used to purchase items held for sale or used during the manufacture of products that will be sold.
Investment Contribution	This is the cash given to an organization for an interest in the ownership of the business (usually stock).
Loans/Borrowing	These are funds received from financial institutions or investors by the issuing of a debt.
Operating Expenses	This is the cash used to pay costs arising from the day-to-day operating of the organization such as salaries, rent, and utilities.

Balance Sheet Terms

The following is a list of terms and their definitions that are used in balance sheets.

Term	Detail
Accounts Payable	Also known as creditors, this is the total amount of money owed by the organization to all suppliers on credit.
Accounts Receivable	Also known as debtors, this is the total amount owed to the organization by suppliers but the cash has not yet been received.
Accruals	These are costs and expenses that have been accumulated against current profits but have not yet been physically paid for.
Assets	This is the value of all cash, land, buildings, equipment, and inventory that an organization owns.
Cash	These are items immediately accessible to be used as cash.
Common Stock	This is money provided to the organization in order to have a piece of ownership by parties who will then become investors in the organization.
Current Assets	This is the total of all cash, accounts receivable, inventory, and any other item that can be converted into cash in less than 12 months.
Current Liabilities	This is the money that is due to the organization during the course of its activities that will be paid within 12 months.
Depreciation	An accounting procedure that puts a valuation on the physical assets of an organization over the assets' useful life.
Fixed Assets	These assets can be land, buildings, furniture and fixtures, equipment, patents, and goodwill.
Inventory	This is the total amount of physical goods owned by the organization intended to generate revenue irrespective of its state (raw or finished) or its location.
Liabilities	This is everything that a company owes to creditors.
Retained Earnings	This is the profit that is kept in the organization and thus has not been allocated to shareholders.
Owner's Equity	This is the difference between assets and liabilities, which in theory is the amount due to shareholders.

APPENDIX

C

Ready-Made Functions

Listed are a number of functions that I have found useful for modeling that you can copy and use. These functions will be beneficial to have in your function library. I have provided a list of these functions and a short brief on how to enter them. Before working with these functions, be sure to read Chapter 18, particularly the section on using the Visual Basic Editor (VBE).

Adding Functions

1. Open the Visual Basic Editor (VBE) from Tools ➤ Macro ➤ VBE (Keys: ALT+F11). In the Project Explorer pane, select VBAProject (Book1). This selects the empty workbook (Figure C-1).

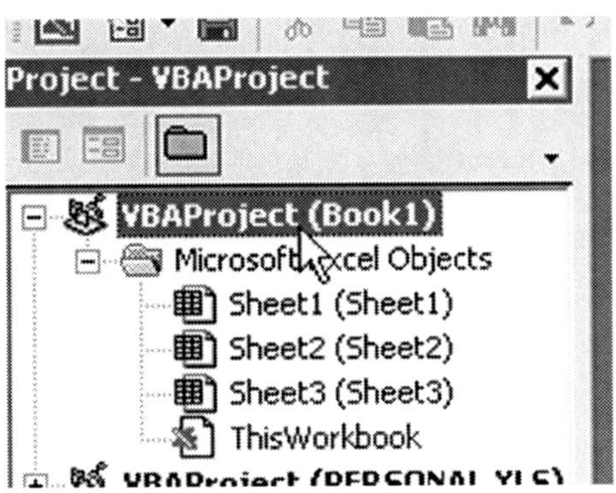

Figure C-1. The VBA Project window has a list of all the worksheet objects in the current workbook

2. If you were already working in Excel, the name might be different. Check the name in the title bar of the Excel window if you aren't sure. If the Project Explorer is not visible, open it by going to View ➤ Project Explorer.
3. From the Insert menu, choose Module (Figure C-2). This adds a new empty code module to the selected workbook. You will also see the module appear in the Project Explorer pane.

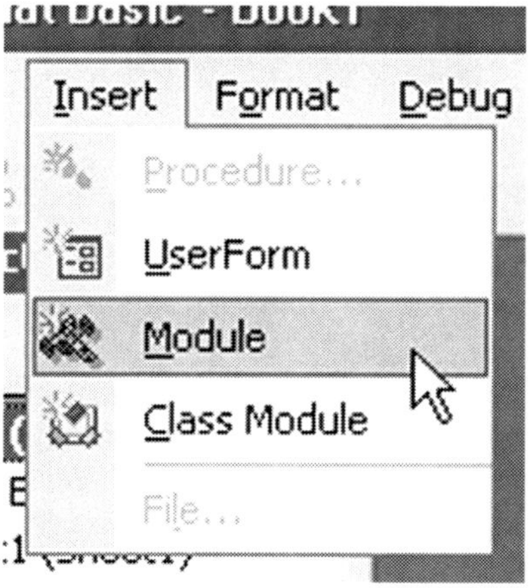

Figure C-2. The Insert menu is where you add the module. This brings up the code windows, where you type the code

Find Saturday

The key feature of this function is not that it finds Saturday but that you can change the weekday to any day that you choose. I use this function when I need a specific weekday to trigger some event.

Here's the code:

```
Public FunctionFindSaturday(InputDate As Date)
' Returns the date of the first Saturday following the Inputdate
   FindSaturday = FormatDateTime(InputDate + (7 - Weekday(InputDate)))
End Function
```

Remove Spaces

This particular function removes spaces from text, but its strongest asset is that it can be modified to remove just about anything simply by changing the strInput " " to whatever you need. This is an extremely useful function when dealing with data, particularly CSV files.[1]

Here's the code:

```
Public Function RemoveSpaces(strInput As String)
' Removes all spaces from a string of text
Test:
   If InStr(strInput, " ") = 0 Then
      RemoveSpaces = strInput
   Else
      strInput = Left(strInput, InStr(strInput, " ") - 1) _
      & Right(strInput, Len(strInput) - InStr(strInput, " "))
      GoTo Test
   End If
End Function
```

Sum Colors

This function calculates totals based on colors. It's very useful when reviewing models as you can color-code specific cells and use this code to check the values based on those colors.

```
Function SumColor(rColor As Range, rSumRange As Range)
'Sums cells based on a specified fill color.

        Dim rCell As Range

        Dim iCol As Integer

        Dim vResult

        iCol = rColor.Interior.ColorIndex
                For Each rCell In rSumRange
                        If rCell.Interior.ColorIndex = iCol Then
                                vResult = WorksheetFunction.Sum(rCell) + vResult
                        End If
```

[1]CSV stands for Comma Separated Values. A CSV file is a text document that can be read by Excel and all the Microsoft office applications.

```
            Next rCell
        SumColor = vResult
End Function
```

Count Colors

This function will count a range of cells based on their fill color. It is activated by choosing a fill color and pointing the formula to the cell and then choosing the range to count, as in Figure C-3.

```
Function CountColor(rColor As Range, rSumRange As Range)
'Counts cells based on a specified fill color
Dim rCell As Range
Dim iCol As Integer
Dim vResult
iCol = rColor.Interior.ColorIndex
   For Each rCell In rSumRange
    If rCell.Interior.ColorIndex = iCol Then
         vResult = vResult + 1
    End If
   Next rCell
CountColor = vResult
End Function
```

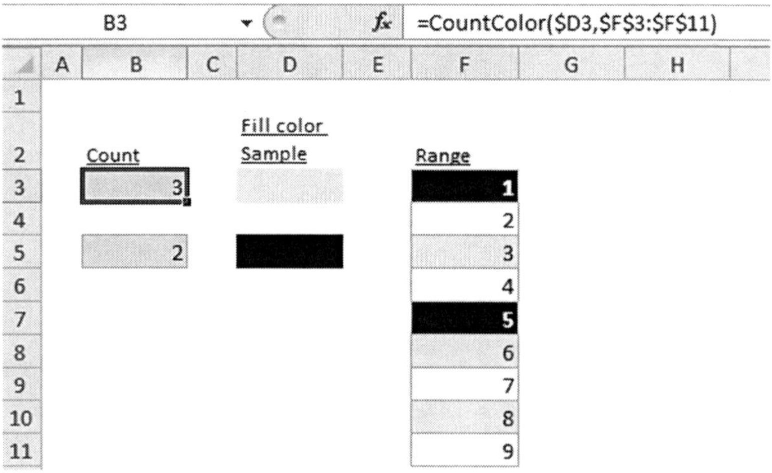

Figure C-3. The CountColor() function used will count the number of cells in a range that conform to the designated color

Sort Using Colors

This is another of the sort functions. With this function, you can apply different colors and assign a sort priority, is useful for checking and testing data.

Here's the code:

```
Function ColorRank(ColorOrder As Range, LookCell As Range)

        Dim i As Integer
        Dim ICol1 As Integer
        Dim ICol2 As Integer
        i = 1
        ICol2 = -1
        ColorRank = 0
        'Loop until match is found
        Do Until ICol1 = ICol2
                'Replace "Interior" with Font to sort by Font color
                ICol1 = ColorOrder(i, 1).Interior.ColorIndex
                ICol2 = LookCell.Interior.ColorIndex

                        If i = ColorOrder.Rows.Count + 1 Then
                                'No Match found place in Text
                                ColorRank = "No color match!!!"
                        Exit Do                 End If

                'Pass the Row number of the color match
                ColorRank = i
                i = i + 1
        Loop
End Function
```

Sum the Bottom and Top Numbers in a Range

I use this function to test the validity of data when it has been copied again or refreshed to test if there have been any changes.

Here's the code:

```
Function SumTopBottomN(rRange As Range, N As Long, Optional bBottomN As
Boolean) As Single
Dim strAddress As String
On Error Resume Next
strAddress = rRange.Address
    If bBottomN = False Then
        SumTopBottomN = Evaluate("=SUMPRODUCT((" _
            & strAddress & ">=LARGE(" & strAddress & "," & X & "))*
(" & strAddress & "))")
```

```
    Else
       SumTopBottomN = Evaluate("=SUMPRODUCT((" _
            & strAddress & "<=SMALL(" & strAddress & "," & X & "))*(" &
strAddress & "))")
    End If
End Function
```

You will use this formula in one of two ways.

=SumTopBottomN($A$2:$A$100,10) For top 10

OR

=SumTopBottomN($A$2:$A$100,10,TRUE) For bottom 10

Remove Formula

This function is used for presentation purposes or when sending a copy of the outputs worksheet by e-mail and you don't want any links or formulas in that copy.

Here's the code:

```
Sub Remove_All_Formulas_In_All_Sheets  'No_formula_Macro()
  'Striping a workbook of formulas
  Dim SH As Worksheet
  For Each SH In Worksheets
    SH.Activate
    Application.ScreenUpdating = False
    Cells.Select
    Selection.Copy
    Selection.PasteSpecial Paste:=xlValues, Operation:=xlNone, _
      SkipBlanks:= False, Transpose:=False
  Next
End Sub
```

Replace External Links with Their Values

I cannot count how many times I have used this function because I use it so often. This function will look at any external links, which can be a real nuisance, and replace them with values.

Here's the code:

```
Sub Tester3()
Dim cell As Range
For Each cell In ActiveSheet.UsedRange.SpecialCells(xlFormulas)
  If InStr(cell.Formula, "[") Then
    cell.Formula = cell.Value
  End If
Next
End Sub
```

Collect Statistics on the Worksheet

I use this function on models that require a review, and I begin with an initial sweep of the model to understand what I am dealing with. This function provides me with enough information to allow me to decide how to approach the review. The type of information this function provides includes the number of formulas, the location's last row or last column, and the number of errors.

Here's the code:

```
Function SheetStats()
'Note in XL97 and above xlcelltypeconstants and xlcelltypeformula
Set rng1 = ActiveSheet.UsedRange
On Error Resume Next
numConstants = rng1.SpecialCells(xlConstants).Count
If Err <> 0 Then numConstants = 0: Err = 0
numerrors = rng1.SpecialCells(xlConstants, xlErrors).Count
If Err <> 0 Then numerrors = 0: Err = 0
numLogical = rng1.SpecialCells(xlConstants, xlLogical).Count
If Err <> 0 Then numLogical = 0: Err = 0
numText = rng1.SpecialCells(xlConstants, xlTextValues).Count
If Err <> 0 Then numText = 0: Err = 0
numNumbers = rng1.SpecialCells(xlConstants, xlNumbers).Count
If Err <> 0 Then numNumbers = 0: Err = 0
numformulas = rng1.SpecialCells(xlFormulas).Count
If Err <> 0 Then numformulas = 0: Err = 0
numBlanks = rng1.SpecialCells(xlBlanks).Count
If Err <> 0 Then numBlanks = 0: Err = 0

Msg = "Address:      " & Chr(9) & rng1.Address & Chr(10) & _
      "Last Row:     " & Chr(9) & rng1.Rows(rng1.Rows.Count).Row & Chr(10) &
_
      "Last Column: " & Chr(9) & rng1.Columns(rng1.Columns.Count).Column &
Chr(10) & _
      "Total Cells: " & Chr(9) & rng1.Count & Chr(10) & _
      "    Formulas: " & Chr(9) & numformulas & Chr(10) & _
      "    Blanks:   " & Chr(9) & numBlanks & Chr(10) & _
      "    Constants:" & Chr(9) & numConstants & Chr(10)
```

```
Mg2 = "Errors:        " & Chr(9) & numerrors & Chr(10) & _
      "Logical:       " & Chr(9) & numLogical & Chr(10) & _
      "Text:          " & Chr(9) & numText & Chr(10) & _
      "Numbers:       " & Chr(9) & numNumbers

 title1 = "SheetStats for " & Application.ActiveSheet.Name & _
      " in " & Application.ActiveWorkbook.FullName

 iANS = MsgBox(Msg & Mg2, , title1)

End Function
```

Look Up Information in All Sheets in an Excel Workbook

This function allows you to look up a specific number or text throughout the workbook. I use this function to check models to see if the inputs are being used correctly or if there are any duplicate inputs in the model.

This function has the same syntax as Excel's VLOOKUP. The only difference is that it will look in all worksheets and stop at the first match.

Here's the code:

```
Function VLOOKAllSheets(Look_Value As Variant, Tble_Array As Range, _
                          Col_num as Integer, Optional Range_look as Boolean)
'Use VLOOKUP to Look across ALL Worksheets and stops at the first match
found.
Dim wSheet As Worksheet
Dim vFound
On Error Resume Next
        For Each wSheet In ActiveWorkbook.Worksheets
                With wSheet
                Set Tble_Array = .Range(Tble_Array.Address)
                        vFound = WorksheetFunction.VLookup _
                        (Look_Value, Tble_Array, _
                        Col_num, Range_look)
                End With
                If Not IsEmpty(vFound) Then Exit For
        Next wSheet
        Set Tble_Array = Nothing
        VLOOKAllSheets = vFound

End Function
```

APPENDIX

D

Sample Outputs

Included in this appendix are some output samples that I have come across in financial models. You should be aware that there are no prescribed or standard outputs for models, although the financial statements such as the income statement, cash flow, and balance sheet are usually required. Much depends on who owns the model and their requirements.

Pricing Summary

This output can be used to summarize revenues, costs, and margins for a pricing model (Figure D-1).

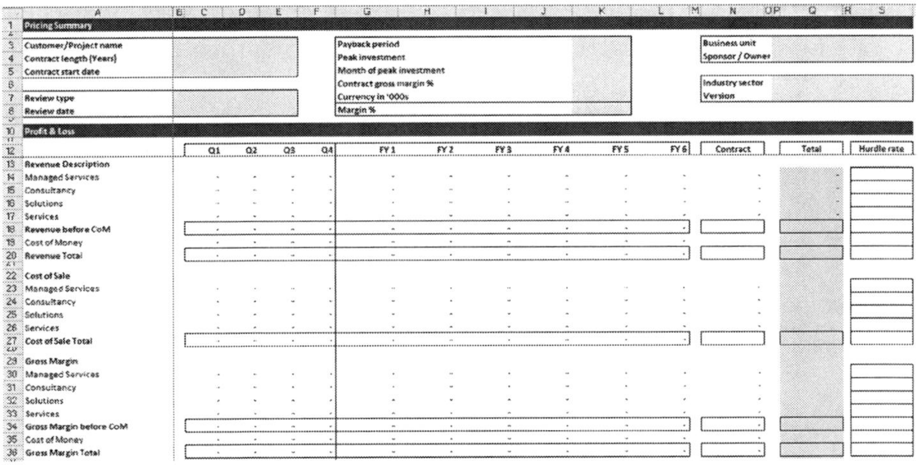

Figure D-1. A pricing summary is shown here

Financial Plan

This output sets out all the key drivers of a financial plan (Figure D-2).

	B	C	D	E
1	**Financial Plan**			
3	**Inputs**			
4	**A) Revenue plan**			
5		**Year 1**	**Year 2**	**Year 3**
6		300,000	600,000	750,000
8	**B) Annual taxation**	30%	30%	30%
11	**Assumptions**			
13	Annual price increase %	-	-	-
14	Annual inflation %	-	-	-
15	Interest rate cash balance %	-	-	-
17	**Interest income**			
18	Loans, including fees	-	-	-
19	Interest and dividends on investment securities	-	-	-
20	Taxable	-	-	-
21	Other	-	-	-
22	**Total Interest income**	-	-	-
24	**Interest Expense**			
25	Interest on deposits	-	-	-
26	Interest on other borrowings	-	-	-
27	Other	-	-	-
28	**Total interest expense**	-	-	-
30	**Noninterest income**			
31	Service charges	-	-	-
32	Loan placement fees	-	-	-
33	Gain on sale of securities	-	-	-
34	Gain on sale of fixed assets	-	-	-
35	Other	-	-	-
36	**Total noninterest income**	-	-	-

Figure D-2. A financial plan is shown here

Balance Sheet Summary

The balance sheet is often shown and summarized over a set number of years. Figure D-3 is part of that summary.

	B	C	D	E	F
1	**Balance Sheet Summary**				
3	**Assets**				
4		**Initial Balance**	**Year 1**	**Year 2**	**Year 3**
5	Cash and due from banks	-	-	-	-
6	**Cash and cash equivalents**	-	-	-	-
8	Securities available for sale	-	-	-	-
9	Securities held to maturity	-	-	-	-
10	**Total investment securities**	-	-	-	-
12	Loans and leases	-	-	-	-
13	Unearned fees	-	-	-	-
14	Allowance for credit losses	-	-	-	-
15	**Total loans**	-	-	-	-
17	Accrued interest receivable	-	-	-	-
18	Premises and equipment	-	-	-	-
19	Other real estate owned	-	-	-	-
20	Intangible assets	-	-	-	-
21	Cash surrender value of life insurance	-	-	-	-
22	Net amortized assets	-	-	-	-
23	Deferred income taxes	-	-	-	-
24	Other assets	-	-	-	-
25	**Total assets**	-	-	-	-
27	**Liabilities and shareholders' equity**				
28	Deposits	-	-	-	-
29	Noninterest-bearing	-	-	-	-
30	Interest-bearing	-	-	-	-
31	**Total deposits**	-	-	-	-

Figure D-3. A balance sheet summary is shown here

The Net Present Value (NPV)

There are several different outputs for the net present value (NPV). However, this is a simple and clear calculation output (Figure D-4).

	A	B
1	NPV	
2		
3	Discount Rate:	10%
4		
5	Time	Cash flow
6	0	(200,000)
7	1	20,000
8	2	22,500
9	3	25,000
10	4	27,500
11	5	30,000
12	6	32,500
13	7	35,000
14	8	37,500
15	9	40,000
16	10	42,500
17		
18	NPV =	(19,880)

Figure D-4. The NPV is calculated here

The Internal Rate of Return (IRR)

Again, just like the NPV, the internal rate of return (IRR) can be shown as a simple table with the calculations (Figure D-5).

	A	B	C	D	E
1	IRR				
2					
3	Cash flow frequency:		12	Monthly	
4					
5	Monthly number	Monthly income flow	Capital flow	Net monthly flow	
6	0	-	(2,000,000)	(2,000,000)	
7	1	50,000		50,000	
8	2	50,000		50,000	
9	3	50,000		50,000	
10	4	50,000		50,000	
11	5	50,000		50,000	
12	6	50,000		50,000	
13	7	50,000		50,000	
14	8	50,000		50,000	
15	9	50,000		50,000	
16	10	50,000		50,000	
17	11	50,000		50,000	
18	12	50,000	2,500,000	2,550,000	
19					
20		IRR of net quarterly flow		4.14958%	monthly
21		IRR p.a.		62.88844%	per annum
22		Check NPV		(0)	

Figure D-5. The IRR is calculated here

APPENDIX

E

Model Housekeeping

In this appendix, I have pulled together a list of helpful tidbits that may prove to be useful in your work with models.

1. **Reserve some preliminary columns on every sheet**. I would advise that you reserve a few columns to the left that you leave blank. If you later decide to add labels or name references, these blank columns will prove themselves to be useful. I use these columns to provide referencing throughout the model.

2. **Hide grid lines**. Over the years, I have grown to detest gridlines, possibly because they are set as the default worksheet view and are pervasive throughout the worksheet. I prefer to have more control over the grid, so I tend to turn them off. They are usually unhelpful and rather distracting. To turn off the grid lines in Excel 2003, go to Tools ➤ Options ➤ View ➤ Grid lines. In Excel 2007, it is under Office Button ➤ Excel Options ➤ Advanced ➤ Display options for this worksheet ➤ Show grid lines. In Excel 2010, you would follow these same steps except the last two locations would be View ➤ Grid lines.

3. **Do not use the white font color.** You should avoid using a white font color along with colorless cell fills to hide data. This advice may seem really obvious, but I have seen this mistake enough times to include it in this list. If you do need to hide data so that no one can read it, then simply do not include that information in the model.
4. **Do not use defined names excessively.** The process of defining and using names to access data is very useful and in fact in some circumstances essential. But when using defined names, sensibility should come into play. Do not spend so much time naming every single formula or range as it is just not practical and will become confusing.
5. **Make templates.** Where there are many similar sheets, design a template that can be applied to all sheets. This makes it far easier to maintain than having to edit multiple sheets individually. By using templates in every sheet, your model will have a consistent feel that will ensure the model has been developed with a high level of professionalism.
6. **Flow the information.** Ideally, information and headings should be entered once and then flow through the file to wherever they are required. This flow makes the file far easier to maintain and reduces the opportunity for errors. The simplest solution is to use range names (defined names).
7. **Use file linking.** In the event you have to link multiple files together, ensure that dependency information is provided in the file to assist with future maintenance.
8. **Work with the model layout.** Use separate sheets for Setup (all standing data for the file), Workings (reference and lookup tables, data storage, and calculations that are not relevant to the user), and About model (details regarding the file's overall purpose, spreadsheet owner, version, changes, and so forth). Keep in mind that Workings should be well-documented to assist with maintainability.
9. **Apply range naming conventions.** Named ranges should be named consistently throughout the file as SourcesheetTypeName, such as inputsTblMonth (or just iTblMonth) shown in E1-1 and E1-2.
10. **Color your tabs.** Use sheet tab colors to assist with visually identifying sheets with a similar function.

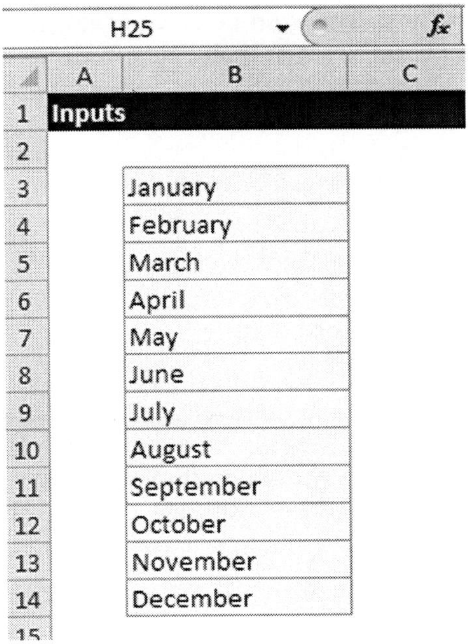

E1-1. The table contains the months of the year

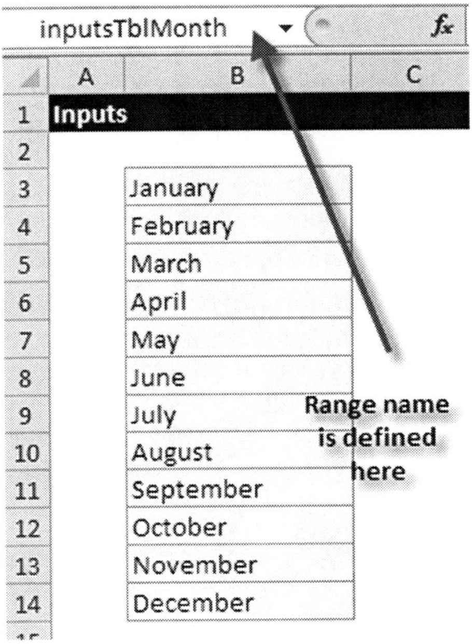

E1-2. The table has now been defined with a range name

11. **Take care with merged cells.** Consider using "Center across Selection" rather than "Merge Cells" as merged cells are very problematic and will cause havoc with lookup functions. In simple terms, avoid using merged cells. If they are absolutely necessary, then do not use them on any data-driven or formula cells.

12. **Use shorter formulas.** Split long formulas into smaller chunks to aid readability. If you have to use a long formula, then document it via a cell note to assist yourself and other users.

13. **Access user-defined functions (UDFs).** Consider using user-defined functions (UDFs) when long, complex formulas are required. This simplifies the readability and maintainability of formulas and allows better documentation, portability, and re-use (see Chapter 3 for more information on UDFs).

14. **Use range names with conditional formatting.** Use range names to aid formula readability and to calculate results by using different cells and/or methods to detect potential errors. Use conditional formatting to provide a visual indication of any errors that exist.

15. **Never use the spacebar as a way to clear cells.** This is another tip that may seem obvious, but under no circumstance should the spacebar be used to clear cells. Use the Delete key instead. The computer will always see the space as a character, so irrespective of whether the character is blank it will still be processed as a character and will therefore produce an error. Following this tip will prevent errors.

16. **Ensure a robust formula.** Build your formulas so that they can handle unusual situations such as zero, negative values, or text values in cells. This is particularly important with formulas using division, as they will produce an error. Using either the data validation error message or handling the error in a formula will give you error assurance.

17. **Use the subtotal function.** Calculate subtotals by using the SUBTOTAL() function rather than the SUM() function to allow easier maintenance. The SUBTOTAL() function is capable of handling interruptions in the columns or rows such as text, while the SUM() function will produce an error.

18. **Be wary of hidden links.** Avoid copying a formula that includes a named range from a spreadsheet in one workbook to a spreadsheet in another workbook. Copying between workbooks creates a hidden link between the workbooks. If you should find the need to copy, then just make sure you break the link in the data links and also be sure to de-link the range name in the name manager. (You can usually spot these because the "Refers to" will show a file path to another file.) Hidden links are capable of changing the data in your workbook if the linked file changes, and so you will end up losing control of the data and will have stability issues.

19. **Establish a VBA style**. If the model is going to contain more than two VBA coding modules, I would suggest establishing a VBA style guide containing rules and details about coding standards that will ease a lot of the pain when the time comes to recode and refresh the VBA.

20. **Using VBA and range names**. Use named ranges in macros rather than absolute cell references so that the file can be amended such as a new row or column being inserted or deleted without requiring amendment to the macro code.

21. **Provide VBA documentation**. VBA code should always be well-documented with proper indentation according to the style manual for that model.

22. **Using the macro recorder**. Use the macro recorder sparingly. The code it produces is lengthy, inefficient, and hard-coded. You can get away with first recording a macro and then going back through the code to make it more efficient through the VBE. Always review and potentially edit all macro recordings. The basic premise here is never permit any macro recordings to remain in the model without some scrutiny.

APPENDIX

F

References

Big Mac Index, *The Economist,* `http://www.economist.com/content/big-mac-index`

Gill, Matthew. *Accountants' Truth: Knowledge and Ethics in the Financial World.* New York: Oxford University Press, 2009.

McConnell, Steve. *Code Complete, Second Edition.* Redmond, VA: Microsoft, 2004.

Panko, Ray. "We Know About Spreadsheet Errors" in the special issue of *Journal of End User Computing* on "Scaling Up End User Development," Volume 10, No 2 (Spring 1998): 15-21.

PriceWaterhouseCoopers (PWC), "Implementing a Process to Ensure Appropriate Controls over Spreadsheets Is a Critical Element of Compliance with Sarbanes-Oxley Section 404," July 2004.

I

Index

G, H

I, J, K

L

M

N

O

P, Q

R

S

T

W, X, Y, Z

Lightning Source UK Ltd.
Milton Keynes UK
UKOW04f0408071213

222539UK00001B/1/P

9 781430 262053